הגדה של פסח בצאתי ממצרים

Departing Egypt Passover Haggada

הגדה של פסח בצאתי ממצרים

Departing Egypt Passover Haggada

INSIGHTS AND COMMENTARY

Rabbi Aryeh A. Frimer

Urim Publications
Jerusalem • New York

Departing Egypt Passover Haggada:
Insights and Commentary
by Rabbi Aryeh A. Frimer

Copyright © 2025/5785 Aryeh A. Frimer

All rights reserved

No part of this publication may be translated, reproduced, stored in a retrieval system, or transmitted, in any form or by any means, electronic, mechanical, photocopying, recording, or otherwise, without express written permission from the publishers.

Typeset by Juliet Tresgallo

Printed in Israel
First Edition
ISBN 978-965-524-385-7

Urim Publications
P.O. Box 52287
Jerusalem 9152102, Israel
www.UrimPublications.com

Cataloging-in-Publication data is available from the Library of Congress.

Table of Contents

Author's Preface	7
Introductory Essays	11
1. Reliving the Exodus	11
2. *Haggada* – הגדה	12
3. The Purpose of the *Seder*	12
4. The Ebb and Flow of the *Haggada*	15
5. *Shabbat ha-Gadol* and a Preparatory Reading of *Maggid*	18
6. The Centrality of the Egypt Experience	20
7. The Unasked Question: Why Were the Israelites Exiled and Why to Egypt?	22
8. The Holiday of Freedom	25
9. The *Pesaḥ* of Lot vs. the *Pesaḥ* in Egypt	27
10. The Number Four at the *Seder*	30
11. Remembering Temple Times – *Zekher le-Mikdash*	31
The *Haggada*	34
Eḥad Mi Yodea – Popular Translations into the Vernacular	388
Additions to the *Haggada*	406

*T*his Haggada is lovingly dedicated
to the memory of our parents

Rabbi Norman E. and Esther M. Frimer z"l
הרב נחמן ב"ר יששכר דב ורייזל חיה בלימה ז"ל
אסתר מרים בת הרב משה זאב הכהן וחוה ז"ל

Rev. Jonas and Libby Neiman z"l
ר' יונתן ב"ר יעקב יהודה ואסתר ז"ל
הינדא ליבא בת הרב מנחם מנדל צבי הכהן ולאה רבקה ז"ל

and to the memory of our son
Yaakov Yehudah Frimer z"l
יעקב יהודה ז"ל בן הרב אריה אברהם ואסתר

by
Rabbi Aryeh A. and Esther A. Frimer

Author's Preface

Throughout my adult life, I have devoured the writings of many different commentators on the *Haggada*, gleaning ideas and insights into these age-old verses. I was intrigued by the authors' creativity, ingenuity, flights of fancy, and probing intellectual, psychological, and emotional analysis. The great expounders were able to bring life experiences to bear on the text and were not afraid to ask tough fundamental questions. I recorded their comments assiduously and filed them away for future use. I found the comments of R. Joseph B. Soloveitchik and R. Jonathan Sacks particularly insightful and relevant to our generation, and I have quoted many of them in this work. Fortunately, many (but not all) of the finest *Haggada* insights of R. Soloveitchik have appeared posthumously in "*Haggada Si'ah ha-Grid,*" "An Exalted Evening," and "Festival of Freedom." R. Sacks published an annotated *Haggada* in his lifetime, while other insights are scattered throughout his Torah Commentary "Covenant and Conversation." There were, of course, a plethora of other insightful and gifted commentators over the generations whose contributions are timeless and whose comments I have included in this work.

As a young rabbi at Harvard Radcliffe Hillel in the early 1970s, and thereafter at the Rabbi Jacob Berman Community Center – Tiferet Moshe Synagogue in Rehovot – I would give a yearly *Haggada* s*hiur* on *Shabbat ha-Gadol*. My organized files continued to swell over the years and stood me in good stead in these classes. This volume, then, is the distillation of many decades of teaching the *Haggada* and a product of the encouragement of congregants, friends, and family. I thank them all for their continued support. The audience often suggested several new directions, and I have included their comments as well.

I have called this work *Be-Tzeiti Mi-Mitzrayim* – "Departing Egypt." The Hebrew title is based on the Torah's instruction to parents to teach the Exodus story as a firsthand experience: "This is what God did for me *be-tzeiti mi-Mitzrayim*, when I departed Egypt" (Ex. 13:8). I pray that this work will help participants see the words of the *Haggada* in a new, fresh light. I've also called it "Insights and Commentary on the *Haggada*," for our commentary not only includes many perceptive comments about the *Haggada*'s structure and text but also focuses on the *Haggada*'s insights into the character of the Jewish People.

In my preparation for these lessons, I paid particular attention to the flow of the *Haggada* from section to section. I have often stopped my commentary to summarize where we have been, what we have learned, and where we are headed. I have also put in particular effort into the post-meal *Hallel-Nirtza* portion of the *Haggada* which is largely ignored by most *Haggada* commentators. The latter phenomenon is a shame. Most *Seder* participants can testify that *Nirtza* proves to be one of the most memorable and meaningful sections of the evening experience for children and adults alike.

As mentioned above, in my annual survey, I relied much on my broad reading and a few of my own insights, but largely focused on the ideas of others. I have credited them but sometimes simply indicated that it comes from their *Haggada* or biblical commentary. Long quotes are often abridged.

This book contains a wealth of material and ideas related to the *Haggada*. Central concepts regarding the servitude and exodus are discussed at length. It certainly cannot be digested on the fly. To get the most out of this work, the reader should study it before the *Seder*. But one who does so will certainly find his *Seder* experience enriched and renewed.

A few personal acknowledgments are in order. I have been blessed to have been born into a family that embodied the finest of the tradition of Torah *u-Madda*. I owe a great debt to my very gifted and loving parents *z"l*, R. Norman E. and Esther Miriam Frimer. They encouraged and inspired their children in all their intellectual pursuits, to be not only serious *bnai Torah*, but also knowledgeable secularly, and conversant with – and involved in – the world around us.

My wife and best friend, Esther, has been a true *ezer ke-negdo*, a full partner in all my endeavors. Striving to be both a *ben Torah* and a Chemistry Professor necessarily required that I would not always be available on the home front. Sharing my values, Esther willingly picked up the slack and I will forever be in her debt.

I want to thank my talented children – Michal and Avi Jacob, Yaakov (*z"l*) and Shira Frimer, Shoshana and Benjamin Dekel, Nechama and Itai Saffer – and their families, for all the pride and *nahat* they have given me over the years. May they continue to grow and prosper, proudly passing the living Torah and a vibrant Jewish Tradition on to the next generation.

In this regard, I remember that as a youth, my father *z"l* described to me the ancient Greek marathon. It was a unique relay race, he explained, in which the runners passed not a simple baton from hand to hand but a lighted torch. And as they ran, they guarded the burning torch closely. This is because the winning team was not necessarily the team that crossed the "Finish Line" first; but rather, the team that crossed the "Finish Line" first with the flame still lit, with the torch still burning bright. That is our goal as Jewish parents – to keep the flame of Torah and Tradition alive! Indeed, that is ultimately the goal of the *Seder* and the *Haggada*!

My brothers, R. Dov I. Frimer and R. Shael I. Frimer have been loyal and challenging study partners and companions throughout my life pursuits. I owe much of my solid spiritual growth to them; deep love and respect bind us.

I would like to express my deep appreciation to Sandy and Paula Colb for more than fifty years of lasting friendship, encouragement, partnership and support.

My profound gratitude to Joel B. Wolowelsky for his guidance and encouragement throughout this undertaking. He was one of the first to review the entire manuscript, suggesting extensive changes and improvements, which helped bring this project to fruition.

I cannot close without acknowledging all those masterful and skilled individuals who have helped me bring this project to its desired conclusion. Kudos to Tzvi Mauer of Urim Publications who oversaw the whole production process, to the astute and experienced Pearl Friedman who served as the editor of this volume, and to Shanie Cooper for the creative and colorful cover design.

And to you our reader, we pray you find this volume insightful, enjoyable and inspiring.

le-Shana ha-ba'ah bi-Yerushalayim – Next year in Jerusalem.

Aryeh A. Frimer

In Memoriam

During the course of writing this work, three close relatives passed away. I would like to remember them here in chronological order of their passing: my brother-in-law – The Honorable Noach Dear *z"l*, נח בן הרב משולם שרגא ויספא דבורה ז"ל; my sister-in-law Rochelle Ann (Shelli) Frimer *a"h*, רחל חנה ע"ה בת מאיר ורבקה ז"ל; and my cousin Rabbi Shael Bellows *z"l*, הרב שאול בן שמואל וחנה לאה ז"ל. Each one has had a long and meaningful impact on my life and those of the members of our family. יהי זכרם ברוך!

Introductory Essays

1. Reliving the Exodus

The *Pesah Haggada* is clearly one of the most beloved books of the Jewish People, irrespective of their religious persuasions or affiliations. With the exception of *siddurim* and *Tanakh*, the *Pesah Haggada* is the most published Jewish book, with about 5,000 editions having appeared since printing was invented. In their commentaries to this volume, authors have given expression to their hopes and aspirations, and allowed their imagination and creativity to soar, combining both mind and heart in their desire not just to **remember** the Exodus, but to **relive** it firsthand. "For Judaism, memory is experiential in nature," says R. Joseph B. Soloveitchik; "one does not simply recollect the past or just remember bygones, but **re-experiences** that which has been. The Passover *Seder* is, of course, the prime example: 'In each generation, a person is required to see himself as if he had gone out of Egypt'" (*Out of the Whirlwind*, p. 14).

Similarly, R. Jonathan Sacks has written:

> There is a profound difference between history and memory. History is *his* story – an event that happened sometime else to someone else. Memory is *my* story, something that happened to me and is part of who I am. To be a Jew is to know that over and above history is the task of memory. More than any other faith, Judaism made this a matter of religious obligation. *Pesah* is where the past does not die, but lives in the chapter we write in our own lives, and in the story we tell our children (*Haggada*).

It is the purpose of the *Haggada* to guide us in making the servitude and Exodus come alive and convert these historical events into a first-hand memory after more than three millennia. It is one of the goals of this commentary to reveal how the *Haggada* does so.

2. *Haggada* – הגדה

The *Haggada* is the liturgy read on the night of the Passover *Seder*. It often contains the text to be read, instructions to the rituals to be performed, illustrations, and commentaries. The word *Haggada* means a declaration or statement and is based on a verse dealing with a parent-child dialog about *Pesaḥ* rituals. The Torah instructs the parent: *ve-higgadeta le-vinkha* – "And you shall tell your child on that day, saying: 'It is because of this that the Lord acted on my behalf when I came forth out of Egypt'" (Ex. 13:8). But, as we shall see, the *Haggada* is more than just "telling"; it is about bearing witness, testimony in action. Interestingly, the body of the *Maggid* section of the *Haggada* is based on four verses (Deut. 26:5–8) which appear in the Torah as the declaration recited by the farmer bringing his basket of first fruit to the Temple. Upon approaching the *kohen*, he says: *Higgadeti hayom* – "I **tell** this day to the Lord your God that I have come unto the land which the Lord swore unto our fathers to give us" (Deut. 26:3). R. Baruch Epstein (*Tosefet Berakha*) notes that *Higgadeti* can't come from the root "to tell" since it is a past tense form, while the sentence is in the present ("this day"). Rather it comes from a related root which means to declare or give testimony (see: Psalms 19:2, 97:6; Samuel I 24:19; Samuel II 19:7). Thus, this verse should be translated as: "I bear witness this day – in words and action – before the Lord your God…" Thus, *ve-higgadeta le-vinkha* means: you should declare or testify – in words and action – before your child, as to the veracity of the Exodus. The *Haggada* is in essence a record of the testimony of the Jewish People's redemption from Egyptian slavery.

3. The Purpose of the *Seder*

At the beginning of the *Haggada*, the child asks: "How different this night is from all other nights?!" But shortly after that, we learn from Rabbi Elazar ben Azariah that there is an obligation to mention the redemption from Egypt *every* night of the year! So what indeed is the unique essence of the *Seder* night?

Some have suggested that on every other night of the year, the obligation is merely *lehazkir*, to mention the Exodus briefly. But on the *Seder* night, the special mitzva is to be *ma'arikh* – extend the discussion substantially. But if that were the case, why does the *Haggada* state "…and all those who relate the Egypt experience at great length are praiseworthy." Why only praiseworthy?! It's what's obligated!

Others have proposed that the mitzva on the night of the fifteenth of *Nissan* is to cultivate a dialogue with one's children – *ve-higadeta le-vinkha* – through question and answer. However, Jewish law ordains the observance of a *Seder* even in the absence of children or a spouse, even when one is alone. Clearly, the dialogue with one's children is an important element in how **best** to fulfill the *Seder* night obligation – but not the essence of the commandment.

Still other scholars suggest that a solution to this can be found in the words of Rabbi Moses ben Maimon (Maimonides, Rambam). As the *Maggid* section of the *Haggada* reaches its climax, we say: "In every generation, one is obligated *lire'ot* – to **envision** oneself as if he/she were redeemed from Egypt." Maimonides, in his classic code (*Yad, Hilkhot Hametz u-Matza*, 7:7), rephrases this slightly differently: "In every generation one is obligated *lehar'ot* (or *lar'ot*) – to **act** as if one were **now** redeemed from the **servitude** of Egypt."

Rambam's reformulation teaches us that the obligation on the *Seder* night is to **re**-enact that uniquely stunning and exhilarating moment of transition from slavery to redemption – "as if oneself were **now** redeemed from the **servitude** of Egypt." On every other night of the year, the obligation is to **remember** the Exodus like an academic studying and analyzing a historical fact. But on the night of the fifteenth of *Nissan*, maintains Maimonides, remembering is not enough; the unique obligation of the *Seder* is to **relive** the Exodus. In the immortal words of Walter Cronkite: "It was a night like any other night – only you are there."

To recreate this experience – not only for oneself but for the whole family – takes teamwork and planning. Good food, good friends, and a good story are not enough; you cannot **relive** the Exodus unless the annual experience is fresh, exciting, and relevant. There has to be a dialogue where all generations are involved. You have to stimulate the children and the adults to challenge and be challenged – to question and be questioned – by the tale and its details. As Maimonides stresses, there is much acting and drama. We not only talk about the bread of oppression and bitter herbs – we eat them. At the same time, we act out freedom with wine, songs that make us smile, and food fit for royalty.

Physical and spiritual redemption is the precious gift that the Passover story describes. But as modern man knows only too well, freedom needs to be properly protected and correctly channeled. The goal of the *Seder* is to sensitize us yearly to the need to guard, cherish, and value this bequest. May we be equal to the challenge.

But the *Seder* has an additional facet to it. Let us begin by asking why the *Seder* is perhaps the most observed ritual in Jewish life? It is after all a ritual which requires a great deal of time and preparation. I believe it is because it touches on a special chord: the issue of identity. It relates to the question of who we were, who we are, and where we are headed. It deals with the handing on of national memory and a proud heritage. Writes R. Jonathan Sacks:

> Imagine you are the leader of a people that is enslaved and oppressed, that has suffered exile for more than two centuries. What will you speak about? If you examine the text in *Parashat Bo* you will see that three times Moshe reverted to the same theme: children, education, and the distant future. So Jews became the only people in history to predicate their very survival on education. The most sacred duty of parents was to teach their children. *Pesaḥ* itself became an ongoing seminar in the handing on of memory. Judaism became the religion whose heroes were teachers and whose passion was study and the life of the mind. The Mesopotamians built ziggurats. The Egyptians built pyramids. The Greeks built the Parthenon. The Romans built the Coliseum. Jews built schools. That is why they alone, of all the civilizations of the ancient world, are still alive and strong, still continuing their ancestors' vocation, their heritage intact and undiminished. (Covenant and Conversation, *Bo* 5781)

So the *Seder* is also an educational seminar. It is about keeping the memory of our special history, lineage, and relationship to God alive. It's about doing *mitzvot*, it's about identifying with Jewish history past, present, and future. It's about us, our parents, and our children.

The *Haggada* is the guidebook through the *Seder*, and concomitantly through the experience of Jewish history.

4. The Ebb and Flow of the *Haggada*

How does the *Haggada* get us to identify Jewishly with our past, and commit ourselves to Judaism's present and future? And how does the whole text hold together? Clearly, it does so slowly and methodically. We begin the *Seder* with *Kiddush* over wine, as we do all festivals. However, we also mention, for the first time, that *Pesaḥ* is the "Time of our Liberation" without yet getting into details. This cup is thus the first "Cup of Redemption." Next, in order to encourage the children to become involved in our subsequent discussion, we pique their curiosity about the *Seder* through several strange acts: washing our hands without a blessing; eating a vegetable dipped in salt water; and breaking the middle of three *Matzot* and hiding one half away. We then begin the *Maggid* or narrative section of the *Haggada*. In order to tell the story properly, the *Seder* participants need to be transported back some 3500 years to the biblical land of the Nile. The *Haggada*'s story of the Exodus, begins with a variation of "Show and Tell." With the *matzot* exposed, the assembled say in Aramaic: *Ha laḥma anya di akhalu avhatana be-ara de-mitzrayim* – "This is the bread of oppression our forefathers ate in Egypt." The use of Aramaic gives the statement an aura of the historic. It sets the mood by putting us in a foreign land, in the midst of the hardship of Egypt. We should have properly switched to Egyptian, but it is a language which no one knows. So we do the next best thing: switch to Aramaic – an ancient cognate language of Hebrew.

We now turn to the children to ask the "Four Questions." Having them do so puts the children in the limelight, allowing them to shine. But it also communicates that they "count" and are an integral part of Judaism and the Seder experience. The questions invite them to pay attention to the strange and special quality of this *Seder* night. These questions also serve as a perfect segue into our night's tale of servitude and redemption.

The immediate response to these questions is a one sentence answer, which goes something like this: "We were slaves and the Almighty miraculously redeemed us; hence, we are all obligated to express our gratitude in word and deed." This response is true, but is far from complete! It perhaps answers why we lean tonight or why we immerse our foods in various dips because we celebrate our being free men and women. But it doesn't answer the child's other specific questions about *Matza* and *Maror*. Nor does it detail what happened during the Exodus or the miracles involved.

But before getting down to the full answer, we take a short detour to briefly discuss how one fulfills this requirement of thanksgiving at the *Seder*. In particular, who specifically is obligated? How much detail and depth is required? What rituals are involved? When must all this be done?

After disposing of these issues, we begin with the long answer which begins with "Initially our forefathers were idolaters…" It takes us from Terah, the idolater father of Avraham, down to Egypt with Yaakov and his sons, followed by centuries of pain, servitude, and suffering. It is via these paragraphs that, through the text, our discussion, amplification, and imagination, we are meant to experience the back-breaking labors in Egypt, the task-masters whip, and the nightmare of the Egyptians' infanticide. We are then astounded by the Ten Plagues and God's outstretched hand, and exhilarated by our ultimate flight to freedom. The song *Dayenu* then lists a plethora of kindnesses spanning the Exodus, crossing the Red Sea and the revelation at Sinai, the forty years in the desert, our conquest of the Land of Israel, and ultimately concluding with the building of the Temple.

In recognition of God's kindness and redemption, we first commit ourselves to happily and enthusiastically fulfill His commandments. After all, when Moshe came to Pharaoh, He said in God's name: "Let my people go – so that they may **serve** me!" (Ex. 7:16, 28; 9:1, 13). So on *Seder* night, we serve him specifically through the *mitzvot* of *Pesah*, *Matza*, and *Maror*. We will eat these foods in a moment, but we first explain their meaning, and in doing so answer the child's questions. We next turn to the Almighty's praises as Israelites leaving Egypt and sing the first two chapters of *Hallel* (Psalms 113 and 114) which focus on the Almighty's role in nature and history. With this song, we end *Maggid* drinking the second "Cup of Redemption."

At this high point of the evening, everyone is smiling. We excitedly begin the business end of the *Seder*, where we sit down to do the *Pesah* commandments of *Pesah*, *Matza*, and *Maror*. However, we are in for a rude awakening, when we prepare our "Hillel *Korekh* Sandwich" and realize that we have Matza and *Maror*, but there is no *Korban Pesah*.

With our *Matza* and *Maror* in hand, all we can say is "This is what Hillel would do when the Temple was standing…." We become painfully aware that we are no longer leaving Egypt, but millennia later in *galut* with the destruction of the Temple, and trying to survive as Diaspora Jews. A modicum of depression sets in. We eat our sumptuous meal, recite *Birkat ha-Mazon* over the third "Cup of Redemption," and pour a special cup for Eliyahu – the prophet of redemption – but he remains a no-show at our *Seder* for the two-thousandth time!

We continue *Hallel* (Psalms 115–118) thanking God for what remains, but this time as Diaspora Jews, fully appreciative of our precarious situation. This part of Hallel reflects both faith and fear, joy and pain, dejection, and exhilaration! Like King David, we have the conviction that God will ultimately redeem us again, but we don't know when or how. Hallel leaves us unsure and insecure.

Hence, our sages, in their wisdom, ordained that we should extend the recitation of *Hallel* with two additional selections. The first is *Hallel ha-Gadol* (Psalms 136) where we see the Almighty as the God of Creation and history, who watches over the People of Israel. But most importantly, it concludes: "He remembered us in our lowly state… and rescued us from our tormentors… He gives food to all living beings…" So God does care about the **individual**, though he is downtrodden and lowly.

This theme is developed in a second addition, the poetic song *Nishmat*. Here we declare: "You are God… who liberates, rescues, sustains, answers, and is merciful in every time of distress and anguish… He Who rouses the sleepers and awakens the slumberers; Who raises the dead and heals the sick, causes the blind to see, and straightens the bent; Who makes the mute speak and reveals what is hidden. To You alone we give thanks!" We affirm that God does indeed care about us throughout history and today! By the end of *Hallel*, our faith is renewed and our spirits are invigorated. Thus, *Hallel* ends hopefully and on an upbeat note, which is as it should be, because we want Jews of all ages to believe that it is worthwhile being a Jew. It is here, at the conclusion of *Hallel*, that the *Seder* as composed by our Sages ends, and we drink the fourth and final "Cup of Redemption."

This buoyant ending would have sufficed if it weren't for the fact that decades, centuries, and millennia have passed and the Jewish people are still suffering. The question then arises: Where is all this leading?

This is where the final section of the *Haggada*, *Nirtza*, comes into play. The overall answer is: "Jews: Hang in there! The Jewish past has been glorious and so will be its future. Stay steadfast, hopeful, and optimistic!" Thus, the songs *va-Yehi ba-Hatzi ha-Layla* and *ve-Amartem Zevah Pesah* demonstrate that the Jewish past has indeed been a dramatic one, full of God's intervention and miracles of salvation. The next pair *Ki Lo Na'eh* and *Adir Hu* emphasizes that the God we put our faith in is awesome, blessed, and great. He is worthy of our faith, trust, and obedience. *Ehad Mi Yode'a* reviews some of the central motifs and principles of the Jewish faith. And, finally, the *Seder* concludes with *Had Gadya*, asserting the Almighty's obvious and manifest mastery over all of creation. While the last two songs seem almost childish in nature, deeper study reveals their true profundity and educational importance. Nevertheless, they lift everyone's spirit!

So we end the *Seder* sated physically with good food, uplifted emotionally, and with a smile on our faces. That's how it is supposed to be. That's how our sages throughout the generations planned it. That's part of the magic of the *Seder* that appeals to children and adults of all ages. It keeps the flame of tradition burning brightly.

5. *Shabbat ha-Gadol* and a Preparatory Reading of *Maggid*

Shabbat ha-Gadol (literally "The Great *Shabbat*") is the name given by Jewish tradition to the *Shabbat* immediately preceding Passover. *Tosafot* (*Shabbat* 87b) teaches that the first *Shabbat ha-Gadol* took place in Egypt on the 10th of Nisan, five days before the Israelite's Exodus. On that date, the Israelites were commanded (Ex. 12:3) to "take a lamb for the household, a lamb for each home" to be later slaughtered as a paschal lamb. A special *haftara* is read on this *Shabbat* from the prophet Malachi. In addition, in preparation for the *Seder*, it is common that the *Haggada* is read from "*Avadim hayinu…*" through "*…al kol avonotenu.*" Interestingly, we leave out the opening "Four Questions" of *Maggid* and the minimal answers as formulated by Rabban Gamliel – which are the central fulfillment of *ve-higadeta le-vinkha* on *Seder* night! These are left for the *Seder* proper. Customarily, the communal rabbi gives a major sermon or *shi'ur* on *Shabbat* afternoon discussing the laws and themes of Passover.

The commentators have struggled with finding a reason for the appellation *Shabbat ha-Gadol*; in what way is this Sabbath particularly "great"? A plethora of answers have been proposed and we cite a few of them.

(1) One approach maintains that *Gadol* refers to *Nes ha-Gadol* – the great miracle. Thus *Shabbat ha-Gadol* is an elliptical phrase meaning the Sabbath of the great miracle. This is because God (in Ex. 12:3) commanded that a lamb, the Egyptian deity, be set aside and tied to the bedpost for four days in anticipation of its sacrifice prior to the plague of the firstborn. The *Talmud* (*Shabbat* 87b) indicates that the Israelite Exodus was on Thursday the fifteenth of Nisan. *Tosafot* calculates from this that the 10th of Nisan – when the Israelites publicly set aside their Paschal lamb as a sacrifice – was the previous *Shabbat*. We find two variants of what exactly happened. *Tosafot* there indicates that the Egyptian firstborn, upon hearing of their pending demise, started an armed rebellion against Pharaoh for not releasing the Israelites. The Tur (OH 430), on the other hand, emphasizes that nothing could have been more abominable to the Egyptians than to know that their deity was about to be slaughtered. Nevertheless, miraculously the Egyptians stood by helplessly as their god was being prepared for sacrifice. Rabbi Chaim Druckman (*Orot Etzion*, 10, 5746) emphasizes the miraculous courage and audacity of the former slaves to set aside a lamb, despite their former masters. The willing endangerment of their lives demonstrated their complete trust and faith in God. This courageous act required us to assert our unique identity and break with the values of the leading culture of the time. It was on *Shabbat ha-Gadol* that we proved we had the mettle to be different, worthy of being redeemed physically and spiritually. It was on this special *Shabbat* that we stopped being passive and became partners in the redemptive process. Clearly, any one of these miracles could well have been the great miracle that gave this *Shabbat* its name.

(2) R. David Abudarham (*Abudarham ha-Shalem*, p. 210) argues that on this Sabbath before *Pesaḥ*, the commandment of setting aside the lamb as a sacrifice was the first mitzva that the Jewish people fulfilled. (Actually, the mitzva of fixing *Rosh Hodesh* was the first mitzva given, but it could not be practically fulfilled at that time in that month.) The fulfillment rendered this Sabbath great, special, and unique. He also points out that it was on this *Shabbat* that the Israelites became like a *gadol* – a halakhic adult – obligated in commandments.

(3) R. Moshe Met of Przemyśl (*Mateh Moshe* 542) cites his mentor

R. Solomon Luria that this *Shabbat* may be named after the concluding words of the penultimate line of the traditional *haftara* read from the prophet Malachi: "Behold, I will send you Eliyahu the prophet before the coming of *Yom Hashem ha-gadol ve-ha-nora*, the great and terrible day of the Lord" (Malachi 3:23). This reason places *Shabbat ha-Gadol* in the same category as *Shabbat Hazon, Shabbat Nahamu,* and *Shabbat Shuva* – each named after a distinctive *haftara*.

(4) Others posit that the adjective *ha-Gadol* refers to the large crowds that gather to hear the great rabbi of the city give the customary lengthy sermon.

(5) Interestingly, some have suggested that the appellation *Shabbat ha-Gadol* is a misnomer and should be *Shabbat Haggada*. This would be related to the custom of reading the opening portion of the *Haggada* on this *Shabbat*. R. Menachem Mendel Kasher (*Haggada Sheleima*, p. 52ff) demonstrates that such a position is untenable since chronologically the name *Shabbat ha-Gadol* long precedes the later custom of reading the *Haggada* on this Sabbath.

(6) If the "great" refers to the Sabbath itself, then it should be *Shabbat ha-Gedola* in the feminine! However, this is less problematic since *Shabbat* may be an abbreviated form of *Yom ha-Shabbat* which is oftentimes treated as male-gendered (see Ex. 20:8, 20:11; Deut. 5:12).

(7) It has been suggested in jest that summertime (first introduced in 1916) is usually initiated just before *Pesah*. With the clock shifted forward, the length of daylight hours of *Shabbat* day is extended, making the day of *Shabbat ha-Gadol* seem particularly long.

6. The Centrality of the Egypt Experience

Before diving into the *Haggada*, it is important to review the reasons for the centrality of the redemption from Egypt in Judaism. Why, indeed, are the Sabbath, the Festivals, and close to fifty other commandments referred to by the Torah and tradition as *zekher le-yetzi'at Mitzrayim* – commemorations of the Egypt experience? Four suggested reasons follow:

(1) It was with the Exodus that God begins to have a continuing and manifest role in history. The Almighty is no longer merely the "God of Creation" – but also the "God of history." He is no longer the God of the Patriarchs, making spot appearances. Henceforth, until the cessation of prophecy, He plays a dominant recognized role on the scene of

human events. And, hence, when the Almighty introduces Himself at Sinai, He does not say: "I am the Lord, thy God, Creator of Heaven and Earth," but rather "I am the Lord, thy God, who took you out of Egypt (Ex. 20:2)." R. Meir Loeb Malbim (Psalms 96:1; 98:1) indicates that this conspicuous role in molding human history is the subject of the "new song of praise" referred to at the end of *Maggid* (the central historical narrative) section of the *Haggada* and the subsequent first two sections of the *Hallel* in which God's praise are sung.

(2) It was through the Almighty's intervention that in Egypt we became a nation, instead of a mere conglomeration of individuals, a slave rabble. In contradistinction to slaves, we were given charge of our destiny and control over our time – with a command to sanctify both.

(3) There is a humanizing quality of the slavery experience: having once been slaves we ought to understand the bitterness of oppression. We are, therefore, expected to empathize with the downtrodden, be they orphans, widows, the poor, the strangers, or the slaves. That is why we are commanded yearly on the *Seder* night to eat bitter herbs: to re-enact and re-identify, to become re-humanized and re-sensitized.

(4) Just as there are physical and spiritual aspects to slavery, so too are there physical and spiritual aspects to redemption. From the perspective of Jewish history, the physical redemption occurs with the Exodus of *Pesah*, while the spiritual redemption and transformation occurs at Sinai on *Shavu'ot*. However, the Egyptian Exodus and the Sinaitic revelation are not to be viewed as two separate points, but as a continuum of freedom. It is for this reason that the Torah links the two events with the "Counting of the Omer." On *Pesah*, God took the Israelites out of Egypt; on *Shavu'ot*, God took Egypt out of the Israelites. It was at Sinai that the Almighty made it eminently clear to us why He freed us and what he expected us to do with our physical freedom. Our task was to sanctify and be sanctified through the mitzva – by fulfilling His commandments. When Moshe came to Pharaoh, he did NOT just say "Let my people go!" But more accurately, *Shalah et ami ve-ya'avduni*, that is "Let my people go so that they may **serve** me!" (Ex. 7:16, 28; 9:1, 13) In the Jewish scheme of things, freedom is not an end in and of itself, but rather a means which enables one to serve his Creator more fully.

7. The Unasked Question: Why Were the Israelites Exiled and Why to Egypt?

R. Jonathan Sacks (*Haggada*) indicates that the *Seder* night is one full of questions, but there is one that we do not ask, and it is significant. Why was there a *Pesah* in the first place? Why the years of exile, suffering, and slavery? Why did God not arrange for Abraham or Isaac or Yaakov simply to inherit the land of Canaan? And if Israel was, for whatever reason, destined to go into exile – why specifically into Egypt? This query may not be asked at the *Seder* – which celebrates our miraculous Exodus, but it is raised by leading Jewish commentaries and thinkers. There are basically two major approaches.

A. The first cadre of scholars maintains that the Egyptian exile was a punishment for a sin of the nation's forefathers.

(1) Ramban (Gen. 12:10) posits that the exile was punishment for our forefather Abraham's sin in fleeing to Egypt during a time of famine in Israel. In the process, he endangered his righteous wife, Sarah – for fear of his own life. He should not have contravened God's original directive to go to the Land of Canaan, and trusted in His protection. Since the transgression was in Egypt, measure for measure his offspring would be punished with exile in Egypt.

(2) Rabbeinu Bahaya ben Asher (Gen. 12:13) agrees that the exile was punishment for a sin of Abraham. However, he points to Abraham's failure of faith regarding the Almighty's promise of the Land of Canaan. When God said (Gen. 15:7): "I am the Lord who brought you out from Ur of the Chaldeans – to assign this land to you as a possession," Abraham responded (Gen. 15:8): "O Lord, how shall I know that I am to possess it?" Abraham's failure was in requiring some concrete sign of this oath. To this, the Almighty retorted (Gen. 15:13): "Know well that your offspring shall be strangers in a land not theirs, and they shall be enslaved and oppressed four hundred years…" As to why the Israelites were exiled specifically to Egypt, Rabbeinu Bahaya (Gen. 12:10) cites the rabbinic principle (*Tanhuma, Lech Lecha*, 40) "The acts of the forefathers is a blueprint for their offspring." Indeed, the exile of Abraham to Egypt (Gen. 12) is mirrored in a great many of its details by what happened to his offspring several generations later.

(3) R. Don Isaac Abravanel (to Gen. 15:12), by contrast, refuses to accept that the Egyptian exile was a punishment to the Israelites for

a sin performed by their righteous forefather Abraham. Rather, Abravanel argues that it was a punishment to the sons of Yaakov for their sin: the sale of Yosef as a slave to Egypt. The Maharal (*Gevurot Hashem* 9) rejects this suggestion of Abravanel because his reading of the text convinces him that the exile in Egypt was planned by God generations before. The sale of Yosef to Egypt and the subsequent famine was, to Maharal's mind, merely the mechanism the Almighty used to bring the Israelites to Egypt.

(4) R. Joseph B. Soloveitchik (*Divrei Hashkafa, va-Yeshev*) proposes that the exile to Egypt resulted from Yaakov's refusal to carry out the divine plan. R. Soloveitchik cites Rashi (Gen. 37:2) who writes: "Yaakov wished to live at ease, but this trouble with Yosef suddenly came upon him. When the righteous desire to live at ease, the Holy One, blessed be He, says to them: 'Are not the righteous satisfied with what is stored up for them in the world to come that they wish to live at ease in this world too?!'" (Gen. Rabba 84:3). R. Soloveitchik explains that when Yaakov returned to Canaan, the Almighty gave Esav the opportunity to leave Canaan and conquer Mt. Se'ir. With Canaan clear, God desired Yaakov to now conquer the entire Land of Israel. Nevertheless, Yaakov was tired of turmoil and wanted to live in peace. As a result, the Divine plan was seemingly stymied – but only temporarily. As we know the crisis with Yosef forced Yaakov back into action and resulted in the family's abandoning Canaan for Egypt.

(5) Finally, Yehuda Kiel (*Da'at Mikra*, Gen. 15) suggests that the slavery was punishment of the Israelites for dallying in Egypt after the famine was over, and not returning home to Canaan. Three challenges have been raised to Kiel's suggestion. (a) Firstly, the fact that the famine ended in Egypt does not necessarily prove that the same was true for Canaan. After all, both at the time of Abraham and Isaac there were periods of famine in Canaan, but not in Egypt. (b) According to Amos Hakham (*Da'at Mikra*, Ex.1:11) Pharaoh instituted bondage to prevent the Israelites from leaving and "rising up from the land." (c) Most convincingly, several biblical verses at the end of Genesis intimate that the Children of Israel were to wait in Egypt until the Lord Himself would return them. (1) Thus, in order to encourage Yaakov to go down to Egypt, the Almighty tells him (Gen. 46:4): "I Myself will go down with you to Egypt, and I Myself will also bring you back…" (2) Then, prior to his demise, Yaakov tells Yosef (48:21): I am about to die, but

God will be with you and bring you back to the land of your ancestors. (3 and 4) Finally, before he dies, Yosef says to his brothers (50:24 and 25): "…God will surely remember you and bring you up from this land to the land promised to Abraham, to Isaac, and to Yaakov. So Yosef made the sons of Israel swear, saying, 'When God remembers you, you shall carry up my bones from here'".

B. The second cadre of scholars proposes that the exile was imposed for an assortment of educational, spiritual, and character-building reasons – to attain goals not easily attainable otherwise.

(1) Thus, R. Meir Simcha of Dvinsk (*Meshekh Hokhma*, Ex. 13:13) proposes that one purpose of the two centuries of servitude was to expose the Israelites to the scientific and cultural knowledge and skills of the most advanced nation of that period. At the same time (ibid., Ex. 7: 3) Egypt and the rest of the world learned of the Creator's existence and dominion over the world through the plagues, miracles, and signs shown by Moshe.

(2) Mazor Levanoni (*Petihta* 7, *Nissan* 5768) in a similar vein suggests several plausible reasons for the servitude in Egypt. Firstly, the fact that all our forefathers married women who were not from Canaan, strongly suggests that the daughters of Canaan lacked the desired traits. God was interested in developing a nation unto itself, with its own unique message – with minimal, if any, Canaanite influence. That goal could only be attained by nurturing and molding them in a hostile (Egyptian) or relatively isolated (Goshen or desert) environment.

(3) Additionally, for nearly all other nations, their identity and culture are an outgrowth of the land in which they dwell. However, it seems that the Almighty was interested in developing a people whose national identity and culture were connected, but, to a large extent, independent of the land which is their designated home. This allowed the Jewish people to survive and maintain their uniqueness despite their often extended exile from the Land of Israel.

(4) Our final reason, proposed by R. Jonathan Saks (*Haggada*), maintains that Israel had to lose its freedom before it could cherish it. Only what we lose do we fully pay attention to. Similarly, Israel had to suffer the experience of slavery and degradation, before it could learn, know, and feel intuitively that there is something morally wrong with oppression. Nor could it, or any other people, carry this message in perpetuity

without reliving it every year, tasting the harsh tang of the bread of oppression and the bitterness of slavery. Thus was created, at the birth of the nation, a longing for freedom that was at the very core of its memory and identity. Had Israel achieved immediate nationhood in the patriarchal age, without the experience of exile and persecution, it would – like so many other nations in history – have taken freedom for granted; and when freedom is taken for granted, it has already begun to be lost. Israel became the people conceived in slavery so that it would never cease to long for liberty – and know that liberty is anything but natural. It requires constant vigilance and unceasing moral struggle. Israel discovered freedom by losing it. May we never lose it again.

8. The Holiday of Freedom

The 15th of *Nissan* initiates a continuum of redemption, beginning with the physical freedom of Passover and culminating with the spiritual freedom of Sinai on *Shavu'ot*. Note, however, that while freedom is a value in both Western and Jewish cultures, R. Sol Roth (*Tradition*, 13:2) points out that their conceptions of freedom differ fundamentally in three areas.

(a) Is Freedom an Individual or National Goal?

From a Western perspective, freedom is an objective of the **individual**. The goal of democracy is to guarantee every person the right to pursue "the good life" – **according to his or her own formula**. The individual has the **right** to choice – even the **right** to be wrong. The Western notion of freedom requires independence, i.e., self-determination. Through the identification of freedom with independence or self-determination, the **human will** is elevated to the highest level of importance. Considerations of truth and morality are subordinated to what "**I want**." The individual is transformed into a legislator of ethical doctrine and this leads naturally to a justification of a "New Morality."

Freedom in Jewish life is a **national** goal. The **right** of the individual to deviate from established norms of belief and action is not included in the traditional Jewish conception of freedom. In short, Judaism seeks the observance of Torah and the commandments, i.e., uniformity in commitment and behavior within the Jewish community. The intent of religion is to describe a specific notion of "the good life," to describe the means of attaining it (via Torah and *mitzvot*), and to inspire the adoption of this program. Traditional Judaism opposes the assignment of primacy to the individual will. It objects to the subordination of classic religious values to acts of volition. One may well have freedom of choice and the *power* to sin, but one does not have the *right* to sin. In absolute terms, Judaism calls one to submit to truth and moral precepts, i.e., the will of God.

(b) "Freedom of" vs. "Freedom for."

This brings us to the second distinction. Freedom in Western culture denotes a **right** – "freedom of." Freedom to a traditional Jew refers mainly to a *power* – "freedom for." "Freedom of" – as in freedom of speech, press, and religion – refers to the right to speak, publish, and preach according to one's conceptions and commitments. "Freedom for" refers to a power. As a prerequisite one needs to achieve "freedom from" want, fear, ignorance, and enslavement – for these are obstacles that stand in the way of "freedom for" – of choosing a desirable pattern of living.

Judaism emphasizes "freedom for" and "freedom from" because its purpose is to guarantee the power to choose. The power to choose is essential to the Jewish conception of freedom for two reasons. First, an act of commitment cannot be performed in a state of coercion. Secondly, an individual cannot be held morally accountable for the violation of a moral precept if he/she did not have the power to do otherwise.

(c) An Ends or a Means?

We move now to the third area of distinction. In political democracy, freedom is an **end**. It is a purpose of the Western form of government to guarantee a life of freedom. This implies that, to attain the Western ideal of freedom, it is necessary to multiply opportunities and, at least preserve a variety of possible commitments. If freedom means the right to choose, the wider the range of choices – be they political, religious, cultural, or economic – the greater the freedom!

By contrast, traditional Judaism's goal is the embodiment within the community of a certain defined way of life. Hence, freedom is merely a means to enable the attainment of that end. Judaism requires freedom – not to preserve or increase the variety of possible experiences – but to enrich life by the introduction of more meaningful ways to experience Judaism.

Based on these distinctions we can understand with greater clarity, a pivotal passage in the Biblical redemption story. When Moshe, in God's name, turns to Pharaoh, he does **not** just say: "Let my people go!" (*Shalah et ami*). That would have suggested that freedom per se is the goal. Rather, Moshe proclaimed (Ex. 7:16): "Let my people go to serve Me" (*Shalah et ami ve-ya'avduni*). Freedom is a means – a means to enable Divine service. The purpose of the physical freedom of Passover is to enable the spiritual freedom of Sinai on *Shavu'ot* and, hence, the two are connected by *Sefirat ha-Omer*.

9. The *Pesah* of Lot vs. the *Pesah* in Egypt

We read in *Parashat Vayera* (Gen. 18) of the three angels who visited Avraham in the heat of the day – two of which continued to Sedom. There they rescued Lot and his family ahead of the city's destruction. The Torah tells us that Lot saw the angels – who appeared as men – and invited them into his home, where he prepared for them a meal and baked *matzot* (19:3). Rashi comments there, *Pesah haya*, that this occurred on the 15th of Nissan – the first day of *Pesah*, which is why Lot prepared *matzot* for his guests. This theme is picked up by the poet R. Elazar ha-Kalir in his song *u-ve-Khen va-yehi ba-Hatzi ha-Layla* appearing in the concluding section of the *Haggada* – *Nirtza*. Rashi's comment draws our attention to more than a subtle parallel that exists between the story of Lot's rescue from Sedom and the story of the night of the Exodus, the redemption from Sedom and the redemption from Egypt. In the table below, R. Yosef Zvi Rimon (https://www2.biu.ac.il/JH/Parasha/pesah/Rimon.doc) shows a comparison of the two stories with emphasis on the points of similarity.

1. In both stories, Matza appears as part of the menu of the central meal.
2. In both stories the major protagonists are in a house whose door (*petah*) is closed
3. The door is also **protected** from evil forces – in the case of Lot by the angels, and by God in Egypt – who **smites** the enemy.
4. There is a common use of the term *le-hashhit* – "to destroy."
5. In both there is a clear command to leave – *kumu u-tze'u*.

6. The story of the redemption goes on for the whole night.
7. Hesitation (*le-hitmahame'ah*) is a critical factor in the story of the exit. Lot hesitates, but the Jews cannot and do not.
8. Intriguingly, in both instances, the rescued group was spared in the merit of Avraham. Thus, in its summary of the destruction of Sedom, the Torah writes, "It happened that when God destroyed the cities of the plain, God remembered Avraham, and he sent Lot from the upheaval…" (19:29). Similarly, the process of the Exodus began when "God remembered His covenant with Avraham, Yitzhak, and Yaakov" (Ex. 2:24). Neither Lot nor *Benei Yisrael* really deserved to be rescued, but they were spared in the merit of Avraham (and, in the Children of Israel's case, also in the merit of the other forefathers).

Pesah in Egypt – Exodus 12	Lot's *Pesah* – Genesis 19	Common Keywords
וְאָכְלוּ אֶת־הַבָּשָׂר בַּלַּיְלָה הַזֶּה צְלִי־אֵשׁ וּמַצּוֹת עַל־מְרֹרִים יֹאכְלֻהוּ (יב:ח).	(ג) וַיַּעַשׂ לָהֶם מִשְׁתֶּה וּמַצּוֹת אָפָה וַיֹּאכֵלוּ.	1 מצות
וְאַתֶּם לֹא תֵצְאוּ אִישׁ מִפֶּתַח־בֵּיתוֹ עַד־בֹּקֶר (יב:כב).	(ו) וַיֵּצֵא אֲלֵהֶם לוֹט הַפֶּתְחָה, וְהַדֶּלֶת סָגַר אַחֲרָיו. (י) וַיִּשְׁלְחוּ הָאֲנָשִׁים אֶת יָדָם וַיָּבִיאוּ אֶת לוֹט אֲלֵיהֶם הַבָּיְתָה וְאֶת הַדֶּלֶת סָגָרוּ:	2 פתח סגור
וּפָסַח ה' עַל־הַפֶּתַח (יב:כג). וְהִכֵּיתִי כָל־בְּכוֹר בְּאֶרֶץ מִצְרַיִם […] בְּהַכֹּתִי בְאֶרֶץ מִצְרַיִם (יב:יב-יג). וַה' הִכָּה כָל־בְּכוֹר בְּאֶרֶץ מִצְרָיִם (יב:כט).	(יא) וְאֶת־הָאֲנָשִׁים אֲשֶׁר־פֶּתַח הַבַּיִת הִכּוּ בַּסַּנְוֵרִים […] וַיִּלְאוּ לִמְצֹא הַפָּתַח.	3 הגנה ומכה

4 משחית	(יג) כִּי־מַשְׁחִתִים אֲנַחְנוּ אֶת־הַמָּקוֹם הַזֶּה. כִּי־גָדְלָה צַעֲקָתָם אֶת־פְּנֵי ה' וַיְשַׁלְּחֵנוּ ה' לְשַׁחֲתָהּ.	וְלֹא יִתֵּן הַמַּשְׁחִית לָבֹא אֶל־בָּתֵּיכֶם לִנְגֹּף (יב:כג).
5 קומו צאו	(יב) וְכֹל אֲשֶׁר־לְךָ בָּעִיר הוֹצֵא מִן־הַמָּקוֹם. (יד) קוּמוּ צְּאוּ מִן־הַמָּקוֹם הַזֶּה, כִּי־מַשְׁחִית ה' אֶת־הָעִיר.	וַיִּקְרָא לְמֹשֶׁה וּלְאַהֲרֹן לַיְלָה וַיֹּאמֶר קוּמוּ צְּאוּ מִתּוֹךְ עַמִּי גַּם־אַתֶּם גַּם־בְּנֵי יִשְׂרָאֵל (יב:לא).
6 כל הלילה	(טו) וּכְמוֹ הַשַּׁחַר עָלָה, וַיָּאִיצוּ הַמַּלְאָכִים בְּלוֹט...	וַיְהִי בְּעֶצֶם הַיּוֹם הַזֶּה הוֹצִיא ה' אֶת־בְּנֵי יִשְׂרָאֵל מֵאֶרֶץ מִצְרַיִם עַל־צִבְאֹתָם (יב:נא).
7 התמהמה	(טז) וַיִּתְמַהְמָהּ [...] וַיֹּצִאֻהוּ [...]	וְלֹא יָכְלוּ לְהִתְמַהְמֵהַּ (יב:לט).
8 זכות אברהם	(כט) וַיְהִי בְּשַׁחֵת אֱלֹהִים אֶת־עָרֵי הַכִּכָּר וַיִּזְכֹּר אֱלֹהִים אֶת־אַבְרָהָם וַיְשַׁלַּח אֶת־לוֹט מִתּוֹךְ הַהֲפֵכָה	וַיִּשְׁמַע אֱלֹהִים אֶת נַאֲקָתָם וַיִּזְכֹּר אֱלֹהִים אֶת בְּרִיתוֹ אֶת אַבְרָהָם אֶת יִצְחָק וְאֶת יַעֲקֹב (ב:כד)

Given that the parallels have been drawn, what is the message that we are to learn from this comparison? R. Yosef Zvi Rimon suggests that there is one further ninth parallel that we have neglected in our table – in each story, the protagonists are surrounded by wicked individuals in a wicked culture. Before the protagonist can be redeemed, he must perform an act of disconnection from that culture. This involves performing a dangerous act that is antithetical to the dominant culture. In the case of Lot, it was *hakhnassat orhim* – opening his home to the angelic guests. In the case of the Israelites, it was setting aside the god of the Egyptians for Korban Pesah and slaughter. Thus, we need a clear element of **self**-redemption before the Almighty is willing to complete the job.

This disconnection was not at all easy for Lot. He hesitates to leave Sodom – and loses his wife and two married daughters in the process. His redemption is only partially successful because he really could not disconnect. The Israelites, however, fulfill God's commands fully, rushing to freedom without hesitation. They leave Egypt behind and become God's people.

Indeed, *Matzot* are at the center of the difference between the *Pesaḥ* of Lot and the *Pesaḥ* of the Israelites in Egypt. Lot only eats Matza at the beginning when he feeds the angels – he is willing to disconnect from some of Sodom's values, but finds it hard to leave Sodom completely. He is only saved because the angels take him by the hand and carry him out of Sodom. The Israelites, on the other hand, eat Matza at the *Pesaḥ Mitzrayim* meal with the *Korban Pesaḥ* and they eat Matza again at the end as they rush to freedom. In order to be redeemed, we must regain our individuality and cut our ties with the dominant detrimental cultures. Matza expresses the disengagement from foreign influences and the establishment of our own unique identity.

10. The Number Four at the *Seder*

The number "four" appears repeatedly in the structure of the *Seder* and *Haggada*. Thus, the *Seder* is punctuated by four cups of wine; four special foods – *Karpas, Ḥaroset, Matza* and *Maror*; four questions; four children – introduced by the paragraph *Barukh ha-Makom barukh Hu…* which contains *barukh* four times; the *Maggid* section of the *Haggada* is based on four verses – *Arami oved avi…, Va-yarei'u otanu ha-Mitzrim…, va-nitzak el Hashem…,* and *va-yotzi'einu Hashem…*; finally, *Shefokh Ḥamatekha* is made up of four verses.

Various reasons have been suggested for the meaningfulness of this number. Most often quoted is the Jerusalem Talmud (*Pesaḥim* 10:1) which asserts that there are four terms of redemption – based on the verses (Ex. 6:6–7):

> Say, therefore, to the Israelite people: I am God. I will **extract**, *ve-hotzeiti*, you from the labors of the Egyptians and **deliver**, *ve-hitzalti*, you from their bondage. I will **redeem**, *ve-ga'alti*, you with an outstretched arm and through extraordinary chastisements. And I will **take**, *ve-lakaḥti*, you to be My people, and I will be your God…

The Gaon of Vilna (Gr"a; cited by R. Asher Weiss, *Tazria-Metzora*, 5780) suggests a different approach. The *Seder* is a meal of praise and thanksgiving – *seudat shĕvah ve-hodaya* – to the Almighty for his miraculous salvation. *Haza"l*, the sages of the Talmud, based on Psalms 107, instituted that individuals have to publicly thank the Almighty by reciting *Birkat ha-Gomel* (*Berakhot* 54a) for their deliverance from the following four life-threatening situations: 1) safe release from prison; 2) recuperation from serious illness; 3) successful crossing of the ocean; and 4) successful crossing of the desert. All four of these categories were present in the Exodus. Thus, the Israelites were released from their Egyptian prison; they were ill following the pre-Paschal lamb circumcision; they crossed *Yam Suf*; and they travelled through the desert.

Thus, the number four pays tribute to the Almighty as redeemer of our nation and the individual.

11. Remembering Temple Times – *Zekher le-Mikdash*

One of the central purposes of the *Seder* is to keep the memory of the *Bet ha-Mikdash* and of Temple practices alive. Below is a list of some of the *Pesah* practices we do in remembrance.

(1 and 2) The *Seder* plate sitting at the center of the *Seder* table includes two cooked items: a *zero'a* (roasted piece of meat) and a *beitza* (roasted egg). These are visual reminders of the meat of the two different sacrifices eaten at the *Seder* during Temple times. One is the *Korban Hagiga* – the holiday sacrifice(s) which is/are consumed for the bulk of the meal. The other is the *Korban Pesah* or Paschal lamb, a small olive-sized portion of which was eaten to commemorate the Almighty's redemption during the Egyptian Exodus.

(3) *u-Rehatz* – the practice of washing our hands before dipping *karpas* into a dip – was instituted to recall the stringencies in effect when eating sacrifices in Temple times. (R. Zvi Pesah Frank *Mikra'ei Kodesh*, *Pesah* II, p. 182).

(4) The custom of wearing a *kittel* (a white linen or cotton robe) at the *Seder* recalls the vision of the High Priest in the Temple and reminds us of the missing *Korban Pesah* (ibid. p. 183).

(5) There is a custom to eat eggs (traditional food of mourners) at the beginning of the *Seder* meal to remember the destruction of the Temple. In addition, the following *Tisha be-Av*, the anniversary of the

destruction of the two Temples, will fall on the same day of the week as *Seder* night.

(6) *Maror* and *Korekh* are not biblically obligated in the absence of a *Korban Pesah*. Yet they were enacted rabbinically in order to keep their memory alive, *zekher le-Mikdash*.

(7) A final piece of Matza, called the *Afikoman*, is eaten at the very end of the *Seder* meal in place of the *Korban Pesah* eaten during Temple times at that point.

(8) Similarly, this *Afikoman* Matza is eaten before *hatzot* (midnight), *zekher le-Mikdash* when the *Korban Pesah* also had to be eaten before then.

(9) The concluding *berakha* of *Maggid* ends with a prayer for the re-establishment of Jerusalem, the Temple, and the Temple service. "*Hasal Siddur Pesah*" ends the formal *Seder* with *le-Shana ha-ba'ah bi-Yerushalayim* – "Next Year in Jerusalem!" Lastly, *Nirtza* includes a repeated chant for the rebuilding of the Temple: *Benei Betkha be-Karov!* – "Build your home (Temple) soon!"

All these are clear attempts by our sages to keep the memory, love, and yearning for Jerusalem and the Temple alive in our collective memory. By reliving the past, we and our children learn to identify with its future. We are instructed not to give up our dreams despite our suffering and tribulations. In a very real sense, it was these memories that facilitated in part the ultimate reestablishment of the State of Israel in our times – two millennia later. May we who have had the privilege of seeing the beginning of the redemption, have the strength and fortitude to see the dream through to its final fruition.

הגדה

בְּדִיקַת חָמֵץ

The search for *Hametz* begins upon nightfall of the fourteenth of Nissan. We must search all areas where *Hametz* may have been brought over the course of the year, even if a thorough cleaning has already been done. Once the blessing below has been recited, the search should not be interrupted by unnecessary conversation until its completion. If the *Seder* falls on Saturday night, the search is performed on Thursday night. Some have the custom of distributing ten pieces of *Hametz* throughout the house prior to the search. In such a case, utmost care should be taken to record the locations of these hidden pieces.

The following blessing is recited before the search for *Hametz*:

בָּרוּךְ אַתָּה יְיָ, אֱלֹהֵינוּ מֶלֶךְ הָעוֹלָם, אֲשֶׁר קִדְּשָׁנוּ בְּמִצְוֹתָיו, וְצִוָּנוּ עַל בִּעוּר חָמֵץ:

After the search, one should wrap the *Hametz* found and put it in a safe place. Then, the following declaration is made. (The paragraph is commonly repeated in English since the declaration must be understood in order to take effect. Any *Hametz* that you still want to use is not included in the declaration.)

כָּל חֲמִירָא וַחֲמִיעָא דְּאִכָּא בִרְשׁוּתִי דְּלָא חֲמִתֵּהּ וּדְלָא בְעַרְתֵּהּ וּדְלָא יְדַעְנָא לֵהּ, לִבָּטֵל וְלֶהֱוֵי הֶפְקֵר כְּעַפְרָא דְאַרְעָא.

THE *HAGGADA*

The Search for Hametz

The search for *Hametz* begins upon nightfall of the fourteenth of Nissan. We must search all areas where *Hametz* may have been brought over the course of the year, even if a thorough cleaning has already been done. Once the blessing below has been recited, the search should not be interrupted by unnecessary conversation until its completion. If the *Seder* falls on Saturday night, the search is performed on Thursday night. Some have the custom of distributing ten pieces of *Hametz* throughout the house prior to the search. In such a case, utmost care should be taken to record the locations of these hidden pieces.

The following blessing is recited before the search for *Hametz*:

Blessed are You, Lord, our God, King of the universe, Who has sanctified us with His commandments and has commanded us to remove all Hametz from our possession.

After the search, one should wrap the *Hametz* found and put it in a safe place. Then, the following declaration is made. (The paragraph is commonly repeated in English since the declaration must be understood in order to take effect. Any *Hametz* that you still want to use is not included in the declaration.)

All leaven and Hametz that is in my possession which I have not seen, have not removed, and do not know about, should be as if it does not exist and should become ownerless, like the dust of the earth.

בִּיעוּר חָמֵץ

On the morning after the search, before five hours into the day, we dispose of (traditionally, burn) all remaining *Hametz* that has not been consumed or sold to a non-Jew. This is followed by reciting the declaration in Aramaic below. The paragraph is commonly repeated in English since the meaning of this declaration must be understood for it to take effect. If the *Seder* falls on Saturday night, this declaration is made on Shabbat morning; however, the burning takes place on Friday morning. Any *Hametz* remaining from the Shabbat morning meal is to be flushed down the toilet. After burning (or on Shabbat, flushing) the following declaration is made:

כָּל חֲמִירָא וַחֲמִיעָא דְּאִכָּא בִרְשׁוּתִי דַּחֲזִיתֵהּ וּדְלָא חֲזִיתֵהּ, דַּחֲמִתֵּהּ וּדְלָא חֲמִתֵּהּ, דְּבִעַרְתֵּהּ וּדְלָא בִעַרְתֵּהּ, לִבָּטֵל וְלֶהֱוֵי הֶפְקֵר כְּעַפְרָא דְאַרְעָא.

עֵרוּב תַּבְשִׁילִין

Outside of Israel, when Passover falls on Thursday and Friday, an *eiruv tavshilin* must be made on Wednesday for it to be permissible to cook on Friday for Shabbat. The *eiruv* indicates that preparations for Shabbat have begun prior to Yom Tov. One takes a baked item (minimally the size of an egg, generally a *matza*) and a cooked food (minimally the size of a large olive, e.g. a hard-boiled egg, a piece of gefilte fish, or a piece of chicken). One then holds the *eiruv tavshilin* and recites the following blessing and text:

בָּרוּךְ אַתָּה יְיָ, אֱלֹהֵינוּ מֶלֶךְ הָעוֹלָם, אֲשֶׁר קִדְּשָׁנוּ בְּמִצְוֹתָיו וְצִוָּנוּ עַל מִצְוַת עֵרוּב:

בַּהֲדֵין עֵרוּבָא יְהֵא שָׁרֵא לָנָא לְמֵפָא וּלְבַשְּׁלָא וּלְאַטְמָנָא וּלְאַדְלָקָא שְׁרָגָא וּלְמֶעְבַּד כָּל צָרְכָנָא מִיּוֹמָא טָבָא לְשַׁבַּתָּא לָנוּ וּלְכָל יִשְׂרָאֵל הַדָּרִים בָּעִיר הַזֹּאת.

The *eiruv* may be stored in the fridge to keep the items fresh to be eaten on Shabbat. If not eaten, the *eiruv* is still valid.

Burning the Hametz

On the morning after the search, before five hours into the day, we dispose of (traditionally, burn) all remaining *Hametz* that has not been consumed or sold to a non-Jew. This is followed by reciting the declaration in Aramaic below. The paragraph is commonly repeated in English since the meaning of this declaration must be understood for it to take effect. If the *Seder* falls on Saturday night, this declaration is made on Shabbat morning; however, the burning takes place on Friday morning. Any *Hametz* remaining from the Shabbat morning meal is to be flushed down the toilet. After burning (or on Shabbat, flushing) the following declaration is made:

All leaven that is in my possession, whether I have seen it or not, whether I have removed it or not, should be as if it does not exist and should become ownerless, like the dust of the earth.

Eiruv Tavshilin

Outside of Israel, when Passover falls on Thursday and Friday, an *eiruv tavshilin* must be made on Wednesday for it to be permissible to cook on Friday for Shabbat. The *eiruv* indicates that preparations for Shabbat have begun prior to Yom Tov. One takes a baked item (minimally the size of an egg, generally a *matza*) and a cooked food (minimally the size of a large olive, e.g. a hard-boiled egg, a piece of gefilte fish, or a piece of chicken). One then holds the *eiruv tavshilin* and recites the following blessing and text:

Blessed are You, Lord, our God, King of the universe, Who has sanctified us with His commandments and commanded us to observe the mitzva of eiruv.

By means of this eiruv it shall be permitted to bake, cook, keep food warm, kindle a flame, and make all necessary preparations on Yom Tov for Shabbat for ourselves and for all Jews who live in this city.

The *eiruv* may be stored in the fridge to keep the items fresh to be eaten on Shabbat. If not eaten, the *eiruv* is still valid.

הַדְלָקַת נֵרוֹת

The candles are lit and the blessings are recited.
(When Yom Tov falls on Shabbat, the words in parentheses are added.)

בָּרוּךְ אַתָּה יְיָ, אֱלֹהֵינוּ מֶלֶךְ הָעוֹלָם, אֲשֶׁר קִדְּשָׁנוּ בְּמִצְוֹתָיו וְצִוָּנוּ לְהַדְלִיק נֵר שֶׁל (בשבת: שַׁבָּת וְשֶׁל) יוֹם טוֹב:

בָּרוּךְ אַתָּה יְיָ, אֱלֹהֵינוּ מֶלֶךְ הָעוֹלָם. שֶׁהֶחֱיָנוּ וְקִיְּמָנוּ וְהִגִּיעָנוּ לַזְּמַן הַזֶּה:

ברכת הבנים והבנות

It is a widespread custom for parents to bless their offspring at the onset of Shabbat or a Holiday before *Kiddush*. The parent places one or both hands on (or above) the child's head and recites a text comprised of an initial gender-specific verse, followed by three more biblical verses (Numbers 6: 24–26) used by the *Kohanim*. The last four verses below are recited in the Frimer Family and selected from Proverbs and Psalms. The parent's blessing generally ends with a loving kiss or embrace.

לְבֵן: יְשִׂמְךָ אֱלֹהִים כְּאֶפְרַיִם וְכִמְנַשֶּׁה (בראשית מד:כ)

לְבַת: יְשִׂמֵךְ אֱלֹהִים כְּשָׂרָה, רִבְקָה, רָחֵל וְלֵאָה

יְבָרֶכְךָ ה' וְיִשְׁמְרֶךָ (במדבר ו:כד)

יָאֵר ה' פָּנָיו אֵלֶיךָ וִיחֻנֶּךָּ (במדבר ו:כה)

יִשָּׂא ה' פָּנָיו אֵלֶיךָ, וְיָשֵׂם לְךָ שָׁלוֹם (במדבר ו:כו)

כִּי אֹרֶךְ יָמִים וּשְׁנוֹת חַיִּים וְשָׁלוֹם יוֹסִיפוּ לָךְ (משלי ג:ב)

אֹרֶךְ יָמִים בִּימִינָהּ, בִּשְׂמֹאולָהּ עֹשֶׁר וְכָבוֹד (משלי ג:טז)

ה' יִשְׁמָרְךָ מִכָּל רָע, יִשְׁמֹר אֶת נַפְשֶׁךָ (תהילים קכא:ז)

ה' יִשְׁמָר צֵאתְךָ וּבוֹאֶךָ, מֵעַתָּה וְעַד עוֹלָם (תהילים קכא:ח)

Candle-Lighting

The candles are lit and the blessings are recited.
(When Yom Tov falls on Shabbat, the words in parentheses are added.)

Blessed are You, Lord, our God, King of the universe, Who has sanctified us with His commandments and commanded us to kindle the light (of Shabbat and) of Yom Tov.

Blessed are You, Lord, our God, King of the universe, Who has kept us alive, sustained us, and enabled us to reach this season.

Blessing for Sons and Daughters

It is a widespread custom for parents to bless their offspring at the onset of Shabbat or a Holiday before Kiddush. The parent places one or both hands on (or above) the child's head and recites a text comprised of an initial gender-specific verse, followed by three more biblical verses (Numbers 6: 24–26) used by the Kohanim. The last four verses below are recited in the Frimer Family and selected from Proverbs and Psalms. The parent's blessing generally ends with a loving kiss or embrace.

For a son: May God make you like Ephraim and Menasheh [Genesis 48:20].
For a daughter: May God make you like Sarah, Rivka, Rachel, and Leah.

May God bless you and protect you [Numbers 6:24].

May God make His countenance shine upon you and be gracious unto you [Numbers 6:25].

May God turn His face toward you and grant you peace [Numbers 6:26].

For [Torah teachings] will lengthen your days, years of life, and well-being [Proverbs 3:2].

In her right hand is length of days; in her left, riches and honor [Proverbs 3:16].

The Lord will guard you from all harm; He will guard your life [Psalms 121:7].

The Lord will guard your going and coming – now and forever [Psalms 121:8].

The Fifteen *Seder* Rituals (*Simanim*)

It is customary that, at the beginning of the *Seder*, participants sing a mnemonic for the order of the 15 constituent rituals/elements of the *Seder*. Many mnemonics have been proposed, but the most popular appears below and it is attributed to the Eleventh Century school of Rabbi Shlomo Yitzhaki (Rashi).

1. **Kadesh** קדש – declare the Sanctity of the day by reciting *Kiddush* and drinking the first of four cups of wine – four cups celebrating redemption.
2. **u-Rehatz** ורחץ – wash one's hands, without a *berakha*.
3. **Karpas** כרפס – dip a vegetable (celery or potato) in salt water.
4. **Yahatz** יחץ – break the middle Matza in half, with the larger piece reserved for the *Afikoman*.
5. **Maggid** מגיד – tell the Passover story and drink the second cup of wine.
6. **Rahtza** רחצה (or רחץ) – wash one's hands again, this time with a *berakha*.
7. and 8. **Motzi, Matza** מוציא, מצה – recite two blessings (*ha-Motsi* and *Al akhilat Matza*) before eating Matza.
9. **Maror** מרור – recite the blessing *Al akhilat Maror* and eat the bitter herbs.
10. **Korekh** כורך – eat the "Hillel-sandwich" made of *Matza*, *Maror* and *Haroset*.
11. **Shulhan Orekh** שלחן-עורך – lit. "table-setting" – serve the holiday meal.
12. **Tzafun** צפון – eat the *Afikoman* – which is the half-Matza set aside or hidden by the leader of the Seder at *Yahatz* (no. 4 above) for this purpose.
13. **Barekh** ברך – recite *Birkat ha-Mazon* and drink the third cup of redemption.
14. **Hallel** הלל – recite the extended *Hallel* and drink the fourth cup of wine.
15. **Nirtza** נרצה – Find favor in God's eyes by concluding the *Seder* with fun educational and inspirational songs.

41 / Insights and Commentary on the Haggada

The fifteen *simanim* make an 8-line poem in which the rhyming scheme is AABB CCCB; see below. Some have suggested that it is likely that the sixth *siman* is רחץ – not רחצה – and the rhyming scheme should be AAAB CCCB.

1. Kadesh קדש Recite the Kiddush	**2. u-Rehatz** ורחץ Wash hands before eating *karpas*
3. Karpas כרפס Eat a vegetable dipped in salt water	**4. Yahatz** יחץ Break the middle matza, and hide the larger half of the *Afikomen*
5. Maggid מגיד Tell the story of Passover	**6. Rahtza (רחץ)** רחצה Wash hands for the meal
7. Motzi מוציא Say the *ha-Motzi* blessing	**8. Matza** מצה Eat *Matza*
9. Maror מרור Eat bitter herbs	**10. Korekh** כורך Eat matza and bitter herbs together
11. Shulhan Orekh שולחן-עורך Eat the festive meal	
12. Tzafun צפון Eat the *Afikomen*	**13. Barekh** ברך Say Grace After Meals
14. Hallel הלל Sing Hallel	**15. Nirtza** נרצה Conclude the Seder

סימנים

This mnemonic, as well as the very name *Seder*, emphasize that this night's rituals have a definite order, in which the ceremonies and practices need to be done. The issue of order, says the Maharal of Prague, is one of the major take-home lessons of the *Haggada*. The *Pesah* story teaches that events in this world are not haphazard. The Almighty is in control not only of the laws of nature and miracles, but also of history, and even what happens to the Jews in the Diaspora. There is order in the *Seder*, there is an order in nature, and there is order in Jewish history. Very often we cannot see the Divine hand as we go through history, but we can often see it as we glance backwards.

1. קַדֵּשׁ

Cover the Matzot, the first cup is poured and the Kiddush is recited.

When the festival begins on Friday night, begin here and include all passages in parentheses.

(בְּלַחַשׁ: וַיְהִי עֶרֶב וַיְהִי בֹקֶר)

יוֹם הַשִּׁשִּׁי (בראשית א:לא).

וַיְכֻלּוּ הַשָּׁמַיִם וְהָאָרֶץ וְכָל־צְבָאָם. וַיְכַל אֱלֹהִים בַּיּוֹם הַשְּׁבִיעִי מְלַאכְתּוֹ אֲשֶׁר עָשָׂה וַיִּשְׁבֹּת בַּיּוֹם הַשְּׁבִיעִי מִכָּל מְלַאכְתּוֹ אֲשֶׁר עָשָׂה. וַיְבָרֶךְ אֱלֹ־הִים אֶת יוֹם הַשְּׁבִיעִי וַיְקַדֵּשׁ אוֹתוֹ כִּי בוֹ שָׁבַת מִכָּל־מְלַאכְתּוֹ אֲשֶׁר בָּרָא אֱלֹהִים לַעֲשׂוֹת (בראשית ב:א-ג).

When the festival begins on a weekday, begin here:

סַבְרִי,

בָּרוּךְ אַתָּה ה', אֱלֹהֵינוּ מֶלֶךְ הָעוֹלָם בּוֹרֵא פְּרִי הַגָּפֶן.

קַדֵּשׁ

It is appropriate that the first ritual of the *Seder* is **Kadesh** – declaring the sanctity of the day by reciting *Kiddush*. This is because, the obligation/responsibility to sanctify time was the first commandment given to the Jewish people just prior to their exodus from Egypt with the words: "This month is for you **to fix** as the beginning of the months" (Ex. 12:2). As stressed by R. Ovadia Seforno (Commentary to Ex.), only fundamentally free individuals can choose to do with their time as they wish; only one liberated can volitionally dedicate his time and actions to the service of the Almighty – the source of sanctity. By sanctifying time, a Jew transforms what the ancient Greeks called *chronos* (simple chronological time) into *chiros* (special moments) of holiness. Thus, Judaism takes twenty-five-hour periods and converts them into what R. Abraham Joshua Heschel (*The Sabbath: Its Meaning for Modern Man*) referred to as "sanctuaries in time" – a Sabbath, a festival, or a Fast of Atonement.

Astonishingly, however, the *Seder* does not begin with a preliminary *berakha* on fulfilling the mitzva of *Sippur Yetzi'at Mitzrayim* or

1. Kadesh – First Cup

Cover the Matzot, the first cup is poured and the Kiddush is recited.

When the festival begins on Friday night, begin here and include all passages in parentheses.

(Quietly: And it was evening and it was morning)
the sixth day (Genesis 1:31).

And the heaven and the earth and all their hosts were completed. And on the seventh day, God finished His work which He had made, and He rested on the seventh day from all His work which He had made. And God blessed the seventh day and made it holy, for on it He rested from all His work which He, God, created to do (Genesis 2:1–3).

When the festival begins on a weekday, begin here:

With your permission, my masters and teachers:
Blessed are You, Lord, our God, King of the universe,
Who creates the fruit of the vine.

---

of *ve-Higadeta le-Vinkha* – discussing and teaching our children about the Exodus. *Haggada Mishnat Moshe* cites a similar discussion as to why there is no *birkat ha-mitzva* before reading *Shema*. Many scholars remind us that *Shema* is the acceptance of *Ol Malkhut Shamayim* – the Yoke of Heaven, while a *birkat ha-mitzva* is the acceptance of the Divine Yoke of *Mitzvot*. The acceptance of the yoke of Heaven is a logical prerequisite to the yoke of *mitzvot* – just as *Shema* needs to be said before *ve-Haya im shamo'a* (*Berakhot* 13a). The purpose of the *Haggada* is to inspire us to accept the yoke of Heaven as a prerequisite for accepting the yoke of commandments and doing the *mitzvot* of *Pesaḥ*, *Matza*, and *Maror*. To say a preliminary *berakha* on the mitzva of telling the tale before reading through the *Haggada* and accepting that yoke of Heaven – would be to put the proverbial cart before the horse.

אֲשֶׁר בָּרָא אֱלֹהִים לַעֲשׂוֹת

This verse seems incomplete: "…that God created **to do**" – to do what?

בָּרוּךְ אַתָּה ה', אֱלֹהֵינוּ מֶלֶךְ הָעוֹלָם אֲשֶׁר בָּחַר בָּנוּ מִכָּל־עָם וְרוֹמְמָנוּ מִכָּל־לָשׁוֹן וְקִדְּשָׁנוּ בְּמִצְוֹתָיו. וַתִּתֶּן לָנוּ ה' אֱלֹהֵינוּ בְּאַהֲבָה (לשבת: שַׁבָּתוֹת לִמְנוּחָה וּ) מוֹעֲדִים לְשִׂמְחָה, חַגִּים וּזְמַנִּים לְשָׂשׂוֹן, (לשבת: אֶת יוֹם הַשַּׁבָּת הַזֶּה וְ) אֶת יוֹם חַג הַמַּצּוֹת הַזֶּה

R. Soloveitchik (*Chumash Mesorat ha-Rav*, Gen. 2:3) posits that God purposely left Creation imperfect and unfinished. He expects man to uncover the rules and secrets of Creation, and to partner with Him in fighting evil, curing illness and disease, and completing the creative process He (the Almighty) started.

אֲשֶׁר בָּחַר בָּנוּ

The Jewish people have been chosen for responsibility – to fulfill Torah and *mitzvot*, not for privilege. Thus we say in *Kiddush*: "...who has chosen us from all the nations... and sanctified us through the commandments..." and in the benedictions before learning Torah: "...who has chosen us from all the nations and given us His Torah." On the subject of "Chosenness," the Talmud reports two famous yet seemingly contradictory rabbinic traditions regarding the giving of the Torah (*Avoda Zara* 2a–b). One indicates that God indeed chose Israel; the Midrash actually proposes that God held up Mount Sinai aloft over the people's heads threateningly and said that they had either "to accept the Torah or here be buried." The second tradition maintains, however, that the people of Israel chose God; it proposes the alternate image of God going around to the nations of the world unsuccessfully trying to give them the Torah as nation after nation rejected it upon hearing of some specific restriction or prohibition (*Sifrei, Devarim*, sec. 343.). Only the people of Israel said, "All that the Eternal has said we will do" (Ex. 19:8).

R. Norman Lamm (*Jewish Action* 65:1) suggests that these two traditions are not irreconcilable. Indeed, at Sinai, God chose the Israelites to receive the Torah and its commandments. Each member of the people of Israel, for better or for worse, is born into a people who have a divine calling. But revelation is of no value unless we willingly accept that calling unless the people of Israel volitionally choose God by

Blessed are You, Lord our God, King of the universe, Who has chosen us from among all people, and exalted us above all tongues, and sanctified us through His commandments. You, Lord our God, have given us with love (Shabbatot for rest and) festivals for happiness, festivals and seasons for joy: (this Shabbat and this) Festival of Matzot,

---

answering affirmatively, unless each Jew responds, like Father Avraham, "I am ready" (Gen. 22:1). I may be a Jew by virtue of God's choice, but only I can determine **what kind of Jew** I choose to be! This reciprocal relationship between God and Israel is reflected in *Devarim Rabba* (to Deut. 6:4), where we read: "You chose Me, and I too choose you." It is an idea made famous by a pair of couplets, one by William Norman Ewer who wrote: "How odd of God, to choose the Jews." To which Leon Roth responded: "It's not so odd – The Jews chose God."

Indeed, there exists a mutual bond of love between God and the Jewish people. God chose Israel out of love, as proclaimed in the benediction recited before the morning recitation of Shema, where the liturgist acclaims God using the words *ha-boḥer be-ammo Yisrael be-ahava* ("who has chosen His people Israel with love"). In almost antiphonal response, the congregation immediately sings out the verse from Deuteronomy (6:5): "You shall love your God with all your heart and with all your soul and with all your might."

חַג הַמַּצּוֹת הַזֶּה

Jewish tradition records two primary names for this holiday: *Hag ha-Pesaḥ* and *Hag ha-Matzot*. R. Isaac Levi of Berdichev (*Kedushat Levi, Parashat Bo*, s.v. *ve-Amaratem*) notes that Jews commonly call the holiday *Pesaḥ* (Passover). We do so in order to praise God and express our love to Him for sparing His people by passing over their homes, when afflicting the first-born Egyptians in Egypt. God, on the other hand, calls the holiday in the Torah *Hag ha-Matzot* in order to praise the people of Israel for their trust in Him, their *hipazon* – "rush to freedom" (Deut. 16:3) which is reflected in the unleavened nature of the *Matzot*. The Torah recounts that upon being notified of their pending departure from Egypt, and urged on by the Egyptians to leave, the people of Israel didn't tarry to prepare food for the trip. Instead, they

זְמַן חֵרוּתֵנוּ. (לשבת: בְּאַהֲבָה) מִקְרָא קֹדֶשׁ זֵכֶר לִיצִיאַת מִצְרָיִם. כִּי בָנוּ בָחַרְתָּ וְאוֹתָנוּ קִדַּשְׁתָּ מִכָּל הָעַמִּים. (לשבת: וְשַׁבָּת) וּמוֹעֲדֵי קָדְשֶׁךָ (לשבת: בְּאַהֲבָה וּבְרָצוֹן) בְּשִׂמְחָה וּבְשָׂשׂוֹן הִנְחַלְתָּנוּ. בָּרוּךְ אַתָּה ה', מְקַדֵּשׁ (לשבת: הַשַּׁבָּת וְ) יִשְׂרָאֵל וְהַזְּמַנִּים.

---

immediately took their dough on their shoulders and followed Moshe into the desert – with complete faith that God would continue to provide for all their needs.

R. Ovadia Yosef (*Haggada Hazon Ovadia*) views the double name as a lesson in modesty. *Hag ha-Pesah* reminds us that God skipped over the Israelite homes in Egypt as he smote the Egyptian firstborn. We should, therefore, remember with pride and gratitude that the Almighty Himself miraculously intervened on our behalf to redeem us from Egypt. We are a nation of value and purpose. On the other hand, *Hag ha-Matzot* recalls our humble slave origins – symbolized by unleavened bread. We memorialize the fact that we did **not** leave Egypt as conquerors, but rushed to freedom – improperly prepared – driven by God's command and the Egyptian's urging.

זְמַן חֵרוּתֵנוּ

As already noted in our "Introductory Essays" # 7, R. Jonathan Sacks (*Haggada*) remarks that although *Pesah* is a night of questions, there is one we do not ask, and it is truly significant. Why was there a *Pesah* in the first place? Why the years of suffering and slavery? Why did God not arrange for our forefathers Avraham or Yitzhak or Yaakov simply to inherit the land of Canaan? If the Israelites had not gone down to Egypt in the days of Yosef, there would have been no servitude, no suffering, and no need for redemption. Furthermore, why is it so important to relive this servitude yearly?

R. Sacks argues that the Hebrew term for freedom, *herut*, refers not only to physical freedom, but, more importantly, to mental, moral, and intellectual redemption as well. We are meant to be independent thinkers with independent values. But the truth is that freedom is not natural. On the contrary, the history of ages has demonstrated that the natural order in human societies, as it is in the animal kingdom, is that

season of our Freedom (in love), a holy convocation in remembrance of the Exodus from Egypt. For You have chosen us and sanctified us from all the nations, and You gave us (the Shabbat and) Your holy festivals (with love and favor), in happiness and joy, as a heritage. Blessed are You, God, Who sanctifies (the Shabbat and] Israel and the festive seasons.

---

the strong prey on and dominate the weak. Nothing is rarer or harder to achieve than a society of equal dignity for all. It would seem therefore that "Israel had to lose its freedom before it could cherish it." Often, it is only to what we lose, that we pay full attention.

Israel had to suffer the experience of slavery and degradation before it could learn, know, and feel intuitively that there was something morally wrong with oppression. Nor could it, or any other people, carry this message in perpetuity without reliving it every year, tasting the harsh tang of the bread of oppression and the bitterness of slavery. Thus, at the birth of the nation, a longing for freedom was created that was at the very core of its memory and identity.

מְקַדֵּשׁ (לשבת: הַשַּׁבָּת וְ) יִשְׂרָאֵל וְהַזְּמַנִּים

The Talmud (*Berakhot* 49a) notes that in this closing *berakha*, there is a specific order of sanctification: God first sanctifies the Sabbath followed by the People of Israel, and only then the holidays. Why this order? After all, all sanctity flows from the Eternal. The answer is that the *Sabbath* was sanctified directly by God long before the Nation of Israel appeared on the stage of history. Israel too was sanctified directly by the Almighty at Sinai. Israel, in turn, was empowered – nay commanded – to fix the date of *Rosh Hodesh* with the verse: "This month was given **to you** as the first of the months" (Ex. 12:2). By setting the time of *Rosh Hodesh*, the People of Israel fix – and thus sanctify – the timing of the *Mo'adim* (holidays and fasts).

Rabbenu Bahya (Ex. 13:4) comments on Haza"l's use of the term *zemanim* (times) for the holidays, rather than the biblical term *mo'adim* (Lev. 23:4). He argues that they did so because the Torah itself describes each holiday as coming at a particular *zeman* (time): *Pesah* in springtime (*aviv*); *Shavu'ot* during wheat harvest time (*ketzir ha-hitim*); and *Sukkot* at harvest time (*asif*).

If the festival falls on Saturday night, the following is recited:

בָּרוּךְ אַתָּה ה', אֱלֹהֵינוּ מֶלֶךְ הָעוֹלָם, בּוֹרֵא מְאוֹרֵי הָאֵשׁ.

בָּרוּךְ אַתָּה ה', אֱלֹהֵינוּ מֶלֶךְ הָעוֹלָם הַמַּבְדִּיל בֵּין קֹדֶשׁ לְחֹל. בֵּין אוֹר לְחֹשֶׁךְ. בֵּין יִשְׂרָאֵל לָעַמִּים. בֵּין יוֹם הַשְּׁבִיעִי לְשֵׁשֶׁת יְמֵי הַמַּעֲשֶׂה. בֵּין קְדֻשַּׁת שַׁבָּת לִקְדֻשַּׁת יוֹם טוֹב הִבְדַּלְתָּ, וְאֶת־יוֹם הַשְּׁבִיעִי מִשֵּׁשֶׁת יְמֵי הַמַּעֲשֶׂה קִדַּשְׁתָּ. הִבְדַּלְתָּ וְקִדַּשְׁתָּ אֶת־עַמְּךָ יִשְׂרָאֵל בִּקְדֻשָּׁתֶךָ. בָּרוּךְ אַתָּה ה', הַמַּבְדִּיל בֵּין קֹדֶשׁ לְקֹדֶשׁ.

On all nights conclude here:

בָּרוּךְ אַתָּה ה', אֱלֹהֵינוּ מֶלֶךְ הָעוֹלָם, שֶׁהֶחֱיָנוּ וְקִיְּמָנוּ וְהִגִּיעָנוּ לַזְּמַן הַזֶּה.

The cup of wine should be drunk while reclining on the left side, symbolizing freedom.

2. וּרְחַץ

The hands are ritually washed without a blessing.

3. כַּרְפַּס

All participants take a piece of *karpas* [a vegetable other than *maror*), less than the size of an olive, dip it in salt water and eat it without reclining after reciting the following blessing. You should have in mind that this blessing includes the *maror* which is eaten later on in the *Seder*.

בָּרוּךְ אַתָּה ה', אֱלֹהֵינוּ מֶלֶךְ הָעוֹלָם. בּוֹרֵא פְּרִי הָאֲדָמָה.

כַּרְפַּס

Now that *Kiddush* is complete, the time has come to set the stage for the "Four Questions," but more importantly for the answers. The Questions and Answers (up to and including the second cup of wine)

If the festival falls on Saturday night, the following is recited:

Blessed are You, Lord our God, King of the universe, Creator of lights of fire.

Blessed are You, Lord our God, King of the universe, Who distinguishes between holiness and secular, between light and darkness, between Israel and nations, between the seventh day and the six days of activity. You have made a distinction between the holiness of Shabbat and the holiness of Ḥag; and You have sanctified the seventh day above the six days of labor. You distinguished and sanctified Your nation, Israel, with Your holiness. Blessed are You, God, Who distinguishes between holiness [of Shabbat] and holiness [of Ḥag].

On all nights conclude here:

Blessed are You, Lord our God, King of the universe, Who has granted us life, sustained us, and enabled us to reach this season.

The cup of wine should be drunk while reclining on the left side, symbolizing freedom.

2. U-Reḥatz

The hands are ritually washed without a blessing.

3. Karpas

All participants take a piece of karpas [a vegetable other than maror], less than the size of an olive, dip it in salt water and eat it without reclining after reciting the following blessing. You should have in mind that this blessing includes the maror which is eaten later on in the Seder.

Blessed are You, Lord our God, King of the universe, Who creates the fruit of the earth.

---

constitute the *Maggid* section of the *Seder*, and it is through them that we recount the Exodus story. To attract the children's attention and pique their interest, we begin by eating *karpas* – vegetables (e.g., parsley, celery, or potatoes) usually immersed in a sauce or dip. (*Tosafot, Pesaḥim*

4. יַחַץ

Break the middle *matza* into two. The larger piece is wrapped, hidden from view, and set aside to serve as the *Afikoman*.

The smaller piece is put back between the two whole *matzot*.

114a, had no particular preference; R. Hananel, Rashi and Rambam used *haroset*; while R. Tam's preference was saltwater – as is the general custom nowadays.) Seeing this, the child thinks that the meal is about to begin since vegetables are an appetizer always accompanied by the main meal (Rashbam, *Pesahim* 114a). But this does not happen and the child is led to ask. (More about this when we discuss the Four Questions.) Parsley and celery are green vegetables symbolizing spring and *Nisan* as *Hodesh ha-Aviv* – the month of spring (Ex. 23:15 and 34:18; Deut. 15:1). In addition, during Roman times parsley was used as a breath freshener at the **end** of the meal. Its use at the **beginning** of the *Seder* may have prodded the child to take note of other strange occurrences at this festive meal. In the cold April climes of Eastern Europe, parsley and celery were unknown or unavailable for *karpas* – so potatoes were commonly used (*Arukh ha-Shulhan*, OH 473:10).

However, prior to eating the *karpas*, we wash our hands without a *berakha* (*u-rehatz*). The major reason given for this washing is that this is an example of *Davar she-tibulo be-mashke* – "something that is immersed into a liquid" (*Mishna Berura*, OH, 473:6 nos. 51 and 52). However, R. Yehiel Michel Epstein (*Arukh ha-Shulhan*, OH 473:18) finds this reason insufficient since we are not stringent all year round about washing before eating immersed foods. Therefore, he posits that we do so specifically tonight – so that the children will ask why this night is so different.

יַחַץ

The Torah writes regarding Matza (Deut. 16:3): "You shall not eat anything leavened; for seven days you shall eat מַצּוֹת לֶחֶם עֹנִי – unleavened bread – for you departed from the land of Egypt בְּחִפָּזוֹן – hurriedly."

4. Yahatz

Break the middle matza into two. The larger piece is wrapped, hidden from view, and set aside to serve as the Afikoman.

The smaller piece is put back between the two whole matzot.

The Gemara (*Pesahim* 36a) indicates that the word עני is written like the word עָנִי (which means poor), but vocalized עֹנִי (meaning distress or recitation). From the use of a word with a multiplicity of meanings, the Talmud derives several intentions. Firstly, the fact that we vocalize the word as *oni* indicates that it is the bread over which many matters are recited. Rashi (ad loc.) indicates that this is an allusion to the Passover *Seder*, at which one recites the *Haggada* and *Hallel* in the presence of Matza. The second inference is that just as a poor person is wont to eat a **piece** of bread, for lack of a whole loaf, so too, here at the *Seder* we should use a broken piece of Matza. As a result of this double inference, prior to reciting the *Haggada*, we break the middle Matza (יחץ) – to prepare a broken piece of Matza. As a result, we assure that the "the bread over which many matters are recited" – לֶחֶם עֹנִי – is at the same time a לֶחֶם עָנִי – a poor person's broken bread (R. Shlomo Zalman Auerbach, *Haggada*).

Tosafot (*Pesahim* 116a, *s.v Ma Darko*) understands that as a result of the above discussion, we set up the *Seder* Table with **three** whole *matzot*. Two *Matzot* are *lehem mishne* for *Hamotzi* like every Shabbat and holiday where we commemorate the double portion of Manna that fell in preparation for Shabbat in the desert. In addition, however, we also need a third broken Matza for לֶחֶם עָנִי – a poor person's bread. It is this third broken Matza that we prepare specifically now – just before *Maggid* – as just discussed. The larger half of the broken Matza is saved/hidden for *Afikoman*. Maimonides (*Hil. Hametz u-Matza*, 8:6) disagrees with *Tosafot*, maintaining that לֶחֶם עָנִי teaches that, instead of two whole loaves on *Pesah* for *lehem mishne*, one-and-a-half suffice. Tradition follows the *Tosafot* (*Shulhan Arukh*, OH 473:6).

The larger half of the broken middle Matza is traditionally wrapped

5. מַגִּיד

Uncover the *matzot* and raise them saying aloud:

---

and saved until *Tzafun* – to be used as the *Afikoman* (*Shulhan Arukh*, *O.H.* 493:6). R. Chaim of Brisk (cited by R. Joseph B. Soloveitchik, *Exalted Evening*, p. 124, and by R. Moshe Shternbuch, *Mo'adim u-Zemanim*, 7, sec. 188) explains that the wrapping and hiding of the *Afikoman* at this juncture is yet another symbolic commemoration of the *Korban Pesah*. The latter, like all sacrifices, had to be slaughtered by day, before sunset. However, *halakha* also requires that one partake of the meat of the *Korban Pesah* – *al ha-sova* – "with a satiated stomach," meaning, after the meal. For this reason, we eat the *Afikoman* – the commemoration of the *Korban Pesah* – after we complete the meal at the *Seder*. The large time gap between the *korban's* slaughtering and consumption necessitated the protection of the sacrificial meat from *tuma* (ritual impurity). People would, therefore, wrap and hide the meat of the *korban* until after the meal. In commemoration, we wrap and hide the *Afikoman* until the time for its consumption.

מַגִּיד

The *Maggid* section is the long narrative section of the *Haggada* where we recount the Exodus story. This pivotal section formally begins with *Ha Lahma Anya* and the Four Questions and concludes with the first two chapters of *Hallel* and the *berakha* of *ga'al Yisrael* prior to the second cup. The goal is to create within each participant a strong sense of **personal** redemption and **personal** indebtedness to the Almighty. R. Joseph B. Soloveitchik suggests that to understand how this goal is accomplished, we need to realize that the *Maggid* section is divided into three parts.

The first part, which stretches from *Avadim hayinu* until *Arami oved avi*, deals in part with the philosophical principles that are the basis of

5. Maggid

Uncover the *matzot* and raise them saying aloud:

Mitzvat Sippur Yetzi'at Mitzrayim – the obligation to tell the story of the Exodus from Egypt. These include:

1. that we were enslaved both physically and spiritually and were ultimately redeemed on both planes;
2. that we are eternally indebted to the Almighty;
3. that we must pass this tradition onto our children – each child in a manner appropriate to him or her.

This first part also deals with the laws and rules of *Mitzvat Sippur Yetzi'at Mitzrayim*. These include: **Who is obligated**? Even the well-educated; **How much**? The more the better; **When**? When Matza and Maror are lying before you; and **Why**? (1) *Avadim hayinu* – We were slaves and are now free. (2) *mi-Tehilla ovdei avoda zara* – Our forebears were initially idolaters and we now have been drawn near God's service; (3) *be-khol dor va-dor* – In every generation, there are those who rise up to destroy us and God saves us from their clutches.

The second part goes from *Arami oved avi* through *Pesah, Matza, u-Maror* and is the formal narrative portion of *Maggid*. It is here that we detail and hopefully **relive** the experience of enslavement and then the ultimate miraculous redemption. It is here that our involvement, imagination, insight, and creativity have the greatest impact on attaining the desired goal of reenacting and reliving the Exodus experience.

The final portion of *Maggid* beginning with *be-Khol dor va-dor* reiterates that it is a Jewish person's obligation to envision himself or herself as having just left Egypt. We are not merely the progeny of those who left Egypt three millennia ago. Rather we ourselves went out and, therefore, feel driven to sing the Almighty's praise. We then recite the first two chapters of the six that comprise *Hallel*.

הָא לַחְמָא עַנְיָא

הָא לַחְמָא עַנְיָא דִּי אֲכָלוּ אַבְהָתָנָא בְּאַרְעָא דְמִצְרָיִם. כָּל דִּכְפִין יֵיתֵי וְיֵיכֹל,

---

הָא לַחְמָא עַנְיָא

We have cited R. Joseph B. Soloveitchik's comment that "[A Jew] does not simply recollect the past or just **remember** bygones, but **re-experiences** that which has been" (*Out of the Whirlwind*, p. 14). Thus at the beginning of *Maggid*, the *Haggada* begins its tale by transporting the *Seder* participants back some 3500 years to the biblical land of the Nile. The *Haggada*'s story of the Exodus begins with a variation of "Show and Tell." With the *matzot* exposed, the assembled say in Aramaic: *Ha lahma anya* – "This is the bread of oppression that our ancestors ate in Egypt." The use of Aramaic – an ancient cognate language of Hebrew – gives the statement an aura of times long past. It sets the mood by putting us in a foreign land. (See the insight of R. Dov Lior in our comment below on לְשָׁנָה הַבָּאָה בְּאַרְעָא דְיִשְׂרָאֵל.) This is why *Ha lahma anya* is an integral part of *Maggid* – not just the answer to the four questions beginning with *Avadim hayinu*.

This declaration raises a plethora of questions. Firstly, the clear implication of *Ha lahma anya* is that we eat Matza to remember the bread of oppression that our forebears ate as slaves in Egypt. Presumably, because of hunger, exhaustion, and time pressure, they did not have the luxury to let their dough rise. What resulted perforce was unleavened Matza bread. Yet, this stands in seeming opposition to a statement recited towards the end of *Maggid*. There, Rabban Gamliel posits that we eat Matza in commemoration of our rush to freedom: "...that we did not have time to allow the bread to rise." This very contradiction actually appears not only in the *Haggada* but more notably in a verse in the Torah (Deut. 16:3): "You shall not eat anything leavened with it; for seven days you shall eat *lehem oni* – unleavened bread and/or bread of oppression – for you departed from the land of Egypt in haste." On the one hand, Matza is referred to as *lehem oni* – the bread of oppression; yet in the next phrase it indicates that Matza commemorates *hipazon* – haste, the rush to freedom.

As a result of this question, R. Samuel ben Meir (Rashbam, *Haggada*)

Ha Lahma Anya

This is the bread of affliction that our fathers ate in the land of Egypt.

posits that the phrase "...that our ancestors ate in Egypt..." refers to the Matza the Israelites ate on the *Seder* night in Egypt, also in haste. The term *lehem oni* appearing in the verse merely refers to the unleavened form of the bread, not when it was eaten.

A perhaps more satisfying answer appears in the Bible commentary of R. Moses ben Nahman (Ramban, Nahmanides) to the above verse (end of Deut. 16:2). He posits that there are indeed **two** reasons for eating Matza, both of which are valid. At the beginning of the *Seder*, we visualize the unleavened Matza as quickly made bread due to hardship and affliction; this transports us back some 3300 years to the Egypt of slavery – ready to start our Exodus tale. But at the end of *Maggid*, following the Ten Plagues, and with the Israelites on the verge of liberation, we now identify the Matza **also** as the bread of haste prepared in our "rush to freedom."

We would like to take Ramban's idea one step further. As we declare in *Ha lahma anya*, Matza was undoubtedly the bread of oppression, affliction, and slavery. But that is not the reason why **we** continue to eat it at the *Seder* in post-Exodus generations. Rather, as stated at the end of *Maggid*, **we** eat unleavened bread with leaning as freed individuals as a **celebrative** festive act, commemorating the haste of our progenitor's "rush to freedom."

R. David Zvi Hoffman (Commentary to Deut. 16:3) asks why this haste is so important. He observes that the key phrase (Ex. 12:39) is *Ki gorshu mi-mitzrayim*, the Israelites were literally driven out. The Egyptians pressured them to leave as fast as possible, presumably for fear of their own lives. But as a result, the Israelites could no longer claim that they left at their leisure as conquerors: that it was their strength and might that won them their freedom.

בְּאַרְעָא דְמִצְרָיִם

We have noted above that the use of Aramaic in *Ha lahma anya*, and have suggested that it sets the mood by putting us in a foreign land, outside Israel, at the start of the *Seder*. Indeed, Aramaic was the Lingua

כָּל דִּצְרִיךְ יֵיתֵי וְיִפְסַח. הָשַׁתָּא הָכָא. לְשָׁנָה הַבָּאָה בְּאַרְעָא דְיִשְׂרָאֵל. הָשַׁתָּא עַבְדֵי. לְשָׁנָה הַבָּאָה בְּנֵי חוֹרִין.

Franca of Mesopotamia outside the Land of Israel from ca. 900 BCE to ca. 650 CE. This 1500 year period includes both the destruction of the First and Second Temples and the corresponding exiles. Some suggest that this paragraph was introduced when Aramaic was widely spoken. The Aramaic was retained in this selection to communicate that the *Haggada* should be intelligible to the participants and may be said in any language. This ruling is cited by R. Moses Isserles in *Shulhan Arukh* (OH, 473:6).

כָּל דִכְפִין יֵיתֵי וְיֵיכֹל

Here, at the beginning of *Maggid*, we issue a proclamation inviting the poor to join us for the observance of the *Seder*. The question naturally arises as to why we include this invitation as we introduce the story of *Yetzi'at Mitzrayim*. R. Joseph B. Soloveitchik (*Haggada Si'ah Ha-Grid*), suggested that inviting needy guests is a display of *herut* (freedom), one of the prominent themes of the *Seder*. A slave does not legally own any property – as a master enjoys ownership over everything in the slave's possession – and thus it is only after achieving freedom that we have the opportunity to perform the mitzva of charity. At the *Seder*, when we are to conduct ourselves in a manner that reflects freedom, we exhibit our status as free men and women by extending an open invitation to the poor – a privilege reserved only for those who are not under any person's rule.

Additionally, R. Soloveitchik observed that concern for the needy members of our nation is integral to the *Pesah* observance. The Rama (O.C. 429:1) famously codified the obligation of *kimha de-pisha*, a communal effort to raise and distribute funds to the poor before *Pesah* to enable them to buy the necessary goods for the holiday. Revealingly, the Rama mentions this halakha in the context of the laws of *Pesah*, and not with the laws of charity in the *Yoreh De'a* section. This is because on *Pesah* we celebrate our national – and not just individual – freedom, and we thus bear a collective responsibility to ensure that all our fellow Jews are truly "free" in the sense of financial viability. By the same token, as

Whoever is hungry, let him come and eat; whoever is in need, let him come and celebrate the Pesaḥ festival. This year we are here [in the exile]; next year – in the land of Israel. This year we are slaves; next year – free people.

---

we sit down to observe the *Seder*, we declare our willingness to assist all those who cannot afford to observe *Pesaḥ* on their own. We proclaim our commitment to our national *ḥerut*, that as part of our *Pesaḥ* observance, we are prepared to share our assets with the needy to ensure that all *Am Yisrael* is truly "free."

R. Pinchas HaLevi Horowitz (*Sefer Hafla'a*) cites his father as pointing out that we first say: "All who are hungry, should come to eat" and only then "All who need, can join us for a paschal meal." This is because, at the time of the Temple, the Paschal lamb had to be eaten *al ha-sova*, on a full stomach. So first comes the meal, followed by a portion of the paschal lamb at the end.

כָּל דִּצְרִיךְ יֵיתֵי וְיִפְסַח

The verse in *Eikha* (Lamentations 1:3) states: *Galta Yehuda me-oni* – Judah has gone into exile because of *oni* (oppression). *Midrash Eikha* homiletically suggests that Judea went into exile because they were not careful of the rules of *leḥem oni* – the laws of *Ḥametz* and Matza. Alternatively, they were exiled because they were lax regarding support for the *ani* – the indigent. R. Chaim Yosef David Azulai (*Haggada Simḥat ha-Regel*), cites scholars who see our passage as a prayerful response to this *Midrash*. If the reason for our exile is laxity in observing *leḥem oni*, then *Ha laḥma anya*! Here is the evidence that we are now properly careful with Matza. If, however, we were careless about the poor and indigent – then let all those in need and hungry come to our table. Thus we conclude this paragraph with the prayer that in the merit of our fulfillment of these *mitzvot*, may we celebrate *Pesaḥ* next year in Israel.

לְשָׁנָה הַבָּאָה בְּאַרְעָא דְיִשְׂרָאֵל

We call attention to the double appearance of the prayer: Next year in Israel or Jerusalem, once at the beginning of *Maggid* and once at the end of the *Seder* by *Ḥasal Siddur Pesaḥ*. R. Dov Lior (*Resp. Devar Ḥevron*,

מַה נִּשְׁתַּנָּה

The matzot are lowered but remain uncovered for the entire reading of the Haggada. The second cup is poured and a child asks "The Four Questions" (After the child, or children recite "The Four Questions," some have the custom that all assembled repeat it.)

Zemanim, p. 109) notes that in the first appearance, the use of Aramaic is meant to signal that at the beginning of *Maggid* the Israelites are in *Galut* (the diaspora); the Jews don't even speak their own language (see הָא לַחְמָא עַנְיָא above). By the end of the *Seder*, we have left Egypt and at that point express our faith that we will eventually return to our country, build our Temple, and converse in our own language. R. David Tamar (*Alei Tamar*, J.T, *Megilla* I:1) points out that in contradistinction to *le-Shana haba'a bi-Yerushalayim* which is said primarily by *Ashkenazic* Jewry at the end of the *Seder*, *le-Shana haba'a be-ar'a de-Yisrael* is said by *Sefaradim* and *Teimanim* as well at the beginning. R. Tamar suggests that this prayer dates back to the Babylonian *amora'im* and is based on the oath Jews took on their way to Babylonia (Psalms 137:5): "If I forget you, O Jerusalem, let my right hand wither" – but was expanded to the Land of Israel as a whole.

הָשַׁתָּא עַבְדֵי. לְשָׁנָה הַבָּאָה בְּנֵי חוֹרִין

R. Moshe Shternbuch (*Haggada Mo'adim u-Zemanim*) indicates that the order of these last sentences suggests that first we arrive in Israel yet remain subject to the "Dominion of the Nations." This will be followed at a later stage by being totally independent. Modern history certainly seems to align with this prophetic wording.

מַה נִּשְׁתַּנָּה

Here we try to involve the children by encouraging them to ask questions. The Torah (Deut. 6:20–21) states: "When your child **asks** you in the future, saying: 'What is the meaning of the testimonies, and the statutes, and the ordinances, which the Lord our God has commanded you?' Then you will declare to your son: 'We were Pharaoh's slaves in Egypt, and the Lord brought us out of Egypt with a mighty hand…'"

Mah Nishtana – The Four Questions

The matzot are lowered but remain uncovered for the entire reading of the Haggada. The second cup is poured and a child asks "The Four Questions" (After the child, or children recite "The Four Questions," some have the custom that all assembled repeat it.)

The sages understood the Torah to be indicating that the retelling of the Egypt story should preferably be part of an intergenerational dialogue. The *Seder* discussion should be initiated by questions asked by the child regarding the reasons behind the outstanding and remarkable practices of the *Pesah Seder*. Indeed, the Mishnah (*Pesahim* 10:4) proposed "Four Questions" (*Matza*, *Maror*, *Korban Pesah* – Paschal lamb, and two dippings) to introduce this discussion of the Exodus, its details, and purpose. (After the destruction of the Temple and the cessation of the *Korban Pesah*, the *Pesah* question was replaced by one about leaning.) Additional questions are encouraged as well.

מַה נִּשְׁתַּנָּה

R. Ovadiah Yosef (*Hazon Ovadia, Pesah* I) asks why four questions are only asked on Passover and not on other holidays. After all, *Sukkot* has the *Sukka* for seven days which is unique and strange. With a wry smile, he points out that over the many years in exile, Jews have become accustomed to leaving their comfortable permanent homes to live in temporary ramshackle structures. But the opposite experience, dining luxuriously at a full table with exotic foods, raises many questions – and the child asks!

R. Elijah Kramer (Vilna Gaon; *Haggada*) focuses on the pivotal phrase *ha-layla ha-zeh* – This night. As a general rule, the central holiday *mitzvot* are performed during the day. But on *Pesah*, it is the *Seder* **night** with all its many *mitzvot* and rituals that stand out. The child then proceeds to cite several examples of these special rites, ceremonies, and traditions: Matza, *Maror*, dipping, leaning. To this, the *Haggada* answers: the miracle of our redemption and liberation began tonight – hence, we celebrate at night.

Many of the commentaries are troubled that of the four questions, one (dipping) is not answered at all, while the others are not addressed

מַה נִּשְׁתַּנָּה הַלַּיְלָה הַזֶּה מִכָּל הַלֵּילוֹת?!
שֶׁבְּכָל הַלֵּילוֹת אָנוּ אוֹכְלִין חָמֵץ וּמַצָּה, הַלַּיְלָה הַזֶּה – כֻּלּוֹ מַצָּה.

specifically until the end of *Maggid*. R. Don Isaac Abravanel (*Haggada Zevah Pesah*) suggests that in truth there is only **one** question with four examples. The one question is: How different is this night – which is full of contradictory themes – from all other nights? On the one hand, at the *Seder* we do actions that symbolize slavery and hardship, like eating unleavened bread and bitter herbs; at other times, we act in a way that reflects freedom and wealth, like leaning and dipping. To this, the *Haggada* answers: *Avadim hayinu… va-yotzi'einu* – Tonight, on the 15th of Nissan, we were both slaves and free men.

But there may well be a pedagogic reason why only three of the questions are answered and only at the end of *Maggid*. Just as we encourage the children to ask good, tough questions, we also want them to learn that many good questions don't have simple answers, and require extensive study before they can be resolved. Other questions don't have answers at all, and one has to learn to "live with questions" – in the hope that an answer may eventually be found. In the particular case of the two dippings, this strange behavior has no real answer. It was introduced by the Rabbis of the Talmud to arouse the child (*hekera le-tinokot*; *Pesahim* 114b) to pay attention to the special quality of the *Seder* night and ask!

חָמֵץ וּמַצָּה

The child's first question about eating Matza resolves an interesting halakhic inquiry. It is rabbinically forbidden to eat Matza on Erev *Pesah* (the 14th of *Nisan*) so that one will eat Matza that night at the *Seder* with zest. R. Chaim Soloveitchik of Brisk (cited by R. Joseph B. Soloveitchik – as brought by R. Michel Shurkin, *Harerei Kedem*, II, sec. 86, end) was asked whether this prohibition begins from the morning of Erev *Pesah* or even the previous evening (the eve of the 14th of *Nisan*). He argued that the wording of the first of the four questions (which appears in Talmud *Pesahim* 116a) resolves this issue simply. The opening of the question reads: "On all other nights, we eat *Hametz* or Matza…" Thus Matza is clearly permitted every night of the year,

How different this night is from all other nights?!

On all other nights we eat hametz or matza, but on this night only matza.

---

including the eve of the 14th of *Nisan*. R. Moshe Meiselman reports a Soloveitchik family tradition that R. Chaim adduced this proof as a precocious child of six (R. Aryeh Leib Lupianski, *Haggada Shirat ha-Leviyim mi-Bet Brisk*).

R. Moshe Blau (*Haggada Mishnat Moshe*) asks why *Hametz* precedes Matza. He responds by citing the Halakhic principle (*Mishna Horayot* 3:6): *Tadir ve-she-eino tadir: tadir ḳodem* – "that which appears more frequently precedes the infrequent."

R. Shaul Lowenstam (*Binyan Ariel, Hadrei Torah, Bet Mo'ed – le-Hag ha-Matzot*) suggests a totally different direction for this question. He observes that the first of the four *Ma Nishtana* questions is normally translated as: "On all other nights we eat *Hametz* or *Matza*; tonight, only *Matza*." Nevertheless, the Hebrew text actually says: "*Hametz u-Matza*" which literally means that every night of the year, we eat *Hametz* **and** Matza*h*. The fact is, however, that rarely, at any given meal, do we eat both *Hametz* and Matza together. If the author of the *Haggada* actually meant "either/or," he should have used the same formulation *she-bekhol ha-leilot anu okhlim* **bein** *Hametz* **u-vein** *Matza* – as used in the last question on leaning? R. Lowenstam suggests that this first question focuses on the *Korban Pesach*, which is a specific case of a *Korban Toda* (a Thanksgiving Offering). Normally when we bring a *Korban Toda*, the animal offering is accompanied by forty *lahmei Toda* (Thanksgiving breads) – ten of which are leavened (*Hametz*) while thirty others are unleavened (Matza). These loaves together with the meat of the sacrifice must be completed during the day it is brought and the following night. On Pesah, of course, only Matza loaves are permissible. The *Binyan Ariel* suggests that the first question in the *Haggada* should be understood as follows: On all other nights when we eat a *Korban Toda*, we do so with *Hametz* and Matza loaves together. On Seder night, we eat the *Korban Pesach* accompanied by **only** Matza loaves.

For completeness, we cite R. Zvi Hirsch of Harodna (*Haggada Zera Gad*) who argues that R. Lowenstam's question is more simply resolved if we note that on other nights of the year, *Hametz* **and** Matza*h* can actually be eaten simultaneously, in one mouthful. By contrast, leaning

שֶׁבְּכָל הַלֵּילוֹת אָנוּ אוֹכְלִין שְׁאָר יְרָקוֹת – הַלַּיְלָה הַזֶּה מָרוֹר.

שֶׁבְּכָל הַלֵּילוֹת אֵין אָנוּ מַטְבִּילִין אֲפִילוּ פַּעַם אֶחָת – הַלַּיְלָה הַזֶּה שְׁתֵּי פְעָמִים.

---

and not-leaning are mutually exclusive, hence, a ***bein … u-ϑein*** terminology is used.

הַלַּיְלָה הַזֶּה מָרוֹר

The preferred translation of this question is: Normally, one acquires for his *Yom Tov* meal, a broad selection of tasty vegetables, and doesn't go out of his way to purchase specifically bitter herbs. Yet that is exactly what we do for *Seder* night.

שְׁתֵּי פְעָמִים

A careful look at this third question raises several problems:

(1) Firstly, the text suggests to the modern reader that it is the very dunking of the items that catches the child's eye. Yet it is well known that, during the Talmudic period, eating generally involved immersing the selected food item in a variety of dips, sauces, dressings, or spreads. Such a practice is still very common today throughout the Middle East – including, the widespread dipping of pita bread or *lafa* in *Humus, Tehina,* or various *salatim* (salads). In response, most *Rishonim* (medieval scholars of the 11th to 15th century including Rashbam, *Tosafot*, Meiri; see *Haggada Sheleima*) suggest that the question really centers on the eating of vegetables (done generally with dipping in some dressing) **by themselves**, and not as a side-dish for the main meal.

(2) Secondly, why are two dippings mentioned (*Karpas* and *Maror*), when there are really three (*Karpas, Maror,* and *Korekh*)? To this query, one can easily respond that the last two dippings are considered one – since they are done one after the other, and are merely two different ways of eating *Maror* (*Haggada Sheleima*).

(3) But this leads us to ask why *Haza"l* instituted only two "dippings" and no more. Why not four – asked my brother R. Shael Frimer – since it is a night of fours?! R. Abraham Danzig (*Haggada Toldot Adam*) insightfully points to the two dippings (*tibulim*) mentioned in the Torah

On all other nights we eat any kind of vegetable, but on this night we eat maror.

On all other nights we need not dip even once, but on this night we do so twice!

---

which relate directly to the Egyptian saga. The first is the dipping of Yosef's colored coat in goat blood (Gen. 37:31) by his brothers. This was to cover up Yosef's sale which eventually brought the whole family down to Egypt. The second is the dipping of hyssop in the blood of the paschal lamb, and the placement of the blood on the lintel and two doorposts of Israelite dwellings (Ex. 12:22) – on the eve of their redemptive Exodus. David Kessler notes that the nature of these two incidents corresponds nicely with the dips traditionally used in *Ashkenazi* homes for the *tibulim*. The Yosef case led us into Egyptian exile and servitude; hence, for the first dipping (*karpas*) we use salt water (symbolic of tears) or sour vinegar. The second incident was the commencement of our Exodus; thus, we dip *Maror* in sweet *haroset*.

(4) More fundamentally, however, why does the child ask about two dippings, when until now he has only seen one? Why do the questions focus on these four themes and not others, like four cups of wine? And lastly, what in the *Seder* at this point sparks his curiosity? Why does the child ask his questions now?

To answer these questions, we need a short preface. *Tosafot* (*Pesahim* 114a) indicates that when the Second Temple was standing (before 70 CE) there were also four questions, with one fundamental difference. Following the two questions on Matza and *Maror*, the third question dealt with the paschal lamb – "On all other nights we eat either roasted, stewed, or cooked meat, but on this night all the meat is roasted." The fourth question dealt with the two dippings. According to Maimonides (*Hil. Hametz u-Matza*, 8:2), the question regarding leaning was the fifth question. Most *Rishonim*, however, maintain that the question on leaning was not recited; this is because, at large parties in Greek and Roman times, it was commonplace – certainly for the rich and noble – to lean on beds and pillows (recumbent dining), with the food served to each participant on small tables. Leaning was something that might not have aroused the child's curiosity. (Upright eating even for the upper class on chairs around large tables was well-established by

שֶׁבְּכָל הַלֵּילוֹת אָנוּ אוֹכְלִין בֵּין יוֹשְׁבִין וּבֵין מְסֻבִּין – הַלַּיְלָה הַזֶּה כֻּלָּנוּ מְסֻבִּין.

the Middle Ages.) Following *Hurban ha-Bayit*, the paschal lamb question was discontinued. Leaning for the aristocracy commonly fell into disuse; however, leaning at the *Seder* (and the related question) was retained as a quaint archaic custom to symbolize freedom and to arouse the children to ask (*Arukh ha-Shulhan* OH 473:21).

The custom at the time of the Talmud was as follows: the waiters would bring in a small table upon which was *karpas* and salt water (or some other dressing) for the first dip. Seeing this, the child thinks that the meal is about to seriously begin since vegetables as an appetizer are always accompanied by the main meal. Instead, the table is removed and the child then asks the *Seder* leader why they have removed the table. The leader reassures the child that the table will be returned with Matza, *Maror*, the roasted *Korban Pesah*, and *Haroset* for the second dipping. The child's curiosity is piqued by this information, and he asks the "Four Questions," relating specifically to the above items.

As to why the child doesn't ask about the abundance of wine (four cups), it is because there is no cue that there will be so many cups. Another answer is that each cup serves a function at the *Seder* (*Kiddush, Maggid, Birkat ha-Mazon,* and *Hallel*) and is not that outstanding. Next, wine was a common beverage – certainly at festive meals. Finally, following Abravanel's approach, cups of wine reflect neither freedom nor bondage.

כֻּלָּנוּ מְסֻבִּין

We had pointed out that leaning or recumbent dining was a dining ritual of the elite class in ancient Greece and Rome. It was practiced at the *Seder* for the ingestion of foods that symbolize freedom, *herut*, such as Matza, *Korban Pesah*, and drinking the four cups of wine – the four cups of redemption.

עֲבָדִים הָיִינוּ

The *Haggada* now begins the process of briefly answering the child's questions. Interestingly, specific answers regarding the messages of

On all other nights we eat sitting upright or reclining, but on this night we all recline.

Pesaḥ, *Matza*, and *Maror* aren't given until the **end** of *Maggid* – a long time from now. The answer(s) actually given at this juncture focus on explaining – in a pithy way – why this night is "different from all other nights."

Two approaches are suggested in the Talmud (*Pesaḥim* 116a):

Mishna: …When teaching his child about the Exodus, the parent begins with the Jewish people's disgrace and concludes with their glory… **Gemara**: What is the meaning of the term: "With disgrace"? Rav said that one should begin by saying: *mi-Teḥilla ovdei avoda zara hayu avoteinu* – "At first our ancestors were idolaters," before concluding with words of glory. And Shmuel said: The disgrace with which one should begin his answer is: *Avadim hayinu* – "We were slaves."

For Shmuel, the crux of the Exodus story is Israel's physical enslavement and their ultimate physical redemption on the fifteenth of *Nisan* – which began on *Seder* night in Egypt. For this reason, the pithy answer to why this night is different and special should focus on our physical redemption – "We were slaves to Pharaoh in Egypt and The Lord our God took us out with a strong hand and an outstretched arm" (based on Deut. 6:21).

Rav, however, believes that the deeper story is the people's spiritual evolution from pagan idolaters to those who worship *Hashem* and fulfill His *mitzvot*. As stressed above, God did not just say to Pharaoh: "Let My people go," but rather Let My people go – so that they may **serve Me**" (Ex. 7:16; 7:26; 9:1; 9:13). Serve Me in the Temple; Serve Me in prayer; Serve Me by learning Torah and doing *mitzvot*. As we pointed out in our discussion of *Kiddush*, only one who is able to act at will can freely dedicate his time and actions to the service of the Almighty. True, the ultimate spiritual redemption occurred at Sinai, seven weeks after Passover. But the Torah consciously linked *Pesaḥ* to *Shavu'ot* with *Sefirat ha-Omer*. Furthermore, the process of spiritual evolution had already started in Egypt a few days prior to their Exodus, at which time God commanded Israel to sanctify time and prepare for *Pesaḥ Mitzrayim*, the special Paschal lamb service performed in Egypt (Ex. 12:2). If so, argues Rav, we should focus on the spiritual dimension

עֲבָדִים הָיִינוּ

All gathered respond aloud:

(1) עֲבָדִים הָיִינוּ לְפַרְעֹה בְּמִצְרָיִם. וַיּוֹצִיאֵנוּ ה' אֱלֹהֵינוּ מִשָּׁם בְּיָד חֲזָקָה וּבִזְרֹעַ נְטוּיָה. (2) וְאִלּוּ לֹא הוֹצִיא הַקָּדוֹשׁ בָּרוּךְ הוּא אֶת אֲבוֹתֵינוּ

– which is the ultimate purpose of the Exodus. The concise answer should therefore be: "Initially our ancestors were idolaters, and now God has brought us close to His service."

Despite Rav and Shmuel's disagreement, Jewish tradition has chosen to incorporate both positions – doing so chronologically, with Shmuel's physical redemption answer preceding Rav's spiritual one.

עֲבָדִים הָיִינוּ

This paragraph begins an information-rich section and we will begin to unpack its various components (see the numbering of the sentences in the text).

(1) As mentioned above, the opening first sentence briefly answers the child's question as to why this night is special. Following the view of Shmuel (*Pesahim* 116a, previous comment) it deals with the **physical** aspects of the redemption: God the Redeemer took us out from Egypt with a strong hand and an outstretched arm. My wife, Esther Frimer noted that this is not the only time in Jewish tradition that four questions are asked and the answer is a single pithy declaration. When the boat the prophet Jonah takes to Tarshish hits a violent storm at sea, the ship's occupants ask Jonah four questions (Jonah 1:8–9): What is your profession? Where are you coming from? Where do you live? What is your nationality? To these four separate questions, Jonah gives but one answer: "I am a Jew who worships the God of the heavens." It tells you my roots, my values, my concerns, and my aspirations.

(2) And if you should correctly ask: "All this occurred more than three millennia ago, why is any of this **relevant** to us?" The second sentence answers that if the Redeemer had not taken us out of Egypt, we would all have still been in some form of bondage to this day.

(3) Starting with the third sentence, we now go on a short tangent to elucidate the **rules** of giving the full answer. We first need to know:

Avadim Hayinu

All gathered respond aloud:

(1) We were slaves to Pharaoh in Egypt, and the Lord, our God, took us out from there with a strong hand and with an outstretched arm. (2) If the Holy One Blessed is He had not taken our fathers out of Egypt,

---

Who is obligated to answer and tell the *Pesaḥ* tale? The *Haggada* here posits that individuals of all ages and all levels of education are obligated to tell the tale. Suppose one has no children to interact with, or perhaps those sitting at the *Seder* are so learned that there is nothing new to learn or teach! Is there still an obligation to recount the *Pesaḥ* story? The *Haggada* answer emphatically in the affirmative.

(4) Now we need to clarify: **How much** detail are we obligated to give in our answer? To this, the fourth sentence responds that ideally, one should discuss the Exodus in great length – the more the better!

לְפַרְעֹה בְּמִצְרָיִם

R. Joseph B. Soloveitchik ("An Exalted Evening") has remarked that in Shmuel's formulation, the *Haggada* emphasizes enslavement of the Israelites by **Pharaoh**. Indeed, there are two types of slave systems: one in which the slaves belong to individuals – as in ancient Greece, the United States, and in Jewish law; while in the other, the slaves work for the State which is the total master – such as in Soviet Russia, Nazi Germany, and China. In ancient Egypt, the Israelite slaves were owned by Pharaoh – by the State. The distinction between these two systems is significant. In private slavery, some kind of relationship can exist between slave and master: sympathy, confidence, responsibility, and trust – like the relationship between Yosef and Potiphar. It's only relative subordination. In corporate slavery, however, no personal relationship or friendship is imaginable. It is a depersonalized prison.

The Vilna Gaon (*Haggada*) posited that the problem in Egypt was threefold: 1) we were slaves – an evil status; 2) to Pharaoh – an evil merciless king; 3) in Egypt – a hard, unfeeling people. In apposition to these, the *Haggada* recounts that: 1) we were redeemed; 2) by a merciful caring God; 3) leaving Egypt for the Land of Israel.

מִמִּצְרָיִם. הֲרֵי אָנוּ וּבָנֵינוּ וּבְנֵי בָנֵינוּ מְשֻׁעְבָּדִים הָיִינוּ לְפַרְעֹה בְּמִצְרָיִם. (3) וַאֲפִילוּ כֻּלָּנוּ חֲכָמִים כֻּלָּנוּ נְבוֹנִים כֻּלָּנוּ זְקֵנִים כֻּלָּנוּ יוֹדְעִים אֶת הַתּוֹרָה מִצְוָה עָלֵינוּ לְסַפֵּר בִּיצִיאַת מִצְרָיִם. (4) וְכָל הַמַּרְבֶּה לְסַפֵּר בִּיצִיאַת מִצְרַיִם הֲרֵי זֶה מְשֻׁבָּח.

בְּיָד חֲזָקָה וּבִזְרֹעַ נְטוּיָה

Translated as "a strong hand and an outstretched arm." This phrase is based on Deut. 6:21; however, the latter verse only has "a strong hand," – not "an outstretched arm." R. Joseph B. Soloveitchik (*Mesorat ha-Rav Siddur*, p. 454) indicates that "a strong hand," refers to the Almighty's one-time forceful action in Egypt. However, the imagery of "an outstretched arm" symbolizes the idea that God's arm is forever outstretched over the nation of Israel to shield them from their enemies. Even after the Jews have been saved from one calamity, his arm remains outstretched to protect them from future troubles. The author of the *Haggada* has intentionally modified this verse in his answer because he wants to emphasize that we have an ongoing personal relationship with God. As a result, **the Almighty protects us as we go through history**. This is one of the fundamental messages of the *Haggada*'s *Pesah* story.

מְשֻׁעְבָּדִים הָיִינוּ לְפַרְעֹה בְּמִצְרָיִם

This verse has sometimes been understood as follows: If the Redeemer had not taken our ancestors out of Egypt, we and our descendants would still be slaves there. But this approach seems too simplistic. After all, too many great empires have fallen, too many cataclysmic events have transpired, and too many political upheavals have been recorded during the last three millennia – to accept any such statement with surety. It is also true that the Exodus story and the revelation of the Torah had a very dramatic impact on mankind's perception of God, personal freedom, and values. Thus, it is hard to divine what the world would have looked like without the Exodus saga concluding at Sinai.

In this light, we observe that the word chosen by the *Haggada* is not *avadim* – "slaves," but *meshu'badim* – "subjugated or indebted." Thus, this verse could well mean that had God not forcefully redeemed us then we, our children and our children's children would still be enslaved to Pharaoh in Egypt. (3) Even if all of us were wise, all of us understanding, all of us elders, all of us versed in the knowledge of the Torah, we would still be obligated to discuss the Exodus from Egypt. And, (4) whoever discusses the Exodus from Egypt at length is praiseworthy.

---

from Egypt, but rather Pharaoh himself, we might well be indebted to Pharaoh to this day. The Israelites may have ultimately left Egypt, but Egypt would remain deeply buried within them. They would have continued to be slaves – not physically, but psychologically, emotionally, culturally, and spiritually. They would be slaves to the past, held captive by the chains of gratitude, unable to build an independent future.

וַאֲפִילוּ כֻּלָּנוּ חֲכָמִים

There are four different types of intellects listed here: (1) *Hakham* – one with a perceptive mind who can organize material, conceptualize and make fine distinctions, referred to in the Talmud as an *Oker Harim*; (2) *Navon* – an individual with a creative mind, referred to in the Talmud as *Mevin davar me-tokh davar* (understands one thing from another; (3) *Zaken* – one who appreciates the realia of life, who combines and tempers wisdom with extensive life experience; and (4) *Yode'a* – a scholar with a retentive and encyclopedic mind, referred to in the Talmud as a *Bor sud she-eino me'abed tippa* ("a tarred well that does not lose a drop"). R. Abraham of Slonim (*Bet Abraham*) offers an insight into the meaning and significance of this ruling – that even knowledgeable scholars are obligated to tell the story of the Exodus on the night of the *Seder*. He explains that every scholar brings his unique talents and emotions to the understanding of the Exodus experience. No two minds or hearts are identical, and thus everyone who learns about the redemption has a unique perspective, a unique feeling, and a unique outlook to contribute. This is why no one is exempt from this mitzva, not even those who are already very familiar with the information; each person adds his unique angle, thus enhancing other participants' understanding of, and appreciation for, the miraculous experience.

מַעֲשֶׂה בִּבְנֵי־בְרַק

מַעֲשֶׂה בְּרַבִּי אֱלִיעֶזֶר וְרַבִּי יְהוֹשֻׁעַ וְרַבִּי אֶלְעָזָר בֶּן־עֲזַרְיָה וְרַבִּי עֲקִיבָא וְרַבִּי טַרְפוֹן שֶׁהָיוּ מְסֻבִּין בִּבְנֵי־בְרַק וְהָיוּ מְסַפְּרִים בִּיצִיאַת מִצְרַיִם כָּל־אוֹתוֹ הַלַּיְלָה. עַד שֶׁבָּאוּ תַלְמִידֵיהֶם וְאָמְרוּ לָהֶם רַבּוֹתֵינוּ הִגִּיעַ זְמַן קְרִיאַת שְׁמַע שֶׁל שַׁחֲרִית.

מִצְוָה עָלֵינוּ לְסַפֵּר בִּיצִיאַת מִצְרַיִם

Though both *le-hagid* and *le-sapper* mean "to tell," the former denotes recounting the details of the story to someone who doesn't know the facts – as in the verse (Ex. 13:8) *ve-higadeta le-vinkha* – "and you shall tell your child." By contrast, *le-sapper* includes recounting material that is known. That is why the *Haggada* uses this term in the sentence when talking about *ḥakhamim* – scholars. The subsequent proof text tells of five scholars who stayed up all night discussing the Egypt story – even though they did so with no pupils present (i.e., with no one to teach), and even though as leading scholars they presumably already knew all the particulars.

But all this raises the obvious question: How can one spend a whole night, year after year, talking about an unchanging one-time historical event – no matter how special or how unique it may have been? If the goal is to merely focus on the details, then we should be spending *Seder* night reading the Book of Exodus!! Interestingly, the language of the *Haggada* is **bi**-*yetzi'at mitzrayim* – not **al** *yetzi'at mitzrayim*. Clearly, the *Haggada's* intent here is that we use the Exodus as the jumping board for our discussion. Thus, the *Haggada* at the end of *Maggid* instructs us: "In every generation, each one of us is obligated to **relive** the enslavement and the redemption from Egypt." We need to bring to the table the various intellectual gifts the Creator has blessed us with, to use our imagination, to relive and re-enact the Egypt experience, to make the ideas and ideals relevant, and to introduce the personal element. However, each generation has different insights, values, experiences, and perspectives. Thus, our discussion is not to be limited to the facts – but also to their import and importance to us as a nation and perhaps to mankind as a whole. Not surprisingly, then, the *Haggada* teaches us: "In

Ma'aseh be-Bnei Berak

It happened that Rabbi Eliezer, Rabbi Yehoshua, Rabbi Elazar ben Azarya, Rabbi Akiva and Rabbi Tarfon sat reclining [at a Seder] in Bnei Brak. They were discussing the Exodus from Egypt all that night, until their students came and told them: "Our Masters! The time has come to recite the morning Shema!"

---

each generation there are those who rise up against us to destroy us, but the Holy One, blessed is He saves us from their clutches." Obviously, we are also bidden to ponder the messages and lessons of Jewish history and *emuna* (faith) –as we proceed through the ages.

Based on the above introduction, we can now answer another question. We started off this sentence by saying that even if we knew all the Torah, we would still have to be involved in discussing the Exodus. This is an astounding statement! Why would I have thought otherwise?! Is there any precedent in Judaism for an instance where if you "know it all" you are exempt from fulfilling the mitzva? Based, however, on what we discussed above, the mitzva of recounting the Exodus is not about learning the details – but rather about re-living them! It is about making the story, messages, and symbols of the *Seder* personal and relevant.

מַעֲשֶׂה בִּבְנֵי־בְרַק

The purpose of this story is to confirm the correctness of the two statements just made at the end of the previous paragraph. Firstly, that even the greatest of scholars are obligated to recount the story of the Exodus. This is exactly what these great *Tana'im* (Mishnaic scholars) did – even in the absence of their students. Secondly, one is bidden to speak at length about the Exodus, and indeed these scholars spoke all night.

שֶׁהָיוּ מְסֻבִּין

R. Naftali Adler (*Haggada*) pointed out that the language of this selection (*mesubin* – leaning) strongly suggests that it is proper to lean even during the reading and discussion of *Maggid*. Several scholars have noted that Rabbi Akiva ben Yosef was the student of R. Eliezer ben Hurcanus and R. Yehoshua ben Hanania (*Avot de-R. Natan* 6:2), which is presumably why they are mentioned first. Then comes R. Elazar ben Azaria who was for a short time the Nasi (*Berakhot* 28a). Interestingly, the Talmud (*Pesahim* 108b) indicates that a student does not lean in the presence of his teacher(s). We must conclude that Rabbi Akiva's teachers set aside their honor because Rabbi Akiva was the city's rabbi (R. Yaakov Meir Padawa, *Haggada Nitfei Mayim*,) or because of Rabbi Akiva's national prestige. This may also explain why the students use the term *Raboteinu* – "our teachers" without discerning between teachers and students (contrary to *Bava Batra* 119b; see Rema, YD, 242:21). Since they saw Rabbi Akiva leaning, they deduced that his teachers had shown him honor – and they did so as well.

בִּבְנֵי־בְרַק

Despite the seeming simplicity of this story, commentators throughout the generations have posed a plethora of questions regarding its details that deserve our attention. For example, as recounted in *Sanhedrin* 32b, Rabbi Eliezer ben Hurcanus had his court in the city of Lod, Rabbi Yehoshua ben Hanania was in Peki'in, while Rabbi Akiva ben Yosef, their student, was in Bnai Brak. Proper protocol would have dictated that Rabbi Akiva should have traveled to spend *Pesah* with his teachers, rather than vice versa! What's more, Rabbi Eliezer was of the opinion that one should spend the *regalim* at home (Sukka 27b). There must have been a compelling reason for him to travel to Rabbi Akiva for the *Seder*.

R. Yechiel Michel ha-Levi Epstein (*Haggada Leyl Shimurim*) sensitively connects this story with one appearing at the end of *Makkot* (24a-b), in which three of the above protagonists Rabbi Elazar ben Azarya, Rabbi Yehoshua, and Rabbi Akiva also appear:

> Rabban Gamliel, Rabbi Elazar ben Azarya, Rabbi Yehoshua, and Rabbi Akiva were once walking along the road, and they heard the sound of the multitudes of Rome from Puteoli at a distance of 120 Persian miles (ca. 120 kilometers). The other Sages began weeping and Rabbi Akiva was laughing. They said to him: Why are you laughing? Rabbi Akiva said to them: And why are you weeping? They said to him: These gentiles, who bow to false gods and burn incense to idols, dwell securely and tranquilly in this colossal city.

But, our Temple is burnt by fire, and shall we not weep? Rabbi Akiva said to them: That is why I am laughing. If for those who violate His will, the wicked, it is so and they are rewarded for the few good deeds they performed, for those who perform His will, all the more so will they be rewarded.

On another occasion they were ascending to Jerusalem after the destruction of the Temple... When they arrived at the Temple Mount, they saw a fox that emerged from the site of the Holy of Holies. They began weeping, and Rabbi Akiva was laughing. They said to him: For what reason are you laughing? Rabbi Akiva said to them: For what reason are you weeping? They said to him: This is the place concerning which it is written: "And a stranger [non-Priest] who approaches shall die" (Num. 1:51), and now foxes walk in it; and shall we not weep? Rabbi Akiva responded to them: That is why I am laughing, as it is written: "And I will take faithful witnesses to attest: Uriah the priest, and Zechariah the son of Jeberechiah" (Isaiah 8:2). ... Until the prophecy of Uriah with regard to the destruction of the city came true, I was afraid that the prophecy of Zechariah about its rebuilding would not be fulfilled, as the two prophecies are linked. Now that the prophecy of Uriah has been fulfilled, it is evident that the prophecy of Zechariah remains valid as well. The Sages said to him, employing this formulation: Akiva, you have comforted us; Akiva, you have comforted us.

We see that during the dark trying times following the destruction of the Second Temple, Rabbi Akiva represented the voice of optimism, encouragement and hope. It is not surprising that these leaders of Israel in search of inspiration, hope and strength, desired to spend the festival of freedom and liberation specifically with him.

R. Reuven Margaliot (*Margaliot ha-Yam, Sanhedrin* 32b) insightfully links the incident in the *Haggada* to one recorded in *Ma'aser Sheni* (5:9), which also includes three of the previous protagonists, Rabbi Elazar ben Azarya, Rabbi Yehoshua, and Rabbi Akiva. In the latter story, Rabban Gamliel and several elders (including the above three) were on a ship presumably returning from a mission to Rome. The context of the Mishna suggests that the timing to this incident was close to *Pesah* (see

אָמַר רַבִּי אֶלְעָזָר בֶּן־עֲזַרְיָה הֲרֵי אֲנִי כְּבֶן שִׁבְעִים שָׁנָה וְלֹא זָכִיתִי שֶׁתֵּאָמֵר יְצִיאַת מִצְרַיִם בַּלֵּילוֹת עַד שֶׁדְּרָשָׁהּ בֶּן זוֹמָא, שֶׁנֶּאֱמַר (דברים טז:ג): "לְמַעַן תִּזְכֹּר אֶת יוֹם צֵאתְךָ מֵאֶרֶץ מִצְרַיִם כֹּל יְמֵי חַיֶּיךָ." יְמֵי חַיֶּיךָ הַיָּמִים. כֹּל יְמֵי חַיֶּיךָ הַלֵּילוֹת. וַחֲכָמִים אוֹמְרִים יְמֵי חַיֶּיךָ הָעוֹלָם הַזֶּה. כֹּל יְמֵי חַיֶּיךָ לְהָבִיא לִימוֹת הַמָּשִׁיחַ:

Ma'aser Sheni 5:6) of either the fourth or seventh year of the *Shmittah* cycle when all tithes need to be distributed. Rabban Gamliel allocated to Rabbi Elazar ben Azarya the *kohen*, Rabbi Yehoshua a Levite, and to Rabbi Akiva a charity collector for the poor – what was due in each category. Rabban Gamliel would not have done so on the ship unless he was seriously concerned that he would not make it home in time for the *Seder*. R. Margaliot hypothesizes that they landed at the Jaffa port just prior to *Pesaḥ*. They presumably had enough time to make it to the nearby town Bnai Brak for *Seder*, as the guests of Rabbi Akiva – where the *Haggada* picks up. Why Rabban Gamliel did not join the others is left to speculation.

Both R. Hayim Joseph David Azulai (Hida, *Simḥat ha-Regel*) and R. Zvi Hirsch Chajes (*Kol Kitvei Maharatz Hayot*, I, *Darkei Hora'ah*, sec. 2, note p. 259) call attention to the lineage of each of the five personalities. Rabbi Eliezer, Rabbi Elazar ben Azarya, and Rabbi Tarfon were all *Kohanim*; Rabbi Yehoshua was a Levite. Thus four of the five scholars were from the tribe of Levi, which according to *Midrash Rabba* (on Ex. 5:4 cited by Rashi), was not enslaved in Egypt. Rabbi Akiva's progenitors were not enslaved either since he was from a family of converts. If these scholars – who had no direct connection to the Egyptian bondage – found it appropriate to talk about *yetzi'at Mitzrayim* all night, how much more should we!

Assorted commentators have raised the following questions: (1) Why did these scholars leave their homes and communities to gather by Rabbi Akiva? (2) Why were the students excluded from the discussions? And, finally, (3) Why were these Torah leaders oblivious to the rising of the sun signaling the time for reciting *Keri'at Shema*? The often-cited suggestion is that this incident may well have taken place during the very harsh Hadrianic period in which Jews were martyred

Rabbi Elazar ben Azarya said: "I am like a seventy-year-old man, yet I did not succeed in proving that the Exodus from Egypt must be mentioned at night – until Ben Zoma explained the verse (Deuteronomy 16:3): 'In order that you may remember the day you left Egypt all the days of your life.' 'The days of your life' would mean only the days; the additional word 'all' indicates the inclusion of the nights!" The Sages, however, say that "the days of your life" would mean only the present world; the addition of "all" includes the days of Mashiah.

---

for keeping tradition. Rabbi Akiva hosted his brave colleagues for the *Seder* in deep secret, but the students remained outside on guard. Some authors (R. Shevah Knevil, *Haggada*) even speculate that the five were perhaps discussing or planning the Bar Kokhba rebellion – which Rabbi Akiva supported, but other scholars (perhaps, Rabban Gamliel) rejected.

הִגִּיעַ זְמַן קְרִיאַת שְׁמַע שֶׁל שַׁחֲרִית

These *Tana'im* were part of a wide discussion as to when is the starting time for reciting *Keri'at Shema*. "Nevertheless," said the students, "irrespective of your positions – it's light enough to read *Shema* according to everyone!"

אָמַר רַבִּי אֶלְעָזָר בֶּן־עֲזַרְיָה

This section appears in *Mishna, Berakhot* (1:5) but was included at this juncture in the *Haggada*, presumably because it remains from the learning of "that" night in Bnai Brak. Indeed, Maimonides in his text of the *Haggada* (*Mishne Torah*, end of *Hametz u-Matza*) has the reading: *Amar **lahem** Rabbi Eliezer ben Azarya*… – "Rabbi Eliezer ben Azarya said to them…." – "to them" clearly refers to his colleagues at the Bnai Brak *Seder*.

Another possibility is that, if there were not an obligation to mention the Exodus from Egypt every night, I might have thought that the special obligation on *Seder* night is merely to **mention** this fact tonight. However, now that we have established that there is an obligation to do so every night of the year, the obligation on *Seder* night is perforce to discuss the Exodus at length and in depth.

כְּנֶגֶד אַרְבָּעָה בָנִים

בָּרוּךְ הַמָּקוֹם. בָּרוּךְ הוּא. בָּרוּךְ שֶׁנָּתַן תּוֹרָה לְעַמּוֹ יִשְׂרָאֵל, בָּרוּךְ הוּא. כְּנֶגֶד אַרְבָּעָה בָנִים דִּבְּרָה תוֹרָה: אֶחָד חָכָם, וְאֶחָד רָשָׁע, וְאֶחָד תָּם, וְאֶחָד שֶׁאֵינוֹ יוֹדֵעַ לִשְׁאוֹל.

עַד שֶׁדְּרָשָׁהּ בֶּן זוֹמָא

Why did Rabbi Elazar ben Azarya not merit to have his derivation accepted until Shimon ben Zoma supported his position? The Babylonian Talmud (*Berakhot* 28a) records that Rabbi Elazar was eighteen (Jerusalem Talmud says sixteen) when he was chosen to be Nasi (Head) of the Sanhedrin. Tradition indicates that he miraculously aged overnight and looked seventy. It would seem that because of his youthfulness, his colleagues were not eager to accept his novel position until it was corroborated by ben Zoma. What is fascinating is that Shimon ben Zoma is the sage who is cited in *Pirkei Avot* (4:1) as espousing the position: "Who is wise? He who learns from everyone." (R. Asher Weiss, *Haggada Minhat Asher*).

כְּנֶגֶד אַרְבָּעָה בָנִים

This section of the *Haggada* continues our discussion of the **rules for giving the full answer**. We are concerned here with **how to answer** the child's question(s). The *Haggada*'s message is that one answer does not fit all! **Each child is unique and requires his or her own response**.

בָּרוּךְ

Abudarham (*Abudarham ha-Shalem*) emphasizes that God is the source of blessing, *mekor ha-berakha*, and cannot be acted upon. Hence, the correct translation is "Blessed **is** the Place, blessed **is** He" – not Blessed **be** the Place, blessed **be** He.

בָּרוּךְ הַמָּקוֹם

Why is God euphemistically referred to as *ha-Makom* – literally, the "place"? Some commentaries cite as a possible source the verse in *Megillat* Esther (4:14): *Revah ve-hatzala yavo la-Yehudim mi-makom aher*

Arba Banim – Four Children

Blessed is the Place [God], blessed is He! Blessed is He who gave the Torah to His people Israel, blessed is He! Concerning four children, the Torah speaks: One is wise, one is wicked, one is simple and one does not know how to ask.

– "Relief and deliverance will arise to the Jews from another place." Thus, *ha-Makom* is an appellation for God emphasizing his Divine providence. Others note that God is literally in every place, omnipresent. Finally, mystics have pointed out that, in Hebrew, God's ineffable name is י-ה-ו-ה. Squaring the numerical value of each letter gives us 100 (10x10) + 25 (5x5) + 36 (6x6) + 25 (5x5) = 186 which is equal to the numerical value of מקום.

R. Joseph B. Soloveitchik (cited by R. Ari Kahn, *Haggada Od Yosef Hai*) observes that the *Haggada* generally refers to God as *ha-Kadosh Barukh Hu* (the Holy One, blessed is He). There are two instances, however, where God is referred to as *ha-Makom* in this work: (1) *Barukh ha-Makom, barukh Hu* – prior to the "Four Children" which speaks of God giving us the Torah; and (2) *ve-Akhshav kervanu ha-Makom le-avodato* – when we mention, based on verses from the Book of Yehoshua, that the Almighty chose us for Divine service. Why are these two places singled out?

Insight into the significance of these two appellations can be derived from their use in the prophecies of the two great prophets Isaiah and Ezekiel. Both prophets have visions of God's heavenly throne surrounded by angels, yet Isaiah responds by noting his sensing of God's holiness: *Kadodsh, kadosh, kadosh Hashem Tzevakot* – "Holy, Holy, Holy is the Lord of Hosts." Isaiah was given prophecy during a time when the First Temple stood in its glory; when the *Shekhina* – the Divine presence was palpable and one could feel His holiness. It is under such enlightened conditions that God is referred to by his usual names, such as *Hashem Tzevakot*. Ezekiel, by contrast, declares, *Barukh kevod Hashem mi-memokmo* – "Blessed is God's honor from His place" – wherever that may be. Ezekiel prophesized from Babylon, the exile, during the period of the Temple's destruction. It was a time of *hester panim* (God's hidden presence) and it was very hard to sense the immediacy of God. It is in such periods that *ha-Makom* appears.

Similarly, in times of mourning and personal *hester panim*, when we console the mourners, we use the term *ha-Makom yenahem etkhem* – may the *Makom* comfort you. Likewise, following the weekday reading of the Torah, we pray for *Aheinu kol Bet Yisrael* – our brethren the entire family of Israel who are in distress and captivity – *ha-Makom yerahem aleihem* – may the *Makom* mercifully redeem them. There is no greater *hester panim*, no greater sense of God's hidden presence and alienation – than in times of tragedy and suffering. (See more in our discussion of שֶׁבְּשִׁפְלֵנוּ זָכַר לָנוּ below.)

Returning now to R. Soloveitchik's question, *ha-Makom* is used in the *Haggada* after Yehoshua indicates that we were chosen for Divine service. This is because our "chosenness" for Torah and Divine service is based on the *Brit bein ha-Betarim* – the Covenant of the Parts (Gen. 15). In this covenant, God casts a deep sleep over Avraham and promises him the Torah and the Land of Israel – but they would be preceded by the difficult process of a 400-year exile in a "foreign land." This period of *hester panim* (hidden presence), continues R. Solovitchik, would not be broken until the redemption and liberation from Egypt had been completed. The *Meshekh Hokhma* (Gen. 46:2) posits that the scheduling of Avraham's vision at nighttime symbolizes the darkness of exile and underscores God's assistance through the terror of exile: "In the end they shall go free with great wealth" (Gen. 15:14).

In preparation for the redemption from Egypt, the *Haggada* below states that the Merciful one "*hishave et hakaytz* – calculated the end." This refers to a calculated reduction in the length and pain of the exile – a lifting of God's alienation. All this led up to the Jews receiving the Torah and their involvement in Divine service. However, R. Soloveitchik observes, that history has not been kind to the Jews. We stubbornly maintain a Torah lifestyle that has led to much suffering, and great difficulties throughout the ages. This tragic record of *hester panim* calls for the *ha-Makom* appellation for God.

R. Soloveitchik does not comment on the use of *ha-Makom* just before and after *Dayenu*. This *piyut* is not recorded in Maimonides *Haggada* (end of *Hil. Hametz u-Matza*) and is presumably a very late addition.

בָּרוּךְ שֶׁנָּתַן תּוֹרָה לְעַמּוֹ יִשְׂרָאֵל

R. Joseph B. Soloveitchik maintains that this reference to the Jews as "His people" is a most appropriate introduction to the "Four Children." This is because the term *amo* (His people) describes the people as a whole, the masses. Thus, the Torah is not meant just for the spiritually and intellectually aristocratic, but also for the *Tam* and the *Eino yodeia li-she'ol* – to the ignorant, limited, and slow individual.

כְּנֶגֶד אַרְבָּעָה בָנִים דִּבְּרָה תוֹרָה

The centrality of children in the *Haggada* stems from the fact that on four occasions in the Torah, we find the text referring to an intergenerational dialog between child and parent regarding an Exodus related ritual.

1. **Ex. 12:26-27** – And it shall come to pass when your **children will say** unto you: What is the meaning of this service to you? And you shall say: "It is the sacrifice of the Lord's Passover, for He passed over the houses of the children of Israel in Egypt when He smote the Egyptians and delivered our houses."
2. **Ex. 13:8** – And you shall **tell your child** on that day, saying: "It is for this [Divine service] – that the Lord acted on my behalf when I came forth out of Egypt."
3. **Ex. 13:14** – And it shall be when your **child asks** you in the future, saying: What is this? Then you shall say to him: With a strong hand the Lord brought us out from Egypt, from the house of bondage.
4. **Deut. 6:20–21** – When your **child asks** you in the future, saying: "What is the meaning of the testimonies, statutes, and ordinances, which the Lord our God has commanded you?" Then you will say to your son: "We were Pharaoh's slaves in Egypt, and the Lord brought us out of Egypt with a mighty hand…"

Haza"l (the sages of the Talmud), who read the Torah text closely, derived many insights from these four verses. Firstly, they learned from Ex 13:8 *ve-Higadeta le-vinkha*… – "And you shall **tell your child**" that there is an explicit mitzva obligation for parents to talk to their children about the experiences and lessons of Egypt. (Although the text uses

חָכָם מָה הוּא אוֹמֵר? "מָה הָעֵדוֹת וְהַחֻקִּים וְהַמִּשְׁפָּטִים אֲשֶׁר צִוָּה ה' אֱלֹהֵינוּ אֶתְכֶם?" (דברים ו:כ). וְאַף אַתָּה אֱמוֹר לוֹ כְּהִלְכוֹת הַפֶּסַח: אֵין מַפְטִירִין אַחַר הַפֶּסַח אֲפִיקוֹמָן:

---

the word *le-vinkha* – which often means "your son," the *Halakhic* literature makes eminently clear that *le-vinkha* in this context means "child." Thus, this obligation includes both male and female children – R. Ovadiah Yosef, *Resp. Hazon Ovadya*, sec. 21 and copious references cited therein.) The texts also emphasize the importance of utilizing various Exodus-related rituals as a form of "show and tell." The parents' goal should be to involve the children, pique their curiosity, and transmit to them, the next generation, our historical heritage and sense of gratitude to the Almighty.

The Rabbis also noted that in three of the four dialogs (verses no. 1, 3, and 4), the child initiates the conversation – each in his own way and with varying levels of sophistication and understanding. Furthermore, in each case, the response given is different. But in one case (verse no. 2), the child does not ask, but the parent is still encouraged not to be complacent, but to discuss the message of the Exodus with him. Clearly, the above four dialogs led the author of the *Haggada* to envision Four Children: *Hakham* (Wise one; no. 4), *Rasha* (Wicked one; no. 1), *Tam* (Simple one; no. 3) and *Eino Yode'a Lishol* (Clueless one; no. 2). Each child is special, each requires a different pedagogic approach.

In order to arouse the child's curiosity on and about the *Seder* night, *Haza"l* instituted several practices whose goal is to get the children to ask. These include, *inter alia*: eating *karpas*; washing before *karpas* (*Arukh ha-Shulhan*, OH 473:18); breaking the middle Matza and hiding/stealing the *Afikoman*; *heseiba* – leaning (*Arukh ha-Shulhan* OH 473:21) when eating foods symbolizing freedom such as the four cups of wine, *motzi Matza*, and *Afikoman*; removing the *Seder* plate before the four questions (*Tosafot, Pesahim* 114a). *Pesahim* (109a) recounts that the famous Rabbi Akiva would hand out nuts and toasted seeds to children on the eve of *Pesah* so that they would be excited about the upcoming *Seder*.

Indeed, children are encouraged to ask questions about novel rituals and to be aware of what is happening in our historical tale. We

The wise one – what does he say? "What are the testimonies, the statutes and the laws which the Lord, our God, has commanded you" (Deuteronomy 6:20)? You, in turn, shall instruct him in the laws of the Pesah offering: one may not eat dessert after the Pesah offering.

---

keep them awake throughout the long evening via dialogue (the four questions), ritual (dipping the *Karpas*, spilling the wine), song (*Hallel*, *Dayenu*, *Ehad mi yode'a* and *Had Gadya*), strange foods (Matza, *Maror*, *Haroset*, and the Hillel sandwich) and even games (e.g., "stealing" the *Afikoman*). This is because the ultimate goal of *Seder* is to stimulate our children to identify with the Exodus, with Sinai, and with the Land of Israel. As my father explained: "On *Pesah*, a child's senses are caught and stirred by the smells, sights, sounds, touches, and tastes of the *Seder*. Through such sensuous stimuli, a young child is conditioned to identify with his people's past, participate in its present, and share its dreams for a distant yet beckoning tomorrow." (R. Norman E. Frimer, Horizon, September 1970). We want to make the *Seder* fascinating, stimulating, and challenging enough – so that all four children will identify as proud Jews. As many have observed (R. Jonathan Sacks Haggada, "The Missing Fifth"), perhaps our greatest existential fear is for the "fifth child" – who doesn't show up to the *Seder* at all!

חָכָם מָה הוּא אוֹמֵר

(a) Note that each of the "Four Children" is introduced with the formula: [*Hakham/Rasha/Tam/she-eino yode'a lishol*] *ma hu omer*? This is translated as: "The [Wise/Wicked/Simple/Clueless] child – what does he say?" A Hassidic tradition suggests parsing the words thusly: "[*Hakham/Rasha/Tam/she-eino yode'a lishol*] *ma hu*? *Omer*!" If you want to know what that child's true essence is – then listen very carefully to **what** he says, and perhaps, **how** he says it.

(b) With this caveat in mind, we turn first to the two children who by far attract the most attention, the Wise and Wicked children. The former is **not** called the "Righteous" child, because he lacks much basic knowledge, and the ignorant can't be righteous (*Lo am ha-aretz hasid*, *Avot* 2:1). But he is "Wise" because his questions about the *Seder* and *Korban Pesah* service show him to be discerning and aware of various types of *mitzvot*: *eidot*, *hukim* and *mishpatim*. Thus, the word *ma* for this child means: "What is the difference between the various categories of rituals? *Eidot* are testimonies – rituals performed to commemorate past events. Hence, eating Matza and *Maror* testifies that God took the Jews out of Egypt into the desert. Similarly, keeping the Sabbath testifies that God created heaven and earth and rested on the seventh day. *Hukim*, or statutes, are *mitzvot* without revealed or rational reason – like not breaking bones of the Paschal lamb. *Mishpatim*, or ordinances, are laws that govern men's dealings with one another – such as not allowing the uncircumcised to eat from one's Paschal lamb. R. Elijah Kramer (The Vilna Gaon, Commentary to *Haggada*) astutely observes that, contrary to the other children, the *Hakham* invokes God's name in his question: *…asher tziva Hashem Elokeinu etkhem* – "which the Lord our God commanded you." R. Yehiel Michel Epstein (*Haggada Leyl Shimurim*) points out that the Torah introduces the *Hakham*'s question (verse no. 4 in previous comment) with the words: "When your child **asks** you in the future saying…." His question is honest and polite.

By contrast, the *Rasha* is a challenging – if not rebellious – "wicked child." On all the points mentioned above, his tack is polar opposite. Like the *Hakham* he sees varied rituals and observances – but to him they are all the same: service, burden, and toil. He finds no meaning or relevance in these practices – not an opportunity for spiritual growth and sanctification. For this child, the word *ma* means: "Of what value are all these practices?" God's name is not mentioned in his statement. Indeed, his question is rhetorical. Thus, the Torah introduces the *Rasha*'s comments (verse no. 1 in previous comment) with the words: "When your children will **say** unto you…" He's not really interested in an answer. On the contrary, he is making a declaration. R. Yehuda Gershuni (*Sha'arei Zedek*, pp. 295–296) notes that the *Hakham* and *Tam* ask their honest questions individually, but the *Rasha*'s declaration is made as a group to challenge, belittle, and perhaps intimidate.

(c) The *Rasha*'s question appears in Exodus 12:26. The Torah there gives us a very specific answer with which to respond to this question: "It is the sacrifice of the Lord's Passover, for He passed over the houses of the children of Israel in Egypt, when He smote the Egyptians, and delivered our houses." Many commentators have asked why the *Haggada* offers a different response to the wicked son's question than that ordained by the Torah. The *Haggada* instead has us scold the *Rasha* and let him know that "were he to have been there, he would not have been redeemed." R. Yisrael Meir Lau (*Haggada Yahel Or*) suggests that the *Rasha*, who is referred to in the *Haggada*, lives in exile, and with his statement, he has totally alienated himself from the Jewish People. He has to be dealt with sternly. But the query of the wicked child of the Torah is preceded by the following verse (Ex. 12:25): "And when you enter the land that the Lord will give you, as promised, you shall observe this [Paschal] rite." Thus, the *Rasha*, while problematic, lives in the Land of Israel and is nevertheless intimately linked to Jewish life in the Hilly Land – he has not rejected Jewish Peoplehood. Such a child needs to be brought close and treated warmly and with respect. R. Zvi Yehezkel Michelson (cited by R. Ovadiah Yosef, *Halakha Yomit, Erev Pesah 5784*) indicates that in the Haggada we are dealing with an individual *Rasha* who comes to the *Seder* with *hutzpa* to challenge his parents and the religious leadership: "*Rasha*, what does **he** say?" – in the singular. Such a child needs to be rejected – his teeth set on edge! However, in the Torah (as also indicated by R. Yehuda Gershuni above) the *Rasha*'s declaration is made by a large group: "When your child**ren** will say unto you…" Here we are dealing with a large number of non-observant Jews, perhaps a majority of the population – as is often the case in modern times, who simply find no value in these "antiquated" rituals. They are in search of meaning and relevance. To such a religious search, you need to respond directly, honestly, and respectfully.

R. Yehuda Gershuni (*Sha'arei Zedek*, p. 297) has a very different and much less conciliatory approach. He points out that the Torah begins its answer to the *Rasha's* question with the words: "And you shall say," – not "And you shall say **to them**." The explanation is not meant for them, since they are not really interested in an answer. The explanation is meant for the other respectful participants at the Seder Table. The only thing we say to him is said with self-pride and as a rejection of his derision. It sets his teeth on edge: "Were he to have been there, he would not have been redeemed."

(d) Three of the children ask a question about the unique ceremonies of the *Seder* night. While the *Hakham* is praised for his query, the *Rasha* is chastised for his. When the *Rasha* asks: *Ma ha-avoda ha-zot* **lakhem** – "What is the meaning of this service to you?" His use of the word **lakhem** – YOU (plural), instead of **lanu** – US, is understood to reveal his underlying rejection of the Jewish people and perhaps even the fundamentals of tradition. Yet, truth be told, the *Hakham*, too, uses a similar formulation. He, after all, asks: *Ma ha-eidot ve-ha-hukim ve-ha-mishpatim asher tziva Hashem Elokeinu* **etkhem** – "What are the various commandments that our God has commanded YOU (plural)?"

R. Yisrael Meir Lau (*Haggada Yahel Or*) quotes the insightful comments of the Blozhover Rebbe. The latter suggests that the crucial difference between the wise and wicked children is their respective choice of the Hebrew word for YOU. The *Hakham* uses the word *etkhem*, while the *Rasha* uses *lakhem*. The two words are synonymous – but each has its own nuance of meaning (see Malbim). The *Hakham* uses the word *etkhem*, which stems from the word *et* (often synonymous with *im*); it is inclusionary in connotation and thus should be translated as "with you." Furthermore, homiletically, *etkhem* is composed of *Aleph* – the first letter of the Hebrew alphabet, *Taf* – the last letter, and *Khaf* and *Mem* – which are two central letters. Each of these letters represents points in Jewish history. The *Hakham* is a Jew who has solid roots in the Jewish past and tradition (*Aleph*), is proudly involved in its present (*Khaf* and *Mem*), and works hard at building a solid foundation for the future (*Taf*). The *Rasha*, on the other hand, uses *lakhem* which is exclusionary in nuance – you, but not me! What's more, it is composed solely of the three central letters in the Hebrew alphabet: *Khaf, Lamed,* and *Mem*. He is concerned only about the present – he has little interest in his people's past and is even less concerned with their future. One who sees no future for the Jewish people – or doesn't see himself as part of that future – has effectively cut himself off from Jewry and the God of history.

Some commentaries have suggested that the *Rasha's* comments are directed to the respected national leadership. "What is the meaning of this service to **you**?" Why are you personally involved with the details of this Paschal sacrifice, setting the animal aside, its slaughtering, and grilling? Wouldn't it be more befitting to leave this to your underlings and workers? To this, we respond: "It is the sacrifice of the **Lord's** Passover, for He passed over the houses of the Children of Israel…" Just as God was **personally** involved in our salvation ("I – and not a messenger"), so are **we personally** involved in this thanksgiving sacrifice to Hashem.

אֵין מַפְטִירִין אַחַר הַפֶּסַח אֲפִיקוֹמָן

The ruling that nothing should be eaten after the Afikoman appears in the next to last *Mishna* in *Masekhet Pesahim*. But what do the rules of the *Afikoman* have to do with the wise child's question? Furthermore, why doesn't the father simply give the Torah's answer which is (Deut. 6:20): "We were Pharaoh's slaves in Egypt, and the Lord brought us out of Egypt with a mighty hand…"

Some commentators suggest that the answer begins with *ve-Af ata emor lo* which means you shall **also** tell him. This suggests that indeed the father gives the Torah's answer of *avadim hayinu* – as we actually do in the *Haggada*, but this has already appeared above following the four questions. Therefore, the *Haggada* instructs the parent to **also** teach his precocious child the *mishnayot* of *Masekhet Pesahim* which concludes with *Ein maftirin ahar ha-Pesah afikomkan*.

Haggada Talmidei ha-Besh"t also mentions the strange formulation of the *Haggada's* statement, but emphasizes another word: *ve-Af ata emor lo ke-hilkhot ha-Pesah…* which means "you shall also tell him **like** the laws of *Pesah*." They suggest that the intention here is to instruct the father that his answers have to be carefully and clearly formulated so they leave a long-term impression on the child. This is analogous to the requirement that the *Afikoman* must be the last food eaten at the *Seder* so that its flavor remains.

Alternatively, we suggest that the author of the *Haggada* is instructing the father: "One should always teach his student in a concise manner" (*Pesahim* 3b). Thus one needs to give a short and to-the-point answer to his inquisitive child. This is similar to the pithy style of various *Mishnayot* of *Masekhet Pesahim*. This is indeed what we do at the *Seder*. The two initial and basic answers to the "Four Questions" of the *Seder* are *Avadim hayinu le-Pharaoh be-Mitzrayim* and *Mi-tehilla ovdei avoda zara hayu avoteinu* – and the rest of *Maggid* is amplification, proof texts, and examples.

רָשָׁע מָה הוּא אוֹמֵר? מָה הָעֲבוֹדָה הַזֹּאת לָכֶם? לָכֶם – וְלֹא לוֹ. וּלְפִי שֶׁהוֹצִיא אֶת עַצְמוֹ מִן הַכְּלָל כָּפַר בְּעִקָּר. וְאַף אַתָּה הַקְהֵה אֶת שִׁנָּיו וֶאֱמוֹר לוֹ: "בַּעֲבוּר זֶה עָשָׂה ה' לִי בְּצֵאתִי מִמִּצְרָיִם" (שמות יג:ח). לִי וְלֹא־לוֹ. אִלּוּ הָיָה שָׁם, לֹא הָיָה נִגְאָל:

מָה הָעֲבוֹדָה הַזֹּאת לָכֶם

As discussed above, the *Rasha* sees the *Pesah* rituals and observances as "service," namely an unnecessary burden and meaningless toil. He finds no meaning or relevance in these practices – not an opportunity for spiritual growth and sanctification. For this child, the word *ma* means: **"Of what value** are all these practices?"

וּלְפִי שֶׁהוֹצִיא אֶת עַצְמוֹ מִן הַכְּלָל - כָּפַר בְּעִקָּר

Kafar (and not *ve-kafar*) *be-ikar* is the standard reading of the text. Accordingly, the *Rasha's* disavowal of any connection to the Paschal "service" is in essence a rejection of the God of Israel. This is first because the plagues reveal that the God of our forefathers is the God of nature – Creator of Heaven and Earth and hence in control of all. The Exodus experience affirms Him to also be the God of History – involved with the world and in control of nations and the forces of history. Finally, God's commandments, beginning with the Egyptian *Seder* and continuing with the Sinaitic revelation, reflects God's concern for man and Israel's Divine mission to serve the Almighty. "Let my people go," said God to Pharaoh, "so that they may serve me!" (Ex. 7:16, 28; 9:1, 13). The *Haggada's* narrator concludes, that because the *Rasha* denies the importance of "serving" God, and refuses to acknowledge the Almighty's role in the Exodus – God would not have redeemed **him** from Egypt.

Judaism has long considered those who separate themselves from the broader Jewish community to be worthy of denigration. In his seminal halakhic work, the *Mishneh Torah*, Maimonides writes that "One who separates himself from the community, ... holds aloof from the congregation of Israel, does not fulfill religious precepts in common with his people, shows himself indifferent when they are in distress...

The wicked one – what does he say? "What is this service to you" (Exodus 12:26)?! He says "to you," thereby excluding himself. By excluding himself, he denies the basic principle of our faith. Therefore you should blunt his teeth and say to him: "It is because of this that the Lord did [all these miracles] for me when I left Egypt" (Exodus 13:8); "for me" – but not for him! Had he been there, he would not have been redeemed!

– such a person has no share in the world to come." R. Jonathan Sacks (*Haggada*) tied Maimonides' description to the *Haggada*'s wicked child, who – by removing himself from the community – "has denied a fundamental principle [of Judaism]." R. Sacks posits that "the mere fact that an individual fails to identify with the collective fate of the Jewish people… is a denial of one of the principles of Judaism, namely that ours is a collective faith. Though many Jews in the modern age found it difficult to believe, they identified with the Jewish people, fought its cause, and gave it their support. Belonging is the first step to believing. What makes the wicked child wicked, according to the *Haggada*, is not that he fails to believe, but that he fails to identify with the people of whom he is a part." (See also the end of our comments on עַל שׁוּם שֶׁפֶּסַח below.)

However, many of the *Rishonim* have the reading: *ve-kafar be-ikar*. Such a reading suggests that the *Rasha* – by saying *Ma ha-avoda ha-zot lakhem?* – has explicitly excluded himself from being part of *Klal Yisrael* (the Nation or People of Israel) and their obligation in *mitzvot*. He therefore denies the God of Revelation. Furthermore, his refusal to invoke God's name, reflects a fundamental issue with his belief in the God of Israel. Our response to him is in kind: *Ilu haya sham, lo haya nigal*. The narrator of the *Haggada* suggests that had the *Rasha* been in Egypt, his disconnection from the People of Israel and their God would have been punished measure for measure. Namely, he would not have been redeemed with the rest of the nation.

וְאַף אַתָּה הַקְהֵה אֶת שִׁנָּיו

R. Reuven Margaliot (*Haggada*) points out that the verse (Ex. 12:43): *Kol ben neikhar lo yokhal bo* excludes those who are estranged from Judaism

תָּם מָה הוּא אוֹמֵר? "מַה זֹּאת" (שמות יג:יד)? וְאָמַרְתָּ אֵלָיו "בְּחוֹזֶק יָד הוֹצִיאָנוּ ה' מִמִּצְרַיִם מִבֵּית עֲבָדִים" (שם).

---

and espouse heretical views – from eating from the Paschal lamb. This rule would apply to the *Rasha* who denies God and his *mitzvot* and is therefore likewise excluded from receiving such a tasty portion of barbequed meat. R. Margaliot points to the phrase in *Shir ha-Shirim Rabba* (1, 12, 3): *ve-Hayeta nafsham koha le-ekhol* which means: "and their souls **craved** to partake of it." Thus, the Hebrew root קהה can also mean to "crave." The *Haggada's* narrator's statement *ve-Af ata hakheh et shinav* means, therefore, that in response to the *Rasha's* rejection "cause his teeth to crave the Paschal meat – by not allowing him to partake of this tasty barbequed meat with everyone else."

בַּעֲבוּר זֶה עָשָׂה ה' לִי בְּצֵאתִי מִמִּצְרָיִם

In his commentary to this verse, R. Abraham Ibn Ezra explains as follows: *ba'avur zeh* – "Because of **this**" refers to the Divine service of the *Seder* night. This includes the positive commandment to eat Matza and a negative commandment to abstain from *Hametz*, which were among the first of the *mitzvot* given to us in Egypt. Because of this Divine Service that I will do in the future, the Almighty did these miracles and wonders for me upon our exiting Egypt. This is because the whole reason for our redemption was only so that we would serve him – as the verse says (Nu. 15:41): "I the Lord am your God, who brought you out of the land of Egypt to be your God…." This then is the response to the *Rasha*: Because you deny the first of the *mitzvot*, you therefore reject the very reason why God redeemed us – namely to do His *mitzvot* and accept Him as God. You, *Rasha*, deny these very fundamentals of our faith and would never have been redeemed.

Others point out that the numerical value (*gematria*) of the word *zeh* is 7+5 or **12**, referring to the 12 central rituals of the *Seder*: 4 cups of wine; 2 washings; 2 dippings; *Korban Pesah*; Matza; *Maror*; and *Korekh*.

לִי וְלֹא־לוֹ

Note that it says *li ve-lo lo* – referring to the wicked child in the third person, not *li ve-lo lekha* in the second person. As a result, some argue

The simple one – what does he say? "What is this" (Exodus 13:14)? Tell him: "With a strong hand did the Lord take us out of Egypt, from the house of bondage." (Ibid.)

---

that this phrase of rejection is not said directly to the *Rasha*, but as an aside to others. One needs to be careful not to push the *Rasha* away irreparably, in the hope that he will eventually find his way. Other commentators, however, suggest that in the long run, it is best not to get into a debate with such heretics – because they are really not interested in an answer. Rather, they should be ignored and, thereby, isolated. All energies should be directed at responding **internally** to their arguments.

לֹא הָיָה נִגְאָל

The question remains as to why the *Rasha* would not have been redeemed. After all, there were many unrighteous people among those who left Egypt. Among the most famous perhaps were Datan, Aviram, Korah, and their supporters. (According to *Midrash Rabba* [Ex 2:15], Datan and Aviram were the ones who made known Moshe's killing of the Egyptian oppressor!) Yet they were all initially redeemed, only to later die because of their sin! We suggest that Datan, Aviram and Korah rebelled against Moshe's authority, but did not challenge God. As commanded, on the night of *Makkat Bekhorot* they placed blood on the lintel and doorpost, and performed the Paschal service with their families. The *Rasha*, on the other hand, makes light of his *Seder* obligation and those of others. Hence he presumably would not have placed blood on the lintel and doorpost – and would not have been saved.

תָּם

For the *Tam*, the word *ma* means "What is all this about?" He doesn't understand the connection between the rituals and the story of the Exodus from servitude. R. David Abudarham (*Abudarham ha-Shalem*) calls attention to the order of the four children as it appears in the *Haggada* (*Hakham, Rasha, Tam* and *Eino Yodea Lishol*) does not correspond to the order as it appears in the Torah (*Rasha, Eino Yodea Lishol, Tam* and *Hakham*). Based on the Torah's ordering, R. Abudarham suggests that there are only two children here – as adults and children: a *Rasha*/

וְשֶׁאֵינוֹ יוֹדֵעַ לִשְׁאוֹל – אַתְּ פְּתַח לוֹ. שֶׁנֶּאֱמַר "וְהִגַּדְתָּ לְבִנְךָ בַּיּוֹם הַהוּא לֵאמֹר. בַּעֲבוּר זֶה עָשָׂה ה' לִי בְּצֵאתִי מִמִּצְרָיִם" (שמות יג:ח).

Eino Yodea Lishol and a *Hakham/Tam*. The *Hakham* and *Rasha* are adult versions of the immature *Tam* and *Eino Yode'a Lishol*, respectively. The *Tam* is intrigued by what he sees at the *Seder* and asks basic queries, but he doesn't yet know enough, nor is he mature enough to ask discerning questions. As he continues to probe and study he develops into the *Hakham*. By contrast, the *Eino Yodea Lishol* is a child who finds the *Seder* boring and irrelevant. Because of his lack of knowledge he belittles the *Seder*'s importance. This in turn leads to detachment, estrangement and ultimately distaste for tradition. This is the child that we have to prod and stimulate so that he won't disengage.

I would suggest that the Four Children in the Torah ask their questions at different times, but the Four Children in the *Haggada* ask their questions in each other's presence one after the other. Thus, in the *Haggada*, the precocious *Hakham* asks first because he surmises quickly how and what to ask. To him, we teach the laws of *Pesah* down to details of the *Afikoman* – which appears at the very end of the *Seder*. We were redeemed to **serve**; Halakha tells us how! The rebellious *Rasha*, upon hearing the detailed list of laws and regulations, belittles their importance and relevance, and challenges: "Of what value is this service to you all?" He, thereby, disconnects himself from the God of Israel, the people of Israel, and their Divine mission. We make it clear to him that we chose to proudly be grateful to the Almighty for the Exodus by fulfilling his *mitzvot*. The *Tam* does not comprehend the Passover laws explicated to the Wise child, nor does he understand the sharp challenges of the *Rasha*. But he nevertheless wants to know what the festive *Seder* is all about. To him, we give a pithy message of gratitude to the Almighty for our miraculous redemption from slavery. While all this commotion is going on, the *Eino Yode'a Lishol* stands on the sidelines totally confused. To the latter, we give a personal message: I do God's will because He acted on **my** behalf, when I came forth out of Egypt."

My son Yaakov Yehudah *z"l* suggested that the Four Children in the *Haggada* reflect the deterioration of the generations (*yeridat ha-dorot*)

As for the one who does not know how to ask [who is clueless] – you must prompt him, as it says: "You shall declare to your child on that day: 'It is because of this that the Lord did [all these miracles] for me when I left Egypt' " (Exodus 13:8).

---

so often observed in modern times. The grandfather raised in learning and steeped in tradition is the *Hakham*. His rebellious child, seduced by modernity, is the *Rasha*. The grandchild still feels the positive influence of the grandparent and can therefore ask basic questions. The great-grandchild has no memory of authentic Judaism and can't ask any informed questions – he is the clueless *Eino Yodea Lishol*.

אַתְּ פְּתַח לוֹ

As indicated above, this fourth child does not ask of his own initiative. So it is **you,** the parents, who have the responsibility to initiate the discussion and education process. Many have noted the *Haggada*'s use here of the second person feminine form for "you," *at* instead of *ata*. Some commentators understand this as a hint at the need for a soft warm loving approach to bring the uneducated *Eino Yode'a Lishol* closer. Alternatively, it may be necessary to teach this child all the fundamentals – from the first Hebrew letter *aleph* to the last *tav*.

R. Yaakov Medan (https://tinyurl.com/fu5t6dp3) suggests that the Four Children are commonly assumed to come in pairs: *Hakham* vs *Rasha* and *Tam* vs the *Eino Yode'a Lishol*. R. Medan points out, however, that in the Jerusalem Talmud (*Pesahim* 10:4), the *Tam* is replaced by a *Tipesh* – commonly translated as a "stupid child" – and it is he who asks *ma zot* – "What is all this about?" If so then it is this stupid child – not the *Rasha* – who is the foil to the *Hakham*. Following this line of reasoning, R. Medan concludes that the *Eino Yode'a Lishol* is the one who contrasts the rebellious Rasha. The *Eino Yode'a Lishol* is a *tzaddik* – a righteous Jew who asks no questions and follows commands unflinchingly and unquestioningly. The *Haggada* instructs us; *ve-at petah lo* – open him up and encourage him to ask questions. The Torah is interested that all gathered understand the meaning and implication of the various mitzvot.

יָכוֹל מֵראשׁ חֹדֶשׁ

יָכוֹל מֵראשׁ חֹדֶשׁ? תַּלְמוּד לוֹמַר "בַּיּוֹם הַהוּא." אִי בַּיּוֹם הַהוּא יָכוֹל מִבְּעוֹד יוֹם? תַּלְמוּד לוֹמַר "בַּעֲבוּר זֶה" – בַּעֲבוּר זֶה לֹא אָמַרְתִּי, אֶלָּא בְּשָׁעָה שֶׁיֵּשׁ [פסח] מַצָּה וּמָרוֹר מֻנָּחִים לְפָנֶיךָ.

יָכוֹל מֵראשׁ חֹדֶשׁ

This section continues our discussion of the **rules** for giving the full answer to the child. We are concerned here with **when** (on what date) is there an obligation to answer the child's question(s). We just derived from Ex. 13:8 that the Torah requires a **parent** of a clueless child to initiate a discussion of the Exodus. What's more, the verse cited states "And you shall recount to your children on that day." Which day is this exactly? When does this obligation of *ve-higadeta le-vinkha* begin? The answer to be given shortly (after a brief analysis) is "When Matza and *Maror* are lying before you," i.e. *Seder* night – the 15th of *Nisan*!

יָכוֹל מֵראשׁ חֹדֶשׁ? תַּלְמוּד לוֹמַר "בַּיּוֹם הַהוּא"

We are discussing the verse (Ex. 13:8): *ve-Higadeta le-vinkha ba-yom hahu* – And you shall explain to your child on that day. Just prior to that verse, the Torah (Ex. 13:5–6) indicates: "When the Lord has brought you into the land of the Canaanites … a land flowing with milk and honey, you shall observe this [Passover] service in this month (*Nisan*)." Because the Torah makes use of "this month," one might have thought that the mitzva of *ve-Higadeta le-vinkha* is applicable anytime during *Nisan* – starting perhaps from *Rosh Hodesh* – the beginning of the month. Therefore, the Torah explicitly says (Ex. 13:8) "And you shall explain to your child on **that day**…" Thus, a specific day is being designated.

יָכוֹל מִבְּעוֹד יוֹם

The *Haggada* now raises the possibility that the word "day" – יום – in the phrase *ba-Yom hahu* refers to a daytime period. The commentators suggest that two daytime periods are possible candidates: either the

Yakhol me-Rosh Hodesh

One might think that from the beginning of the month there is an obligation to discuss the Exodus. The Torah therefore says (Exodus 13:8): "On that day." "On that day," however, could be understood to mean only during the daytime; therefore the Torah specifies, "It is because of this." The expression "because of this" can only be said when [Pesach,] matza and maror are placed before you.

---

afternoon of the 14th of *Nisan* – when the Paschal lamb is sacrificed; or on the 15th of *Nisan* around midday – when the Israelites exited Egypt (Ex. 12:41 and 12:51). The *Haggada*, however, rules this suggestion out, by noting that the complete verse (Ex. 13:8) states: *ve-Higadeta le-vinkha ba-yom hahu leimor:* **ba'avur zeh** *asa Hashem li be-tzeiti mi-Mitzrayim.* – **Because of this** [Divine service] God redeemed me." There is something in front of the speaker to which he is referring. The *Haggada* asserts and these are the *mitzvot* of the *Seder*: Matza and Maror (and *Pesah* in Temple times) – whose obligation is on *Seder* night. Hence, *ba-yom hahu* is the night of the 15th of *Nisan*.

מִתְּחִלָּה עוֹבְדֵי עֲבוֹדָה זָרָה הָיוּ אֲבוֹתֵינוּ

Let us now stop for a moment to summarize what we have accomplished thus far in *Maggid* and see where we are headed next. In response to the "Four Questions," we give a suitably concise reply to the children's queries as to the uniqueness of this night – namely, *Avadim hayinu*. This short account authored by Shmuel (*Pesahim* 116a, see our comments on עֲבָדִים הָיִינוּ) emphasizes our physical redemption and contains all the essential elements of the Exodus story: (1) *Avadim hayinu* – that we were lowly slaves in Egypt; (2) that we were miraculously redeemed by the Almighty; and finally (3) that each generation must see itself as if they themselves were part of the Egypt experience. But before proceeding with the full treatment of our redemption, we first presented a few ground rules regarding **who** should recite the *Haggada*, **how much** of a discussion is required, and **when** exactly we are obligated to recite the tale. We now complete our cursory introduction by recording Rav's alternative short answer to the *Ma nishtana* which emphasizes not the

מִתְּחִלָּה עוֹבְדֵי עֲבוֹדָה זָרָה הָיוּ אֲבוֹתֵינוּ

מִתְּחִלָּה עוֹבְדֵי עֲבוֹדָה זָרָה הָיוּ אֲבוֹתֵינוּ. וְעַכְשָׁיו קֵרְבָנוּ הַמָּקוֹם לַעֲבֹדָתוֹ. שֶׁנֶּאֱמַר (יהושע כד:ב-ד): וַיֹּאמֶר יְהוֹשֻׁעַ אֶל־כָּל־הָעָם, כֹּה אָמַר ה' אֱלֹהֵי יִשְׂרָאֵל: בְּעֵבֶר הַנָּהָר יָשְׁבוּ אֲבוֹתֵיכֶם מֵעוֹלָם, תֶּרַח אֲבִי אַבְרָהָם וַאֲבִי נָחוֹר, וַיַּעַבְדוּ אֱלֹהִים אֲחֵרִים. וָאֶקַּח אֶת־אֲבִיכֶם אֶת־אַבְרָהָם מֵעֵבֶר הַנָּהָר וָאוֹלֵךְ אוֹתוֹ בְּכָל־אֶרֶץ כְּנָעַן, וָאַרְבֶּה אֶת־זַרְעוֹ וָאֶתֶּן לוֹ אֶת־יִצְחָק, וָאֶתֵּן לְיִצְחָק אֶת־יַעֲקֹב וְאֶת־עֵשָׂו. וָאֶתֵּן לְעֵשָׂו אֶת־הַר שֵׂעִיר לָרֶשֶׁת אֹתוֹ. וְיַעֲקֹב וּבָנָיו יָרְדוּ מִצְרָיִם.

---

physical redemption but the spiritual transformation of the Israelites from idolaters (like Terah) to the servants of God at Sinai. The proof text from Yehoshua (24:2–4) serves, at the same time, as a seamless entree into a more detailed account of the Egyptian bondage and the miraculous liberation therefrom – which follows next.

Before continuing though, we need to clarify why Yehoshua refers to Terah as one of our nation's *Avot* – "forefathers" – even though the latter was an idolater! R. Yaakov Medan (https://www.youtube.com/watch?v=2uxcMf_hswo) suggests that this accolade was given to Terah not only because he was Avraham's father, but also because all four Jewish Matriarchs – Sarah (Yiska; Rashi to Gen. 11:29), Rivka (Gen. 22:23), Rahel, and Leah (Gen. 29:10) – were his offspring.

וְעַכְשָׁיו קֵרְבָנוּ הַמָּקוֹם לַעֲבֹדָתוֹ

We were now brought close **to serve**, i.e., chosenness for responsibility. (See our discussion above in *Kiddush*.) "We were **now** brought close" – as commented on in the previous note the "now" reflects the idea stated later in the *Haggada* that each generation must feel as if they were part of the Exodus experience and how relevant it is to them!

וְיַעֲקֹב וּבָנָיו יָרְדוּ מִצְרָיִם

The verses from the Book of Yehoshua do more than just explain how the Exodus completed the spiritual transformation of the Israelites.

Mi-Tehilla Ovdei Avoda Zara

In the beginning, our ancestors were idol worshipers; but now God has brought us close to His service, as it is said (Joshua 24:2): "Yehoshua said to all the people: 'Thus said the Lord, the God of Israel, "Your fathers used to live on the other side of the river – Terah, the father of Avraham and the father of Nahor, and they served other gods. And I took your father Avraham from beyond the river, and I led him throughout the whole land of Canaan. I increased his seed and gave him Yitzhak, and to Yitzhak I gave Yaakov and Eisav. To Eisav I gave Mount Seir to inherit, and Yaakov and his sons went down to Egypt."'"

As R. Isaac Zev Soloveitchik (*Hiddushei ha-Gri"z al Tanakh*, no. 158) has pointed out, it also explains why – of all Avraham's offspring who were promised the Land of Israel – only the children of Yaakov/Israel were entitled to inherit it. To explain this, Gri"z cites *Mishna Nedarim* (3:11) which reads: "One who forswears pleasure from the children of Avraham is forbidden to derive pleasure from Israelites, but may derive benefit from the other nations of the world." Maimonides (*MT, Hil. Nedarim* 9:21) indicates that Ishmaelites are excluded from the category of "Abrahamic progeny" because the verse (Gen. 21:12) clearly states: "It is Yitzhak's issue that will be called your seed." But this does not seem sufficient, since Yitzhak had twin sons, Yaakov and Esav (also known as Seir); nevertheless, only Yaakov is considered a true inheritor. The answer, says Maimonides in his Commentary to the Mishna (*Nedarim* 3:11), is found in the *Brit bein ha-Betarim* – "Covenant of the Parts" (Gen. 15) mentioned in the next paragraph of the *Haggada*. In this covenant, God promises the Land of Israel to Avraham and his progeny (verses 7 and 18). However, there is a stipulation that the right to this inheritance is conditional on the exile of Avraham's offspring (verse 13).

> **Genesis 15:7** And He said to him: "I am the Lord that brought you out of Ur of the Chaldees, to give you this land to inherit it…" **13** And He said to Avram: "Know that your seed will be a stranger in a land not theirs, and shall serve them; and they shall afflict them four hundred years. **14** But I will execute judgment on

בָּרוּךְ שׁוֹמֵר הַבְטָחָתוֹ לְיִשְׂרָאֵל. בָּרוּךְ הוּא. שֶׁהַקָּדוֹשׁ בָּרוּךְ הוּא חִשַּׁב אֶת־הַקֵּץ. לַעֲשׂוֹת כְּמוֹ שֶׁאָמַר לְאַבְרָהָם אָבִינוּ בִּבְרִית בֵּין הַבְּתָרִים.

the nation they shall serve, and in the end, they shall go free with great wealth. **16** And in the fourth generation, they shall come back hither...". **18** On that day the Lord made a covenant with Avram, saying: "Unto thy seed have I given this land."

Exactly where this exile would take place is not revealed in this vision; nor do we know why the Almighty felt this exile necessary. However, as the story of Yaakov and his sons plays out at the end of Genesis and the beginning of Exodus, we know that the site was Egypt. Maimonides concludes, this exile condition of the enslavement was only fulfilled through Yaakov. Esav, after all, left the Land of Israel to **inherit** the Mt. Seir region; it was only Yaakov and his sons who went down into Egyptian exile and torment. As the verse from Yehoshua (24:4) emphasizes: "And I gave unto Yitzhak, Yaakov, and Esav; and I gave unto Esav Mt. Seir, to possess it; and Yaakov and his children went down into Egypt." Hence, the Israelites are the only true inheritors of the land promised to Avraham.

בָּרוּךְ שׁוֹמֵר הַבְטָחָתוֹ לְיִשְׂרָאֵל

Having now just stated that Yaakov and his sons went down to Egypt, the *Haggada* narrator makes it clear that this exile was prophesied generations before in the *Brit bein ha-Betarim* – Covenant of the Parts," Gen. 15:13–21 immediately cited in the *Haggada* text. As Yehoshua indicates, of the two sons of Yitzhak, **only** Yaakov and his sons went down into Egyptian exile – and, hence, only they are rightfully deserving of inheriting the Land of Canaan (Israel) – which they indeed ultimately receive. For that we now give praise: "Blessed is He who kept his **promise** to Israel, blessed is He." What promise? Presumably the promise of the Land of Israel. On second thought, though, this praise is highly surprising! After all, are we to be surprised when God keeps his explicit promise?! Several possible answers have been proposed.

(a) The first resolution posits that the emphasis in "Blessed is He who kept his promise to Israel" is not on keeping His promise, but on

Blessed is He Who keeps His promise to Israel, blessed is He! For the Holy One Blessed is He calculated the end [of the bondage], in order to do as He had said to our father Avraham at the "Covenant between

---

doing so to "Israel." We thank the Creator for having Esav choose voluntarily to leave Israel and settle in Se'ir. After all, the text in Yehoshua emphasizes that it was the Almighty who enabled Esav to conquer the Land of Se'ir: "And I gave to Esav Mt. Seir as an inheritance." Therefore, of the progeny of Yitzhak, God only had to keep His promise of the Land of Avraham to Israel – the children of Yaakov.

(b) Alternatively, the reference to "Israel" is to our forefather Yaakov. To encourage Yaakov to go down to Egypt, despite his qualms and fears, the Lord committed himself to escort him down to Egypt and personally supervise the redemption: "… Fear not to go down to Egypt, for I will make you there into a great nation. I Myself will go down with you to Egypt, and I Myself will also bring you back…." (Gen. 46:3–4)

(c) According to the majority of the *Rishonim*, *Barukh shomer havtahato le-Yisrael* here and *ve-Hi she-amda la-voteinu* in the next paragraph are a single unit. Thus, the intent of *ve-hi* (and She) in the present paragraph is to the *havtaha* (a feminine word in Hebrew) – the promise that God made in the *Brit bein ha-Betarim* **to** redeem the Israelites from Egypt. This verse appears in Gen 15:14 where God says: *ve-Aharei khen yetze'u bi-rekhush gadol* – "And then they will go out – with great wealth." The latter verse is a double promise: to extract them after the period of servitude and to have them released with tremendous wealth. In this section, we praise God for "saving" us then, but more so for applying this commitment in **every** generation. As we say in the next paragraph: *ve-Hi she-amda la-avoteinu ve-lanu*. *ve-Hi* (a feminine pronoun) refers to the above *havtaha* (also feminine in Hebrew) – meaning a promise of redemption. Furthermore, posits the Haggada: *ve-Hakadosh Barukh Hu matzileinu mi-yadam* – the salvation of the Holy One Blessed is He can indeed be observed in every generation.

(d) Many commentators find the answer in the paragraph itself. Why is the Almighty to be praised? Because God did a special calculation to determine the *ketz* – "end" – i.e. when the Egyptian servitude would end. After all the *Brit bein ha-Betarim* stipulates that the Israelites would

שֶׁנֶּאֱמַר: "וַיֹּאמֶר לְאַבְרָם. יָדֹעַ תֵּדַע כִּי־גֵר יִהְיֶה זַרְעֲךָ בְּאֶרֶץ לֹא לָהֶם. וַעֲבָדוּם וְעִנּוּ אֹתָם אַרְבַּע מֵאוֹת שָׁנָה. וְגַם אֶת־הַגּוֹי אֲשֶׁר יַעֲבֹדוּ דָּן אָנֹכִי. וְאַחֲרֵי־כֵן יֵצְאוּ בִּרְכֻשׁ גָּדוֹל" (בראשית טו:יג-יד).

be in bondage for 400 years (Gen. 15:13), and only then be redeemed (see also Ex. 12:40 and 42). But, from the combined ages (347 including overlap) of grandfather Kehat (130) – who came to Egypt, his son Amram (137) and Moshe (80 at Exodus) it is clear that the Israelites were not in Egypt for four centuries (Rashi on Gen. 15:13). Indeed, *Shemot Rabba* (sec. 91; cited in Rashi, ibid.) asserts that the Israelites were in Egypt for only 210 years – 190 years shy of the quota required! Nevertheless, the Almighty delivered us from bondage, and for that we give praise. Interestingly, *ketz* in *gematria* is 190; thus, *hishev et ha-**ketz*** implies that God calculated how to overcome the missing 190 years. Commentators have proposed several ways of hurdling this deficiency (*Parashat Derakhim* by R. Judah b. Samuel Rozanes).

(1) One approach distinguishes between different starting points for the various calculations. Rashi (Gen. 15:13) famously argues that the count of "Know that your **seed** will be a stranger in a land that is **not theirs** ... 400 years...." starts when Yitzhak (Avraham's seed) was born. Yitzhak was forced at a time of famine to go into exile to Gerar, the land of the Philistines (Gen. 26:6). From Yitzhak to the Exodus was 400 years. That is why the Torah cryptically says: "in a land not theirs" – and does not specify Egypt.

(2) The second approach is to distinguish between quantitative and qualitative time. Quantitatively, the Israelites were in Egypt for only 210 years. However, the Torah (Ex. 1:13–14) states that the Israelites did particularly backbreaking labor *avodat parekh* – work that crushes body and soul. The Almighty calculated that they effectively accomplished 400 years of work in only 190 years. Alternatively, they were enslaved day and night, thus, working double-time. Finally, because the Israelites multiplied at such a rapid rate, the amount of work the people accomplished in 210 years was what should have taken 400.

יָדֹעַ תֵּדַע כִּי־גֵר יִהְיֶה זַרְעֲךָ

In his *Haggada* commentary, R. Reuven Margaliot notes that God

the Pieces," as it says (Genesis 15:13) "And He said to Avraham, 'Know for certain that your seed will be strangers in a land that is not theirs, and they [Bnai Yisrael] will serve them and they [the Egyptians] will oppress them for 400 years. But I shall also judge the nation that they shall serve, and after that they will come out with great wealth'" (Genesis 15:13–14).

---

promised Avraham that his offspring, though exiled for several generations, would remain *gerim* – strangers, and not assimilate in the foreign land. This is further emphasized when the *Haggada* states: *va-Yehi sham le-goi: melamed she-hayu metzuyanim sham* – "The Israelites remained outstanding there," in other words, a nation unto itself.

וְגַם אֶת־הַגּוֹי אֲשֶׁר יַעֲבֹדוּ דָּן אָנֹכִי

In the *Brit bein ha-Betarim* – "Covenant of the Parts" (Gen. 15:13–14), God foretells to Avraham that his offspring will be enslaved and afflicted in a "foreign land" for four hundred years but will be ultimately redeemed and the tormenters punished. The obvious question arises: If Egypt fulfilled God's will, why are they to be punished?

1. Maimonides (*Hil. Teshuva* 6:5) suggests that even though God stated that the Israelites would be enslaved, He did not specify who would do it. All it says is "a land not theirs" (Gen. 15:13). It was Egypt's own wicked choice and they would be severely punished for it.
2. Ra'avad (ibid.) posits that the Egyptians in cruelty went far beyond what God had minimally ordained. This is analogous to the prophecy of Zekharia (1:14–15) who writes: "Thus says the Lord of Hosts: I am jealous for Jerusalem and for Zion with a great jealousy; and I am very displeased with the nations that are at peace; for I was but a little displeased, and they did join in enthusiastically."
3. Ra'avad (ibid.) further observes that once Moshe warned them of punishment, they were now aware of God's displeasure and could have ceased their enslavement and affliction without repercussions. Once they continued with temerity, they were deserving of chastisement.

וְהִיא שֶׁעָמְדָה

The *matzot* are covered momentarily while the cup of wine is raised:

וְהִיא שֶׁעָמְדָה לַאֲבוֹתֵינוּ וְלָנוּ. שֶׁלֹּא אֶחָד בִּלְבָד עָמַד עָלֵינוּ לְכַלּוֹתֵנוּ. אֶלָּא שֶׁבְּכָל דּוֹר וָדוֹר עוֹמְדִים עָלֵינוּ לְכַלּוֹתֵנוּ, וְהַקָּדוֹשׁ בָּרוּךְ הוּא מַצִּילֵנוּ מִיָּדָם.

Although the oppression inflicted by the Egyptians may have followed Pharaoh's lead, the text (Ex. 1:9–10) reveals that Pharaoh discussed his motives and planned actions with the people in advance. The text then states (Ex. 1:13): "And the Egyptians enslaved the Israelites with rigor," suggesting that the people fully acquiesced and carried out the plan vigorously. Later the Torah records (Ex. 2:11): "…and he [Moshe] saw an Egyptian smiting a Hebrew, one of his brethren." The verse again implies that this was a personal action rather than a royal injunction or initiative. In the case of the fundamentally immoral oppressive actions like those of Pharaoh or the Nazis, silence is not an out.

וְאַחֲרֵי־כֵן יֵצְאוּ בִּרְכֻשׁ גָּדוֹל

The importance of the *rekhush gadol* is not only that it represents partial payment for centuries of labor and servitude. More importantly, argues R. Joseph B. Soloveitchik (*Haggada Si'ah ha-Grid*), it was a tangible symbol of the Israelites' recognized freedom, since only free men can own property. R. Yaakov Tzvi Mecklenburg (*ha-Ketav ve-ha-Kabbala*) takes a spiritual approach to the phrase *bi-rekhush gadol*. The Torah says *rekhush gadol* which refers to the qualitative nature of someone or something rather than *rekhush rav* which refers to a quantitative measure. In a word, *bi-rekhush gadol* refers to the holy Torah that our ancestors were now fully ready to receive. Following R. Mecklenburg's general approach, R. Soloveitchik (*Yemei Zikaron*, pp. 93–95) suggested that the *rekhush gadol* referred to is their *amimut* (nationhood). Simply, in Egypt, they had become a distinct people. Similarly, the Zohar refers to the Israelites becoming a *goy gadol*. Finally, some commentators suggest that the wealth the Israelites exited with was merely bait to draw the Egyptians (irrationally) after them to the *Yam Suf* – Red Sea. Had they thought clearly about the situation, the Egyptians would never have

Ve-Hi she-Amda

The matzot are covered momentarily while the cup of wine is raised:

This [promise] has sustained our fathers and us! For not only one enemy has risen against us to destroy us, but in every generation they rise against us to destroy us; and the Holy One Blessed is He saves us from their hand.

---

challenged God yet again. But as *Haza"l* say (*Pesahim* 11b): *Adam bahul al mamono* – one is agitated, anxious and irrational about his money.

The story is told that R. Joseph B. Soloveitchik asked his young son, Haym, why we have so many aids reminding us of the bitterness and slavery of Egypt. Thus, we eat *Maror* like the *Hakhomim* and then like Hillel. And we use *haroset* to remember the mortar. But we do little if anything to commemorate the *rekhush gadol*? To this young Haym responded that sadly the bitterness of the exile and the dominion of foreign nations has remained prominently with us; however, the *rekhush gadol* has been long forgotten! Actually, R. Ovadiah Yosef (*Hazon Ovadya*) suggests that the *Seder* Table should be decorated with beautiful expensive tableware in commemoration of the *rekhush gadol*.

וְהִיא שֶׁעָמְדָה לַאֲבוֹתֵינוּ וְלָנוּ

It is **this** that stood by (and preserved) our forebears and us." What exactly does "this" refer to?

(a) A majority of the *Rishonim* (see our comments above re: בָּרוּךְ שׁוֹמֵר הַבְטָחָתוֹ לְיִשְׂרָאֵל) indicate that *ve-Hi* (a feminine pronoun) refers to the *havtaha* – the promise of the *Brit bein ha-Betarim* referred to in the previous paragraph. Thus, the Almighty foretells the Egyptian bondage but promises to redeem the Israelites from their subjugation, punish the oppressors, and free the persecuted. The *Rishonim* cite *Genesis Rabba* (44:15, 17 and 19) which notes the extra inclusionary term *ve-gam* in the previous paragraph. The latter comes to teach that Jews, throughout history – not only in Egypt – can rely on God's saving intervention to prevent the decimation of the Jewish people.

(b) Alternatively, the promise may be found in another verse in *Brit bein ha-Betarim*. In Gen. 15:18, Scripture says: *le-Zarakha natati et ha-aretz ha-zot*. Nahmanides (ad loc.) points out that this promise of the

אֲרַמִּי אֹבֵד אָבִי

The wine cup is put down and the *matzot* are uncovered:

צֵא וּלְמַד מַה בִּקֵּשׁ לָבָן הָאֲרַמִּי לַעֲשׂוֹת לְיַעֲקֹב אָבִינוּ: שֶׁפַּרְעֹה לֹא גָזַר אֶלָּא עַל הַזְּכָרִים. וְלָבָן בִּקֵּשׁ לַעֲקֹר אֶת־הַכֹּל. שֶׁנֶּאֱמַר:

---

land of Israel is further expanded in Gen. 17:8 making it an *ahuzat olam* – "an **eternal** inheritance." Nahmanides explains that *ahuzat olam* means that if they are exiled from the land, they will surely return to it. As a result of this promise, the Jewish people need to be physically present on the land; hence, they cannot be destroyed.

(c) The 14th century *Kol Bo* (*Haggada Shel Pesah Otzar Perushim*, Eisenstein ed.) suggests that even if there is no explicit promise for the future, the promise of the *Brit bein ha-Betarim* inspired an expectation and faith that God could and might well show up in other cases of oppression to save the Jews, just like he did in Egypt.

(d) Others indicate that *ve-Hi* is an acrostic for the ingredients of Jewish survival:

ו' – ששה סדרי משנה: ה' – חמישה חומשי תורה: י' – עשרת הדברות:
א' – ה' אחד ושמו אחד

(e) R. Marcus Lehman (*Haggada*) comments that this very persecution – *she-bekhol dor va-dor kamim aleinu le-khaloteinu* – is sadly the guarantor of Jewish identity and eternity. Anti-Semitic hatred won't allow Jews to assimilate or forget who they are. Thus, if we should ask: What is it exactly that has kept the Jewish people from assimilating – *ve-Hi she-amda la-avoteinu ve-lanu*? The answer is: *she-Lo ehad bilvad amad aleini le-khaloteinu*!

וְהַקָּדוֹשׁ בָּרוּךְ הוּא מַצִּילֵנוּ מִיָּדָם

People often wish they could live in times of miracles, a time when one could experience the ten plagues, the splitting of the sea, the *manna* falling from heaven, and God's voice on Mount Sinai. And yet R. Yaakov Emden (Introduction, *Siddur Bet Yaakov*, *Sulam Bet El*) maintains that the very existence of the Jewish people is a bigger miracle than all of the

Arami Oved Avi

The wine cup is put down and the matzot are uncovered:

Go and learn what Lavan the Aramean wanted to do to our father Yaakov. For Pharaoh had issued a decree only against the male children, but Lavan wanted to uproot everyone.

---

miracles described in the Torah. As stated here in the *Haggada*: *ve-Hi she-amda la-avoteinu ve-lanu* – the very existence of the Jewish people is the hand of God, because as a people the Jews really shouldn't be here anymore. By any of the normal laws of history and sociology, we should have been long gone. What's left of the ancient Babylonian, Greek, Roman, or Persian Empires that oppressed us? Where is the mighty Roman Empire that controlled the world? Nothing. And yet we are here today. *She-Lo eḥad bilvad amad aleinu le-khaloteinu, ela she-bekhol dor va-dor omdim aleinu le-khaloteinu*, "for not only one nation has stood against us, but in every generation, they rise up against us."

R. Warren Goldstein has pointed out (http://www.youtube.com/watch?v=0eVMfNQskWc) that these words of the *Haggada* are a remarkable prophecy. Look how they have been fulfilled: there has been a relentless, savage pursuit by enemy after enemy to eradicate the Jewish people. Forget not the savagery of Europe, the Spanish Inquisition, the Khmelnitsky massacres, the pogroms, culminating with the horrors of the Holocaust, and the more recent pogrom of October 7, 2023. And after all that, here we are; and that is why R. Yaakov Emden said that to see the Jewish people alive and well and thriving is to witness a greater miracle than even the splitting of the sea. *ve-ha-Kadosh Barukh Hu matzileinu mi-yadam*: God has looked after us, protected us, and ensured that we would survive, outlive, and outlast every single one of our enemies.

אֲרַמִּי אֹבֵד אָבִי

We are now ready to begin the central section of *Maggid*. Following the instructions of *Mishna Pesaḥim* (10:4), the narrative is based on the first **four** verses (Deut. 26:5–8) of the **six**-verse formula known as *Vidui Bikkurim* or "The Declaration of The First Fruits" (Deut. 26:5–10). During Temple times, this declaration was recited as written by those bringing their first fruits to the Temple. As Deut. 26 makes clear, the purpose of the historical introduction to *Vidui Bikkurim* is to explain how we came to be in the Land of Israel and why we owe the Almighty a great debt of gratitude – *hakarat ha-tov* – symbolized by the first fruit of the land. With his basket of first fruits in front of him, the farmer says the following text:

(5) My father was a wandering Aramean. He went down to Egypt with meager numbers and sojourned there; but there he became a great and very populous nation.

(6) The Egyptians dealt harshly with us and oppressed us; they imposed heavy labor upon us.

(7) We cried to the Lord, the God of our fathers, and the Lord heard our plea and saw our plight, our misery, and our oppression.

(8) The Lord freed us from Egypt by a mighty hand, by an outstretched arm and awesome power, and by signs and portents.

(9) He brought us to this place and gave us this land, a land flowing with milk and honey.

(10) Which is why I now bring the first fruits of the soil which You, Lord, have given me.

Regarding this law, R. Jonathan Sacks (*Covenant and Conversation*) explained:

What makes this law remarkable is this: We would expect, when celebrating the soil and its produce, to speak of the God of Nature. But this text is not about nature. It is about history. It is about a distant ancestor, a "wandering Aramean." It is the story of our ancestors. It is a narrative explaining why I am here, and why the people to whom I belong is what it is and where it is. There was nothing remotely like this in the ancient world, and there is nothing quite like it today. As Yosef Hayim Yerushalmi said in his classic book *Zakhor: Jewish History and Jewish Memory* (1982): "Jews were the first people to see God in history, the first to see an overarching meaning in history, and the first to make memory a religious duty."

The function of *Arami Oved Avi* in the *Haggada*, however, is much more than *hakarat ha-tov* – remembering the past – our roots – and being thankful. Indeed, if the main purpose of reading this selection is merely to tell the story of the Exodus, why don't we simply read the sections in the Torah from the portions of *Shemot, Va-Era,* and *Bo* – which tell the story of the Exodus in detail? After all, the *Haggada* in general, and *Arami Oved Avi* in particular – does not contain extensive details of the servitude and Exodus.

In "The Nine Aspects of The *Haggada*" (Yeshiva University *Haggada*), R. Joseph B. Soloveitchik has identified various elements that explain why the Rabbis of the Talmud chose these four verses (Deut. 26:5–8) as the backbone of the *Haggada*. Interestingly, each of the four verses (in bold in the *Haggada* text above) is first cited in full, and then examined and analyzed phrase by phrase. *Derashot* (rabbinic analysis, derivations, and extension) are cited which expand on various points. Thus, on *Pesah, Arami Oved Avi* serves as the catalyst for group **Torah learning** of the written Torah text – *Torah she-bi-khtav*, and this is coupled with a systematic exegesis and elaboration of each word and phrase – a fulfillment of studying *Torah she-be-al peh* – the Oral Torah. Through questions and answers, all present become involved in **teaching Torah** – *limud ha-Torah*. This reflects the point we made earlier, that the purpose of the Israelites' redemption was to serve God, as the Torah itself says: *Shalah et ami ve-ya'avduni* – Let My people go so that they may **serve Me**! Serve Me in the Temple; Serve Me in prayer; Serve Me by learning Torah and doing *mitzvot*.

The text of *Arami Oved Avi* is in many ways ideal for the *Seder* since it is written in first person which allows – indeed, encourages – all gathered to relive and re-experience the Exodus from their own personal perspective. The limited text allows the *Seder* to be short or long depending on time constraints, and on the creativity and imagination of the participants – *ve-Khol ha-marbeh le-sapper bi-yetzi'at Mitzrayim harei zeh meshubah*. It is drafted in a minimal and pithy style – thus encouraging questions and begging for amplification. These verses serve, therefore, as a jumping board for a broad intergenerational exchange and analysis of the Egypt experience and miraculous Exodus – way **beyond** what the short text describes. Most importantly, the text is flexible enough to be used as a medium for identifying with the rich

Jewish past, its dynamic present, and beckoning future.

R. Joseph B. Soloveitchik (*An Exalted Evening*) furthermore hypothesized, as did R. David Zvi Hoffman (Resp. *Melamed le-Ho'il*, III, 65) before him, that, at the time of the Temple, the fifth verse of *Arami Oved Avi* (Deut. 26:9) was also said at the *Seder* and analyzed. However, with the destruction of the Temple and the scattering of the Jews throughout the diaspora, this verse was no longer relevant to the overwhelming majority of Jewry, and no longer said. R. David Mescheloff has suggested that this verse and its *derashot* should be reinstituted now that close to half of the world's Jewish population lives in the Land of Israel. He has composed a possible text for this purpose which can be found at the end of this *Haggada* in the "Additions to the *Haggada*," section 1.

מַה בִּקֵּשׁ לָבָן הָאֲרַמִּי לַעֲשׂוֹת לְיַעֲקֹב אָבִינוּ

If the *Haggada* here is merely trying to teach us that there were other oppressors of our nation even before Egypt, why is Lavan cited as the principal example. After all, Esav's plan to kill Yaakov (Gen. Chap. 27:41) preceded Lavan's. The truth, however, is that Esav's plan is less problematic since Yaakov himself brought this on by stealing Esav's blessing. In any case, the *Haggada* could have recounted the actions of Pharaoh of Egypt (Gen. Chap. 12) and Avimelekh, King of Gerar (Gen. Chap. 20), who abducted Sarah, before the birth of Yitzhak. There must be something very special about Lavan's actions. R. Moshe Alshikh (Deut. 26:5) suggests that Lavan, by switching Leah for Rachel, was ultimately responsible for the jealousy between Yosef and his brother. This dissension eventually led to the sale of Yosef and the exile of the Israelites in Egypt. R. Ovadia Yosef (*Haggada Hazon Ovadia*) and R. Shevah Kenevil (*Haggada*) posit that the lesson here is that we must always be on guard. We are sometimes persecuted by those who were initially benevolent to us, called us family, and treated us as brothers and equals. Jewish history teaches us that assimilation is no protection against antisemitism. My friend Arnold Schwartz suggested that *Yaakov Avinu* was indentured for three periods of seven years to Lavan. Thus, Yaakov could be considered the first example of an *eved Ivri* followed by his offspring – *Ma'aseh avot siman le-banim*.

וְלָבָן בִּקֵּשׁ לַעֲקֹר אֶת־הַכֹּל

It is not clear when and how Lavan attempted to destroy us, and commentators have made various suggestions. Many point to the chase in which Lavan catches up with Yaakov. They stress the verse (Gen. 31:29): "I have the power to do you harm, but last night the God of your father told me saying, 'Take care from speaking to Yaakov from good to bad.'" According to this interpretation, Lavan intended to wipe out Yaakov and his entire family. The difficulty with this interpretation is that Yaakov's wives and children were Lavan's daughters and grandchildren. In addition, Lavan was upset because he felt cheated out of his flock. Wouldn't it have been sufficient to simply take back the sheep?

R. Moshe Feinstein posits that Lavan attempted to wipe out monotheistic Judaism when he said (Gen. 31:53): "May the God of Avraham and the god of Nahor" – their ancestral deities – "judge between us." This implies that all is the same, and there are multiple valid deities. Besides, as a child, Avraham was raised as an idolater. However, Yaakov was careful and rejected that formula, as it says at the end of the above verse: "And Yaakov swore by the Fear of his father Yitzhak." Avraham may have been an idolater as a child, but his son Yitzhak believed purely in the one God from birth – the one God of the *Akeida*.

R. Shlomo Yosef Zevin (*Mo'adim be-Halakha*) and R. Chaim Kanievsky (*Haggada*) cite the Talmudic ruling (*Gittin* 64a, *Nazir* 12a) regarding one who says to his agent: Go out and betroth a woman for me, and he did not specify which woman. If his agent died without informing him whether he betrothed a woman or the identity of the woman he betrothed, it is prohibited for him to marry all the women in the world. This is because there is a presumption that an agent performs his assigned agency. Hence, one must be concerned with regard to all women; perhaps they are relatives of the woman whom the agent betrothed on his behalf. R. Zevin and R. Kanievsky mention that the *Yalkut Shimoni* (Gen. 24:33) indicates that Lavan wanted to kill Eliezer for his possessions. Had his plans succeeded, Yitzhak would have been forbidden to marry and his line would have come to an end.

R. Meir Yehoshua Krofman (*Hosheiv Mahashavot*), offers a different approach. He draws attention to Yaakov's description of the dreadful conditions under which he worked for Lavan (Gen. 31:40): "During the day, I was consumed by heat, and by frost at night, and my eyes

אֲרַמִּי אֹבֵד אָבִי, וַיֵּרֶד מִצְרַיְמָה וַיָּגָר שָׁם בִּמְתֵי מְעָט, וַיְהִי שָׁם לְגוֹי גָּדוֹל, עָצוּם וָרָב (דברים כו:ה).

וַיֵּרֶד מִצְרַיְמָה. אָנוּס עַל פִּי הַדִּבּוּר.

---

were deprived of sleep." For twenty years, Yaakov hardly slept and was exposed to the harsh elements. It stands to reason, R. Krofman writes, that Yaakov did not voluntarily work under these conditions, but was rather compelled to by Lavan's insistence. Lavan treated Yaakov as a disposable utensil, with utter disregard for his health and wellbeing. This, then, might be the meaning of *Arami oveid avi* – that Lavan relegated Yaakov to the status of an object under his control. Lavan's mistreatment of Yaakov highlights the great miracle of the emergence of *Am Yisrael*. Yaakov, a foreigner treated as a mere object, would eventually become the patriarch of a large, strong, proud nation with a beautiful, flourishing country.

R. Ari Kahn (Explorations, 2001, p. 373) suggests that Lavan never planned on physically killing Yaakov and his family. Rather, as the *Haggada* exactly states, Lavan attempted to "uproot everything" by never allowing them to return to Canaan. When Lavan challenges Yaakov and asks why he ran away, Yaakov responds, "Because I said, 'lest you steal your daughters from me.'" Yaakov's fears are substantiated by Lavan's revealing response: "The girls are my daughters, the boys are my sons, and the flocks are my flocks; and all that you see belongs to me" (Gen. 31:43). According to Lavan, Yaakov and his family (descendants of Nahor and Avraham), belonged in Padan Aram. Allowing them to leave Aram was tantamount to a retrospective legitimization of Avraham's journey to Canaan. It was only because of the warning Lavan received from God in his dream that he agreed to allow Yaakov and his family to return to Canaan.

אֲרַמִּי אֹבֵד אָבִי

The majority of classic Biblical commentaries (on Deut. 26:5) understand the verse to mean "A wandering Aramean was my father" – and refer to our forefather Yaakov who wandered to Aram Naharayim. (See, for example, R. Abraham Ibn Ezra, R. Hezekiah ben Manoah

As it says: "The Aramean sought to destroy my father; and he went down to Egypt and sojourned there, few in number; and he became there a nation, great and mighty and numerous" (Deuteronomy 26:5).

"And he went down to Egypt" forced by Divine decree.

(*Hizkuni*), R. Ovadya Seforno, R. David Kimchi, R. Joseph Kara, R. Joseph Bekhor Shor, and R. David Zvi Hoffman.) Rashbam prefers Avraham as the verse's subject. Nevertheless, *Haza"l* in the *Sifrei* and *Haggada* had a tradition that Lavan attempted to wipe out Yaakov and they attempted to read it homiletically in this verse. *Targum* Onkelus, Rashi, and R. Elijah Mizrahi (on Deut. 26:5) followed in their footsteps.

אָנוּס עַל פִּי הַדִּבּוּר

The *Haggada* here is answering an implicit question. After all, Yaakov had experienced first-hand the precarious nature of living in a foreign land; even his uncle Lavan wanted to destroy him. God Himself told him to leave Padan Aram and return to "the land of his fathers" (Gen. 31:3). Why then did Yaakov acquiesce to Yosef's entreaties that he come down to Egypt (Gen. 45). To this the narrator responds: "He felt compelled to do so by the word" – that is the word of God. The 13th-century *Shibbolei ha-Leket* explains: Initially Yaakov only had thoughts of seeing his long-lost son Yosef in Egypt. But the night before his trip he has a prophetic vision (Gen. 46:2–4):

(2) God called to Israel in a vision by night: "Yaakov! Yaakov!" He answered, "Here I am."
(3) And He said, "I am God, the God of your father. Fear not to go down to Egypt, for I will make you there into a great nation.
(4) I Myself will go down with you to Egypt, and I Myself will also bring you back; and Yosef's hand shall close your eyes."

It is clear that this move to Egypt was in accord with **God's** will. What's more, God wishes Yaakov to remain in Egypt until his peaceful death. Indeed, "He felt compelled to do so by the word of God."

R. Menashe Klein (*Haggada Maggid Mishne*) creatively posits that

וַיָּגָר שָׁם. מְלַמֵּד שֶׁלֹּא יָרַד יַעֲקֹב אָבִינוּ לְהִשְׁתַּקֵּעַ בְּמִצְרַיִם אֶלָּא לָגוּר שָׁם. שֶׁנֶּאֱמַר: וַיֹּאמְרוּ אֶל־פַּרְעֹה, לָגוּר בָּאָרֶץ בָּאנוּ, כִּי אֵין מִרְעֶה לַצֹּאן אֲשֶׁר לַעֲבָדֶיךָ, כִּי כָבֵד הָרָעָב בְּאֶרֶץ כְּנָעַן. וְעַתָּה יֵשְׁבוּ־נָא עֲבָדֶיךָ בְּאֶרֶץ גֹּשֶׁן (בראשית מז:ד).

Yaakov was forced by his **own** words, his own prediction. When young Yosef came to his father to tell him of his dreams, Yaakov himself says (Gen. 37:10): "What is this dream you have dreamed? Are we to come, I and your mother and your brothers, and bow low to you to the ground?" Thus Yaakov's own interpretation of the dream confirms that Yosef was divinely destined for royalty and that the entire family is destined to come before Yosef (in Egypt) and show obeisance. That time had now come!

שֶׁלֹּא יָרַד... אֶלָּא לָגוּר שָׁם

R. Menashe Klein (*Haggada Maggid Mishne*) is troubled by the lack of novelty of this *derasha*. After all, the Israelite's homeland was Canaan, where they always intended to return. Who would have thought otherwise? To this, R. Klein stresses that Yosef tells his brothers to leave their possessions behind in Canaan since he would supply them with anything they needed – "And never mind your belongings, for the best of all the land of Egypt shall be yours" (Gen. 45:18–20). Nevertheless, when Yosef presents his brothers to Pharaoh, he states (Gen. 46:32): "The men are shepherds; they have always been breeders of livestock, and they have brought with them their flocks and herds and all that is theirs." Nevertheless, the brothers say to Pharaoh (Gen. 47:4): **la-Gur ba-aretz banu** – "We have come **to sojourn** in this land." We've come temporarily. Perforce, posits R. Klein, the reason they brought all their livestock was so they could remain independent of the Egyptians and leave anytime they wanted to!

This of course leads to the question of why the Israelites didn't leave after the years of famine were over. (1) Yehuda Kil (*Da'at Mikra*, Summary, Gen. 15, p. 427) posits that this is indeed the reason why the Israelites were punished with slavery. This charge is to my mind unfounded; the fact that the famine ended in Egypt is no proof that it was

"And he sojourned there" – This teaches that our father Yaakov did not go down to Egypt to settle, but only to live there temporarily. As it says: "They said to Pharaoh: 'We have come to sojourn in the land, for there is no pasture for your servants' flocks because the famine is severe in the land of Canaan; and now, please, let your servants dwell in the land of Goshen'" (Genesis 47:4).

---

no longer raging in Canaan. (2) Amos Hakham (*Da'at Mikra*, Ex. 1:10) posits that it was Pharaoh who was afraid of losing them, as implied by the verse (Ex. 1:10): "[And Pharaoh said to his people]: Let us deal shrewdly with them, so that they may not … leave from the land." He, therefore, hindered their departure and ultimately enslaved them. (3) In my humble opinion, they stayed because that seemed to them to be the Divine will. Indeed, in four verses the text intimates that God Himself will redeem them:

> Gen. 46:4 – "[God called to Israel…] I Myself will go down with you to Egypt, and I Myself will also bring you back…"
> Gen. 48:21 – "Then Israel said to Yosef, 'I am about to die; but God will be with you and bring you back to the land of your ancestors.'"
> Gen. 50:24 – "Yosef said to his brothers, 'I am about to die. God will surely remember you and bring you up from this land to the land promised on oath to Avraham, to Yitzhak, and to Yaakov.'"
> Gen. 50:25 – "So Yosef made the sons of Israel swear, saying, 'When God has remembered you, you shall carry up my bones from here.'"

כִּי אֵין מִרְעֶה לַצֹּאן אֲשֶׁר לַעֲבָדֶיךָ

Nahmanides (Gen. 47:4) proposes that even though famine was equally fierce in both Egypt and Canaan, Yosef's brothers explain the fundamental difference between Egypt and Canaan. In Egypt, there is food saved up for the people; hence the grass can be used by the animals. But in Canaan, all the grass has been eaten by the people and, therefore, there is no grazing land left for the livestock.

בִּמְתֵי מְעָט. כְּמָה שֶׁנֶּאֱמַר: בְּשִׁבְעִים נֶפֶשׁ יָרְדוּ אֲבוֹתֶיךָ מִצְרָיְמָה, וְעַתָּה שָׂמְךָ ה' אֱלֹהֶיךָ כְּכוֹכְבֵי הַשָּׁמַיִם לָרֹב (דברים י:כב).

וַיְהִי שָׁם לְגוֹי. מְלַמֵּד שֶׁהָיוּ יִשְׂרָאֵל מְצֻיָּנִים שָׁם.

גָּדוֹל עָצוּם. כְּמָה שֶׁנֶּאֱמַר: וּבְנֵי יִשְׂרָאֵל פָּרוּ וַיִּשְׁרְצוּ וַיִּרְבּוּ וַיַּעַצְמוּ בִּמְאֹד מְאֹד. וַתִּמָּלֵא הָאָרֶץ אֹתָם (שמות א:ז).

וָרָב. כְּמָה שֶׁנֶּאֱמַר: רְבָבָה כְּצֶמַח הַשָּׂדֶה נְתַתִּיךְ. וַתִּרְבִּי וַתִּגְדְּלִי וַתָּבֹאִי בַּעֲדִי עֲדָיִים. שָׁדַיִם נָכֹנוּ וּשְׂעָרֵךְ צִמֵּחַ, וְאַתְּ עֵרֹם וְעֶרְיָה (יחזקאל טז:ז). וָאֶעֱבֹר עָלַיִךְ וָאֶרְאֵךְ מִתְבּוֹסֶסֶת בְּדָמָיִךְ, וָאֹמַר לָךְ בְּדָמַיִךְ חֲיִי, וָאֹמַר לָךְ בְּדָמַיִךְ חֲיִי (יחזקאל טז:ו).

שֶׁהָיוּ יִשְׂרָאֵל מְצֻיָּנִים שָׁם

R. Samson Raphael Hirsch (Commentary on Deut. 26:5) suggests that the import of this verse is that they became a nation unto themselves: that is how the Egyptians saw them and how they presumably viewed themselves. Indeed, Pharaoh himself was the first to describe the Israelites as a nation unto themselves (Ex. 1:9): "And [Pharaoh] said to **his people**, 'Look, the **Israelite people** are much too numerous for us.'" *Midrash Rabba* (Lev. 32:5 and *Shir ha-Shirim* 4:24) cites four ways in which the Israelites stood out: they changed neither their names nor their language; they refrained from gossip, and they refrained from sexual immorality. Other aggadic traditions speak of the Israelites unique or modest dress. The message here is clear: Jews remain great by maintaining their unique culture and identity – not by assimilating! My maternal grandfather *zt"l*, R. Moshe Zev Kahn, would repeat yearly (with a smile, a wink, and in a *litvishe* accent) the following quip: *Metzuyanim* – "They were *tziyoynim* (Zionists) there!"

פָּרוּ וַיִּשְׁרְצוּ וַיִּרְבּוּ וַיַּעַצְמוּ בִּמְאֹד מְאֹד

R. Samson Raphael Hirsch (Commentary to Ex. 1:7) cites the Exodus Rabba (1:8) that the Israelite women gave birth to six at a time. R. Hirsch suggests that this tradition is based on the presence of six

"Few in number" as it says: "Your fathers went down to Egypt with seventy persons, and now, the Lord your God, has made you as numerous as the stars of heaven" (Deuteronomy 10:22).

"And he became there a nation" – This teaches that Israel was distinctive there.

"Great and mighty" as it says: "And the children of Israel were fruitful and increased and multiplied and became very mighty, and the land became filled with them" (Exodus 1:7).

"And numerous" as it says: "I caused you to thrive like the plants of the field, and you increased and grew and became very beautiful, with perfect breasts and your hair grown long. But you remained naked and bare (Yehezkel 16:7). And I passed over you and saw you downtrodden in your blood, and I said to you, 'By your blood you shall live.' And I said to you, 'By your blood you shall live'" (Yehezkel 16:6).

---

synonyms for multiplied and increased (*paru, va-yishretzu, va-yirbu, va-ya'atzmu, bi-me'od, me'od*) which refer to this exceptional fertility. He notes that the simple meaning of the word *va-yishretzu* is to give birth like insects – many to a litter. But you may ask: Perhaps many died in the birthing process? To this the Torah responds: *va-yirbu*. But perhaps many were weak and sickly due to multiple births? To this the Torah adds: *va-ya'atzmu bi-me'od me'od*. What's more, they multiplied rapidly, and *va-timalei ha'aretz otam* – the land was filled with them. That is why the Egyptians saw them as a threat.

Interestingly, the verse says **bi**-*me'od me'od*, with a *bet* prefix, rather than the usual *me'od me'od*. This opens up the possibility that **bi**-*me'od* here is like *u-vekhal me'odekha* (Deut. 6:5) in *Keri'at Shema* – which refers to one's wealth and resources. Thus, *paru, va-yishretzu, va-yirbu* refers to the Israelite nation's outstanding population growth, while *va-ya'atzmu, bi-me'od, me'od* focuses on the Israelite's rapid increase in financial assets.

וָרָב. כְּמָה שֶׁנֶּאֱמַר

The two verses cited in this section are from Chapter 16 of the Book of Ezekiel, but they actually appear here in inverted order, with v. 7

וַיָּרֵעוּ אֹתָנוּ הַמִּצְרִים וַיְעַנּוּנוּ, וַיִּתְּנוּ עָלֵינוּ עֲבֹדָה קָשָׁה (דברים כו:ו).

וַיָּרֵעוּ אֹתָנוּ הַמִּצְרִים – כְּמָה שֶׁנֶּאֱמַר: "הָבָה נִתְחַכְּמָה לוֹ פֶּן יִרְבֶּה, וְהָיָה כִּי תִקְרֶאנָה מִלְחָמָה וְנוֹסַף גַּם הוּא עַל שֹׂנְאֵינוּ וְנִלְחַם־בָּנוּ, וְעָלָה מִן־הָאָרֶץ" (שמות א:י).

---

appearing before v. 6. To understand their importance, let us briefly review the context of this chapter. God chastises Israel for being disloyal. The Children of Israel were like a newborn and deserted baby who is still covered in blood and whose umbilical cord has not been cut and tied. No one really cared about the child – but God did. Passing by and seeing the naked blood-stained baby, the Merciful One commanded the child to live in spite of its blood – *va-omar lakh be-damayikh ḥayi*. And, indeed, the infant grew into a beautiful alluring woman, with whom God made a covenant of marriage, adorned, bejeweled, clothed and fed. But she was disloyal and became a harlot – following other gods and beliefs. *Haza"l* understood this baby as being *Klal Yisrael* (the Israelite nation) in Egypt, covered with the blood of slavery. God commands them to live despite the blood and become a beautiful nation. The verses in the *Haggada* from the prophecy of Yeḥezkel are inverted because the narrator of the *Haggada* wants to use *revava* to explain *rav*. So the narrator starts with verse 7. But then, he wants to assure us that the Israelites flourished despite the torment of *va-yare'u* described in the next verse in the *Haggada*. This is analogous to *ve-Ka'asher ya'anu oto ken yirbeh ve-khen yifrotz* (Ex. 1:12). The more they were tormented, the more they multiplied and thrived!

Haza"l in the *Mekhilta* (*Parashat Bo*, 4) note that the word used by the prophet Yeḥezkel is *be-damayikh* which is in the plural and not the singular *be-damakh*. From this, *Haza"l* derived that before their redemption from Egypt God gave the Israelites **two** *mitzvot* to fulfill: circumcision and the Paschal lamb. Both *mitzvot* involved the letting of blood and both have an element of self-endangerment. It was because of their fulfillment that they merited the Exodus.

"And the Egyptians did evil to us and they oppressed us, and they imposed hard labor upon us" (Deuteronomy 26:6).

"And the Egyptians did evil to us" as it says: "Come, let us deal cunningly with them lest they multiply and, if a war breaks out, they will join our enemies and fight against us, and escape from the land" (Exodus 1:10).

רְבָבָה כְּצֶמַח הַשָּׂדֶה נְתַתִּיךְ

Revava means numerous. However, Maharal (*Haggada Divrei Negidim*) points out that the verse states they became numerous like the plants in the field – which all tend to blossom at approximately the same time. The same was true for the Israelite women: all gave birth at approximately the same time. And despite the great numbers, each plant was attractive and complete.

וַיָּרֵעוּ אֹתָנוּ הַמִּצְרִים

These words are usually understood to mean: "And the Egyptians did evil **to** us." But if that were so, the phrase should have been worded: *va-yare'u* **lanu** *ha-Mitzrim*. Interestingly, elsewhere we find that Moshe gives the King of Edom a similar precis of the Exodus saying (Num. 20:15–16): *va-yare'u* **lanu** *Mitzrayim*. *va-Yare'u* **otanu** *ha-Mitzrim* literally means "and the Egyptians **made** us evil." Thus, the *Sifri* (ad loc.) interprets this verse to mean that the Egyptians **considered** us evil and conniving – though we were neither. In order to oppress the Israelites, Pharaoh had to belittle the Israelites and turn them into a potential threat, if not real danger. This is consistent with the proof text: "*Hava nithakma lo… ve-nosaf gam hu al soneinu* – Let us outsmart them…and he will join our enemies." Thus, Pharaoh charged them with being a fifth column. (See also R. Barukh Epstein, *Barukh She-Amar*, on *Hallel*, *me-Am Loez*.) Others suggest that the Egyptians justified their poor treatment of the Israelites by claiming that the Israelites were ungrateful for the hospitality shown them; worse, they were parasites and disloyal. Many other commentators (*Shelah – Pesah* 189; *Hida – Haggada Simhat Regel*; *Ohr ha-Hayim* and *Ha'amek Davar ad loc.*) suggest that living among the decadent Egyptians had a negative effect on our moral fiber

וַיְעַנּוּנוּ. כְּמָה שֶׁנֶּאֱמַר: "וַיָּשִׂימוּ עָלָיו שָׂרֵי מִסִּים לְמַעַן עַנֹּתוֹ בְּסִבְלֹתָם. וַיִּבֶן עָרֵי מִסְכְּנוֹת לְפַרְעֹה. אֶת־פִּתֹם וְאֶת־רַעַמְסֵס" (שמות א:יא).

and behavior. The text intimates that to survive, many chose to serve as *shotrim* or Jewish police, to supervise and punish their fellow Jews (reminiscent of the Jewish Kapos in the Nazi concentration camps).

In April 1986, when my brother R. Dov Frimer and I visited Leningrad to give *shi'urim* to Refuseniks, Elimelech Rochlin suggested a novel interpretation of this verse based on the Russian experience. He suggested that *va-Yare'u* meant that the Egyptians tried to make **us think** that we were fundamentally evil; thus, there was no reason to be proud of our heritage. It should not be surprising, then, that when Moshe informed the Israelites of their impending redemption – they didn't show excitement or enthusiasm. And so it was with Soviet Jewry, continued Elimelech Rochlin, for so many decades they had been taught that being Jewish was shameful and odious. One should hide and run away from such an identity. One should refrain from making *aliya*, since it merely strengthens one's detestable heritage. (See also the last paragraph in the next comment).

הָבָה נִתְחַכְּמָה לוֹ

At first blush, it is hard to understand why "Let us deal shrewdly with them…" is an appropriate proof text for "And the Egyptians did evil to us." After all, nothing had yet been done! One possibility is that from what follows in the text we see that Pharaohs plan was not a simple whim, but all worked out to the finest detail. That is truly evil. Interestingly, Maimonides (M.T., *Hil. Teshuva* 6:3 – cited below in our comments on דְּצַ"ךְ עַדַ"שׁ בְּאַחַ"ב, para. f2) argues that, as a punishment for repeated disobedience in the five earlier plagues, the Almighty took away Pharaoh's freedom of choice during the later plagues. R. Yosef Sorotzkin, in his *Megged Yosef*, observes that Rambam quotes this very verse of Pharaoh to prove the heinous nature of this plan. To Rambam's mind, the sins which receive such a unique punishment as loss of free will are those which stem from a calculated, resolute decision

"And they oppressed us," as it says: They placed taskmasters over them in order to oppress them with their burdens, and they built store cities for Pharaoh, Pitom and Ramses" (Exodus 1:11).

---

to perpetrate evil. Pharaoh's words demonstrate that the King ordered persecution and murder with a clear mind, with his rational faculties fully functioning, without the slightest bit of moral struggle. For this flagitious and heinous act, Pharaoh lost the ability to repent.

R. Menashe Klein (*Haggada Maggid Mishne*) posits that the real danger is not when our adversaries plan to treat us badly – **that** we can prepare for and resist. The true danger is when our enemies come to us in seeming friendship and try to convince us that what they are imposing upon us is for our benefit. Ramban (ad loc.) expresses a similar idea in describing how the Israelites were ultimately enslaved. Pharaoh began by introducing a large-scale draft for the building of new communities of Pitom and Ra'amses as an economic development project; this eventually escalated into full-fledged slavery.

Alternatively, our clever enemies may initially offer us all sorts of benefits – be they civil, financial, social, or educational. But their ultimate goal is to cause us to assimilate and forsake our Jewish values. Following such an approach and based on the word *rei'a* – which means "friend," Leonard Gamms has proposed that we interpret *va-Yare'u otanu ha-mitzrim* – the Egyptians befriended us. Finally, *Hava nithakma lo* might mean: Let us try to reeducate them by initially treating them well.

וַיָּשִׂימוּ עָלָיו שָׂרֵי מִסִּים

R. Samson Raphael Hirsch (Commentary to Ex. 1:11) points out the gradual buildup of the intensity of the torment. First their fiscal officers harass them and tax them. Next people were drafted for building projects, but that seems to have been under their control. Subsequent verses move them into slavery, as it says (v. 12 and 13): "But the more they were oppressed…and they imposed upon them hard crushing labor."

וַיִּתְּנוּ עָלֵינוּ עֲבֹדָה קָשָׁה. כְּמָה שֶׁנֶּאֱמַר: "וַיַּעֲבִדוּ מִצְרַיִם אֶת־בְּנֵי יִשְׂרָאֵל בְּפָרֶךְ" (שמות א:יג).

וַנִּצְעַק אֶל־ה' אֱלֹהֵי אֲבֹתֵינוּ, וַיִּשְׁמַע ה' אֶת־קֹלֵנוּ, וַיַּרְא אֶת־עָנְיֵנוּ וְאֶת עֲמָלֵנוּ וְאֶת לַחֲצֵנוּ (דברים כו:ז).

וַיַּעֲבִדוּ מִצְרַיִם אֶת־בְּנֵי יִשְׂרָאֵל בְּפָרֶךְ

Rashi (Ex. 1:13) defines *avodat parekh* as hard labor which crushes (*mefarekhet*) the body and shatters it. Interestingly, *Haza"l* (*Sota* 11a) suggest that the particularly difficult element of this work was that they "assigned work typically done by males to females, and vice versa." This suggests both a conscious physical and psychological element to the torment of the servitude.

However, another approach is possible, based on the following ruling of Rambam (*M.T., Hil. Avadim* 1:6): "It is forbidden to work a Hebrew slave ruthlessly (*be-farekh*). What is meant by ruthless work? It is work that has no definite time or limit, or needless work designed only to keep the slave working and occupied." [We would call such work: "busy work."] A good example of this is what the Gemara (*Sota* 11a) tells us regarding the construction of the cities of Pitom and Ra'amses. The Talmud records that they were built on land unsuitable for building, and the structures would often readily collapse and require demolition. This being so, why didn't the Egyptians have their cities built elsewhere? R. Abraham Pam explains that in every task that a human being performs, no matter how degrading and lowly the work may be, there is a fundamental degree of satisfaction that is achieved from the knowledge that the task being performed will provide some benefit. There is a story told of an imprisoned man whose duty was to push a heavy stone wheel around all day long. He was told that his energy was pushing a mill on the other side of the prison wall which was crushing wheat and barley. With the knowledge that his toil would benefit so many people, the man continued in his labor for many years, encouraging himself by thinking of the young children eating bread baked as a result of his

"And they imposed hard labor upon us," as it says: "The Egyptians made the children of Israel work with rigor" (Exodus 1:13).

"And we cried out to the Lord, the God of our fathers, and the Lord heard our voice and saw our suffering, our labor, and our oppression" (Deuteronomy 26:7).

---

hard work. After many years, the man was freed, and he went to see the product of his labor, only to discover that there was no mill, no wheat, and no barley. All of his years of hard labor were of no value to anyone! He became bitterly enraged and demoralized to the point of losing his mind. This was Pharaoh's goal in the crushing labor of Bnei Yisrael. R. Abraham Pam suggested that Pharaoh was not content to break Israel's body, he wanted to break its spirit as well by subjecting it to *avodat parekh* – the purposeless task of constructing doomed buildings.

וַנִּצְעַק אֶל־ה' אֱלֹהֵי אֲבֹתֵינוּ

The *Hovot ha-Levavot* (cited by R. Joseph Elias, *Artscroll Haggada*) remarks that because of the generations of servitude, the Israelites were alienated from God and suffered from *hester panim* – God's hidden presence. They had no direct relationship with God other than what they heard from their ancestors. Hence, out of desperation, their prayer was directed to the God of their **fathers**. R. Barukh ha-Levi Epstein (*Haggada Barukh She-Amar*) observes that the Israelites did not believe themselves to be worthy of God's intervention in their own right. Nevertheless, the text makes clear: *va-yishma Hashem et koleinu* – that the Almighty indeed responded because of their merits, their modesty, and their suffering. The verse is abbreviated because it doesn't really say what they cried out or what God heard. *Tzidkat Yosef* (cited in *Haggada Pilpula Harifta*) creatively suggests that what they cried out was *Elokei avoteinu* [analogous to the Yiddish *Gott fun Avraham*]. Thus, the verse should be parsed as follows; "We cried out to God: 'Oh God of our fathers!'"

וַנִּצְעַק אֶל־ה' אֱלֹהֵי אֲבֹתֵינוּ – כְּמָה שֶׁנֶּאֱמַר: "וַיְהִי בַיָּמִים הָרַבִּים הָהֵם וַיָּמָת מֶלֶךְ מִצְרַיִם. וַיֵּאָנְחוּ בְנֵי־יִשְׂרָאֵל מִן־הָעֲבוֹדָה וַיִּזְעָקוּ. וַתַּעַל שַׁוְעָתָם אֶל־הָאֱלֹהִים מִן הָעֲבֹדָה" (שמות ב:כג).

וַיְהִי בַיָּמִים הָרַבִּים הָהֵם

Several interpretations have been given for the meaning of the adjective *rabim* – "many." This statement appears after a variety of incidents: the flight of Moshe from Egypt to Midyan; Moshe's wedding to Zippora; and the birth of the couple's eldest son, Gershom. Thus, Rashi and Seforno understand the phrase as referring to the many days Moshe tarried in Midyan. Alternatively, the Torah may be speaking psychologically, since days of suffering "drag on." Finally, *rabim* could be referring to the 210 years of Egyptian servitude which were **qualitatively** *yamim rabim* – i.e. 400 years.

וַיָּמָת מֶלֶךְ מִצְרַיִם

Haza"l report a tradition that Pharaoh at this point did not actually die, but rather was stricken with the serious skin disease called *tzora'at*, homiletically considered equivalent to death. R. Elijah of Vilna (Gra, cited by *Ketav ve-Kabala*) asks: What was it that dissuaded *Haza"l* from accepting the verse at face value? The Gra answers, by King David the text writes (Kings I, 2:10): "So David slept with his fathers." Note that after his passing, the text does not call him King David, because there is no kingship after death. But by Pharaoh it says: "The King of Egypt died." The honorifics suggest that the Pharaoh was still alive.

וַיֵּאָנְחוּ בְנֵי־יִשְׂרָאֵל

What was the connection between the death of the Egyptian King and the people's groaning? *Haggada Sha'arei Shamayim* suggests that as slaves the Israelites were even forbidden to complain – which was tantamount to rebellion. Instead, they groaned quietly and secretly.

"And we cried out to the Lord, the God of our fathers," as it says: "And it came to pass during that long period that the king of Egypt died, and the children of Israel groaned because of the servitude, and they cried out. And their cry for help from their servitude rose up to God" (Exodus 2:23).

However, when the Pharaoh died, the Egyptians cried in sorrow, and the Israelites could finally do so as well – from their servitude. R. Samson Raphael Hirsch (Ex. 2:23) suggests that when one tyrant dies and his successor is equally wicked, cruelty has become a national tradition. This is something to groan about!

מִן־הָעֲבוֹדָה

The corresponding verse in Exodus (1:14) reads: "[The Egyptians] made life bitter for [the Israelites] with harsh labor, with mortar and bricks, and with all sorts of tasks in the field." From the latter verse, it seems clear that they had assorted tasks to carry out and were constantly being reassigned. This too could have been a form of psychological pressure placed upon the Israelites: (1) They couldn't get used to one job and do it most efficiently; (2) They couldn't make friendships which would help them cope psychologically with stress and difficulties; (3) Because of the constant moving from job to job, they were constantly insecure – new tasks, new surroundings, new methods to learn. All this seems to have been part of the mental stress consciously applied to them. In Ex. 5:10–11: "Thus says Pharaoh: I will not give you any straw. You must go and get the straw yourselves wherever you can find it, but there shall be no decrease whatever in your work." Pharaoh could have made the Israelites work harder by increasing the quota of the number of bricks. Why did he choose instead to take away the straw? The Rebbi of Alexander suggests that making more bricks would have been more work, but work they knew already. Hunting for straw also involved uncertainty about finding enough, resulting in physical and mental suffering. Pharaoh sadistically preferred the latter.

וַיִּשְׁמַע יקוק אֶת קֹלֵנוּ. כְּמָה שֶׁנֶּאֱמַר: "וַיִּשְׁמַע אֱלֹהִים אֶת־נַאֲקָתָם, וַיִּזְכֹּר אֱלֹהִים אֶת־בְּרִיתוֹ אֶת־אַבְרָהָם, אֶת־יִצְחָק וְאֶת־יַעֲקֹב" (שמות ב:כד).

וַתַּעַל שַׁוְעָתָם... מִן הָעֲבֹדָה

In this verse, the phrase *Min ha-avoda* – "from the work" appears twice. At first, the ruthless work caused them to groan and cry out. But at a later stage, the unbearable situation led them to raise up prayerful cries to the Almighty for salvation. As observed above, they were alienated from their Creator by the years of servitude – and turned to Him out of desperation. At the end of our comments to בָּרוּךְ שׁוֹמֵר הַבְטָחָתוֹ לְיִשְׂרָאֵל, we indicated that many commentaries believe that the excruciating difficulty of the labors in Egypt was taken into consideration by God to reduce the term of bondage from four hundred to two hundred ten years. This is intimated by the double emphasis of *Min ha-avoda* – "from the work." The 210 years were qualitatively *yamim rabim* – i.e. 400 years (*Haggada Mishkenot Yaakov* cited by *Haggada Pilpulei Harifta*).

וַיִּשְׁמַע יקוק אֶת קֹלֵנוּ

R. Joseph Elias (*Artscroll Haggada*) points out that God's name used in this verse (Deut. 27:7) is *yud-heh-vav-heh* which reflects the Almighty's attribute of mercy. The proof text cited (Ex 2:24) uses אֱלֹקִים which describes God as the dispenser of justice. R. Elias suggests the following resolution for this seeming contradiction. In Exodus, we are reading the story as it is occurring. The Egypt experience involved slavery, pain, and suffering, and God's actions don't seem particularly merciful; we, therefore, use *Elokim*. The retrospective in the Deuteronomy *Bikkurim* Declaration sees the whole gamut of the Almighty's action – ultimately leading the Israelites into the Promised Land. The overall picture includes the pain, but also the miracles, the redemption, and the great wealth – and overall, this is indeed merciful and protective.

וַיִּזְכֹּר אֱלֹהִים אֶת־בְּרִיתוֹ

Exactly which covenant, made with all three forefathers, are we referring too? If we are speaking of the *Brit bein ha-Betarim*, that covenant

"And the Lord heard our voice," as it says: "And God heard their moaning, and God remembered His covenant with Avraham, Yitzhak, and Yaakov" (Exodus 2:24).

---

was formally made with Avraham alone. Furthermore, what is the connection between the people's groan and God's remembering? R. Elijah Mizrahi (Ex. 6:4–5) explains the verse as follows. As discussed above, the Almighty made the *Brit bein ha-Betarim* in which both Egyptian enslavement of Avraham's progeny (Gen 15:13), and subsequent retribution and redemption (Gen 15:14) are mentioned. At the same time, God promised Avraham's offspring inheritance of the land of Canaan (Gen 15:18): "On that day the Lord made a further covenant with Avraham, saying: 'Unto thy seed have I given this land…" This second covenant was later reconfirmed with Yitzhak (Gen 26:3): "… I will assign all these lands to you and to your heirs, fulfilling the oath that I swore to your father Avraham." This promise was reconfirmed again to Yaakov (Gen 35:12): "The land that I gave to Avraham and Yitzhak, I assign to you; and to your future offspring will I allocate the land." R. Mizrahi explains that the covenant that God remembered was the covenant regarding the **inheritance of the land**; but no inheritance is possible if the Israelites are still slaves to Pharaoh! Hence, redemption became necessary.

Maharal of Prague (*Gur Aryeh*, Ex. 6:4–5) dissents, because the text (Ex. 2:23) states clearly that the Israelites cried about their labors: "And their cries rose up to God from their toil" (Ex. 2:23). God heard their cry which was about their **toil**, not about the promised **inheritance** of the land. To resolve these issues, Maharal parses the next verse and the sequence of events is as follows. (1) Firstly, the Israelites call out to God about their labors and He hears their desperate cries. (2) This led the Lord to recall His promise to Avraham – wherein He said (Gen. 15:14) "But I will execute judgment on the nation they shall serve…" (3) Finally, having remembered the first part of the *Brit bein ha-Betarim*, by association, God is, in turn, reminded of the second part of that covenant, dealing with the inheritance of the Land which had been reconfirmed with Yitzhak and Yaakov.

וַיַּרְא אֶת־עָנְיֵנוּ. זוֹ פְּרִישׁוּת דֶּרֶךְ אֶרֶץ. כְּמָה שֶׁנֶּאֱמַר: "וַיַּרְא אֱלֹהִים אֶת בְּנֵי־יִשְׂרָאֵל וַיֵּדַע אֱלֹהִים" (שמות ב:כה).

וְאֶת־עֲמָלֵנוּ. אֵלּוּ הַבָּנִים. כְּמָה שֶׁנֶּאֱמַר: "כָּל־הַבֵּן הַיִּלּוֹד הַיְאֹרָה תַּשְׁלִיכֻהוּ וְכָל־הַבַּת תְּחַיּוּן" (שמות א:כב).

וַיַּרְא אֶת־עָנְיֵנוּ. זוֹ פְּרִישׁוּת דֶּרֶךְ אֶרֶץ

Most commentators understand that the *Haggada* here is reading between the lines. The verse's use of *va-Yeda Elokim* – "God knew" – hints that the subject of God's knowledge was related to intimate relations since the verb *yedi'a* sometimes refers to carnal knowledge (see, for example, Gen 4:1; 19:8). The abstention from sexual relations is generally not something one talks about publicly. It is something God "saw," not "heard."

It is unclear though whether this refraining from relations was forced upon them or was voluntary in nature. This actually seems to be a dispute between two Midrashic traditions. One Midrash recounts that when Amram (Moshe's father and communal leader) heard of Pharaoh's decree (Ex. 1:22): "All male newborns should be cast into the Nile," he divorced Yocheved his wife – and the other men followed in kind. Miriam his daughter pointed out that in doing so Amram had gone beyond Pharaoh on three accounts: (1) Pharaoh had passed an edict only against the males, while Amram's action affected the birth of women as well; (2) Pharaoh's decree affected only this world, while Amram's actions affected also the world to come; (3) Pharaoh's edict might be carried out, perhaps not. But Amram's edict of celibacy would most definitely prevent the birth of any children! Hearing this, the men recanted (*Sota* 11b) and Moshe was consequently born.

While the above source suggests the separation was voluntary, other sources imply that it was forced upon them. The Talmud (*Sota* 11b; *Midrash Rabba* Ex. 1:12) indicates that at the end of a hard day, the men were told to sleep out in the fields (to conserve their energy). Nevertheless, their loving wives took the initiative to come out to them with clean water to wash up, food to give them strength, and encouraging

"And He saw our suffering" – This refers to the separation of husband and wife, as it is said: "God saw the Children of Israel and God took note" (Exodus 2:25).

"Our burden" – these are the sons, as it says: "Every boy that is born, you shall throw into the river, and every girl you shall keep alive" (Exodus 1:22).

---

words. These "righteous women" – *nashim tzidkaniyot* – then modestly made love to their husbands – in faith that God would indeed redeem His people. They wanted to assure that there would be a nation to take out from Egypt. Indeed, they surreptitiously birthed their children – undetected by the Egyptians – under the scent of the *tapu'ah* blossoms (Song of Songs 8:5).

R. Yosef Dov Soloveitchik (*Bet Halevi*, Exodus, 2:25), suggests an alternate interpretation to this verse. He indicates that in *Yalkut Shimoni* (*be-Shalah*, *Remez* 234), Satan attempts to dissuade God from intervening on behalf of the Israelites at the Red Sea, noting that they, like the Egyptians, are idolaters. To this, the Almighty responds that the Egyptians acted volitionally, while the Israelites were placed in an impossible situation by their crushing bondage, and hence acted abnormally – if not irrationally. Following this approach, the present line in the *Haggada* should be translated as follows: "The Lord saw their suffering" (Deut. 26:7) – This relates to their departure from normal rational behavior, as it is written "God saw the [abject suffering of the] Children of Israel, and God understood [what was really happening to them, responding accordingly]" (Ex. 2:25).

וְאֶת־עֲמָלֵנוּ. אֵלּוּ הַבָּנִים

Amal is best defined as laboring for naught, travail without value, like the famous verse (Kohelet 1:3): *Ma yitron ha-adam be-khol amalo she-ya'amol tahat ha-shamayim?* – "What real value is there for a man in all his travail beneath the sun?" Therefore, the narrator cites the Egyptian decree to drown newborn babies in the Nile – nine months and a birth for naught. (See also the Abravanel, in the next comment.)

וְאֶת־לַחֲצֵנוּ. זֶה הַדְּחַק, כְּמָה שֶׁנֶּאֱמַר: "וְגַם־רָאִיתִי אֶת־הַלַּחַץ אֲשֶׁר מִצְרַיִם לֹחֲצִים אֹתָם" (שמות ג:ט).

וַיּוֹצִאֵנוּ ה' מִמִּצְרַיִם בְּיָד חֲזָקָה, וּבִזְרֹעַ נְטוּיָה, וּבְמֹרָא גָּדֹל, וּבְאֹתוֹת וּבְמֹפְתִים (דברים כו:ח).

וַיּוֹצִאֵנוּ ה' מִמִּצְרַיִם. לֹא עַל־יְדֵי מַלְאָךְ, וְלֹא עַל־יְדֵי שָׂרָף, וְלֹא עַל־יְדֵי שָׁלִיחַ, אֶלָּא הַקָּדוֹשׁ בָּרוּךְ הוּא בִּכְבוֹדוֹ וּבְעַצְמוֹ. שֶׁנֶּאֱמַר:

וְאֶת לַחֲצֵנוּ

Abravanel notes a seeming redundancy. After Deut. 26:6 says: *Va-Yareʾu… va-yaʿanunu, va-yitnu aleinu avoda kasha*, why does the next verse (Deut. 26:7) say *va-Yar et onyeinu ve-et amaleinu ve-et lahatzenu*? After all, *va-yaʿanunu* and *onyeinu* are from the same root; furthermore, after saying *Va-Yareʾu* and *va-yitnu aleinu avoda kasha*, aren't *onyeinu*, *amaleinu*, and *lahatzenu* unnecessary? As a result of these and other questions, the Abravanel suggests that verse 6 deals with public torment, while verse 7 focuses on the private tribulations – things that at times only God truly perceives and appreciates. Thus, the frustration resulting from abstention from sexual relations is generally not something one talks about publicly. *Amal* refers to throwing the newborn sons into the Nile because of the hardship of bearing, rearing, and hiding a child with Egyptians all around. Finally, *lahatzenu* deals with the psychological pressure and mental stress that a slave undergoes with a ruthless master.

זֶה הַדְּחַק

Lahatz can be translated as pressure or oppression and can refer to either physical or mental cruelty. The Gra (cited by R. Reuven Margaliot, *Haggada*) suggests that Pharaoh forced the Israelites to live under poor cramped living conditions. Similarly, *Rabbenu* Hananel (Steinzaltz *Haggada*) suggested that when the Israelites first came to Egypt their numbers were limited and they lived in spacious homes. With their torment they multiplied, but they were forced to remain in the same living quarters under overcrowded conditions. As *Haza"l* commented: Spacious living quarters give one a sense of inner peace (*Berakhot* 57b).

"And our oppression" – This refers to the pressure, as it says: "I have seen the oppression with which the Egyptians are oppressing them" (Exodus 3:9).

"And the Lord took us out of Egypt with a strong hand and an outstretched arm, and with great awe, and with signs and wonders" (Deuteronomy 26:8).

"The Lord took us out of Egypt" – Not through an angel, not through a seraph. And not through a messenger. The Holy One Blessed is He did it in His glory by Himself. As it says: "In that night

כְּמָה שֶׁנֶּאֱמַר

What does this proof-text in Ex. 3:9 teach us that we didn't already know before from Deut. 26:7? The answer seems to be that we learn that the pressure was consciously applied by the Egyptians. It was a malicious tactic to increase the Israelite suffering and demoralization.

וַיּוֹצִאֵנוּ

We just read at the beginning of the third verse of *Viduy Bikkurim* (Deut. 26:7) that even though God **heard** the Israelites cry, He did not yet remove them from Egypt. This occurred (here in this fourth verse) only after the **end** of the third verse records that the Merciful One **saw** their suffering. R. David Cohen (*Haggada Simchat Yaavetz*) writes that after hearing their anguished cries, God undoubtedly had mercy on them. But that did not require that He take them out of Egypt. It would have sufficed for them to no longer be in crushing servitude. True, the covenant with the forefathers required them to eventually come to Israel – but perhaps a bit later. They might have remained in exile somewhat longer. However, once God perceived their *prishut derekh eretz* – abstention from procreation, and the pending drowning of male children – He knew that if He tarried, there might not be a generation left to take out of Egypt. Hence, He acted immediately.

וַיּוֹצִאֵנוּ ה' מִמִּצְרַיִם

The importance of this section is that, with the Exodus, the role of the Almighty in the world undergoes a major transformation. He is no longer just the "God of Creation" or even the "God of our forefathers." By personally stepping in to redeem Israel, and by changing the course of history publicly, visibly, and miraculously – He thereby becomes the "God of Israel" (*Elokei Yisael*) and the "God of History." He is recognized by Egypt. Indeed, when Moshe first comes to Pharaoh in the name of Hashem, the God of Israel, demanding to set the Israelites free, Pharaoh responds by saying (Ex 5:2): "Who is Hashem that I should heed His voice." To this God responds (Ex. 7:5): "Egypt shall know that I am Hashem," followed by (Ex. 7:17): "So says Hashem: 'With this you will know that I am Hashem." This transformation occurs gradually, but conclusively at the smiting of the Firstborn, as outlined in Exodus 12:12: Firstly, "I will pass through Egypt on this night" – God hasn't taken dramatic action yet, but He cares and His presence is felt. Next, "I will strike down every firstborn in the land of Egypt, both human and beast." God starts taking game-changing action. Finally, "I will mete out punishments to all the gods of Egypt, I am Hashem" – He not only takes action; He takes total control.

וַיּוֹצִאֵנוּ ה' מִמִּצְרַיִם. לֹא עַל־יְדֵי מַלְאָךְ

(a) The emphasis here is on the seemingly superfluous mention of the Almighty's name. Its mention stresses that God himself intervened in *Makat Bekhorot*. No form of messenger, intermediary, or go-between was involved. Since God Himself was personally involved in Israel's redemption, we owe Him a particular debt. As a result of this special relationship, He is not just *Elokei Avoteinu* – The God of our forefathers but also *Elokeinu ve-Elokei Avoteinu* – **Our** God **and** the God of our forefathers.

(b) Abravanel finds the assertion that there were no messengers in the redemption process astounding, in light of the prominent role of Moshe Rabbenu in the plagues and throughout! Furthermore, there is an explicit verse to the contrary! Moshe gives the King of Edom a precis of the Exodus, similar to *Vidui Bikkurim*, which invokes the presence of an intercessor who took us out of Egypt (Num. 20: 15–16):

(15) Our ancestors went down to Egypt, and we dwelt in Egypt for a long time, and the Egyptians dealt harshly with us and our

ancestors. (16) We cried to God, and **He** heard our plea, and **He** sent a messenger, and **he/He** freed us from Egypt.

Abravanel distinguishes between two types of intermediaries. There are messengers that act independently, and it is these that our verse comes to exclude. But there are messengers who only do as they are told. They are like a hand-held sword which is clearly an extension of the wielder. That was Moshe – and, hence, he does not have an independent status. More simply, Num. 20:16 can be understood such that each verb is attributed to the Almighty – including the last one (freed) – as follows:

"We cried to God, [and God] heard our plea, [and God] sent a messenger**,** [and God] freed us from Egypt."

Another approach argues that the verse under discussion "and God took us out of Egypt" (Deut. 26:8) refers specifically to the night of the plague of the firstborn in which Pharaoh allowed the Israelites to leave. **That** night there was no intercessor and God was in full control. The verse "and He sent a messenger, and he freed us from Egypt" (Num. 20:16) is referring to the overall process in which Moshe was clearly involved as God's emissary.

Haggada Ma'aseh Yedei Yotzer (cited in *Pilpula Harifta*) resolves the problematics of this *derasha*, by citing Rashi (Ex. 14:6). The text indicates that Pharaoh led his troops in their pursuit of Israel to the Red Sea. Therefore, when the verse says (Ex. 14:10): And Pharaoh drew near," it doesn't mean that others didn't accompany him; rather it was Pharaoh who led the chase. Similarly, when God says: "And I passed through the land of Egypt on this night – I and not a messenger," it means that He personally will be the **first** to pass through Egypt, kill the firstborn, and pay retribution to their gods.

(c) The *Haggada*'s assertion that no messenger was involved in smiting the *Bekhorot* troubles the Gra (Vilna Gaon, *Haggada – ha-Gra ve-Talmidav*) because of a different verse. The Torah writes regarding the 10th plague (Ex. 12:23): "For the Almighty, when going through to smite the Egyptians, will see the blood on the lintel and the two doorposts, and God will pass over the door and not let the Destroyer enter and smite your home." The verse states the Destroyer/Angel of

"וְעָבַרְתִּי בְאֶרֶץ מִצְרַיִם בַּלַּיְלָה הַזֶּה, וְהִכֵּיתִי כָל־בְּכוֹר בְּאֶרֶץ מִצְרַיִם מֵאָדָם וְעַד בְּהֵמָה, וּבְכָל אֱלֹהֵי מִצְרַיִם אֶעֱשֶׂה שְׁפָטִים. אֲנִי ה'" (שמות יב:יב). "וְעָבַרְתִּי בְאֶרֶץ מִצְרַיִם בַּלַּיְלָה הַזֶּה" - אֲנִי וְלֹא מַלְאָךְ; "וְהִכֵּיתִי כָל בְּכוֹר בְּאֶרֶץ־מִצְרָיִם" - אֲנִי וְלֹא שָׂרָף; "וּבְכָל אֱלֹהֵי מִצְרַיִם אֶעֱשֶׂה שְׁפָטִים." "אֲנִי" וְלֹא הַשָּׁלִיחַ; "אֲנִי ה'." אֲנִי הוּא וְלֹא אַחֵר.

בְּיָד חֲזָקָה. זוֹ הַדֶּבֶר. כְּמָה שֶׁנֶּאֱמַר: הִנֵּה יַד־ה' הוֹיָה בְּמִקְנְךָ אֲשֶׁר בַּשָּׂדֶה, בַּסּוּסִים, בַּחֲמֹרִים, בַּגְּמַלִּים, בַּבָּקָר וּבַצֹּאן, דֶּבֶר כָּבֵד מְאֹד (שמות ט:ג).

Death was prevented from plaguing Israelite homes. The verse does intimate that into Egyptian homes he did have entry on this night. Three answers have been proposed: (1) The Gaon himself proposes that if it were not for God's direct command, there would have been two kinds of death transpiring on *Makat Bekhorot* night – natural deaths and unnatural firstborn deaths. But the Redeemer wanted to prevent all natural deaths so as to eliminate any possible claims among the Egyptians as to an Israelite death. Therefore, God did not allow the Destroyer to carry out natural deaths either. Firstborn deaths God took care of Himself. (2) *Haggadat Simhat Yaavetz*, cites R. Akiva Eiger who maintains that the Destroyer killed only those firstborn who were from the mother and public knowledge, while only the Almighty would kill the firstborn from the father which required private secret knowledge. (3) Finally, Abravanel creatively posits that the Destroyer is Egypt itself! God prevented them from entering Israelite homes on the night of *Makkat Bekhorot* to attack the Israelites as they sacrificed the Paschal lamb – an Egyptian God.

וְעָבַרְתִּי בְאֶרֶץ מִצְרַיִם בַּלַּיְלָה הַזֶּה

It is important to mention that *Makkat Bekhorot* occurred at midnight of the 15th of *Nisan* and Pharaoh's approval to let the Israelite slaves free occurred somewhat thereafter. Nevertheless, the Israelites did not leave Egypt until the following day, as the verse says (Ex. 12:51; see also 12:41): In the midst of that very day, God freed the Israelites from the land of Egypt, in an orderly fashion. The text (Ex. 12:33) tells us that

I will pass through the land of Egypt, and I will smite every firstborn in the land of Egypt, from man to beast, and I will carry out judgments against all the gods of Egypt, I am the Lord" (Exodus 12:12). "I will pass through the land of Egypt," I and not an angel. "And I will smite every firstborn in the land of Egypt" – I and not a seraph – "And I will carry out judgments against all the gods of Egypt" – I and not a messenger – "I am the Lord" – it is I and no other.

"With a mighty hand" – This refers to the dever [pestilence] as it says: The hand of the Lord will strike your livestock which are in the field – the horses, the donkeys, the camels, the oxen and the sheep, with a very severe pestilence" (Exodus 9:3).

---

all that night the Egyptians pressured the Israelites to quickly leave – to the point that the Torah says (Ex. 12:39) that the Israelites were "chased out of Egypt." The lesson for the Israelites was important. On the one hand, they did not flee from Egypt surreptitiously at night – but in full view of day. On the other hand, they didn't leave Egypt as conquerors – but were hurried out! Clearly, the Israelites should never think they were calling the shots; God was!

בְּיָד חֲזָקָה. זוֹ הַדֶּבֶר

Why, of all the plagues, is *dever* – "pestilence" singled out and considered emblematic of a *yad hazaka* – "the Almighty's strong hand"? (a) R. Yisroel Belsky proposed that during this plague of pestilence, sheep – the Egyptian idol – died. This was a stunning blow – "a strong hand" – because it proved that it was God who was in control, and not the god of the Egyptians. (b) R. Ovadiah Yosef (*Haggada Hazon Ovadia*) observes that Pharaoh's magicians referred to the plague of lice as the "finger of God." (Ex. 8:15). If one plague is a finger of God, then *dever* – which was the completion of five plagues – is a hand. Continuing with this line of thinking, the last five plagues which culminate in *Makkat Bekhorot* is referred to in the next *derasha* as a *zero'a netuya* – an outstretched arm bearing a sword. (c) The Abravanel comments that while the Redeemer killed both with a *yad* (animals) and with a *zero'a* (humans – first born), the damage caused by an outstretched arm is greater. (d) R. Azarya

וּבִזְרֹעַ נְטוּיָה. זוֹ הַחֶרֶב. כְּמָה שֶׁנֶּאֱמַר: "וְחַרְבּוֹ שְׁלוּפָה בְּיָדוֹ, נְטוּיָה עַל־יְרוּשָׁלָיִם" (דברי הימים א. כא:טז).

וּבְמוֹרָא גָּדֹל. זוֹ גִּלּוּי שְׁכִינָה. כְּמָה שֶׁנֶּאֱמַר. "אוֹ הֲנִסָּה אֱלֹהִים לָבוֹא לָקַחַת לוֹ גוֹי מִקֶּרֶב גּוֹי בְּמַסֹּת בְּאֹתֹת וּבְמוֹפְתִים וּבְמִלְחָמָה וּבְיָד חֲזָקָה וּבִזְרוֹעַ נְטוּיָה וּבְמוֹרָאִים גְּדֹלִים כְּכֹל אֲשֶׁר־עָשָׂה לָכֶם ה' אֱלֹהֵיכֶם בְּמִצְרַיִם לְעֵינֶיךָ" (דברים ד:לד).

Berzon (*Hadarom* 53, *Nisan* 5744) points out that both *yad hazaka* and *zero'a netuya* appear in Deut. 26:8 which opens with the assertion that God redeemed us alone with no intercessors. Indeed, by the pestilence the Torah states (Ex. 9:3): "The hand of God will strike your livestock in the fields." Thus, this plague was carried out by the Almighty Himself and is therefore referred to as a *yad hazaka* – the Almighty's strong hand. Similarly, *Makkat Bekhorot* was carried out by God Himself and called *zero'a netuya* – the Almighty's outstretched arm.

וּבִזְרֹעַ נְטוּיָה. זוֹ הַחֶרֶב

The sword referred to here is presumably the figurative sword wielded by God in *Makkat Bekhorot* to kill the Egyptian firstborn (see also the end of the last comment). Other commentaries, however, point to *Tosafot* (*Shabbat* 87b), *Midrash Shohar Tov* (Psalms 136), and *Shemot Rabba* (*Bo*) which describe a rebellion of the Egyptian firstborn upon hearing Moshe's warning regarding the pending *Makkat Bekhorot* if the Israelites are not set free. The intransigence of Pharaoh and their elders led the firstborn to raise their swords against them in the hope of forcing the issue. Hundreds of thousands perished in this civil war. According to this, the sword referred to is the sword of the firstborn themselves. These Midrashim posit that the line in Psalm 136:10 (*Hallel ha-Gadol*) *le-Makkeh Mitzrayim bi-vekhoreihem* – "Who struck Egypt through their firstborn," refers to the killing of the Egyptians **by** their firstborn. Similarly, *Makkat Bekhorot* does not mean the plague wrought **to** the firstborn, but **by** the firstborn.

"And with an outstretched arm" – This refers to the sword, as it says: "His sword was drawn in His hand, stretched out over Jerusalem" (Chronicles I: 21:16).

"And with great awe" – This refers to the revelation of the Divine Presence, as it says: "Has God ever tried to take unto Himself a nation from the midst of another nation, with trials, signs and wonders, with war, with a mighty hand and an outstretched arm, and with awesome revelations, like all that the Lord your God did for you in Egypt before your eyes" (Deuteronomy 4:34)

וּבְמוֹרָא גָּדֹל. זוֹ גִּלּוּי שְׁכִינָה

According to R. Joseph B. Soloveitchik (*Haggada Si'ah ha-Grid*), *Gilui Shekhina* – the revelation of God's presence as a sensory experience is a fundamental element of the miracles experienced in Egypt. They generated great awe and fear. After all, why did the Redeemer need to do all the miracles and plagues described in the Torah just to convince Pharaoh to release the Israelites? Why didn't he simply force Pharaoh to let them free from the get-go? The answer is that the dragged-out process of miracles and plagues was not just about redemption. It was on one hand, an educational process of reintroducing the "God of Israel" to the Children of Israel – as God declares (Ex. 6:7) "And you shall know that I, Hashem, am your God who freed you from the labors of the Egyptians." More importantly, however, the redemptive process is about revealing God to Pharaoh and the world.

Pharaoh had no knowledge of Hashem, the God of Israel – as Pharaoh himself says: (Ex. 5:2): "I do not know Hashem." The Almighty is now the God of history, recognized and manifest in history. As Moshe declares before the first plague (Ex. 7:17): "Thus says Hashem, 'By this you shall know that I am Hashem.'" I shall strike the water in the Nile with the rod that is in my hand, and it will be turned into blood." This declaration is thereafter repeated in the Torah. The double educational role of this revelation to Israel and Egypt (the World) is repeated in the proof text (Deut. 4:34): "All that God did to **Egypt** before **your** eyes."

The *Bet HaLevi* (R. Joseph B. Soloveitchik's namesake and great-grandfather) explains that prophecy doesn't normally mean that

וּבְאֹתוֹת. זֶה הַמַּטֶּה, כְּמָה שֶׁנֶּאֱמַר: "וְאֶת הַמַּטֶּה הַזֶּה תִּקַּח בְּיָדֶךָ, אֲשֶׁר תַּעֲשֶׂה־בּוֹ אֶת הָאֹתֹת" (שמות ד:יז).

וּבְמֹפְתִים. זֶה הַדָּם, כְּמָה שֶׁנֶּאֱמַר: "וְנָתַתִּי מוֹפְתִים בַּשָּׁמַיִם וּבָאָרֶץ: דָּם וָאֵשׁ וְתִימְרוֹת עָשָׁן" (יואל ג:ג).

Remove one drop of wine for each of the previous 3 calamities.

דָּבָר אַחֵר: בְּיָד חֲזָקָה שְׁתַּיִם, וּבִזְרֹעַ נְטוּיָה שְׁתַּיִם, וּבְמֹרָא גָּדֹל – שְׁתַּיִם, וּבְאֹתוֹת – שְׁתַּיִם, וּבְמֹפְתִים – שְׁתַּיִם.

God is located in the location of the **prophecy**, merely that He is spiritually linked to the **prophet**. But on the night of *Makkat Bekhorot*, God made Himself palpably present as He passed through Egypt. This is what is called *Gilui Shekhina* – God's presence is revealed. It was this presence that is described in the verse (Ex. 12:12): "On that night I will go through the land of Egypt" that led to the next step which is "I will mete out punishments to all the gods of Egypt." According to the Midrash (*Yalkut Shimoni*, *Remez* 200; cited by Rashi ad loc.), what this means is that the idols underwent self-destruction – stone melted, wood rotted, metals rusted. This is because there cannot be a revelation of God's presence in a location tainted by the impurity of idolatry; the latter therefore disintegrates.

דָּם

This verse comes from the Prophet Yoel and refers to the redemption from Gog and Magog in the Messianic period (not the Egyptian Exodus). It is brought to prove that *mofet* refers to blood, i.e., that blood is a wonder – not necessarily a punishment. The signs refer to the snake, *tzara'at* (a skin ailment) and blood (see Ex. Chap. 4) that God had Moshe perform so that the Israelites and the Egyptians would become aware of Him.

"And with signs" – This refers to the staff, as it says: "Take into your hand this staff with which you shall perform the signs" (Exodus 4:17).

"And with wonders" – This refers to the blood, as it says: "And I shall show wonders in the heavens and on the earth: **blood, fire and columns of smoke**." (Joel 3:3).

Remove one drop of wine for each of the previous 3 calamities.

Another interpretation [of the preceding verse]: "With a mighty hand" – two [plagues]. "And with an outstretched arm" – two. "And with great awe" – two. "And with signs" – two. "And with wonders" – two.

Remove one drop of wine

When we recite the three wonders mentioned by the Prophet Yoel, we remove some wine from our cup. The same is done at the mention of each of the Ten Plagues, and their three abbreviations by R. Yehuda. Some remove the wine with their finger, others with a spoon, yet others by spilling off a bit from their cup. The method used may depend on the reason for the custom. R. Moses Isserles (*Darkei Moshe*) suggests that a finger is used to remind us that the plagues are *etzba Elokim* – "the finger of God. (Ex. 8:15)." Abravanel indicates that wine represents joy and happiness, and the goal of the custom is to lessen our joy as we read of the travail of our enemies. This is based on the verse in Proverbs 24:17: "If your enemy falls, do not exult." Hence any method is acceptable. While we undoubtedly rejoice at the salvation of the Israelites, and recite *Hallel* in thanks and praise – we are not insensitive to the loss of life, even of the wicked.

וּבְאֹתוֹת – שְׁתַּיִם

For this count *be-yad ḥazaka*, *bi-zro'a netuya*, *be-mora gadol* are each considered two, because they are two-word phrases, while *otot* and *moftim* are in the plural – so they also count for two each as well.

אֵלּוּ עֶשֶׂר מַכּוֹת שֶׁהֵבִיא הַקָּדוֹשׁ בָּרוּךְ הוּא עַל־הַמִּצְרִים בְּמִצְרַיִם. וְאֵלּוּ הֵן:

As each of the Ten Plagues is mentioned, a drop of wine is removed from the cup.

כִּנִּים	צְפַרְדֵּעַ	דָּם
שְׁחִין	דֶּבֶר	עָרוֹב
חֹשֶׁךְ	אַרְבֶּה	בָּרָד

מַכַּת בְּכוֹרוֹת

אֵלּוּ עֶשֶׂר מַכּוֹת

We have essentially completed our analysis of the fourth and last verse of *Viduy Bikurim* (Deut. 26:8) which is the backbone of the *Maggid* section of the *Haggada*. We are about to list the ten plagues, but before doing so, let us review how *Haza"l* expanded upon this last verse and used it to summarize all the important elements of the Exodus story. The complete verse reads as follows: *va-Yotzi'enu mi-Mitzrayim be-yad hazaka, u-vi-zero'a netuya, u-ve-mora Gadol, u-ve-otot u-ve-moftim.*

va-Yotzi'enu mi-Mitzrayim – God Himself was personally involved in Israel's redemption and we owe him a particular debt of gratitude. As a result of this special relationship, He is not just the God of our forefathers but also *Elokeinu ve-lokei avoteinu* – **our** God.

be-yad hazaka – corresponds to the first five plagues through pestilence, while *u-vi-zero'a netuya* – represents the second five plagues culminating with *Makkat Bekhorot*. These ten plagues, particularly the last one, resulted in *mora Gadol* which refers to the palpable revelation of Hashem as the God of history both by the Israelites and the Egyptians.

Finally, *u-ve-otot u-ve-moftim* refers to all the miracles and signs (see Ex. Chap. 4) that God performed so that the Israelites and the Egyptians would become aware of Him.

וְאֵלּוּ הֵן

R. Dovid Cohen (*Haggada Simhat Ya'avetz*) maintains that recounting the *Makkot* is a fundamental element of telling the story of the Exodus, as the verse says (Ex. 10:2): "So that you may recount into your

These are the Ten Plagues which the Holy One Blessed is He brought upon the Egyptians in Egypt, and they are as follows:

As each of the Ten Plagues is mentioned, a drop of wine is removed from the cup.

Blood.   **Frogs.**   **Lice.**
Wild Beasts.   **Pestilence.**   **Boils.**
Hail.   **Locusts.**   **Darkness.**
Slaying of the Firstborn.

---

child's ears and those of your child's child how I made a mockery of the Egyptians and how I displayed My signs among them – in order that you may know that I am God." Here we fulfill this detail. For, after all, the liberation of the Israelites occurred only with *Makkat Bekhorot*, and God could have begun with it. But He decided that nine plagues should precede it, toying with Pharaoh and thereby getting the educational message out to the Israelites and the Egyptians, as to who really is in control of the world, history, and the forces of nature. We should point out that in addition to the **educational components** of the plagues, they also served as **punishment** for the Egyptians for their maltreatment and enslavement of the Israelites. This is already stated in the *Brit bein ha-Betarim* (Covenant of the Pieces) made between the Almighty and Avraham (Gen. 15:13–14): "And He said to Avram: 'Know that your seed will be a stranger in a land not theirs, and shall serve them; and they shall afflict them four hundred years. But I will execute judgment on the nation they shall serve….'"

דָּם

R. Dovid Cohen (*Haggada Simhat Ya'avetz*) remarks that the major reason that the Egyptians refrained from drinking from the Nile was not because it had turned to blood. After all, the Torah had to repeatedly warn Jews not to drink blood, though this was the custom of the world around them. Blood was considered the life force and healthy! Rather, the Egyptians abstained from doing so because of the stench of the Nile water, caused by the putrefaction of the dead fish. This is explicitly stated in the Torah – but usually missed (Ex. 7:21): "And the fish in the Nile died, and the Nile stank so that the Egyptians could not drink water from the Nile."

צְפַרְדֵּעַ

Abravanel and Seforno posit that the *tzfarde'a* were "crocodiles." Indeed, the Nile crocodile is ca. 16 ft. (4.9 m) long, weighs 500 lbs (227 kg) and is known to attack human beings.

שְׁחִין

R. Yehuda Herzl Henkin (*Hiba Yeteira*) indicates that the verse (Ex. 9:9) records that both humans and animals were stricken with *shkhin* – boils. What was Hashem's message in doing so? What extra punishment is there by having both animals and humans receive the same disease? R. Henkin posits that the take-home lesson from this zoonotic disease is that man – even a Pharaoh – is not much above the animals. Alternatively, since the disease was passed on by men and animals alike, it presented a greater threat, spreading the suffering rapidly.

אַרְבֶּה

(a) The Torah describes the uniqueness of the locust plague (Ex. 10:14) as follows: "Locusts invaded all the land of Egypt and settled within all the territory of Egypt in a thick mass; never before had there been so many, nor will there ever be so many again." This statement is seemingly contradicted by a similar verse describing a locust plague during the time of the Prophet Yoel (2:2): "A vast, enormous horde – nothing like it has ever happened, and it shall never happen again..." The statements seem to be mutually exclusive. Rashi (Ex. 10:14) argues that the locust of Yoel had a greater total number, but it was made up of four types of locusts (*arbeh, yelek, hasil,* and *gezem*). By contrast, the *arbeh* of Moshe may have been less numerous overall but was made up of only a single type. (Rashi's answer seems problematic since in Psalms 78:46 and Psalms 105:34, quoted below in our comments to דְּצַ"ךְ עֲדַ"שׁ בְּאַחַ"ב, the locust plague is mentioned as containing in addition to *arbeh*, either *hasil* or *yelek*. *Siftei Hakhamim* responds that the other types were only mentioned as synonyms for poetic beauty.) *Da'at Zekenim mi-Ba'alei ha-Tosafot* suggests that in both cases there were various types. However, in Exodus, they all came together, while in Yoel they came one after the other. Finally, *Ba'al ha-Turim* and *Agra de-Kalla* propose that the plague in the time of Moshe was unique in that the locusts rested from eating on *Shabbat*. This follows those traditions that the Ten Plagues did not function on *Shabbat*. *Ba'al ha-Turim* derives this from the *Mesora* which points out that the word *va-yanaḥ* appears twice in *Ḥumash*: once by the locusts: *va-yanaḥ be-khol gevul Mitzrayim* (Ex. 10:14), and once by *Shabbat*, *va-yanaḥ ba-yom ha-shevi'i* (Ex. 20:11). By contrast, in the case of the Prophet Yoel, the locusts did not rest on *Shabbat*.

(b) At the request of Pharaoh that the locusts be removed, "God caused a shift in a very strong west wind, which lifted the locusts and hurled them into the Red Sea; not a single locust remained in all the territory of Egypt" (Ex. 10:19). R. Yehuda Herzl Henkin (*Hiba Yeteira*) suggests that the Almighty drove the locusts into the sea so that they would not migrate elsewhere and present a future threat to Egypt or to other neighboring countries.

חֹשֶׁךְ

(a) In the Plague of Darkness, the verse says (Ex. 10: 22–23): "… A thick darkness descended upon all the land of Egypt for three days. People could not see one another, and for three days no one could move about…" Rashi (ad loc.) comments that this plague lasted six days: "There was pitch darkness when no man saw another during those three days, and there was an additional period of three days' darkness, twice as thick as this, when no man rose from his place…." As Moshe is leaving Pharaoh following the six days of darkness, he warns Pharaoh (Ex. 11:4, see also *Berakhot* 11b) that the following night (15th of *Nisan*) would be the Plague of the Firstborn.

In our discussion of *Shabbat ha-Gadol* above, we noted that the Talmud (*Shabbat* 87b) fixes the Israelite Exodus to Thursday the fifteenth of *Nisan*. *Tosafot* (ad loc., s.v. *ve-Oto*) calculates from this that the previous *Shabbat* was the 10th of *Nisan* when the Israelites publicly set aside their Paschal lamb as a sacrifice. *Midrash Rabba* (*Bo*) indicates that this designation was done at great personal risk because the lamb was the god of the Egyptians. Indeed, miraculously the Israelites proceeded without fear and the Egyptians did not harm them. R. Yaakov Yehoshua Falk (*Pnei Yehoshua*, cited in *Moriah*, Vol. 18, issue 5–6, *Nisan* 5752, p. 35) asks why there should have been any danger in the lamb selection. After all, based on the above discussion, the 10th of *Nisan* fell within the six days of darkness that preceded the 15th of *Nisan*, and the Egyptians simply would not have **seen** any selection of a lamb! R. Falk cleverly resolves the query by noting – as we did above – that the 10th fell on *Shabbat*, and there are traditions that the plagues did not function on *Shabbat* (see the discussion of the locust – אַרְבֶּה above). Hence, the Egyptians could well have seen the lamb selection.

(b) We have a clear sense that each of the ten plagues increased in intensity over those before it. While there is no question that the Plague of Darkness was a horrifying, enervating experience, in what way was this plague more traumatic than the previous eight plagues had been? R. Shabsi Yudelewitz (https://tinyurl.com/yf4kakj6), the venerable *Maggid* of Yerushalayim, answers this question as follows. As we saw above, during *Makkat Hoshekh*, the Egyptians were engulfed in thick darkness, but the loneliness made it worse. As the text itself says (Ex. 10:23): "People could not see one another, and for three days no one could move about." Thus, they could not share their feelings of fear, anger, grief, and frustration with anyone else. This is why *Hoshekh* was so devastating. True, the earlier plagues had caused great destruction, almost ruining the entire country, but each Egyptian had not suffered alone. They all suffered collectively, and this gave them a measure of comfort and eased their pain. One can accede to the most ruinous plague as long as he is not alone, as long as he can share his travail with his fellow man. In *Makkat Hoshekh*, as just quoted: "People could not see one another." They had no one to commiserate with. This added "feature" rendered the plague nigh unbearable. (This aspect of isolation explains much of the psychological suffering experienced during the Corona pandemic. All this occurred despite the fact that we have phones, WhatsApp, Zoom, radio, TV, etc. – which despite social distancing – allowed one to stay virtually connected and in touch.)

מַכַּת בְּכוֹרוֹת

(a) R. Joseph B. Soloveitchik (*Haggada Si'ah ha-Grid*) asks why the firstborn of all the children were selected for punishment. He suggests that one nation cannot subjugate another just by the decree of the king, unless the leadership, its governors, and priests aid in the process. We know that in many cultures the firstborn was *in loco parentis*, receiving a double portion or more of the inheritance, a power figure in the family, and, hence, considered the future communal and national leaders – both secular and religious. When God comes to punish the Egyptians, he takes revenge on its heads and leadership, and on the firstborn destined to take over.

(b) The *Pesaḥ Seder* in Egypt was also the night of *Makkat Bekhorot*. The Torah records that one of the truly eerie events of that *Seder* was that no dogs barked all night – *Lo yeḥeratz kelev leshono* (Ex. 11:7) – despite all the wailing and commotion in the Egyptian homes. Some commentaries propose that the lack of barking was done to prevent the Israelites from being frightened (R. Abraham ben ha-Rambam; Shadal). Alternatively, the silence emphasized the *Gilui Shekhina* – the sensation of awe that even the canines sensed as God passed through Egypt (see our comments above on וּבְמוֹרָא גָּדֹל. זוֹ גִּלּוּי שְׁכִינָה). This reminds one of the wonderful quote from Arthur Conan Doyle (*The Adventure of Silver Blaze*): "I draw your attention," he said to Dr. Watson, "to the curious incident of the dog at night." "But the dog did nothing at night," said Watson. "That," said Holmes, "is the curious incident."

(c) Two things are unique about the midnight of *Makkat Bekhorot*. The first is that the Torah (Ex. 12:29) records that it occurred exactly at midnight: *va-Yehi ba-ḥatzi ha-layla ve-Hashem hikka kol bekhor be-Eretz Mitzrayim*…. Midnight does not mean twelve on the clock, but halfway through the night between sunset and sunrise – when the sky is the blackest and metaphorically hope is the bleakest. Interestingly, there is one other place in the Bible where this phrase appears, in *Megillat Ruth* (3:8): *va-Yehi ba-ḥatzi ha-layla va-yeḥerad ha-ish va-yilafet, ve-hinei isha shokhevet le-margelotav*. Here Ruth seeks out Boaz, as Naomi had urged. In both cases, what happens at *ḥatzot ha-layla* is the source of their salvation and that of *Klal Yisrael*.

The other curious thing is that although *Makkat Bekhorot* was carried out precisely at midnight – **ba**-*ḥatzi ha-layla*, Moshe warns Pharaoh that God will kill the country's firstborn at **around** midnight –*ka-ḥatzot ha-layla*. The Gemara (*Berakhot* 4a) explains that Moshe feared the possibility of a miscalculation on the part of the Egyptian astronomers.

רַבִּי יְהוּדָה הָיָה נוֹתֵן בָּהֶם סִמָּנִים:

Remove a drop of wine for each acronym:

דְּצַ"ךְ עֲדַ"שׁ בְּאַחַ"ב.

If the plague does not take place at the moment they expect based on their incorrect computation, they might deny the authenticity of Moshe's prophecy and accuse him of making it all up. He, therefore, intentionally predicted that the plague would take effect "at **around** midnight," so that they could not accuse him of inaccuracy. The obvious question arises as to why Moshe feared the skepticism of the Egyptian scientists. After all, they had already seen the Almighty's power; would a few seconds change their perspective? After the first nine plagues, would this feared slight discrepancy actually have had a detrimental effect on Moshe's credibility?

R. David Silverberg cites many explanations that have been offered for this Gemara (http://gush.net/archive/salt-shemot/15-6bo.htm). R. Eliyahu Meir Bloch of the Telshe Yeshiva posits that indeed even a perceived delay in the onset of the plague could potentially diminish *kĕvod Shamayim* (God's honor). If the plague would occur several minutes after the expected moment, this would be the time during which the Egyptian scientists questioned the Almighty's power. Even though the discrepancy would be later shown to be the astronomer's error, the skepticism would remain.

R. Silverberg proposes that one of the declared purposes of the plagues was not only to free the Israelites but also to ensure that "Egypt shall know that I am the Lord" (Ex. 7:5). Pharaoh denied the existence of an authority higher than himself and therefore felt justified in subjugating the Israelites. The release of Hebrews had to teach Pharaoh and the world about the existence and power of God. To that end, Moshe left his prediction ambiguous, so that the astrologers had no possibility of questioning the accuracy of his prophecy, and they would indeed come to "know that I am the Lord."

Finally, R. Ovadiah Yosef (*Me'or Yisrael, Berakhot* 4a) suggests that Moshe was forced to say *ka-hatzot ha-layla*, because the discrepancy would perforce be large! God was referring to midnight **Israel** time (Jerusalem: tinyurl.com/ypzwz5n4) which at *Pesah* time (15th of *Nisan*,

Rabbi Yehuda abbreviated them by their [Hebrew] initials:

Remove a drop of wine for each acronym:

DeTzaKh **ADaSh** **BeAHaV**
blood, frogs, lice   wild beasts, pestilence, boils   hail, locusts, darkness, slaying of the firstborn.

---

mid-April) is about 16 minutes earlier than midnight **Egypt** time (Cairo: tinyurl.com/37hayvbz). Midnight Israel time was chosen since according to *Shemot Rabba* (*Bo, Parasha* 18) the midnight hour was the result of an agreement between Avraham and God. Avraham took the first half of the fifteenth of *Nisan* for his battle against the four kings (Gen. 14:15) to recover Lot, while God took the second half of the night for the Plague of the Firstborn. Since the halving of the night for Avraham occurred in Canaan (according to Israel-time), the second half (though occurring in Egypt) by necessity began according to Israel-time as well.

דְּצַ"ךְ עֲדַ"ש בְּאַחַ"ב

(a) The obvious question is why R. Yehuda felt it important to impart this mnemonic? Assorted answers have been proposed: (1) The simple answer is that *Haza"l* taught us that (*Pesah*im 3b): "One should always teach his student in a concise manner." And this is, of course, exactly what R. Yehuda did. (2) Another possibility is that R. Yehuda wanted to remind us of what appears in *Midrash Rabba* (Ex. 5:6; cited by Ramban to Ex. 4:21), namely, that this acronym is important since it was engraved on Aharon's staff which was used to perform the plagues. (3) Alternatively, R. Yehuda may have been hesitant to invoke the full names of ten terrible illnesses, plagues, and suffering (along the lines of *al tiftah peh le-Satan*). Nevertheless, the majority opinion maintains that detailing the plagues is a praise of the Redeemer, an integral part of the Egyptian Exodus tale, and incorporates many important theological lessons (R. Menashe Klein, *Haggada Maggid Mishne*). (4) R. Yehuda may have wanted to emphasize that the tenth plague is *Bekhorot* (thus בְּאַחַ"ב) – that the firstborn were killed by God, and not *Makkat Bekhorot* (thus בְּאַחַ"מ). The armed uprising of the Egyptian firstborn upon hearing Moshe's warning regarding their pending death is described in *Midrash Shohar Tov* (Psalms 136) and *Shemot Rabba* (Bo). The intransigence of Pharaoh and their elders led the firstborns themselves to raise their swords against the leadership in the hope of forcing the issue and hundreds of thousands perished in this civil war. (5) Finally, R. Yehuda may have wanted to leave us with an official concise list of the ten plagues and their proper order. This is because Psalms 78:44–51 and 105:28–36 give two different poetic presentations of the plagues. In these Psalms, the plagues are incorporated and ordered based on poetic considerations – not necessarily based on historical tradition. Thus, in Psalm 78, only seven plagues appear and their order is: *dam, arov, tzefarde'a, arbeh, barad, dever,* and *bekhorot* – with *kinim, shehin* and *hoshekh* missing. By contrast, in Psalm 105, eight plagues are included and their order is: *hoshekh, dam, tzefarde'a, arov, kinim, barad, arbeh,* and *bekhorot* – with *dever* and *shehin* missing].

תהלים פרק עח פסוקים מג-נב

(מג) אֲשֶׁר שָׂם בְּמִצְרַיִם אֹתוֹתָיו וּמוֹפְתָיו בִּשְׂדֵה צֹעַן:
(מד) וַיַּהֲפֹךְ לְדָם יְאֹרֵיהֶם וְנֹזְלֵיהֶם בַּל יִשְׁתָּיוּן:
(מה) יְשַׁלַּח בָּהֶם עָרֹב וַיֹּאכְלֵם וּצְפַרְדֵּעַ וַתַּשְׁחִיתֵם:
(מו) וַיִּתֵּן לֶחָסִיל יְבוּלָם וִיגִיעָם לָאַרְבֶּה:
(מז) יַהֲרֹג בַּבָּרָד גַּפְנָם וְשִׁקְמוֹתָם בַּחֲנָמַל:
(מח) וַיַּסְגֵּר לַבָּרָד בְּעִירָם וּמִקְנֵיהֶם לָרְשָׁפִים:
(מט) יְשַׁלַּח בָּם חֲרוֹן אַפּוֹ עֶבְרָה וָזַעַם וְצָרָה מִשְׁלַחַת מַלְאֲכֵי רָעִים:
(נ) יְפַלֵּס נָתִיב לְאַפּוֹ לֹא חָשַׂךְ מִמָּוֶת נַפְשָׁם וְחַיָּתָם לַדֶּבֶר הִסְגִּיר:
(נא) וַיַּךְ כָּל בְּכוֹר בְּמִצְרָיִם רֵאשִׁית אוֹנִים בְּאָהֳלֵי חָם:

תהלים פרק קה פסוקים כז-לו

(כז) שָׂמוּ בָם דִּבְרֵי אֹתוֹתָיו וּמֹפְתִים בְּאֶרֶץ חָם:
(כח) שָׁלַח חֹשֶׁךְ וַיַּחְשִׁךְ וְלֹא מָרוּ אֶת דְּבָרוֹ:
(כט) הָפַךְ אֶת מֵימֵיהֶם לְדָם וַיָּמֶת אֶת דְּגָתָם:
(ל) שָׁרַץ אַרְצָם צְפַרְדְּעִים בְּחַדְרֵי מַלְכֵיהֶם:
(לא) אָמַר וַיָּבֹא עָרֹב כִּנִּים בְּכָל גְּבוּלָם:
(לב) נָתַן גִּשְׁמֵיהֶם בָּרָד אֵשׁ לֶהָבוֹת בְּאַרְצָם:
(לג) וַיַּךְ גַּפְנָם וּתְאֵנָתָם וַיְשַׁבֵּר עֵץ גְּבוּלָם:
(לד) אָמַר וַיָּבֹא אַרְבֶּה וְיֶלֶק וְאֵין מִסְפָּר:
(לה) וַיֹּאכַל כָּל עֵשֶׂב בְּאַרְצָם וַיֹּאכַל פְּרִי אַדְמָתָם:
(לו) וַיַּךְ כָּל בְּכוֹר בְּאַרְצָם רֵאשִׁית לְכָל אוֹנָם:

(b) Most commentaries, however, see a yet deeper significance in R. Yehuda's mnemonic device. These commentaries understand from R. Yehuda that the ten *Makkot* are to be divided into three unique sets – from which particular lessons are to be learned. Both Abravanel (*Haggada Zĕvah Pesah*) and R. Meir Loeb Malbim (on Ex. 7:14) posit that there are three sets of three: דְּצַ"ךְ עֲדַ"שׁ בְּאַ"חֲ and then one: "ב". The purpose of each of the three sets was not to free the Israelites, since God actually hardened Pharaoh's heart in each case; indeed, to free the Israelites was the purpose of only the tenth plague. Rather each of the three sets comes to teach an important theological lesson to Pharaoh and the world/Egyptians – which is stated clearly in the first plague of each set. (1) The first set publicizes that **the God of Israel exists** – as is stated in *Makkat Dam* (Ex. 7:17): "Thus says God: 'By this you shall know that I am God.'" (2) The second set teaches that He is the **God of history**; and is concerned and involved in what happens on Earth, as it says in *Makkat Arov* (Ex. 8:18): "...that you may know that I God am in the midst of the land. (3) The final set demonstrates that **He is omnipotent**, as it says in *Makkat Barad* (Ex. 9:14): "...in order that you may know that there is none like Me in all the world." And again, two verses later (9:16): "Nevertheless, I have spared you for this purpose: in order to show you My power, and in order that My fame may resound throughout the world." All this comes in response to Pharaoh's taunting words to Moshe (Ex. 5:2): "Who is Hashem that I should heed what He says."

(c) *Hagahot Maimoniyot, Shibbolei ha-Leket*, and Abravanel all point out that the first two plagues in each set come with a warning to Pharaoh, while the third in the set appears as a punishment without warning. The Malbim detects yet a deeper pattern. The first of the warned plagues in each set comes in the morning, with Moshe standing confrontationally (*hityatzvut*) before Pharaoh, by the Nile (a god of the Egyptians). This body language communicates self-confidence, opposition to the Ruler, and denial of the Egyptian deity. The second of the warned plagues in each set begins *Bo el Par'oh* – "Come to Pharaoh" suggesting that Moshe and Aharon came later in the day, to the palace, when the royal court was in session packed with courtiers and advisers. All present saw the dramatic entrance and heard the warning as it was given.

(d) Ra'avya (*Pesahim*, sec 424) proposes that the first set was performed by Aharon, the second by God – with the exception of *shehin* (boils) which was carried out by Moshe and Aharon, and the third set was executed by Moshe. Additionally, to demonstrate that God's power is in Heaven and Earth, דְּצַ"ךְ came from the Earth, עֲדַ"שׁ was mixed, and בְּאַחַ"ב came from the sky.

(e) R. Yaakov Medan has suggested (https://www.youtube.com/watch?v=aOVVDIaXMqU) that R. Yehuda's mnemonic comes to teach us that the *Makkot* are divided into two groups: a set of six (דְּצַ"ךְ and עֲדַ"שׁ) natural, scientifically explicable plagues, and another set of four (בְּאַחַ"ב) inexplicable supernatural ones. The first of the plagues was *Dam* – that the Nile turned to blood. R. Medan argues that the male babies thrown into the Nile did not die by drowning but were eaten by the crocodiles known to inhabit the Nile River. (Indeed, one of the Egyptian gods was the crocodile Sobek, and mummified crocodile remains have been found.) As "measure for measure" punishment God began with the Nile and its crocodiles. When Aharon hit the Nile with his staff (Ex. 7:20), the resulting shock wave killed the crocodiles whose **blood** colored the river. The decaying crocs and their blood caused the fish to die, the Nile to stink, and ultimately drove the **frogs** to the land – infesting Egypt. Realize, however, that while the latter step was the natural entrée to the next plague, it only occurred when Moshe said it would. The frogs may have been a natural outcome of the blood and decay, but it was still strictly controlled both in its onset and ending (Ex. 8:5): "And Moshe said to Pharaoh, "For what time shall I plead on your behalf…to remove the frogs." The decay and putrefaction of the piles of dead frogs caused the land of Egypt to stink (Ex. 8:5) and brought in its wake four plagues: lice, *arov* **(**which R. Medan understands as rats**)**, pestilence, and boils – all steps were natural but closely regulated by the Almighty**.** However, the last four plagues (hail, locust, darkness, and firstborn) have no scientific connection to the previous six, or to one another. They are clearly the hand of Heaven. Indeed, it is after the plague of hail that Pharaoh for the first time admits (Ex. 9:27): *Hatati ha-pa'am* – "I stand guilty this time. God is in the right, and I and my people are in the wrong."

We should point out that the unspoken underlying premise of the above discussion is that God, even in performing miracles, works as much as possible through the laws of nature that He Himself set up. This view is explicitly stated by R. Hezekiah ben Manoah (*Hizkuni*, Ex. 15:25) Similar ideas appear in the works of Maimonides (Guide to the

Perplexed, Book II, Chaps. 25 and 29) Gersonides (R. Levi ben Gerson, *Milḥamot Adon-ai*, final chapters) and other Jewish philosophers and commentaries. These scholars posit that miracles are more often a matter of "timing" than of the acts themselves. Divine intervention – just when needed – does not necessarily require a supernatural tour de force.

(f) Finally, it would seem that each plague comes as a punishment for Pharaoh's previous hardening of his heart to the Israelite's liberation. The first refusal was when the king stiffened his heart after the transformation of Aharon's rod to a serpent (Ex. 7:13). This was followed by the first plague of blood. Similarly, prior to each of the subsequent plagues of דָּצַ"ךְ and עַדַ"שׁ it says *va-yakhbed* or *va-yeḥezak lev Paroh* (or some related formulation: see Ex. 7:22, 8:11, 8:15, 8:28, and 9:7). At the end of the sixth plague *sheḥin* – boils, we find the seventh refusal which states: *va-Yeḥazek Hashem et lev Paroh* (9:12). This signals a change with God hardening Pharaoh's heart. Moshe now announces the coming of hail – the first of the בְּאַחַ"ב. In each subsequent case, the hardening is effected by God (Ex. 10:1; 10:20, and 10:27). (There is one seeming exception: after hail [Ex. 9:35] where it says *va-Yeḥezak lev Paroh* but the truth is immediately revealed [Ex. 10:1] with God saying: "It was I who hardened his heart.") Thus, before דָּצַ"ךְ and עַדַ"שׁ the King of Egypt had freedom of choice, while prior to the last four plagues he did not.

(g) These last comments raise a fundamental question as to whether one can lose his or her freedom of choice. Can one lose the ability to repent? And if such is possible, how can such an individual (or nation, for that matter) be judged and punished for misdeeds carried out under such conditions? Several answers have been proffered: (1) *Haza"l* (B.T. *Ḥagiga* 15b; J.T. *Ḥagiga* 2:1) also struggled with this issue when dealing with the possibility of repentance for the one-time *Tanna*-turned-apostate, Elisha ben Avuya, also known post-heresy as *Akher* ("Another"). Although *Akher* himself maintained that heaven had declared that he could not be penitent, his disciple R. Meir forcefully dissented that Elisha ben Avuya could – and ultimately did do *Teshuva*. (2) Maimonides (M.T., *Hil. Teshuva* 6:3; see also *Shemot Rabba* 11 at the end) argues that as a punishment for repeated disobedience in the five earlier plagues, the Almighty indeed took away Pharaoh's free will during the later plagues. He did this in order to punish the king properly and fully

רַבִּי יוֹסֵי הַגְּלִילִי אוֹמֵר: מִנַּיִן אַתָּה אוֹמֵר שֶׁלָּקוּ הַמִּצְרִים בְּמִצְרַיִם עֶשֶׂר מַכּוֹת וְעַל הַיָּם לָקוּ חֲמִשִּׁים מַכּוֹת? בְּמִצְרַיִם מַה הוּא אוֹמֵר? "וַיֹּאמְרוּ הַחַרְטֻמִּם אֶל פַּרְעֹה: אֶצְבַּע אֱלֹהִים הִוא," וְעַל הַיָּם מָה הוּא אוֹמֵר? "וַיַּרְא יִשְׂרָאֵל אֶת־הַיָּד הַגְּדֹלָה אֲשֶׁר עָשָׂה ה' בְּמִצְרַיִם, וַיִּירְאוּ הָעָם אֶת־ה', וַיַּאֲמִינוּ בַּה' וּבְמֹשֶׁה עַבְדּוֹ" (שמות יב:לא).

---

for the earlier offenses. Pharaoh was not punished, however, for the later refusals stemming from a God-hardened heart. (3) Seforno (*Ex.* 7:3) argues that God hardened Pharaoh's heart so that he could **resist** the coercive quality of the plagues. His freedom of choice was thereby maintained throughout, and the King could therefore make a purely willing and volitional decision unaffected by pressure. Making Pharaoh strong enough to resist the pain and suffering of the plagues, increased his stature so that he would continue to be viewed as a strong powerful leader. Concomitantly, the king's downfall would send a message that even the mightiest rulers and despots are powerless before God Almighty.

רַבִּי יוֹסֵי הַגְּלִילִי אוֹמֵר

The next three paragraphs represent an aggadic attempt to enhance God's glory by increasing the number of plagues brought upon Egypt beyond the basic ten (Maharits Chajes). It does this by suggesting that the Egyptians suffered multiple plagues (or variants) both in Egypt and during their drowning at the Red Sea. R. Elijah of Vilna (*Haggada – ha-Gra ve-Talmidav*) cites the verse (Ex. 15:26): "I will not bring upon you any of the diseases that I brought upon the Egyptians." Thus, by heaping on the Egyptians more disease, one hopefully limits the susceptibility of the Jewish People to illness. Finally, my father, R. Norman Frimer z"l, was wont to say that this is an example of Jewish "Give it to them!" Jews working out centuries of historic frustration – something akin to *Shefokh Hamatekha*. For once Jews are on top! This discussion is followed by the poem *Dayenu* which praises the Almighty for subsequent miracles leading up to the giving of the Torah, Israel's conquest of the Land of Israel, and the building of the Temple.

Interestingly, in the Rambam's text of the *Haggada* (end of M.T., *Hil.*

Rabbi Yossi the Galilean says: How do you know that the Egyptians were struck by ten plagues in Egypt, and then were struck by fifty plagues at the sea? About the plagues in Egypt, what does it say? "The sorcerers said to Pharaoh, 'It is the finger of the Lord'" (Exodus 8:15). But of the events at sea, it says, "Israel saw the great hand that the Lord laid against Egypt, and the people feared the Lord. And they believed in the Lord, and in His servant Moshe" (Exodus 14:31).

Hametz u-Matza) the three paragraphs and *Dayenu* are absent. R. Joseph B. Soloveitchik (*Si'ah ha-Grid*) suggested that Rambam is consistent with his view (*Hil. Hametz u-Matza.* 7:1) that we are commanded on *Seder* night to describe the occurrences of the fifteenth of *Nisan*, as it is written (Ex. 13:3), "Remember **this** day that you went out of Egypt." Hence, Maimonides refrained from including in his *Haggada* text a discussion of miracles that occurred after the fifteenth – such as those of the **seventh** day of *Pesah* at *Yam Suf* and thereafter. (We should mention for completeness that in the Venice edition of the *Ma'aseh Roke'ah* on the Rambam's *Haggada* text, a comment is cited from R. Abraham, the son of the Rambam, indicating that his father's custom was to indeed say R. Yossi ha-Galili through *Dayenu*. Nevertheless, Maimonides felt these sections were not required, and, hence, did not include them in his authorized *Haggada* text.) For the same reasoning, suggests R. Soloveitchik, *Hallel* at the *Seder* does not include *Shirat ha-Yam* (*Az Yashir*).

Nevertheless, our custom is to include the text of R. Yossi ha-Galili through *Dayenu*. R. Moses Joseph Walkin (cited in *Haggada Pilpulei Harifta*) argues that our tradition bases the obligation to recount the details of the Exodus on the verse (Ex. 13:8): "And you shall declare (or state) before your child on that day, saying: 'It is because of this – that the Lord acted on my behalf when I came forth out of Egypt.'" This verse may well include recounting the whole process of redemption – both physical and spiritual – including events that occurred after the fifteenth of *Nisan*, such as the splitting of the Red Sea.

וַיַּאֲמִינוּ בַּה' וּבְמֹשֶׁה עַבְדּוֹ

What was it about the splitting of the Red Sea that caused the Israelites to finally believe that Moshe was God's true messenger and agent.

כַּמָּה לָקוּ בְאֶצְבַּע? עֶשֶׂר מַכּוֹת. אֱמוֹר מֵעַתָּה: בְּמִצְרַיִם לָקוּ עֶשֶׂר מַכּוֹת וְעַל הַיָּם לָקוּ חֲמִשִּׁים מַכּוֹת.

רַבִּי אֱלִיעֶזֶר אוֹמֵר: מִנַּיִן שֶׁכָּל־מַכָּה וּמַכָּה שֶׁהֵבִיא הַקָּדוֹשׁ בָּרוּךְ הוּא עַל הַמִּצְרִים בְּמִצְרַיִם הָיְתָה שֶׁל אַרְבַּע מַכּוֹת? שֶׁנֶּאֱמַר (תהילים עח:מט): "יְשַׁלַּח־בָּם חֲרוֹן אַפּוֹ – עֶבְרָה, וָזַעַם, וְצָרָה, מִשְׁלַחַת מַלְאֲכֵי רָעִים." עֶבְרָה – אַחַת, וָזַעַם – שְׁתַּיִם, וְצָרָה – שָׁלֹשׁ, מִשְׁלַחַת מַלְאֲכֵי רָעִים – אַרְבַּע. אֱמוֹר מֵעַתָּה: בְּמִצְרַיִם לָקוּ אַרְבָּעִים מַכּוֹת וְעַל הַיָּם לָקוּ מָאתַיִם מַכּוֹת.

רַבִּי עֲקִיבָא אוֹמֵר: מִנַּיִן שֶׁכָּל־מַכָּה וּמַכָּה שֶׁהֵבִיא הַקָּדוֹשׁ בָּרוּךְ הוּא עַל הַמִּצְרִים בְּמִצְרַיִם הָיְתָה שֶׁל חָמֵשׁ מַכּוֹת? שֶׁנֶּאֱמַר (תהילים עח:מט): "יְשַׁלַּח־בָּם חֲרוֹן אַפּוֹ, עֶבְרָה וָזַעַם, וְצָרָה, מִשְׁלַחַת מַלְאֲכֵי רָעִים." חֲרוֹן אַפּוֹ – אַחַת, עֶבְרָה – שְׁתַּיִם, וָזַעַם – שָׁלוֹשׁ, וְצָרָה – אַרְבַּע, מִשְׁלַחַת מַלְאֲכֵי רָעִים – חָמֵשׁ. אֱמוֹר מֵעַתָּה: בְּמִצְרַיִם לָקוּ חֲמִשִּׁים מַכּוֹת וְעַל הַיָּם לָקוּ חֲמִשִּׁים וּמָאתַיִם מַכּוֹת.

Hadn't they seen the ten plagues?! R. Dovid Cohen (*Haggada Simhat Ya'avetz*) suggests that during the period of the ten plagues, a large percentage of the Israelites were located in Goshen – which was largely unaffected by the plagues. These Israelites may have only heard about them and the havoc they engendered. When it comes to God's might: "seeing **is** believing." The Malbim and Netziv (on Ex. 14:31) suggest that until now there were still those who maintained that Moshe was merely the best magician of his time! The miraculous splitting of the Red Sea and the sudden drowning of the entire elite Egyptian army – all in response to Moshe's outstretched arm, convinced all that Moshe was the true messenger of God.

יְשַׁלַּח־בָּם חֲרוֹן אַפּוֹ עֶבְרָה, וָזַעַם...

The dispute between R. Eliezer and R. Akiva relates to a verse from *Psalms* 78:49 which (as cited above) deals with the ten plagues. They

How many plagues did the Egyptian receive from one finger? Ten. From here we can conclude that if they suffered ten plagues in Egypt, they suffered fifty at the sea.

Rabbi Eliezer says: How do we know that each and every plague which the Holy One Blessed is He brought upon the Egyptians in Egypt, consisted of four plagues? For it says (Psalms 78:49): "He sent upon his fierce anger; wrath, fury and trouble, and a team of hostile angels." Wrath is one. Fury is two. Trouble is three. And a team of hostile angels is four. Thus, from here we can conclude that in Egypt they were struck by forty plagues, and at the sea they were struck by 200 plagues.

Rabbi Akiva says: How do we know that each individual plague which the Holy One Blessed is He brought upon the Egyptians in Egypt consisted of five plagues? For it says (Psalms 78:49): "He sent upon them his fierce anger; wrath, fury, trouble, and a team of hostile angels." Fierce anger is one, wrath is two, fury is three, trouble is four and a team of hostile angels is five. From here we can conclude that in Egypt they were struck by 50 plagues, and at the sea they were struck by 250 plagues.

---

disagree as to whether *haron apo* in the cited proof text is a general description of the **four** categories that follow, like this: *Yeshalah ba-hem haron apo:* *evra, va-za'am*... with a colon after *haron apo*. Alternatively, *haron apo* could be one of **five** categories of plagues, like this: *Yeshalah ba-hem: haron apo, evra, va-za'am*... with a colon after *bahem*. Possible proof for the former position of R. Eliezer can be found in the fact that there is no connecting *vav* (*vav ha-hibbur*) at the beginning of *evra* – suggesting that **it** is the beginning of the list. R. Akiva, on the other hand, could well argue that this is inconclusive proof since regarding the taking of the four species on *Sukkot* (Lev. 23:40) we read: "On the first day you shall take the fruit of a *hadar* tree, branches of palm trees, and boughs of leafy trees, and willows of the brook...." Here we have a list of four species with no connecting *vav* at the beginning of the second element.

דיינו

כַּמָה מַעֲלוֹת טוֹבוֹת לַמָּקוֹם עָלֵינוּ!

אִלּוּ הוֹצִיאָנוּ מִמִּצְרַיִם וְלֹא עָשָׂה בָהֶם שְׁפָטִים, דַּיֵּנוּ.

אִלּוּ עָשָׂה בָהֶם שְׁפָטִים, וְלֹא עָשָׂה בֵאלֹהֵיהֶם, דַּיֵּנוּ.

אִלּוּ עָשָׂה בֵאלֹהֵיהֶם, וְלֹא הָרַג אֶת־בְּכוֹרֵיהֶם, דַּיֵּנוּ.

דַּיֵּנוּ

In this poem, following the mention of each significant kindness Hashem did for us upon leaving Egypt, we recite the refrain *Dayenu!* – "It would have been enough! It would have sufficed!" But how can we possibly say such a thing, asks Abravanel (*Zevaḥ ha-Pesaḥ*)? Had the Almighty not completed the process, of what value would the earlier stages have been? Of what worth is bringing us to Mt. Sinai, if the Lord had not given us the Torah?! (Indeed, in jest, some have suggested the reading *Dayenu?* – meaning: "Would that have sufficed?") Abravanel posits that even if each stage doesn't complete the process, it nevertheless creates an obligation of praise since it brings us closer to the final goal. **It would have sufficed to obligate our giving praise!** Indeed, R. Menachem Liebtag ("The *Hashkafa* of *Dayenu*," https://tanach.org/special/dayenu.htm) develops this latter idea further to teach an important lesson relevant to our generation: Each significant stage in the process of redemption deserves our recognition and requires that we praise God for it, even though it is really "not enough!" *Ge'ulat Yisra'el* – the redemption of Israel – even in our time, is a process that is comprised of many stages. Every significant step in this process, be it simply sovereignty, partial borders, victory in battle, or freedom to study Torah, even without complete redemption, requires our gratitude and praise to Hashem.

כַּמָה מַעֲלוֹת טוֹבוֹת לַמָּקוֹם עָלֵינוּ

This opening phrase is perhaps best translated as: "How manifold are the levels of goodness for which we owe a debt of gratitude to the Omnipresent." The choice of the word *ma'alot* (steps) well reflects the

Dayenu

How manifold are the levels of goodness for which we owe a debt of gratitude to the Omnipresent!

Had He brought us out from Egypt, and not executed judgment against the Egyptians, **it would have been enough for us!**

Had He executed judgments against them, and not against their gods, **it would have been enough for us!**

Had He executed judgment against their gods, and not smitten their firstborn, **it would have been enough for us!**

---

structure of the *piyut* which moves from kindness to kindness in a step-like fashion.

אִלּוּ הוֹצִיאָנוּ מִמִּצְרַיִם וְלֹא עָשָׂה בָהֶם שְׁפָטִים

In contradistinction to Abravanel (see above comments on דַּיֵּנוּ), Rashbam (*Haggada Torat Hayim*) suggests that each step has value since God performed each of the various miraculous stages with tremendous flair – and it is for that, that we owe God special praise. Thus, for example, God could have brought judgment on only some of our oppressors, yet he brought it on all. He gave us Egyptian wealth both in Egypt **and** on the sea. He could have saved us by protecting us without splitting the sea. We could have crossed the sea in mud, yet the ground beneath the Israelites was perfectly dry. The Almighty could have closed the waters behind us and forced the Egyptian army to retreat; yet he chose to drown them. The Israelites had flocks and money, yet God miraculously supplied all their needs in the desert. God personally gave us the Torah. All those who were below twenty and saw the Egyptian miracles also entered the Land of Israel. Finally, in addition to building the Temple, there were ten regular miracles (*Avot* 5:7).

אִלּוּ עָשָׂה בֵאלֹהֵיהֶם, וְלֹא הָרַג אֶת־בְּכוֹרֵיהֶם

This verse suggests that the Redeemer struck down the Egyptian idols and only later plagued the first-born. Yet the Biblical verse says (Ex.

אִלּוּ הָרַג אֶת־בְּכוֹרֵיהֶם וְלֹא נָתַן לָנוּ אֶת־מָמוֹנָם, דַּיֵּנוּ.

אִלּוּ נָתַן לָנוּ אֶת־מָמוֹנָם וְלֹא קָרַע לָנוּ אֶת־הַיָּם, דַּיֵּנוּ.

אִלּוּ קָרַע לָנוּ אֶת־הַיָּם וְלֹא הֶעֱבִירָנוּ בְּתוֹכוֹ בֶּחָרָבָה, דַּיֵּנוּ.

אִלּוּ הֶעֱבִירָנוּ בְּתוֹכוֹ בֶּחָרָבָה וְלֹא שִׁקַּע צָרֵנוּ בְּתוֹכוֹ, דַּיֵּנוּ.

אִלּוּ שִׁקַּע צָרֵנוּ בְּתוֹכוֹ וְלֹא סִפֵּק צָרְכֵּנוּ בַּמִּדְבָּר אַרְבָּעִים שָׁנָה, דַּיֵּנוּ.

אִלּוּ סִפֵּק צָרְכֵּנוּ בַּמִּדְבָּר אַרְבָּעִים שָׁנָה וְלֹא הֶאֱכִילָנוּ אֶת־הַמָּן, דַּיֵּנוּ.

אִלּוּ הֶאֱכִילָנוּ אֶת־הַמָּן וְלֹא נָתַן לָנוּ אֶת־הַשַּׁבָּת, דַּיֵּנוּ.

12:12): "For that night I will go through the land of Egypt and strike down every firstborn in the land of Egypt, both human and beast; and I will meteced out punishments to all the gods of Egypt, I am the Lord." This suggests that the firstborns were smitten and then the gods. It would seem, however, that both processes occurred simultaneously as God passed through the land.

וְלֹא שִׁקַּע צָרֵנוּ בְּתוֹכוֹ

The Biblical text states (Ex. 14:28): "The waters turned back and covered the chariots and the riders – Pharaoh's entire army that followed them into the sea; **not one of them remained**." *Yalkut Shimoni* (Ex. *Remez* 238) cites the view of R. Nehemia, that Pharaoh (the leader) alone survived. This may seem to be an aggadic interpretation – indicating that Pharaoh survived in order to bear witness to the events. Nevertheless, this may actually be the *peshat* (simple meaning) of the verse. This would be based on a similar language usage appearing in the Book of Judges (4:16) where Sisera's army is vanquished by Barak and Devorah the Prophetess: "All of Sisera's camp fell by the sword; **not one** of them remained." Yet, this is immediately followed by (Judges 4:17): "Sisera fled on foot…" We should also add that naturally some of the physically fit Egyptian soldiers should have been able to swim to shore. Yet the churning turbulent waters miraculously prevented this from occurring and all drowned.

Had He slain their firstborn, and had not given us their wealth,
it would have been enough for us!

Had He given us their wealth, and not split the sea for us,
it would have been enough for us!

Had He split the sea for us, and not led us through it on dry land,
it would have been enough for us!

Had He led us through on dry land, and not drowned our tormenters in it, **it would have been enough for us!**

Had He drowned our tormenters in it, and not provided for our needs in the desert for forty years, **it would have been enough for us!**

Had He provided for our needs in the desert for forty years, and not fed us the manna, **it would have been enough for us!**

Had He fed us the manna, and not given us the Shabbat,
it would have been enough for us!

וְלֹא סִפֵּק צָרְכֵּנוּ בַּמִּדְבָּר אַרְבָּעִים שָׁנָה

The delay in the desert was because of the Sin of the Spies; hence God was not really obligated to feed them all. This was especially true in light of the people's wealth in livestock and gold acquired both in Egypt and at the Red Sea. This is the connection between the drowning of Pharaoh's army and why God's supplying their needs for forty years was such an act of graciousness.

אִלּוּ הֶאֱכִילָנוּ אֶת־הַמָּן וְלֹא נָתַן לָנוּ אֶת־הַשַּׁבָּת

The Talmud (B.T. *Sanhedrin* 56b) indicates that the Sabbath was first commanded to Israel at Marah (Ex. 15:25) immediately after the splitting of the Red Sea. Manna was given a short time afterward (Ex. 16:4). Hence, why is Manna mentioned before *Shabbat* in the present verse? One approach, suggested by R. Dovid Cohen (*Haggada Simchat Yaavetz*), is that the pre-Sinaitic Sabbath of Marah was kept from sunrise to sunrise – in the same manner that days are counted by non-Jews. The Sabbath mentioned in *Dayenu* is the Sabbath commanded at Sinai

אִלּוּ נָתַן לָנוּ אֶת־הַשַּׁבָּת, וְלֹא קֵרְבָנוּ לִפְנֵי הַר סִינַי, דַּיֵּנוּ.

אִלּוּ קֵרְבָנוּ לִפְנֵי הַר סִינַי, וְלֹא נָתַן לָנוּ אֶת־הַתּוֹרָה. דַּיֵּנוּ.

אִלּוּ נָתַן לָנוּ אֶת־הַתּוֹרָה וְלֹא הִכְנִיסָנוּ לְאֶרֶץ יִשְׂרָאֵל. דַּיֵּנוּ.

אִלּוּ הִכְנִיסָנוּ לְאֶרֶץ יִשְׂרָאֵל וְלֹא בָנָה לָנוּ אֶת־בֵּית הַבְּחִירָה, דַּיֵּנוּ.

---

in the fourth commandment which was to be observed from nightfall to nightfall – in the same manner days are counted by Jews. A second possibility – suggested by R. Pinchas Shapiro of Koretz (cited in *Haggada Pilpulei Harifta*) – is that this verse in its entirety refers to the Manna and should be translated as follows: If the Almighty had given us the Manna and not given us the special "double portion" on Friday in honor of *Shabbat* which stayed fresh and tasty – *Dayenu*!

אִלּוּ קֵרְבָנוּ לִפְנֵי הַר סִינַי, וְלֹא נָתַן לָנוּ אֶת־הַתּוֹרָה

This is perhaps the most perplexing verse in *Dayenu*. Of what value would there be in bringing 3 million Israelites through the desert to Sinai and not revealing the Torah to them? How could one say *Dayenu*?! Many answers have been proposed. (a) My brother R. Shael Frimer pointed out that when the Israelites arrived at Sinai the verse says (Ex. 19:2): "Israel encamped there opposite the mountain." Importantly, the Hebrew word used for the verb "encamped" is *va-Yihan* and is in the singular. This leads Rashi ad loc. to comment: "Israel encamped there – as one man and with one mind." It is about this moment of unity that we declare *Dayenu*. (b) My brother R. Dov Frimer suggested that the very experience of revelation alone warrants saying *Dayenu*, even if we never received a tangible written Torah. (c) R. Chaim Yaakov Goldvicht argues that the key word here is *lanu* – "to us." Indeed, we would be missing the transmission of a **written** Torah. However, Moshe was taught the Torah **orally** while atop Mount Sinai for 40 days as well as the 13 hermeneutical principles. The Rabbis were also authorized to extrapolate and derive new laws – and this could serve as the basis for further development. (d) There is also a Midrashic

Had He given us the Shabbat, and not brought us before Mount Sinai, **it would have been enough for us!**

Had He brought us before Mount Sinai, and not given us the Torah, **it would have been enough for us!**

Had He given us the Torah, and not brought us into the Land of Israel, **it would have been enough for us!**

Had He brought us into the Land of Israel, and not built the Holy Temple, **it would have been enough for us!**

---

tradition (*Midrash Tanhuma Yitro* 8, *Devarim Rabba* 1:1; *Zohar, vaEra*, p. 25b; Rashi, *Shabbat* 146a, s.v. *Mazalaihu havu*) that assorted illnesses were cured at Mount Sinai – including the blind and the lame. This was certainly worthy of praise. (e) R. Jerome Herzog notes that at the burning bush (Ex. 3:12) the Almighty promised that the People of Israel would "worship God on this mountain." At that time this oath was quite astonishing. God's promise was kept when the nation traveled to Sinai following the Exodus. Thus, even if we had not received the Torah, we praise our Redeemer for indeed keeping His amazing commitment. (f) R. Yerucham Levovitz, *Mashgiah* of Mir (cited by R. Mordechai Schwab, *Ma'amar Mordechai* III, sec. 66) emphasizes the three days of preparation the Israelites underwent before arriving at Sinai. As a result, they achieved sanctity, prophecy, and spirituality – all worthy of a heartfelt *Dayenu*. (g) R. Azariah Berzon (*Hadarom*, 53, *Nisan* 5744) points out that Jewish tradition going back to the Rabbis of the Talmud views *Ma'amad Har Sinai* (the Sinaitic stand) as a wedding between a bride (People of Israel) and a groom (God). Indeed, several customs stem from this imagery (see R. Yaakov Werdiger, *Eidut le-Yisrael*). Thus, the three days the Israelites camped around the mountain morphed into the bride circling the groom three times (later expanded to seven); marching down the bride and groom with candles stems from the thunder and lightning; the recitation of the Song of Songs is a love story between God and Israel. Thus, it is for this love relationship that we sing *Dayenu*.

עַל אַחַת, כַּמָּה וְכַמָּה, טוֹבָה כְפוּלָה וּמְכֻפֶּלֶת לַמָּקוֹם עָלֵינוּ: (1) שֶׁהוֹצִיאָנוּ מִמִּצְרַיִם, (2) וְעָשָׂה בָהֶם שְׁפָטִים, (3) וְעָשָׂה בֵאלֹהֵיהֶם, (4) וְהָרַג אֶת־בְּכוֹרֵיהֶם, (5) וְנָתַן לָנוּ אֶת־מָמוֹנָם, (6) וְקָרַע לָנוּ אֶת־הַיָּם, (7) וְהֶעֱבִירָנוּ בְתוֹכוֹ בֶּחָרָבָה, (8) וְשִׁקַּע צָרֵנוּ בְּתוֹכוֹ, (9) וְסִפֵּק צָרְכֵּנוּ בַּמִּדְבָּר אַרְבָּעִים שָׁנָה, (10) וְהֶאֱכִילָנוּ אֶת־הַמָּן, (11) וְנָתַן לָנוּ אֶת־הַשַּׁבָּת, (12) וְקֵרְבָנוּ לִפְנֵי הַר סִינַי, (13) וְנָתַן לָנוּ אֶת־הַתּוֹרָה, (14) וְהִכְנִיסָנוּ לְאֶרֶץ יִשְׂרָאֵל, (15) וּבָנָה לָנוּ אֶת־בֵּית הַבְּחִירָה לְכַפֵּר עַל־כָּל־עֲוֹנוֹתֵינוּ.

פסח מצה ומרור

רַבָּן גַּמְלִיאֵל הָיָה אוֹמֵר: כָּל שֶׁלֹּא אָמַר שְׁלֹשָׁה דְבָרִים אֵלּוּ בַּפֶּסַח, לֹא יָצָא יְדֵי חוֹבָתוֹ, וְאֵלּוּ הֵן:

פֶּסַח, מַצָּה, וּמָרוֹר.

לֹא יָצָא יְדֵי חוֹבָתוֹ

After a lengthy discussion of the Egypt experience, we now finally turn to answer the children's questions asked, at the beginning of *Maggid*, about the message of the central foods of the *Seder*. These are: *Pesah* (the Paschal lamb – when the Temple was standing); Matza (the unleavened bread); and *Maror* (the Bitter Herbs) (*Shibbolei ha-Leket*, 218). We begin our answer by citing the comments of *Rabban* Gamliel (*Mishna, Pesahim* 10:5; 116a) who emphasized the centrality of this discussion of *Pesah, Matza,* and *Maror* to the fulfillment of our *Seder* obligation. Some like Maimonides (*Hametz u-Matza*, 7:5) take this statement literally; others (Ran on Rif, *Tiferet Yisrael* to *Mishna*) maintain that the **optimal** fulfillment (*mitzva min ha-muvhar*) is referred to here. In any case, several further questions have been raised:

There is some dispute between the commentators as to the identity of Rabban Gamliel. Some maintain that he was the Nasi Rabban Gamliel "The Elder" (*ha-Zaken*; d. ca. 52 C.E.) who was active while the Temple was still standing. This is consistent with the fact that in

Thus how much more so should we be grateful to God for the manifold goodness that He has showered upon us: (1) for He brought us out of Egypt, (2) and executed judgments against them, (3) and against their gods, (4) and slew their firstborn, (5) and gave us their wealth, (6) and split the sea for us, (7) and led us through it on dry land, (8) and drowned our tormentors in it, (9) and provided for our needs in the desert for forty years, (10) and fed us the manna, (11) and gave us the Shabbat, (12) and brought us before Mount Sinai, (13) and gave us the Torah, (14) and brought us into the land of Israel, (15) and built for us the Holy Temple to atone for all our sins.

Pesah, Matza, Maror

Rabban Gamliel used to say: Whoever does not discuss the following three things on Pesah has not fulfilled his obligation, and these are:

Pesah. Matza. And Maror.

---

the original version (*Mishna*, *Pesahim* 116a) the words "…that our ancestors ate when the Temple was standing" are absent. It was presumably inserted into the *Haggada* only after Rabban Gamliel had already passed away and after the Temple was destroyed. Others continue to insist that Rabban Gamliel here refers to Rabban Gamliel II of Yavne (d. 118) or a later descendant in whose time "…our ancestors ate when the Temple was standing" was relevant.

Secondly, what does Rabban Gamliel mean by "One who has not said…"? After all, *Pesah*, *Matza*, and *Maror* are mentioned repeatedly in the *Haggada*! Rashbam on this *Mishna* explains that the reason and importance must be explained. *Tosafot* emphasizes that it's not enough to **know** the reason – the reason must be **verbalized**. *Nimukei Yosef* suggests that it refers to citing the relevant *Torah* verse.

We next need to clarify to which obligation is *Rabban* Gamliel referring. One group of *Rishonim* (e.g., Rashbam, *Tosafot*, and Ramban *Milhamot Hashem ad loc.*) maintains that he is referring to the obligation of eating *Pesah, Matza*, and *Maror*. Thus, it's not enough to eat these foods; we must first explain why we were commanded to do so! *Tosafot* maintains that the source of this obligation are the verses (Ex.

12:26–27) which state: "And when your children ask you 'What do you mean by this rite?' You shall say: 'It is the Passover sacrifice to God, who passed over the houses of the Israelites in Egypt when smiting the Egyptians, but saved our houses.'" Thus, "This rite" namely, eating the Paschal lamb – must be accompanied by an explanation of your actions, to wit: "You shall say: 'It is the Passover sacrifice to God, etc.'" Since the Torah requires eating the three foods together (Ex. 12:8), Matza and *Maror* also require an explication of their reason. We fulfill this obligation before the culmination of *Maggid* – just before transitioning into the first part of *Hallel*. (As we shall see, the recitation of *Hallel* is not only praise for the miracles recounted in *Maggid*, but also a prerequisite for eating the *Korban Pesah*.)

The second school of commentators (R. Zedekiah ben Abraham Anav, *Shibbolei ha-Leket*, 218; Rambam, *Hil. Hametz u-Matza*, 7:5) maintains that Rabban Gamliel is referring to the obligation of *Sippur Yetzi'at Mitzrayim* – recounting the Exodus story. Thus Rambam, after writing that one is obligated to explain *Pesah*, *Matza*, and *Maror*, adds: "And these things are called *Haggada* (recounting)." In other words, is **Maggid in action!** Similarly, R. Abraham Danzig (*Hayei Adam*, *Kelal* 130; cited in *Mishne Berura*, sec. 473, no. 64*)* stresses the importance of translating Rabban Gamliel to the non-educated maid, so she can minimally fulfill her obligation of *Maggid*. What would be the source of this school? Exodus 13:8 states: *Ba'avur zeh…* – "It is because of **this** – that the Lord acted on my behalf, when I came forth out of Egypt." Rashi on the word "this" writes: "so that I should fulfill these *mitzvot*." We've already seen above that the *Haggada* uses this text to determine when there is a mitzva of recounting the Exodus story. "When [*Pesah*,] Matza, and *Maror* are set before you." But at the same time, it highlights what we should talk about: the three central foods! We fulfill this obligation just before the culmination of *Maggid*, with the statement of Rabban Gamliel becoming the summary statement of *Maggid* before we transition into the first part of *Hallel*.

Several practical outcomes have been suggested between these approaches. Firstly, the Talmud (*Pesahim* 95a) states that only those *halakhot* pertaining to the actual Paschal lamb on the first *Pesah* – apply equally to the Paschal lamb on *Pesah Sheni* – the make-up *Pesach* on the 14th *Iyar* at twilight (Num. 9:1–14). Thus, if Rabban Gamliel's requirement of explaining *Pesah*, *Matza*, and *Maror* is connected to the mitzva of eating the *Korban Pesah*, then it applies to both. If, however, it is part of *Maggid*, there is no mitzva of *Maggid* except on the night of the fifteenth of *Nisan*. Interestingly, Rambam (*Hilkhot Hametz u-Matza*, 7:5) writes: "Anyone who has not said these three things **on the night of the fifteenth** has not fulfilled his obligation, and these are: *Pesah*, *Matza*, and *Maror*… And these statements are all called *Haggada*." Note that the *Mishna* (*Pesahim* 116a) cites Rabban Gamliel as it appears in the *Haggada*: "Anyone who has not said these three things on *Pesah*." Yet, Maimonides replaced *Pesah* with the "fifteenth (of *Nisan*)" – to exclude *Pesah Sheni*, and furthermore, dubs Rabban Gamliel's *Pesah*, *Matza*, *Maror* as "*Haggada*" i.e., *Sippur Yetzi'at Mitzrayim*. Another distinction is that if *Pesah*, *Matza*, *Maror* is part of *Sippur Yetzi'at Mitzrayim* it needs to be said to one's children. If, however, it is part of the mitzva of eating, recitation to one's self is sufficient.

One can argue that these two schools argue as to the central focus and goal of the *Seder*. One position is that it is the pivotal story of the Exodus – and the accompanying praise and debt of gratitude we owe the Almighty as a result. This explains why the *Maggid* section ends with the first two paragraphs of *Hallel*. A second school cites the verse "Let my people go **so that they may serve me!**" (Ex. 7:16). This indicates that the central focus of the *Haggada* should be the *mitzvot ma'asiyot – the* mitzva actions of the *Seder*: *Pesah*, *Matza*, and *Maror*. It is also consistent with the verse in the closing benediction of *Maggid* which reads: "…Who has redeemed us and our ancestor from Egypt and brought us to this night to eat Matza and *Maror*."

The fact is, however, that these two approaches are not mutually exclusive. *Pesah*, *Matza*, *Maror* may serve as a transition both to *lefikhakh anahnu hayavim* and *Hallel*, as well as to the eating of (*Pesah*,) *Matza*, and *Maror*. Thus, the placement of the statement of *Rabban* Gamliel between *Maggid* and the eating of (*Pesah*,) *Matza*, and *Maror* comfortably accommodates both these views – which may well be its real intention!

פֶּסַח שֶׁהָיוּ אֲבוֹתֵינוּ אוֹכְלִים בִּזְמַן שֶׁבֵּית הַמִּקְדָּשׁ הָיָה קַיָּם. עַל שׁוּם מָה? עַל שׁוּם שֶׁפָּסַח הַקָּדוֹשׁ בָּרוּךְ הוּא עַל בָּתֵּי אֲבוֹתֵינוּ בְּמִצְרַיִם. שֶׁנֶּאֱמַר (שמות יב. כז): וַאֲמַרְתֶּם זֶבַח פֶּסַח הוּא לַה׳. אֲשֶׁר פָּסַח עַל בָּתֵּי בְנֵי יִשְׂרָאֵל בְּמִצְרַיִם בְּנָגְפּוֹ אֶת־מִצְרַיִם. וְאֶת־בָּתֵּינוּ הִצִּיל וַיִּקֹּד הָעָם וַיִּשְׁתַּחֲווּ.

פֶּסַח. מַצָּה. וּמָרוֹר

One wonders why the order is *Pesah, Matza, Maror*? Chronologically it should have been: *Maror* (slavery), *Pesah* (beginning of salvation), *and* Matza ("rush to freedom" – end of redemption). It may be true that *Rabban* Gamliel was relying on the biblical verse (Ex. 12:8) וּמַצּוֹת עַל מְרֹרִים יֹאכְלֻהוּ. The subject of the verse is *Pesah*, and it is to be eaten with Matza and *Maror*. While this may be true, it doesn't answer the question as to the rationale of the non-chronological order. My daughter Shoshana Dekel suggested that Jewish tradition wanted the moral/educational lessons to be learned from our experience of oppression. Hence, slavery (*Maror*) should remain with us as the central take-home lesson of *Maggid*.

פֶּסַח... עַל שׁוּם מָה

As mentioned in our comments to לֹא יָצָא יְדֵי חוֹבָתוֹ, we now finally turn to answer the children's four or five questions in *Ma Nishtana* (*Shibbolei ha-Leket*, 218). Interestingly, we don't relate to the inquisitive child's query regarding the double dipping. This is because this strange behavior was done merely to arouse the child (*hekera le-tinokot*; *Pesahim* 114b) to pay attention to the special quality of the night and ask questions. Hence the query really has no answer! As to "Leaning" – like affluent Romans, this was resolved almost immediately by saying: "We were slaves and are now free." The question *Pesah al shum ma?* and the two subsequent queries regarding Matza and *Maror*, are all rhetorical. This is as if to say: "Remember you asked me earlier about why the Paschal lamb was so special? I haven't forgotten. Here's why! The question-and-answer format of the *Seder* is maintained.

The Pesaḥ sacrifice that our fathers ate, during the period of the Holy Temple – what is its meaning? It is because the Holy One blessed is He passed over our fathers' houses in Egypt, as it says: "You shall say, 'It is a Pesaḥ sacrifice to the Lord Who passed over the houses of the Children of Israel in Egypt when He smote the Egyptians and saved our houses.' And the people bowed down and prostrated themselves" (Exodus 12:27).

עַל שׁוּם שֶׁפָּסַח

Several interpretations for the verb *pasaḥ* have been proffered. *Targum Onkelus* understands it to mean spare and have mercy, while *Targum Jonathan ben Uziel* suggests that it means to protect. However, the most accepted understanding is that of Rashi (to Ex. 12:13) who posits that *pasaḥ* means to leap, spring, or pass over. Thus, the word *pasaḥ* in the verse (Ex. 12:27) cited by the *Haggada* indicates that the Israelite homes were interspersed among the Egyptians. The Almighty passed over the houses of the Israelites when He reached them – without entering, continuing onto the adjacent houses of the Egyptians. The sacrifice thankfully commemorates or celebrates this merciful and life-preserving act. What is remarkable is that *Pesaḥ* is fundamentally different from Matza and *Maror*. Matza – as we shall shortly see, represents *ge'ula* – the redemption which occurred in haste, in a rush to freedom. *Maror* represents *galut* – exile and bitter enslavement. These are indelible historical experiences worthy of commemoration! *Pesaḥ*, however, represents neither exile nor freedom; the skipping occurred during *makkat bekhorot* – before they left. If anything, it represents the **method** by which the redemption was eventually attained. This raises the question as to why this method is so centrally important to Judaism that it too is memorialized?

In order to answer this question, we need to determine whether the *Korban Pesaḥ* is a *Korban Yaḥid* – a personal sacrifice, or a *Korban Tzibbur* – a communal sacrifice. A private sacrifice, like an *olah*, *shelamim* or *ḥatat* cannot be brought on *Shabbat*, while a communal sacrifice, like the *Tamid* or *musafim*, is brought despite the restrictions of the Sabbath. Many of the laws of the *Korban Pesaḥ* reflect its private nature. Thus, it is in essence a private family-centered sacrifice (Ex. 12:3) "a lamb to a family, a lamb to a household." No other sacrifice requires *minuyin* – knowing exactly who will be eating the lamb. No unexpected guests are allowed, nor can the meat be shared outside the group. This is a very private affair. On the other hand, it is a very public sacrifice in that everyone brings it, it represents the redemption of the nation from Egypt, and, like communal sacrifices, the Paschal lamb is brought on *Shabbat*! How are we to understand this unique dual identity of the *Korban Pesah*?

There is the communal redemption represented by the Matza. All the Israelites gathered in the town square and in their common rush to freedom, baked and ate Matza. But there is the private redemption which is represented by the *Korban Pesah*. I'm not part of the community because we all gathered together – after all I am in my home surrounded by Egyptian homes. The next Israelite house might be blocks, perhaps miles away. I am part of the community because I identify spiritually and experientially with all of the Children of Israel. All Israelites, wherever they may have been throughout Egypt, put blood on the lintel and doorposts of their homes, circumcised their males, ate the *Korban Pesah*, and identified with all other Israelites. A Jew can sit alone in a village in Egypt and be the only door in the city with blood on the lintel and doorposts – and he/she is intimately part of *Klal Yisrael*. We are joined together by our observance of God's commandments, and by his protective skipping over our home. The *Korban Pesah* is indeed a *Korban Yahid*; but it is also a *Korban Tzibbur* which binds all Jews together.

At the *Seder*, we emphasize this lesson of the two types of "Community." One type is the togetherness that results from a common shared group experience. Thus, Matza and *Maror* memorialize the fact that all Israelites were enslaved together in Egypt, and in their miraculous rush to freedom, baked unleavened bread. But the *Korban Pesah* teaches us of another type of togetherness that has been so critical to Jewish identity and survival. A lone Jew in Montana with a *Mezuza* on his door is intimately connected to the Breslov Hassid in New York or Zefat. I may dwell alone, but I am not alone. We are bound together through a common commitment, a common dedication, a common vision of the future, and a common faith in the guiding hand of the Almighty.

In light of the above discussion, let us return to the *Rasha* of the "Four Children." The latter asks his parent (Ex. 12:26) "What is the meaning of this service to you?" To this, the *Haggada* responds: "to **you**" (plural) – but not "to **us**" (including him). Because he has excluded himself from the community, he has rejected the central principal… "Were he there (in Eqypt), **he would not have been redeemed**." The rationale behind the *Haggada*'s conclusion becomes clear. Of course, he would not have been redeemed! After all, he is the disconnected Israelite who does not identify with the community and would not have put blood on his doorposts! He wants to mesh with the Egyptians around him – not stand out.

We can now answer another question regarding the *Rasha*. Surprisingly, the *Haggada*'s response to the *Rasha* is seemingly not identical to the Torah's answer, which reads (Ex 12:27): "And you shall say: 'It is the sacrifice of the Lord's Passover, for He passed over the houses of the children of Israel in Egypt, when He smote the Egyptians and delivered our houses.'" The fact is, however, that the Torah's answer to the *Rasha* is the very verse that teaches us here about *Pesah*: that community and togetherness are central to what it is to be Jewish. Thus, the Torah's answer to the *Rasha* and that of the *Haggada* are essentially the same – except that the *Haggada* makes explicit what the Torah implies. To wit: rejecting community is a disconnection from God's guiding hand: "Were he there [in Egypt], he would not have been redeemed."

וַיִּקֹּד הָעָם וַיִּשְׁתַּחֲווּ

R. Azaria Berzon (*Hadarom*, **53**:52, *Nisan* 5744) wonders why the last words of this verse –"The people bowed and prostrated themselves" – is cited as well. The answer is that if one reads the six previous verses (Ex. 12: 21–26) which culminate in our proof text (v. 27), one sees that the people received three good tidings: redemption, the Promised Land, and future progeny. To this, they bowed in thanks. All this is to emphasize the importance of gratitude and is a natural preparation for the next and last topic of *Maggid* (once we conclude *Rabban* Gamliel's required explanations): *Hallel*.

Lift up or point to the *matza* and recite the following:

מַצָּה זוּ שֶׁאָנוּ אוֹכְלִים. עַל שׁוּם מַה? עַל שׁוּם שֶׁלֹּא הִסְפִּיק בְּצֵקָם שֶׁל אֲבוֹתֵינוּ לְהַחֲמִיץ עַד שֶׁנִּגְלָה עֲלֵיהֶם מֶלֶךְ מַלְכֵי הַמְּלָכִים. הַקָּדוֹשׁ בָּרוּךְ הוּא. וּגְאָלָם. שֶׁנֶּאֱמַר (שמות יב:לט): וַיֹּאפוּ אֶת־הַבָּצֵק אֲשֶׁר הוֹצִיאוּ מִמִּצְרַיִם עֻגֹת מַצּוֹת. כִּי לֹא חָמֵץ. כִּי גֹרְשׁוּ מִמִּצְרַיִם וְלֹא יָכְלוּ לְהִתְמַהְמֵהַּ. וְגַם צֵדָה לֹא עָשׂוּ לָהֶם.

מַצָּה זוּ שֶׁאָנוּ אוֹכְלִים

Why does the *Haggada* say *Matza* **zo** *she-anu okhlin al shum ma* – "**This** Matza that we eat, what does it recall?" Shouldn't it have said more simply: *Matza al shum ma* – "Matza, what does it recall?"

(a) One possibility is that this section is a form of "Show and Tell." Following the Temple's destruction, there is no Paschal lamb to point to, so with *Pesaḥ* no **zeh** can be used. But with Matza and *Maror* we can point to them, and we do – for the greater pedagogic effect.

(b) A second approach suggests that *zeh* – this refers back to the *Haggada's* discussion as to the timing of the mitzva of *ve-higadeta le-vinkha* – instructing the children regarding the Exodus. The *Haggada* answers that the proper time for this conversation is when one can say (Ex. 13:8): *Ba'avur zeh asa li Hashem be-tzeiti mi-Mitzrayim* – "It was for **this** [the fulfillment of *Pesaḥ*, *Matza*, and *Maror*] that the Almighty redeemed me from Egypt." Referring to this verse, the parent here is therefore effectively saying: "My child, because of the destruction of the Temple, one can no longer perform *Pesaḥ*; but "this" is the Matza and "this" is the *Maror* – for whose fulfillment we were redeemed."

(c) R. Menashe Klein (*Haggada Maggid Mishne*) reminds us that we've already mentioned that Matza can be a reminder of **slavery** – as we said at the *Seder's* beginning: *Ha Laḥma Anya*. But this Matza that we eat is a reminder of **freedom**, while **this** *Maror* reminds us of the bitter servitude.

מַצָּה זוּ שֶׁאָנוּ אוֹכְלִים. עַל שׁוּם מַה?

The role of Matza in the redemption story requires a good deal of elucidation. But let us first review selected verses from Exodus Chapter

Lift up or point to the matza and recite the following:

This Matza that we eat – what is its meaning? It is because our fathers' dough did not have time to rise before the King of kings: the Holy One Blessed is He revealed Himself to them and redeemed them. As it says: "They baked the dough which they had brought out of Egypt into cakes of matza, for it had not leavened; because they were driven out of Egypt and could not delay, nor had they prepared provisions for themselves" (Exodus 12:39).

---

12 relating to the baking of Matza. The Torah tells us about the *Pesah* observed in Egypt (*Pesah Mitzrayim*):

> **12:3.** Speak to the community of Israel and say that on the tenth of this month (*Nisan*) each of them shall take a lamb for a family, a lamb for a household. **6.** You shall keep watch over it until the fourteenth day of this month; and all the assembled congregation of the Israelites shall slaughter it at twilight. 8. They shall eat the flesh that same night – roasted over the fire, with Matza, and with bitter herbs. 12. On that night I will go through the land of Egypt and strike down every firstborn in the land of Egypt, both human and beast; and I will mete out punishments to all the gods of Egypt, I am Hashem.

The Narrative then switches to discuss *Pesah Dorot* – the Passover to be observed in future years in commemoration of the Exodus.

> **12:14.** This day shall be to you one of remembrance: you shall celebrate it as a festival to *Hashem* throughout the ages; you shall celebrate it as an institution for all time. **15.** Seven days you shall eat Matza; on the very first day you shall remove leaven from your houses, for whoever eats leavened bread from the first day to the seventh day, that person shall be cut off from Israel. **20.** You shall eat nothing leavened; in all your settlements you shall eat unleavened bread.

Finally, details are recounted of what actually happened in Egypt on *Pesah* night.

12:29. In the middle of the night Hashem struck down all the first-born in the land of Egypt... **30.** And Pharaoh arose in the night, with all his courtiers and all the Egyptians – because there was a loud cry in Egypt; for there was no house where there was not someone dead. **31.** He summoned Moshe and Aharon in the night and said, "Up, depart from among my people, you and the Israelites with you! Go, worship Hashem as you said! **33.** The Egyptians urged the people on, impatient to have them leave the country, for they said, "We shall all be dead." **34.** So the people took their dough before it was leavened, their kneading bowls wrapped in their cloaks upon their shoulders. **37.** The Israelites journeyed from Rameses to Succoth... **39.** And they baked the dough that they had taken out of Egypt as "Matza cakes," for it was not leavened, because they were driven out of Egypt and could not delay; nor had they prepared any provisions for themselves.

Question 1: The *Haggada* cites 12:39 as proof that we eat Matza (in *Pesah Dorot*) in commemoration of the Matza baked in the rush to freedom. And while this verse indeed proves that Matza during this Exodus was baked in haste – it does not prove that **this is the reason** why we eat Matza yearly at the *Seder*. After all, in the *Seder* held in Egypt prior to their departure from Egypt (*Pesah Mitzrayim*) they also ate Matza (see 12:8).

The answer is that this very point is explicitly mentioned in Deut. 16:3.
1. Observe the month of the Spring (*Nisan*) and offer a Passover sacrifice to your God Hashem... **3.** You shall not eat with it anything leavened; for seven days you shall eat Matza, bread of distress – for you departed from the land of Egypt hurriedly (*be-hipazon*) – so that you may remember the day of your departure from the land of Egypt as long as you live.

This suggests then that when the Torah commanded eating Matza at *Pesah Dorot* (12:15) it was based on a reason only to be revealed in the future (*al shem ha-atid*). Thus, the Matza of *Pesah Mitzrayim* is in commemoration of the Matza of slavery, while the Matza of the seven days of *Pesah Dorot* is in memory of the *hipazon* – the Matza baked in the rush to freedom.

Question 2: If the real proof text is Deut. 16:3, why did the *Haggada* cite Ex. 12:39?! The answer would seem to be that the latter verse is close enough and supplies more facts and details. It is, therefore, more appropriate for telling a story – *Sippur Yetzi'at Mitzrayim*.

Question 3: Verse 8 above makes clear that there is an obligation to eat Matza on *Pesah Mitzrayim*. However, the Talmud in *Pesahim* 36b cites R. Yossi *ha-Gelili* that there was also a prohibition of *Hametz* on that whole day of *Pesah Mitzrayim*. What then does 12:39, cited by the *Haggada*, mean when it says: "And they baked the dough that they had taken out of Egypt as 'Matza cakes,' for it was not leavened because they were driven out of Egypt and could not delay…." The clear implication is that had they not been driven out, they **would** have delayed and they **would** have allowed the dough to rise! How so? According to *Pesahim* 36b, there was a prohibition of *Hametz* even on *Pesah Mitzrayim*! We will cite three of the answers proposed:

(a) Ramban (Ex. 12:39) proposes that, because of the prohibition of *Hametz*, the Israelites from the get-go intended to bake Matza. That's why they kept the dough in arm's reach – "in their cloaks upon their shoulders" (Ex. 12:34) – so they could work the dough when necessary. According to this, which the *Haggada* says: "that the dough of our ancestors did not have time to rise" means that everything proceeded so miraculously fast that the dough did not have a chance to rise and leaven. The phrase "because they were chased out of Egypt" explains why they baked the dough on the road rather than in Egypt (– not why it didn't rise).

(b) Rashi (on Ex. 12:34) and Ran (on Rif to *Pesahim* 116b, s.v. Matza) both assert that the Israelites would have preferred to let the dough rise. Ran explains that while they were forbidden on the 15th of *Nisan* to eat *Hametz*, they weren't forbidden in *bal yira'e u-bal yimatzei* – to bake or possess leavened bread. They need the leavened bread for the next day (16th of *Nisan*), as the verse cited says "nor did they prepare food for the trip." Because of the rush – they couldn't even do that.

(c) Malbim (12:34) creatively suggests that before the giving of the Torah, a day was from morning to morning. Subsequent to Sinai, Jews observed a day from evening to evening. (See also our comments to אִלּוּ הֶאֱכִילָנוּ אֶת־הַמָּן וְלֹא נָתַן לָנוּ אֶת־הַשַּׁבָּת above.) Thus, the one-day prohibition of *Hametz* on *Pesah Mitzrayim* was from the morning on the 14th of *Nisan* to the morning of the 15th. When they left Egypt on the 15th they were already permitted to bake and eat *Hametz*.

Question 4: How is it possible that the dough did not become *Hametz*? Halakhically, if flour is mixed with water and not worked every 18 minutes, the dough becomes *Hametz*. A simple calculation suggests that there were ca. 3 million people who left Egypt (600,000 males aged 20–50; an equal number of women – another 600,000; and children below 20 and elders above 50 – another 2 million.) These ca. 3 million traveled from all over Egypt to Rameses and from there to Succoth (Ex. 12:37). With all that, how could the dough not have leavened? Here too several answers have been suggested:

(a) *Mekhilta* of R. Shimon bar Yohai (to Ex. 12) posits that the absence of leavening was simply miraculous; *Mekhilta* of R. Yishmael (*Bo, Masekhet de Pisha, Parasha* 14) posits that it was the speed at which they traveled that was the miracle.

(b) Ramban (Ex. 12:39), *Or ha-Hayim* and *Ketav ve-Kabala* maintain that, because of the prohibition of *Hametz*, the Israelites kept the dough in arm's reach – "in their cloaks upon their shoulders" – so they could work the dough when necessary.

(c) R. Samson Raphael Hirsch (Ex. 13:39) and Amos Hakham (*Da'at Mikra*) suggest that the people's very swift pace kept the dough continually bouncing around – which was equivalent to working it.

Question 5: A final question concerns the importance of the *hipazon* – the haste, the rush to freedom. Why was it important to have the Israelites driven out by the populace from Egypt? Here too several answers have been put forward:

(a) One traditional answer (*Zohar Hadash*, Beginning of Yitro) is that the Israelites had sunk deeply into the corrupt Egyptian lifestyle, culture, and idolatry (referred to by *Haza"l* as the "49th level of impurity"). Hence it was imperative to remove them hastily.

(b) So that the Egyptians would not be able to claim that the Israelites fled.

(c) So the Israelites could not claim they were conquerors. On the contrary, the Israelites were **forced** into freedom; they were driven out of Egyptian bondage. The significance of this *hipazon* (hurriedness), R. Samson Raphael Hirsch explains (Deut. 16:3), is that at the moment of the Exodus, no one was truly free – not even the emancipated slaves. They did not leave Egyptian bondage into freedom. Rather, God freed them from the yoke of Egypt so that they would take upon themselves the yoke of Heaven.

(d) The Egyptians felt the hand of God and the presence of God in Egypt. There was *Gilui Shekhina* (Divine Revelation) and fulfillment of the verse (Ex. 7:17): "By this, you shall know that I am Hashem." This may well be the explanation for the Haggada's statement: "Until the King of Kings revealed Himself and redeemed them." All finally recognized God's dominion: Egyptians, Pharaoh, and Israelites! The goal had been attained.

Lift up or point to the maror and recite the following passage:

מָרוֹר זֶה שֶׁאָנוּ אוֹכְלִים. עַל שׁוּם מַה? עַל שׁוּם שֶׁמֵּרְרוּ הַמִּצְרִים אֶת־חַיֵּי אֲבוֹתֵינוּ בְּמִצְרָיִם. (שמות א:יד) שֶׁנֶּאֱמַר: וַיְמָרְרוּ אֶת חַיֵּיהֶם בַּעֲבֹדָה קָשָׁה, בְּחֹמֶר וּבִלְבֵנִים וּבְכָל־עֲבֹדָה בַּשָּׂדֶה אֵת כָּל עֲבֹדָתָם אֲשֶׁר עָבְדוּ בָהֶם בְּפָרֶךְ.

בְּכָל־דּוֹר וָדוֹר חַיָּב אָדָם לִרְאוֹת אֶת־עַצְמוֹ כְּאִלּוּ הוּא יָצָא מִמִּצְרָיִם.

(e) Finally, Maharal indicates that the leavening of bread is a natural process and requires time. But the *hipazon* – haste involved in the origin of Matza reflects the fact that the salvation of the Exodus was **super**natural and occurred speedily; as Haza"l tell us: *Yeshu'at Hashem ke-heref ayin* – "God's salvation can occur in the blink of an eye" (*Midrash Lekah Tov, Pesikta Zutreta*, Esther 4:17). Similarly, the essence of the salvation and extraction of "a nation from the midst of another nation" (Deut. 4:34) is the reversal of 210 years of assimilation in one fell swoop.

כִּי גֹרְשׁוּ מִמִּצְרָיִם

In response to the *Tam* – the simple child– who asks why we celebrate Passover, the Torah (Ex. 13:14) instructs us: "Then you shall say to him: 'With a strong hand the Lord brought us out from Egypt, from the house of bondage.'" It is generally assumed that the "strong arm" refers to the punishing plagues of the Almighty that led to our redemption. It is possible that it also refers – at least in part – to the Egyptians who chased/drove the Israelites out of Egypt, as it says in the proof text (Ex: 12:39): *Ki gorshu mi-Mitzrayim*. Similarly, in Ex. 12:33 we read: "The Egyptians forced the people on, urging them to leave the country...."

כְּאִלּוּ הוּא יָצָא מִמִּצְרָיִם

This final portion of *Maggid* reiterates that it is a Jew's obligation *Seder* night to envision himself or herself as having just left Egypt. We are not merely the progeny of those who left Egypt three millennia ago.

Lift up or point to the *maror* and recite the following passage:

This bitter herb that we eat – what is its meaning? It is because the Egyptians embittered our fathers' lives in Egypt, as it says: "They made their lives bitter with hard labor, with mortar and with bricks, and with all manner of labor in the field; whatever they made them do was with rigor" (Exodus 1:14).

In every generation, it is one's duty to see himself as though he had personally come out from Egypt, as it says: "You shall tell your child

---

Rather we ourselves went out and, therefore, have to give praise to the Almighty. We then recite the first two chapters of the six that comprise *Hallel*.

Former Israeli Chief R. Shlomo Goren asked why the Jewish tradition requires each of us to relive the Exodus experience yearly, while we are not required to do the same when it comes to the giving of the Torah or our entering the Land of Israel. To this R. Goren answered that both Torah and the Land of Israel are referred to in the Torah as a *Morasha* (an heirloom). Concerning Torah it is written (Deut. 33:4): "Moshe bequeathed to us the Torah, an heirloom of the congregation of Yaakov;" while regarding the Land of Israel (Ex. 6:8) it states: "And I will bring you in unto the land, concerning which I lifted up My hand to give it to Avraham, to Yitzhak, and to Yaakov; and I will give it you for an heirloom: I am the Lord." Both Torah and the Land of Israel are heirlooms to be shared by both, cherished, and passed on from generation to generation. By contrast, the fact that my parents were free does not guarantee my rights – unless I appreciate them, guard them, and fight for them; unless I appreciate what I stand to lose. This requires yearly sensitization at the *Seder* table.

An eloquent modern reformulation of this imperative was declared by Israeli President Ezer Weizmann in a speech he gave to the German Bundestag (January 16, 1996):

Every Jew, in every generation, is obligated to see himself as if he was in Egypt, and also as if he was in the places *and took part in the events of all prior generations*. Two hundred generations have passed

שֶׁנֶּאֱמַר (שמות יג:ח): וְהִגַּדְתָּ לְבִנְךָ בַּיּוֹם הַהוּא לֵאמֹר, בַּעֲבוּר זֶה עָשָׂה ה' לִי בְּצֵאתִי מִמִּצְרָיִם. לֹא אֶת־אֲבוֹתֵינוּ בִּלְבָד גָּאַל הַקָּדוֹשׁ בָּרוּךְ הוּא,

in the history of my people yet they appear, in my eyes, as several days. Only two hundred generations have passed since a man arose whose name was Avraham. He left his land and his birthplace and went to a land that today is mine. Only two hundred generations passed between Avraham's purchase of the Machpelah Cave in the city of Hebron and the murderous attacks against Jews in my own generation in that same city. From the Pillar of Fire in the Exodus from Egypt – to the pillars of smoke in the Holocaust... I, born from the seed of Avraham in the land of Avraham, was part of it all.

I was a slave in Egypt. I received the Torah at Mount Sinai. Together with Yehoshua, I crossed the Jordan River. I entered Jerusalem with David, was exiled from it with Zedekiah, and did not forget it by the rivers of Babylon. When the Lord returned the exiles of Zion, I dreamed among those who rebuilt its ramparts. I fought the Romans and was banished from Spain. I was bound to the stake in Mainz. I studied Torah in Yemen and lost my family in Kishinev. I was incinerated in Treblinka, rebelled in Warsaw, and immigrated to the Land of Israel, the country from which I had been exiled and where I had been born, from which I come and to which I return.

Just as it is demanded of us, by the power of memory, to live through each day and each experience of our past, so too it is demanded of us, by the power of hope, to look expectantly toward each day of our future.

שֶׁנֶּאֱמַר (שמות יג:ח)

This citation is a bit problematic. After all, in an attempt to prove that a parent must relate to their progeny their first-hand tale of the Exodus, the *Haggada* cites the verse from Exodus (13:8): "And you shall recount to your child on that day, 'It is because of this that Hashem acted for me when I went free from Egypt.'" So why is it necessary to bring a second proof text from Deuteronomy (6:23): "And [God] freed **us** from

on that day: 'It was because of this that the Lord did [all these miracles] for me when I went out of Egypt'" (Exodus 13:8). Not only our fathers did the Holy One Blessed is He redeem from Egypt, but He

---

there…" The answer would seem to be that the verse in Exodus is speaking to the Israelites of the first generation, those actually redeemed from Egypt. (Although Exodus 13:5 begins "When the LORD brings you into the land…," they fully expected to be in Canaan in several months – not 40 years!) It is in reference to this first generation that the verse says: "And you shall explain to your child…" But how do I know that this obligation refers to subsequent generations as well? For this reason, the *Haggada* cites the verse of Deuteronomy which is focused on the second generation. But if I had only the latter verse, I would have thought that there is only an obligation to tell the Exodus story if the child asks, because that section (Deut. 6:20) begins: "When your child asks you…. Exodus teaches that there is an obligation to discuss the redemption, even if there is no spontaneous question – even if the parent initiates the discussion. We now better understand the *Haggada*'s choice of repetitive language: "In generation after generation…" It comes to include not only the generation of the redeemed parents (Exodus) but also the generation of the sons who entered the Land of Canaan/Israel (Deuteronomy).

We note that this motif of the relevance of the redemption story to all generations is repeated thrice in the *Haggada*. The first time follows the "Four Questions" when we say *Avadim hayinu*: "We were slaves to Pharaoh in Egypt … and had the Holy One, blessed is He, not brought our ancestors out from Egypt, **we and our children and our grandchildren** would still be enslaved in Egypt." The second time appears in connection to the passage *ve-Hi she-Amda* which states: "And it is this that has stood for our ancestors and for us. For it is not just one that has stood against us to destroy us. Rather **in each generation**, they stand against us to destroy us – but the Holy One, blessed is He, rescues us from their hand." And thirdly, we find the same theme here in the passage *be-Khol dor va-dor*, where we say: "In generation after generation, an individual is obligated to see oneself leaving Egypt…" In each case, the message is that the Egyptian experience remains relevant. In *Avadim Hayinu* at the beginning of *Maggid*, we explain why we are

אֶלָּא אַף אוֹתָנוּ גָּאַל עִמָּהֶם, שֶׁנֶּאֱמַר (דברים ו:כג): וְאוֹתָנוּ הוֹצִיא מִשָּׁם, לְמַעַן הָבִיא אוֹתָנוּ, לָתֶת לָנוּ אֶת־הָאָרֶץ אֲשֶׁר נִשְׁבַּע לַאֲבֹתֵינוּ.

---

telling the 3300-year-old tale of the Exodus. We are free because our ancestors were freed, and this redemption obligates all future beneficiaries to retell the story. But note that for this indebtedness I don't have to feel personally redeemed. Then at *ve-Hi she-Amda* we recall the *Brit bein ha-Betarim*, in which the Egyptian exile of our forebears is foretold; but so is a promise to keep our nation alive through that oppression and all subsequent generations. This too is deserving of our praise, but it doesn't require that I personally have lived under Egyptian oppression. Finally, this motif appears here at the end of *Maggid* to explain why we loudly sing *Hallel*. Here, through the medium of *Seder*, we **personally** experience a taste of the bitterness and slavery (*Haggada* and *Maror*), and the exhilaration of the redemption (*Pesah, Matza*, and *Hasaba*). We are personally moved to sing – with joy and passion – the Almighty's praises. In his halakhic guide to the *Seder* (MT, Hil. *Hametz u-Matza*, 7:6), Maimonides emphasizes the proper state of mind at this juncture by slightly changing the usual formula of *be-Khol dor va-dor* and uses the following language (bold words are not in the standard text): *be-Khol dor va-dor hayav adam* **le-harot** *et atzmo ke-ilu hu* **be-atzmo** *yatza ata me-shi'abud Mitzrayim* – "In generation after generation, one must **act** as if he **personally** has **just now** come out from **the subjugation of** Egypt." This is then followed by the paragraph beginning "Therefore, we are obligated to thank and praise…" followed by the recitation of *Hallel*. Ideally, argues Rambam, the *Hallel* is meant to be a spontaneous song of praise stemming from one's strong sense of **personal** redemption and indebtedness to the Almighty.

My father, R. Norman Frimer z"l, pointed out that Halakha often uses mitzva actions to generate emotion, aura, and mood – as the *Hinukh* (*Mitzva* 15) says: "Emotions follow our actions." Thus, the Torah commands *ve-Samahta be-hagekha* – "rejoice on your holidays." However, are emotions something that can be commanded? That is why *Haza"l* in their wisdom required Jews to fulfill *ve-Samahta be-Hagekha* by doing those things that normally cause them joy. Hence, men are required to eat meat and wine; women should purchase jewelry and festive clothing; while children should be given candies and snacks. When

redeemed us with them as well, as it says: "It was us that He brought out from there, so that He might bring us to give us the land that He promised to our fathers" (Deuteronomy 6:23).

---

it comes to mourning, *aveilim* are required to do those things that normally cause them sadness: avoid pleasurable bathing, new clothing, joyous music, and leather shoes; sit on low chairs; avoid social gatherings and parties, etc. The same applies to the obligation to see yourself as if you just left Egypt. Jewish tradition requires me to do those actions which create a sense of being liberated and feeling noble: dress in festive garments (*kittel*), eat several courses (*shnei tavshilin*), drink multiple cups of wine, wash excessively, eat leaning, use your finest dishes and silver, set the table early and beautifully as you would for rich dinner parties (*Arukh ha-Shulhan* 472:2), and surround yourself with lots of family and friends. If you act like nobility, you will feel noble. R. Chaim Palagi (*Chaim le-Rosh*, p. 25a) suggests that expensive clothing and table settings remind us of (Ex. 3:22): "Each woman shall borrow from her neighbor and the lodger in her house objects of silver and gold, and clothing, and you shall put these on your sons and daughters…" It also reminds us of the *rekhush Gadol* – "great wealth" with which they ultimately left Egypt, as promised to Avraham (Gen. 15:14).

אֶלָּא אַף אוֹתָנוּ

The greater impact of first-hand testimony, we all appreciate when listening to a survivor speak about their holocaust experiences. It's hard to gainsay such a witness. In 1953, my second-grade teacher at *Yeshiva Ohel Moshe* in Brooklyn, NY was Mrs. Sawyer. She would teach us world history by briefly discussing the background of the event, and then recount her "first-hand" experiences and the conversations "she had" with the major protagonists: Moshe, Abravanel, Shakespeare, George Washington, and Abraham Lincoln. We suspended any disbelief and listened with rapt and focused attention. After all, she "was there" and what she told us must be accurate. We looked forward eagerly each week to the next testimonial. It would seem to me that this is the model *Haza"l* desired for *Maggid* as well: *Af otanu ga'al imahem… ve-otanu hotzi mi-sham.* – "We too were redeemed with them…and He took us out from there as well."

הקדמה לאמירת ההלל

Raise the cup of wine.

לְפִיכָךְ אֲנַחְנוּ חַיָּבִים לְהוֹדוֹת. לְהַלֵּל. לְשַׁבֵּחַ. לְפָאֵר. לְרוֹמֵם. לְהַדֵּר. לְבָרֵךְ. לְעַלֵּה וּלְקַלֵּס לְמִי שֶׁעָשָׂה לַאֲבוֹתֵינוּ וְלָנוּ אֶת־כָּל־הַנִּסִּים הָאֵלּוּ: הוֹצִיאָנוּ מֵעַבְדוּת לְחֵרוּת. מִיָּגוֹן לְשִׂמְחָה. וּמֵאֵבֶל לְיוֹם טוֹב. וּמֵאֲפֵלָה לְאוֹר גָּדוֹל. וּמִשִּׁעְבּוּד לִגְאֻלָּה. וְנֹאמַר לְפָנָיו שִׁירָה חֲדָשָׁה: הַלְלוּיָהּ.

הקדמה לאמירת ההלל

The previous section, *be-Khol dor va-dor*, reiterates that it is a Jew's obligation on *Seder* Night to envision himself or herself as having just left Egypt. We are not merely the progeny of those who left Egypt three millennia ago. Rather we ourselves went through the experience and, therefore, have to give praise to the Almighty. Upon salvation, Jews historically sang *Hallel* as recorded in *Pesahim* 117a: "The song [at the Sea] (Ex. 15:1–19): Moshe and the Jewish people recited it when they ascended from the sea. And who said this *Hallel* (Psalms 113–118)? The Prophets among them established this *Hallel* for the Jewish people, that they should recite it on every appropriate occasion; and for every trouble... When they are redeemed, they recite it over their redemption." In contradistinction to *Hallel ha-Gadol* (Psalms 136 with the repeated *ki le'olam hasdo* refrain), Psalms 113–118 is dubbed by *Haza"l* as *Hallel ha-Mitzri*. This is either because it was first recited at the Red Sea (*Pesahim* 117a citing R. Eliezer) or because the second paragraph is *be-Tzeit Yisrael mi-Mitzrayim*.

Regarding the *Hallel* recited at the *Seder*, we should ask: "How is this *Hallel* different from the *Hallel* recited throughout the rest of the year?"

(1) All other times, *Hallel* is said at home or in Shul; why is this *Hallel* declaimed specifically at the *Seder* Table?
(2) All other times, *Hallel* is recited during the day; why is this *Hallel* said specifically at night?
(3) All other times, *Hallel* is preceded with a *berakha*; why is this *Hallel* said without an opening *berakha*?

Introduction to Hallel

Raise the cup of wine.

Therefore it is our duty to thank, praise, hail, glorify, exalt, honor, bless, extol and celebrate the One Who did all these miracles for our fathers and us. He brought us forth from slavery to freedom, from sorrow to joy, and from mourning to festivity, and from darkness to great light, and from servitude to redemption. Let us therefore recite before Him a new song: Halleluyah!

---

(4) All other times, *Hallel* is recited standing; why is this *Hallel* said sitting around the *Seder* Table?

(5) Why is the *Hallel* recited in a split fashion, two paragraphs before eating the *mitzvot* and meal, and the remainder afterward?

In order to answer these questions, I'd like to introduce a distinction first formulated by *Rav* Hai Gaon and more recently by R. Yitzhak Zev (Velvel) Soloveitchik (*Haggada Bet ha-Levi*). These scholars explain that there are two types of *Hallel*. The first is *Hallel shel Simha* – *Hallel* of Rejoicing. This is the complete *Hallel* which we read in Israel on the 18 days of the *shalosh regalim* (*Pesah* – 1, *Shavu'ot* – 1 and *Sukkot* – 8) and *Hanukah* (8) (see Maimonides MT, *Hil. Hanukah* 3:6). However, the *Hallel* we say on *Seder* Night is fundamentally different. This second kind of *Hallel*, says R. Velvel, is a *Hallel* of *Shira* – *Hallel* of Salvation. This is a spontaneous song of praise that one says when he/she is rescued from peril. One of the fundamental differences between these two types of *Hallel*, is that *Hallel* of Rejoicing can be said by all who rejoice in *simhat Yom Tov* – the joy of the holiday. *Hallel* of Salvation, on the other hand, can only be said by one who experienced the deliverance. Since the *Hallel* recited at the *Seder* is in the second class of *Hallel of Shira*, the goal of *Seder* is to enable us to feel that "We were there!" In our comments to שֶׁנֶּאֱמַר (שמות יג:ח) above, we have already cited the special language used by Maimonides (MT, Hil. *Hametz u-Matza*, 7:6) to describe the state of mind one is to experience at the end of

Maggid as he moves into *Hallel*: "In generation after generation, one must act as if he personally has just now come out from the subjugation of Egypt…" Thus, the recital of *Hallel* stems from the *Seder* participants strong sense of personal redemption and deep sense of indebtedness to the Almighty.

In light of the fact that *Hallel* at the *Seder* is meant to be a spontaneous personal expression of gratitude, the above five questions can be answered as follows:

(Questions 1, 2, and 4) The *Hallel* intended by *Haza"l* can only be said at **home**, at **night**, while we **sit** reading the *Haggada*. This is because it is through the *Haggada* narrative that we come to feel that we were slaves and are now being miraculously redeemed.

(Question 3) By the same token, how could we recite a **berakha** "… who commanded us to recite the *Hallel*"? Wouldn't a *berakha* obligation be the exact opposite of spontaneity and the outpouring of song?

(Question 5) As to why the *Hallel* is **split** so that only the first two chapters of *Hallel* are recited as part of *Maggid*, R. Joseph B. Soloveitchik ("An Exalted Evening") explains that these chapters are completely dedicated to thanksgiving and praise. They contain no request or petition. These first sections deal with the Almighty as the one in control of creation and His selection of the Children of Israel as the "Chosen People." The rest of *Hallel* does indeed contain many requests (e.g., *Ana Hashem Malta Nafshi* – "Please God deliver my soul;" *Ana Hashem hoshi'a na* – "Please God save us") mixed with praise. But at the present point in the *Seder*, having just been redeemed, we have an obligation to praise Hashem in a format that is pure tribute without plaint and petition. (See our comments to שִׁירָה חֲדָשָׁה below for an alternate suggestion of the Malbim).

The next issue worthy of our attention concerns a Gemara (*Megilla* 10b, *Sanhedrin* 39b) which recounts that during the episode at the Red Sea, the heavenly angels wanted to sing the Almighty's praises. He forbade them saying: *Ma'asei yadai tovim ba-yam ve-atem omrim shira?!* – "My handiwork is drowning in the sea, and you want to sing in praise?!" The implication of this statement is that the angels were silenced because, though the Israelites were being miraculously saved, the Egyptians – God's handiwork – were being drowned. How then do we sing *Hallel* at the *Seder*, when the Israelites' redemption came at the Egyptians' expense? R. Joseph B. Soloveitchik (*Haggada Si'ah ha-Grid*) cites R. Chaim Volozhin to the effect that while the angels were silenced, this was because they were uninvolved third parties. However, the Israelites themselves, for whom the miracle of salvation was performed, could certainly have sung *Shira* upon their redemption. And on *Seder* night, **since we view ourselves as having been redeemed** from Egypt, we too can sing *Hallel* of *Shira*.

Based on the above discussion, R. Soloveitchik (ibid.) asks why the Israelites **themselves** did not sing *Hallel* immediately when they left Egypt? Why did they wait until after the Red Sea was split? He answers that the Israelites were not truly free men until they saw their Egyptian taskmasters lying dead at their feet at the water's edge. Only then did they fathom the full implications of the Almighty's "strong arm" and became physically and spiritually free of Egyptian influence. Only **then** could they sing *Shira* – song and praise.

Raise the cup of wine

It should be remarked that when saying the introductory paragraph to *Hallel* – *le-Fikhakh* – there are two customs. One is to cover the *Matzot* upon completing *Pesah*, *Matza*, and *Maror*. Then, as we begin *le-Fikhakh*, we raise our cups and hold them through the first two chapters of *Hallel* and through the final *berakha*. This *minhag* follows Maimonides, that *Maggid* formally ends with *Pesah*, *Matza*, *Maror* and, thereafter, we cover the *Matzot* – signaling that *Maggid* has essentially ended. Starting from *le-Fikhakh* we transition into *Hallel* – *shira* – song and praise, so we raise our cup to recite the chapters of *Hallel* and finish up with the concluding *berakha of Ga'al Yisrael*.

Others cover the *Matzot* upon completing *Pesah*, *Matza*, and *Maror* – stopping *Maggid* temporarily. We pick up the cup for *le-Fikhakh*. The cup is put down and the *matzot* uncovered for the saying of the first two chapters of *Hallel*. The premise of this second custom is that these two chapters of praise and *Hallel* are also an integral part of the story we are recounting in *Maggid*. We are reliving what our forebears experienced on their redemption – spontaneous song! The cup is raised again for the final *berakha* of *Ga'al Yisrael* said over the cup.

לְבָרֵךְ. לְעַלֵּה וּלְקַלֵּס

We have here 9 synonyms for praise plus the concluding phrase … ve-nomar le-fanav shira hadasha, halleluya. This gives 10 praises counting halleluya (as different from le-hallel) or shira. The Vilna Gaon (Haggada – ha-Gra ve-Talmidav) suggests that these 10 praises correspond to the 10 plagues. In truth however, different Rishonim have a different number of terms in their list of praises ranging from five to ten (Maimonides, MT, Hil. Hametz u-Matza, 8:5 has eight terms). The real point is the exuberance – the chant of acclaim and adulation. The list creates a crescendo of energy culminating with u-le-kales!

Interestingly, Maimonides does not have le-kales, and instead of le-varekh, le-aleh u-le-kales has le-gadel u-le-natze'ah. Indeed, Ritva is of the opinion that le-kales should not be used since in Tanakh it means derision (see Psalms 79:4 – la'ag va-keles). Nevertheless, in the later Rabbinic Midrashic literature we find the use of keles to mean praise. R. Shaul Lieberman (Alei Ayin – In honor of Zalman Shoken, p. 75f) has noted that the Greek word kalos (καλος) means beautiful, praiseworthy, and noble. Hence, le-kales may have taken on a new meaning based on a Greek root.

לְמִי שֶׁעָשָׂה לַאֲבוֹתֵינוּ וְלָנוּ אֶת־כָּל־הַנִסִּים הָאֵלּוּ

Pesah, like Purim and Hanukah, is a holiday whose purpose is to publicize the Almighty's miraculous salvation of the Israelites from oppression. Hence, the berakha, she-asa nisim la-avoteinu – "who performed miracles to our ancestors" should also be recited at the beginning of the Haggada. But, says Rav Amram Gaon (as explained by R. Menahem Kasher, Haggada Sheleima, p. 88), it couldn't have been said there, since we were still slaves! By contrast, at this point in the storyline, at the end of Maggid, we have been liberated and can declare: He who has done miracles to our ancestors and us…."

הוֹצִיאָנוּ מֵעַבְדוּת לְחֵרוּת

There are five pairs of redemption terms which Abravanel (Haggada Zevah Pesah) suggests corresponds to the five nations of exile (Egypt, Babylonia, Persians/Medes, Greece and Rome) or the five languages of redemption (ve-hotzeiti, ve-hitzalti, ve-ga'alti, ve-lakahti, ve-heveiti).

We point out that the terms *me-avdut le-herut* and *me-shi'abud li-ge'ula* seem redundant; however, *me-avdut le-herut* may refer to a physical plane, while *me-shi'abud li-ge'ula* may refer to the spiritual-cultural dimension. This would be consistent with what we wrote above on the phrase: *me-shu'abadim hayinu le-Pharaoh be-Mitzrayim*. Similarly, *herut* is "freedom from," but it doesn't direct me in any particular direction. By contrast, *ge'ula* is "freedom for" with a spiritual direction – in particular, "Let My people go to serve Me" (Ex. 7:16).

R. Velvel Soloveitchik (*Haggada Bet ha-Levi*) notes that in each of these five terms, there is a double miracle. Thus, *mi-yagon le-simha* involves not just the removal of one from a deeply sad situation, but its replacement by a joyous one. The same is true for *me-afeila le-or gadol* – one proceeds from a negative situation into a positive one. Even in the case of *me-shi'abud li-ge'ula*, this can be understood as "from subservience to spiritual redemption" – namely, an obligation in *mitzvot*. However, in the case of *me-avdut le-herut*, it would seem to mean "from slavery to freedom" – the absence of slavery, a single miracle, the removal of the negative. R. Velvel notes the verse (Lev. 25:55): "For unto Me the children of Israel are servants; they are My servants…" On this verse the Talmud (*Kiddushin* 22b; *Bava Metzi'a* 10a) famously states: "My servants – but not servants to servants." We were transformed from the servants of Pharaoh to the servants of the Almighty. As such we are **inherently** free, possessing eternal freedom. Thus, even if our body becomes enslaved, our spirit, mentality, and intellect will remain free.

שִׁירָה חֲדָשָׁה

Why is this recitation of this *Hallel* a new song? One simple answer would be that the miracle for which we are singing didn't happen three millennia ago, but just now! Hence it is new and fresh. Malbim (Psalms 96:1; 98:1) suggests that our new song is that the Almighty is not merely the **God of Creation**, as it says: "The sea saw and fled; the Jordan turned back." Now, after Egypt, He is also the **God of history**, as it also says in these chapters: "High above all nations is the Lord" and "When Israel came out of Egypt." Hence, we sing only the two first two chapters of the six chapters of *Hallel* which focus on these two attributes.

הלל

(תהלים פרק קיג): הַלְלוּיָהּ הַלְלוּ עַבְדֵי ה׳. הַלְלוּ אֶת־שֵׁם ה׳. יְהִי שֵׁם ה׳ מְבֹרָךְ מֵעַתָּה וְעַד עוֹלָם. מִמִּזְרַח שֶׁמֶשׁ עַד מְבוֹאוֹ מְהֻלָּל שֵׁם ה׳. רָם עַל־כָּל־גּוֹיִם ה׳. עַל הַשָּׁמַיִם כְּבוֹדוֹ. מִי כַּה׳ אֱלֹהֵינוּ הַמַּגְבִּיהִי לָשָׁבֶת. הַמַּשְׁפִּילִי לִרְאוֹת בַּשָּׁמַיִם וּבָאָרֶץ? מְקִימִי מֵעָפָר דָּל. מֵאַשְׁפֹּת יָרִים אֶבְיוֹן, לְהוֹשִׁיבִי עִם־נְדִיבִים. עִם נְדִיבֵי עַמּוֹ. מוֹשִׁיבִי עֲקֶרֶת הַבַּיִת. אֵם הַבָּנִים שְׂמֵחָה. הַלְלוּיָהּ.

(תהלים פרק קיד): בְּצֵאת יִשְׂרָאֵל מִמִּצְרָיִם. בֵּית יַעֲקֹב מֵעַם לֹעֵז, הָיְתָה יְהוּדָה לְקָדְשׁוֹ, יִשְׂרָאֵל מַמְשְׁלוֹתָיו. הַיָּם רָאָה וַיָּנֹס. הַיַּרְדֵּן יִסֹּב לְאָחוֹר.

תהלים פרק קיג

Haggada Me'am Lo'ez posits that in the opening chapter of *Hallel*, the Psalmist wants to clarify four fundamental issues. (1) Who is fit to sing the Almighty's praises? (2) Whom are we to praise? (3) When are we to praise Him? (4) Where is He to be praised?

(1) To the first query, "Who is fit to sing Hashem's praises?" the Psalmist responds: *Hallelu et shem Hashem*. Praise of God is hollow unless we view God as our master. Furthermore, we are affirming that we are no longer the servants of Pharaoh, but only to the Almighty.

(2) With all that said, we recognize that we cannot truly appreciate the Infinite; hence we cannot accurately praise Him. We can only praise His name – His outward expression – but not His essence. Hence the Psalmist says: *Hallelu et shem Hashem*.

(3) As to when to praise Him, the answer is: *Yehi shem Hashem mevorakh me-ata ve-ad olam*, His name is blessed from the Exodus and henceforth. Until the generation of the Egyptian redemption, we have no record of anyone singing *shira* or *Hallel* to the Almighty. No nation acknowledged God's ability to do miracles contrary to nature. This all changed

Hallel ha-Mitzri – Part 1

Halleluyah! Praise His mighty deeds, you servants of the Lord, praise the Name of God. Blessed is the Name of the Lord from now and forever. From the rising of the sun to its setting, praised be the Name of the Lord. Supreme above all nations is the Lord, above the heavens is His glory. Who is like the Lord, our God, Who is enthroned on high, yet looks down upon the heaven and the earth? He raises the poor from the dust, from the trash heaps He lifts the pauper – to seat them with nobles, with the nobles of His people. He transforms a childless woman into a joyful mother of children. Halleluyah (Psalms 113).

When Israel went out from Egypt, the House of Yaakov from a people of a foreign tongue, Judah became His holy one, Israel His dominion. The sea saw and fled; the Jordan turned backward. The mountains

---

with the Ten Plagues where both Israel and Egypt observed God as being in total control of nature, as it says: "From the sun's rising to its setting, blessed be the name of the Lord."

(4) Finally, the nations also observed that the Almighty was in control of history and their fate: "High is God above all the nations," in addition to the forces of nature. He is concerned with man: "He raises the poor from the dust and the needy from the refuse heap." He is manifest everywhere: "From the sun's rising to its setting, blessed be the name of the Lord;" hence, *Hallel* can be said anywhere. In the language of the philosophers, God is both transcendent and imminent.

מֵעַם לֹעֵז

This phrase is commonly translated as "a people of a foreign/strange/alien tongue." The question is why the Psalmist chose such a non-descriptive term to depict the Egyptian oppressors. It would have been appropriate for just about any nation. One possibility is that the Psalmist wanted to emphasize that the Israelites in Egypt were not assimilated and did not speak Egyptian. As *Haza"l* say (*Midrash Rabba*, Deut. 13:20): The Israelites were redeemed from Egypt because of three good qualities – they didn't change their names, they didn't change their

הֶהָרִים רָקְדוּ כְאֵילִים, גְּבָעוֹת כִּבְנֵי צֹאן. מַה לְּךָ הַיָּם כִּי תָנוּס, הַיַּרְדֵּן –
תִּסֹּב לְאָחוֹר, הֶהָרִים – תִּרְקְדוּ כְאֵילִים, גְּבָעוֹת כִּבְנֵי־צֹאן. מִלִּפְנֵי אֲדוֹן
חוּלִי אָרֶץ, מִלִּפְנֵי אֱלוֹהַּ יַעֲקֹב. הַהֹפְכִי הַצּוּר אֲגַם־מָיִם, חַלָּמִישׁ לְמַעְיְנוֹ־
מָיִם.

---

language, and they guarded themselves against licentiousness. R. Barukh Epstein (*Barukh she-Amar, Hallel*) suggests that *lo'ez* here means "disparaging language" as in *le-hotzi la'az* (see *Shabbat* 77a). This verse suggests that the Egyptians spoke deridingly of the Israelites – as we discussed earlier regarding the verse *va-Yare'u otanu ha-Mitzrim*.

הַיָּם רָאָה וַיָּנֹס, הַיַּרְדֵּן יִסֹּב לְאָחוֹר

(a) This verse recounts that as the Israelites exited Egypt, the *Yam Suf* "fled" (i.e., split). The Midrash (*Tanhuma*, Naso, 34; *Yalkut Shimoni, Psalms* 114, 873) indicates the sea did so when it saw the casket of Yosef. The latter's great trait was his ability to overcome his nature. (1) He resisted the temptations of the seductive wife of Potiphar. (2) He forgave his brothers despite their cruel mistreatment of him. (3) Finally, many of the commentaries (Ramban and *Rabbenu* Bahya to *Gen* 45:27; *Da'at Zekenim, Gen* 48:1) maintain that during the 17 years that Yaakov was in Egypt, Joseph avoided being alone with his father, lest the latter ask Yosef how he arrived in Egypt – lest his father come to curse the brothers as a result. This school maintains that Yaakov never found out the whole story about Yosef (Rashi dissents; see: Gen. 49:5 and 50:16–17). Because Yosef conquered his nature in the above three instances, he merited that the waters of the Red Sea did the same. Just as Yosef fled from the wife of Potiphar, so did the waters of the sea. Rashi suggests that the Jordan and all water sources "turned back" at the same time. Other commentaries (Rashbam, Ibn Ezra, Metzudot) assert that the turning back of the Jordan occurred in the time of Yehoshua (Yehoshua 3:13–17).

I am always amazed by some of the playful creativity catalyzed by Jews' love for the *Haggada*. Here is one example involving *gematria*. R. Yaron Halbertal suggests that there is a hint to the splitting of the Jordan River by Yosef's casket in *gematria*. If we take

skipped like rams, the hills like young sheep. What ails you, sea, that you flee, Jordan, that you turn backward? Mountains, why do you skip like rams, hills, like young sheep? Tremble O earth before the God of Yaakov, Who turns the rock into a pool of water, the flint into a flowing fountain (Psalms 114).

---

the word: ה-י-ר-ד-ן and "turn back" each letter by one – we get: ד-ט-ק-ג-מ which has a numerical value of 40+3+100+9+4 = **156**. Amazingly, this is also the numerical value of the name = י-ו-ס-ף **156** = 80+60+6+10.

(b) To my mind, the image of the casket of Yosef – the powerful Viceroy of Egypt, the man who was thought of as Egyptian to the core by Pharaoh and all of Egypt – leading the Exodus, is very powerful. It communicates his true identity and values and the importance of the land of his forefathers. R. Joseph B. Soloveitchik (Mesorat ha-Rav Chumash, Gen. 50:5) has recounted a moving story regarding Baron Edmond de Rothschild. This well-known philanthropist passed away around the time of the 1948 War of Independence. He wanted to be buried in Israel but because of the war taking place at that time his remains could not be sent over and he was buried in France. When conditions permitted the exhumation and reinterment in Israel, his children made a request to the interior ministry to send his remains to Israel. When some time passed and they did not receive a reply, they inquired and were told that Charles De Gaulle himself was holding up their request. They were wondering why De Gaulle himself would be interested in this matter. When asked, he responded that he was troubled by the request. He had always thought of Rothschild as first and foremost a Frenchman. To be a Frenchman means that one is born, lives, dies, and is buried on French soil. He could not understand why he would want his remains removed to non-French soil. Such a request would imply that he was not a true Frenchman. Eventually, De Gaulle acceded to the family's request and allowed the exhumation and transportation to Israel; however, his opinion of the Rothschild family as Frenchmen was forever diminished. Indeed, Yosef, like his distinguished father Yaakov, may have lived and died in Egypt – but it was important for them to signal to all future generations that the Israelite future would be in the "Promised Land."

כוס שני – ברכת אֲשֶׁר גְּאָלָנוּ

The *matzot* are covered and the cup is filled and lifted.

בָּרוּךְ אַתָּה ה' אֱלֹהֵינוּ מֶלֶךְ הָעוֹלָם, אֲשֶׁר גְּאָלָנוּ וְגָאַל אֶת־אֲבוֹתֵינוּ מִמִּצְרַיִם, וְהִגִּיעָנוּ הַלַּיְלָה הַזֶּה לֶאֱכָל־בּוֹ מַצָּה וּמָרוֹר.

ברכת אֲשֶׁר גְּאָלָנוּ

We have now come to the conclusion of *Maggid* – the narrative section of the *Seder*. In our first-hand historical tale, we have been through the slavery of Egypt, experienced the Ten Plagues, left Egypt, crossed the Red Sea, and even begun to sing *Hallel*. The *berakha*, *Asher Ga'alanu*, allows us to look back for one last moment and take stock of how far we've come – and where we are headed. We then transition into the "business end" of the *Seder*, namely the eating of [*Pesaḥ*,] Matza, and *Maror*.

אֲשֶׁר גְּאָלָנוּ וְגָאַל אֶת־אֲבוֹתֵינוּ מִמִּצְרַיִם

(a) Looking carefully at the language of this *berakha*, we see that it can be broken down into three sections: (1) *Asher ga'alanu ve-ga'al et avoteinu mi-Mitzrayim* – is set in the past; (2) *ve-higianu ha-layla hazeh le-ekhol bo Matza u-Maror* – is in the present; (3) *Ken… yagianu le-mo'adim ve-li-regalim akherim* – looks hopefully to the future. The *Mishna* (*Pesaḥim* 116b) teaches us that sections 1 and 2 alone were said by R. Tarfon without a concluding benediction – because the text was relatively short. Indeed, his text seems to be a contraction of two short benedictions *she-Asah nissim la'avoteinu* and *she-Heḥiyanu, ve-kiyemanu, ve-higi'anu*. The lengthy future-looking section 3 was added by R. Akiva, who – as a result of the added length – pinned on a concluding *berakha* of *Ga'al Yisrael* (see *Tosafot*, *Pesaḥim* 116b, s.v. *ve-Ḥotem*). When Maimonides (MT, *Ḥametz u-Matza*, 8:5) discusses this *berakha*, he indicates that R. Akiva's third section was added "in our times," a euphemism for post-*ḥurban* (following the destruction of the Temple). Abravanel (*Haggada Zevaḥ Pesaḥ*) clarifies the picture as follows: R. Tarfon was a *kohen* born before the *Ḥurban*, and he actually served and *duchaned* in the Temple. Before the *Ḥurban* the text

Asher Ga'alanu Blessing – Second Cup

The matzot are covered and the cup is filled and lifted.

Blessed are You, Lord our God, King of the universe, Who has redeemed us and redeemed our fathers from Egypt, and enabled us to reach this night that we may eat matza and maror on it.

---

of the *berakha* –*Asher ga'alanu* – went like this: *Asher ga'alanu ve-ga'al et avoteinu mi-Mitzrayim ve-higi'anu ha-layla hazeh le-ekhol bo Pesah, Matza, u-Maror*. Following the Temple's destruction, however, the word *Pesah* was removed. For his student R. Akiva this was not enough! We needed a benediction with optimism for the future – looking toward a time when we would eat from the *Korban Pesah*! So R. Akiva added: *Ken… yagi'anu le-mo'adim ve-li-regalim akherim …ve-nokhal sham min ha-zevahim u-min ha-Pesahim….* It is not at all surprising that the concluding upbeat and hopeful section was authored by R. Akiva, for this was his personality – as seen in the story brought in *Makkot* (24a–b), cited at length in our discussion of מְסִבִּין בִּבְנֵי־בְרַק above. Even his spiritual leadership of the Bar Kokhba Revolution was not out of character.

(b) We have already indicated that the opening of this *berakha* seems to be a contraction of two well-known short benedictions *she-asa nisim la-avoteinu* and *she-hehiyanu*. Indeed, Rav Amram Gaon (as explained by R. Menahem Kasher, *Haggada Sheleima*, p. 88) asks why the *berakha* – *she-asa nisim la-avoteinu* – is not recited at the end of *Kiddush* – at the very beginning of *Maggid*. After all, like *Purim* and *Hanukah*, the element of Divine miracles is so fundamental to the *Pesah* story. Nevertheless, posits Rav Amram Gaon, at the beginning of *Maggid*, the *she-asa nisim la-avoteinu* benediction would have been completely inappropriate, since we were still slaves then! We need to wait until a point in the *Haggada* more suitable – and that is at the close of *Maggid*.

As on *Hanukah* and *Purim* in this *berakha*, we speak of our salvation by God. However, by *Hanukah* and *Purim* we speak **only** of our ancestors: *she-asa nisim la-avoteinu*, but here by *Pesah* we say: *Asher ga'alanu ve-ga'al et avoteinu* – "the Almighty redeemed us **and** our forebears." What's more, **we** the descendants are mentioned first! The answer to both these questions would seem to be one. On *Hanukah* and *Purim* we

כֵּן ה' אֱלֹהֵינוּ וֵאלֹהֵי אֲבוֹתֵינוּ יַגִּיעֵנוּ לְמוֹעֲדִים וְלִרְגָלִים אֲחֵרִים הַבָּאִים לִקְרָאתֵנוּ לְשָׁלוֹם. שְׂמֵחִים בְּבִנְיַן עִירֶךָ וְשָׂשִׂים בַּעֲבוֹדָתֶךָ. וְנֹאכַל שָׁם מִן הַזְּבָחִים וּמִן הַפְּסָחִים אֲשֶׁר יַגִּיעַ דָּמָם עַל קִיר מִזְבַּחֲךָ לְרָצוֹן, וְנוֹדֶה לְךָ שִׁיר חָדָשׁ עַל גְּאֻלָּתֵנוּ וְעַל פְּדוּת נַפְשֵׁנוּ. בָּרוּךְ אַתָּה ה', גָּאַל יִשְׂרָאֵל. בָּרוּךְ אַתָּה ה', אֱלֹהֵינוּ מֶלֶךְ הָעוֹלָם בּוֹרֵא פְּרִי הַגָּפֶן.

The second cup is drunk while leaning on the left side.

---

remember and celebrate what happened to our ancestors thousands of years ago; but we were not participants, merely secondary beneficiaries. But as we have shown, *Pesaḥ* is different. It is through the re-enactment of the *Seder* that we experience the bondage of Egypt and the redemption – not vicariously, not as mere secondary beneficiaries – but **first-hand**. We emphasize the personal quality of this experience by mentioning ourselves first.

As neat as the above presentation would seem, one issue remains. In the section *Lefikhakh* just before *Hallel*, we praise the Almighty's miracles by saying: *le-Mi she-asa la-avoteinu ve-lanu et kol haNissim et kol ha-nissim ha-elu*. Here we are speaking of the miraculous *me-Avdut le-Ḥerut ... u-me-shi'abud li-ge'ula* that we just relived at the *Seder* – yet our forebears are mentioned first! The answer seems to be that since we went out **together**, the order is inconsequential – sometimes our forebears are mentioned first, and sometimes we are. My brother R. Shael Frimer further indicates that the thrust and focus of the present *berakha* – *asher ga'alanu* – is on **our** actions – past, present, and future; hence **we** are given priority.

וְהִגִּיעָנוּ הַלַּיְלָה הַזֶּה

After reciting *she-heḥiyanu ve-kiyemanu ve-higi'anu la-zeman ha-zeh* at the close of *Kiddush*, why do we repeat *ve-higi'anu ha-layla ha-zeh* here again? Many Rishonim (cited in R. Menaḥem Kasher's *Haggada Sheleima*) indicate that the *she-Heḥiyanu* in *Kiddush* (like the *she-Heḥiyanu*

So too, Lord our God and God of our fathers, enable us to reach future holidays and festivals in peace, rejoicing in the rebuilding of Your city and ecstatic in Your service. And there we will partake of the sacrifices and Pesah offerings [on Saturday night say: of the Pesah offerings and of the sacrifices] whose blood shall be sprinkled on the wall of Your altar for gracious acceptance. We will then thank You with a new song for our redemption and for the deliverance of our souls. Blessed are You, God, Redeemer of Israel. Blessed are You, Lord our God, King of the universe, Who creates the fruit of the vine.

The second cup is drunk while leaning on the left side.

---

recited at candle lighting) goes on the joy of celebrating *Yom-Tov*. On the other hand, the *she-Hehiyanu* in the *berakha* of *Asher Ga'alanu* goes on the joy of fulfilling the mitzva of eating Matza and *Maror*. Indeed, the benediction says: *ve-higi'anu ha-layla ha-zeh le-ekhol bo Matza u-Maror*. The question arises, however, why can't the *she-Hehiyanu* recited in *Kiddush* apply to all three: the day, Matza, and *Maror*? After all, on *Sukkot*, the *she-Hehiyanu* recited in *Kiddush* applies both to the day of Yom Tov and the mitzva of eating in a *Sukka!* The answer is rather straightforward: eating in the *sukka* occurs a very short time after *Kiddush*. Eating Matza and *Maror* generally takes place a long time, even several hours, after *Kiddush*; hence, a separate *she-Hehiyanu* is required.

לֶאֱכָל־בּוֹ מַצָּה וּמָרוֹר

We have now come to what I believe is one of the most pivotal statements of the *Haggada*! I sense that most *Seder* participants believe that the primary goal of *Maggid* is to recite *Hallel* out of a sense of exhilaration resulting from a personal sense of redemption – as the *Haggada* says: *li-Re'ot et atzmo ke-ilu hu yatza mi-mitzrayim*. While it is true that this is an intermediary goal, this sense of uplifting joy is a **means** – not the ultimate goal! As the *berakha* of *Asher ga'alanu* itself says, we are here at the *Seder* – why? *ve-higi'anu ha-layla ha-zeh le-ekhol bo Matza u-Maror*. We are at the *Seder* to do *mitzvot*! Sure, we need to feel a sense of elation and thankfulness to the Almighty for the Exodus and the redemption. But all this is meant as motivation, to create a sense of gratitude and indebtedness to God leading to **a commitment** to fulfill God's commandments. This is the whole point of the redemption story from the get-go! As mentioned repeatedly above, God did not just say to Pharaoh: "Let my people go," but *Shalah et ami ve-ya'avduni* – "Let my people go so that they may **serve Me**" (Ex. 7:16; 7:26; 9:1; 9:13). Serve Me in the Temple; Serve Me in prayer; Serve Me by learning Torah and by doing *mitzvot*. Thus, the *berakha* of *Asher ga'alanu*, which is the summary statement of *Maggid*, clearly states: *ve-higi'anu ha-layla ha-zeh le-ekhol bo Matza u-Maror* – we are here to do *mitzvot*. We will return to this crucial point in our summary of *Birkat Asher ga'alanu* below.

וַגִּיעֵנוּ לְמוֹעֲדִים וְלִרְגָלִים אֲחֵרִים הַבָּאִים לִקְרָאתֵנוּ לְשָׁלוֹם

In Talmud *Rosh ha-Shana* (11a), there is a dispute as to whether the future messianic redemption will occur in *Tishre* (R. Eliezer) or in *Nisan* (R. Joshua). According to the tradition of R. Joshua "In (the month of) *Nisan* they were redeemed (from Egypt), and in *Nisan* they will be redeemed (once more with the coming of the Messiah)" – it seems that the future redemption will come *Seder* night. This is because as the source for R. Joshua's tradition, the Gemara cites Exodus 12:42: "**A night of vigil** it is for the Lord to bring them out of the land of Egypt." The Talmud (*Rosh ha-Shana* 11b) explains this verse as follows *Leyl Shimurim* – "A night of [watching/vigil/protection] – This teaches that this night of vigil [for the Exodus] is a night that has been set aside for the purpose of redemption, from the six days of Creation **and on** (i.e., it will remain so until the final redemption)." Following this tradition, if the future redemption does not occur on *Seder* night, when will it happen? Only the following *Pesah*! So how do we say here: "May [God] bring us to other seasons and festivals… happy in the building of Your city and rejoicing in Your service." This would suggest that the Messiah will come after *Pesah*, before the next festival!?

Two approaches have been suggested: (a) R. Isaiah di Trani (*Tosafot* Rid, *Haggada Torat Hayim*) suggests that when we say that the redemption will come in *Nisan* or on *Pesah* – that doesn't mean that everything will be complete. What we are referring to is the good tidings of the Messiah's arrival or pending arrival. Indeed, in the case of the *Pesah* in Egypt, only the news of their pending salvation was declared at night of the fifteenth of *Nisan*. The actual Exodus did not occur until "that very day" (Ex. 12:41) – noon of the following day, but the process had started at midnight.

(b) R. Aryeh Leib Gunzberg (*Turei Even, Rosh ha-Shana* 11a) notes that the Talmud *Sanhedrin* 98a cites the verse in Isaiah (60:22) *be-Ita ahishena* – "In its time I will hasten the process." It explains that the rule, "In *Nisan* they were redeemed, and in *Nisan* they will be redeemed" applies under normal conditions (*be-Ita*) when Jews are not particularly worthy. However, when Jews are particularly worthy, final redemption can happen rapidly and at any time (*ahishena*). About this, *Ani Ma'amin* says: …*ahakeh lo be-khol yom she-yavo* – "I will await for the Messiah whenever he should come." In this *berakha*, we are praying that God should redeem us speedily. In this regard, R. Yaakov ben Yakar (*Haggada Torat Hayim*) draws attention to the strange terminology in this *berakha*: "May [God] bring us to other seasons and festivals that are coming to us…" How do we say regarding the holidays that they are moving toward us – when man moves towards them? He suggests that we are praying for a period of *ahishena* – when time is contracting and the Messianic period will arrive earlier than expected.

Haggada Gedolei Yisrael stresses that the text here states: *ha-ba'im likrateinu* **le**-*shalom* (to peace) rather than **be**-shalom (**in** peace). This choice of preposition is based on Biblical precedent as noted in *Berakhot* 64a: "Rabbi Avin HaLevi said: One who takes leave from another should not say to him: Go in peace (*be*-shalom), but rather, he should say: Go to peace (*le-shalom*). For we find that Yitro said to Moshe: "Go to peace" (Ex. 4:18), and Moshe ascended and was successful. By contrast, David said to his son, Absalom: "Go in peace" (Samuel II 15:9), and Absalom went and was ultimately hanged." The Gaon of Vilna insightfully remarks that when the Torah describes Yosef's brothers it states (Gen. 37:4): They hated him and could **not** [wish him to go **to** peace]. On the contrary, Yosef held no grudge against his brothers, and when he spoke to them, he twice (Gen. 43:27 and 44:17) used "Go to peace."

Haggada Gedolei Yisrael also points out that the term *mo'adim* can include *Rosh ha-Shana* and *Yom ha-Kippurim*. *Regalim* refers to *Pesah, Shavu'ot*, and *Sukkot*. But what does *aherim* – "others" refer to? He cites the verse (Zekharia 8:19): "Thus said the Lord of Hosts: The fast of the fourth month (17th of Tammuz), the fast of the fifth month (9th of Av), the fast of the seventh month (Fast of Gedalia), and the fast of the tenth month (10th of Tevet) shall become occasions for joy and gladness, happy festivals for the House of Judah…" Thus, we see that in the time of the ultimate redemption, the fast days will be converted into **additional** "happy festivals."

שְׂמֵחִים בְּבִנְיַן עִירֶךְ וְשָׂשִׂים בַּעֲבוֹדָתֶךְ

R. David Abudarham (*Abudarham ha-Shalem*) suggests that the joy and rejoicing described here regarding the rebuilding of Jerusalem and Zion is based on the *pasuk* in Isaiah 51:3: "The Lord has truly comforted Zion, comforted all her ruins. He has made her wilderness like Eden, her desert like the Garden of the Lord. Gladness and joy shall abide there, thanksgiving and the sound of music."

R. Judah Leib Diskin (cited in *Siddur ha-Gra Ishei Yisrael, Perush Si'ah Yitzhak* to *Mussaf le-Shalosh Regalim*) posits that in the *berakha* of *Asher Ga'alanu*, the focus is on the future **rebuilding of Jerusalem**: *Semeihim be-vinian irekha* – "Happy in the rebuilding of **Your city**." The same is true for the *Al ha-gefen* benediction following the fourth cup of wine: *u-venei Yerushalayim irekha* – "and build Jerusalem Your city." By contrast, the Mussaf prayer for the festivals places more focus on the rebuilding of the **Temple** and we say: *Benei veitkha ke-vatehilla ve-khonen mikdashekha al mekhono* – "Rebuild **Your house** as it was and reestablish **Your Temple** on its foundations." Furthermore, why do we say by the building of the Temple: *ve-hareinu be-vinyano ve-sameheinu be-tikuno* – "Let us **see** the building, and rejoice in the **fixing**." The redundancy here is troubling. Why does the "fixing" cause joy, and why is this worthy of special mention?!

In response, R. Diskin cites Rashi to *Sukka* (40a. s.v. *I nami*) who maintains that the future third *Bet ha-Mikdash* will come down from Heaven in an almost complete state. That is the meaning of *ve-hareinu be-vinyano* – namely, that we will see the Temple come down from heaven, but we will not yet be involved in its construction. However, it seems that some fixing-up and human intervention on the final touches will still be required, as the text states: *ve-sameheinu be-tikuno*. Thus, because of these later actions, we will rejoice in taking part in the mitzva of *Binyan Bet ha-Mikdash* – building the Temple. Thus, even according to Rashi's approach that the Third Temple will descend from Heaven, man will still be required to do some finishing up; thus, the mitzva of *Binyan Bet ha-Mikdash* (*Sefer ha-Mitzvot* of Maimonides, *Eseh* 20) is still relevant. (See more below in our discussion of אַדִּיר הוּא יִבְנֶה בֵּיתוֹ בְּקָרוֹב).

וְנֹאכַל שָׁם מִן הַזְּבָחִים וּמִן הַפְּסָחִים

This particular phrase is one of the most discussed by the commentaries on this *berakha*. In some *Haggadot* it states that on *Motza'ei Shabbat* (*Motzash*), the order is reversed and one should say: *ve-Nokhal sham min ha-Pesahim ve-ha-Zevahim*. Other *Haggadot* are resoundingly silent. In order to understand what all the "heat" is about, we need a few introductions:

(a) The term *Pesahim* refers to the Paschal lamb sacrifice (*Korban Pesah*) which was eaten broiled (*tzli esh*). Together with Matza and *Maror*, this was the centerpiece of the *Seder*. There was normally other meat at the *Seder* (see below) and this came from the *Hagiga* holiday sacrifices referred to as *Zevahim*, and these too were broiled. At the *Seder*, the *Zevahim* (*Hagiga* holiday sacrifices) were eaten first until everyone was moderately full – and then each would eat a final olive-sized piece (*kezayit*) of the *Korban Pesah* to conclude the meal.

(b) The preparation of the קרבן פסח (פְּסָחִים), but not the קרבן חגיגה (זְבָחִים), deferred the prohibitions of *Shabbat*. Thus, when *Seder* night fell on *Motzash*, the Paschal lamb could be prepared (sacrificed and broiled) on *Shabbat Erev Pesah*, but not the *Hagiga* sacrifices; hence, at that *Seder*, only meat from the *Korban Pesah* was eaten. The *Hagiga* holiday sacrifices could only be brought the next day.

(c) Although the text of the *Asher Ga'alanu* benediction appears in the *Mishna*, there are various traditions as to what the proper reading is: *ve-Nokhal sham min ha-Zevahim u-min ha-Pesahim* or *min ha-Pesahim u-min ha-Zevahim*. However, we find no one who made a distinction between *Motzash* and any other night. *Tosafot* suggests that *zevahim* should come first because, as pointed out above, they are normally eaten before the *ke-zayit* of the *Korban Pesah*. In the mid-15th century, R. Yaakov Weil suggested that when the *Seder* falls on *Motzash*, *min ha-Pesahim u-min ha-Zevahim* should be said since only קרבן פסח meat is eaten at the *Seder* and זבחים are eaten the next day. It was based on his comment that many *Poskim* (Bach, *Magen Avraham*, *Hok Yaakov*, and *Arukh ha-Shulhan* on OH 473) and *Haggadot* changed their text for Saturday night *Seders*.

(d) Nevertheless, other leading scholars posit that the text should be maintained uniform for all years – as it had before the mid-15th century with the acquiescence of all leading *Rishonim*. The text as set by *Tosafot* as *min ha-Zevahim u-min ha-Pesahim* is the most reasonable. What's more, R. Weil's suggestion may well be wrong for a host of reasons. For example, the *berakha* is talking about the future – not tonight's *Seder*! (*Responsa Knesset Yehezkel*). On *Motzash* there are no *zevahim* at all, and should, therefore, not be mentioned at all (R. Jacob Emden, *Siddur Bet Yaakov*). Finally, the terms *min ha-Zevahim* and *min ha-Pesahim* may refer to the holiday sacrifices brought throughout *Pesah* – and not necessarily on *Seder* night. The order is thus inconsequential! (*Haggada Imrei Shefer* of the Netziv).

עַל קִיר מִזְבַּחֲךָ לְרָצוֹן

This is seemingly a strange and unusual request, one which does not appear elsewhere. R. Isaac Zev Soloveitchik (Gri"z; cited by R. Yehudah Prero, https://tinyurl.com/3rc3yuw5) explains that in the Talmud (*Zevahim* 26b) we learn that if the blood of a sacrifice was not sprinkled on its proper place on the altar, one may not eat the sacrifice. Nevertheless, one does achieve atonement. One can fulfill the obligation despite improper sprinkling and without consuming the meat. However, when it comes to the *Korban Pesah*, the sacrifice had to be eaten *al ha-sova* – with a sense of being comfortably full and satisfied. As we have said above, this was accomplished by first eating the *Korban Hagiga* until one was nearly full and then eating an olive-sized portion of a *Korban*

Pesaḥ to cap off the meal. Thus, generally speaking, one needs to partake of **both** sacrifices – *min ha-Zevahim u-min ha-Pesahim* – to fulfill his obligation of *al ha-sova*. Therefore, we ask Hashem that we should merit a Temple and an Alter – upon which the blood of the *Zevahim* and *Pesahim* will be sprinkled properly. This will then allow us to eat from the sacrifices and fulfill our central *Seder* obligation.

וְנוֹדֶה לְךָ שִׁיר חָדָשׁ

This is the second time we refer to a redemption engendering a "new song" – just before *Hallel* in the section beginning *Lefikhakh anahnu hayavim* before Hallel. According to the Malbim (Psalms 96:1; 98:1), the "new song" engendered by the Exodus is that the Almighty is not merely the God of Creation but also the God of History. R. Yehuda ben Yakar (*Haggada Torat Hayim*) suggests that, here in *Birkat Asher Ga'alanu*, R. Akiva is speaking of the future messianic redemption. This will involve the miraculous ingathering of dispersed Jewry from around the globe back to the Land of Israel – as prophesied by Jeremiah (23:7–8) millennia ago. This will be so awesome that it will eclipse even the Egyptian Exodus, as Jeremiah says:

(7) Indeed, a time is coming – declares the Lord – when it shall no more be said, "As the Lord lives, who brought the Israelites out of the land of Egypt,"
(8) But rather, "As the Lord lives, who brought out and led the offspring of the House of Israel from the northland and from all the lands to which I have banished them." And they shall dwell upon their own soil.

עַל גְּאֻלָּתֵנוּ וְעַל פְּדוּת נַפְשֵׁנוּ

Two types of redemption are referred to here: *ge'ula* – redemption; *pedut nefesh* – salvation of our souls. Along the lines of the previous comment, R. Yehuda ben Yakar (*Haggada Torat Hayim*) suggests that *ge'ulateinu* refers to the future Messianic redemption, while *pedut nafsheinu* refers to the past – the Egyptian Exodus. Alternatively, both refer to the Egyptian Exodus; however, *ge'ulateinu* connotes our physical redemption, the liberation of the body; and *pedut nafsheinu* signifies our spiritual redemption. Thus, just as *Maggid* focused on these two aspects in *Avadim hayinu le-Pharaoh be-Mitzrayim* and *mi-Tehilla ovdei avoda zara hayu avoteinu*, respectively – so do we close the narrative with them. Our tale has come full circle.

בָּא"י גָּאַל יִשְׂרָאֵל

The closing *berakha* of *Asher Ga'alanu* and that of the third *Berakha* of *Keri'at Shema* is *Barukh Ata Hashem Ga'al Yisrael* – which is suggestive of the past tense. By contrast, the seventh benediction of the weekday *Shemoneh Esrei* ends *Barukh Ata Hashem Go'el Yisrael*. This is suggestive of the present continuous tense which in Hebrew can be equivalent to a future tense. This is problematic. After all, we have seen that the first two verses (by R. Tarfon) of *Asher Ga'alanu* deal with the past (Egyptian Exodus) and our commemoration of that experience by eating Matza and *Maror*. The whole lengthy concluding section (by R. Akiva) focuses on the future! So in *Birkat Asher Ga'alanu*, why don't we use the present continuous form *Go'el Yisrael*?!

Rashba (to *Berakhot* 11a) maintains that even though the *berakha* ends with a prayer for the future, this was only added by R. Akiva following the *Hurban*. The central thrust of the benediction is in the past – as the conclusion to our historical narrative of *Maggid*, and requires the more suitable *Ga'al Yisrael* ending. R. Yehuda ben Yakar (in the previous comment) points out that just before the final *berakha*, the text ends with two salvations: *Al ge'ulateinu ve-al pedut nafsheinu. Ge'ulateinu* refers to the future Messianic redemption, while *pedut nafsheinu* refers to the past – the Egyptian Exodus. The concluding *berakha* then also ends in the past – with *Barukh Ata Hashem Ga'al Yisrael*.

Our analysis of this ending is not truly complete yet. For if גָּאַל is truly a verb form, correct Hebrew usage would have required the benediction to end: *Barukh Ata Hashem* **asher** *Ga'al Yisrael* – Blessed are you Hashem **who** redeemed Israel. The same would be true for the seventh benediction of the weekday *Shemoneh Esrei*, it should have been *Barukh Ata Hashem* **asher** *Go'el Yisrael* – Blessed art you Hashem **who** redeems Israel. Without going into too much grammatical detail (See Rashbam to Ex. 21:11), the answer is that both *Go'el* and *Ga'al* are synonymous nouns (in a *semikhut* form) whose meaning is "redeemer of." Both their benedictions should be translated similarly as: Blessed are you Hashem Redeemer of Israel. These two nouns *Go'el* and *Ga'al* merely *sound* like verbs in the present and past tense, respectively! One or the other is picked for usage based on the context or content of the *berakha*.

גָּאַל יִשְׂרָאֵל

We have finally come to the conclusion of *Maggid*. In our first-hand historical tale, we have been through the servitude of Egypt, experienced the ten plagues, and left Egypt. Miraculously, we crossed the Red Sea and began to sing Hashem's praises with *Hallel*. And now we do something very strange indeed! After reciting the first two sections of *Hallel*, we prematurely stop our song, recite the *berakha* of *Asher Ga'alanu*, eat Matza and *Maror* and the rest of the meal – and only after *Birkat ha-Mazon* do we complete *Hallel*.

This order of things is strange for several reasons (though it wouldn't be the only strange thing we do tonight!) **Firstly**, if we start with *Hallel*, the Redeemer's praise, why shouldn't we complete it? Isn't giving God our thanks and praise for our providential salvation the whole purpose of *Seder* night? Isn't the purpose of *Maggid* to relive the bondage and truly appreciate the exhilaration of the *ge'ula*?!

To sharpen the point a bit more: When Moshe *Rabbenu* came before Pharaoh before the first plague (and several times thereafter) he repeats (Ex. 7:17): "Through this [plague] you shall know that I am Hashem…" As Rashbam comments (ad loc.): Pharaoh himself claimed (Ex 5:2) "I don't know Hashem" – I am unaware of God's existence. But the truth is that Moshe says the same thing to the enslaved Israelites (Ex. 6:7): "And you shall know that I, Hashem, am your God who freed you from the labors of Egypt." Thus, the purpose of the miracles was so that both Egypt and Israel should recognize the Almighty as the God of Creation – in control of the forces of nature – **and** the God of History, who can change the course of nations. Is not *Hallel* an expression of this recognition – "And you shall know that I am your God." Shouldn't *Hallel* have central importance? If we start *Hallel*, why not say it all?

Secondly, let's now take a look at the closing *berakha* of *Maggid*, *Asher Ga'alanu*. The benediction can be divided into three basic sections: (a) The first part mentions the "salvation from Egypt" without detail – not even the ten plagues are mentioned; (b) the second part focuses on the present eating of Matza and *Maror* – no mention is made of *Hallel*; (c) the third section is centered on the future sacrifices of the *Zevahim* and *Pesahim*. Is this an accurate presentation of *Maggid?!* No back-breaking slavery, no miraculous plagues, no redemption, no song! Just *Pesah, Matza,* and *Maror*!

The answer would thus seem to be that the purpose of the miracles was indeed (Ex. 6:7): "And you will know that I am God." However, that was not the objective of the salvation! As pointed out repeatedly above, the purpose of the redemption was clearly stated by Moshe when he said to Pharaoh: *Shalah et ami ve-ya'avduni* – "Let my people go so that they may **serve** me" (Ex. 7:16; 7:26; 9:1; 9:13). The purpose of the redemption was not freedom per se – but freedom to serve the Creator. "Serve Me" in the Temple; serve Me in prayer; serve Me by learning Torah; and serve Me by doing *mitzvot*. This idea is repeated in Exodus (13:8) "Because of **this** God redeemed me from Egypt." Rashi (ad loc.) comments: "I was redeemed from Egypt so that I would fulfill God's commandments like these – *Pesah, Matza,* and *Maror*." This, of course, is why the *Haggada* says that the *Seder* should only be performed "when [*Pesah,*] *Matza,* and *Maror* are there before you." If they are the purpose of the salvation, they need to be the centerpiece of our discussion. If you don't explain them, says R. Gamliel, you are missing the point of the Exodus and, hence, have not fulfilled your obligation. This is also why "Because of **this** God redeemed me from Egypt" is the answer the *Haggada* gives to both the *rasha* and the clueless son. These are the two children who have the hardest time understanding why we fulfill the rituals at the *Seder*. Do you want to know why I am bound to carry out these rituals? The answer is that the Almighty redeemed me **for this purpose** and I owe him a debt of loyalty and gratitude.

This insight also answers the question raised by several commentaries. Why doesn't the *berakha* that summarizes *Maggid* begin as follows: *Barukh Ata…she-asa nissim lanu ve-la'avotenu ve-ga'alanu…*? Weren't the miracles of *Pesah* greater than those of *Hanukah* and *Purim*?! The answer is that the miracles of *Hanukah* and *Purim* are extolled because of the expressions of God's involvement and intervention. But on *Pesah*, *Haza"l* wanted us to realize that the miracles were not the **goal** of the salvation, but merely a **means** by which: (1) we and Egypt learned to recognize the Almighty as the God of Creation and History; and (2) to effect our physical and spiritual redemption so that we would be able and motivated to fulfill His *mitzvot*.

There is one more piece of the puzzle left. The *Mishna* in *Pesahim* (9:3) states: "What is the difference between 'What is the difference between the first *Pesah* Paschal lamb and the second?'… The first *Pesah* Paschal lamb requires the recitation of *Hallel* as it is eaten while the second does not. However, both require the recitation of *Hallel* as they are sacrificed." Since the fulfillment of the *mitzvot* is the purpose of the redemption, *Haza"l* ordained that *Hallel* be recited **during** their fulfillment – in particular, the eating of the *Korban Pesah*. However, notes R. Nachum Rabinovitch, *Halakha* forbids conversation while your mouth is full: *Ein mesihin bi-seuda* (BT, *Ta'anit* 5b; JT, *Berakhot* 6:6; *Shulhan Arukh*, *OH*, 170:1). Hence, we say the first two chapters of *Hallel* before eating (*Pesah*) Matza and *Maror* and the remainder of *Hallel* after eating the *Afikoman* and *Birkat ha-Mazon*. Why only two chapters before? As suggested above (Malbim, Psalms 96:1; 98:1) these two paragraphs emphasize the role of the Almighty as the God of Creation – in control of forces of nature, and the God of History – in control of the fate of nations. They are also pure praise without requests (R. Joseph B. Soloveitchik, see our comments to הקדמה לאמירת ההלל – answer to question no. 5).

This splitting up the *Hallel* to "sandwich" the eating *mitzvot* of the *Seder*, sends a very important message about the role of *Hallel* and our redemption. *Haza"l* emphasized that we recite these Psalms of praise not only on the *Shalah et ami* – on our physical redemption, but also, and more importantly, on the *ve-ya'avduni* – our spiritual salvation through the fulfillment of God's *mitzvot* and divine service.

6. רָחְצָה

The participants wash their hands and then recite the following blessing:

בָּרוּךְ אַתָּה ה'. אֱלֹהֵינוּ מֶלֶךְ הָעוֹלָם.
אֲשֶׁר קִדְּשָׁנוּ בְּמִצְוֹתָיו וְצִוָּנוּ עַל נְטִילַת יָדַיִם.

One should not speak until after making the following two blessings and eating the *matza*.

7. מוֹצִיא

The *matzot* are taken in the order that they are placed on the tray – the broken piece between the two whole *matzot* – and the following blessing is recited:

בָּרוּךְ אַתָּה ה'. אֱלֹהֵינוּ מֶלֶךְ הָעוֹלָם הַמּוֹצִיא לֶחֶם מִן הָאָרֶץ.

מוֹצִיא

The Jerusalem Talmud (*Pesahim*, Chap. 10:1) cites Rabbi Levi who forbids eating Matza on the day before *Pesah* – so that Matza on *Seder* night will be eaten with zest. Rabbi Levi compares eating Matza prematurely to a bride and groom who consummate their relationship before the wedding benedictions. R. Isaac of Narvona (13th century Spain; *Haggada Sheleima*, p. 148) suggests that the comparison stems from the fact that Jewish law permits a bride to her beloved only after the recitation of nine benedictions at the wedding ceremony: two from the *Kiddushin* and seven from the *Nisu'in*. Similarly, Matza can be eaten only after nine benedictions at the *Seder*: (1) *ha-Gafen*; (2) *Kiddush*; (3) *she-Hehiyanu*; (4) *ha-Adama* (*karpas*); (5) *Ga'al Yisrael*; (6) *ha-Gafen*; (7) *Yadayim*; (8) *ha-Motzi*; and (9) *Al Akhilat Matza*. R. Joseph B. Soloveitchik concludes that this analogy indicates that Israel's redemption – symbolized by Matza – is to be viewed as a marriage. Indeed, the Almighty describes their pending redemption with the words (Ex. 6:7): "And I will take you (*ve-lakahti*) to Me for a people, and I will be to you a God; and you shall know (*vi-yeda'atem*) that I am the LORD your God." R. Joseph B. Soloveitchik argues that the term *ve-lakahti* can well be a euphemism for wedlock as in the verses in Deuteronomy

6. Rahtza

The participants wash their hands and then recite the following blessing:

Blessed are You, Lord our God, King of the universe, Who has sanctified us with His commandments and commanded us concerning the washing of the hands.

One should not speak until after making the following two blessings and eating the *matza*.

7. Motzi

The *matzot* are taken in the order that they are placed on the tray – the broken piece between the two whole *matzot* – and the following blessing is recited:

Blessed are You, Lord our God, King of the universe, Who brings forth bread from the earth.

(22:13 and 24:1): *Ki yikah ish isha* – "If a man takes a wife." Similarly, *vi-yeda'atem* recalls the verse (Gen. 4:1) *Ve-ha-Adam yada et Ḥava ishto* – "And Adam knew Eve his wife" which in the latter verse refers to carnal knowledge. That is why tradition dictates the reading of *Shir ha-Shirim* on *Shabbat Hol ha-Moed Pesah*. Passover is God's expression of his love for Israel. Throughout the Prophets we see the People of Israel referred to as the Almighty's spouse, and when Israel is idolatrous, Israel is referred to as an adulterous wife. Many of the Jewish wedding customs are based on the Sinai experience (e.g., candles recall the thunder and lightning at Sinai; the bride circling the groom recalls the 3 days the Israelites camped around the mountain) – the spiritual continuation of the Exodus.

We have noted that Matza in the Torah (Deut. 16:3) is referred to as *lehem oni*, which can be understood as *lehem ani* – a poor person's broken loaf. Tosafot (*Pesahim* 116a, s.v *Ma Darko*) understands that as a result, we make *Hamotzi* on two whole *Matzot* as *lehem mishne* like every other holiday. In addition, we also need a third broken Matza for *lehem ani*. Maimonides (*Mishne Torah, Hil. Hametz u-Matza*, 8:6) disagrees maintaining that *lehem ani* teaches that instead of two whole

8. מַצָּה

The bottom whole *matza* is lowered to the table, the broken middle *matza* is now moved above the remaining whole *matza*, and the following blessing is recited over them. (This blessing also covers the subsequent eating of the *Korekh* and the later eating of the *Afikoman*):

בָּרוּךְ אַתָּה ה', אֱלֹהֵינוּ מֶלֶךְ הָעוֹלָם,
אֲשֶׁר קִדְּשָׁנוּ בְּמִצְוֹתָיו וְצִוָּנוּ עַל אֲכִילַת מַצָּה.

Following the blessing, *matza* "the size of an olive" should be eaten from both the whole and broken *matzot* together, while leaning on one's left side.

9. מָרוֹר

The *maror* (bitter herbs) "the size of an olive" is dipped in *haroset* and eaten after reciting the following blessing:

בָּרוּךְ אַתָּה ה', אֱלֹהֵינוּ מֶלֶךְ הָעוֹלָם,
אֲשֶׁר קִדְּשָׁנוּ בְּמִצְוֹתָיו וְצִוָּנוּ עַל אֲכִילַת מָרוֹר.

---

loaves on *Pesah* for *lehem mishne* like every other holiday, one and a half suffices. Tradition follows the *Tosafot* (*Shulhan Arukh*, OH 473:6).

The members of the Mussar Movement derived a moral message even from the *Simanim* of the *Seder*. *Hametz* represents haughtiness, an over-inflated ego, and the evil inclination. Matza, by contrast, symbolizes humility and subservience to the Almighty. *Maror* represents the evil inclination, the *yetzer ha-ra*. Thus, the *siman*, Motzi Matza, hints that we are commanded to bring to the front our subservience to God. *Maror Korekh* instructs us to envelop the evil inclination with our subservience to God – and serve the Creator with both our inclinations (*Berakhot*, Chapter 9, *Mishna* 5).

עַל אֲכִילַת מַצָּה

We have mentioned above (comments to וְהִגִּיעָנוּ הַלַּיְלָה הַזֶּה) that we do not say the *she-Hehiyanu* blessing prior to eating either Matza or *Maror* for two possible reasons: (1) The *she-Hehiyanu* in *Kiddush* covers all the rituals in the *Seder*; (2) *she-Hehiyanu* was effectively just recited in the

8. Matza

The bottom whole *matza* is lowered to the table, the broken middle *matza* is now moved above the remaining whole *matza*, and the following blessing is recited over them. (This blessing also covers the subsequent eating of the *Korekh* and the later eating of the *Afikoman*):

Blessed are You, Lord our God, King of the universe, Who has sanctified us with His commandments and commanded us concerning the eating of matza.

Following the blessing, *matza* "the size of an olive" should be eaten from both the whole and broken *matzot* together, while leaning on one's left side.

9. Maror

The *maror* (bitter herbs) "the size of an olive" is dipped in *haroset* and eaten after reciting the following blessing:

Blessed are You, Lord our God, King of the universe, Who has sanctified us with His commandments and commanded us concerning the eating of maror.

---

concluding *berakha* of *Maggid Asher Ga'alanu* where we say: *ve-higi'anu ha-layla ha-zeh le-ekhol bo Matza u-Maror.*

מָרוֹר

Matza appears in Exodus 12 in two ways. In verse 8 it appears in conjunction with *Maror* and *Korban Pesah*: "And they shall eat the meat (of the Paschal lamb) that night, roasted by fire, and **with unleavened bread and bitter herbs they shall eat it**" – *al matzot u-merorim yokhluhu*. This would suggest that fulfillment of the Biblical commandment of Matza requires the presence of both the paschal lamb and *Maror*. Subsequently, however, in verse 18, Matza appears alone: "In the first month, on the fourteenth day of the month at evening, you shall eat unleavened bread…" Thus, eating Matza is Biblically obligated even when there is no Temple and no *Korban Pesah* in force. By contrast, *Maror* only appears in verse 8 above, together with Matza and *Korban Pesah*. No Biblical obligation to eat bitter herbs exists in their absence.

Haza"l, nevertheless, instituted a rabbinical obligation to eat *Maror* – *zekher la-Mikdash* – to remember how it once was when the Temple stood and will prayerfully soon be again!

R. Norman Lamm ("The Royal Table") suggests that the fact that *Maror* is not an independent mitzva, but contingent on *Korban Pesah*, is of fundamental importance. It suggests that the experience of *Korban Pesah* – of freedom – is somehow intimately and unavoidably linked to *Maror* – the bitterness of struggle and pain. This is true with much of life: without prior darkness, we do not seem to appreciate the light. As a rule, strenuous effort is a prerequisite to the mastery of Torah; labor and frustration are the price of later success. So too is it with the **bitterness** we often experience in the Land of Israel. It would seem to be the tragic, but unavoidable and necessary introduction to a life of security and safety in the Jewish State. But once the *Maror* has been tasted, we pray that the way is prepared for the full enjoyment of freedom and its blessings.

Although the *Seder* is a celebration of freedom, *Maror* plays an important role because Jewish history needs to be transmitted to the next generation in its entirety, and this is for four reasons: (1) Jews are a product of their history and we need to understand our history in all its complexity in order to understand us as a people. We are a rich, diverse, and complicated people because our long history has been varied, multinational, and at times multicultural. (2) To do justice to those who have preceded us, it is imperative to appreciate what exactly they lived through: their sacrifice and how they succeeded in surviving – against all the rules of history and logical odds. (3) An understanding of the past puts our present troubles, trials, and tribulations in perspective. Jews can survive despite the fact that in each generation there are attempts to destroy us – *be-khol dor va-dor kamim alenu lekhalotenu* – because ultimately *ha-Kadosh Barukh Hu matzilenu mi-yadam*. As mentioned by R. Jacob Emden (see our comments above on וְהַקָּדוֹשׁ בָּרוּךְ הוּא מַצִּילֵנוּ מִיָּדָם), the very existence of the Jewish people is a bigger miracle than all of the miracles described in the Torah. (4) Finally, we must remain sensitive to our past adversity and affliction to ensure that it doesn't happen again. We must be forever vigilant, for as noted historian George Santayana (The Life of Reason, 1905) has said: "Those who cannot remember the past are condemned to repeat it." We need to value our physical and spiritual freedom so that these gifts are not taken for granted and lost. This is the central role of the *Maror*. If we appreciate our ultimate debt to and dependence on the Almighty, we will fulfill our part of the covenant with God through keeping the *mitzvot*.

Haroset

Haroset was introduced already in the times of the *Mishna* to attenuate the sharpness of the bitter herbs (*Pesahim* 116a). Recipes for *haroset* vary from community to community and family to family. The *Tur* (OH 473) and *Arukh ha-Shulhan* (OH 473:17) prescribe several characteristics for *haroset* and offer a rationale for each. Its texture should be paste-like to remind us of the mortar the Israelites worked with in Egypt. Red wine is to remind us of the blood of the infants thrown into the Nile. Almonds are used because the Hebrew name *shaked* can also mean to accelerate – indicating that the Almighty accelerated their redemption. Cinnamon is added to give the *Haroset* a brownish color to resemble the bricks produced during the Egyptian slavery. Another common ingredient is apples, presumably based on the verse in Song of Songs (8:5): "Under the *tapu'ah* tree I aroused you." This verse is cited in *Sota* 11b to indicate that the pregnant Israelite women surreptitiously birthed their children – undetected by the Egyptians – under the scent of the *tapu'ah* blossoms (see our comments above to וַיַּרְא אֶת־עָנְיֵנוּ. זוֹ פְּרִישׁוּת דֶּרֶךְ אֶרֶץ). The identity of the biblical *tapu'ah* is no little matter of dispute, ranging from apple (widely accepted; Prof. Yehuda Felix on *Shir ha-Shirim*) and pomegranate, to etrog (R. *Tam, Shabbat* 88a, *s.v. Perav*) or other citrus fruit (R. Hershel Schachter, *Nefesh ha-Rav*, p. 209–210).

10. כּוֹרֵךְ

Maror "the size of an olive" is dipped in *haroset* and placed between two pieces of the remaining bottom *matza* "the size of an olive." It is eaten as a "sandwich" in a reclining position following the recitation of the following:

זֵכֶר לְמִקְדָּשׁ כְּהִלֵּל. כֵּן עָשָׂה הִלֵּל בִּזְמַן שֶׁבֵּית הַמִּקְדָּשׁ הָיָה קַיָּם. הָיָה כּוֹרֵךְ [פֶּסַח] מַצָּה וּמָרוֹר וְאוֹכֵל בְּיַחַד, לְקַיֵּם מַה שֶׁנֶּאֱמַר: עַל מַצּוֹת וּמְרוֹרִים יֹאכְלֻהוּ (במדבר ט:יא).

Korekh

The importance of the *Korekh* "Hillel wrap or sandwich" at the *Seder* is the product of a discussion in the Talmud (*Pesahim* 115a) and an extensive give-and-take among the *commentaries*. We will try to present a straightforward explanation of the resulting procedure based on *Tosafot* in *Pesahim*. In particular, we need to understand why Matza and *Maror* are each first eaten alone and then again together – emphasizing the minority view of Hillel.

We begin by pointing out that the verse regarding the *Korban Pesah* (Paschal lamb) (Num. 9:11) reads: *Al Matzot u-Merorim yokhluhu* – "…together with *Matzot* and bitter herbs you shall eat it [the Paschal lamb]." According to the view of Hillel, this *pasuk* indicates that the basic biblical obligation is to eat *Korban Pesah* together *in the same mouthful* with Matza and *Maror*. According to this position, the word *al* means "together with or simultaneously;" hence, a sandwich or wrap of the three is called for. The majority view of the *Hakhamim* dissents, however, arguing that *al* only requires "the same general time period." Thus, *Hakhamim* allow for some flexibility: *Pesah, Matza,* and *Maror* **can** be eaten either separately or simultaneously. But all this is true because in Temple times *Pesah, Matza,* and *Maror* were each Biblically obligated.

Complications began in post-Temple times when there was no *Korban Pesah*. We have already pointed out above (comments to מָרוֹר) that in the absence of the *Korban Pesah*, eating Matza remains biblical, but *Maror* – which is mentioned only in conjunction with the Paschal lamb – is rabbinic. Hence, according to both *Hakhamim* and *Hillel*, in

10. Korekh

Maror "the size of an olive" is dipped in *haroset* and placed between two pieces of the remaining bottom *matza* "the size of an olive." It is eaten as a "sandwich" in a reclining position following the recitation of the following:

In remembrance of the Temple, we do as Hillel did at the time when the Temple was standing. He would wrap [Pesah] matza and maror and eat them together, to fulfill what is written in the Torah, "with matzot and bitter herbs shall they eat it" (Numbers 9:11).

---

order to fulfill one's biblical Matza obligation, one cannot simply eat Matza with *Maror* – as one might have done when the Temple was standing. This is because the rabbinic *Maror* flavor will interfere with the higher biblical experience of eating Matza. Hence, according to **all views, one must first eat the Matza alone** to fulfill one's Biblical Matza obligation. Remaining now is a rabbinic obligation to eat *Maror* in commemoration of the Temple (*zekher le-Mikdash*; *Shulhan Arukh ha-Rav*, OH, 475:15). **According to the *Hakhamim*,** even at the time of the Temple, one could have always eaten *Maror* alone. But this is now required since *Maror* is only rabbinically obligated. Since we have already fulfilled our Matza obligation, the Matza is now optional and would result in a clash of flavors of foods of differing levels of obligation. Optional Matza would nullify the fulfillment of rabbinic *Maror*. Hence *Maror* according to the *Hakhamim* must be eaten alone. Turning now to **Hillel**, the **biblical** commandment requires eating Matza and *Maror* together. The rabbinic commandment to eat *Maror* instituted in commemoration of the Temple – not only rabbinically requires the *Maror* to be eaten but to be eaten **with** Matza together, *zekher le-Mikdash*. Hence, unlike the *Hakhamim*, accompanying Matza is not optional but rabbinically obligated. Thus, the *Maror* and the Matza are both rabbinically ordained and the flavors do not clash.

The Talmud records that contrary to the normative situation, no decision was made as to which halachic opinion was to be followed. Indeed, tradition teaches that in this specific case, we try to accommodate both the *Hakhamim* and *Hillel*. Thus, **to accommodate all opinions**, we first eat Matza alone to fulfill the biblical obligation of Matza according to everyone. Then we eat *Maror* alone *zekher le-Mikdash* following the *Hakhamim's* position. Finally, we wrap Matza and *Maror* together – *zekher le-Mikdash* following *Hillel's* opinion.

The question remains as to why the minority position of Hillel has become so central. Generally, following the *Hakhamim's* majority position should have sufficed. One possibility is that we do so to encourage the children to ask. Additionally, following the *Hakhamim* alone does not emphasize the *zekher le-Mikdash* element; after all, according to the *Hakhamim* we don't really change our practice from that performed when the Temple was standing. The Hillel sandwich, on the other hand, is unique and attracts attention. It also emphasizes the lack of a *Korban Pesah* which created this novel situation and practice in the first place.

Eaten as a "sandwich"

In a moment we will say: "He [Hillel] would wrap up *Pesah*, *Matza*, and *Maror* together…." With what do you wrap? *Rabbenu* Hananel suggests that Hillel wrapped the *Pesah* and *Matza* with the leaves of *Maror* (lettuce). Others have proposed that the Matza was soft unleavened bread much like Israeli *laffa* bread, resulting in a wrap.

Following the recitation

The custom of making a declaration before eating the "Hillel wrap" is recorded in *Shulhan Arukh* (*OH* 475:1). But this procedure is surprising on several accounts. Firstly, nowhere does the Talmud require or even mention that this or any other text should be recited! Secondly, we are in the midst of fulfilling our *Maror* obligation by eating bitter herbs two different ways: once like the *Hakhamim* and the other like Hillel. The *berakha* "*al akhilat Maror*" goes on both variations, thus saying a non-obligatory introductory text to *Korekh* would be an interruption (*hefsek*) between the mitzva benediction and the mitzva action according to Hillel. (We note that there are indeed some authorities – see *Mishna Berura*, OH sec. 475, *Be'ur Halakha*, s.v. ןכ*ve-Omer*, *Arukh ha-Shulhan*, OH sec. 475:5 – who maintain that one should not speak between *al akhilat Maror* and eating *Korekh*. (According to these latter authorities, *Zekher le-Mikdash ke-Hillel*, etc. is said only after completing the *Korekh* sandwich. Nevertheless, this is only a minority practice.)

(a) In order to understand this practice, let us first focus on the famous verse from Psalms (137:6): "Let my tongue cleave to the roof of my mouth, if I remember thee not; if I set not Jerusalem above my greatest joy." R. Shmuel Eidels (Maharsha, *Hiddushei Aggadot, Bava Batra* 60b) posits that it is this verse that requires us not only to remember Jerusalem but to involve our tongue – to verbalize it. R. Joseph Engel (*Gilyonei ha-Shas, Megilla* 18a, s.v. *Zakhor*) and R. Joseph Kohen (in R. Zvi Pesah Frank *Mikra'ei Kodesh, Pesah*, Part II, sec. 52, p. 178, *Harerei Kodesh*, note 1) suggests that this then is the source for the practice of reciting *Zekher le-Mikdash ke-Hillel* before *Korekh* at the *Seder*. Since the recitation is part of the *zekher le-Mikdash*, it is not a *hefsek*.

We still have to fine-tune the Maharsha's verbalization rule a bit more. *Tosafot* (Megilla 20b, s.v. *Kol ha-layla*), as explained by R. Joseph B. Soloveitchik ("An Exalted Evening"), indicates that there are two types of *zekher le-Mikdash*. One is a reenactment of exactly what was done in the Temple – like shaking *lulav* and *etrog* all seven days of *sukkot* – as a **remembrance** of the past and as a **preparation** for the future. It is a joyous act because one is in training, looking forward to doing the same act in the Almighty's presence *lifnei Hashem Elokeikhem* (Lev 23:40) in the rebuilt *Bet ha-Mikdash*. In these types of *mitzvot*, we don't have to verbalize the *zekher le-Mikdash*. The other type of *zekher le-Mikdash* which does require verbalization – is when I am not in training, because I am not doing the act as it was done in the Temple. Thus, in *sefirat ha-omer*, I lack the bringing of the *Omer* offering. Here I must say: *ha-Rahaman yahazir lanu et avodat Bet ha-Mikdash li-mekoma bi-mehera be-yamenu. Amen Selah.* – "May the Merciful One return to us the Temple service speedily in our day. Amen." In the case of *Korekh*, the *Korban Pesah* is absent – and one must, therefore, say: *Zekher le-Mikdash ke-Hillel*. In both cases, one needs the statement of *zekher le-Mikdash* to complete the action. In addition, since I am sad, *she-Hehiyanu* cannot be said.

(b) A second reason why *Zekher le-Mikdash ke-Hillel* is not a *hefsek* was proposed by R. Elyakim Getsel Horowitz (*Zikhron Yerushalayim*). It is related to the special practice at the *Seder* of explaining the meaning of the various special foodstuffs found at the *Seder* Table: *Pesah zeh…, Matza zo…. Maror zeh… al shum ma?* These explanations are based on the verse: *ve-Amartem Zevah Pesah hu la-Shem* (Exodus 12:27) – a biblical mandate to explain the various components of the *Seder* to

11. שֻׁלְחָן עוֹרֵךְ

The festive meal is eaten. It is a custom to eat a hard-boiled egg at the beginning of the meal. Ashkenazi Jews do not eat roasted meat at the Seder for this might be mistaken for the Pesah sacrifice, which is forbidden to be offered in exile. One should try to recline throughout the meal.

---

the children. The same is true for *Korekh*; its explanation is part of this fulfillment, and hence not a needless interruption.

(c) A final reason suggested by R. Joseph B. Soloveitchik is that Hillel only required *Korekh* when there was a *Korban Pesah*. In its absence, even Hillel admits that one can eat Matza and *Maror* separately, with separate *berakhot*. *Korekh* is done, only as a *zekher* – not as a rabbinic obligation. Hence, *al akhilat Maror* does not go on *Korekh*, and there is no *hefsek* problem.

זֵכֶר לְמִקְדָּשׁ כְּהִלֵּל

R. Gedaliah Silverstone (cited by R. Avrohom Yisroel Rosenthal, *Haggada ke-Motzei Shallal Rav*) commented to the members of his household how outstanding it is that the Jewish people associate *Korekh* with Hillel. How unfortunate it is that many don't accept with the same zeal many of the other of Hillel's ways and qualities: his love, respect, and patience towards all people; his modesty; and his commitment and sacrifice for Torah and scholarship.

עַל מַצּוֹת וּמְרוֹרִים יֹאכְלֻהוּ

It is somewhat surprising that Hillel cites a verse appearing by *Pesah Sheni* (Num. 9:11): *Al Matzot u-Merorim yokhluhu* – "Together with Matzot and bitter herbs you shall eat it [the Pascal lamb]." Why cite this verse rather than a comparable one appearing by *Pesah Rishon* (Ex. 12:8) *u-Matzot al Merorim yokhluhu* – "*Matzot* together with bitter herbs you shall eat it." R. Samuel Strashun (Rashash, *Pesahim* 115a) cleverly observes that the answer is found in the Torah cantillations (*trop* or *ta'amei ha-mikra*). These musical notes function much like punctuation, guiding us in how to parse the Torah sentences into phrases. Here are both verses with their cantillation notes:

11. Shulhan Orekh

The festive meal is eaten. It is a custom to eat a hard-boiled egg at the beginning of the meal. Ashkenazi Jews do not eat roasted meat at the Seder *for this might be mistaken for the* Pesah *sacrifice, which is forbidden to be offered in exile. One should try to recline throughout the meal.*

שמות יב:ח – וְאָכְלוּ אֶת־הַבָּשָׂר בַּלַּיְלָה הַזֶּה צְלִי־אֵשׁ וּמַצּוֹת עַל־מְרֹרִים יֹאכְלֻהוּ

במדבר ט:יא – בַּחֹדֶשׁ הַשֵּׁנִי בְּאַרְבָּעָה עָשָׂר יוֹם בֵּין הָעַרְבַּיִם יַעֲשׂוּ אֹתוֹ עַל־מַצּוֹת וּמְרֹרִים יֹאכְלֻהוּ

In the verse from Exodus, there is a major stop (*etnahta*) on *hazeh*, and a minor stop (*zakef katan*) on the word *u-Matzot* – such that this sentence can be understood as follows: "And they shall eat the meat on this night: fire-roasted and *matzot*, with bitter herbs they shall eat it." It is not at all implied by this punctuation that all three – *Pesah*, *Matza*, and *Maror* – have to be eaten **together** in one mouthful. By contrast, in the verse from Numbers cited by Hillel, dealing with *Pesah sheni*, the second half of the verse after the major stop (*etnahta*) can only be understood as follows: "…with *matzot* and bitter herbs you shall eat it [the Pascal lamb]." For Hillel, this clearly suggests that all three – *Pesah*, *Matza*, and *Maror* – must be eaten in one mouthful! Importantly, a later verse in this very chapter (*Num.* 9:18) declares: *ke-Khol hukat ha-Pesach ya'asu oto* – "You shall prepare it (*Pesah Sheni*) following all the rules of the *Pesah*" – thus equating the rules of *Pesah Sheni* sacrifice with *Pesah Rishon*.

שֻׁלְחָן עוֹרֵךְ

A priori, it is somewhat astounding that one of the 15 *simanim* of the *Seder* is appropriated by *Shulhan Orekh* – eating and drinking – a function that is seemingly totally physical in nature. The answer is that in the Jewish view of things, the physical can very much be part of *avodat Hashem* – Divine worship. After all, it is only the body that can do *mitzvot* and serve as the major agent for Divine service. In this regard, former Chief R. Yisrael Meir Lau *(Haggada Yahel Or)* points out that there were four large ritual objects in the Temple sanctuary: (1) The *Aron* (Ark) containing the Tablets of the Covenant, representing the centrality of the Torah. (2) The Menorah (Candelabra) which gives

12. צָפוּן (אפיקומן)

At the end of the meal, an olive-sized amount of matza should be eaten for the Afikoman in a reclining position by all of the participants. The Afikoman should be eaten before the midpoint of the night. No food or drink, other than the last two cups of wine, should be consumed after the eating of the Afikoman.

---

light and incorporates the *Ner Tamid* (eternal light) signifying God's perpetual presence. (3) The *Mizbe'ah* (Alter) for sacrifices, which is the locus of Divine service. (4) Finally, there is the *Shulḥan* (Table) which carried the twelve showbread loaves – eaten by the *Kohanim* who were in Temple service. The concern for the body involved in *avodat Hashem* (Divine service) is interconnected with spirituality. Mainstream Judaism rejects the view that the soul is good and the body bad, for it is the body that does *ḥessed* and *tzedaka*. It is only the body that can fulfill *mitzvat ona* (marital intimacy) and *Peru' u-Revu* (procreation). Only in Judaism is there a concept of *se'udat mitzva* – a meal that is a religious sanctified experience. These include *Sabbath* and Yom Tov meals, meals celebrating a *siyum*, wedding, *Brit Mila* or *Pidyon ha-Ben*, and a *Se'udat Shevaḥ ve-Hodaya* – a celebrative meal of thanks and praise for the occurrence of an act of Divine grace or a life-saving event. Here too at the *Seder, Shulḥan Orekh* is not just "half-time" – but a *Seudat Shevaḥ ve-Hodaya* for our people's miracle of redemption and salvation. As such it is a *seudat mitzva* – an integral part of our *avodat Hashem* on *Seder* Night!

The festive meal is eaten.

There is a widespread custom to eat eggs (a traditional food of mourners) at the beginning of the *Seder* meal to remember the destruction of the Temple. In addition, the following *Tisha be-Av* (the anniversary of the two Temples' destruction) will fall on the same day of the week as the *Seder* night. In a very real sense, the 9th of Av is the antithesis of the *Seder*, as can be seen by comparing the requirements of the *Seder* meal, with those of the *seuda ha-mafseket* (the separation meal) – the last meal before the *Tisha be-Av* Fast. **At the Seder:** (1) We eat like rich nobility, leaning on couches; (2) we drink four cups of wine; (3) consume meat; (4) eat at least two cooked dishes; (5) gather joyously with friends and family. **At the *seuda ha-mafseket*:** (1) we eat like mourners on the floor or low stool; (2 and 3) we are forbidden from drinking wine or eating

12. Tzafun (Afikoman)

At the end of the meal, an olive-sized amount of matza should be eaten for the Afikoman in a reclining position by all of the participants. The Afikoman should be eaten before the midpoint of the night. No food or drink, other than the last two cups of wine, should be consumed after the eating of the Afikoman.

---

meat; (4) we eat only one cooked dish; (5) we sit somberly alone (without a *mezuman*). This is a clear attempt by *Haza"l* to keep the memory, love, and yearning for Jerusalem and the Temple alive in our collective memory. By associating the sadness of *Tisha be-Av* with the joy of the *Seder* and its dream for the future, we and our children learn to identify with this promising future. We are taught not to give up our dreams despite our suffering and tribulations.

Interestingly, R. Yaakov Leiner of Izhbitz (*Haggada Sefer ha-Zemanim, Shulhan Orekh*) suggests that the custom to eat eggs at the *Seder* is because an egg appears to be a complete creation when in reality it is the preparatory stage for a new life. Similarly, while the Exodus appeared to be salvation as an end in and of itself, it was, in fact, only the means for the future spiritual redemption at Sinai. As the Torah says repeatedly: "*Shalah et ami ve-ya'avduni* – Let my people go - **so that** they may **serve Me**" (Ex. 7:16; 7:26; 9:1; 9:13). The purpose of the physical redemption from Egypt was not freedom per se – but freedom to serve the Creator. "Serve Me" in the Temple; serve Me in prayer; serve Me by learning Torah; and serve Me by doing *mitzvot*.

צָפוּן (אפיקומן)

The Hebrew word *Tzafun* means hidden. It indicates that at this point of the *Seder* we "reveal" the large half of the middle Matza, which was broken at *Yahatz* (at the beginning of the *Seder*) and set aside or "hidden" by the leader of the Seder. This hidden Matza was set aside to be eaten as the *Afikoman*, the last *ke-zayit* of Matza consumed at the *Seder* at this point. Since the Matza set aside by the *Seder* leader will not suffice for all present, other pieces of Matza will perforce be used. (As to why the *Afikoman* is hidden, see the explanation of R. Chaim Soloveitchik at the end of our comments on יחץ).

In order to understand the significance of what is being done, let us ask a fundamental question. What did the *Seder* meal look like at the time of the *Bet ha-Mikdash* (following the majority view of *Hakhamim*)? Based on Rambam (*Hametz u-Matza* 8:6, 7 and 9), one started off by eating, in turn, Matza, *Maror*, *Korban Hagiga* and *Korban Pesah* – each with their own appropriate *berakha* and each a *ke-zayit* size volume. At this point the main meal was brought out (e.g., gefilte fish, chicken soup with kneidelach, salad, more meat (*hagiga*), sponge cake, etc.). When one was full but not "over-stuffed" (dubbed *al ha-sova*) – he/she ate a final *ke-zayit* of *Korban Pesah*. [There are *Rishonim* (see Maharam Halava) who maintain that the *Korban Pesah* was **only** eaten at the end.] No dessert should be eaten following the final *ke-zayit* of *Korban Pesah* – as the *Mishna* (*Pesahim* 10:8) states: "One does not conclude after the final portion of Paschal lamb with an *Afikoman*" (provisionally defined as dessert, but see more below).

Despite the above description, the Talmud (*Pesahim* 119b) indicates that nowadays, when there is no Paschal lamp, we eat a *ke-zayit* of Matza at the end of the meal with no food following it – "One does not conclude after the final Matza with an *Afikoman*." Some *Rishonim* (Rashi and Rashbam) suggest that there must have been Matza that was eaten with the final *Korban Pesah*, and we re-enact that eating now. Other *Rishonim* (Rosh) dissent, suggesting that no Matza was eaten with the final *ke-zayit Pesah*; the final Matza eaten post-Temple times is merely a rabbinic reminder/replacement for the *Korban Pesah*. (As a result of the above dispute, some meticulous halakhists eat **two** *ke-zetim* of Matza for *Afikoman*.) In any case, the Afikoman should properly be consumed before midnight following the stringent position of R. Elazar ben Azarya (*Pesahim* 120b), just as the *Korban Pesach* was eaten before midnight during the days of the Temple in Jerusalem (*Shulhan Arukh* O.H. 477:1).

Let's now focus on the word *Afikoman*. This is not a Hebrew word and sounds Aramaic or Greek in origin. Nevertheless, as noted above, it does appear in the *Mishna* (*Pesahim* 10:8): *Ein maftirin ahar ha-Pesah Afikoman*. Indeed, this *Mishna* was cited above in the *Haggada*'s answer to the Wise Son. Not only is the meaning and etymology of this word unclear today, two millennia after the *Mishna*, but so it was to the *Amoraim* (*Pesahim* 119b) who lived only a few hundred years after the passing of its author, R. Judah the Prince (ca. 217 CE). The suggested explanations break down into two schools: (1) One group understood

Afikoman to be some sort of food, dessert, or delicacy that was forbidden for consumption after the final *ke-zayit* of *Korban Pesah*. The reason for this ruling is so that the taste of the *Korban Pesah* should remain in one's mouth following the *Seder* (Rambam, MT, *Hametz u-Matza*, 8:9). (2) The second group of *Amoraim* understands *Afikoman* as some sort of after-dinner social activity – common among the Greeks and Romans. On this basis, modern scholars have suggested that *Haza"l* feared that the *Seder night* – with its singing, rejoicing, friends, good food and plentiful wine – would degenerate into lewd and raucous behavior of the Greek/Hellenistic "Symposia" or *Epikomazein*. (For discussion see: R. Joseph Tabory, https://www2.biu.ac.il/JH/Parasha/eng/Pesah/tabori.html). On this basis *Haza"l* forbade post-*korban Pesah* desserts, going from house to house and excessive wine drinking.

As noted above, after the destruction of the Temple, Matza replaced the *Korban Pesah* as the last food eaten at the *Seder*. Ironically, because the last *korban* meat or Matza eaten at the *Seder* became the officially sanctioned "dessert," it was dubbed by Jews as the *Afikoman*. *Afikoman* thus moved from being the **forbidden** dessert in the *Mishna*, to the halakhicly **required** dessert of *Tzafun*!

A comment is in place regarding the Ashkenazi custom of having the children "steal the *Afikoman*" from the *Seder* leader and then having the latter "redeem" it before *Tzafun* for consumption. This custom is mentioned in the writings of R. Moshe Halava (1290–1370), though we have no details of how this game was actually played. In most homes, the negotiations are carried out with love, and quite often more than one *Afikoman* is available. In the home of my parents, we were notified from the get-go that if the "ransom price" became unreasonable, my father would simply remove another piece of *Matza shemura* from the box! The purpose of this distraction was obviously to keep the children awake throughout the majority if not all, the *Seder* – and has proven its success over the generations. Like the *Ma Nishtana* at the beginning of the *Seder*, acting out the Ten Plagues in the middle, and singing *Ehad Mi Yodea* and *Had Gadya* at the end – these ploys keep the children awake and involved throughout. In a very real sense, they are all a fulfillment of the biblical imperative (Ex. 13:8): "And you shall tell your child on that day, saying: 'It is because of "this," that the Lord acted on my behalf when I came forth out of Egypt.'" Our history must become

13. בָּרֵךְ

The third cup is poured and *Birkat ha-Mazon* is recited.

---

our children's story, as well. That will only occur if they feel involved and relevant when we recount it.

One further custom, I observed in the home of my in-laws, Rev. Jonas and Libby Neiman z"l. He would make a small circle of Matza from the *Afikoman* and store it visibly in the breakfront until the burning of the *Hametz* the next year. This custom appears in the responsa literature (see, e.g., R. Jacob Reischer, *Resp. Shevut Yaakov*, sec. 52 and *Hok Yaakov*, OH 477:3) and is presumably based on the Torah's directive to remember the Exodus year-round – in fulfillment of (Deut. 16:3): "So that you may remember the day of your departure from the land of Egypt all the days of your life."

בָּרֵךְ

We are about to conclude the "*mitzvot* section" of the *Seder* by reciting *Birkat ha-Mazon* which is composed of three biblically based *berakhot*, and one rabbinic benediction. The first three biblical *berakhot* are grounded on the verse (Deut. 8:10): *ve-Akhalta ve-savata u-verakhta* (1) *et Hashem Elokekha* (2) *al ha-aretz* (3) *ha-tova asher natan lakh* – "When you have eaten your fill, give thanks: (1) to your God (2) for the land (3) which is good, given to you." Section 1 of the verse is the basis for the first *berakha Birkat ha-Zan* and refers to the Almighty's gift of food and sustenance. Section 2 is the basis for *Birkat ha-Aretz* (*Nodeh lekha...*) – God's gift of the Land of Israel. Finally, Section 3 of this verse is the basis for *Birkat Yerushalayim* (*Rahem na*) – the Creator's special gift of Jerusalem. This benediction ends with Amen (*Boneh be-rahamav Yerushalayim. Amen.*) to emphasize that it concludes the biblical series of *berakhot*. The fourth *berakha*: *ha-Kel Avinu Malkenu... ha-Melekh ha-Tov ve-ha-meitiv...le-olam al yehasrenu* – is rabbinic in origin and was established following the destruction of Beitar at the culmination of the Bar Kokhba revolution (135 CE).

R. Jonathan Sacks (*Haggada*) observes that if we focus on the three core Biblical *berakhot*, there are, in fact, three concentric circles of holiness here. The outer circle is the topic of the first blessing which

13. Barekh (Birkat ha-Mazon)

The third cup is poured and *Birkat ha-Mazon* is recited.

---

focuses on the world as a whole: – *ha-Zan et ha-olam kulo be-tuvo*.... Here we speak as citizens of the world and acknowledge His universal mercy. The middle circle is referred to in the second blessing, *Nodeh lekha*, which focuses on the Land of Israel and God's special providence over it. The third *berakha* focuses on Jerusalem and emphasizes the Almighty's special presence and relationship with us – which gives Jerusalem its unique status and holiness. R. Meir Simha of Dvinsk (*Meshekh Hokhma*, Deut. 8:10) focuses on the fourth rabbinic *berakha*. He argues that the latter teaches us that – even after the destruction of Jerusalem, even when they are in *galut* (the diaspora) – God's providence continues to watch over His people Israel, though He now often does so surreptitiously.

The *Birkat ha-Mazon* is recited over the third of the *Arba Kosot*. It is important to appreciate that each of these four cups celebrates *herut* – freedom and redemption. This is why we are obligated to lean (like Roman nobility) when drinking them. The first cup, *Kiddush*, celebrates man's ability to sanctify time and fix the calendar and months. That's why the Sabbath and Holidays are each a commemoration of the Egyptian exodus. The second cup at the conclusion of *Maggid* celebrates the Almighty "who redeemed us and our ancestors from Egypt." This cup is also connected to redemption and freedom. The fourth cup is the one over which we recite a much-expanded *Hallel* – praises for *Hashem's* salvation. But the third cup over which we thank the Creator for our sustenance, in what way is it a cup of *ge'ula* – salvation? The answer is the thanksgiving list appearing at the beginning of the second benediction of *Birkat ha-Mazon*: *Nodeh Lekha* – "We thank you Lord… for taking us out us from the Land of Egypt and for redeeming us from the house of slavery.…"

R. Joseph B. Soloveitchik (as cited by R. Stewart Weiss, https://mizrachi.org/hamizrachi/israel-the-partnership-between-man-and-g-d/) notes that at the *Seder* we recite both *Birkat ha-Mazon* over the third cup of the *Arba Kosot*, and *Al ha-Gefen* after the last cup at the end of *Hallel*. *Al ha-Gefen* is also known as *Berakha me-ein shalosh* – or "the one *berakha* digest of the three" – because it briefly summarizes the

שִׁיר הַמַּעֲלוֹת, בְּשׁוּב ה' אֶת שִׁיבַת צִיּוֹן הָיִינוּ כְּחֹלְמִים. אָז יִמָּלֵא שְׂחוֹק פִּינוּ וּלְשׁוֹנֵנוּ רִנָּה. אָז יֹאמְרוּ בַגּוֹיִם: הִגְדִּיל ה' לַעֲשׂוֹת עִם אֵלֶּה. הִגְדִּיל ה' לַעֲשׂוֹת עִמָּנוּ, הָיִינוּ שְׂמֵחִים. שׁוּבָה ה' אֶת שְׁבִיתֵנוּ כַּאֲפִיקִים בַּנֶּגֶב. הַזֹּרְעִים בְּדִמְעָה, בְּרִנָּה יִקְצֹרוּ. הָלוֹךְ יֵלֵךְ וּבָכֹה נֹשֵׂא מֶשֶׁךְ הַזָּרַע, בֹּא יָבֹא בְרִנָּה נֹשֵׂא אֲלֻמֹּתָיו.

When three or more men say Birkat ha-Mazon together, the following zimmun (invitation) is said. When three or more women say Birkat ha-Mazon together, substitute "Friends" (חברותי) for "Gentlemen" (רבותי) in the zimmun. When a male quorum of ten or more is present, the words in parentheses are added in the zimmun: If there are neither three or more men, or three or more women, the Birkat Hamazon begins below with בָּרוּךְ אַתָּה ה' –"Blessed are You...":

Leader	רַבּוֹתַי נְבָרֵךְ:
Others	יְהִי שֵׁם ה' מְבֹרָךְ מֵעַתָּה וְעַד עוֹלָם.
Leader	יְהִי שֵׁם ה' מְבֹרָךְ מֵעַתָּה וְעַד עוֹלָם. בִּרְשׁוּת מָרָנָן וְרַבָּנָן וְרַבּוֹתַי, נְבָרֵךְ [אֱלֹהֵינוּ] שֶׁאָכַלְנוּ מִשֶּׁלּוֹ.
Others	בָּרוּךְ [אֱלֹהֵינוּ] שֶׁאָכַלְנוּ מִשֶּׁלּוֹ וּבְטוּבוֹ חָיִינוּ.
Leader	בָּרוּךְ [אֱלֹהֵינוּ] שֶׁאָכַלְנוּ מִשֶּׁלּוֹ וּבְטוּבוֹ חָיִינוּ.
All say	בָּרוּךְ הוּא וּבָרוּךְ שְׁמוֹ.

themes of the first three *berakhot* of the *Birkat ha–Mazon*. R. Soloveitchik was intrigued by the fact that after bread one biblically recites three full benedictions, but after wine (and similarly, grain products, or the special fruit of the Land of Israel) only a single digest *berakha* is said. After all, when it comes to wine, man does very little. Most of the processing is accomplished by *Hashem*. The fruit grows by itself yearly – all one has to do is collect the fruit, squeeze it, and allow it to ferment into wine. In the case of bread, the investment of man is maximal. He plows, then sews, reaps, winnows, grinds, sifts, kneads, and bakes – and only then can he eat. Thus, Man's time and effort in bread–making

A song of Ascents. When the Lord returns the captives of Zion, we will be like dreamers. Then our mouth will be filled with laughter, and our tongue with joyous song. Then will they say among the nations, "The Lord has done great things for these." The Lord has done great things for us, we were joyful. Lord, return our captivity like water-springs in the southern desert. Those who sow with tears will reap with great joy. Though he goes on his way weeping as he carries the seeds through the field, he will return singing, bearing his sheaves.

> When three or more men say Birkat ha-Mazon together, the following zimmun (invitation) is said. When three or more women say Birkat ha-Mazon together, substitute "Friends" (חברותי) for "Gentlemen" (רבותי) in the zimmun. When a male quorum of ten or more is present, the words in parentheses are added in the zimmun: If there are neither three or more men, or three or more women, the Birkat Hamazon begins below with "Blessed are You...":

LEADER: Gentlemen, let us say Grace!

OTHERS: May the name of the Lord be blessed from now and forever.

LEADER: Blessed is the name of the Lord from now and forever. With the permission of the masters, teachers and gentlemen, let us bless (our God), from Whose abundance we have eaten.

OTHERS: Blessed is (our God), from Whose abundance we have eaten and through Whose goodness we live.

LEADER: Blessed is (our God), from Whose abundance we have eaten and through Whose goodness we live.

ALL: Blessed is He and blessed is His name.

---

would seem to be primary as compared to the Almighty's, while the opposite is the case in wine production. Why then is the benediction on wine so relatively short as compared to bread? Shouldn't the length of the benediction correlate to the debt of gratitude to Heaven?

The answer, says R. Joseph B. Soloveitchik (*Chumash Mesorat ha-Rav*, Gen 2:3; *Halakhic Man* p. 101), is that God wants man to be a **partner**

בָּרוּךְ אַתָּה ה', אֱלֹהֵינוּ מֶלֶךְ הָעוֹלָם, הַזָּן אֶת הָעוֹלָם כֻּלּוֹ בְּטוּבוֹ בְּחֵן בְּחֶסֶד וּבְרַחֲמִים. הוּא נוֹתֵן לֶחֶם לְכָל בָּשָׂר כִּי לְעוֹלָם חַסְדּוֹ. וּבְטוּבוֹ הַגָּדוֹל תָּמִיד לֹא חָסַר לָנוּ, וְאַל יֶחְסַר לָנוּ מָזוֹן לְעוֹלָם וָעֶד. בַּעֲבוּר שְׁמוֹ הַגָּדוֹל. כִּי הוּא אֵל זָן וּמְפַרְנֵס לַכֹּל וּמֵטִיב לַכֹּל, וּמֵכִין מָזוֹן לְכָל בְּרִיּוֹתָיו אֲשֶׁר בָּרָא. בָּרוּךְ אַתָּה ה', הַזָּן אֶת הַכֹּל.

נוֹדֶה לְךָ ה' אֱלֹהֵינוּ עַל שֶׁהִנְחַלְתָּ לַאֲבוֹתֵינוּ אֶרֶץ חֶמְדָּה טוֹבָה וּרְחָבָה, וְעַל שֶׁהוֹצֵאתָנוּ ה' אֱלֹהֵינוּ מֵאֶרֶץ מִצְרַיִם. וּפְדִיתָנוּ מִבֵּית עֲבָדִים. וְעַל בְּרִיתְךָ שֶׁחָתַמְתָּ בִּבְשָׂרֵנוּ. וְעַל תּוֹרָתְךָ שֶׁלִּמַּדְתָּנוּ. וְעַל חֻקֶּיךָ שֶׁהוֹדַעְתָּנוּ. וְעַל חַיִּים חֵן וָחֶסֶד שֶׁחוֹנַנְתָּנוּ. וְעַל אֲכִילַת מָזוֹן שָׁאַתָּה זָן וּמְפַרְנֵס אוֹתָנוּ תָּמִיד, בְּכָל יוֹם וּבְכָל עֵת וּבְכָל שָׁעָה:

---

in Creation – not an observer! That is why the verse says (Gen. 1:28): *Peru u-revu u-mile'u et ha-aretz* **ve-kivshuha** – "Be fertile and multiply, fill the earth **and master it**." This is also the meaning of the verse that concludes the Creation story (Gen. 2:3): *Ki vo shavat mi-kol melakhto asher bara Elokim* **la'asot** – "because He rested on the Sabbath] from all the work He had created **to do**." "To do" is meant to be understood as: "that was yet to be done." The Creator left the world incomplete – on purpose, for man to complete! (See also comments to שְׁמוֹנָה יְמֵי מִילָה.) When man joins God as His partner, as in making bread, he is elevated by this partnership and deserves the maximal blessing and praise. If he is only an observer, as in the case of fruit, that deserves a minimal benediction – since man has been minimally elevated in the process.

אֶרֶץ חֶמְדָּה טוֹבָה וּרְחָבָה

We began our discussion of the second *berakha* of *Birkat ha-Mazon* at the end of the previous comment. This second benediction of *Birkat ha-Mazon* contains a long thanksgiving list: *Nodeh Lekha* – "We thank you Lord" for giving us the Land of Israel and taking us out of the Land of Egypt. But as we've emphasized so many times before, tradition typically tells us straightaway **why** we were given this freedom: *al britkha she-hatamta bi-vesarenu, ve-al toratkha she-limadetani*,

Blessed are You, Lord our God, King of the universe, Who, in His goodness, nourishes the whole world with grace, with kindness, and with compassion. He gives nourishment to all flesh, for His kindness is eternal. And through His great goodness we have never lacked, and may we never lack food forever – for the sake of His great name. For He is a God Who provides and sustains all, does good to all, and prepares food for all His creatures whom He has created. Blessed are You, Lord, Who provides food for all.

We thank You, Lord our God, for having given as an inheritance to our fathers a desirable, good and spacious land; for having brought us out, Lord our God, from the land of Egypt and redeemed us from the house of slavery; for Your covenant which You have sealed in our flesh; for Your Torah which You have taught us; for Your statutes which You have made known to us; for the life, favor and kindness which You have graciously bestowed upon us; and for the food which You provide for us and sustain us with constantly, in every day, in every season, and in every hour.

---

ve-al ḥukekha she-limadetanu. We were redeemed to do God's calling and fulfill his mitzvot: circumcision, learning Torah, and observing His laws. We thank Hashem for this as well. We don't forget, of course, to thank the Creator for the basic elements of a good life: *ve-al ḥayim ḥen va-ḥessed she-ḥonantanu, ve-al akhilat mazon…*

Interestingly, the list of topics for thanks referred to in this *berakha* seems to be totally out of sequence: (1) *naḥala* – inheritance of the Land of Israel came in Yehoshua's time, while (2) redemption from Egypt was in Moshe's period. (3) *brit* – circumcision goes back to Avraham and (4) *Torah* – was given to us by Moshe following the Exodus. The list closes with a reference to (5) God's ongoing sustenance. So chronologically the order should be 3, 2, 4, 1, 5! We suggest that (1) *naḥala* here refers to the inheritance of the Land of Canaan/Israel promised to our forefather Avraham at the *Brit Bein ha-Betarim* (Gen. 15:13–21; see our comments above to וְיַעֲקֹב וּבָנָיו יָרְדוּ מִצְרָיִם and בָּרוּךְ שׁוֹמֵר הַבְטָחָתוֹ לְיִשְׂרָאֵל). This was followed by (2) the Exodus from Egypt. At the culmination of the latter, comes the Paschal lamb

וְעַל הַכֹּל ה' אֱלֹהֵינוּ. אֲנַחְנוּ מוֹדִים לָךְ וּמְבָרְכִים אוֹתָךְ. יִתְבָּרַךְ שִׁמְךָ בְּפִי כָּל חַי תָּמִיד לְעוֹלָם וָעֶד. כַּכָּתוּב (דברים ח:י): וְאָכַלְתָּ וְשָׂבָעְתָּ וּבֵרַכְתָּ אֶת ה' אֱלֹהֶיךָ עַל הָאָרֶץ הַטֹּבָה אֲשֶׁר נָתַן לָךְ. בָּרוּךְ אַתָּה ה'. עַל הָאָרֶץ וְעַל הַמָּזוֹן:

רַחֵם נָא ה' אֱלֹהֵינוּ עַל יִשְׂרָאֵל עַמֶּךָ וְעַל יְרוּשָׁלַיִם עִירֶךָ וְעַל צִיּוֹן מִשְׁכַּן כְּבוֹדֶךָ וְעַל מַלְכוּת בֵּית דָּוִד מְשִׁיחֶךָ וְעַל הַבַּיִת הַגָּדוֹל וְהַקָּדוֹשׁ שֶׁנִּקְרָא שִׁמְךָ עָלָיו: אֱלֹהֵינוּ אָבִינוּ. רְעֵנוּ זוּנֵנוּ פַּרְנְסֵנוּ וְכַלְכְּלֵנוּ וְהַרְוִיחֵנוּ, וְהַרְוַח לָנוּ ה' אֱלֹהֵינוּ מְהֵרָה מִכָּל צָרוֹתֵינוּ. וְנָא אַל תַּצְרִיכֵנוּ ה' אֱלֹהֵינוּ, לֹא לִידֵי מַתְּנַת בָּשָׂר וָדָם וְלֹא לִידֵי הַלְוָאָתָם. כִּי אִם לְיָדְךָ הַמְּלֵאָה הַפְּתוּחָה הַקְּדוֹשָׁה וְהָרְחָבָה, שֶׁלֹּא נֵבוֹשׁ וְלֹא נִכָּלֵם לְעוֹלָם וָעֶד.

The following paragraph is included on Shabbat:

רְצֵה וְהַחֲלִיצֵנוּ ה' אֱלֹהֵינוּ בְּמִצְוֹתֶיךָ וּבְמִצְוַת יוֹם הַשְּׁבִיעִי הַשַּׁבָּת הַגָּדוֹל וְהַקָּדוֹשׁ הַזֶּה. כִּי יוֹם זֶה גָּדוֹל וְקָדוֹשׁ הוּא לְפָנֶיךָ לִשְׁבָּת בּוֹ וְלָנוּחַ בּוֹ בְּאַהֲבָה כְּמִצְוַת רְצוֹנֶךָ. וּבִרְצוֹנְךָ הָנִיחַ לָנוּ ה' אֱלֹהֵינוּ שֶׁלֹּא תְהֵא צָרָה וְיָגוֹן וַאֲנָחָה בְּיוֹם מְנוּחָתֵנוּ. וְהַרְאֵנוּ ה' אֱלֹהֵינוּ בְּנֶחָמַת צִיּוֹן עִירֶךָ וּבְבִנְיַן יְרוּשָׁלַיִם עִיר קָדְשֶׁךָ כִּי אַתָּה הוּא בַּעַל הַיְשׁוּעוֹת וּבַעַל הַנֶּחָמוֹת.

אֱלֹהֵינוּ וֵאלֹהֵי אֲבוֹתֵינוּ. יַעֲלֶה וְיָבֹא וְיַגִּיעַ וְיֵרָאֶה וְיֵרָצֶה וְיִשָּׁמַע וְיִפָּקֵד וְיִזָּכֵר זִכְרוֹנֵנוּ וּפִקְדוֹנֵנוּ. וְזִכְרוֹן אֲבוֹתֵינוּ, וְזִכְרוֹן מָשִׁיחַ בֶּן דָּוִד עַבְדֶּךָ, וְזִכְרוֹן יְרוּשָׁלַיִם עִיר קָדְשֶׁךָ. וְזִכְרוֹן כָּל עַמְּךָ בֵּית יִשְׂרָאֵל לְפָנֶיךָ,

---

which required all males to be (3) circumcised (as explicitly stated in Exodus 12:48). This was followed by (4) the giving of the Torah at Sinai. Finally, if the Israelites keep the Torah, God promises them, as a nation, (5) sustenance and financial security (Lev. 26, 3–5). Hence, the list is in historical sequence!

For all this, Lord our God, we thank You and bless You. May Your name be blessed by the mouth of every living being, constantly and forever. As it is written: "When you have eaten and are satiated, you shall bless the Lord your God, for the good land which He has given you." Blessed are You, Lord, for the land and for the food.

Have mercy, Lord our God, upon Israel Your people, upon Jerusalem Your city, upon Zion the abode of Your glory, upon the kingship of the house of David, Your anointed; and upon the great and holy House upon which Your Name is called. Our God, our Father, our Shepherd, tend us, provide for us, sustain us, support us, and speedily grant us, Lord our God, relief from all our troubles. Lord our God, please do not make us dependent upon the gifts of mortal men nor upon their loans, but only upon Your full, open, holy and generous hand, that we may not be shamed or disgraced forever and ever.

The following paragraph is included on Shabbat:

May it please You, God, our Lord, to give us rest, through Your commandments and through the commandment of the seventh day, this great and holy Shabbat. For this day is great and holy before You, to refrain from work on it and to rest on it with love, in accordance with Your will. May it be Your will, God our Lord, to grant us rest, that there shall be no distress, grief or moaning on this day of our rest. And show us God our Lord, the consolation of Zion Your city, and the rebuilding of Jerusalem Your holy city, for You are the Master of salvation and the Master of consolation.

Our God and God of our fathers, may the remembrance and consideration of us; the remembrance of our fathers; the remembrance of Mashiah; son of David, Your servant; the remembrance of Jerusalem, the city of Your holiness; the remembrance of all Your people, the House of Israel, ascend, come and reach, be seen and accepted, heard,

לִפְלֵיטָה לְטוֹבָה לְחֵן וּלְחֶסֶד וּלְרַחֲמִים. לְחַיִּים וּלְשָׁלוֹם בְּיוֹם חַג הַמַּצּוֹת הַזֶּה. זָכְרֵנוּ ה' אֱלֹהֵינוּ בּוֹ לְטוֹבָה וּפָקְדֵנוּ בּוֹ לִבְרָכָה וְהוֹשִׁיעֵנוּ בּוֹ לְחַיִּים. וּבִדְבַר יְשׁוּעָה וְרַחֲמִים חוּס וְחָנֵּנוּ וְרַחֵם עָלֵינוּ וְהוֹשִׁיעֵנוּ. כִּי אֵלֶיךָ עֵינֵינוּ. כִּי אֵל מֶלֶךְ חַנּוּן וְרַחוּם אָתָּה.

וּבְנֵה יְרוּשָׁלַיִם עִיר הַקֹּדֶשׁ בִּמְהֵרָה בְיָמֵינוּ. בָּרוּךְ אַתָּה ה'. בּוֹנֵה בְרַחֲמָיו יְרוּשָׁלַיִם. אָמֵן.

בָּרוּךְ אַתָּה ה'. אֱלֹהֵינוּ מֶלֶךְ הָעוֹלָם. הָאֵל אָבִינוּ מַלְכֵּנוּ אַדִּירֵנוּ בּוֹרְאֵנוּ גּוֹאֲלֵנוּ יוֹצְרֵנוּ קְדוֹשֵׁנוּ קְדוֹשׁ יַעֲקֹב רוֹעֵנוּ רוֹעֵה יִשְׂרָאֵל הַמֶּלֶךְ הַטּוֹב וְהַמֵּטִיב לַכֹּל שֶׁבְּכָל יוֹם וָיוֹם הוּא הֵטִיב. הוּא מֵטִיב. הוּא יֵיטִיב לָנוּ. הוּא גְמָלָנוּ הוּא גוֹמְלֵנוּ הוּא יִגְמְלֵנוּ לָעַד. לְחֵן וּלְחֶסֶד וּלְרַחֲמִים וּלְרֶוַח הַצָּלָה וְהַצְלָחָה. בְּרָכָה וִישׁוּעָה נֶחָמָה פַּרְנָסָה וְכַלְכָּלָה וְרַחֲמִים וְחַיִּים וְשָׁלוֹם וְכָל טוֹב. וּמִכָּל טוּב לְעוֹלָם עַל יְחַסְּרֵנוּ.

הָרַחֲמָן הוּא יִמְלוֹךְ עָלֵינוּ לְעוֹלָם וָעֶד.
הָרַחֲמָן הוּא יִתְבָּרַךְ בַּשָּׁמַיִם וּבָאָרֶץ.
הָרַחֲמָן הוּא יִשְׁתַּבַּח לְדוֹר דּוֹרִים. וְיִתְפָּאַר בָּנוּ לָעַד וּלְנֵצַח נְצָחִים. וְיִתְהַדַּר בָּנוּ לָעַד וּלְעוֹלְמֵי עוֹלָמִים.
הָרַחֲמָן הוּא יְפַרְנְסֵנוּ בְּכָבוֹד.

וּמִכָּל טוּב לְעוֹלָם עַל יְחַסְּרֵנוּ

The words: *le-olam al yehasreinu* conclude the rabbinic fourth *berakha* of *Birkat ha-Mazon* as established by *Haza"l*. Nevertheless, most traditions include a series of additional non-obligatory supplications – referred to as the *ha-Rahaman*s. The optional list grew slowly and spontaneously, with different supplications recited in different localities. In *Nusah Ashkenaz* there are nine *ha-Rahaman*s on weekdays, and

and be considered, and be remembered before You, for deliverance, for goodness, for grace, for kindness, for compassion, for life, and for peace, **on this day of the Festival of Matzot**. Remember us, Lord our God, on this day for goodness, consider us on it for blessing; and save us on it for life. And with Your word of salvation and mercy, pity us and be gracious and compassionate with us, and save us, for our eyes are turned to You, because You are a gracious and compassionate God and King.

Rebuild Jerusalem, the holy city, speedily in our days. Blessed are You, Lord, Who in His mercy rebuilds Jerusalem. Amen.

Blessed are You, Lord our God, King of the Universe, God our Father, our King, our Sovereign, our Creator, our Redeemer, our Maker, our Holy One, the Holy One of Yaakov, our Shepherd, the Shepherd of Israel, the King Who is good and Who continually does good to all, each and every day. He has done good for us, He does good for us, and He will do good for us; He was bountiful to us, He is bountiful to us, and He will be bountiful to us forever, with grace, kindness and with mercy, and with relief, salvation and success, blessing and help, consolation, sustenance and support, and with compassion and life and peace, and all goodness; and may He never deprive us of all good things.

May the Merciful One reign over us forever and ever.
May the Merciful One be blessed in heaven and on earth.
May the Merciful One be praised for all generations, and be glorified through us forever and all eternity, and be honored through us forever and ever.
May the Merciful One sustain us in honor.

---

additional ones said on *Shabbat* and *Yom Tov*. While some of these are prayers for divine protection and sustenance, five of the *ha-Rahaman*s deal with the distant future/end of days (see the following comment).

הָרַחֲמָן הוּא יִשְׁבּוֹר עֻלֵּנוּ מֵעַל צַוָּארֵנוּ, וְהוּא יוֹלִיכֵנוּ קוֹמְמִיּוּת לְאַרְצֵנוּ. הָרַחֲמָן הוּא יִשְׁלַח לָנוּ בְּרָכָה מְרֻבָּה בַּבַּיִת הַזֶּה, וְעַל שֻׁלְחָן זֶה שֶׁאָכַלְנוּ עָלָיו.

וְהוּא יוֹלִיכֵנוּ קוֹמְמִיּוּת לְאַרְצֵנוּ

As just clarified above, in *Nusah Ashkenaz* there are nine *ha-Rahaman*s on weekdays and additional ones said on *Shabbat* and *Yom Tov*. While some of these are prayers for divine protection and sustenance, five of the *ha-Rahaman*s deal with the messianic period (*Yemot ha-Mashi'ah*), the "World-to-Come" (*Olam ha-Ba*), or the "days to come" (*le-Atid Lavo*). But before we can proceed, we need a crash course in Jewish eschatology. The latter is the branch of theology that is concerned *inter alia* with death and judgment, the afterlife, Heaven and Hell, messianism, resurrection, and the end of the world. There are essentially two schools in this matter: (1) the Rationalist School represented by Maimonides (Rambam, MT, *Hilkhot Melakhim*, 11:1 and 12:1–2; *Hilkhot Teshuva* 8:2 and elsewhere); and the Mystical School represented by Nahmanides (Ramban, *Torat ha-Adam, Sha'ar ha-Gemul*).

(1) **Rationalist School:** Our temporal world is referred to as "this world" – *Olam ha-Zeh*. According to the school of Maimonides, many of the descriptions of the various future periods by the prophets and *Haza"l* are to be understood allegorically. Thus, when a person dies, his soul moves into a purely spiritual existence known as "the world to come" – *Olam ha-Ba*, with the righteous located close to God, comprehending the universe and enjoying the Almighty's radiance – *Nehenim me-ziv ha-Shekhina*. As stated by Rav (*Berakhot* 17a): "In the World-to-Come there is no eating, no drinking, no procreation, no business negotiations, no jealousy, no hatred, and no competition. Rather, the righteous sit with their crowns upon their heads, enjoying the splendor of the Divine Presence." The wicked suffer enormously by being distanced far from this radiance. Those who are punished with *Karet* are cut off and have no spiritual existence whatsoever.

In the meantime, in *Olam ha-Zeh*, history continues. There will ultimately be a war of Gog, with his nation Magog, against Israel culminating with the arrival of the Messiah (*Bi'at ha-Mashi'ah*) – foretold by the prophet Eliyahu. The Messiah will assure Israel's salvation and judge

May the Merciful One break the yoke of exile from our neck and may He lead us upright to our land.

May the Merciful One send abundant blessing into this house and upon this table at which we have eaten.

---

the oppressing nations of the world. He and his sons will rule the world for hundreds of years. There will be peace and prosperity, and Jews will be primarily occupied doing *mitzvot*, learning *Torah*, and studying the ways of the Creator. This period will be perfectly natural, as Samuel opined (*Pesahim* 68a): "There is no difference between this world and the days of the Messiah – except for the absence of subjugation by foreign kingdoms." Sometime during the Messianic period, there will be an ingathering of all the exiles (*Kibbutz Galuyot*), the resurrection of the righteous (*Tehiyat ha–Metim*), and the reestablishment of the Temple in Jerusalem – but the timing and details are unknown. People will live, have children, and die, and this utopian period will continue for many hundreds of years.

At some point the physical world and history will come to an end – again the timing and details are unknown. We will not have bodies, eat or die, or do *mitzvot*. This spiritual world is actually a continuation of *Olam ha–Ba* – but is often referred to as "The days to come" (*le–Atid Lavo*) – because it is the point at which history, time, decay, death, and all physicality come to an end. The souls will eternally bask in the Almighty's radiance – *Nehenim mi-Ziv ha-Shekhina*.

(2) **Mystical School:** According to the second **Mystical School** led by Nahmanides, many of the descriptions of the various future periods by the prophets and *Haza"l* are to be understood literally. This school holds that the Messianic period is an unnatural miraculous era. What's more, *Yemot ha-Mashi'ah* and the *Olam ha-Ba* of *le-Atid Lavo* are a continuum. The Messiah will come and do miracles, gather those in exile, resurrect the dead, and reestablish the Temple. Some time thereafter, mankind will move into a spiritual world – with their bodies. Despite the absence of eating, human bodies will be preserved and not decay. There will no longer be *Mitzvot* as we know it, but we will continue learning Torah and Theology.

Let us now return to the *ha-Rahamans* dealing with the future. The verse: *ha-Rahaman Hu yishbor uleinu me-al tzavareinu, ve-Hu yolikhenu*

הָרַחֲמָן הוּא יִשְׁלַח לָנוּ אֶת אֵלִיָּהוּ הַנָּבִיא זָכוּר לַטּוֹב. וִיבַשֶּׂר לָנוּ בְּשׂוֹרוֹת טוֹבוֹת יְשׁוּעוֹת וְנֶחָמוֹת.

---

komemiyut le-artzeinu – deals with the ingathering of the exiles which is part of the messianic process. Next is the coming of Eliyahu the Prophet: *ha-Rahaman Hu yishlah lanu et Eliyahu ha-navi zakhur latov, vi-yevasser lanu besorot tovot yeshu'ot ve-nehamot*. The third future-focused verse is said on *Shabbat*: *ha-Rahaman Hu yanhilenu yom she-kulo Shabbat u-menuhah le-hayei olamim*. This refers to "the days to come" discussed above, a purely spiritual existence of endless peace, where physical time essentially stops. On a standard *Yom Tov*, we say: *ha-Rahaman Hu yanhilenu yom she-kulo tov* – which also refers to this same endless peaceful period of "the days to come." But at the *Seder* this particular *ha-Rahaman* is often expanded as follows: *ha-Rahaman Hu yanhilenu yom she-kulo tov, yom she-kulo arokh, yom she-tzaddikim yoshvim ve-atroteihem be-rasheihem, ve-nehenim mi-ziv ha-Shehina – vi-yehi helki imahem!* This last section is a paraphrasing of Rav (*Berakhot* 17a) which we cited above and refers to the fact that the righteous (pictured as wearing crowns) will be in total communion with the Almighty. The fifth *ha-Rahaman* in this set is: *ha-Rahaman Hu yezakeinu li-yemot ha-Mashi'ah u-le-hayei ha-olam ha-ba* – a supplication to be present to actually see the events of the Messianic era and the end of days.

From all the above, it should be clear then, that a sharp turn in focus of the *Haggada* has occurred from the past to the future. The first hint of this turn occurred in the latter part *Birkat Asher Ga'alanu*, where, following R. Akiva, we pray for the rebuilding of the Temple (see our comments above to אֲשֶׁר גְּאָלָנוּ וְגָאַל אֶת־אֲבוֹתֵינוּ מִמִּצְרַיִם). This prayer is repeated throughout the third *berakha of birkat ha-Mazon* culminating in *u-Veneh Yerushalayim*. But this turn becomes more pronounced during the *ha-Rahamans*. We will have more to say about how this dynamic plays out when we reach *Shefokh Hamatekha*.

הָרַחֲמָן הוּא יִשְׁלַח לָנוּ אֶת אֵלִיָּהוּ הַנָּבִיא זָכוּר לַטּוֹב

This *ha-Rahaman* uses the verb *yishlah* because it is basing itself on the words of the Prophet Malakhi (3:23) *Hineh anokhi* **shole'ah** *lakhem et Eliyahu ha-navi...* – "Lo, I will send you Elijah the prophet before

May the Merciful One send us Eliyahu the Prophet, and let him bring us good tidings, salvation and consolation.

---

the coming of the awesome, fearful day of the LORD [when God judges the oppressor nations]." R. Yehuda ben Yakar (*Peirush ha-Tefillot ve-ha-berakhot*) asks why Eliyahu is referred to as *zakhur la-tov* – remembered for good? He answers simply that this is because Eliyahu will announce good news and comforting tidings: the coming of the Messiah. But this does not explain why Eliyahu, of all Jewish personalities, was chosen to sound the voice of redemption. R. Yisrael Rosenson points to the *Midrash Pesikta Rabati* (Piska 4) which gives a very long list of traits shared by Moshe, the first redeemer, and Eliyahu, the final one. A sampling follows: by both, the verb *shalah* was used (Ex. 3:10 vs. Malakhi (3:23); both are referred to as *Ish ha-Elokim* – "Man of God" (Deut. 33:1 vs Kings I, 17:18); Moshe ascended on high as did Eliyahu (Kings II, 2:1); Moshe gathered the Israelites at Mount Sinai, while Eliyahu did so at Mt. Carmel; both rid Israel of idolaters; both were zealots (Ex. 32:226 vs. Kings I, 18:30); both pleaded on behalf of Israel (Deut. 9:26 vs Kings I, 18:37). Hence, maintains the *Pesikta*, they were equally worthy to serve as redeemers.

R. Moshe Shulman suggests a different rationale. Throughout his career as a dynamic prophet, Eliyahu attempted to conquer idolatry and foreign culture by force: bringing a three-year drought and famine (Kings I, 17), then by a miraculous stand on Mount Carmel which concluded with the execution of the Prophets of Ba'al (ibid., 18). In style, he copied Moshe's career in his miraculous and forceful conquest of the idolatry of Egypt, the Golden Calf, and the daughters of Mo'av. But despite some momentary success, in the long run, his sensationalism and force proved unsuccessful in effecting any permanent change in the people's observance. In a subsequent meeting with God in the barren desert of *Horev* (ibid., 19), Eliyahu reveals that despite all his zealous efforts, the people of Israel have continued to sin, and he has given up on them. The Almighty reveals to Eliyahu, that religious belief cannot be imparted through force (represented by mighty winds, earthquake, and fire), but only by discussion and dialog via a "quiet still voice" – *kol demama daka* (ibid., 19:12). Jews in the future would have to redeem themselves and bring themselves back. As is clear from the *Horev* desert

הָרַחֲמָן הוּא יְבָרֵךְ אֶת (אָבִי מוֹרִי) בַּעַל הַבַּיִת הַזֶּה. וְאֶת (אִמִּי מוֹרָתִי) בַּעֲלַת הַבַּיִת הַזֶּה. אוֹתָם וְאֶת בֵּיתָם וְאֶת זַרְעָם וְאֶת כָּל אֲשֶׁר לָהֶם.

הָרַחֲמָן הוּא יְבָרֵךְ אוֹתִי (וְאֶת בַּעֲלִי / אִשְׁתִּי, וְאֶת זַרְעִי) וְאֶת כָּל אֲשֶׁר לִי, אוֹתָנוּ וְאֶת כָּל אֲשֶׁר לָנוּ, כְּמוֹ שֶׁנִּתְבָּרְכוּ אֲבוֹתֵינוּ אַבְרָהָם יִצְחָק וְיַעֲקֹב בַּכֹּל מִכֹּל כֹּל, כֵּן יְבָרֵךְ אוֹתָנוּ כֻּלָּנוּ יַחַד בִּבְרָכָה שְׁלֵמָה, וְנֹאמַר, אָמֵן.

בַּמָּרוֹם יְלַמְּדוּ עֲלֵיהֶם וְעָלֵינוּ זְכוּת שֶׁתְּהֵא לְמִשְׁמֶרֶת שָׁלוֹם. וְנִשָּׂא בְרָכָה מֵאֵת ה', וּצְדָקָה מֵאֱלֹהֵי יִשְׁעֵנוּ. וְנִמְצָא חֵן וְשֵׂכֶל טוֹב בְּעֵינֵי אֱלֹהִים וְאָדָם.

בשבת: הָרַחֲמָן הוּא יַנְחִילֵנוּ יוֹם שֶׁכֻּלּוֹ שַׁבָּת וּמְנוּחָה לְחַיֵּי הָעוֹלָמִים.

הָרַחֲמָן הוּא יַנְחִילֵנוּ יוֹם שֶׁכֻּלּוֹ טוֹב [יש מוסיפים: יוֹם שֶׁכֻּלּוֹ אָרוּךְ. יוֹם שֶׁצַּדִּיקִים יוֹשְׁבִים וְעַטְרוֹתֵיהֶם בְּרָאשֵׁיהֶם וְנֶהֱנִים מִזִּיו הַשְּׁכִינָה, וִיהִי חֶלְקֵנוּ עִמָּהֶם].

הָרַחֲמָן הוּא יְזַכֵּנוּ לִימוֹת הַמָּשִׁיחַ וּלְחַיֵּי הָעוֹלָם הַבָּא. מִגְדּוֹל יְשׁוּעוֹת מַלְכּוֹ וְעֹשֶׂה חֶסֶד לִמְשִׁיחוֹ לְדָוִד וּלְזַרְעוֹ עַד עוֹלָם (שמואל ב. כב:נא). עֹשֶׂה שָׁלוֹם בִּמְרוֹמָיו, הוּא יַעֲשֶׂה שָׁלוֹם עָלֵינוּ וְעַל כָּל יִשְׂרָאֵל וְאִמְרוּ, אָמֵן.

יְראוּ אֶת ה' קְדֹשָׁיו, כִּי אֵין מַחְסוֹר לִירֵאָיו. כְּפִירִים רָשׁוּ וְרָעֵבוּ, וְדֹרְשֵׁי ה' לֹא יַחְסְרוּ כָל טוֹב. הוֹדוּ לַה' כִּי טוֹב כִּי לְעוֹלָם חַסְדּוֹ. פּוֹתֵחַ אֶת יָדֶךָ, וּמַשְׂבִּיעַ לְכָל חַי רָצוֹן. בָּרוּךְ הַגֶּבֶר אֲשֶׁר יִבְטַח בַּה', וְהָיָה ה'

May the Merciful One bless (my father and teacher) the master of this house, and ([my mother and teacher) the mistress of this house – them, their household, their children, and all that is theirs.

May the Merciful One bless me, (my wife / husband, and my children) and all that is mine, us and all that is ours – just as our forefathers, Avraham, Yitzhak and Yaakov were blessed in everything, from everything, and with everything. So may He bless us all together with a perfect blessing, and let us say, Amen.

In heaven, may their merit and our merit be invoked as a safeguarding of peace. May we receive blessing from the Lord, and righteousness from the God of our salvation, and may we find favor and understanding in the eyes of God and man.

On Shabbat add: May the Merciful One cause us to inherit the day which will be completely Shabbat and rest for eternal life.

May the Merciful One cause us to inherit the day which is all good. [Some add: that everlasting day, the day when the just will sit with crowns on their heads, enjoying the reflection of God's Majesty – and may our portion be with them.]

May the Merciful One grant us the privilege of reaching the days of the Mashiah and the life of the World to Come. He is a tower of salvation to His king, and bestows kindness upon His anointed, to David and his descendants forever [Shmuel Bet 22:51]. He Who makes peace in His heights, may He make peace for us and for all Israel; and say, Amen.

Revere the Lord, you His holy ones, for those who revere Him lack nothing. Young lions are in need and go hungry, but those who seek the Lord shall not lack any good (Psalms 34:10–11). Give thanks to the Lord for He is good, for His kindness is everlasting (Psalms 118:1). You

מִבְטַחוֹ. נַעַר הָיִיתִי גַם זָקַנְתִּי, וְלֹא רָאִיתִי צַדִּיק נֶעֱזָב, וְזַרְעוֹ מְבַקֶּשׁ לָחֶם. ה' עֹז לְעַמּוֹ יִתֵּן, ה' יְבָרֵךְ אֶת עַמּוֹ בַשָּׁלוֹם.

כוס שלישי

The blessing over wine is recited and then the third cup is drunk while reclining on the left side.

בָּרוּךְ אַתָּה ה', אֱלֹהֵינוּ מֶלֶךְ הָעוֹלָם בּוֹרֵא פְּרִי הַגָּפֶן.

---

conversation, Eliyahu was too hurt by the people's rejection to curb his zealotry. He had effectively given up on them. He did not understand God's message or was too hurt by the people's rejection to internalize Hashem's message. He was, therefore, replaced by the younger and less frustrated Elisha. But when the future redemption comes, Eliyahu will be given another chance, as is clearly described by the Prophet Malakhi (3:23–24): "Lo, I will send Elijah the prophet to you before the coming of the awesome, fearful day of the Lord. He shall reconcile parents with children and children with their parents" – *ve-Heshiv lev avot al banim, ve-lev banim al avotam*. His function then will be to bridge the generations engendering love and respect, discourse and dialog. We will have more to say about Eliyahu *ha-Navi* below.

נַעַר הָיִיתִי גַם זָקַנְתִּי

This verse from Psalms (37:25) appearing at the close of *benching* (*Birkat ha-Mazon*) is an astonishing statement by King David. Was he not aware of the problem of theodicy – that bad things happen to righteous people (*Tzaddik ve-ra lo*)? Are we not acutely aware that during the Holocaust, the righteous were seemingly forsaken and their children wanted for sustenance? In his Haggada, former British Chief R. Sacks cites a beautiful explanation of one of the great leaders of Boston, R. Moshe Feuerstein. The key phrase is *ve-lo ra'iti* – but I have never seen."

open Your hand and satisfy the desire of every living thing (Psalms 145:16). Blessed is the man who trusts in the Lord, and the Lord will be his trust (Jeremiah 17:7). I was a youth and also have aged, and I have not seen a righteous man forsaken and his children begging for bread (Psalms 37:25). God will give strength to His people, God will bless His people with peace (Psalms 29:11).

Third Cup

The blessing over wine is recited and then the third cup is drunk while reclining on the left side.

Blessed are You, Lord our God, King of the universe, Who creates the fruit of the vine.

Interestingly, the verb *ra'iti* appears twice in Megillat Esther (8:6) where Esther says to Ahashveirosh: *Ki eikhakha ukhal ve-ra'iti ba-ra'ah asher yimtza et ami*, ve-*eikhakha ukhal ve-ra'iti be-ovdan moladeti*. Says R. Feuerstein, this memorable verse should be translated thusly: "How can **I stand idly by and watch** while disaster befalls my people! And how can **I stand idly by and watch** while my birthplace is destroyed!" Queen Esther was attempting to explain to the King why she had to risk her life and become involved. So too here: King David declared that he could not stand idly by and watch; he could not be a passive witness or a disengaged spectator seeing the righteous suffer and his children begging for bread. He too had to get involved. Read this way, not only does the verse make sense, but ends the *Birkat ha-Mazon* with a model commitment. Yes, we have eaten and are satisfied – but that doesn't mean that we are indifferent to the needs of others. Interestingly, we start the *Seder* with the declaration: *Kol dikhfin yeitei ve-yeikhol* – "all who are hungry should come and eat." And this message is repeated at the end of *bentching* (*Birkat ha-Mazon*). In Jewish tradition, there can be no true *simha* unless one includes the indigent. It is this commitment to the social welfare of all that we conclude the *Birkat ha-Mazon* and drink the third cup of redemption.

שפוך חמתך (כוס של אליהו)

The fourth cup is now poured for the recitation of *Hallel*. In addition, a special "Fifth Cup" is poured in honor of the Prophet Eliyahu. The door is then opened and everyone rises, saying: "*Barukh ha-ba* – Blessed be he who arrives!" This is followed by the following paragraph:

שְׁפֹךְ חֲמָתְךָ אֶל־הַגּוֹיִם אֲשֶׁר לֹא יְדָעוּךָ וְעַל־מַמְלָכוֹת אֲשֶׁר בְּשִׁמְךָ לֹא קָרָאוּ.

כִּי אָכַל אֶת־יַעֲקֹב וְאֶת־נָוֵהוּ הֵשַׁמּוּ (תהלים עט:ו-ז).

שְׁפֹךְ־עֲלֵיהֶם זַעְמֶךָ וַחֲרוֹן אַפְּךָ יַשִּׂיגֵם (תהלים סט:כה).

תִּרְדֹּף בְּאַף וְתַשְׁמִידֵם מִתַּחַת שְׁמֵי ה' (איכה ג:סו).

Following the verses of *Shefokh Hamatekha*, the song *Eliyahu haNavi* is sung and the fourth cup should be raised for completion of the Hallel.

שפוך חמתך (כוס של אליהו)

Now that we have completed the third cup, the next *Siman*, or item, on the *Seder* agenda is completing *Hallel*, which is recited over the fourth cup of wine. Surprisingly, however, we first do the following **six** sequential actions: (1) The fourth cup is filled in preparation for the recitation of *Hallel*. (2) We then fill up a special (fifth) cup of wine, dubbed the Cup of Eliyahu – *Kos shel Eliyahu*, from which we do not intend to drink. This is not a personal cup, but one for all those gathered. (3) The front door is opened, and some have the custom of saying *Barukh ha-ba* – "Blessed be he who arrives!" as if to greet someone, presumably Elijah the Prophet. (4) We then say – not *Hallel*, but a series of quite belligerent vengeful verses, beginning with the words: *Shefokh Hamatekha* – "Pour out your wrath." (5) This is followed by the singing of *Eliyahu ha-Navi* as we do on *Motza'ei Shabbat*. (6) We then start to recite the third paragraph of *Hallel Lo lanu* – continuing our recital of *Hallel*. Why is all this done, and why here?

(a) One simple "unified answer" is that towards the end of *Birkat ha-Mazon*, the focus of the *Seder* has made a sharp and dramatic turn from the past to the future. As we saw above, of the ten or so

Shefokh Hamatekha (Eliyahu's Cup)

The fourth cup is now poured for the recitation of Hallel. In addition, a special "Fifth Cup" is poured in honor of the Prophet Eliyahu. The door is then opened and everyone rises, saying: "Barukh ha-ba – Blessed be he who arrives!" This is followed by the following paragraph:

Pour out Your wrath upon the nations that do not acknowledge You and upon the kingdoms that do not call upon Your Name.

For they have devoured Yaakov and destroyed his habitation
(Psalms 79:6–7).
Pour out Your anger upon them, and let Your wrath overtake them
(Psalms 69:25).
Pursue them with wrath and annihilate them from beneath the heavens of the Lord (Eikha 3:66).

Following the verses of Shefokh Hamatekha, the song Eliyahu haNavi is sung and the fourth cup should be raised for completion of the Hallel.

---

*ha-Rahaman*s, two deal with the Messianic period (*Yemot ha-Mashi'ah*), another two with the world to come (*hayei ha-olam ha-ba*), and one more *ha-Rahaman* with **both** periods: *ha-Rahaman Hu yezakeinu li-yemot ha-Mashi'ah u-le-hayei ha-olam ha-ba*.

We finish *benching* and declare in words and deed: We are ready! Bring the Messiah on! Our expectation that on *Seder* night Eliyahu will reveal himself – to announce the coming of the Messiah and the future redemption – is not unreasonable. After all, this is the anniversary of our first redemption from Egypt. As the Talmud says, *Pesah* is referred to in the Torah as a *Leyl shimurim* (Ex. 12:42). In *Rosh ha-Shana* (11b) the Talmud says: "In the month of *Nisan* our ancestors were redeemed; in the month of *Nisan* our people are destined to be redeemed (once again). What is the source? *Leyl shimurim* – 'A night of watching/vigil/protection' (Ex. 12:42) a night set aside for the future redemption from the six days of Creation." (See comments regarding יַגִּיעֵנוּ לְמוֹעֲדִים וְלִרְגָלִים אֲחֵרִים הַבָּאִים לִקְרָאתֵנוּ לְשָׁלוֹם above.)

In anticipation of Eliyahu's arrival, we pour a fourth cup of wine to recite *Hallel*. (According to this approach, this is not a special fifth cup – merely the fourth cup for Eliyahu, should he arrive at our *Seder*.)

David Tannor suggests that the moment of redemption in Egypt, *Makkat Bekhorot*, was at midnight – the moment, according to R. Eliezer, that the Paschal meal was concluded. (See comments to צָפוּן – אפיקומן above). We too hope for redemption when the Passover meal ends before midnight. We open the door after *benching* – in the hope that *Eliyahu ha-Navi* will be there and we will greet him happily. We show our deep faith that he certainly **could** be there – and "even if he should be tardy we will await him!" (*Ani Ma'amin*; see: *Mishna Berura, OH*, 480:10.) (This would be an example of "Prayer in Action" – analogous to going to the *mikva* and wearing white on the High Holidays; eating *Simanim* and reciting *Tashlikh* on *Rosh ha-Shana*; doing *Kapparot* on *Yom Kippur*, and many other customs.)

Bryna Jocheved Levy (in "Battle Fatigue and Deliverance") suggests a further reason for calling upon Eliyahu *ha-Navi* after *benching*. At this point in the *Seder*, the spirits of all present are at their highest. The several generations gathered have been intellectually challenged: the children have starred in reciting the Four Questions and retelling the tale of redemption; there has been "show and tell" with *Pesah, Matza*, and *Maror;* all have enjoyed a sumptuous meal – concluding with haggling over the *Afikoman*. All are relaxed, full, and happily satisfied. Now is the best time to call on Eliyahu to appear and bridge the generation gap – as stated by the Prophet Malakhi (3:23–24): "Lo, I will send the prophet Eliyahu to you before the coming of the awesome, fearful day of the Lord. **He shall reconcile parents with children** and children with their parents." If we have done our job well at the *Seder*, we have gone a long way to attaining that very goal; the *Seder* has been a stimulating, interesting, inspiring, and fun family evening – spanning the generation gap. It's not by accident that from this point on, the *Seder* is full of singing and less intellectual discussion. We let our hair down. It's meant to be uplifting and fun. We sing our way through *Hallel*, *Shokhen ad*, and *Nirtza* concluding with fun songs like *Ehad Mi Yodea* and *Had Gadya*. For the nations of the world, *Eliyahu ha-Navi* heralds the coming of "the awesome, fearful day of the Lord" a day of judgment and dread. But for the Jews, it is a day of rebirth and rebuilding of the family and the nation. It is a job we start at the *Seder* and pray that Eliyahu will help us complete.

Completing our presentation of the "unified approach," as just mentioned, part of the function of the Messiah will be to judge and punish those nations that have unjustifiably oppressed us. In this spirit, we call on the Almighty to avenge our persecution by reading the passage *Shefokh Hamatekha*. We then sing in honor of Eliyahu's eventual arrival and continue with the *Seder* by completing *Hallel*, which – as we shall see – deals in part with the Messianic period and the World-to-Come.

(b) Interestingly, there is a widespread folk tradition that on *Pesah* night Eliyahu actually attends every *Seder* – whether we see him there or not. A similar tradition indicates that Eliyahu is the *Malakh ha-Brit* – Angel of the Covenant, and tasked with being spiritually present at every circumcision. In addition, throughout the Talmud, we find stories about *Gilui Eliyahu* – the appearance of Eliyahu to various prominent personalities to teach an important lesson. In Hassidic tales, Eliyahu shows up as a savior, benefactor, or teacher who suddenly appears in times of need – and equally suddenly disappears. This fluidity in appearance seems to be suggested by the verses (II Kings, 2:11–12) that describe Elisha's vision of Eliyahu's departure from this world: "As [Elisha and Eliyahu] kept on walking and talking, a fiery chariot with fiery horses suddenly appeared and separated one from the other; and Eliyahu went up to heaven in a whirlwind."

There are essentially three approaches to this matter in *Haza"l*: (1) One maintains that Eliyahu died much the way that Moshe *Rabbenu* did, but his death is portrayed more dramatically. What Elisha saw was a prophetic vision. All subsequent sightings of Eliyahu are prophetic visions as well (Radak, II Kings 2:1). (2) The second school holds that Eliyahu went straight into *Gan Eden* with his body – never dying, living in *Gan Eden* like Adam before the sin. (3) The third school posits that Eliyahu has a dual existence. Most of the time he is a spirit – like an angel – and as such he comes to a circumcision (see below) and the *Seder*. On the other hand, sometimes he assumes a physical form and this is known as *Gilui Eliyahu*. According to all positions, when he comes in a physical form, he is bound by *the* commandments and Jewish law (*Encyclopedia Talmudit, Eliyahu*).

Continuing this line of thinking, why was Eliyahu the Prophet, of all Jewish personalities, tasked with the responsibility of coming to *Britot* and *Pesah Sedarim*. We know that Eliyahu was replaced by Elisha because the former was a zealot. But more fundamentally, Eliyahu erred when he gave up on the Jewish People and on his mission of bringing them back to belief and observance. In his desert conversation with the Almighty, he explains that he left the people because (ibid., verses 10 and 14): "I have been zealous for the Lord, the God of Hosts, **for the Israelites have forsaken Your covenant**...." Tradition asserts that this blanket charge was false, and as a result, Eliyahu was tasked with being present at every circumcision (*brit* = covenant); he is present to bear witness that he erred when he lost faith in the Jews and in their future. The Jews are indeed a frustratingly stubborn stiff-necked nation; but they act this way not only **against** God – but also **for** Him, as Jewish history testifies time and again! Similarly, Eliyahu is tasked with coming to each *Seder* in order to encourage the Jews: "Hang in there! Never give up the way I did! The redemption will eventually come and I will be there to notify you of its coming." Even if he should be tardy – await him. Eli Wiesel (1979) has written: "To be a Jew is to have all the reasons in the world not to have faith… but to go on telling the tale, to go on carrying on the dialogue, and to have my own silent prayers and quarrels with God." As we will see, "Hang in there!" is also the overall theme of the final section of the *Haggada – Nirtza*.

The final question is why we have to **open** the door to invite Eliyahu into our home and to our *Seder*. If he has a spiritual essence, the doors should not serve as a barrier?! The answer is straightforward. He is waiting for us to make the first move. Until we welcome him in, until we make it clear that we are ready for redemption – he will honor us with his arrival, but will not enter. We have to be willing partners in accepting and heralding the redemptive process. A similar idea was expressed by the Hassidic Rebbe Naftali Zvi Horowitz of Ropshitz who used to invite all the *Seder* participants to pour wine from their personal cups into the Cup of Eliyahu. This symbolizes the fact that everyone has to make his contribution to the coming of the Messiah and strengthen the divine forces of redemption by being involved in *Tikun Olam* – by improving the world physically and spiritually. In Kabbalistic terminology, there won't be an "awakening from above," until there has been an "awakening from below." Thus, for the Ropshitzer Rebbe, the Cup of Eliyahu was not just a matter of faith – it was a call to action! The Redeemer wants us to make the first step – to open the door. Alternatively, perhaps the symbolism of opening the door is a call to us – those who have undergone the indoctrination of the *Haggada*, to reach out to our fellow Jews who are not at the *Seder*. We have to start the *ķiruv* which *Eliyahu ha-Navi* will complete.

(c) As indicated above, in addition to the "unified approach," other scholars have suggested an assortment of intriguing explanations for the various actions performed following the third cup. 1) Regarding the custom of opening the door on *Seder* night, we have noted above that according to the "unified approach," we do so in anticipation and hope of the arrival of Eliyahu *ha-Navi*. 2) Another explanation given by commentaries is that the Torah refers to *Pesah* as *Leyl Shimurim* – "A night of vigil/watching/protection" (Ex. 12:42). In the Talmud (*Rosh ha-Shana* 11b) one rationale for this name is that *Pesah* is a night on which Jews are watched over and protected from harm. Opening the door would be another example of "Prayer in Action" affirming this hope and supplication. 3) An additional reason suggested by some scholars is that *Seder* night regularly coincides with Easter and was rife with "Blood Libels." Jews would open their doors after the meal to make sure that there were no spies or attempts to plant evidence. 4) Finally, opening the door may be reminiscent of practices observed during the days of the Temple. Thus, the Paschal lamb was eaten with a pre-designated group; each group would keep their doors locked while eating the sacrificial meat so that others would not wander in and partake of it. After the sacrifice was eaten (before midnight; see comments to (צָפוּן - אפיקומן), the doors would be opened so that the participants could ascend to the rooftops of their homes to sing *Hallel* with their neighbors (end of *Pesahim* 85b in Rashi; see: R. Gil Student, "Seder on Rooftops," *TorahMusings.com*, March 27, 2017). Josephus (*Antiquities* 18:2:2) also mentions the custom of opening the gates of the *Bet Ha-Miķdash* on *Seder* night after midnight – by which time the eating of the Paschal lamb had to be completed (Rambam, *Ķorban Pesah*, 8:15). It is possible, therefore, that we are reenacting this custom at our *Seder*s.

(d) Turning to the filling of a *Kos shel Eliyahu*, the Gaon of Vilna (Gra, R. Elijah Kramer, *Divrei Eliyahu*, *va-Era*,) suggests that while this special cup symbolizes Eliyahu's eventual coming, it is not one for him to drink but rather for him to adjudicate. To understand this better, we point out that R. Tarfon (cited in *Pesahim* 117b–118a) disagreed with the *Mishna* and held that there are **five** cups of wine, not just four. According to him, *Hallel ha-Mitzri* (Psalms 113–118) is said over the fourth cup, while *Hallel ha-Gadol* (Psalms 136) is recited over a separate fifth cup. From the subsequent halakhic discussion, it is not clear whether R. Tarfon disagrees with the *Mishna* or is merely adding a fifth **optional** cup. Argues the Gra, we pour the fifth cup now to symbolize that when Eliyahu comes, he will resolve this doubtful issue like many others left hanging in the Talmud. Is this fourth cup of limited scope, covering only *Hallel ha-Mitzri* (Psalms 113–118) – and, hence, we will also need a fifth cup for *Hallel ha-Gadol* (Psalms 136)? Or does this fourth cup also cover the whole *Hallel* section, including *Hallel ha-Gadol*? In the meantime, we pour the fifth cup but do not use it, because of the doubt.

In honor of the Prophet Eliyahu

Malakhi (3:23) prophesizes that "Lo, I will send you the prophet Eliyahu before the coming of the awesome, fearful day of the Lord." This refers to "Judgement Day" when the Almighty will judge and punish the oppressors of the Jews. This is the lead-in to the verses of *Shefokh Hamatekha*. As the Talmud (*Pesahim* 118a) clarifies: "And since we recite the great *Hallel* (Psalms 136), what is the reason that one also recites this *Hallel* (of Psalms 113–118)? The reason is that the latter contains the following five matters: a) The Exodus from Egypt (*be-Tzeit Yisrael mi-Mitzrayim* – "When Israel came out of Egypt," Psalms 114); b) The splitting of the Red Sea (*ha-Yam ra'a va-yanos* – "The sea saw and fled," ibid.); c) The giving of the Torah (*he-Harim rakdu ke-eilim* – "The mountains skipped like rams,"ibid.); d) The resurrection of the dead (*ki hilatzta nafshi me-mavet* – "For You rescued me from death"...*Ethalekh lifnei Hayim* – "I shall walk before Hashem in the land of the living," Psalms 116; and e) The pre-Messianic pangs (*Lo lanu* – "Not to us," Psalms 115)." Since it mentions these five key concepts, recitation of the complete *Hallel ha-Mitzri* was considered essential on *Seder* night.

שְׁפֹךְ חֲמָתְךָ

In nearly all Jewish communities, the custom of opening the door is followed by the recitation of *Shefokh Hamatekha* – four verses in

Ashkenazic tradition, but a different number in others. The *pesukim* call on the Almighty to take vengeance and destroy those nations who have attempted over the generations to destroy us. Please pay attention that it is not man who is being called to vengeance – but God himself, the true judge of action and motivation. Furthermore, it is not aimed at all non-Jews, only "those who do not know you." But I am in no way belittling the depth of the wrath and the acerbity of the curse. Its recitation is documented as being early 12th Century and is mentioned in the Tosafot (*Berakhot* 14a) and Mahzor Vitri. This is the period of the Crusades, where Jewish communities were mercilessly wiped out. The Crusaders were presumably marching against the Moslems in the Holy Land – but as they marched, they raped and killed the Jewish infidels along the way! Indeed, the militant tone of *Shefokh Hamatekha* is strongly reminiscent of the *Av ha-Rahamim* prayer said most *Shabbatot* before *Mussaf* in Ashkenazic synagogues. The latter prayer was written to memorialize the German communities of Speyer, Worms, and Metz which were similarly destroyed around *Shavu'ot*-time by Crusader mobs in the massacres of 1096.

אָב הָרַחֲמִים ... הוּא יִפְקֹד ... קְהִלּוֹת הַקֹּדֶשׁ שֶׁמָּסְרוּ נַפְשָׁם עַל קְדֻשַּׁת הַשֵּׁם.....
וְיִנְקֹם לְעֵינֵינוּ נִקְמַת דַּם עֲבָדָיו הַשָּׁפוּךְ. כַּכָּתוּב בְּתוֹרַת מֹשֶׁה אִישׁ הָאֱלֹהִים.
הַרְנִינוּ גוֹיִם עַמּוֹ כִּי דַם עֲבָדָיו יִקּוֹם וְנָקָם יָשִׁיב לְצָרָיו וְכִפֶּר אַדְמָתוֹ עַמּוֹ. וְעַל יְדֵי
עֲבָדֶיךָ הַנְּבִיאִים כָּתוּב לֵאמֹר. וְנִקֵּיתִי דָּמָם לֹא נִקֵּיתִי וַה׳ שֹׁכֵן בְּצִיּוֹן: וּבְכִתְבֵי
הַקֹּדֶשׁ נֶאֱמַר לָמָּה יֹאמְרוּ הַגּוֹיִם אַיֵּה אֱלֹהֵיהֶם. יִוָּדַע בַּגּוֹיִם לְעֵינֵינוּ נִקְמַת דַּם
עֲבָדֶיךָ הַשָּׁפוּךְ: ... וְאוֹמֵר. יָדִין בַּגּוֹיִם מָלֵא גְוִיּוֹת מָחַץ רֹאשׁ עַל אֶרֶץ רַבָּה.
מִנַּחַל בַּדֶּרֶךְ יִשְׁתֶּה עַל כֵּן יָרִים רֹאשׁ:

Father of mercy ... remember ... the holy communities, who laid down their lives for the sanctification of His name... May He avenge the spilled blood of His servants as it is written in the Torah of Moshe the man of God (Deut. 32:43): "O nations, make His people rejoice for He will avenge in our sight the blood of His servants. He will retaliate against His enemies and appease His land and His people." And through Your servants, the prophets, it is written (Joel 4:21): "Though I forgive, their bloodshed I shall not forgive When God dwells in Zion." And in the Holy Writings, it says (Psalms 79:10): "Why should the nations say,

'Where is their God?' Let it be known among the nations in our sight that You avenge the spilled blood of Your servants." ... And it says (Psalms 110:6–7): "He will execute judgment among the corpse-filled nations crushing the rulers of the mighty land; from the brook by the wayside, he will drink then he will hold his head high."

Why were the verses of *Shefokh Hamatekha* placed here after pouring the fourth cup and prior to the third paragraph of *Hallel* – beginning *Lo lanu* (Psalms 115)? The Gaon of Vilna (*Be'ur ha-Gra* to OH 480:1) cites the Talmud (*Pesahim* 118a) that *Lo lanu* refers to the pre-Messianic troubles and turmoil (*Hevlei Mashi'ah*). (See end of previous comments.) We ask the Almighty to spare us and duly punish those who have persecuted us. In addition, the second verse of *Lo lanu* says: *Lama yomru ha-goyim: Ayei Elokeihem* – "Why should the nations say: 'Where now is their God?'" Similarly, *Shefokh Hamatekha* states: *Shefokh hamatekha all ha-goyim asher lo yeda'ukha* – "Pour out Your wrath on the nations that do not know You!" R. Avigdor Nebenzahl (*Yerushalayim be-Mo'adeha*) suggests an alternate explanation. He proposes that the verses of *Shefokh Hamatekha* come to answer why we are completing *Hallel*, even though we have not yet eaten from the *Korban Pesah*. The answer is: *Shefokh hamatekha all ha-goyim asher lo yeda'ukha*. It is not our fault, but that of those non-Jews who do not know you. *Ki akhal et Yaakov, ve-et naveihu heshamu* – "They have devoured Yaakov and destroyed his Temple, your dwelling place."

Many individuals are bothered by the belligerency of this selection of *pesukim*. They argue that we should not teach our children to hate. Indeed, the Torah (in Deut. 23:8) warns us against hating Egyptians and Edomites. Some even cite a positive formulation *Shefokh Ahavatekha* presumably found in a 1521 manuscript:

שפך אהבתך על הגויים אשר ידעוך. ועל ממלכות אשר בשמך קוראים.
Pour out your love on the nations that know you, and on the kingdoms that call on your name.

בגלל חסדים שהם עושים עם זרע יעקב. ומגינים על עמך ישראל מפני אוכליהם.
Because of the kindness they do to Yaakov's seed, and protect your people Israel from their devourers.

יזכו לראות בטובת בחיריך. ולשמוח בשמחת גוייך.
May they see the favor of your sons, and rejoice in
the joy of your nations.

This manuscript (first publicized by R. Chaim Bloch, *Heikhal le-Divrei Haza"l u-Pitgamehem*, New York, 1948) has been determined to be a forgery by several noted scholars (see *inter alia*: R. Joseph Tabory, *Shefokh Hamatekha: Mashma'uto, ve-Nisyonot le-Shanoto*, 2012).

In response, it should be mentioned that nowhere does the liturgy say that **we** should take vengeance. Rather we ask the Almighty to take just vengeance for us. Furthermore, it would seem to me that we have no reason to be apologetic following the Holocaust when six million of our brethren were murdered and the world, for the most part, stood silent! Again in recent times, on Simhat Torah (October 7th) 2023 some 1200 Israelis were barbarically massacred by Hamas terrorists in southern Israel –much of the world refused to condemn this carnage, nor the accompanying beastly actions. Jews are not taught to turn the other cheek, and we will not let Jewish life be cheap. That is why we have the Israel Defense Forces. It is also one of the fundamental lessons of the *Sho'ah* – and why *Yom ha-Sho'ah* is critical to the identity of the Modern Jewish State. *Shefokh Hamatekha* is an expression of Jewish pride. Throughout the millennia – be it during the crusades, Spanish Inquisition, expulsions, pogroms, and the holocaust – Jews stood proud when reciting this paragraph because of their unshakeable faith that justice will ultimately prevail; evil will be eradicated. What's more, *Shefokh Hamatekha* is the fulfillment of the imperatives formulated by Jewish philosopher and Holocaust survivor Emil Fackenheim ("The Jewish Return to History," 1978):

> [The 614th Commandment:] Jews are forbidden to grant posthumous victories to Hitler. They are commanded to survive as Jews, lest the Jewish people perish. They are commanded to remember the victims of Auschwitz, lest their memory perish… They are forbidden to despair of the God of Israel, lest Judaism perish.

Thus we affirm that we will continue to survive as a people. We will not forget or forgive the atrocities perpetuated against us. And we call on

14. הַלֵּל

the Almighty to set the record straight. We may justifiably doubt Man, but we certainly have not given up on God.

הַלֵּל

We have described the splitting of the reading of *Hallel* above (at the end of our comments to גָּאַל יִשְׂרָאֵל), and we now begin the second half. *Tosafot* (*Sukka*, 38a, *s.v Mi she-Haya*) indicates that *Hallel* at the *Seder* is **not** the same as the *Hallel* recited following *Shaharit* on the Holidays. On the latter, Hallel is said as an expression of *simha yeteira* – the special quality of joy present on these special days. Here at the *Seder*, says Tosafot, *Hallel* was mandated *al ha-nes* because of the miraculous *Makkat Bekhorot* and the Egyptian Exodus. All this is symbolized by the *Korban Pesah* and, hence, *Hallel* was recited **during its sacrifice** in the Temple and again during the *Seder* **when it is eaten** (see: *Mishna, Pesahim* 95a). However, in a private conversation, R. Nachum Rabinovitch explained that this cannot be fulfilled literally because *Halakha* forbids conversation while your mouth is full: *Ein meisihin bi-se'uda* (BT, *Ta'anit* 5b; JT, *Berakhot* 6:6; *Shulhan Arukh*, *OH*, 170:1). As a consequence, we say the first two chapters of *Hallel* before eating [*Pesah,*] Matza and *Maror* and the remainder of *Hallel* after *Afikoman* and *Birkat ha-Mazon*.

At this juncture we should ask: what do we mean when we say *Hallel*? We know that on Holidays it includes Psalms 113–118 (dubbed *Hallel ha-Mitzri*) and concludes with the *Yehalelukha* benediction. By contrast, *Hallel* at the *Seder* includes **three** components: 1) The first is indeed *Hallel ha-Mitzri* said on the *regalim* and *Hanukah* which appropriately for *Pesah* includes *be-Tzeit Yisrael mi-Mitzrayim*. 2) The second element is *Hallel ha-Gadol*, Psalms 136 with its 26 verses ending *Ki le-olam hasdo* – "His lovingkindness is everlasting." Of the 26 verses in this Psalm more than half focus on God's role in the Egyptian redemption, the crossing of the Yam Suf, and the conquest of Canaan. 3) The third part is *Birkat ha-Shir* – "The Blessing of Song," which is the beautifully poetic *Nishmat kol hai* including *Shokhen ad* through *Yishtabah* – which we regularly say on *Shabbat* and *Yom Tov*. While it is predominantly

14. Hallel

universalistic in nature, it does indeed contain several verses dealing with our bondage and redemption from Egypt and sustenance in the desert. At the *Seder*, the fancy *berakha* ending *Yishtabah* supplements (and in other traditions replaces) the simple *Yehalelukha* ending of *Hallel*. Thus, the *Hallel* we say at the *Seder* is a much-expanded *Hallel* with an appropriately celebrative ending.

R. Joseph B. Soloveitchik (quoted by R. Ari Kahn, *Haggada Od Yosef Hai*; http://arikahn.blogspot.com/2013/03/blog-post_8.html) asks, why don't we sing the *Shirat ha-Yam* (*Az Yashir*) at the *Seder* as the song that celebrates Hashem's deliverance from slavery? Why did *Haza"l* choose *Hallel* as the celebratory song of the *Seder*? He answers based on Rashi's commentary to II Samuel 23:1 which describes David *ha-Melekh* as the "sweet singer of Israel." Rashi explains "The Jewish people do not sing songs of praise to the Almighty in the *Bet ha-Mikdash* unless it was composed by David *ha-Melekh*." R. Soloveitchik observes that the same applies to *Pesukei de-Zimra*, where we say in *Barukh she-Amar* that we will sing David *ha-Melekh*'s songs of praise to the Creator. Indeed, it is for this reason that Maimonides (*Hilkhot Tefilla* 7:13) records a custom to recite *Shirat ha-Yam* in our daily prayers only **after** the *berakha* of *Yishtabah* is recited. He believes that since David *ha-Melekh* did not compose the *Shirat ha-Yam*, its place is not in the *Pesukei de-Zimra* that is recited between *Barukh she-Amar* and *Yishtabakh*. Similarly, R. Soloveitchik suggests that at the *Seder* we utilize only songs composed by David *ha-Melekh* to sing praise to *Hashem* for redeeming us from *Mitzrayim*.

For completeness, we should clarify that *Haza"l* refer to Psalms 145–150 as *Hallel she-be-Khol Yom*. These are the Psalms that were chosen for *Pesukei de-Zimra* because they deal with praising God as the omnipotent Creator – in control of Nature – and the God of History. The themes are universal and, hence, not completely appropriate for *Seder* night, since they don't emphasize the unique relationship between God and the People of Israel.

הלל המצרי (המשך, תהלים פרקים קטו-קיח)

(תהלים פרק קטו): לֹא לָנוּ. ה'. לֹא לָנוּ. כִּי לְשִׁמְךָ תֵּן כָּבוֹד. עַל חַסְדְּךָ עַל אֲמִתֶּךָ. לָמָּה יֹאמְרוּ הַגּוֹיִם אַיֵּה נָא אֱלֹהֵיהֶם. וֵאלֹהֵינוּ בַשָּׁמַיִם. כֹּל אֲשֶׁר חָפֵץ עָשָׂה. עֲצַבֵּיהֶם כֶּסֶף וְזָהָב מַעֲשֵׂה יְדֵי אָדָם. פֶּה לָהֶם וְלֹא יְדַבֵּרוּ. עֵינַיִם לָהֶם וְלֹא יִרְאוּ. אָזְנַיִם לָהֶם וְלֹא יִשְׁמָעוּ. אַף לָהֶם וְלֹא יְרִיחוּן. יְדֵיהֶם וְלֹא יְמִישׁוּן. רַגְלֵיהֶם וְלֹא יְהַלֵּכוּ. לֹא יֶהְגּוּ בִּגְרוֹנָם. כְּמוֹהֶם יִהְיוּ עֹשֵׂיהֶם. כֹּל אֲשֶׁר בֹּטֵחַ בָּהֶם. יִשְׂרָאֵל בְּטַח בַּה'. עֶזְרָם וּמָגִנָּם הוּא. בֵּית אַהֲרֹן בִּטְחוּ בַה'. עֶזְרָם וּמָגִנָּם הוּא. יִרְאֵי ה' בִּטְחוּ בַה'. עֶזְרָם וּמָגִנָּם הוּא.

הלל המצרי

Hallel ha-Mitzri is in many ways radically different from *Hallel she-be-Khol Yom* and *Hallel ha-Gadol* – both in tone and content. While the other *Hallel*s focus on God almost exclusively, *Hallel ha-Mitzri* places a major emphasis on man and his relationship with God. Thus, the first two chapters (Psalms 113–114) said at the end of *Maggid*, talk about the Almighty's omnipotence and introduces Him as the God of Nature and History (see our comments to שִׁירָה חֲדָשָׁה). In this second part (Psalms 115–118), following *Shefokh Hamatekha*, the Psalmist introduces his varied life experiences, emotions, fears, and hopes – and he uses the first person. The content is almost always autobiographical, and realistic but we are not sure of the incident. In contradistinction to the other *Hallels*, the second part of *Hallel ha-Mitzri* is full of personal prayer, request, and praise. A few examples follow:

> I love the Lord, for he hears my voice, my pleas (Psalms 116:1).
> Lord, I pray, save my life (ibid. 4).
> In my distress I called on the Lord. The Lord answered me and set me free (Psalms 118:4).
> The Lord is my strength and my song. He has become my salvation (ibid. 25).

The psalmist is afraid of suffering and death but at the same time expresses faith in the Almighty's salvation.

Hallel ha-Mitzri – Part 2

Not for us, Lord, not for us, but for Your Name's sake give honor, for Your kindness and Your truth. Why should the nations say, "Where is their God?" Our God is in the heavens, whatever He wills, He does. Their idols are of silver and gold, the product of human hands. They have a mouth, but cannot speak; they have eyes, but cannot see. They have ears, but cannot hear; they have a nose, but cannot smell; their hands cannot feel; their feet cannot walk; they can make no sound with their throat. Let those who make them become like them, whoever trusts in them! Israel, trust in the Lord! He is their help and their shield. House of Aaron, trust in the Lord! He is their help and their shield. You who fear the Lord, trust in the Lord! He is their help and their shield (Psalms 115:1–11).

> For you have rescued me from death, my eyes from weeping, my feet from stumbling (Psalms 116:8).
> I will not die, but live, and tell the world what the Lord has done (Psalms 118:17).
> The Lord has chastened me severely, but He has not given me over to death (ibid. 18).

To paraphrase R. Joseph B. Soloveitchik, *Hallel ha-Mitzri* is not only a shout of joy, but also an outcry of pain – there is an inner contradiction. We say: "This is the day that *Hashem* has made. Let us rejoice and be glad in it," while in the same breadth we say, *Ana Hashem hoshi'a na!* – "Please, Lord, save us!"

This is very important, because starting with the fourth cup of wine, we are acutely aware of the *Hurban ha-Bayit* – the destruction of the Temple, and reminded that we are deep in the exile waiting for the future redemption. We no longer experience the Almighty's public miracles and clear intervention in human affairs. On the contrary, we suffer from *hester panim* – a hidden God or *Deus Absconditus*. This was the very experience of King David who from his anointing as King suffered nothing but challenges, trials, and tribulations. It was these experiences that gave birth to *Hallel*. Indeed, *Hallel ha-Mitzri*, with its mixture of fear and faith, trepidation and trust, helplessness and hope, desperation and devotion – is the most appropriate selection of *Psalms* for the insecure *galut* Jew who is buffeted by the changing winds of history. Such a Jew thanks the Almighty for personal or communal miracles, while clearly remembering the pain and dread. Thus, even though *Hallel* was written three millennia ago it remains relevant to those sitting around the *Seder* table.

Nechama Leibowitz (*Leaders Guide to the Book of Psalms*, 1971) tackles the question of the relevance of *Psalms* from a different perspective: "[Do not] read these Psalms as documents from an ancient time, as records of Israel in olden days, but rather as poetry which transcends time. The "I" who speaks in these chapters is not the "I" of King David, Asaph, or Ben-Korah. The "I" who speaks, weeps, expresses joy, offers thanks to God, and cries for help, is the "I" of the reader at that very moment of reading. For indeed, all great literature is contemporaneous with the reader of any time...Each generation brought to the words of Psalms its own experiences, joys and tribulations, problems and tensions, faith and trust, and hopes and disappointments."

R. Kalman Farber (Itamar Levin, *Haggada Dam va-Esh ve-Timrot Ashan*) describes the recitation of *Hallel* on *Seder* Night in the Vilna Ghetto in 1942. The relevance of the *Hallel* was obvious.

> It was not a regular prayer but more of a heated conversation with the Almighty. You sensed that you were setting forth before the Heavenly throne valid claims, which rose from the depths of your heart – and which could cut right through all disinterest. *Lo lanu Hashem lo lanu – ki le-shimkha ten kavod* – We also raised the issue of God's holy name being defiled. *Lama yomru ha-goyim: ayei elokeihem.* And, of course, we presented the argument that: *Lo ha-meitim yehallelu Ka, ve-lo kol yordei duma.* Our spirits were cleansed and uplifted by what we intuited was an intimate conversation and heart-to-heart discussion with the Creator who could no longer remain indifferent.

As indicated above, the *Hallel* recited in the *Haggada* is not simply *Hallel ha-Mitzri*; this is because the *Haggada*'s goal is to leave *Seder* participants with hope and happiness. To this end, *Haza"l* chose to expand the scope of *Hallel ha-Mitzri* at the *Seder* with *Hallel ha-Gadol*.

The latter talks about *Pesaḥ* themes: *Makkat Bekhorot*, the splitting of the Red Sea, and the conquest of the Land of Israel – but also the creation of Heaven and Earth and the luminaries. Thus, we thank God on this night of *Pesaḥ* not only for the miracles of Egypt, but also for the miracles of our very existence, the miracles of Creation. But most notable for the Jew in Exile waiting for Messiah are verses 23 and 24 of *Hallel ha-Gadol* (Psalm 136) which reads: *she-be-Shifleinu zakhar lanu… va-yifrekeinu mi-tzareinu* – "in our lowliness He remembers us … and redeems us from our tormentors." And then we conclude *Hallel* at the *Seder* with *Nishmat*. This beautifully poetic piece emphasizes God's omnipotence and beneficence and we are informed that the Almighty really does care about us. All this bolsters our hopes for a truly promising future as foretold by the prophets and tradition. As we shall see, the ultimate message of the *Seder* is: "Jews, hang in there! Redemption and salvation are coming."

לֹא לָנוּ

The transitions in the *Haggada* are not always obvious or clear. So let us review why the transition from *Shefokh Hamatekha* into *Lo lanu* and the second part of *Hallel* is really quite natural and appropriate for the *Seder*. One of the central themes of the Egyptian redemption is God's revelation to the world as the God of Nature and History. When Moshe and Aharon first come to Pharaoh demanding the release of the Hebrews. Pharaoh says (Ex. 5:2): "Who is Hashem that I should heed him and let Israel go? I do not know Hashem …." To this God responds (Ex. 7:5): "Egypt shall know that I am Hashem …" And then again (Ex. 7:17): "Thus says Hashem, 'By this (Plague of Blood) you shall know that I am Hashem …'"

As we have mentioned above, this fourth cup expresses a yearning for the era of Eliyahu and the Messiah, when all nations will come to know the God of Israel and acknowledge His existence and dominion. Thus, *Shefokh Hamatekha* – "Pour out your rage upon the nations that do not know You" – flows seamlessly into *Lo lanu* and "Why should the nations say: 'Where now is their God?'" It is a call to the Almighty to once again reveal Himself to the world so that our detractors will stop taunting us and defaming God. As the Prophet Isaiah states (Isaiah

11:9) regarding the end of days: "For the land shall be filled with the knowledge of the Lord as water covers the sea."

Lo lanu goes on to emphasize that our God is not like the gods of the other nations. Their idols do not see, do not speak, do not hear, and so on, whereas the God of Israel is described as doing all of these things. Rav Shimshon Refael Hirsch explains (Deut. 4:28) that pagans had two different concepts of their idols. There were the common, simple people who believed that some divine spirit resided in the wood and stone that had been crafted for them by other men. The more educated pagans realized that the idols were but mere representations of some higher forces that existed in the world, and it was those higher forces that they were worshipping. Either way, our statements here in *Hallel* refer to both of these groups. Obviously, the dead stone and wood had no sensory powers, but even the forces of nature that were believed to be represented by the graven images were also powerless to help mankind in any way befitting of a true deity. These forces have no true freedom of choice since they too are bound by laws and the will of the God of Israel.

לֹא לָנוּ, ה', לֹא לָנוּ

R. Abraham Twerski (*Haggada Mi-Shi'abud li-Geula* – A Psychological Approach to the *Haggada*) explains this passage as follows. Often we feel unworthy of God's grace, and hence, incapable of turning to Him in prayer in our time of need. To this, the Psalmist responds that each of us has been created in the image of God – with a spark of God's spirituality (*ḥelek eloka mi-ma'al*) embedded in each of us. When our esteem is at an all-time low, man hesitates to ask his Creator a favor for his own sake. Hence, we say: *Lo lanu, Hashem, lo lanu* – "Save us not for our sake but for God's essence that lies within us." "I was created," says Man, "in the image of God. Hence, what happens to me reflects on Your Honor. Therefore, I come to You, O' Lord, in prayer to defend Your name and honor. Grant me Your blessing."

אַיֵּה נָא אֱלֹהֵיהֶם

What is the meaning of the word *na* in this context? There are three possibilities: 1) *Na* could mean please as it usually does, but in a taunting tone of voice as if to say: Pretty **please**! Could we see your God?" 2)

It could be a word of emphasis as in (Gen. 27:2) *Hineh na zakanti* – "I am **indeed** old." Thus, this verse could mean: "Could we indeed see your God?" 3) Finally, many commentaries, including *Targum Onkelos*, translate *Na* as **now**. Thus, this verse would mean: So where is your God now? Why isn't he intervening on your behalf now? (A fourth meaning – raw – is not relevant here.)

עֲצַבֵּיהֶם כֶּסֶף וְזָהָב

The verse *Atzabeihem kesef ve-zahav* is usually understood as their gods are **made from** silver and gold. R. Don Yitzhak Abravanel, the scholarly mid-fifteenth-century treasurer of Ferdinand and Isabella of Spain, insightfully suggests that we translate this verse literally: Their gods **are** silver and gold. Quite often the idolaters **worshipped** their money of silver and gold – viewing it as the all-powerful ends, not just a means. How modern this interpretation seems!

פֶּה לָהֶם וְלֹא יְדַבֵּרוּ

There are several points in the next three verses that deserve comment. Firstly, there is a great deal of redundancy. It should have said: "Their gods are from silver and gold made by human hands. They cannot speak, see, hear, smell, feel or walk." The point is that a worthy god should be able to do all this even without the appropriate limbs. But these idols are so lacking in value that they actually have a mouth, eyes, ears, and nose and still can't do anything! (*Haggada Talelei Orot*). Secondly, the Gaon of Vilna (cited by R. Reuven Margaliot, *Haggada*) points out that when it comes to a mouth, eyes, ears, and nose, the verse says **lahem** – "belongs to them." But when it refers to arms or legs *lahem* does not appear. The Gra resolves this discrepancy based on a *Mishna* in *Avoda Zara* (41a) which reads: "One who finds unidentifiable fragments of statues, these are permitted (i.e., one may derive benefit from them). If, however, one found an object in the figure of a hand or a foot, these are forbidden, as objects similar to these are worshipped." Thus, a mouth, eyes, and ears are only forbidden if they are *lahem* – connected to the idol. While arms or legs broken off from the idol – not *lahem* – are still forbidden. (Many other scholars have suggested this novel idea.)

ה' זְכָרָנוּ יְבָרֵךְ. יְבָרֵךְ אֶת בֵּית יִשְׂרָאֵל. יְבָרֵךְ אֶת בֵּית אַהֲרֹן, יְבָרֵךְ יִרְאֵי ה'. הַקְּטַנִּים עִם הַגְּדֹלִים. יֹסֵף ה' עֲלֵיכֶם. עֲלֵיכֶם וְעַל בְּנֵיכֶם. בְּרוּכִים אַתֶּם לַה'. עֹשֵׂה שָׁמַיִם וָאָרֶץ. הַשָּׁמַיִם שָׁמַיִם לַה' וְהָאָרֶץ נָתַן לִבְנֵי אָדָם. לֹא הַמֵּתִים יְהַלְלוּ יָהּ וְלֹא כָּל יֹרְדֵי דוּמָה. וַאֲנַחְנוּ נְבָרֵךְ יָהּ מֵעַתָּה וְעַד עוֹלָם. הַלְלוּיָהּ.

כְּמוֹהֶם יִהְיוּ עֹשֵׂיהֶם

R. Abraham Twerski (*Haggada Mi-Shi'abud li-Ge'ula*) notes that one has to be very careful as to what or whom he chooses as his god, because one tends to emulate it. If one chooses a god of silver or gold – then like that mute, inanimate, and uncaring god – he/she too will lack the aspirations to communicate and empathize with their fellow. As the verse says, "Those who make them will become like them." By contrast, the People of Israel trust in Hashem. By doing this we emulate a Divine Being which enhances our spiritual nature. This is known as (Deut. 28:9) *ve-Halakhta bi-derakhav* (in Latin: Emulatio or Imitatio Dei) – "walking in God's footsteps" (*Sota* 14a): "One should follow the attributes of the Holy One, Blessed be He: Just as He clothes the naked... visits the sick... consoles mourners... buries the dead... so too, should you."

יִשְׂרָאֵל בְּטַח בַּה'

In this paragraph (first half of Psalms 115), we find three subdivisions of the worshipers: *Yisrael*, *Bet Aharon*, and *Yirei Hashem*. In the next paragraph (second half of Psalms 115), we find: *Bet Yisrael*, *Bet Aharon*, and *Yirei Hashem*. In Psalms 118, we have: *Yisrael*, *Bet Aharon*, and *Yirei Hashem*. Finally, in *Pesukei de-Zimra* of *Shabbat* (Psalms 135) we have four divisions: *Bet Yisrael*, *Bet Aharon*, *Bet ha-Levi*, and *Yirei Hashem*. *Bet Yisrael* – House of Israel is presumably the general populace, *Klal Yisrael*. *Bet Aharon* – House of Aharon is undoubtedly the *Kohanim*, while *Bet ha-Levi* – House of Levy, are the Levites. But who are the *Yirei Hashem* – those that fear the Lord? There seems to be a gradation here and the *Yirei Hashem* is at the top of the list! (They can't be the Levites since the latter are explicitly mentioned in Psalms 135!)

Interestingly, Rashi suggests that this top position is held by converts

The Lord, Who has been mindful of us, will bless – He will bless the House of Israel; He will bless the House of Aaron; He will bless those who revere the Lord, the small with the great. May the Lord increase you, you and your children. Blessed are you to the Lord, Maker of heaven and earth. The heavens are the heavens of the Lord, but the earth, He has given to mankind. The dead cannot praise God, nor any who go down into the silence of the grave. But we will bless God, from now to eternity. Halleluyah (Psalms 115:12–18).

---

who have never experienced normative Judaism as a way of life, yet have decided to tie their lot with Israel. Similarly, *Ibn Ezra* posits that they are the righteous of the nations – *Hasidei umot ha-olam*. Radak suggests that the *Yirei Hashem* are scholars who study God's Torah and contemplate God's ways. Following this approach, Leeor Gottlieb (personal conversation) clarifies that while *Yisrael* and *Bet Aharon* are each an inherited status, *Yirei Hashem* is open to anyone who devotes himself to study God's ways and his Torah. This is indeed the highest religious level. Finally, the Maharal *mi-Prague* views these three categories as different ways individuals approach God. The first group, *Bet Yisrael*, are those who serve God out of love like a father. The second group, *Bet Aharon*, are those whose love leads them to be totally devoted to God's service like *Kohanim*. The *Yirei Hashem*, are those who serve the Almighty out of awe. By each group, the Psalmist says: "He is their help and their shield," because each group has different spiritual and emotional needs, and God tailors his response accordingly.

ה' זְכָרָנוּ יְבָרֵךְ

This paragraph is the second half of Psalm 115 and also a thematic continuation. We just said that *Yisrael, Bet Aharon*, and *Yirei Hashem* trust in the Almighty who helps and protects them. But He not only defends us, He is proactive and blesses us. He can do this because as the God of Creation, He is the maker of Heavens and Earth. Hence, He is in control. This is not the God of the Greek philosophers, who set the world spinning and is no longer involved. Rather, the Jewish God is one who creates, cares, commands, and is also involved. Only such a God is worthy of praise!

This paragraph begins: *Hashem zekharanu, yevarekh* – "Hashem who has remembered us, will bless us." But how can an omniscient God "remember" – if He cannot forget? In a *shiur* given in 1958, R. Joseph B. Soloveitchik argued that the purpose of memory in Judaism is to effect change. The word *zakhor* does not denote the mere recollection of past events – but rather becoming involved with another. Indeed, whenever the Bible says *va-Yizkor Hashem,* the verse means that the Almighty became actively involved in their lives. Thus, when God remembered Noah in the Ark (Gen. 8:1), it was to bring him to dry land. And when God remembered the matriarchs (Gen. 21:1 and 30:22) and Chana (I Samuel, 1:19), it was to enable them to conceive. When God recalled his covenant with the patriarchs, it was to redeem their progeny from the travails of Egypt.

In this light, when we are commanded to "Remember the Sabbath day to keep it holy (Ex. 20:8)," the goal is not the memory. Rather, we are bidden to become involved in some small way in the process of Creation. Just as the Almighty sanctified the seventh day, we too are empowered to convert "chronos" into "chiros": a neutral 24-hour period into an event of holiness. Similarly, when we "Remember this day of Exodus from Egypt" (Ex. 13:3), the goal is that "In every generation, each Jew should feel as if he himself had been released from Egypt." The purpose of the *Seder* is to transport us back in time so that the Egypt experience and its lessons become incorporated into our lives. Thus, in the *Hallel,* when we say *Hashem zekharanu, yevarekh* we are acknowledging that when God remembers us and becomes involved in our life – it is a source of blessing. This is true not only for us but also for the entire nation: *Bet Yisrael, Bet Aharon,* and *Yirei Hashem.*

יְבָרֵךְ אֶת בֵּית יִשְׂרָאֵל

R. Barukh Epstein (*Barukh she-Amar, Hallel*) asks why the Psalmist uses the term *Bet Yisrael* and not *Bet Avraham* or *Bet Yitzhak.* The answer is that *Bet* connotes nobility of birth – but Avraham had Yitzhak and Yishmael, while Yitzhak had Yaakov and Esav. Only Yaakov/Yisrael's progeny was pure; only his home was complete enough for *Bet Yisrael.* R. Epstein also wonders why we find *Bet Aharon* but not *Bet Yirei Hashem.* He suggests that *Bet* suggests a familial connection, while

Yirei Hashem is a self-selected group from throughout Israel and the righteous of the nations.

הַשָּׁמַיִם שָׁמַיִם לַה' וְהָאָרֶץ נָתַן לִבְנֵי אָדָם

The Talmud (*Berakhot* 35a,b) cites R. Levi who questions the meaning of our verse: "R. Levi contrasted two texts. It is written: 'The heavens are the Lord's, but the earth He has given over to mankind.' (Psalms 115:16) [This implies that the Earth belongs to mankind.] But it is also written, 'The earth is the Lord's, and the fullness thereof (Psalms 115:16).' [To whom then does the earth belong, to God or to man?] [The Talmud responds:] There is no contradiction: in one case, it is before a *berakha* has been said, in the other case, after."

The usual interpretation explains that before one makes a *berakha*, everything belongs to God; hence, partaking of something without a blessing is in effect a theft from the Creator. But as a result of the *berakha*, the Almighty grants us permission to partake of the physical world. In effect, before the blessing, the world is God's, and after the blessing, He gives the world's bounty to us to enjoy and use.

In a unique twist, R. Ahron Soloveichik turns this interpretation on its head: "The heavens are the Lord's, but the earth He has given over to mankind [Psalms 115:16]" is the description of the world before blessings, and the verse, "The earth is the Lord's and the fullness thereof," is after the blessing! Why? A world devoid of blessings is a world without any Divine connection or spiritual content. Under such conditions, the spiritual belongs to the heavenly domain, to God, while the physical is the sphere of humanity. But once a human being utters a blessing, humanity is suffusing the physical sphere with Divine spirituality. If the Torah has one urgent message, it's the importance of sanctifying our physical world by connection to God.

R. Ben Zion Nesher (*Haggada Shir Zion*) and R. Reuven Margaliot (*Haggada*) read R. Soloveitchik's idea into the text: The Heavens are the heavens of God, but the Earth was given to the children of man – to sanctify it and covert it into *shamayim*. *Lo ha-Metim yehallelu Kah* – The dead can do nothing to correct the situation. *Ve-Anahnu nevarekh Kah* – but we the living can bless God the Creator – and thereby sanctify the world.

(תהלים פרק קטז): אָהַבְתִּי כִּי יִשְׁמַע ה' אֶת קוֹלִי תַּחֲנוּנָי. כִּי הִטָּה אָזְנוֹ לִי וּבְיָמַי אֶקְרָא. אֲפָפוּנִי חֶבְלֵי מָוֶת וּמְצָרֵי שְׁאוֹל מְצָאוּנִי. צָרָה וְיָגוֹן אֶמְצָא. וּבְשֵׁם ה' אֶקְרָא: אָנָּא ה' מַלְּטָה נַפְשִׁי. חַנּוּן ה' וְצַדִּיק. וֵאלֹהֵינוּ מְרַחֵם. שֹׁמֵר פְּתָאיִם ה'. דַּלּוֹתִי וְלִי יְהוֹשִׁיעַ. שׁוּבִי נַפְשִׁי לִמְנוּחָיְכִי. כִּי ה' גָּמַל עָלָיְכִי. כִּי חִלַּצְתָּ נַפְשִׁי מִמָּוֶת. אֶת עֵינִי מִן דִּמְעָה. אֶת רַגְלִי מִדֶּחִי. אֶתְהַלֵּךְ לִפְנֵי ה' בְּאַרְצוֹת הַחַיִּים. הֶאֱמַנְתִּי כִּי אֲדַבֵּר. אֲנִי עָנִיתִי מְאֹד. אֲנִי אָמַרְתִּי בְחָפְזִי כָּל הָאָדָם כֹּזֵב.

Returning to "The heavens are the Lord's," R. Aharon Lichtenstein in an Essay entitled "Rav Soloveitchik's Approach to Zionism," comments:

> The Rav [R. Joseph B. Soloveitchik] had no patience for philosophies that glorified passivity and reliance on miracles. At the beginning of the 1960s, a few years after the launch of Sputnik, I had occasion to talk with the Rav about those people who claimed that man should not reach out for the heavens, for "the heavens are the heavens of God," and only "the earth is given to human beings." The Rav heaped scorn upon them. One of those present jumped up to protest: "But Rabbi, the Ramban in *be-Hukotai* (*Lev.* 26:11) speaks about how a person should have faith in the Holy One, and not to delve into matters that are too wondrous for him." [The discussion there refers to disease.] The Rav replied, "I heard from my father, in the name of my grandfather, that the Ramban never uttered that statement!"

לֹא הַמֵּתִים יְהַלְלוּ יָהּ וְלֹא כָּל יֹרְדֵי דוּמָה

For David *ha-Melekh*, the greatest tragedy of being dead is the inability to be an *Oved Hashem* – one who serves the Almighty, which is the primary purpose of man on this earth. It is only through the body that we can do *mitzvot* and that ability is gone when we die. This is also a loss for the Almighty, since only those alive can praise God and publicize His works, as we declare here: *Lo ha-meitim yehallelu Kah*… (This theme appears several times in *Psalms*; see, e.g., Psalms 30:10:

I love it when the Lord hears my voice, my prayers. For He has inclined His ear to me; and in my own days I will call upon Him. The pains of death encompassed me, and the confines of the grave have found me, trouble and sorrow I encountered. And I called upon the Name of the Lord: "Please, Lord, deliver my soul!" The Lord is gracious and just, our God is compassionate. The Lord watches over the simple; I was brought low, but He saved me. Return, my soul, to your resting place, for the Lord has dealt kindly with you. For You have delivered my soul from death, my eyes from tears, my feet from stumbling. I shall walk before the Lord in the land of the living. I had faith even while speaking of how I suffer so much [even though] I said in haste, "All mankind is deceitful." (Psalms 116:1–11).

"What is to be gained from my death, from my descent into a grave? Can dust praise You? Can it declare Your faithfulness?") Unfortunately, however, there are those who are physically alive, but spiritually dead. These are the …*Kol Yordei Duma* – "those who descend into silence" and are equated with the dead because they too remain silent and don't praise *Hashem* in word or deed.

וַאֲנַחְנוּ נְבָרֵךְ יָהּ מֵעַתָּה וְעַד עוֹלָם. הַלְלוּיָהּ

In the way of introduction, I should point out that the importance of many Hassidic homilies (*vertilakh*; singular *vort*), is not necessarily in the correctness of their understanding of the text. Rather it is in the correctness of the insight they impart! R. Abraham Weinberg (the first Rebbi of Slonim, cited by R. Reuven Margaliot in his Haggada) insightfully points out that when one comes to pray to his Creator, he often feels unworthy because of his sins or lack of spirituality. He hasn't spent enough time learning or doing *mitzvot*. That feeling of inadequacy, says R. Abraham, comes from the *Yetzer ha-Ra* (evil inclination) who wants you to give up without trying. The critical thing is that – in the *va-anahnu nevarekh Kah* – in coming close to Hashem in prayer, there is an honest commitment to the future, to *me-ata ve-ad olam, Halleluya*.

אָהַבְתִּי כִּי יִשְׁמַע ה' אֶת קוֹלִי תַּחֲנוּנָי

We just concluded the previous Psalm by noting that the deceased cannot praise God – but we the living can! In this next chapter, David ha-Melekh – representing the paradigmatic Jew – asserts that the All-Merciful hears our prayers. Because the Almighty cares, this attention creates an intimate relationship with Him. At the same time, King David knows that just because God hears, doesn't, therefore, mean that He will answer affirmatively. "No," after all is also an answer, but at least there is hope. I can trust in God because He prefers me alive serving Him and doing His *mitzvot*. By contrast, I cannot truly trust in man – because he is fickle and ephemeral.

The commentaries, as a rule, understand the opening line as if it were written: *Ahavti [et Hashem] ki yishma et koli tahanunai* – "I love [**God**] because He hears my voice and supplications." But this would imply that my love of the Almighty is dependent on His hearing my prayers. By contrast, Abravanel suggests parsing the sentence as follows: *Ahavti – ki yishma Hashem et koli – tahanunai*. Namely, "I love my **supplications** because God hears my voice. I value my prayers because I know the Infinite hears my plea!

R. Shneur Zalman of Liadi (the first Lubavitcher Rebbi) is quoted as saying the following Hassidishe Vort: If you want God to love **you** and listen to **your** prayers – *Ki yishma Hashem et koli tahanunai*, then begin your prayers by saying: *Ahavti* – "I love my fellow Jews." Indeed, R. Hayim Vital cites his teacher R. Isaac Luria (Arizal) as urging all to say before their morning prayers – *Hareni mekabbel alai mitzvat asei shel ve-Ahavta le-reakha ka-mokha* (Lev. 19:18) – "I accept upon myself the positive commandment of loving my fellow Jew."

וּבְשֵׁם ה' אֶקְרָא

As posited above, this chapter (Psalms 116, which is comprised of both *Ahavti* and *Ma Ashiv*) is a statement of faith that God hears our prayers. What's more, He cares about me, leans towards me, and figuratively cups His ear – *Ki hita ozno li* – to hear me better. The chapter records three instances in particular where the Psalmist called out to Hashem: (1) *Afafuni hevlei mavet… **u-ve-shem Hashem ekra*** – In the first case, I call out to Hashem when my life is in **danger** and I am surrounded by trouble. This response is natural and expected since man does not have too many options! (2) *Kos yeshu'ot esa,* **u-ve-shem Hashem ekra** – The second instance is a moment of **triumph** and victory when I could have taken credit for my resilience and ingenuity – I, nevertheless, thank the Almighty and give Him credit for my victory. And (3) *Lekha ezbah zevah toda,* **u-ve-shem Hashem ekra** – **I thank God generally** for all the good He has bestowed. In every life situation, be it trouble, victory, or thanksgiving, the Jewish response is always the same – call out in the Name of God.

אָנָּא ה' מַלְּטָה נַפְשִׁי

Commentaries have proposed that *Ana* might mean please, indeed, or thank you, as discussed above.

הֶאֱמַנְתִּי כִּי אֲדַבֵּר. אֲנִי עָנִיתִי מְאֹד

This verse can be translated as: I have faith and trust in Hashem, even though I declare that I am deeply suffering. In this regard, R. Jonathan Sacks ("A Message for Yom Kippur," 2006) asks "What is faith?" To which he profoundly answers:

> Faith is the belief that life has a purpose, that we are not here by accident, that history is not meaningless, and that it is not merely wishful thinking that we live by ideals. The Almighty is not deaf to our prayers, blind to our hopes, or indifferent to our existence.
>
> My faith as a Jew tells me that our ancestors were not wrong to pledge themselves, in the Sinai desert thirty-three centuries ago, to a code of conduct, the Torah, that seeks to create communities based on justice, charity, compassion, and the sanctity of life. They were not wrong to believe that every human being – not just those who think like us – is made in God's image and thus entitled to dignity and respect.
>
> My faith tells me that it is not wrong to question, argue, debate, or wrestle with God. Our first request in the weekday *Amidah* is for "knowledge, understanding, and wisdom" – this is not a faith that asks us to sacrifice our intellect.
>
> Faith is not a certainty. Faith is the courage to live with

מָה אָשִׁיב לַה' כָּל תַּגְמוּלוֹהִי עָלָי. כּוֹס יְשׁוּעוֹת אֶשָּׂא וּבְשֵׁם ה' אֶקְרָא. נְדָרַי לַה' אֲשַׁלֵּם נֶגְדָה נָּא לְכָל עַמּוֹ. יָקָר בְּעֵינֵי ה' הַמָּוְתָה לַחֲסִידָיו. אָנָּה ה' כִּי אֲנִי עַבְדֶּךָ, אֲנִי עַבְדְּךָ בֶּן אֲמָתֶךָ, פִּתַּחְתָּ לְמוֹסֵרָי. לְךָ אֶזְבַּח זֶבַח תּוֹדָה וּבְשֵׁם ה' אֶקְרָא. נְדָרַי לַה' אֲשַׁלֵּם נֶגְדָה נָּא לְכָל עַמּוֹ. בְּחַצְרוֹת בֵּית ה'. בְּתוֹכֵכִי יְרוּשָׁלָיִם. הַלְלוּיָהּ.

---

uncertainty. Faith is the voice within us that says, "Though I walk through the valley of the shadow of death, I will fear no evil, for You are with me." Faith is the ability to live through catastrophe and yet not lose hope. Without faith, we would never take a risk. Without faith, we would never have a child. Without faith, we would never undertake anything great.

It was faith that led the Jewish people – only three years after standing eyeball to eyeball with the angel of death at Auschwitz – to proclaim the State of Israel, with its national anthem, *Od lo avda tikvatenu*, "Our hope is still not lost."

אֲנִי אָמַרְתִּי בְחָפְזִי כָּל הָאָדָם כֹּזֵב

We have noted that one of the things that makes *Psalms* so difficult is that many of the chapters have tremendous mood swings between desperation and faith, praise of God and exasperation. We find many examples of such swings in *Ahavti*. King David finds himself in constant trials and tribulations and life-threatening situations. He has often had to rely on individuals who at times mislead and betray him. In the end, it is God, not man, who comes through. Hence, he declares in anguish and frustration that one cannot rely on man! All men are liars and deceitful! The question is: Why is this conclusion considered to be an unfortunate generalization, one said rashly and in haste? The simple answer is that the assertion that *Kol ha-adam kozev* is inaccurate. Life experiences teach us that there are certainly some people that you **can** rely on, even if they are few and far between.

Da'at Mikra suggests that *kozev* is not deceitful but ephemeral, not lasting. King David seeing his precarious position asks: "What is man good for? If he is not lasting, one can't rely on them to be around when you really need them in the future." But even David realizes that this

How can I repay the Lord for all His kindnesses to me? I will raise the cup of salvation and call upon the Name of the Lord. I will pay my vows to the Lord in the presence of all His people. Precious in the eyes of the Lord is the death of His devout ones. Thank You, Lord, for allowing me to be Your servant; I am Your servant the son of Your handmaid: You have released my bonds. To You I will bring an offering of thanksgiving, and I will call upon the Name of the Lord. I will pay my vows to the Lord in the presence of all His people, in the courtyards of the House of the Lord, in the midst of Jerusalem. Halleluyah (Psalms 116:12–19).

---

statement was made in haste because man has some value; through *mitzvot* and Divine service, man can link himself to the Almighty – *ethalekh lifnei Hashem be-eretz ha-hayim* – and thus be connected to the Eternal.

R. Joseph B. Soloveitchik (in *Family Redeemed*) posits a very modern approach. He suggests that *kozev* should not be understood as deceitful but disappointing – not what they seem. man is a very complicated and complex creation, with conscious and unconscious mental processes. Hence, it is nigh impossible for a man to fully know **himself**. When one makes a commitment, it is not that he is consciously lying; rather he does not know the whole truth even about himself.

מָה אָשִׁיב לַה׳. כֹּל תַּגְמוּלוֹהִי עָלָי

As is clear from this chapter, King David has just survived another life-threatening experience and was redeemed by God. He feels a debt of gratitude to his Divine Savior but doesn't know how to pay Him properly. (1) R. Ben-Zion Nesher (*Haggada Shir Zion*) posits that the simple understanding of this verse is that there is a question (with an understood preposition) and answer here. The question is: *Ma ashiv la-Shem* [***bishvil***] *kol tagmulohi alai* – How can I repay Hashem [**for**] all the kindness He has done to me? The answer is: *Kos yeshu'ot esa* – I will repay him in public by raising a cup acknowledging His salvation, and invoking and publicizing His name in gratitude – *u-veshem Hashem ekra*.

(2) However, suggests R. Nesher, a better explanation of this verse understands *Kol tagmulohi alai* as the point of the question. The question now becomes: *Ma ashiv laShem* [**ka-asher**] *kol tagmulohi alai* – How can I repay God [**when**] all that I have to use – be it time, money, or resources – are in actuality from Him in the first place!? If I get a windfall profit and bring a *korban* or donation in thanks, then all I have done is give back to the Almighty what He has given me! If I sing a song of God's praises, it is God who has given me that breath, that song, the life spirit to thank Him. In effect, I've given Him nothing. This theme reminds one of the words of the Slonimer Niggun *Ki hirbeita tovot elai* (renewed by Abraham Fried) – and based on the *Shir ha-Yihud* for Sunday:

For you have done me many favors,	כִּי הִרְבֵּיתָ טוֹבוֹת אֵלָי.
and been generous in your kindnesses.	כִּי הִגְדַּלְתָּ חַסְדְּךָ עָלָי.
How can I repay you? All is yours!	וּמַה אָשִׁיב לְךָ וְהַכֹּל שֶׁלָּךְ
Yours is Heaven, even the Earth.	לְךָ שָׁמַיִם אַף אֶרֶץ לָךְ.
We are Your people and Your sheep,	וַאֲנַחְנוּ עַמְּךָ וְצֹאנֶךָ.
who desire to do Your will.	וַחֲפֵצִים לַעֲשׂוֹת רְצוֹנֶךָ.

Reiterating the question: How can I properly repay God **when** all that I have to use in showing my appreciation is, in actuality, from Him in the first place!? The answer is: *Kos yeshu'ot esa, u-ve-shem Hashem ekra. Nedarai LaShem ashalem* **negda na le-khol amo**. When I give my thanks, I do so publicly (*pirsumei nisa*), thereby multiplying my single hour of praise by all those present. This is equivalent to giving a one-hour *shiur* to 25 participants, which becomes 26 hours of *Torah* learning.

(3) It would seem to me, though, that all the Almighty wants is an honest appreciative "Thank You!" Like a loving parent, He has no qualms about doing kindness to his children and loved ones. That's the nature of love – to give, share, and make your beloved happy. All the lover wants is a "Thank You" said heartily and meaningfully. Raising a cup of gratitude and singing the Lord's praises is the essence of the *Seder* Night.

יָקָר בְּעֵינֵי ה' הַמָּוְתָה לַחֲסִידָיו

The word *yakar* means that it comes at great expense or cost. It is hard, difficult, and grievous to *Hashem* when His righteous ones die. We have already commented on the verse לֹא הַמֵּתִים יְהַלְלוּ יָהּ וְלֹא כָּל יֹרְדֵי דוּמָה that only the living can serve and praise Hashem, and only those alive can do *mitzvot*. Hence, King David's clear presumption is that God wants His righteous ones vital and full of life.

אָנָּה ה' כִּי אֲנִי עַבְדֶּךָ

This is a very multifaceted verse. The first problem is the meaning of the word *ana* – spelled: *aleph nun heh*. Some commentators (Rashbam, Ibn Ezra, and Malbim) suggest that *ana* with a final *heh* is like *ana* with a final *aleph* – and means "please." This is problematic in this verse since David *ha-Melekh* is not requesting anything specific. He is merely giving praise and declaring his willingness to serve the Almighty. (Malbim does indicate, however, that a request for salvation from his enemies is implied.)

Alternatively, some interpret *ana* with a final *heh* as: "indeed" or "truly." This verse would then be translated as: "Indeed Hashem, I am Your servant… because You have undone the cords of my bondage." We, as Jews, are God's servants – both legally and morally – because it was He who freed us from Egyptian slavery. This is the implication of the verse (Lev. 25:55): "For it is to Me that the Israelites are servants, they are My servants, whom I freed from the land of Egypt" (David Kessler).

However, to our mind, the most likely meaning (Radak and Metzudot) is that *ana* with a final *heh* regarding God means "Thank you." Thank you, God, for allowing me to be an *Eved Hashem* – to be God's servant. In contrast to being the slave of man, being the Almighty's servant does not require the loss of personal autonomy or freedom of choice. It means that I have made a commitment to carry out the **commands** of God, the *mitzvot*, as the highest priority in my life. Sadly, people think that they can attain "instant" spirituality without service. They delve into *Kabbala* and mysticism because it doesn't require any specific action. As seen from *Parashat Kedoshim* (Lev. Chaps. 19–20), *kedusha*

(תהלים פרק קיז): הַלְלוּ אֶת ה' כָּל גּוֹיִם. שַׁבְּחוּהוּ כָּל הָאֻמִּים. כִּי גָבַר עָלֵינוּ חַסְדּוֹ. וֶאֱמֶת ה' לְעוֹלָם. הַלְלוּיָהּ.

(sanctity) comes from fulfilling *mitzvot*! Furthermore, even individuals who are willing to do God's commandments and follow *halakha*, often want to be selective. They want to do those *mitzvot* that "speak to them," or "that are relevant to them." But Judaism, says R. Yehuda Amital (*Bein Hithabrut le-Mehuyavut*), speaks of commitment and obligation. In this light, Rav Amital explained the significance of forming the silver *adanim* foundation of the *Mishkan* (Tabernacle) specifically from the compulsory half-shekel tax – the only compulsory contribution imposed upon *Benei Yisrael*. All the other materials needed for the *Mishkan* were supplied through voluntary donations. This symbolizes the fact that, while there is certainly room for creativity and ingenuity in *avodat Hashem*, the basis of religious observance is subservience, obeying the divine command. If we serve God strictly voluntarily, how and when we see fit, and only when we are so inspired, then we are essentially serving ourselves, not God. Volunteerism in religious life must come only on top of the *adanim*, after one has built a firm foundation of unconditional compliance and obedience (cited by R. David Silverberg in *Surf a Little Torah*, *Va-Yakhel Pekudei* 5769).

The Ba'al Shem Tov (Besh"t cited by R. Norman Lamm, *The Royal Table*) asks how King David could refer to himself as an *Eved Hashem* – a servant of the Lord. After all, it was Moshe, the modest of all men whom the Torah refers to as an *Eved Hashem* (Deut. 34:5): *Va-Yamot sham Moshe **Eved Hashem***. How could King David refer to himself with this very term: *Avdekha* – Your servant. The Besh"t replied that this is the very reason why David *ha-Melekh* immediately added: *Ani avdekha ben amatekha* – "I am Your servant, the son of your maidservant." He was saying: "I didn't come to this status in my own right – like Moshe Rabbenu – but rather I was raised to be a slave, with my mother's milk. It came naturally and instinctively."

Speaking from his own experience, R. Joseph B. Soloveitchik notes that there is something unique about the *Avodat Hashem* one learns from one's mother. A father commonly teaches his children how to think and how to act, while a mother teaches us the living experience

Praise the Lord, all nations! Extol Him, all peoples! For His kindness has overwhelmed us, and the truth of the Lord is everlasting. Halleluyah (Psalms 117).

---

of the commandments – their flavor, scent, and warmth. From her, we learn "to feel the presence of the Almighty." From our father, we learned much of the laws of *Shabbat*, but from our mother we learned how to live and experience *Shabbat*, to perceive its warmth, beauty, and splendor. (R. Joseph B. Soloveitchik, "A Tribute to the *Rebbitzen* of Talne," Tradition 17:2, Spring 1978, p. 77.)

R. Asher Weiss (*Haggada Minhat Asher*) recounts that the second Gerer Rebbe, R. Yehuda Leib Alter (better known as the *Sefat Emet*) mentioned to his *Hassidim* at the end of a *fahrbrengen* that it is particularly important to say *Ana Hashem...* in *Hallel*, with *kavana* (proper intention). After the *Rebbe* left, the *Hassidim* discussed among themselves whether the *Rebbe* meant *Ana Hashem hoshi'a na* or *Ana Hashem hatzliha na*. The next morning there was no opportunity to ask the *Rebbe* what he meant before *Hallel*, so some had particular *kavana* while reciting the first verse, and some while reciting the second. When asked after davening to which *Ana* he was referring, the *Rebbe* said "Neither. The main thing is *Ana Hashem ki ani avdekha*. Once a person realizes that he is an *eved Hashem*, other things fall in place." Supplication is important, but even more essential is the sense of subjugation to the Divine.

הַלְלוּ אֶת ה' כָּל גּוֹיִם. שַׁבְּחוּהוּ כָּל הָאֻמִּים

This chapter continues the theme that mankind has a great debt of thanks to the Almighty for his ongoing kindness – Jew and non-Jew alike. Radak comments that this is the shortest chapter in the Bible, and posits that the unity and simplicity of world order portrayed, suggests that it is referring to the Messianic Era. R. Samson Raphael Hirsch (Commentary to Psalms 117) concurs based on the fact that **all** nations and **all** peoples are united in the belief in God.

The next question is why the nations of the world would give praise to the Lord for the good that was done to **us** – the Jews. R. Chaim of Volozhin and R. Zvi Elimelech Shapiro of Dinov (*Bnei Yissachar*)

(תהלים פרק קיח): הוֹדוּ לַה' כִּי טוֹב כִּי לְעוֹלָם חַסְדּוֹ.

יֹאמַר נָא יִשְׂרָאֵל כִּי לְעוֹלָם חַסְדּוֹ.

יֹאמְרוּ נָא בֵית אַהֲרֹן כִּי לְעוֹלָם חַסְדּוֹ.

יֹאמְרוּ נָא יִרְאֵי ה' כִּי לְעוֹלָם חַסְדּוֹ.

---

explain that, throughout the ages, countless anti-Semitic schemes have been planned to destroy us. But our Merciful God manages to foil many of these public and secret plots. Only the non-Jewish schemers know clearly how much of a miracle our salvation was, and how God's "kindness to us was overwhelming." Therefore, only they can praise Him adequately! In addition, *Midrash Shokher Tov* (Psalms 105:35) emphasizes that the Egyptians had suffered so much on account of the Israelites that they rejoyced when Pharaoh let them go. The same will happen at the end of days; the nations of the world will be relieved when the Jews are finally redeemed.

כִּי גָבַר עָלֵינוּ חַסְדּוֹ

R. Moshe Sofer (*Derashot Hatam Sofer*, II, 277a) suggests that non-Jewish nations are impressed only when the Almighty does great miracles: *Ki gavar alenu hasdo* – "when *hessed* is shown with force, overwhelmingly." But Israel acknowledges the daily natural miracles, the continuous laws of nature – as we say in the *Modim* blessing in the *Amida*: "We gratefully acknowledge You… for the daily miracles that are with us and for Your wonders and favors that we experience at all times." That is also why the Psalm goes on in the next verse to point out that Israel says: *Hodu la-Shem ki Tov, ki le-olam hasdo* – "Give thanks to the Lord for He is good: His kindness is everlasting." This refers to the regular miracles and God's eternal kindness.

הוֹדוּ לַה' כִּי טוֹב

There is an important distinction between **doing** good and **being** good, and this Psalm praises God for the latter – *Ki tov* – "for He **is** good." R. Don Isaac Abravanel (Gen. 1:14), however, suggests that the Psalmist

Give thanks to the Lord for He is good: His kindness is everlasting.

Let Israel say: His kindness is everlasting.

Let the House of Aaron say: His kindness is everlasting.

Let those who revere the Lord say: His kindness is everlasting.

---

argues that God **is** inherently good because *Ki le-olam ḥasdo* – because He **eternally** does good. The nature of good is to do good! Alternatively, this connection could be understood as a statement of faith: *Kol de-avid raḥmana le-tav avid* – "All that the merciful God does is ultimately for good" (*Berakhot* 60b; *Shulḥan Arukh*, *OH* 230:5) – even though, at the moment, this assertion seems highly problematic. This position is first stated here in *Hallel ha-Mitzri*, but is more fully developed in *Hallel ha-Gadol* (Psalms 136).

כִּי לְעוֹלָם חַסְדּוֹ

One way of translating *le-olam* is "forever" (Metsudot David and Abravanel). Alternatively, it might indicate that The Almighty does not do good for His own benefit, but *le-olam* – for the world. (*Siddur Otzar ha-Tefilot, Etz Yosef.*)

יֹאמְרוּ נָא יִרְאֵי ה׳

Before proceeding on to *Min ha-Meitzar*, we point out that the opening chapters of *Hallel* (Psalms 113–115) are in the plural. Then, in *Ahavti* and *Ma Ashiv* (Psalms 116), when the author speaks of his own fear and torment we switch back to the singular. The next chapters, *Hallelu* (Psalms 117) and *Hodu* (opening of Psalms 118), switch back to the plural. Then from *Min ha-Meitzar* (Continuation of Psalm 118) to the end of the *Hallel*, where the author again speaks of his own fear and torment and his hopes for the future, it is again in the singular – a more intimate relationship with God.

In order to understand this ebb and flow, we need to remember that the *Korban Pesaḥ* is a form of *Korban Toda* – an offering of thanksgiving for the Almighty's beneficence, salvation, or miracle. The *korban* was followed by a large meal of praise and thanks (*Se'udat shevaḥ ve-hodaya*)

מִן הַמֵּצַר קָרָאתִי יָּהּ, עָנָנִי בַמֶּרְחָב יָהּ. ה' לִי, לֹא אִירָא – מַה יַּעֲשֶׂה לִי אָדָם. ה' לִי בְּעֹזְרָי וַאֲנִי אֶרְאֶה בְשֹׂנְאָי. טוֹב לַחֲסוֹת בַּה' מִבְּטֹחַ בָּאָדָם. טוֹב לַחֲסוֹת ב בַּה' מִבְּטֹחַ בִּנְדִיבִים. כָּל גּוֹיִם סְבָבוּנִי, בְּשֵׁם ה' כִּי אֲמִילַם.

---

to describe and publicize the special kindness or miracle, with much food shared by family, friends, the needy, and even passers-by. Likewise at the *Seder*, we invite many to our table and recount the miracle(s) of the Exodus through the *Haggada* and *Hallel*. As we read *Hallel*, we have to picture ourselves at the Psalmist's *seuda* of thanksgiving in which he recounts what happened to him, his fears, his dangers, his hopes, his prayers – and ultimately God's salvation. When he speaks of his personal feelings and thoughts, it is in the singular. Then there are moments when he gives praise – and in this, he involves the community using the plural.

Halakha (*Shulhan Arukh OH* 479:1) dictates that sections of *Hodu la-Shem Ki Tov* and *Ana Hashem Hoshi'a na* should preferably be read in a *zimmun* of at least three individuals (of either gender; *Mishna Berura OH* 479, note 9). And it should be read as we do in the synagogue – responsively (referred to in *Halakha* as: *keri'a ve-aniya*). The leader of the *Seder* serves the role of *Hazan* representing the one to whom the miracle occurred (*ba'al ha-nes*) – with the others at the *Seder* responding.

מִן הַמֵּצַר קָרָאתִי יָּהּ, עָנָנִי בַמֶּרְחָב יָהּ

The major theme of this section is the importance of trust in the Lord, because He ultimately determines what will happen with man. Regarding this verse, R. Barukh Epstein (*Barukh she-Amar*) asks regarding the meaning of *ya* in *merhav ya*. He cites *Gemara Pesahim* (117a) to the effect that *ba-merhav ya* is actually a single (perhaps hyphenated) word and not holy. Creatively, R. Epstein suggests that in this context, the word *ya* means "great." Thus *ba-merhav ya* means "a large broad expanse." Similarly, *shalhevetya* (Song of Songs 8:6) would mean a great flame; *halleluya* is a great loud praise; and *hasin ya* (Psalms 89:9) would be a great protective force. According to this, the present verse could be translated as "From tight straits I called out to the Lord. He answered me in a broad expanse." The Psalmist might also be referring

From tight straits I called out to the Lord. He answered me in a broad expanse. The Lord is with me, I will not fear – what can man do to me? The Lord is with me, through my helpers, and I can face my enemies. It is better to rely on the Lord than to trust in man. It is better to rely on the Lord than to trust in nobles. All the nations surround me; in

---

to a broad expanse that is stirring like a clear view of a star-studded sky, looking down on the Grand Canyon, or the vista from the top of a majestic mountain. It is awe-inspiring, generates a sense of wonder, and makes you sensitive to the Creator's presence. In this vein, are the following moving words of Holocaust Concentration camp survivor Viktor Frankl (*Man's Search for Meaning*, Part I: "Experiences in a Concentration Camp"):

> One day, a few days after the liberation, I walked through the country past flowering meadows, for miles and miles, toward the market town near the camp. Larks rose to the sky and I could hear their joyous song. There was no one to be seen for miles around; there was nothing but the wide earth and sky and the larks' jubilation and the freedom of space. I stopped, looked around, and up to the sky – and then I went down on my knees. At that moment there was very little I knew of myself or of the world – I had put one sentence in my mind – always the same: "I called to the Lord from my narrow prison and he had answered me in the freedom of space." How long I knelt there and repeated this sentence, memory can no longer recall. But I know that on that day, in that hour, my new life started. Step by step I progressed, until I again became a human being.

טוֹב לַחֲסוֹת בַּה' מִבְּטֹחַ בָּאָדָם. טוֹב לַחֲסוֹת בַּה' מִבְּטֹחַ בִּנְדִיבִים

The Gra (*Haggada Peirushei ve-Likutei ha-Gra*, ed. R. Yosef Eliyahu Movshovitz) notes that in this couplet, there is a contrast made between two verbs *la-ḥasot* vs. *li-vto'aḥ*, and two nouns *adam* vs. *nadiv*. The verb *la-ḥasot* means to take refuge by your own choice, even though nothing was promised. By contrast, *li-vto'aḥ* means trusting in, or relying on, someone else's promise. In the first verse, David *ha-Melekh* argues that

סַבּוּנִי גַם סְבָבוּנִי. בְּשֵׁם ה' כִּי אֲמִילַם. סַבּוּנִי כִדְבֹרִים. דֹּעֲכוּ כְּאֵשׁ קוֹצִים. בְּשֵׁם ה' כִּי אֲמִילַם. דָּחֹה דְחִיתַנִי לִנְפֹּל. וַה' עֲזָרָנִי. עָזִּי וְזִמְרָת יָהּ וַיְהִי לִי לִישׁוּעָה. קוֹל רִנָּה וִישׁוּעָה בְּאָהֳלֵי צַדִּיקִים: יְמִין ה' עֹשָׂה חָיִל, יְמִין ה' רוֹמֵמָה, יְמִין ה' עֹשָׂה חָיִל. לֹא אָמוּת כִּי אֶחְיֶה, וַאֲסַפֵּר מַעֲשֵׂי יָהּ. יַסֹּר יִסְּרַנִּי יָּהּ, וְלַמָּוֶת לֹא נְתָנָנִי. פִּתְחוּ לִי שַׁעֲרֵי צֶדֶק, אָבֹא בָם, אוֹדֶה יָהּ. זֶה הַשַּׁעַר לַה'. צַדִּיקִים יָבֹאוּ בוֹ.

---

it is better to trust in the Almighty's protection than in man's promise. In the second half of the couplet, he further posits that even if the promiser is a *nadiv* – a proven generous individual, God is still preferable since only He is truly in control.

R. Joseph B. Soloveitchik has indicated that the idea that man is unreliable is very troubling. After all, a properly functioning society is based on man's presumed dependability. Testimony in court, contracts, Kashrut supervision, rabbis, medical staff, etc. are all based on the assumption that people are reliable. Nevertheless, Jewish history has taught us always to be skeptical. The Holocaust in particular shook man's faith in his fellow. The world as a whole stood by silently as the Jews were wiped out. Men of stature including the Pope and President Franklin Delano Roosevelt were great disappointments. The following are relevant comments of R. Joseph B. Soloveitchik ("The Rav – Thinking Aloud," p. 162.):

> Having confidence and trust in our fellow man is a fundamental duty of every one of us in Judaism. Certain laws depend on this approach, such as *Eid ehad ne'eman be-issurim* (the testimony of one is accepted by *kashrut*) … [Despite this,] ultimate dependence is not warranted with regard to humans, because they are only finite beings. Our faith and unqualified trust is only justified in relation to God. A historical example of this is found in the Jewish relationship to President Roosevelt… [He] had two accomplishments to his credit: that he saved hundreds of thousands of people from starvation; and that he crushed Nazism. As a result, the Jews worshipped Roosevelt, bordering almost on the ecstatic. This overconfidence in him bordering on paganism was wrong, [since]

the name of the Lord I cut them down! They encircle me like bees, but they are quenched like a fire of thorns; in the Name of the Lord I cut them down. You pushed me again and again that I might fall, but the Lord helped me. The Lord is my strength [during the attack] and my song [my praise thereafter], and He is my salvation. The sound of joyous song and salvation is in the tents of the righteous: "The right hand of the Lord performs deeds of valor." The Lord's right hand is exalted; the right hand of the Lord performs deeds of valor! I shall not die, but I shall live and relate the deeds of God. God has chastised me, but He did not let me die. Open for me the gates of righteousness – I will enter them and thank God. This is the gate of the Lord, the righteous will enter it.

---

he could have stopped the mass deportation and extermination of Jews in the bleak years of 1943–1944.

R. Yitzchok Hutner ("Holocaust," *Jewish Observer*, XII:8, p. 5, Oct. 1977) wrote: "The end result of this period [*Sho'ah*] for the Jewish psyche was a significant – indeed, crucial – one. From trust in the gentile world, the Jewish nation was cruelly brought to a repudiation of that trust. In a relatively short historical period, disappointment in the non-Jewish world was deeply imprinted upon the Jewish soul." R. Joel B. Wolowelsky ("Observing Yom ha-Sho'ah," Tradition 24 (4) Summer 1989) points out that: "R. Hutner saw great significance in this shift. This repudiation, he argues, is the necessary first step for reaching *Aharit ha-Yamim* (the end of days).... For R. Hutner, the Holocaust has become an "orienting event," one that changes the way we (Jews) view the world. To wit: You can't trust the *goyim* (nations of the world) – we can only trust in ourselves and the Almighty. This is indeed one of the cornerstone principles of the Israeli state's national security – and it is why Israel refuses to rely on anyone else for its security. R. Zvi Yehuda Kook stated that *Yom ha-Atzma'ut* was a great miracle, primarily because the Israeli leadership relied on themselves (and Heaven) in declaring the new State of Israel despite the advice and objections of leading nations of the world and the threat of war. Had they listened, Israel may never have been born.

R. Yehuda Amital [("A Kaddish for the Martyrs of the Holocaust" (1990) (https://etzion.org.il/en/holidays/asara-betevet/kadish-martyrs-holocaust)] made the following insightful comments: "[We are] facing a world … that stood by as the blood of millions was shed … It is not an easy test to maintain our faith after all that, and to say, *Yitgadal ve-yitkadash shmei rabba* – "May God's great name be exalted and sanctified." But my heart goes out to those Jews who have no faith, who say, 'I believe in man,' and that is what gives them strength. For we have seen how far a man can degenerate. [Fortunate] are we … that we believe in the Holy One, blessed is He, concerning Whom it is written, *Ki lo mahshevotai ke-mahshevotekhem* – 'My thoughts are not your thoughts' (Isaiah 55:8), even with all of our questions."

Almost a decade later (*Confronting the Holocaust*, 1998) (https://etzion.org.il/en/holidays/asara-betevet/confronting-holocaust) R. Amital reveals: "I once had a conversation with Abba Kovner, may he rest in peace, leader of the Vilna Ghetto revolt and an important Hebrew poet. I said to him, "I don't know whose test was greater, mine or yours. Your banner was faith in man. After the *Sho'ah*, can you still believe in **man**? I believe in God, Whom I cannot understand. But man should be fathomable – so what do you believe in now?!"

I don't know what the final answer is to King David's challenge. Ultimately, no man is an island – so we have to rely on others. We just have to choose wisely and carefully. Notice that David *ha-Melekh* writes: *Tov la-hasot ba-Shem* – "It is **good/better** to take refuge in the Lord." This is a dilemma with no simple answers. Perhaps, the choice is not either-or, but both-and. Josh Weinstein has brought to my attention two relevant verses in the Book of Jeremiah (17:5 and 7). The first verse reads, "Thus says the Lord: Cursed be the man who trusts in man… and turns his heart from God." While the second says: "Blessed is the man who trusts in the Lord, and whose hope the Lord is." R. David Kimhi (Radak) comments (on verse 5): "If man does not 'turn his heart from God,' he is not wrong in trusting that humans will help him – if his intention is that **with God's help,** the person can help him." Similar comments are made by R. Shlomo ibn Aderet in his discussion regarding relying on physicians (*Resp. Rashba*, I, sec. 413).

כָּל גּוֹיִם סְבָבוּנִי... סַבּוּנִי כִדְבֹרִים... סַבּוּנִי גַם סְבָבוּנִי....

The Gra (*Haggada Peirushei ve-Likutei ha-Gra*, ed. R. Yosef Eliyahu

Movshovitz) observes that in this triplet of verses we have the same root *sāvov* repeated, but with different implications. *Kol goyim sĕvāvuni* suggests that the nations are gathering around but at a distance. *Sabuni gam sĕvāvuni* suggests a closer, tighter circle. Finally, *Sabuni ki-dĕvorim* indicates that he is surrounded on all sides – top and bottom as well – like an attacking swarm of bees. In all these three cases, he was eventually able to cut them down in God's name.

Abravanel suggests that the struggle with the nations continues into the next verse: *Daho dehitani li-npol ve-Hashem azarani* – "They (the nations) pushed me so hard that I almost fell, but the Lord assisted me to drive them off." Abravanel further suggests that these four verses represent four nations that came to wipe out Israel. The first was the Assyrian King Sennacherib who exiled the 10 tribes, though his army was eventually destroyed. The second was the Babylonian King Nebuchadnezzar who attacked **repeatedly** during the times of Kings Jehoiakim, Jehoiachin, and Zedekiah – which is why it says: *Sabuni gam sĕvāvuni*. The Babylonians captured Jerusalem, but were eventually destroyed by the Persians and the Jews returned to Israel. The third were the Persians, Medes, and Greeks who came one after the other like a swarm of bees – but the Greeks were eventually driven off by the Hasmoneans. The fourth is the attack of the Romans (which morphs into the Christians), and the exile they brought about has lasted for two millennia. This exile almost destroyed us – *Daho dehitani li-npol* – were it not for the assistance of the Almighty. And thus, the Jewish nation lives on.

Interestingly, R. Haim Sabato in his autobiographical novel *Adjusting Sights* (2003) describes his experiences during the Yom Kippur War (1973). He cites his grandfather as interpreting these four verses as a more modern prophecy. Thus, *Kol goyim sĕvāvuni* – refers to the War of Independence (1948); *Sabuni gam sĕvāvuni* – denotes Operation Kadesh (1956); *Sabuni ki-dĕvorim* – describes the Six Day War; and finally, the fourth verse *Daho dehitani li-npol ve-Hashem azarani*, which has a *ve-Hi she-Amda* flavor, refers to the Yom Kippur War. Here, there was no final victory, and the outcome could have been catastrophic. Yet, we made it through with the Almighty's assistance. Nevertheless, R. Sabato indicates that, to his mind, the next verse points to the messianic era: *Ozi ve-zimrat yah va-Yehi li li-yeshu'a* – "The Lord is my strength and my song; He has become my salvation."

אוֹדְךָ כִּי עֲנִיתָנִי וַתְּהִי לִי לִישׁוּעָה. אוֹדְךָ כִּי עֲנִיתָנִי וַתְּהִי לִי לִישׁוּעָה. אֶבֶן מָאֲסוּ הַבּוֹנִים הָיְתָה לְרֹאשׁ פִּנָּה. אֶבֶן מָאֲסוּ הַבּוֹנִים הָיְתָה לְרֹאשׁ פִּנָּה. מֵאֵת ה' הָיְתָה זֹּאת הִיא נִפְלָאת בְּעֵינֵינוּ. מֵאֵת ה' הָיְתָה זֹּאת הִיא נִפְלָאת בְּעֵינֵינוּ. זֶה הַיּוֹם עָשָׂה ה'. נָגִילָה וְנִשְׂמְחָה בוֹ. זֶה הַיּוֹם עָשָׂה ה'. נָגִילָה וְנִשְׂמְחָה בוֹ.

עָזִּי וְזִמְרָת יָהּ וַיְהִי לִי לִישׁוּעָה

This famous verse first appears in Exodus 22:25 after the crossing of the Red Sea, and later – with mild changes – in *Isaiah* 12:2–3 (and from there into *Havdala*). The *kamatz* under the *ayin* of *Ozi* is a *kamatz katan* since the word comes from *Oz* – strength. Structurally the verse is somewhat complex because the word *Yah* refers to what appears before it and after it. In addition, *zimrat* is short for *zimrati* with the *yud* of *Yah* going "up and down." Thus, this *pasuk* should be understood as if it said: *Yah ozi ve-zimrati, va-Yehi Yah li li-yeshu'a* – The Lord is my strength (during the attack) and my song (the subject of my praise thereafter), and the Lord is my salvation. (Amos Hakham, commentary to *Da'at Mikra* on *Psalms* 118:14).

The Gra (*Haggada Peirushei ve-Likutei ha-Gra*, ed. R. Yosef Eliyahu Movshovitz) notes that here David *ha-Melekh* uses the term *yeshu'a* for salvation, while in the first *berakha* of *Shemoneh Esrei*, three terms are used to describe God as savior: *ozer*, *moshi'a* and *magen* – to be translated as "helps, saves and protects." **Ozer** means that God **helps** you when you go to battle or in a life crisis; you do your share and the Almighty assists. **Moshi'a** means that he is your **savior**, and your role is sometimes minor, if at all. Finally, ***magen*** indicates that God **protects** you in the first place and prevents the crisis or battle from occurring.

לֹא אָמוּת כִּי אֶחְיֶה. וַאֲסַפֵּר מַעֲשֵׂי יָהּ

As already indicated above, even in his darkest moments, King David had faith that the Almighty would ultimately preserve him. This is because he believed that man was of greater value to God alive – doing God's *mitzvot* and singing His praises – than dead. That is why King David asserts with confidence in the next verse: "God may chasten

I thank You for You have answered me, and You brought me salvation. I thank You, for You have answered me and become my salvation. The stone scorned by the builders has become the cornerstone. The stone scorned by the builders has become the cornerstone. This thing is from the Lord, it is wondrous in our eyes. This thing is from the Lord, it is wondrous in our eyes. This is the day that the Lord has made, let us be glad and rejoice on it. This is the day that the Lord has made, let us be glad and rejoice on it.

---

me, but He will not hand me over to Death." The Gra (*Aderet Eliyahu*, Deut. 33:6) has a very different take on this *pasuk*. He understands that David *ha-Melekh* is consoling himself with the belief that even if he dies it will not be final – there will be a resurrection (*tehiyat ha-meitim*) and an afterlife (*olam ha-ba*). He reads this verse as follows: "I will not die – forever, but live – after resurrection."

פִּתְחוּ לִי שַׁעֲרֵי צֶדֶק, אָבֹא בָם, אוֹדֶה יָהּ

The commentaries suggest that the "Gates of Righteousness" referred to are those of Jerusalem, about which the Prophet Isaiah (1:21) states that "Righteousness dwelled therein." Alternatively, it refers to the gates of the Temple where the God of Righteousness dwells. R. Joseph Hertz (*The Authorized Daily Prayer Book*, pp. 770–771) asserts that in Judaism the ultimate criterion for entrance into the dwelling of the Lord is righteousness and sensitivity, not celebrity and fame. Judaism deems all worship by wicked or cruel men an insult to God – unless it be a prayer of repentance." This was a repudiation of the Greek view – as recorded in the Talmud (*Tamid* 32b). There it is recounted that Alexander the Great demanded entrance to Paradise because he is the famous conqueror of the world! To Alexander's shock, the attending angels rejected his petition, as it says in the next verse: "This is the Lord's Gate; only the righteous may pass through."

אוֹדְךָ

When reading *Hallel* in prayer or at the Seder, the practice is to repeat the verses beginning with *Odekha* until the end. This is a very old custom already recorded in the *Mishna* (Sukka 3:11). Rashi (Sukka 38a, s.v.

likhpol) suggests that the custom stems from the fact that *Hallel* until this point was full of repetitions and synonyms, which seems to cease at this point. R. Joseph B. Soloveitchik (cited by R. Hershel Schacter, *Divrei ha-Rav*, p.144) proposed that the repetition is meant to indicate that we lack the verbal skills to say enough of God's praises – so we start to repeat. This phenomenon appears elsewhere, as well. Thus, in *Pesukei de-Zimra* at the end of Psalm 150, the last chapter of *Psalms*, we repeat the last verse: *Kol ha-ha-neshama tehallel yah, Halleluya*. This again is to indicate that we should be saying more – but lack the ability. Similarly, at the end of *Az Yashir* (Ex. 15:1–19) – both in prayer and in the Torah reading – we repeat the last verse of praise (Ex. 15:18): *Hashem yimlokh le-olam va'ed*. Similarly, in *Shaharit*, before reciting the *Shema*, we repeat synonyms in describing the Heavenly Angels' praise of the Almighty: *u-mevarkhin, u-meshabehin, u-mefa'arim, u-ma'aritzim, u-makdishin, u-mamlikhim*. All this to imply innumerable praise.

אוֹדְךָ כִּי עֲנִיתָנִי וַתְּהִי לִי לִישׁוּעָה

We say in this *pasuk*, "I thank You [Lord] *ki anitani* and for being my salvation" (Psalms 118:21). Most translate *ki anitani* as "for You have **answered** me." Surprisingly, perhaps, *Midrash Psalms* and several later sources understand *anitani* to stem from the word *inui* or affliction – as if it were written *initani*. The verse therefore means: "I thank You [Lord] because You have **afflicted** me and [thereby] have been my salvation." But how are we to understand gratitude for having been afflicted? R. Abraham Joshua Twerski, the noted psychiatrist and specialist in substance abuse, points out in his *Haggada* "From Bondage to Freedom" that it is not easy to attain spiritual growth – which I take to mean the ability to go beyond the demands of the body towards some higher ideal. In R. Twerski's words:

> It calls for self-sacrifice and for denying oneself many of the things people consider to be the pleasures of life…. People instinctively avoid pain and may avoid spiritual growth because of the discomfort it entails. But an addict has no choice: if he is to recover, he must improve the quality of his spirituality, otherwise, he will relapse. This is why recovered addicts may be grateful for

their suffering because it was the only stimulus that could bring them to spirituality."

Our verse, therefore, means: "I thank You Lord **because** Your **affliction** has directly led to my salvation."

Allow me to suggest a slightly different approach to that of R. Twerski which pivots on the conjunction *ki*, a word with multiple meanings in Hebrew (Talmud, *Rosh ha-Shana* 3a). *Ki* can sometimes mean "because" – and this is how R. Twerski understands it. But it can also mean "even though." Both meanings appear in a single verse (Ex. 13:18) which reads: "When Pharaoh sent the people out, the Lord did not lead them along the main road that runs through Philistine territory, *even though* that was the shortest route to the Canaan, *because* God said, 'If the people are faced with a battle, they might change their minds and return to Egypt.'" Similarly, I would prefer to interpret this verse as: "I thank You [Lord], **even though** You have afflicted me, for giving me the strength to survive and persevere."

Of course, no one willingly chooses suffering – even if it results in spiritual growth. This is analogous to the rabbinic dictum (*Midrash Tanhuma, Balak*, sec. 6) about the bee: "Give me neither of your honey nor your stinger" – we would forego your honey if it means that we could forgo your stinger. Nevertheless, life does not always give us choices. Those who have suffered – and reconstructed their lives in a positive and creative fashion – have acquired a unique strength, a certain credibility that others lack. Indeed, my wife Esther and I lost a gifted child (Yaakov Yehudah *z"l*) to cancer when he was just 24 years old. But we made a willed decision not to wallow in our sadness – but to go on with the business of life, devoting our energies towards strengthening our family, being creative and communally involved. Having lost a child, I know that I can turn to grieving parents, testify about my loss, and describe my life before and after. I can then tell them that *if they will it*, there is a good productive life after and notwithstanding death. Despite the gaping hole that forever remains, there is much good in life to live for – personal growth, family and community, vocation or avocation.

I'm sure that each of us has asked ourselves: Why did the Redeemer deem it necessary to send us down to Egypt to be enslaved and suffer, in the first place? Perhaps, He felt that there were national lessons to

אָנָּא ה'. הוֹשִׁיעָה נָּא.   אָנָּא ה'. הוֹשִׁיעָה נָּא.

אָנָּא ה'. הַצְלִיחָה נָא.   אָנָּא ה'. הַצְלִיחָה נָא.

בָּרוּךְ הַבָּא בְּשֵׁם ה'. בֵּרַכְנוּכֶם מִבֵּית ה'. בָּרוּךְ הַבָּא בְּשֵׁם ה'. בֵּרַכְנוּכֶם מִבֵּית ה'. אֵל ה' וַיָּאֶר לָנוּ. אִסְרוּ חַג בַּעֲבֹתִים עַד קַרְנוֹת הַמִּזְבֵּחַ. אֵל ה'

---

be learned that could not be imparted any other way (see "Introductory Essays" #7). Many of the lessons of life are experiential. Indeed, the Egypt experience is the underlying rationale for more than 50 *mitzvot* and observances. On the *Seder* night we are obligated to re-experience the bitterness of the bondage and the exhilaration of the freedom. Every year we are required to become re-sensitized to the suffering of the downtrodden by eating *Maror*. By reliving the Egypt experience yearly, we can transmit the various moral, historical, and national messages to the next generation in a more personal and, hence, credible fashion. Jews didn't choose to go down to Egypt to be enslaved. But in the process, we have learned a great many lessons that need to be transmitted to our children. And on *Pesah* night we can do so from a personal vantage point. That's what the *Seder* is all about.

Should Jews be thankful for suffering in the Egyptian exile? I think not. But should we be thankful for what we learned from it and for the type of nation we have become? Most definitely! I thank You, Lord, **even though** You have afflicted me, for giving me the strength to survive, persevere, and grow.

זֶה הַיּוֹם עָשָׂה ה'. נָגִילָה וְנִשְׂמְחָה בוֹ

The meaning of the first part of this verse is clear: "This is the day the Lord made." The problem is with the second half: the word *vo* is an indefinite pronoun. Does *vo* refer to the **day** or to "the **Lord**." The fundamental question raised is whether the essence of the day is to rejoice in the physical attributes of the **holiday** with good food and good friends. Or, perhaps, *vo* refers to God – with the proper emphasis placed on the spiritual qualities and endeavors of the holiday experience (like learning God's Torah and doing His *mitzvot*)? *Shir ha-Shirim*

O Lord, please save us!   O Lord, please save us!

O Lord, please grant us success!   O Lord, please grant us success!

Blessed is he who comes in the Name of the Lord; we bless you from the House of the Lord. Blessed is he who comes in the Name of the Lord; we bless you from the House of the Lord. The Lord is Almighty, He gave us light; bring the festival offering, bound with cords to the

---

Rabba (*Parasha* 1:4) resolves this issue by citing a similar verse in *Shir ha-Shirim* (1:4) which reads *Nagila ve-nismekha Bakh* – "Let us exult and rejoice in **You** (God)." "Rabbi Avin said: We do not know regarding what to rejoice, whether in the day or in the Holy One, blessed is He. Solomon came and specified: 'Let us exult and rejoice in You,' in the Holy One, blessed is He. In You: in Your salvation; in You: in Your Torah; in You, in fear of You."

Strangely, the ecstatic joy of "This is the day the Lord made, let us exult and rejoice in Him" is immediately followed by the pain, fear, and helplessness of "Please Lord save us! Please Lord grant us success!" R. Sholom Gold has emphasized that these verses of *Hallel* require us to appreciate the importance of recognizing and thanking Hashem for his past benevolence. The life of a Jew is a tenuous one, and as discussed above, King David is acutely aware that the only one he can truly rely on is the Almighty (see comments to טוֹב לַחֲסוֹת בַּה' מִבְּטֹחַ בָּאָדָם above). But it is only **after** the Psalmist fully and properly acknowledges God's central role in previous kindness – by declaring: *Zeh ha-Yom asa Hashem, nagila ve-nismeha Vo* – that he can turn to God to ask for future salvation and assistance – by repeatedly pleading: *Ana Hashem hoshi'a na! Ana Hashem hatzliha na!*

אָנָּא ה', הוֹשִׁיעָה נָּא. אָנָּא ה', הַצְלִיחָה נָא

The commentaries have suggest two possible differences between *hoshi'a* and *hatzliha*. One possibility is that *hoshi'a* is spiritual success, while *hatzliha* is physical attainment. The other possibility is that *hoshi'a* is salvation from present difficulties, while *hatzliha* is success in moving forward.

וַיֶּאְסְרוּ לָנוּ. אִסְרוּ חַג בַּעֲבֹתִים עַד קַרְנוֹת הַמִּזְבֵּחַ. אֵלִי אַתָּה וְאוֹדֶךָּ, אֱלֹהַי – אֲרוֹמְמֶךָּ. אֵלִי אַתָּה וְאוֹדֶךָּ, אֱלֹהַי – אֲרוֹמְמֶךָּ. הוֹדוּ לַה' כִּי טוֹב, כִּי לְעוֹלָם חַסְדּוֹ. הוֹדוּ לַה' כִּי טוֹב, כִּי לְעוֹלָם חַסְדּוֹ.

(סיום): יְהַלְלוּךָ ה' אֱלֹהֵינוּ כָּל מַעֲשֶׂיךָ, וַחֲסִידֶיךָ צַדִּיקִים עוֹשֵׂי רְצוֹנֶךָ, וְכָל עַמְּךָ בֵּית יִשְׂרָאֵל בְּרִנָּה יוֹדוּ וִיבָרְכוּ, וִישַׁבְּחוּ וִיפָאֲרוּ, וִירוֹמְמוּ וְיַעֲרִיצוּ, וְיַקְדִּישׁוּ וְיַמְלִיכוּ אֶת שִׁמְךָ, מַלְכֵּנוּ. כִּי לְךָ טוֹב לְהוֹדוֹת וּלְשִׁמְךָ נָאֶה לְזַמֵּר. כִּי מֵעוֹלָם וְעַד עוֹלָם אַתָּה אֵל.

יְהַלְלוּךָ

As we transition from *Hallel ha-Mitzri* to *Hallel ha-Gadol*, there are three leading customs as to how to conclude the former. *Minhag* Ashkenaz is to say the paragraph of *Yehalelukha* at this juncture as we would every holiday *Hallel* – but without a final *berakha* of *melekh mehulal be-tishbahot*. This is because we are not finished yet singing Hashem's praises and will be continuing with *Hallel ha-Gadol* and concluding with *Nishmat* and the *berakha* of *Yishtabah*. The second *minhag* is that of the Gra which is not to say *Yehalelukha* at all. The third custom is that of the *Sefaradim* and *Hasidim* which is **not** to say *Yehalelukha* here, but to put off its recitation until the end of *Nishmat* (– the *berakha* at the end of *Yishtabah* is not said). There are also other minor variations. A discussion of the origins of this dispute is beyond the scope of this *Haggada*.

corners of the altar. The Lord is Almighty, He gave us light; bring the festival offering, bound with cords to the corners of the altar. You are my God and I will thank You; my God and I will exalt You. You are my God and I will thank You; my God and I will exalt You. Give thanks to the Lord, for He is good; His kindness is everlasting. Give thanks to the Lord, for He is good; His kindness is everlasting (Psalms 118).

Lord our God, all Your creations shall praise You; Your devout ones, the righteous who do Your will, and Your entire nation the House of Israel, with joyous song will thank and bless, laud and glorify, exalt and adore, sanctify and proclaim the sovereignty of Your Name, our King. For it is good to thank You, and befitting to sing to Your Name, for in this world and for eternity You are Almighty God.

יְהַלְלוּךָ ה' אֱלֹהֵינוּ כָּל מַעֲשֶׂיךָ

Abravanel points out that there are two readings in this *berakha*. One reads: *Yehalelukha Hashem Elokenu kol ma'asekha* – which means: All Your works, *Hashem*, will praise You. The second reading is: *Yehalelukha Hashem Elokenu **al** kol ma'asekha* – which means: They will praise You, *Hashem*, **because** of all Your works.

הלל הגדול (תהלים קלו)

GOD'S OMNIPOTENCE

(א) הוֹדוּ לַה' כִּי טוֹב. כִּי לְעוֹלָם חַסְדּוֹ:

(ב) הוֹדוּ לֵאלֹהֵי הָאֱלֹהִים. כִּי לְעוֹלָם חַסְדּוֹ:

(ג) הוֹדוּ לַאֲדֹנֵי הָאֲדֹנִים. כִּי לְעוֹלָם חַסְדּוֹ:

(ד) לְעֹשֵׂה נִפְלָאוֹת גְּדֹלוֹת לְבַדּוֹ. כִּי לְעוֹלָם חַסְדּוֹ:

הלל הגדול

We have completed *Hallel ha-Mitzri*, but we sense that we have not completed our possible praise of the Almighty. In *Hallel ha-Mitzri* we talked primarily about a God of History and also about a God who relates to the individual and hears his prayer. But we have not emphasized the role God plays in Creation. This is where *Hallel ha-Gadol* (The Great *Hallel*; Psalms 136) comes in. The Talmud (*Pesahim* 118a) indicates that this passage is referred to by this notable title because of the verse (Psalms 136:25) "Who gives food to all flesh, for His kindness is everlasting." That the Almighty sustains the whole world is a great matter. The Talmud (*Berakhot* 4b) also states that a similar verse (Psalms 145:16) "You give sustenance openhandedly, feeding every creature to its heart's content" partially explains the importance of *Tehilla le-David* (better known as *Ashrei*) – which is recited thrice daily.

Hallel ha-Gadol can be broken down into four sections: 1) the first four verses talk of God's omnipotence; 2) the next five focus on the Almighty as the God of Creation; 3) the next 13 of the God of History – but more specifically his special relationship with the Nation of Israel; 4) the last section of four verses remind us of Hashem's continual *hashgaha* (supervision). It is for this reason that *Haza"l* expanded the *Hallel* said at the *Seder* with *Hallel ha-Gadol*. The latter talks about *Pesah* themes: *Makkat Bekhorot*, the splitting of the Red Sea, and the conquest of the Land of Israel – but also the creation of Heaven and Earth and the luminaries. Thus, we thank God on this night of *Pesah* not only for the miracles of Egypt but also for the miracles of our very existence, the miracles of Creation. But most notably for the Jew in

Hallel ha-Gadol (Psalms 126)

God's Omnipotence

(1) Give thanks to the Lord, for He is good
for His kindness is everlasting.
(2) Give thanks to the God of Gods
for His kindness is everlasting.
(3) Give thanks to the Master of Masters
for His kindness is everlasting.
(4) Who alone does great wonders
for His kindness is everlasting.

---

exile waiting millennia for the Messiah are verses 23 and 24 of *Hallel ha-Gadol* (Psalm 136) which reads: *she-be-Shifleinu zakhar lanu… va-Yifrekeinu mi-tzareinu* – "in our lowliness, He remembers us… and delivered us from our oppressors." The Almighty is concerned about our trials and tribulations. This is a tremendous statement of faith and hope – so appropriate for the *galut* Jew and the fourth cup of hope for Eliyahu the prophet and redemption. With this hope we conclude this Psalm with verse 26: "Give thanks to the Lord for He is good: His kindness is everlasting."

לְעֹשֵׂה נִפְלָאוֹת גְּדֹלוֹת לְבַדּוֹ

Why does the Psalmist stress that the Almighty does His miracles **alone**? R. Reuven Margaliot (*Haggada*) responds that Moshe Rabbenu, Eliyahu and Elisha all did grand miracles, but they did it as messengers to God. God doesn't need assistants. Besides, the *Hatam Sofer* (*Derashot* II, 253a) and the *Sefat Emet* (R. Yehuda Aryeh Leib of Gur, *Sefat Emet le-Pesah*, 5653, s.v. *Avadim hayinu*) suggest that the miracles performed by Moshe, Eliyahu, and Elisha were for a limited time. By contrast, the miracles done by the Creator – like the Laws of Nature – are not only by Him alone – *levado* – but are also timeless and forever – *ki le-olam hasdo*! *Sefat Emet* (*va-Yikra, Pesah* 18, 5647) further suggests that *levado* here means: alone, without anybody being aware of it. God often intervenes in the world and in our lives without any individual being

God of Creation

(ה) לְעֹשֵׂה הַשָּׁמַיִם בִּתְבוּנָה. כִּי לְעוֹלָם חַסְדּוֹ:

(ו) לְרוֹקַע הָאָרֶץ עַל הַמָּיִם. כִּי לְעוֹלָם חַסְדּוֹ:

(ז) לְעֹשֵׂה אוֹרִים גְּדֹלִים. כִּי לְעוֹלָם חַסְדּוֹ:

(ח) אֶת הַשֶּׁמֶשׁ לְמֶמְשֶׁלֶת בַּיּוֹם. כִּי לְעוֹלָם חַסְדּוֹ:

(ט) אֶת הַיָּרֵחַ וְכוֹכָבִים לְמֶמְשְׁלוֹת בַּלָּיְלָה. כִּי לְעוֹלָם חַסְדּוֹ:

God of History

(י) לְמַכֵּה מִצְרַיִם בִּבְכוֹרֵיהֶם. כִּי לְעוֹלָם חַסְדּוֹ:

(יא) וַיּוֹצֵא יִשְׂרָאֵל מִתּוֹכָם. כִּי לְעוֹלָם חַסְדּוֹ:

---

cognizant of it. Sometimes we become aware of His intervention, but only long after it is performed.

לְעֹשֵׂה הַשָּׁמַיִם בִּתְבוּנָה

The phrase that attracts our attention is "was made *bi-tevuna*, with wisdom and intelligence." R. Samson Raphael Hirsch (Commentary to Psalms 136:5) suggests that *bi-tevuna* emphasizes the complexity and miraculous nature of the creation. All this despite the enormity of the countless galaxies and suns and celestial bodies. This theme reminds me of the following joke. The story is told that Sherlock Holmes and Dr. John Watson went on a camping trip. After sharing a good meal and a good bottle of wine, they retired to their tent for the night. At about 3 AM, Holmes nudges Watson and asks, "Watson, look up into the sky and tell me what you see." Watson responds, "I see millions of stars." "And, what does that tell you?" Holmes asks. Watson replies, "**Astronomically**, it tells me that there are millions of galaxies and potentially billions of planets. **Theologically**, the expansiveness of the sky tells me that God is great and we are small and insignificant. It is a humbling experience. Yet I am inspired by the fact that the Creator made all this

God of Creation

(5) Who made the heavens with understanding
for His kindness is everlasting.
(6) Who spread out the earth upon the waters
for His kindness is everlasting.
(7) To Him Who made great lights
for His kindness is everlasting.
(8) The sun, to rule by day
for His kindness is everlasting.
(9) The moon and stars, to rule by night
for His kindness is everlasting.

God of History

(10) Who smote Egypt through their firstborn
for His kindness is everlasting.
(11) And brought Israel out of their midst
for His kindness is everlasting.

---

for us to ponder, study, and observe. And, Holmes, what does the starlit sky tell you?" Holmes retorts, "Ah, the sky… It tells me someone stole our tent!"

לְמַכֵּה מִצְרַיִם בִּבְכוֹרֵיהֶם

This verse is a double entendre: It could mean that Egypt was smitten **in** their firstborn, or **by** their first-born. Indeed, *Tosafot* (*Shabbat* 87b and several *midrashim*) cites a tradition indicating that the Egyptian firstborn, upon hearing of their pending demise, started an armed rebellion against Pharaoh and the elders for not releasing the Israelites. This led to the loss of many Egyptians. R. Baruch Epstein suggests that this explains why the last plague is called *Makkat Bekhorot* and not simply: *Bekhorot*. It alludes to the fact that not only were the firstborn smitten but they also smote!

(יב) בְּיָד חֲזָקָה וּבִזְרוֹעַ נְטוּיָה. כִּי לְעוֹלָם חַסְדּוֹ:

(יג) לְגֹזֵר יַם סוּף לִגְזָרִים. כִּי לְעוֹלָם חַסְדּוֹ:

(יד) וְהֶעֱבִיר יִשְׂרָאֵל בְּתוֹכוֹ. כִּי לְעוֹלָם חַסְדּוֹ:

(טו) וְנִעֵר פַּרְעֹה וְחֵילוֹ בְיַם סוּף. כִּי לְעוֹלָם חַסְדּוֹ:

(טז) לְמוֹלִיךְ עַמּוֹ בַּמִּדְבָּר. כִּי לְעוֹלָם חַסְדּוֹ:

(יז) לְמַכֵּה מְלָכִים גְּדֹלִים. כִּי לְעוֹלָם חַסְדּוֹ:

(יח) וַיַּהֲרֹג מְלָכִים אַדִּירִים. כִּי לְעוֹלָם חַסְדּוֹ:

בְּיָד חֲזָקָה וּבִזְרוֹעַ נְטוּיָה

R. Joseph B. Soloveitchik (*Mesorat ha-Rav Siddur*, p. 454) indicates that *be-Yad hazaka*, "with a strong hand" refers to the Lord's one-time forceful actions in Egypt. However, the imagery of *u-vi-zero'a netuya*, "and with an outstretched arm" symbolizes the idea that God's arm is forever outstretched over the nation of Israel to shield them from their enemies. Even after the Jews have been saved from one calamity, his arm remains outstretched to protect them from future troubles. R. Yaakov Emden writes (Introduction to his "Siddur Bet Yaakov") in this regard: "One who thinks about the fact that we [Jews] are standing in exile among nations who persecute us and cause us trouble, and yet cling to God, recognizes the great wonder that we have survived since the destruction of the Holy Temple until today. By my Life! When I consider the existence of our people in exile, one sheep surrounded by seventy wolves, it is greater in my eyes than all the miracles that were done for our ancestors in Egypt, on the Red Sea, and in the Land of Israel." This is a very important message for Jews in precarious positions throughout the diaspora, and one of the fundamental take-home messages of the *Haggada*.

לְגֹזֵר יַם סוּף לִגְזָרִים

(1) Amos Hakham in his *Da'at Mikra* commentary to Psalms suggests that *li-gezarim* means "cut into two parts." Indeed, in the well-known dispute between the two prostitutes over the live baby (Kings I, 3:16ff), King Solomon rules: *Gizru et ha-yeled ha-hai li-shenayim...* – "Cut the live child in two, and give half to one and half to the other."

(12) With a strong hand and outstretched arm
for His kindness is everlasting.
(13) Who split the Red Sea into sections
for His kindness is everlasting.
(14) And led Israel through it
for His kindness is everlasting.
(15) Cast Pharaoh and army into the Red Sea
for His kindness is everlasting.
(16) Who led His people through the wildnerness
for His kindness is everlasting.
(17) Who smote great kings
for His kindness is everlasting.
(18) And slew mighty kings
for His kindness is everlasting.

---

(2) Nevertheless, *li-gezarim* can be interpreted as several slices, and Rashi (based on *Pirkei de-Rabbi Eliezer*, Chap. 42) indicates that *Yam Suf* was split into 12 lanes, one for each tribe. The question then becomes why was such a miracle necessary? (a) The first answer suggests that it was a simple logistics problem. With 2–3 million individuals fleeing the Egyptians, the throughput via 12 channels moving forward simultaneously is greater and easier. (b) Since there was water on each side, they could see the miracle up close. (c) R. Reuven Margaliot (citing the *Sefat Emet*) indicates that this way no Tribe could claim they are more worthy since they were upfront. No tribe could say to the others: You were saved because of my merit!

(3) Rabbenu Bahya ben Asher (Ex. 13:17) creatively posits that the miracle of the Red Sea was a "rolling" one. Thus, the water waited for the Israelites to progress. As they moved forward through the sea, another "slice" of the front slowly receded before them. As the verse says in *Hallel* (Psalms 114:3) *ha-Yam ra'a va-yanos* – "the sea saw and fled." Thus, the Israelites were actively involved in this ongoing miracle.

לְמַכֵּה מְלָכִים גְּדֹלִים... וַיַּהֲרֹג מְלָכִים אַדִּירִים

The six verses 17–22 seemingly deal with the conquest of the Promised Land; hence many commentaries understand these lines to refer to the

(יט) לְסִיחוֹן מֶלֶךְ הָאֱמֹרִי. כִּי לְעוֹלָם חַסְדּוֹ:

(כ) וּלְעוֹג מֶלֶךְ הַבָּשָׁן. כִּי לְעוֹלָם חַסְדּוֹ:

(כא) וְנָתַן אַרְצָם לְנַחֲלָה. כִּי לְעוֹלָם חַסְדּוֹ:

(כב) נַחֲלָה לְיִשְׂרָאֵל עַבְדּוֹ. כִּי לְעוֹלָם חַסְדּוֹ:

God's Continual Supervision

(כג) שֶׁבְּשִׁפְלֵנוּ זָכַר לָנוּ. כִּי לְעוֹלָם חַסְדּוֹ:

---

vanquishing of the Kings of Canaan (Yehoshua 12). There are however various stylistic questions regarding these verses:

(1) Verses 17 and 18 talk about subduing "great kings" and then "mighty kings." The two verses seem redundant.

(2) Verses 19 and 20 talk specifically about Kings *Sihon* and *Og*. Aren't they already included in verses 17 and 18?

(3) Regarding verses 21 and 22: *ve-natan artzam* **nahala** (inheritance)... **nahala** *le-Yisrael avdo*..., why repeat *nahala*? Simply say one verse of five words: *ve-natan artzam nahala le-Yisrael avdo* ("He gave their land as an inheritance to His servant Israel.") The need for two lines can't be a result of a four-word limit to each verse (excluding *ki le-olam hasdo*), since both verses 9 and 15 have five words each!

R. Hayim Joseph David Azulai (Hida, *Simhat ha-Regel*), R. Baruch Epstein (*Barukh she-Amar*), and R. Ben Zion Nesher (*Haggada Shir Zion*) suggest verses 17–22 deal with Moshe's conquest of the Kings on the Eastern bank of the Jordan. As we will see shortly, this novel suggestion resolves and clarifies the above issues, and gives us a new understanding of the meaning and flow of these six lines. But first some words of introduction.

We need to remember that because of the family connection between Avraham and Lot, it was forbidden for the Israelites to conquer the land of *Mo'av* and *Amon* (Deut. 2:9 and 19) – Lot's children were born through incest (Gen. 19:37–38). However, God nevertheless arranged that substantial portions of these lands would be captured by Kings *Sihon* and *Og* (Num. 21:24; Judges 11:13–21) and were, henceforth, considered the conquerors' legal possession (*Gittin* 38a). Once ownership changed hands, Israel could now attack these lands and make

(19) Sihon, king of the Amorites
for His kindness is everlasting.
(20) Og, king of Bashan
for His kindness is everlasting.
(21) And gave us their land as an inheritance
for His kindness is everlasting.
(22) An inheritance to Israel, His servant
for His kindness is everlasting.

GOD OF CONTINUAL SUPERVISION

(23) Who remembered us in our lowliness
for His kindness is everlasting.

---

them their own. R. Azulai, R. Epstein, and R. Nesher suggest that it is to the first stage that verses 17 and 18 refer. God arranged for the defeat of the great and strong Kingdoms of *Amon* and *Mo'av* by *Sihon* and *Og*. In the second stage (verses 19–20), God gave the lands of *Sihon* and *Og* (including the subdued portions of *Amon* and *Mo'av*) over to the hands of the Israelites. The next verses 21 and 22 explain why it happened this way. Verse 21 *ve-natan artzam nahala* goes back to verses 17 and 18 and asserts the Lord gave away **their** *nahala* – i.e., the land of *Mo'av* and *Amon* – presumably to *Sihon* and *Og*. The following verse 22 *nahala le-Yisrael avdo* explains that this inheritance was transferred to *Sihon* and *Og* so that they would pass it on to Israel.

שֶׁבְּשִׁפְלֵנוּ זָכַר לָנוּ

This verse is one of the central take-home messages of the *Seder*. Though we are lowly and downtrodden, the All-Merciful is mindful of us. Mankind, by contrast, tends to pay attention to celebrities, the prominent and powerful, the victor, the rich and the famous. But this verse asserts that God also takes notice of the lowly; even if we are downcast, in a state of confusion, feeling distant from God, suffering the anguish of doubt – God is fully aware of us (see R. Norman Lamm, *The Royal Table: A Passover Haggadah*, 2021). This is very different from

(כד) וַיִּפְרְקֵנוּ מִצָּרֵינוּ. כִּי לְעוֹלָם חַסְדּוֹ:
(כה) נוֹתֵן לֶחֶם לְכָל בָּשָׂר. כִּי לְעוֹלָם חַסְדּוֹ:
(כו) הוֹדוּ לְאֵל הַשָּׁמָיִם. כִּי לְעוֹלָם חַסְדּוֹ:

נשמת (ברכת השיר)

(1) נִשְׁמַת כָּל חַי תְּבָרֵךְ אֶת שִׁמְךָ, ה' אֱלֹהֵינוּ, וְרוּחַ כָּל בָּשָׂר תְּפָאֵר וּתְרוֹמֵם זִכְרְךָ, מַלְכֵּנוּ, תָּמִיד. מִן הָעוֹלָם וְעַד הָעוֹלָם אַתָּה אֵל.

(Psalms 145:18): *Karov Hashem le-khol korav* where those who call out to the Lord, feel close to Him – and He reciprocates with closeness. In s*he-be-Shiflenu*, we are talking about feelings of alienation, that God is distant, unresponsive, and uncaring. These are the feelings of one who is downtrodden and tormented by physical suffering, or who is in mourning for a dear one. *she-be-Shiflenu zakhar lanu* asserts that this is incorrect and the Almighty does care.

Interestingly, the term *ha-Makom* appears four memorable times in Jewish liturgy: (1) By the *Seder* – Barukh **ha-Makom** Barukh Hu; (2) At the beginning of Yom Kippur: Al da'at **ha-Makom** ve-al da'at ha-kahal; (3) When comforting mourners sitting *shiva*: **ha-Makom** yenahem etkhem; and (4) On Mondays and Thursdays in a prayer for those in suffering, distress or captivity: **ha-Makom** yerahem aleihem. In the first two cases, God's presence is palpable: we sense it on Yom Kippur in the solemnity and sanctity; we sense it on *Pesah* in the majesty and joy. But in mourning and suffering, man feels alienated, God seems distant and hidden. It seems to me that this is why we use the same term for God, *ha-Makom*, on all four occasions – to signal that, in truth, the All-Merciful is nigh.

שֶׁבְּשִׁפְלֵנוּ זָכַר לָנוּ... וַיִּפְרְקֵנוּ מִצָּרֵינוּ... נוֹתֵן לֶחֶם לְכָל בָּשָׂר... הוֹדוּ לְאֵל הַשָּׁמָיִם...

R. Yehuda Samet (https://ohr.edu/yhiy/article.php/806) suggests that these last four verses of *Hallel Ha-Gadol* can be seen as paralleling the four cups we drink tonight. Over the first cup, we make *Kiddush* and

(24) And delivered us from our oppressors
for His kindness is everlasting.
(25) Who gives food to all flesh
for His kindness is everlasting.
(26) Give thanks to the God of heavens
for His kindness is everlasting.

Nishmat (Birkat ha-Shir)

(1) The soul of every living being shall bless Your Name, Lord, our God; the spirit of all flesh shall always glorify and exalt Your remembrance, our King. In this world and for eternity You are God,

---

declare, "You chose us from all the nations." Why did God choose us? The Sages explain that He chose the Jewish people because of their humility. *She-be-Shiflenu zakhar lanu* – "In our lowliness (our humility) He remembered us" and chose us. The second cup goes together with the *Haggada*, where we tell how *va-Yifrekenu mi-tzarenu* – "God redeemed us from our oppressors." The third cup is used for *Birkat ha-Mazon*, where we recognize that *Noten lehem le-khol basar* – "He gives food to all flesh." And with the fourth cup, we sing *Hallel…Hodu le-Kel ha-Shamayim* – "Praise the Lord of the heavens!"

With these four verses, we have moved from extolling the God of Creation and History in *Hallel ha-Mitzri and Hallel Ha-Gadol,* to glorifying the God of the Everyday, the God who works through the Laws of Nature. This then serves as a natural transition into *Nishmat* which deals with this very theme in its first section, as it beautifully praises a God "who guides His world with loving-kindness and His creatures with compassion."

נשמת (ברכת השיר)

This magnificent poem evolved over several hundred years and is comprised of three parts. The first section, according to the first-generation *Amora* R. Yohanan (died ca. 280 C.E.), is the *birkat ha-Shir* mentioned in the *Mishna* (*Pesahim* 117b) as the conclusion to *Hallel* at the *Seder*. The second part, *amoraic* in origin and beginning with *Ilu pinu malei*

וּמִבַּלְעָדֶיךָ אֵין לָנוּ מֶלֶךְ גּוֹאֵל וּמוֹשִׁיעַ. פּוֹדֶה וּמַצִּיל וּמְפַרְנֵס וּמְרַחֵם בְּכָל עֵת צָרָה וְצוּקָה. אֵין לָנוּ מֶלֶךְ אֶלָּא אָתָּה. אֱלֹהֵי הָרִאשׁוֹנִים וְהָאַחֲרוֹנִים. אֱלוֹהַּ כָּל בְּרִיּוֹת. אֲדוֹן כָּל תּוֹלָדוֹת. הַמְהֻלָּל בְּרֹב הַתִּשְׁבָּחוֹת. הַמְנַהֵג עוֹלָמוֹ בְּחֶסֶד וּבְרִיּוֹתָיו בְּרַחֲמִים. וַה׳ לֹא יָנוּם וְלֹא יִישָׁן – הַמְעוֹרֵר יְשֵׁנִים וְהַמֵּקִיץ נִרְדָּמִים, וְהַמֵּשִׂיחַ אִלְּמִים וְהַמַּתִּיר אֲסוּרִים וְהַסּוֹמֵךְ נוֹפְלִים וְהַזּוֹקֵף כְּפוּפִים. לְךָ לְבַדְּךָ אֲנַחְנוּ מוֹדִים.

(2) אִלּוּ פִינוּ מָלֵא שִׁירָה כַיָּם. וּלְשׁוֹנֵנוּ רִנָּה כַּהֲמוֹן גַּלָּיו, וְשִׂפְתוֹתֵינוּ שֶׁבַח כְּמֶרְחֲבֵי רָקִיעַ. וְעֵינֵינוּ מְאִירוֹת כַּשֶּׁמֶשׁ וְכַיָּרֵחַ. וְיָדֵינוּ פְרוּשׂוֹת כְּנִשְׁרֵי שָׁמַיִם. וְרַגְלֵינוּ קַלּוֹת כָּאַיָּלוֹת – אֵין אֲנַחְנוּ מַסְפִּיקִים לְהוֹדוֹת

shira kha-yam, is mentioned in *Berakhot* 59b as a thanksgiving prayer for rain. Finally, the third section, starting with *Al ken evarim she-pilagta banu* down to *avdekha meshihekha*, was composed in the Gaonic period.

To place *Nishmat* in context, we need to remember that we have thus far spoken of the Almighty as the God of Creation, the God of History; a God who has a covenant with the People of Israel, and the God of the everyday, who cares about the individual, even the downtrodden. This last theme continues into Section 1 of *Nishmat*. All this makes man awestruck, so much so that he becomes speechless – because he can't possibly do God justice with his simple praise (as described in Section 2). If so, why does man sing God's acclaim? Says R. Joseph B. Soloveitchik that this is because we cannot help ourselves. All we can do is say "Wow"! And we do it in every way possible, with every limb.

גּוֹאֵל וּמוֹשִׁיעַ. פּוֹדֶה וּמַצִּיל

We have here two sets of synonyms. The first compares *ge'ula* (redemption) to *yeshu'a* (salvation). According to the Gra (*Haggada ha-Gra ve-Talmidav*), in **ge'ula** – God takes one out of a bad situation, while in **yeshu'a** – He saves us so that we don't get into the bad situation in the first place. Regarding *podeh u-matzil*, the Gra (*Be'ur ha-Gra*, Proverbs 14:28) proposes that **podeh** means that we are redeemed – saved with the consent of the tyrant, while **matzil** implies that we were saved without the consent of the tyrant, by a strong hand and an outstretched arm.

and besides You we have no King, Redeemer and Savior Who delivers, rescues, saves, sustains, and is merciful in every time of trouble and distress; we have no King but You. You are the God of the first and of the last, God of all creatures, Lord of all generations, Who is extolled with manifold praises, Who directs His world with kindness and His creatures with compassion. Behold, the Lord neither slumbers nor sleeps. He arouses the sleepers and awakens the slumberous, gives speech to the mute, releases the bound, supports the falling and raises up those who are bowed. To You alone we give thanks.

(2) Were our mouths as full of song as the sea, and our tongues with joyous singing like the multitudes of its waves, and our lips with

---

צָרָה וְצוּקָה

The Gra (*Be'ur ha-Gra*, Proverbs 1:27) proposes that **tzara** is sorrow and mourning, where there are clear external factors, like the loss of property or a loved one. **Tzuka,** on the other hand, is sadness, anguish, and deep concern.

הַמְהֻלָּל בְּרֹב הַתִּשְׁבָּחוֹת

The word *rov* in modern Hebrew can mean "majority." But in Biblical Hebrew, it is synonymous with *harbeh* or many, and that is its meaning here (R. Yaakov Emden, *Siddur Bet Yaakov*). (See also the discussion of Amos Hakham to *Da'at Mikra* on Esther 10:3, note 17.)

וְעֵינֵינוּ מְאִירוֹת כַּשֶּׁמֶשׁ וְכַיָּרֵחַ. וְיָדֵינוּ פְּרוּשׂוֹת כְּנִשְׁרֵי שָׁמַיִם. וְרַגְלֵינוּ קַלּוֹת כָּאַיָּלוֹת

What would the eyes, hands, and feet do to give praise to the Almighty? R. Joseph Hertz (*Siddur*) suggests that the eyes would light up creation and the hands and feet would run to do God's will. In other words, doing His will is also a form of praise to the Almighty. I would suggest that the verse is talking about **dance** – praise given in motion. Dance in praise of Hashem is mentioned by King David as they brought the Holy Ark to the City of David. It is also mentioned in *Mishna Sukka* (5:1) by the rejoicing of the *Simhat Bet ha-Sho'eva*. The hyperbolic style of *Nishmat* is strongly reminiscent of *Akdamot*, read on *Shavu'ot*.

לָךְ. ה' אֱלֹהֵינוּ וֵאלֹהֵי אֲבוֹתֵינוּ. וּלְבָרֵךְ אֶת שִׁמְךָ עַל אַחַת מֵאָלֶף, אַלְפֵי אֲלָפִים וְרִבֵּי רְבָבוֹת פְּעָמִים הַטּוֹבוֹת שֶׁעָשִׂיתָ עִם אֲבוֹתֵינוּ וְעִמָּנוּ. מִמִּצְרַיִם גְּאַלְתָּנוּ. ה' אֱלֹהֵינוּ. וּמִבֵּית עֲבָדִים פְּדִיתָנוּ. בְּרָעָב זַנְתָּנוּ וּבְשָׂבָע כִּלְכַּלְתָּנוּ. מֵחֶרֶב הִצַּלְתָּנוּ וּמִדֶּבֶר מִלַּטְתָּנוּ. וּמֵחֳלָיִם רָעִים וְנֶאֱמָנִים דִּלִּיתָנוּ. עַד הֵנָּה עֲזָרוּנוּ רַחֲמֶיךָ וְלֹא עֲזָבוּנוּ חֲסָדֶיךָ. וְאַל תִּטְּשֵׁנוּ. ה' אֱלֹהֵינוּ. לָנֶצַח.

(3) עַל כֵּן אֵבָרִים שֶׁפִּלַּגְתָּ בָּנוּ וְרוּחַ וּנְשָׁמָה שֶׁנָּפַחְתָּ בְּאַפֵּינוּ וְלָשׁוֹן אֲשֶׁר שַׂמְתָּ בְּפִינוּ – הֵן הֵם יוֹדוּ וִיבָרְכוּ וִישַׁבְּחוּ וִיפָאֲרוּ וִירוֹמְמוּ וְיַעֲרִיצוּ וְיַקְדִּישׁוּ וְיַמְלִיכוּ אֶת שִׁמְךָ מַלְכֵּנוּ. כִּי כָל פֶּה לְךָ יוֹדֶה, וְכָל לָשׁוֹן לְךָ תִשָּׁבַע. וְכָל בֶּרֶךְ לְךָ תִכְרַע. וְכָל קוֹמָה לְפָנֶיךָ תִשְׁתַּחֲוֶה, וְכָל לְבָבוֹת יִירָאוּךְ. וְכָל קֶרֶב וּכְלָיוֹת יְזַמְּרוּ לִשְׁמֶךָ. כַּדָּבָר שֶׁכָּתוּב (תהלים לה:י). כָּל עַצְמוֹתַי תֹּאמַרְנָה, ה' מִי כָמוֹךָ, מַצִּיל עָנִי מֵחָזָק מִמֶּנּוּ וְעָנִי וְאֶבְיוֹן מִגֹּזְלוֹ. מִי יִדְמֶה לָּךְ וּמִי יִשְׁוֶה לָּךְ וּמִי יַעֲרָךְ לָךְ הָאֵל הַגָּדוֹל. הַגִּבּוֹר וְהַנּוֹרָא. אֵל עֶלְיוֹן, קֹנֵה שָׁמַיִם וָאָרֶץ. נְהַלֶּלְךָ וּנְשַׁבֵּחֲךָ וּנְפָאֶרְךָ וּנְבָרֵךְ אֶת שֵׁם קָדְשֶׁךָ. כָּאָמוּר: לְדָוִד, בָּרְכִי נַפְשִׁי אֶת ה'. וְכָל קְרָבַי אֶת שֵׁם קָדְשׁוֹ.

עַל כֵּן אֵבָרִים שֶׁפִּלַּגְתָּ בָּנוּ... הֵן הֵם יוֹדוּ וִיבָרְכוּ וִישַׁבְּחוּ...

We have already pointed out the seeming contradiction between two sections of *Nishmat*. In section 2 we describe how we lack the ability to appropriately praise the Almighty. Nonetheless, in section 3 we go ahead and do it! R. Joseph B. Soloveitchik answered that while it is true that we lack the proper ability, we can't help ourselves. It's involuntary. R. Ovadia Yosef suggested that after man realizes his limitations and inadequacy, he also comprehends that he was made this way by the Creator. Hence, he declares: "Therefore, the limbs **You** formed within us, and the spirit and soul **You** breathed into our nostrils, and the tongue **You** placed in our mouth...." You God created them all and hence cannot expect more. Therefore, we will sing Your praises with all that You have placed at our disposal.

praise like the expanse of the sky; and our eyes shining like the sun and the moon, and our hands spread out like the eagles of heaven, and our feet swift like deer we would still be unable to thank You Lord, our God and God of our fathers, and to bless Your Name, for even one of the thousands, and myriads of favors which You have done for us and for our fathers before us. Lord our God. You have redeemed us from Egypt, You have freed us from the house of bondage, You have fed us in famine and nourished us in times of plenty; You have saved us from the sword and delivered us from pestilence, and rescued us from evil and lasting diseases. Until now Your mercies have helped us, and Your kindnesses have not forsaken us; and do not abandon us, Lord our God, forever!

(3) Therefore, the limbs which You have formed for us, and the spirit and soul which You have breathed into our nostrils, and the tongue which You have placed in our mouth all shall thank, bless, praise, glorify, exalt, adore, sanctify and proclaim the sovereignty of Your Name, our King. For every mouth shall offer thanks to You, every tongue shall swear loyalty to You, every knee shall bend to You, all who stand erect shall bow down before You, all hearts shall fear You, and every innermost part shall sing praise to Your Name, as it is written (Psalms 35:10): "All my bones will say, Lord, who is like You; You save the poor from one stronger than he, the poor and the needy from one who would rob him!" Who can be likened to You, who is equal to You, who can be compared to You, the great, mighty, awesome God, God most high, Possessor of heaven and earth! We will laud You, praise You and glorify You, and we will bless Your holy Name, as it says: "A Psalm of David; bless the Lord, O my soul, and all that is within me bless His holy Name."

כָּל עַצְמוֹתַי תֹּאמַרְנָה. ה' מִי כָמוֹךָ

This verse reflects the fundamental position of Judaism that the body is equally important to the soul in the service of the Creator. This is because the body is the only real agent for the fulfillment of *mitzvot*. At a *Shabbat* gathering I attended in the home of R. Elimelech Bar-Shaul in 1964, the Rehovot Chief Rabbi remarked that this verse is cited (in the

הָאֵל בְּתַעֲצֻמוֹת עֻזֶּךָ. הַגָּדוֹל בִּכְבוֹד שְׁמֶךָ. הַגִּבּוֹר לָנֶצַח וְהַנּוֹרָא בְּנוֹרְאוֹתֶיךָ. הַמֶּלֶךְ הַיּוֹשֵׁב עַל כִּסֵּא רָם וְנִשָּׂא.

שׁוֹכֵן עַד מָרוֹם וְקָדוֹשׁ שְׁמוֹ. וְכָתוּב: רַנְּנוּ צַדִּיקִים בַּה׳, לַיְשָׁרִים נָאוָה

Mishna Berura, O.H., sec. 95, sub-sec. 7) as the source for *shokeling* – the traditional swaying back in forth in prayer. "You see," said R. Bar Shaul, "prayer is primarily the service of the heart. The body too wants to be involved – so it *shokels*." The critical point is that, in contradistinction to many other faiths, mainstream Judaism does not consider the *neshama* (soul) as good and the body as bad. How could the body be bad? It was made by the Creator Himself! What's more, it is only through the body that we can reach out to and serve the Almighty. This idea was also presented by my father, R. Norman E. Frimer z"l, in *A Jewish Quest for Religious Meaning* (Ktav, 1993):

> Judaism is more than a "spiritual" or "intellectual" religion. It does not direct its call to the soul or mind of man alone. When man stands over against God in a one-to-one relationship (as all of us must ultimately do in our existential aloneness), the relationship is not partial, but total; not fragmentary, but full – involving the whole person. In this linkage, the body is a partner with divinity. God created it. It is not profane unless man deliberately makes it so. Like the ark housing the Torah, the body enshrines the soul in an inextricable life-union. Neither can meet its maker without the other. The soul remains mute and helpless without the body; the body is cold and cloddish without the soul. As a divinely joined composite they can aspire to fulfill the liturgical task enunciated in the *Nishmat* hymn, "All my limbs declare, O Lord who is like unto Thee!"

Auschwitz survivor R. Zvi Hirsch Meisels (Introduction to his *Resp. Mekadshei Hashem*, p. 19) has a different take on this verse: "In light of the beatings and tortures we have endured at the hands of the murderers – may their memory be erased – the fact that *Kol atzmotai* ("our bones

You are the Almighty God in the power of Your strength; great in the glory of Your Name; mighty forever, and awe-inspiring in Your awesome deeds; the King Who sits upon a lofty and exalted throne.

He Who dwells for eternity, exalted and Holy is His name. And it is written: "Exult, righteous ones, before God; for the upright praise is

---

remained intact") *tomarna* ("bears witness to") *Hashem mi khamokha* ("the incomparable power of the Almighty")."

רָם וְנִשָּׂא

This is based on Isaiah (6:1): *va-Ereh et Ado-nai yoshev al kisei ram ve-nisa* – "I beheld my Lord seated on a throne high and lofty." There is a dispute among the commentaries whether the *ram ve-nisa* – "high and lofty" refers to the chair upon which God sits (Radak, Alshikh, and Amos Hakham in *Da'at Mikra*; Artscroll Siddur) or to the King/God himself who is high and lofty (Malbim; the cantillations (*Ta'amei ha-Mikra*); *Koren Sacks Siddur*). Normally on *Shabbat*, the *Hazan* for *Shaharit* begins with **Shokhen ad** which emphasizes that God is Creator of the world and time, and has existed for all eternity. On *Yom Tov*, we emphasize God's miracles and his absolute power and control. Hence, we start with **ha-Kel be-ta'atzumot uzekha.** Finally, on the *Yamim Noraim*, we emphasize God as **ha-Melekh** – King of the Universe.

שׁוֹכֵן עַד

This is based on Isaiah 57:15. Here too there is some discussion as to how to set the words. (1) One approach is to say: *Shokhen ad/ marom/ ve-kadosh shemo*. Here *ad* means *la-ad* – "for eternity." *Marom*, "exalted," refers back to *shokhen*. So the verse means: God inhabits eternity – (God dwells) in an exalted location and Holy is His name. (2) Another approach is to read it: *Shokhen ad/ marom ve-kadosh shemo*. *Marom* refers to *Shemo* or His name. Put together this becomes: God inhabits eternity, exalted and Holy is His name. And that is how most translations render this verse. (3) The third approach is: *Shokhen ad marom/ ve-kadosh shemo*. Here *ad marom* means: on high. Thus, the verse means: God who dwells on high, and Holy is His name.

תְּהִלָּה. בְּפִי יְשָׁרִים תִּתְהַלָּל. וּבְדִבְרֵי צַדִּיקִים תִּתְבָּרַךְ. וּבִלְשׁוֹן חֲסִידִים תִּתְרוֹמָם, וּבְקֶרֶב קְדוֹשִׁים תִּתְקַדָּשׁ.

וּבְמַקְהֲלוֹת רִבְבוֹת עַמְּךָ בֵּית יִשְׂרָאֵל בְּרִנָּה יִתְפָּאֵר שִׁמְךָ, מַלְכֵּנוּ. בְּכָל דּוֹר וָדוֹר. שֶׁכֵּן חוֹבַת כָּל הַיְצוּרִים לְפָנֶיךָ, ה' אֱלֹהֵינוּ וֵאלֹהֵי אֲבוֹתֵינוּ, לְהוֹדוֹת לְהַלֵּל לְשַׁבֵּחַ. לְפָאֵר לְרוֹמֵם לְהַדֵּר לְבָרֵךְ, לְעַלֵּה וּלְקַלֵּס עַל כָּל דִּבְרֵי שִׁירוֹת וְתִשְׁבָּחוֹת דָּוִד בֶּן יִשַׁי עַבְדְּךָ מְשִׁיחֶךָ.

יִשְׁתַּבַּח שִׁמְךָ לָעַד מַלְכֵּנוּ. הָאֵל הַמֶּלֶךְ הַגָּדוֹל וְהַקָּדוֹשׁ בַּשָּׁמַיִם וּבָאָרֶץ, כִּי לְךָ נָאֶה, ה' אֱלֹהֵינוּ וֵאלֹהֵי אֲבוֹתֵינוּ, (1) שִׁיר (2) וּשְׁבָחָה, (3) הַלֵּל (4) וְזִמְרָה, (5) עֹז (6) וּמֶמְשָׁלָה, (7) נֶצַח, (8) גְּדֻלָּה (9) וּגְבוּרָה, (10) תְּהִלָּה (11) וְתִפְאֶרֶת, (12) קְדֻשָּׁה (13) וּמַלְכוּת, (14) בְּרָכוֹת (15) וְהוֹדָאוֹת מֵעַתָּה וְעַד עוֹלָם. בָּרוּךְ אַתָּה ה', אֵל מֶלֶךְ גָּדוֹל בַּתִּשְׁבָּחוֹת. אֵל הַהוֹדָאוֹת, אֲדוֹן הַנִּפְלָאוֹת. הַבּוֹחֵר בְּשִׁירֵי זִמְרָה, מֶלֶךְ אֵל חֵי הָעוֹלָמִים.

בְּפִי יְשָׁרִים תִּתְהַלָּל

R. Zvi Yehuda Kook (https://meirtv.com/alon-1341/) pointed out that most people believe that there are four levels of righteous individuals described in *Shokhen ad*, namely: *yesharim* – the upright, *tzaddikim* – the righteous, *hassidim* – the devout, and *kedoshim* – the holy. He, however, maintains that the highest level is *be-makhelot* – where all Jewry unites together to sing God's praise. After all, the responsibility to appreciate and praise the Almighty does not fall on the religious elite – they are merely the teachers of Israel – but on the Jewish people as a whole, who are meant to be the teachers of the rest of the world!

וּלְקַלֵּס

This is the same crescendo of synonyms for praise that appeared just before the start of *Hallel* at the end of *Maggid*.

fitting." By the mouth of the upright You are praised; by the word of the righteous You shall be blessed; by the tongue of the devout You shall be exalted; and among the holy ones You shall be sanctified.

And in the assembled multitudes of Your people, the House of Israel, with joyous song Your Name, our King, is glorified in every generation. For such is the obligation of all creatures before You, Lord our God and God of our fathers, to thank, to laud, to praise, to glorify, to exalt, to adore, to bless, to elevate and to honor You, even beyond all the words of songs and praises of David son of Yishai, Your anointed servant.

May Your name be praised forever, our King, the great and holy God and King in heaven and on earth. For You, Lord, our God and God of our fathers, forever befits (1) song (2) and praise, (3) laud (4) and hymn, (5) strength (6) and dominion, (7) victory, (8) greatness and (9) might, (10) glory, (11) splendor, (12) holiness (13) and sovereignty; (14) blessings and (15) thanksgivings for now and forever. Blessed are You, Lord, Almighty God, King, great and extolled in praises, God of thanksgivings, Lord of wonders, Who takes pleasure in songs of praise; King, God, the Life of all worlds.

יִשְׁתַּבַּח שִׁמְךָ לָעַד מַלְכֵּנוּ

The word *la-ad* – "forever," refers back to *Yishtabah*. Thus, this phrase should be parsed *Yishtabah shimkha la-ad/ malkenu* – "May Your name be praised forever, our King" and not as it is commonly and wrongly done *Yishtabah shimkha/ la-ad malkenu*. This is followed by fifteen expressions of praise from *Shir u-shevaha* to *berakhot ve-hoda'ot*. Indeed, in addition to the numbers 4 and 10, 15 is one of the central numbers of the *Seder*. Thus, there are the above fifteen expressions of praise in ישתבח, 15 words in the closing *berakha* of *Yishtabah* (excluding *Barukh Ata Hashem*), 15 *simanim* of the *Seder*, 15 verses in *Dayenu*. Fifteen corresponds to the numerical value of God's name *yud heh (Kah)*; the 15 steps leading from the outer court to the inner court of the Temple; the number of generations from Avraham – who recognized his Creator, to King Solomon – who built Him the *Bet ha-Mikdash*; and, finally, the number of words in the *Kohanim*'s blessing.

R. Barukh Epstein (*Barukh she-Amar*) asks how we are permitted to say so many terms of praise, in light of the following story about Rabbi Ḥanina in *Masekhet Berakhot* (33b):

> A particular individual descended before the ark as the prayer leader in the presence of Rabbi Ḥanina. He extended his prayer and said: "God, the great, mighty, awesome, powerful, mighty, awe-inspiring, strong, fearless, steadfast and honored." Rabbi Ḥanina waited for him until he completed his prayer. When he finished, Rabbi Ḥanina asked him: "Have you concluded all of the praises of your Master? Why do I need [to say] all of this superfluous praise? Even these three praises that we recite [the great, mighty, and awesome,] had Moshe our teacher not said them in the Torah and had the members of the Great Assembly not come and incorporated them into the *Amida* prayer, we would not be permitted to recite them. And you went on and recited all of these. It is comparable to a king who possessed many thousands of golden dinars, yet they were praising him for silver ones. Isn't that deprecatory?"

Thus, we see that reciting a litany of praise does not enhance God's honor. R. Epstein suggests two possible resolutions. Firstly, the problem is only in listing a long list of praises or extending the content or number of examples. In *Yishtabah* we are only describing the many techniques or styles in which God's praise is rendered: "...song and praise, hymn and psalm..." – but not the praises themselves, as occurred in the case of R. Ḥanina. Secondly, suggests R. Epstein, this problem only exists in *Shemoneh Esrei*, which is comprised of *shevah* – praise, *bakasha* – request, and *hodaya* – thanks (see Maimonides, MT, *Hil. Tefilla* 1:4). Hence, increasing the praise is problematic because it can easily be misunderstood as a sort of "bribery" or flattery in anticipation of the subsequent requests. Such excessive praise is deprecatory – as if one is praising for a benefit. However, in *Yishtabah*, we have pure praise and no requests. The synonyms are part of the prayer's rich poetic beauty – and certainly permissible.

הַבּוֹחֵר בְּשִׁירֵי זִמְרָה

The word *ha-boher* literally means to choose or prefer. The question is: What are the choices? I understand *ha-boher be-amo Yisrael be-ahava* – "Who chooses His people Israel in love" which we recite before *Keri'at Shema*. After all, God could have chosen to give the Torah to one of the other nations of the world. I also understand *ha-boher ba-Torah, u-ve-Moshe avdo u-vi-nevi'ei ha-emet ve-ha-tzedek* – "Who chooses the Torah, Moshe His servant, His nation Israel and the prophet of truth and righteousness" – which we say before reading the *haftara* from the prophets. Again, God could have chosen non-Jewish prophets, yet he chose Moshe and the Jewish prophets that followed him. What is the Almighty choosing here?

The answer is that God could have chosen to listen to the Angelic Heavenly Choir – and what a unified beautiful song that would be! Yet he chose to listen to Israel. The verse in *Psalms* (22:4) reads: *ve-Ata kadosh yoshev tehillot Yisrael* – You Holy One are enthroned upon the praises of Israel." Rashi understands *yoshev* to mean – "sit and wait." Thus, he renders this verse: You, Holy One, have made it your wont from time immemorial to sit waiting for the Praise of Israel. Amos Hakham in his *Da'at Mikra* commentary explains this verse similarly: You, God, are sanctified by the angels [who declare your holiness by publicly declaring: Holy! Holy! Holy!]. Nevertheless, You wait to hear the daily praise of Israel. This explanation is based on Hullin 91b which reads:

> The Jewish people are dearer to the Holy One, blessed is He, than the ministering angels. The Jewish people may recite a song of praise to God at any time, but ministering angels recite a song of praise only one time per day... Furthermore, the Jewish people mention the name of God after two words, as it is stated (Deut. 6:4): *Shema Yisrael* **Hashem** *Elokeinu Hashem Ehad*. But the ministering angels mention the name of God only after three words, as it is written (Isaiah 6:3): *Kadosh, Kadosh, Kadosh* **Hashem** *tze-va'ot melo khol ha-aretz kevodo* ... And the ministering angels do not recite their song above until the Jewish people recite their song below on earth...

כוס רביעי

The following blessing is recited before drinking the fourth cup in a reclining position:

בָּרוּךְ אַתָּה ה', אֱלֹהֵינוּ מֶלֶךְ הָעוֹלָם בּוֹרֵא פְּרִי הַגָּפֶן.

It would seem that this preference for the song of Israel is a result of man's free will. The Heavenly angels were created to sing Hashem's praises and they undoubtedly do so exquisitely. But they have no freedom of choice – only man does! So when *Klal Yisrael* praises the Almighty it comes from their deep appreciation of God and His works. Since we choose to sing to the Creator, God **chooses** to listen to us preferentially. *ha-Boher be-shirei zimra* communicates that God has a special relationship with Israel. He listens to our prayers and waits for our songs and praises. He even prefers them over those of the angels. We play a special role in God's scheme of things, and hence He wants us around. King David knew this well.

In this light, we can understand the special role played by *Hallel ha-Gadol* and *Nishmat* and why they were chosen to conclude the *Haggada* as ordained by *Haza"l*. The reason is that these selections give us hope and inspiration as the Jew wanders through history. *Hallel ha-Gadol* and *Nishmat* communicate to us that God cares about us and that we need to "hang in there" for a bright future initiated by the final redemption. Despite all the above, we have to admit though that two millennia is a long time to wait. For this reason, Jewish tradition has added to the *Haggada*, following *Hallel*, the *Nirtza* collection of selected medieval songs whose purpose is to educate, entertain, and inspire – to describe in part what the bright future is all about. No wonder the *Haggada* succeeds in leaving us upbeat and smiling.

ברכת על הגפן

Before we begin *Nirtza*, there is one more piece of *halakhic* business to take care of, namely the recitation of *Al ha-Gefen* after drinking the last of the four cups of wine. *Al ha-Gefen* is one variation of the *Birkat Me-ein Shalosh* – or "the one *berakha* digest of the three." This is because it briefly summarizes the themes of the first three *berakhot* of the *Birkat ha-Mazon* (see our comments above בָּרֵךְ). Other variations of

Fourth Cup

The following blessing is recited before drinking the fourth cup in a reclining position:

Blessed are You, Lord, our God, King of the universe,
Who creates the fruit of the vine.

---

this *Birkat Me-ein Shalosh* are said after eating products made from the seven special fruit of the Land of Israel: wheat, barley, grapes (including wine), figs, pomegranates, olives, and dates. We note that *Al ha-Gefen* is made only after one drinks a volume of a *revi'it* (86 mL or 2.9 fl. oz.) of wine or grape juice, though to fulfill one's obligation of the fourth cup, one only needs to drink the **majority** of a *revi'it*. Nevertheless, the codes (see, e.g.: *Arukh ha-Shulhan* 480:3) indicate that it is proper to drink a full *revi'it* to obligate ourselves to recite *Al ha-Gefen* – and the question is "Why"?

It would seem to us that the text of *Al ha-Gefen* is perfectly suited for the transition into *Nirtza*. We remarked at the end of our previous comment, that as we approach the end of the *Haggada*, Tradition has attempted to communicate to us that God will continue to care for His people until the final redemption. Indeed, *Al ha-Gefen* (and *Birkat Me-ein Shalosh* in general) sings the praises of the Land of Israel that can sustain us and provide for our needs: In *Al ha-gefen* we say: "Blessed art Thou… for the vine and the fruit of the vine and for the precious, good, and spacious land which You have graciously given as a heritage to our ancestors, to eat of its fruit and to be satiated with its goodness." We then pray that *Eretz Yisrael* will be fully rebuilt agriculturally, culturally, nationally, and religiously: "Have mercy, Lord, our God, on Israel Your people, on Jerusalem Your city, on Zion the abode of Your glory, on Your altar, and on Your Temple." We then pray for the ingathering of the exile, the rebuilding of Jerusalem and the Temple: "Rebuild Jerusalem, the holy city, speedily in our days. Bring us up into it and gladden us in its rebuilding, and let us eat from its fruit, and be satisfied with its goodness, and bless You upon it in holiness and purity." It would seem, therefore, that because of this strong sense of hope generated by *Al ha-Gefen*, tradition strongly urged the draining of the entire *revi'it* of the fourth cup in order to **obligate** us to recite this upbeat future focussed prayer.

If the fourth cup of wine contained at least 86 ml (2.91 oz) of wine and was drained, the following blessing is recited:

ברכת על הגפן

בָּרוּךְ אַתָּה ה' אֱלֹהֵינוּ מֶלֶךְ הָעוֹלָם. עַל הַגֶּפֶן וְעַל פְּרִי הַגֶּפֶן, וְעַל תְּנוּבַת הַשָּׂדֶה וְעַל אֶרֶץ חֶמְדָּה טוֹבָה וּרְחָבָה שֶׁרָצִיתָ וְהִנְחַלְתָּ לַאֲבוֹתֵינוּ לֶאֱכוֹל מִפִּרְיָהּ וְלִשְׂבּוֹעַ מִטּוּבָהּ. רַחֶם נָא ה' אֱלֹהֵינוּ עַל יִשְׂרָאֵל עַמֶּךָ וְעַל יְרוּשָׁלַיִם עִירֶךָ וְעַל צִיּוֹן מִשְׁכַּן כְּבוֹדֶךָ וְעַל מִזְבְּחֶךָ וְעַל הֵיכָלֶךָ וּבְנֵה יְרוּשָׁלַיִם עִיר הַקֹּדֶשׁ בִּמְהֵרָה בְיָמֵינוּ וְהַעֲלֵנוּ לְתוֹכָהּ וְשַׂמְּחֵנוּ בְּבִנְיָנָהּ וְנֹאכַל מִפִּרְיָהּ וְנִשְׂבַּע מִטּוּבָהּ וּנְבָרֶכְךָ עָלֶיהָ בִּקְדֻשָּׁה וּבְטָהֳרָה (בשבת: וּרְצֵה וְהַחֲלִיצֵנוּ בְּיוֹם הַשַּׁבָּת הַזֶּה) וְשַׂמְּחֵנוּ בְּיוֹם חַג הַמַּצּוֹת הַזֶּה, כִּי אַתָּה ה' טוֹב וּמֵטִיב לַכֹּל. וְנוֹדֶה לְּךָ עַל הָאָרֶץ וְעַל פְּרִי הַגֶּפֶן (על יין מא"י אומר: פְּרִי גַפְנָהּ). בָּרוּךְ אַתָּה ה'. עַל הַגֶּפֶן וְעַל פְּרִי הַגֶּפֶן (על יין מא"י אומר: פְּרִי גַפְנָהּ).

וְעַל אֶרֶץ חֶמְדָּה טוֹבָה וּרְחָבָה

The importance of *Birkat Me-ein Shalosh*, results from its focus on the rebuilding of *Eretz Yisrael*. The late Chief R. of Rehovot, R. Simcha haKohen Kook cited the Talmudic statement (*Berakhot* 37a) that for wheat and barley products (other than bread) one recites *borei minei mezonot* before and *Birkat Me-ein Shalosh* (*Al ha-Mihya*) thereafter. By contrast, before eating cooked or baked rice, one recites *borei minei mezonot*, but "nothing" afterward. Rashi comments that indeed *Borei nefashot* is said after cooked rice; but the latter is referred to as a "nothing" benediction because – in contradistinction to *Birkat Me-ein Shalosh* – the Land of Israel is not mentioned!

וְנֹאכַל מִפִּרְיָהּ וְנִשְׂבַּע מִטּוּבָהּ

The Tur (OH, sec 208; see also *Torah Temima*, Deut. 3:25, note 6) was troubled by this phrase: "Let us eat from its fruit, and be satisfied with its goodness." This is because it gives the impression that we love the Land of Israel for its physicality and the pleasures it supplies, rather

If the fourth cup of wine contained at least 86 ml (2.91 oz) of wine and was drained, the following blessing is recited:

Final Blessing Over Wine

Blessed are You, Lord our God, King of the universe for the vine and the fruit of the vine, and for the produce of the field, and for the precious, good and spacious land which You have favored to give as an inheritance to our fathers, to eat of its fruit and be satiated by its goodness. Have mercy, Lord our God, on Israel Your people, on Jerusalem Your city, on Zion the abode of Your glory, on Your altar and on Your Temple. Rebuild Jerusalem, the holy city, speedily in our days, and bring us up into it, and make us rejoice in its rebuilding, that we may eat of its fruit and be satiated by its goodness, and we will bless You in holiness and purity. (On Shabbat: May it please You to strengthen us on this Shabbat day) and let us rejoice on this day of the Festival of Matzot. For You, Lord, are good and continually do good to all, and we thank You for the land and for the fruit of the (in Israel: of its) vine. Blessed are You, Lord, for the land and for the fruit of the (in Israel: of its) vine.

---

than for its spirituality – the *mitzvot* associated with the land. To this R. Joel Sirkis (*Bayit Hadash*, ad loc.) responds that *Eretz Yisrael* is infused with sanctity, and hence one should desire to eat its fruit because they will be ingesting its *kedusha*. The physicality of the Land of Israel is infused with sanctity. In this regard, R. Simcha Kook recounted the story of the Belzer Hassid who brought his Rebbe a beautiful large red *Amerikanishe* apple. Despite the Hassid's repeated urging, the Rebbe politely but forcefully refused the Hassid's gift explaining (in his deep Galitsianer accent): *Ayn pyros ke-pyros Eretz Yisruel* [*Ein peirot ke-peirot Eretz Yisrael*] – "There are no fruits like those of the Land of Israel!"

R. Velvel Soloveitchik (*Haggada Im Peirushei Geonei Lita*) comments regarding *ve-Nokhal mi-piryah* – "Let us eat from **its** fruit." Like the previous pronouns, "its" refers to Jerusalem. Yet, the Talmud (*Bava Kama* 82b; *Avot de-Rabi Natan* 35:2) indicates that orchards and gardens were not planted in Jerusalem. Nevertheless, as stated in the next

15. נִרְצָה

verse, we are referring to fruit that needs to be eaten "in holiness and purity." Hence, it is likely that we are talking about the fruit of *Neta Revai* and *Ma'aser Sheni* – which are brought in from outside Jerusalem and eaten therein "in holiness and purity."

נִרְצָה

R. Joseph B. Soloveitchik (*The Seder Night: An Exalted Evening: The Passover Haggadah*, KTAV, 2009) points out that *ritzui* (finding acceptance with the Almighty) is a concept not found by regular *mitzvot* like *shofar* or *lulav*. If God said to do an action and I did it, I have fulfilled my obligation. *Ritzui* is a unique concept of sacrifices, where it is not enough to do the act itself properly. This is because in sacrifices the "human element" is taken into consideration. The Almighty weighs in on our thoughts, motivations, and concerns before He accepts our sacrifice. This is the essence of Isaiah's (1:11) criticism of the sinning Jews: "What need have I of your abundance of sacrifices, sayeth the Lord." R. Chaim Soloveitchik indicates that since our prayers come to replace the Temple sacrifices (based on Hosea 14:3 "Let the utterance of our lips replace the bulls"), prayer also needs *ritzui*. This is why the closing set of three *berakhot* in *Shemoneh Esrei* begins with *Retzei* – "Please accept our prayers favorably..." In actuality, in the weekday *Shemoneh Esrei*, we ask God to accept our prayers twice: once in the sixteenth benediction – *Shema Kolenu*, and a second time immediately afterward in the seventeenth *berakha* – *Retzei*. But there is a difference in the term used for acceptance in the former – *kabbala*, and the term used in the latter – *ritzui*. In *Shema Kolenu*, I ask the Almighty to hear my personal prayers and petitions and to do as I request. God may decide to do so, but I have turned myself into a bit of a "nudnick." In *ritzui*, however, I ask that my prayers should find "favor" in his eyes. In such a case, he would be happy to do what I ask for; there is no negative fallout. So too in the case of the *Pesah Seder*, which comes in part to replace the *Korban Pesah*. We ask God to accept it willingly in anticipation of the real thing.

Some commentators indicate that all the other *simanim* of the *Seder* refer to actions we are supposed to do, e.g., *Kadesh, u-Rehatz, Yahatz*,

15. Nirtza

Maggid, Raḥtza, Shulḥan Orekh, Barekh, Hallel – or describe the object of an action, e.g., *Karpas, Motzi, Matza, Maror, Korekh, Tzafun*. However, *Nirtza* does not seem to require any action; rather it is the **goal** of the other *simanim*: if you do the first fourteen *simanim* properly, the outcome, we pray, will be to find favor and acceptance in the Redeemer's estimation. The Maharal (R. Judah Loew of Prague, *Divrei Negidim*) and Hida (R. Ḥayim Yosef David Azulai, *Simḥat Regel*) both suggest that perhaps there are only fourteen, not fifteen, *simanim* with the last *siman* being *Hallel-Nirtza*. Thus, the purpose of *Hallel* said at the end of the *Seder* is to engender *Nirtza* – appeasement. We are attempting to appease and assuage God's anger which brought about the destruction of the Temple, by demonstrating how much we appreciate God's ongoing (though often hidden) role in the universe. Prayerfully, this will transition us out of *galut* into an era of redemption. This is in contradistinction to the first *Hallel* said at the end of *Maggid*, which is all praise of the Almighty for the miracles of the Exodus. Poetically speaking, if *Hallel-Nirtza* is a two-word *siman*, then it nicely parallels *Shulḥan-Orekh*, another two-word *siman*:

סימנים

קדש	ורחץ	מרור	כורך
כרפס	יחץ	שולחן-עורך	
מגיד	רחצה (רחץ)	צפון	ברך
מוציא	מצה	הלל-נרצה	

I would like to suggest an alternate approach. The word *Nirtza* could be a command: Do that which will make the *Seder*: *ratzui lifnei Hashem* – desirable before the Almighty. How do we accomplish this? By demonstrating that our actions were performed with love and joy! This we do by singing through the *piyutim* of *Nirtza* in which we identify with Jewish history, Jewish principles of faith, and the hope of a bright Jewish tomorrow. In our family, we tend to have long *Sedarim*, but everyone fights to stay awake for "Who Knows One?" and *Ḥad Gadya*. Many recite *Shir ha-Shirim* after the *Seder* as an expression of the mutual love

חֲסַל סִדּוּר פֶּסַח כְּהִלְכָתוֹ. כְּכָל מִשְׁפָּטוֹ וְחֻקָּתוֹ.
כַּאֲשֶׁר זָכִינוּ לְסַדֵּר אוֹתוֹ. כֵּן נִזְכֶּה לַעֲשׂוֹתוֹ.
זָךְ שׁוֹכֵן מְעוֹנָה. קוֹמֵם קְהַל עֲדַת מִי מָנָה.
בְּקָרוֹב נַהֵל נִטְעֵי כַנָּה. פְּדוּיִים לְצִיּוֹן בְּרִנָּה.

לְשָׁנָה הַבָּאָה בִּירוּשָׁלָיִם

לְשָׁנָה הַבָּאָה בִּירוּשָׁלָיִם (הַבְּנוּיָה)!

---

between God and Israel. In the estimation of many, *Nirtza* may well be the most important part of the *Seder* since it leaves us with a smile on our faces and the lasting feeling that it's good to be a Jew! A true fulfillment of (*Psalms* 100:2) *Ivdu et Hashem be-simha* – "Serve God in joy!"

חסל סידור פסח

The custom of extending the *Seder* with song and *piyutim* can be documented back to at least the 1200s in Italy. But each community would say a different selection. Among the *Ashkenazi* communities, seven selections became more or less standard. The first *piyut* was seen as a declaration that the formal/Halakhic *Seder* was over. This *piyut* is the final section of a much longer work written by 11th-century French Talmudist R. Yosef Tuv-Elem (Bonfils) to be said on *Shabbat ha-Gadol*. This poem went through the laws of the *Korban Pesah*. The author and this *piyut* were highly respected. The first line of this concluding section reads: *Hasal siddur Pesah ke-hilkhato* – which originally meant: "We have completed **detailing** the proper order of how to **perform the Korban Pesah** properly – according to all its laws and rules. Just as we have merited to delineate all its (**the Korban's**) laws, so should we merit to perform it." Around the 1300s, this *piyut* found its way into Ashkenazi *Haggadot* and the words *Hasal Siddur* took on a new meaning of "**performing the Seder.**" Thus, the opening section was now understood to mean: "We have finished **performing** the *Pesah Seder* properly – according to the *Seder's* laws and rules."

We note that the custom of Lubavitch (Chabad) is not to recite *Hasal Siddur Pesah* – except for *le-Shana ha-Ba'ah bi-Yerushalayim*. This

We have finished performing the Pesaḥ Seder properly – according to the Seder's laws and rules. Just as we were found worthy to perform it, so may we be worthy to do so in the future. O pure one, Who dwells on high, raise up the congregation that is without number. Soon may You guide the offshoots of Your plants to Zion, redeemed with song.

NEXT YEAR IN JERUSALEM!
Next Year in (Rebuilt) Jerusalem!

---

is because the first Lubavitcher Rebbi, R. Schneur Zalman of Liadi, did not include the passage *Ḥasal Siddur Pesaḥ* in his *Haggada*. To his mind, the *Seder* never concludes and its message endures throughout the year. As the verse says (Deut. 16:3): "So that you will remember the day you left Egypt all the days of your life." Based on this rationale, it is not clear why the Chabad custom precludes the recital of any of the subsequent *piyutim* of *Nirtza*.

לְשָׁנָה הַבָּאָה בִּירוּשָׁלָיִם

In nearly all *Haggadot*, at the end of *Ḥasal Siddur Pesaḥ*, appears *le-Shana ha-ba'ah bi-Yerushalayim* – "Next year in Jerusalem." Indeed, most think that this famous phrase was actually authored by R. Yosef Tuv-Elem, the author of *Ḥasal Siddur Pesaḥ*, although manuscript research makes it clear that it actually entered the *Haggada* separately *circa* the end of the 10th century. *le-Shana ha-ba'ah bi-Yerushalayim* appears in classical Jewish liturgy twice a year – at the end of *Ne'ila* and again at the end of the *Seder*. (In the modern period, *le-Shana ha-ba'ah bi-Yerushalayim* is also included at the end of *Ma'ariv* on *Yom ha-Atzma'ut* evening.) Several explanations for this double mention of a return to Jerusalem have been proposed. (1) Interestingly, the first is in *Tishrei*, while the other is in *Nisan*. Thus, the double recitation may be related to a dispute between R. Eliezer and R. Yehoshua (*Rosh ha-Shana* 10b–11a) as to whether the messianic redemption will be in *Tishrei* (R. Eliezer) or *Nisan* (R. Yehoshua); hence, *le-Shana ha-ba'ah bi-Yerushalayim* is mentioned in both. (2) R. Joseph B. Soloveitchik posited that the return to Jerusalem is referred to on those occasions where the central mitzva of the day cannot be performed because of the absence of the Temple. On

Yom Kippur, it is the two *Se'irim* (goats) of the *Mussaf* service, while on *Pesah* it is the *Korban Pesah*. Thus, *le-Shana ha-ba'ah bi-Yerushalayim* is a form of *zekher le-Mikdash* (remembrance of the Temple) mentioned at the height of the day: in the acceptance of the Divine yoke (*kabbalat ol malkhut Shamayim*) at the end of *Ne'ila* on *Yom Kippur*, and at the end of the *Seder* (*Hasal Siddur Pesah*). (3) Finally, R. Eliyahu Kitov suggests that *Seder* and *Ne'ila* are the happiest nights of the year. On *Seder* night we were freed from slavery and the idolatry of Egypt, while by *Ne'ila* our burden of sin has been removed. As a result, we are at the pinnacle of happiness and oath-bound to remember Jerusalem (Psalms 137:6). Sadly, we remember that we have fulfilled the ritual correctly – but, in the absence of the Temple, not completely. On *Yom ha-Atzma'ut*, *le-Shana ha-ba'ah bi-Yerushalayim* comes to remind us that the establishment of an independent state is not the ultimate goal. It is only *Reshit tzemihat ge'ulatenu* – the beginning of the flowering of our redemption. The culmination is the rebuilding of Jerusalem and ultimately the *Bet ha-Mikdash*.

Interestingly, this famous phrase is almost universally rendered in English as "**Next** year in Jerusalem!" The truth, however, is that the Hebrew word *ba-ah* is a bit tricky. The tense of the word changes depending on which of its two syllables is accented. If you accent the first syllable (called *mi-le'el*) ***BA**-ah*, then it is in the past tense; while accenting it on the second syllable (called *mi-lera*) *ba-**AH***, converts it to the present tense (see for example, Gen. 29:6 vs 29:9). Both the Lubavitcher and Satmar Rebbis have been recorded as suggesting that we should accent the word *ha-ba'ah* in *le-Shana ha-ba'ah bi-Yerushalayim* on the first syllable (*ha-**BA**-ah*) so that it means: **This** (i.e., the current one that already arrived in Tishre) year in Jerusalem!

As intriguing as this suggestion may be, it can be readily challenged because *le-Shana ha-ba'ah bi-Yerushalayim* – or at least a variation of it – actually appears twice in the *Haggada!* (See our comments above regarding לְשָׁנָה הַבָּאָה בְּאַרְעָא דְיִשְׂרָאֵל.) The first time is at the beginning of *Maggid*, at the end of הָא לַחְמָא עַנְיָא, which reads: *Hashata hakha; le-shana ha-ba'ah be-arah de-Yisra'el*. This Aramaic formulation is properly translated as: **This** year we are here (in the exile); **next** year in the Land of Israel. Hence, it is likely that *le-Shana ha-ba'ah bi-Yerushalayim*, like its predecessor, means "**Next** year in Jerusalem!" as commonly rendered (David Kessler).

Regarding this double appearance of "Next year in Jerusalem," R. Dov Lior (*Resp. Devar Hevron, Zemanim,* p. 109) stresses that in its first appearance in the Haggada, the use of Aramaic is meant to signal that at the beginning of *Maggid* the Israelites are in *galut*; the Jews don't even speak their own language. By the end of the *Seder*, we have left Egypt and express our faith that we will eventually return to our country, build our Temple, and converse in our own language.

לְשָׁנָה הַבָּאָה בִּירוּשָׁלָיִם

(a) This declaration is iconic because it represents many things to many people: (1) Firstly, it is **a prayer** where we turn to the God of History stating: "You have redeemed us in the past; please do so now, as well." This would make *le-Shana ha-ba'ah* analogous to *u-Venei Yerushalayim ir ha-kodesh bi-mehera ve-yamenu*. (2) Secondly, it is **a statement of faith** in which we affirm that the Almighty will eventually redeem us. This would be analogous to *Ani Ma'amin* which says: "…*ahakeh lo be-khol yom she-yavo* – I will wait for the Messiah whenever he should come." It has kept our spirits up during the darkest days of our exile. On *Tisha be-Av* when we record our profound sadness about the *Hurban*, we also recite the Zionide elegies (*Kinnot Tziyoniyot*) and our faith in returning to Zion and Jerusalem. (3) Finally, for many, *le-Shana ha-ba'ah bi-Yerushalayim* is **a goal – a calling** to each of us, individually and communally, to concretize the dream, make *aliya* and build Jerusalem. Interestingly, the Jewish people for two thousand years have been asking God to please rebuild Jerusalem. But we sat in the *galut* (diaspora) and did nothing. Yet it was only at the beginning of the 20th century that the Jews finally decided to go out and become involved in the historical process. As a result, the new state eventually became a reality. The God of Creation and History wants partners, he wants our *hishtadlut* – our involvement and efforts. When we get involved, things begin to happen.

There is an aspect of *le-Shana ha-ba'ah bi-Yerushalayim* that is at times very inspiring for a *galut* Jew, but also very challenging. On the one hand, it expresses the hope of *kibbutz galuyot* – the ingathering of the exile – and *Yemot ha-Mashi'ah* – the coming of the Messiah. On the other hand, it challenges us to be honest with ourselves. Why aren't we already on our way to the Land of Israel, and if we are there, why do we ever leave? R. Dr. Rafi Posen was very close to the preeminent and internationally renowned Israeli *Humash* teacher Dr. Nechama Leibowitz. When he was offered a position to serve as a *shali'ah* (one sent abroad to teach Torah and Zionism) in Toronto, R. Posen went to say goodbye to his revered mentor, but she just told him not to go! He went anyway and was very successful. He wrote Nechama a long letter explaining his successes, and she wrote back criticizing his decision to go in the first place: "My only hope is that your children feel miserable there, experience the inauthentic life of those who pray for the return of Zion, who declaim unthinkingly at the end of the *Seder* and on *Yom Kippur* after all the confessions, 'Next year in Jerusalem' and dare to pronounce this utter falsehood before God!" [Yael Unterman, *Nehama Leibowitz: Teacher and Bible Scholar*, p. 264–265].

For the Prisoner of Zion Natan (Anatoly) Sharansky, on the other hand, "Next Year in Jerusalem" was the call that kept him focused. It gave his life meaning and direction despite the Soviet authorities' continuous threats and misdeeds. Clearly, certain ideas carry a person more than he/she carries them. What follows is a short selection from Anatoly Sharansky's final statement to the Soviet Court presented before being sentenced to Siberia on July 14, 1978:

> For more than two thousand years the Jewish people, my people, have been dispersed. But wherever they are, wherever Jews are found, every year they have repeated: "Next year in Jerusalem." Now, when I am further than ever from my people, from (my wife) Avital, facing many arduous years of imprisonment, I say, turning to my people, my Avital: "Next Year in Jerusalem."

The sense that certain values, dreams, and ideas carry a person more than he carries them was expressed by Natan Sharansky himself. The following is a post by Dr. Yael Ziegler, on November 20, 2014:

> This morning I was in a bakery in Jerusalem when I noticed that I was standing behind Natan Sharansky. I summoned up my courage and told him that I had just cited from his book this week in a class I was teaching on *Sefer Psalms*. I explained that I told my students the inspiring story of how he had kept a tiny book of *Psalms* with him at all times, even when he had to struggle with

the authorities to get it back. At that point, Sharansky smiled, reached into his shirt pocket, and pulled out a tiny (palm-sized) tattered book of *Psalms*. I was stunned, and I asked him "Do you carry that wherever you go?" Sharansky didn't even pause and he replied: "Actually, it carries **me**!" I love Jerusalem the city where Jewish heroes walk the streets.

Clearly, *le-Shana ha-ba'ah bi-Yerushalayim* has carried the Jewish people for millennia giving them hope and focus. Another former "prisoner of Zion" Yosef Begun, also a "refusenik" for many years, said the following, when he was already living in Israel (https://bneiakiva.org.il/act/limod-lyom-yeroshalaim/; translation by R. Yaakov Meir).

> Some people say that there's more depth when you're in the Diaspora. I, too – during the long nights in prison, on the *Pesah* nights – used to ask myself, "Nu, so when I get to Jerusalem – what then? What significance will there be to the words of the *Haggada* there, in *Eretz Yisrael*?" And here I am now, in Jerusalem, and I still utter with the same intention in my heart, with the same passionate hope and prayer: Next year in the rebuilt Jerusalem. Because a "rebuilt Jerusalem" means the Temple, it means the Sanhedrin; it means a fully Jewish life. And it is specifically here, since I made *aliya*, that I see and am more conscious of the deficiencies and delays in our lives. It is specifically here that I understand better the spiritual content, not the physical, geographical aspiration towards the rebuilt Jerusalem. And on the *Seder* night I am able to utter these words with the heartfelt prayer that I, too, shall be able to make my contribution towards the rebuilding of this Jerusalem – may it be rebuilt soon."

For Begun, coming to Jerusalem is only the first step in rebuilding it in the full sense of the word.

(b) One last comment is in order regarding the vernacular translation of *le-Shana ha-ba'ah bi-Yerushalayim*. In a fascinating article appearing in *Segula: The Jewish History Magazine* (*Nisan* 5783/March 2023, Issue 64, pp. 42–55), the noted American historian Jonathan D. Sarna indicates that *le-Shana ha-ba'ah bi-Yerushalayim* has appeared in *Haggadot* ever since the end of the 10th century. Yet, in *Haggadot* translated into

German and English through the 19th century, it appeared prominently in the Hebrew text but was missing from the accompanying translation. It was generally understood that printing the words "Next Year in Jerusalem" in the vernacular would court danger – by implying that Jews considered themselves not truly at home where they lived in the Diaspora. Indeed, many non-Jews learned of the problematic phrase and reviled it, resenting its implication that Jews maintained fealty to another nation. Literary giants like the American Herman Melville expressed this animosity clearly in his epic poem *Clarel* published in 1876, where he wrote with bitter scorn: "Some zealous Jews on alien soil / Who still from Gentile ways recoil, / And loyally maintain the dream, / Salute upon the Paschal day – with Next year in Jerusalem!"

In the first *Haggada* published in the United States, in 1837, by Solomon Henry Jackson, *le-Shana ha-ba'ah bi-Yerushalayim* appears in prominent Hebrew letters. The accompanying English translation reads: "The year that approaches, O bring us to Jerusalem." This translation placed the burden squarely upon the Almighty; Jews would depart for Jerusalem only if God personally led them there. The Zionist movement at the turn of the century restored *le-Shana ha-ba'ah bi-Yerushalayim* to a position of respect. In 1911, a popular *Haggada* published yearly added *Hatikva* on its final page. However, no major *Haggada* yet used "Next year in Jerusalem." In 1932 when Maxwell House Coffee Company began distributing free *Haggadot* with its Kosher for Passover Coffee, the translation they used read: "The following year, **grant us** to be in Jerusalem." This guarded translation still leaves the hint that any move to Jerusalem is up to Heaven. (As an aside, we remind the reader that over the years, Maxwell House has published 50 million copies of its *Haggada* and the translation has remained unchanged.) Finally, in 1934, the noted British historian Cecil Roth broke the taboo in his edition, prominently showing "Next year in Jerusalem" alongside *le-Shana ha-ba'ah bi-Yerushalayim*.

As Nazism rose and European Jewry's prospects continued to darken in the 1930s and '40s, "Next year in Jerusalem" transformed from a mere phrase into an urgent necessity, a matter of life and death. Tellingly, a *Haggada* was prepared in 1944 by R. David de Sola Pool, and his wife Tamar and distributed at government expense by the Jewish Welfare Board to a third of a million American soldiers. Not only did it boldly translate *le-Shana ha-ba'ah bi-Yerushalayim* as "Next year in Jerusalem," it also included the text of *Hatikva*. In the midst of the Holocaust and war, the "old phrase" regained full respectability and had come to signify life and hope.

לְשָׁנָה הַבָּאָה בִּירוּשָׁלַיִם הַבְּנוּיָה

Outside of Israel, the most common formulation of this phrase is: *le-Shana ha-ba'ah bi-Yerushalayim* – Next year in Jerusalem. However, in Israel, the prevalent formulation is *le-Shana ha-ba'ah bi-Yerushalayim* **ha-benuya** – Next year in the built up (or rebuilt) Jerusalem. Indeed, the formulation *Yerushalayim ha-benuya* appears prominently in Psalms 122:3: *Yerushalayim ha-benuya ke-ir she-hubra la Yahdav* – "Jerusalem built up, like a city joined together." Several anti-Zionist Rabbis, including R. Yitzhak Zev (Velvel) Soloveitchik (*Haggada Bet ha-Levi – Brisk*), opposed adding *ha-benuya* since they felt it had a Zionist flavor of building the Land – a central theme of modern Zionism. The facts are, however, that this formulation is found in *Haggadot* dating back close to 150 years ago, long before Zionism appeared on the scene. (R. Yosef Zvi ha-Levi Dinar's *Minhagei Maharitz ha-Levi, Mo'adim*, p. 163, note 104.)

R. Simcha Raz (*Malakhim ki-Venei Adam*, p. 221) records a story told about R. Abraham Isaac Kook who went to fundraise in America. A wealthy man offered him a significant donation on the condition that Rav Kook would explain to him why *Yerushalami* Jews say *le-Shana ha-ba'ah bi-Yerushalayim* at the end of the *Seder* and also the end of *Ne'ila* if they are already there! Rav Kook responded with three answers. First, the custom in Israel is to add the word *ha-benuya*, and there is still time until this is fulfilled completely. Second, we are praying for all *Klal Yisrael* to be there. And finally, he added wryly, when we say *le-Shana haba'ah bi-Yerushalayim*, our intention is that our whole being should merit to be in *Yerushalayim*, physically, spiritually, and mentally. Unfortunately, continued R. Kook, nowadays some of us live in *Yerushalayim*, but our minds are elsewhere, thinking about trips abroad to collect money.

Let us return to Psalms 122:3: "Jerusalem built up, like a city joined together." Many of the commentaries have struggled to explain this joining together. Some suggest that Jerusalem is the joining of two

ספירת העומר

For those in the Diaspora making a second Seder: whoever did not count the *Omer* after *Ma'ariv* on the second night of Passover should count now.

ancient cities: Jerusalem and Zion. Others suggest that the city is based on separate portions from the tribes of Benjamin and Judah which were seamlessly joined together through brotherly love. The Mystics talk about a "double Jerusalem": *Yerushalayim shel ma'ala* – the heavenly spiritual Jerusalem, and *Yerushalayim shel mata* – the earthly physical Jerusalem, which have combined to become one. For two millennia, we Jews have succeeded in keeping the heavenly spiritual Jerusalem alive in our collective memories. The challenge of today is to combine it with the physical cosmopolitan Jerusalem of today so that they somehow join seamlessly "like a city joined together." Not a simple task!

ספירת העומר

(a) It is a common custom among Hassidim and some Sephardic communities (see; Hida, *Birkei Yosef*, 489:5); to recite *Sefirat ha-Omer* at the end of the second *Seder* following *Hasal Siddur Pesah*, rather than in *shul* at the end of *Ma'ariv*. The *minhag* is attributed to the *Ba'al Shem Tov (Besh"t)* himself (though there are some conflicting reports). There are several problems with this custom, including: (1) Counting at the end of the *Seder* violates the principle of *zerizin makdimin le-mitzvot* – of fulfilling mitzva obligations as early as possible. (2) One is not allowed to eat before fulfilling pending obligations. (3) Counting *sefirat ha-omer* occurs 49 times each year, while the *Seder* comes twice in the *galut*. A well-known rule states (Pesahim 114a): *Tadir ve-she-eino tadir, tadir kodem* – the more frequently performed ritual gets priority. (4) Fulfilling a mitzva publicly (ברוב עם) in *shul* has priority over doing so privately at home. (5) Finally, counting *Sefira* at the end of the *Seder* after you have drunk four cups of wine is highly problematic – not the least because you are likely to fall asleep before fulfilling your obligation.

R. Joseph B. Soloveitchik's *mi-Peninei ha-Rov*, *Kuntress Sefirat ha-Omer*, sec. 12 (p. 243–244; 5761 ed.) suggests the following rationale for this mode of action. *Sefirat ha-Omer* is a countdown to *Shavu'ot* and *Matan Torah* (the giving of the Torah). But at the *Seder*, our focus is supposed to be on the Exodus from Egypt. As the *Hinukh* (*Mitzva*

Counting the Omer

For those in the Diaspora making a second Seder: whoever did not count the Omer after Ma'ariv on the second night of Passover should count now.

306) posits, that is the reason why God commanded us (Lev. 23:15) to start counting the *Omer mi-Maharat ha-Shabbat* – on the second day of Passover so that we would stay focused on the importance of *Yetzi'at Mitzrayim*. For the same reason, suggests R. Joseph B. Soloveitchik, *Hassidim* don't mention *Sefirat ha-Omer* on the second day of *Pesah* until the *Seder* is officially over. Thus, the focus on the Exodus remains complete until *Hasal Siddur Pesah*, and only then do we turn our focus to the counting up to *Matan Torah*.

R. David Silverberg, citing R. Joseph B. Soloveitchik, suggests a second approach to explain the Hassidic tradition. Performing the *Seder* indicates that the day is holy, it is still *Yom Tov*. Indeed, we even say *she-Heḥiyanu*. But counting *Sefira* signals that it is *mi-Maharat ha-Shabbat* – the day after *Yom Tov*, *Hol ha-Moed*. This is self-contradictory. Hence, the *Mitzvot* of *Yom Tov*: *Pesah, Matza, Maror,* and *Hallel* are first completed, and only then do we turn to the *Hol ha-Mo'ed* mitzva of *Sefirat ha-Omer*. R. Silverberg suggests yet another reason why the Hassidim wanted the counting of the *Omer* at the end of the *Seder*. This is because the count up to *Matan Torah* teaches us the purpose of our Exodus and redemption. The purpose of *Pesah* is *Shavu'ot*! "Let my people go – and serve me!"

One last modern insight by R. Yaakov Meir regarding the period of *Sefirat ha-Omer*. During this time of year, we experience two interrelated periods each linking two festivals – the period between *Pesah* and *Shavu'ot*, and the period between *Yom ha-Atzma'ut* and *Yom Yerushalayim*. The fact that the biblical pair (*Pesah-Shavu'ot*) and the modern pair (*Yom ha-Atzma'ut-Yom Yerushalayim*) – both related to modern-day Israel – occur during the same period, is no coincidence. These two intermediary periods, share a profound connection. *Pesah* commemorates the Exodus from Egypt; then on *Shavu'ot* – fifty days later – we received the Torah. The transition during the intermediate days is one of ascent: beginning with a physical redemption (on *Pesah*), from slavery, "upwards," as it were, towards spiritual redemption (on *Shavu'ot*). *Shavu'ot* explains why we were freed. "Let my people go – to

[ויש אומרים: הִנְנִי מוּכָן וּמְזֻמָּן לְקַיֵּם מִצְוַת עֲשֵׂה שֶׁל סְפִירַת הָעֹמֶר כְּמוֹ שֶׁכָּתוּב בַּתּוֹרָה (ויקרא כג:טו-טז): "וּסְפַרְתֶּם לָכֶם מִמָּחֳרַת הַשַּׁבָּת מִיּוֹם הֲבִיאֲכֶם אֶת עֹמֶר הַתְּנוּפָה שֶׁבַע שַׁבָּתוֹת תְּמִימֹת תִּהְיֶינָה: עַד מִמָּחֳרַת הַשַּׁבָּת הַשְּׁבִיעִית תִּסְפְּרוּ חֲמִשִּׁים יוֹם וְהִקְרַבְתֶּם מִנְחָה חֲדָשָׁה לַה' ": וִיהִי נֹעַם ה' אֱלֹהֵינוּ עָלֵינוּ וּמַעֲשֵׂה יָדֵינוּ כּוֹנְנָה עָלֵינוּ וּמַעֲשֵׂה יָדֵינוּ כּוֹנְנֵהוּ:]

בָּרוּךְ אַתָּה ה', אֱלֹהֵינוּ מֶלֶךְ הָעוֹלָם. אֲשֶׁר קִדְּשָׁנוּ בְּמִצְוֹתָיו וְצִוָּנוּ עַל סְפִירַת הָעֹמֶר.

הַיּוֹם יוֹם אֶחָד בָּעֹמֶר.

הָרַחֲמָן הוּא יַחֲזִיר לָנוּ עֲבוֹדַת בֵּית הַמִּקְדָּשׁ לִמְקוֹמָהּ, בִּמְהֵרָה בְיָמֵינוּ, אָמֵן סֶלָה.

---

serve me" (Ex. 7:16). The period between *Yom ha-Atzma'ut* and *Yom Yerushalayim* can be characterized in a similar way. On *Yom ha-Atzma'ut* we celebrate something akin to *Pesaḥ*, but on a national level. This day commemorates, principally, the attainment of our physical and political independence – our exodus from subjugation to foreign nations. *Yom Yerushalayim* is more akin to *Shavu'ot*. It represents our national spiritual calling and mission.

לְקַיֵּם מִצְוַת עֲשֵׂה... כְּמוֹ שֶׁכָּתוּב בַּתּוֹרָה

This simple phrase is problematic in the case of the counting of the *Omer* since following the destruction of the Temple, the consensus of *Poskim* is that *Sefirat ha-Omer* is only rabbinic in nature. Indeed, R. Ovadia Yosef has ruled that the phrase *...kemo she-katuv ba-Torah: 'u-Sefartem...'* – "...as it is written in the Torah: 'and you shall count...'" should be omitted for this reason. David Kessler has suggested that perhaps the thrust of the verse is as follows: "Almighty: I am prepared to fulfill a Biblical commandment of counting. There is, however, a problem because the Temple is destroyed. Kindly enable us to build the *Bet ha-Mikdash* and reinstate this mitzva."

[Some say: I am ready and prepared to perform the positive command concerning the Counting of the Omer, as it is written in the Torah (Leviticus 23:15–16): "You shall count from the day following the day of rest, from the day you brought the Omer sheaf of the wave-offering, seven whole weeks shall be counted, you shall count fifty days, to the day following the seventh week you shall count fifty days; and you shall offer a new offering to the Lord."]

Blessed are You, Lord our God, King of the Universe, Who has sanctified us with His commandments and commanded us to count the Omer.

Today is the first day of the Omer.

The Compassionate One shall return the service of the Holy Temple for us, speedily in our days, Amen.

וְצִוָּנוּ עַל סְפִירַת הָעֹמֶר

Many scholars have wondered why the *she-Hehiyanu* benediction is not recited the first time we count the Omer yearly. Among the leading reasons are the following four: (1) *she-Hehiyanu* is only recited when one derives some pleasure from the mitzva. By *Sukka* we enjoy the shade, *Lulav* is part of our expression of *simha* – joy. There is no *simha* in the counting of the Omer (*Ittur*, end of *Matza u-Maror*); (2) Counting the *Omer* causes sadness because it reminds us of what we can no longer do biblically because of the destruction of the Temple (*Ba'al ha-Ma'or*, end of *Pesahim*); (3) Since the counting of the *Omer* is dependent on the date of *Pesah*, the *she-Hehiyanu* of *Pesah* covers *Sefira* as well (*Shibbolei ha-Leket*, sec 234; (4) *Sefirat ha-Omer* involves no action, merely a verbal counting; hence the *she-Hehiyanu* benediction is not recited (*Minhagei ha-Maharil, Seder Birkat ha-Omer*).

פיוטי נרצה

(Outside of Israel, this song is for the first night of *Pesaḥ* only.)

וּבְכֵן וַיְהִי בַּחֲצִי הַלַּיְלָה

אָז רוֹב נִסִּים, הִפְלֵאתָ בַּלַּיְלָה
בְּרֹאשׁ אַשְׁמוֹרֶת, זֶה הַלַּיְלָה
1. גֵּר צֶדֶק נִצַּחְתּוֹ, כְּנֶחֱלַק לוֹ לַיְלָה.
וַיְהִי בַּחֲצִי הַלַּיְלָה.

פיוטי נרצה

We have stated repeatedly above that one of the functions of the components of *Nirtza* is to create and cultivate "hope" for a bright Jewish future. I would like to cite the insightful comments of R. Jonathan Sacks distinguishing between "Hope" and "Optimism" (https://www.youtube.com/watch?v=zoCu9JNX758; at 34:10).

> I want to make a distinction that is absolutely fundamental between two ideas that are often confused. One is called optimism and the other is hope. "Optimism" is the belief that things are **going** to get better. "Hope" is the belief that, if we work hard enough together, we can **make** things better. It needs no courage, only a sort of naivety, to be an optimist. But, at times, it requires a great deal of courage to have hope. No Jew, knowing what we do about history, can be an optimist. But no Jew – worthy of the name – ever lost hope… Hope needs courage. Hope needs working together. But it is hope that changes the world.

Indeed, as we will see, the songs of *Nirtza* talk about our glorious Jewish past, our interaction with an amazing caring God of History, and the prospects of a bright Jewish future. *Nirtza* is composed of six *piyutim* (liturgical poems) which can easily be subdivided into three pairs. (1) The first two: *va-Yehi ba-Hatzi ha-Layla* and *ve-Amartem Zevaḥ Pesaḥ* are historical poems that document God's involvement throughout the generations. In *va-Yehi ba-Hatzi ha-Layla* our focus is on events that occurred on *Seder* night. On the other hand, *ve-Amartem Zevaḥ Pesaḥ*

Songs of Nirtza

(Outside of Israel, this song is for the first night of *Pesah* only.)

And it Came to Pass at Midnight!

Then in times of old, You performed many wonders by night,
At the beginning of the watches of this night.

1. The righteous convert [Avraham] You gave victory by dividing for him the night.
   And it came to pass at midnight!

---

reviews events that occurred on the 15th of *Nisan* during the night or day and may have even spilled over to subsequent days during the *Pesah* holiday. Reading them is an inspirational, educational, and intellectual experience. (2) The next pair of songs, *Adir bi-Melukha* and *Adir Hu*, extol the praises of an omnipotent, miraculous God who will change the course of history, return us to Jerusalem and build the Temple. The experience here is an emotional one, excitedly waiting for Hashem's intervention speedily in our days! (3) The final couple of *piyutim*, *Ehad Mi Yode'a* and *Had Gadya* deal with principles of faith and are meant to be didactic and fun for children and adults alike, using riddles and puzzles. Indeed, if you end the *Seder* educated, inspired, and with a smile on your face, the *Haggada* has succeeded in its mission!

וַיְהִי בַּחֲצִי הַלַּיְלָה

This *piyut* was written by Yannai, who lived in the late fifth or early sixth century in the Galilee in Israel (Byzantine-Palaestina Syria), and the verses are arranged alphabetically. He was presumably a prolific *paytan* (author of *piyutim*), but most of his hundreds of poems were lost, except for works that were discovered in the Cairo Geniza. He was highly respected by R. Sa'adya Gaon and subsequent *Rishonim* and he was the teacher of the noted *paytan* R. Elazar ha-Kalir. Two works attributed to him are *Va-Yehi ba-Hatzi ha-Layla* said on *Seder* Night and *Ve-khol Ma'aminim* said in *Mussaf* of the *Yamim Nora'im*. The *piyut Va-Yehi ba-Hatzi ha-Layla*, which follows the *aleph-bet*, was originally written for *Shabbat ha-Gadol*, but was then moved into the *Haggada*.

Yannai assumes that his audience has a mastery of both *Tanakh* and Rabbinic literature.

In this poem, the *paytan* follows *Haza"l*'s lead in attributing to the 15th of *Nisan*, *Seder* night, and the night of *makat bekhorot*, special redemptive powers. This is based on Exodus 12:42 which refers to *Seder* night as *leyl shimurim* – one of vigil and careful watching. The Talmud in *Rosh ha-Shana* (11b) cites R. Joshua that *leyl shimurim* means "a night set aside" and indicates that the 15th of *Nisan* was designated from Creation as a day for redemption from Egypt and from future oppression as well. Hence, it is R. Joshua who maintains: *be-Nisan nigalu, be-Nisan atidin le-higa'el* – "The Israelites were redeemed in *Nisan*, and in *Nisan* they will be redeemed in the future as well." Thus, *Midrash Rabba* (Ex. Bo, *Parasha* 18:12) asks: "Why did the Torah see fit to call the 15th of *Nisan*, *Leyl Shimurim*? This is because the Almighty did great acts for the righteous – just as he had done for the Jews in Egypt. Thus, on this night, He rescued Hizkiyahu [from Sennacherib], …He rescued Chanania and his fellows [Mishael and Azariah], … He rescued Daniel from the lion's den, and on it [this night] Eliyahu and the Messiah will become great…" Other *midrashim*, cited below, mention various other events.

This *piyut* recounts in chronological order thirteen miraculous biblical events that occurred at night (see numbered verses). Each line of this poem begins with a successive letter of the Hebrew alphabet. With the exception of the Plague of the First-Born, there is no mention of the 15th of *Nisan* in the biblical text of each event – only "night." Nevertheless, the *Midrash Rabba* (Numbers, *Parasha* 20, no. 12) asserts that since the 15th of *Nisan* is referred to (Ex. 12:42) as *Leyl Shimurim* – a night of vigil/watching, it is a night on which God watches over us. Furthermore, all salvations of Israel from the wicked – taking place at night – occurred specifically on (or over) *Seder* Night. This view also appears in the writings of R. Jacob Molin (*Sefer Maharil – Minhagim, Seder Leyl Sheni Shel Pesah*, end of par. 1, p. 123). Thus, the *paytan* writes in the second line: *be-Rosh ashmoret zeh ha-layla* – "at the beginning of the watch on **this** night." The first twelve events occurred in the past, while the last occurrence will be the coming of the *Mashi'ah* and the future redemption. The poem is formatted today into 7 stanzas such that we repeat the refrain *va-Yehi ba-hatzi ha-layla* – taken from *Makat*

Bekhorot (Ex. 12:29) – after every three verses. This gives the impression that all these events – like the plague of the firstborn – occurred at midnight (see comments above regarding) מַכַּת בְּכוֹרוֹת. The original *piyut* found in the Cairo *Geniza* did not have this verse as a refrain, and there is no evidence that indeed all these events occurred (or in the case of the thirteenth, **will** occur) at midnight. The present formatting also leads to an incorrect division of the two verses dealing with Haman (numbered 12א and 12ב) into two different stanzas.

R. Joseph B. Soloveitchik (cited by R. Ari Kahn, *Haggada Od Yosef Hai*) maintained that the *piyut va-Yehi ba-Hatzi ha-Layla* has an important *hashkafic* message. The night is normally a time of fear and dread. *Haza"l* posit that man is more sensitive to pain, aloneness, hopelessness, and helplessness at night. This is expressed at the very beginning of *Eikha* (1:2): *Bakho tivke ba-layla* – "Bitterly she weeps in the **night**," and again (2:19): *Kumi roni ba-layla* – "Arise, cry out in the **night**." The purpose of this *piyut* is to show that even in the depth of night, we are not alone (Psalms 121:4): "The Guardian of Israel neither slumbers nor sleeps!" This is all the more so on *Pesah* night, where we have cases documenting that the Almighty is with us.

אָז

"Then" refers to the 15th of *Nisan* in Egypt. Just like in *Megillat Esther* (5:11), here the word *rov* means *harbeh* – many.

בְּרֹאשׁ אַשְׁמוֹרֶת

Two interpretations of this line are possible: (1) According to the first suggestion, this second line is a continuation of the previous one, noting that midnight – *hatzi ha-layla* – is the beginning of the **third** watch (of four night-watches, *Berakhot* 3b). Consequently, the two first lines are an introductory couplet, and there should be a comma at the end of the first line and a period following the second. (2) Alternatively, this second line is connected to the next/third one (marked event 1), which describes Avraham's victory over the four kings (Gen. 14:15). This event occurred during the first half of the night of the 15th of *Nisan* (as discussed further in the next comment). This second line explains that this first half started with the beginning of the **first** night

הַלַּיְלָה.	דַּנְתָּ מֶלֶךְ גְּרָר, בַּחֲלוֹם	2.
לַיְלָה.	הִפְחַדְתָּ אֲרַמִּי, בְּאֶמֶשׁ	3.
לַיְלָה.	וַיָּשַׂר יִשְׂרָאֵל לְמַלְאָךְ, וַיּוּכַל לוֹ	4.

וַיְהִי בַּחֲצִי הַלַּיְלָה.

---

watch – at the **beginning** of the night. According to this, lines 2 and 3 are a couplet (describing event 1) and there should be no period at the end of the second line.

גֵּר צֶדֶק נִצַּחְתּוֹ

The first event recorded is the victory of the "righteous convert" Avraham in his campaign against the "Four Kings" (Gen. 14:14–15) in order to retrieve his captured nephew Lot. According to *Shemot Rabba* (*Bo, Parasha* 18), this event occurred on the eve of the 15th of *Nisan*. The biblical verse regarding Avraham's forces reads: *va-Yeḥalek alehem layla hu ve-avadav va-yakem*, which literally means "And he divided up his force against them at night, he and his servants, and smote them." The *Midrash* interprets this verse homiletically to mean "And this *miraculous* night was divided for them…" – "them" being the Almighty and Avraham. God "suggested" that Avraham use just the first half of the *miraculous* night (before midnight) to defeat the four kings (– that would be time enough), while He, the Almighty, would save the remaining second half – starting from midnight, some generations later, to redeem Avraham's progeny (by carrying out the Plague of the First-Born).

דַּנְתָּ מֶלֶךְ גְּרָר

The incident referred to is described in Genesis 20. Avraham and Sarah go into the Philistine city of Gerar, and Sarah is held captive by King Avimelekh. In a dream, God warns the king not to harm either. Although there is no mention of the 15th of *Nisan* in the text, we have cited above that *Midrash Rabba* (Num. *Parasha* 20, no. 12) asserts that since the 15th of *Nisan* is referred to as (Ex. 12:42): *Leyl shimurim* – "a night of vigil," we may conclude that **all salvations** of Israel from the wicked taking place at night occurred on **this** (Seder) night. Among

2. You judged the king of Gerar [Avimelekh] in a dream at night.
3. You frightened the Aramean [Lavan] in the dark of the night.
4. Yisrael fought an angel and overcame him at night.
   And it came to pass at midnight!

---

the examples cited explicitly are Avraham with the four kings (Gen. 14:15), Avraham with King Avimelekh (Gen. 20:3), and Yaakov with Lavan (Gen. 31:24), discussed below.

הִפְחַדְתָּ אֲרַמִּי

After 20 years of servitude to his uncle Lavan "the Aramean," Yaakov surreptitiously attempts to go back home to Canaan with his family and possessions. Lavan attempts to forcefully prevent Yaakov from doing so, but the night before (*Emesh*) Lavan catches up, the Almighty warns "the Aramean" not to harm Yaakov in any way (Gen. 31:24 and 29). The rabbinic source that Lavan's prophetic dream occurred on Seder night is *Midrash Rabba* (Num. *Parasha* 20, no. 12) cited in the previous comment.

וַיָּשַׂר יִשְׂרָאֵל לְמַלְאָךְ

There is no hint in the text (Gen. 32:28) that the nighttime struggle of Yaakov with the angel occurred specifically on *Seder* night. The *Paytan* presumably relied on the aforementioned generalization of *Num. Rabba* (*Parasha* 20, no. 12; see comments above regarding וַיְהִי בַּחֲצִי הַלַּיְלָה) that **all salvations** of Israel from the wicked taking place at night – occurred specifically on the 15th of *Nisan*. (A similar argument is made by the Abravanel.) Ariela Klein Kosowitz has pointed out that, according to Yannai, both the story of Yaakov's confrontation with Lavan (Gen. Chap. 31) (which concludes with a morning departure), and Yaakov's subsequent wrestling with the angel one chapter later (Gen. Chap. 32) – occurred on the night of the 15th of *Nisan*. This requires that, despite their close proximity in the *Humash*, they took place at least a year apart.

5א. זֶרַע בְּכוֹרֵי פַתְרוֹס מָחַצְתָּ, בַּחֲצִי הַלַּיְלָה,

5ב. חֵילָם לֹא מָצְאוּ, בְּקוּמָם בַּלַּיְלָה,

6. טִיסַת נְגִיד חֲרֹשֶׁת, סִלִּיתָ בְּכוֹכְבֵי לַיְלָה,

וַיְהִי בַּחֲצִי הַלַּיְלָה.

זֶרַע בְּכוֹרֵי פַתְרוֹס מָחַצְתָּ

That the Egyptian firstborn were "crushed" at midnight is explicitly stated in Ex. 12:29. In Jeremiah (44:1) and Ezekiel (29:14 and 30:14) "Patros" is used as a synonym for Egypt.

חֵילָם לֹא מָצְאוּ

Hayil can be translated as multitudes or strength. With the death of all the firstborn, the Egyptians lost their natural leaders, elite soldiers, and/or army officers.

בְּקוּמָם בַּלַּיְלָה

An alternate line for the letter *Het* has been located in the Cairo Geniza manuscript of this *piyut* (see: *Piyutei Yannai* by Menahem Zulay, 1938). This verse reads:

חִלְחַלְתָּ מִדְיָן וַחֲבֵרָיו בִּצְלִיל לֶחֶם בַּחֲלוֹם לַיְלָה

You frightened the army of Midian with a soldier's nightmare about a tumbling barley cake destroying their tents.

This alternate line refers to the incident of Gideon (Judges Chapter 7) who, at God's behest, leads a select group of 300 soldiers into battle against a Midianite army. To allay Gideon's fears, the Almighty encourages him to sneak into the camp of Midian and listen to the soldier's conversation. As the new line recounts, Gideon hears a soldier recount his nightmare of a tumbling barley cake (*tzlil lehem se'orim*) destroying

5A. You crushed the firstborn of Patros [Egypt] at midnight.
5B. They did not find their multitudes upon arising at night.
6. The army of the prince of Haroshet [Sisera] You swept away with the stars of the night.

And it came to pass at midnight!

---

their tents, which panics their forces. The text states (Judges 7:9): "**That night** (*ba-Layla hahu*) God said to Gideon, 'Come, attack the (Midianite) camp, for I have delivered it into your hands.'" The phrase *ba-Layla hahu* is identified as the 15th of *Nisan* by *Midrash Panim Aherim*, Second Version, Chapter 6 – specifically applying it to Gideon. See also *Targum* to *Megillat Esther* (6:1) and our comments above to שְׂנֵאָה נָטַר אֲגָגִי. וְכָתַב סְפָרִים בַּלַּיְלָה and יָעַץ מְחָרֵף לְנוֹפֵף אִוּוּי. *Leviticus Rabba* (*Emor, Parasha* 25:6), however, adds that the *tzlil lehem se'orim* (barley cake) suggests that the battle was won because of the Israelites' sacrifice of the barley *Omer* on the 16th of *Nisan* (which presumably occurred in the course of the battle). This story of Gideon is also included in the poem of Yannai's student, R. Elazar ha-Kalir, *ve-Amartem Zevah Pesah*; see comments on נִשְׁמְדָה מִדְיָן בִּצְלִיל שְׂעוֹרֵי עֹמֶר פֶּסַח below.

טִיסַת נְגִיד חֲרֹשֶׁת

Haroshet was the hometown of Sisera, the general of Canaanite king Yavin (Judges 4:2), who oppressed Israel for 20 years. Heavenly stars miraculously went to battle for Debora the Prophetess and Barak ben Avinoam who headed the Israelite army (Judges 5:20). Although nothing is stated in the text about the timing of the wondrous victory, Yannai presumably assumes that, since this salvation involved stars, it must have occurred at night. Again, following *Midrash Rabba* (Num. *Parasha* 20, no. 12; see comments above on וַיְהִי בַּחֲצִי הַלַּיְלָה), this salvation occurred specifically on the 15th of *Nisan*. (This is indeed explicitly stated in *Midrash Panim Aherim*, Second Version, Chapter 6.)

7. יָעַץ מְחָרֵף לְנוֹפֵף אִוּוּי. הוֹבַשְׁתָּ פְגָרָיו בַּלַּיְלָה,
8. כָּרַע בֵּל וּמַצָּבוֹ. בְּאִישׁוֹן לַיְלָה,
9. לְאִישׁ חֲמוּדוֹת נִגְלָה רָז, חֲזוֹת לַיְלָה,
וַיְהִי בַּחֲצִי הַלַּיְלָה.

10. מִשְׁתַּכֵּר בִּכְלֵי קֹדֶשׁ, נֶהֱרַג בּוֹ בַּלַּיְלָה,

יָעַץ מְחָרֵף לְנוֹפֵף אִוּוּי

The Assyrian King Sancherib came to conquer Judean King Hezekiah in Jerusalem. Sancherib is referred to as "the blasphemer" since he first sent his envoy Ravshakeh to demoralize the Judeans by standing next to the city walls cursing and denigrating the God of Israel (Kings II, Chap. 18). The Bible (Kings II, 19:35) then relates: "And it occurred **that night** (va-Yehi ba-Layla hahu) that an angel of the Lord went out and struck down one hundred and eighty-five thousand in the Assyrian camp, and the following morning they were all dead corpses." "That night" is identified as the 15th of *Nisan* by *Midrash Panim Aherim*, Second Version, Chapter 6; see also *Targum* to *Megillat Esther* (6:1) and comments to "שְׁנַאת נָדַד אֲגָגִי. וְכָתַב סְפָרִים בַּלַּיְלָה" below.

כָּרַע בֵּל וּמַצָּבוֹ

In the nightmare of Nevuchadnezzar, described in the Book of Daniel (Chap. 2), the King sees the collapse of a great idol, whom the *Paytan* identifies as Bel – the Babylonian National deity. This is a prophecy of the fall of Bavel before Persia, leading ultimately to the return of Israel from exile. Since this prophecy of salvation occurred at night, Yannai again assumes that it occurred on the 15th of *Nisan* following *Midrash Rabba* (Num. *Parasha* 20, no. 12; see comments re: וַיְהִי בַּחֲצִי הַלַּיְלָה above). See more in the next comment.

לְאִישׁ חֲמוּדוֹת נִגְלָה רָז

The tale of the previous verse is continued here. God revealed to Daniel (referred to as *ish hamudot* in Daniel 10:11) not only the exact details of

7. The blasphemer [Sanheirev] planned to raise his hand against Jerusalem; but You made him into dry corpses in the night.
8. Bel with its pedestal was overturned in the darkness of the night.
9. To the man You delighted in [Daniel] was revealed the secret of the visions of the night.
And it came to pass at midnight!
10. He who became drunk from the holy vessels [Belshazzar] was killed that very night.

Nevuchadnezzar's dream but also its resolution (Daniel Chap. 2) which greatly pleased the King. As a result, Daniel was given a very prominent position at the King's court, and his friends Hanania, Mishael, and Azaria were appointed high up in the administration of Babylon. Though the Jews remained for the meantime in the Babylonian exile, the administration was very favorably disposed towards them – and for many generations to come. (This may explain why Yannai counts this incident of Daniel as **two** salvations – one related to the eventual return of part of the exile to Israel, and the second regarding the gilded *galut* in Babylonia in which Judaism thrived.)

מִשְׁתַּכֵּר בִּכְלֵי קֹדֶשׁ

The very night that the last Babylonian King Belshazzar sinned by using the First Temple goblets at his royal feast, he was assassinated by Persian conquerors (Daniel 5). The end of his kingdom was predicted by a mysterious writing appearing on the party room wall which read: *mene mene tekel u-farsin*, and which was correctly interpreted by Daniel (Daniel 5:25). That this event occurred on the 15th of *Nisan* may be based on wording of the Aramaic verse in the Book of Daniel (5:30) which reads: *Bei be-leyla ketil Belshatzar* – "**On that night**, Belshazzar was assassinated." (Yannai in the present line uses the Hebrew בּוֹ בַּלַּיְלָה). R. Daniel Ernst Goldschmidt (cited in *Otzar Meforshei ha-Haggada*) has suggested that since *Bei be-leyla* is the Aramaic equivalent of *ba-Layla Hahu*, it too indicates that this event occurred on the 15th of *Nisan* (see above). This event is also discussed by R. Elazar ha-Kalir in *Va-Amartem* below.

11. נוֹשַׁע מִבּוֹר אֲרָיוֹת. פּוֹתֵר בְּעִתּוּתֵי	לָיְלָה,
12א שִׂנְאָה נָטַר אֲגָגִי. וְכָתַב סְפָרִים	בַּלָּיְלָה,

וַיְהִי בַּחֲצִי הַלָּיְלָה.

נוֹשַׁע מִבּוֹר אֲרָיוֹת

The salvation of Daniel from the Lion's den is recorded in the Book of Daniel (6:19–23). The text states explicitly that he was brought to the Lion's den after sunset (v. 15) and kept there all night (v. 19) until removed. That it occurred on *Seder* night is mentioned explicitly in *Midrash Rabba (Ex. Bo, Parasha* 18:12; see comments to וַיְהִי בַּחֲצִי הַלָּיְלָה above).

פּוֹתֵר בְּעִתּוּתֵי לָיְלָה

Daniel is referred to here as the "interpreter of the nightmares," a well-earned reputation he acquired with several Babylonian kings (see instances 8, 9 and 10) described in the Book of Daniel, Chapters 2 and 5.

שִׂנְאָה נָטַר אֲגָגִי. וְכָתַב סְפָרִים בַּלָּיְלָה

This line and the next in the *piyut* deals with the Jews' salvation from Haman the Agagite – which interestingly occurred in part over *Pesah*. The question is why Yannai wrote two verses regarding this incident. As we will also see, this couplet is problematic because of the difficult chronology proposed by the *paytan* for various events. All this requires us to briefly review the *Purim* tale, highlighting several crucial events. The first verse of this couplet relates that because of his hatred for Mordechai who refused to bow, Haman decides to wipe out all the Jews (Esther 3:6ff), picking the 13th of Adar via a lottery as the day for extermination (v. 7). After receiving King Ahashverosh's approval (v. 11), the orders were written and disseminated by horseback on the 13th of *Nisan* (v. 12 and 13). Mordechai immediately notifies Esther of Haman's plan (Chap. 4:1), and she suggests a three-day fast – *Layla va-yom* (day and night; verse 16), during which she will approach the King. The *Megilla* in Chapter 5 opens with Esther's appearance before Achashverosh "on the third day" to invite him and Haman to a party "that day" (Chap. 5:4), which is followed by another invite for a second follow-up party

11. Saved from the lion's den was he [Daniel] who interpreted the horrors of the night.

12A. The Aggagi [Haman] nursed hatred and wrote edicts by night.
And it came to pass at midnight!

---

with Haman on the morrow (v. 8). On the night between the parties, the verse says (Chap. 6:1): *ba-Layla hahu nadeda shenat ha-Melekh* – "On that night the King suffered sleeplessness" and from that point on, Haman's fate takes a nosedive.

It is with this restless night that the second line of Yannai's Haman couplet begins. It is clear throughout this *piyut* that Yannai relied on the tradition of the *Targum* to *Megillat Esther* (6:1) and *Midrash Panim Aherim* (Second Version, Chapter 6), that *ba-Layla Hahu* – "**On that night**" occurred on the 15th of *Nisan*, *Seder* night, like the other acts of salvation in this song. As indicated above, these *Midrashim* understand the expression *ba-Layla Hahu* as referring to that special night of *va-Yehi ba-hatzi ha-layla* – the night of *Makkat Bekhorot*, the 15th of *Nisan*. This assertion is difficult because Haman's edict was only transcribed and publicized on the 13th of *Nisan* – as explicitly stated in the *Megilla* (Esther 3:12–13). This would require that the earliest that Mordechai could have discovered the plot was immediately on the 13th of *Nisan* at night when it was first promulgated. Let us now argue that Esther's 72-hour fast also began that night on the 13th of *Nisan* and continued through the 14th and 15th. (This is suggested by *Pirkei de-Rabbi Eliezer*, Chap. 50 and *Esther Rabba*, 8:7. Rashi to *Esther* 5:17 and *Megilla* 16a dissents, maintaining that the fast began on the 14th). Esther then went to the King on the 15th and the first party was held that day (see the *Haggada* of R. Reuven Margaliot). With all this, the king's sleeplessness night would still only have been that night at the beginning of the 16th! Indeed, because of these and other questions, a variety of other dates have been proposed by various commentaries. Our goal here, however, is to resolve the view of our *paytan* and the related *Midrashim*.

Two solutions are possible. One is that Queen Esther's daring entrance to Ahashverosh "on the third day" (Chap. 5:4) was not the third day from the **fast** (as assumed above) – but the third day from Haman's **lottery**, whose exact date in *Nisan* is not mentioned in the text. It may have well been one day before he excitedly approached the King –

12ב. עוֹרַרְתָּ נִצְחֲךָ עָלָיו בְּנֶדֶד שְׁנַת	לַיְלָה.
13א. פּוּרָה תִדְרוֹךְ, לְשׁוֹמֵר מַה	מִלַּיְלָה,
13ב. צָרַח כַּשּׁוֹמֵר, וְשָׂח אָתָא בֹקֶר וְגַם	לַיְלָה,
וַיְהִי בַּחֲצִי הַלַּיְלָה.	

on the 12th of *Nisan*. Esther's appearance before Ahashverosh would then have fallen on the 14th of *Nisan* (corresponding to the second day of the fast), and the sleepless night of Ahashverosh would then indeed have occurred on the fifteenth. Another possibility is that the whole story of Israel's salvation from the edict's approval, publication, and dissemination on the 13th of *Nisan*, through the three-day fast, the parties, sleepless nights, and Haman's hanging on the 16th of *Nisan* occurred over several very busy days – with the fifteenth of *Nisan* at its epicenter, considered the night of salvation. It is perhaps for this reason that Yannai wrote two lines for this protracted process.

עוֹרַרְתָּ נִצְחֲךָ עָלָיו

The King's sleepless night initiates a precipitous decline in Haman's fate requiring Haman to parade Mordechai gloriously through Shushan. The true import of these events was correctly understood by Haman's wife Zeresh (Esther 6:13).

פּוּרָה תִדְרוֹךְ

In the last six verses, the *Paytan* relates to the thirteenth future event to occur on *Seder* Night – the coming of the Messiah and the concomitant redemption. We already saw in our comments that *Midrash Rabba* (Ex. *Bo, Parasha* 18:12) states that on the 15th of *Nisan* "Eliyahu and the Messiah will become great…" The prophets (Isaiah, Joel, Amos, Ovadiah, Zephania, and Ezekiel) indicate that as part of the Messianic era, there will be a Judgement Day referred to by the prophets as *Yom Hashem* – "Day of the Lord." The latter is a period in which the Almighty judges and punishes those nations that have oppressed the Jews prior to the redemption. The phrase *Pura Tidrokh* is based on Isaiah (63:3) where the prophet describes God's punishment of His enemies like one who treads the grapes in a winepress: *Pura darakhti lěvadi…* – "I alone have trodden [the oppressors under] like a winepress [which crushes and squeezes

12B. You began Your victory over him with disturbing [Ahashveirosh's] sleep at night.
13A. Trample the winepress for those who ask the watchman, "What will come of the night?"
13B. He will shout like a watchman, and say: "Morning shall came and also night."

And it came to pass at midnight!

---

the grapes]...." This scene of pending punishment is in preparation for the ultimate redemption described in the second half of this verse. The anticipation of redemption is described in Isaiah (21:11–12) where a passerby asks a guard, serving as the watchman on the wall: *Shomer ma milel* – "Watchman, what of the night?" Night is a metaphor for exile and Jewish suffering. Thus, the passerby is asking the watchman as to when sunrise – the redemption – will finally come. (The watchman's response appears in the next verse of this *piyut*; explained in the next comment).

The expression *derikhat pura* – "treading the winepress" is quite rare and appears only twice in Tanakh: Isaiah 63:3 and Haggai 2:16. In addition to the *Haggada*, it appears twice more in Jewish liturgy as a catchphrase for God's future punishment and redemption: (1) in the popular *Shabbat* song *Deror Yikra* in the verse: *Derokh pura be-tokh Botzra* – Tread the winepress in Botsra; and (2) in *Anim Zemirot* in the line: *Pura be-dorkho be-vo'o me-Edom* – When he tramples as in a winepress when he comes from Edom. Interestingly, Isaiah's metaphor of "treading the winepress" to mean God's punishment of his enemies – is best known to Americans from Julia Ward Howe's *The Battle Hymn of the Republic* (*The Atlantic Monthly*, February 1862): "Mine eyes have seen the glory of the coming of the Lord; He is **trampling out the vintage where the grapes of wrath** are stored." This American Civil War song of the Union Forces viewed the crushing of the South as God's retribution against evil and part of the realization of God's Kingdom on Earth.

צָרַח כַּשּׁוֹמֵר. וְשָׂח אָתָא בֹקֶר וְגַם לָיְלָה

This line is a direct continuation of the end of the previous verse, dealing with the prophecy of Isaiah (21:11–12). The watchman declares aloud that the morning (redemption) will indeed arrive for the Jews,

13ג. קָרֵב יוֹם. אֲשֶׁר הוּא לֹא יוֹם וְלֹא לַיְלָה,
13ד. רָם הוֹדַע. כִּי לְךָ הַיּוֹם. אַף לְךָ הַלַּיְלָה,
13ה. שׁוֹמְרִים הַפְקֵד לְעִירְךָ. כָּל הַיּוֹם וְכָל הַלַּיְלָה,
13ו. תָּאִיר כְּאוֹר יוֹם. חֶשְׁכַת לַיְלָה.
וַיְהִי בַּחֲצִי הַלַּיְלָה.

---

while night (retribution) will come for their enemies. Poetically, in this and the next four concluding verses Yannai emphasizes a combination of the themes of day and night.

קָרֵב יוֹם. אֲשֶׁר הוּא לֹא יוֹם וְלֹא לַיְלָה

The prophet Zekharia (14:7) described the beginning of the Messianic era as "neither day nor night." "And there shall be one day which shall be known to the Lord, not day and not night; but it shall come to pass, that at evening time there shall be light." Both R. Chaim Druckman and R. Shlomo Aviner note the many sources in *Haza"l* indicate that the future redemption will NOT come in one fell swoop, but rather as stated in the Jerusalem Talmud (*Berakhot* 1:1): "So will be the deliverance of Israel: it starts very slowly and grows stronger the longer it continues." Indeed, these scholars understand the words of the prophet to be a fitting description of our era, a period of partial redemption and partial oppression. Zekharia's prophecy assures us that eventually, this will lead to complete salvation.

רָם הוֹדַע. כִּי לְךָ הַיּוֹם. אַף לְךָ הַלַּיְלָה

Continuing with the theme of day and night, Yannai prays: Almighty reveal Yourself as the one in control of day and night – the forces of Nature and History.

13C. Bring close the day that is neither day nor night.
13D. Exalted One, make known that Yours is the day and Yours is also the night.
13E. Appoint guards for Your city, all day and all night.
13F. Brighten like the light of the day the darkness of night.
   And it came to pass at midnight!

שׁוֹמְרִים הַפְקֵד לְעִירְךָ. כָּל הַיּוֹם וְכָל הַלַּיְלָה

In the messianic era the Temple will be built and there will be guards watching and protecting it out of love day and night, as described in yet another prophecy of Isaiah (62:6): *Al homotayikh Yerushalayim hifkadeti shomrim kol ha-yom ve-khol ha-layla...* – "I have set watchmen upon thy walls, O Jerusalem, all day and all night..."

תָּאִיר כְּאוֹר יוֹם. חֶשְׁכַת לַיְלָה

Bring the exile and oppression to an end, and light up the world with our redemption.

וַיְהִי בַּחֲצִי הַלַּיְלָה

Two additional verses have been written by Yael Levine describing events that occurred to women on *Seder* night. See below: "Additions to the *Haggada*," Sec. 2.

Outside of Israel, this song replaces the previous one on the second Seder night.

וַאֲמַרְתֶּם זֶבַח פֶּסַח (בחו"ל בליל שני)

וּבְכֵן וַאֲמַרְתֶּם זֶבַח פֶּסַח.

אֹמֶץ גְּבוּרוֹתֶיךָ הִפְלֵאתָ	בַּפֶּסַח
בְּרֹאשׁ כָּל מוֹעֲדוֹת נִשֵּׂאתָ	פֶּסַח
גִּלִּיתָ לְאֶזְרָחִי חֲצוֹת לֵיל	פֶּסַח,

וַאֲמַרְתֶּם זֶבַח פֶּסַח.

וַאֲמַרְתֶּם זֶבַח פֶּסַח

The present song was written by a student of Yannai, the noted *paytan* and elegist R. Elazar ha-Kalir, who lived in Israel from approximately 570–640 C.E. The verses are arranged alphabetically. In contradistinction to the previous *piyut* ṿa-Yehi ba-Hatzi ha-Layla which deals with events occurring on the 15th of *Nisan* at night, the present song ṿe-Amartem Zevah Pesah includes incidents that took place on both the day and night of the 15th of *Nisan*. In addition, as we shall see, it also relates in passing to events that occurred on the 16th of *Nisan*, such as: (1) the destruction of Sedom and the saving of Lot (the letters *Zayin* and *Het*); (2) the mention of the *Omer* sacrifice (the letter *Nun*); and (3) the hanging of Haman (the letter *Resh*). Some suggest that this distinction is the reason that in the diaspora ṿa-Yehi ba-Hatzi ha-Layla is read at the first *Seder* (Eve of the 15th of *Nisan*), while ṿe-Amartem Zevah Pesah is read in the diaspora at the second *Seder* (16th of *Nisan*). R. Menachem Mendel Kasher (*Haggada Sheleima*) posits that a more likely reason is that ṿa-Yehi ba-Hatzi ha-Layla was part of the *Kerova* (*Piyut* for the *Hazan*) for the first day of *Pesah*, while ṿe-Amartem Zevah Pesah originally appeared as the *Kerova* for the second day of *Pesah*.

וַאֲמַרְתֶּם זֶבַח פֶּסַח

R. Asher Weiss (*Haggada Minhat Asher*) suggests that the title and chorus of this poem is based on the words of the *Humash* in Exodus (12:26–27): "And when your children ask you, 'What do you mean by this rite?' You shall say: 'It is the Passover sacrifice to Hashem (ṿe-Amartem

Outside of Israel, this song replaces the previous one on the second Seder night.

AND YOU SHALL SAY: THIS IS THE PESAH SACRIFICE.

You displayed Your mighty powers wondrously on Pesah.
Above all seasons of delight You elevated Pesah.
You revealed the Exodus to the Oriental [Avraham] at the midnight of Pesah.

And you shall say: this is the Pesah sacrifice.

Zevah Pesah hu la-Shem), who passed over the houses of the Israelites in Egypt when smiting the Egyptians, but saved our houses.' Those assembled then bowed low in homage." The *Mekhilta* de-Rabi Yishmael (*Bo, Masekhta de-Pisha*, 12) notes the bowing at the end of the previous verse. It indicates that upon hearing of God's miracles of salvation to be performed on *Pesah*, the Hebrews in Egypt were obligated to bow in thanks. We too are obliged to acknowledge all the wonderful deeds that the Almighty did for us over the generations – which the *paytan* will now begin to enumerate.

אֹמֶץ גְּבוּרוֹתֶיךָ הִפְלֵאתָ בַּפֶּסַח

It was on *Pesah* that the Almighty revealed His wondrous mightiness as the God of Nature and History.

פֶּסַח בְּרֹאשׁ כָּל מוֹעֲדוֹת נִשֵּׂאתָ

You raised *Pesah* to the position of first of the *Mo'adim*.

גִּלִּיתָ לְאֶזְרָחִי חֲצוֹת לֵיל פֶּסַח

The opening verse of *Psalms* 89 indicates that it was composed by Eitan the *Ezrahi. Haza"l* (*Bava Batra* 14b–15a; *Midrash Psalms*, Chap. 54) indicate that Eitan the *Ezrahi* is a pseudonym for Avraham *Avinu* where *Ezrahi* means *Mizrahi* – i.e., from the East (*Aram Naharayim*). This verse thus means: You revealed to Avraham *Avinu* the wonders of the salvation that would take place on *Pesah* at midnight. This could refer to two different possibilities: (1) The first is the *Brit bein ha-betarim* – "Covenant of the Parts" (Gen. 15:13–21; see our discussion above to

בְּפֶסַח.	דְּלָתָיו דָּפַקְתָּ כְּחֹם הַיּוֹם
בְּפֶסַח.	הִסְעִיד נוֹצְצִים עֻגוֹת מַצּוֹת
פֶּסַח.	וְאֶל הַבָּקָר רָץ זֵכֶר לְשׁוֹר עֵרֶךְ

וַאֲמַרְתֶּם זֶבַח פֶּסַח.

(בָּרוּךְ שׁוֹמֵר הַבְטָחָתוֹ לְיִשְׂרָאֵל and וְיַעֲקֹב וּבָנָיו יָרְדוּ מִצְרָיִם) in which Avraham was informed of the future enslavement of the Israelites in Egypt and their subsequent glorious redemption. In this regard, the *Mekhilta de-Rabbi Yishmael* (*Massekhta de-Pisha, Parasha* 14) says:

> "And it was at the end of four hundred and thirty years" (Ex. 12:41): We see that when the time has arrived [the 15th of *Nisan*], the Lord did not delay [their redemption] for one moment. On the 15th of *Nisan* God spoke to Avraham regarding the Covenant of the Parts; on the 15th of *Nisan* the angels came to Avraham to apprise him [that Yitzhak would be born]; and on the 15th of *Nisan* Yitzhak was born."

(2) The second possibility is Avraham's victorious battle against the Four Kings to retrieve Lot which occurred on *Seder* night – as we discussed previously in the song *va-Yehi ba-Hatzi ha-Layla*. The Midrash maintains that God "suggested" that Avraham use just the first half of the night (before midnight) to defeat the four kings (– that would be time enough), while He, the Almighty, would save the remaining second half – starting from midnight (*hatzot*), some generations later, to redeem Avraham's progeny (by carrying out the plague of the first-born).

דְּלָתָיו דָּפַקְתָּ כְּחֹם הַיּוֹם

In order to understand the next three lines in this poem, let us read a selection of verses in the beginning of Genesis 18. We note several key points referred to by the *paytan*:

> (1) The **Lord appeared** to him (Avraham) by the terebinths of Mamrei; he was sitting at the entrance of the tent **in the heat of the day**. (2) Looking up, he saw **three men** standing near him.

You knocked at his door in the heat of the day on Pesah.
He gave the angels cakes of matza to dine on during Pesah.
He ran to the herd, harbinger of the sacrificial feast of the Pesah.
And you shall say: this is the Pesah sacrifice.

> Perceiving this, he ran from the entrance of the tent to greet them and bowed to the ground. ... (6) Avraham hastened into the tent to Sarah, and said, "Hasten three seahs of choice flour! Knead and **make cakes**!" (7) Then **Avraham ran to the herd**, took a calf, tender and choice, and gave it to a servant-boy, who hastened to prepare it. ... (10) Then one said, "I will return to you **a year from today, and your wife Sarah shall have a son**!" ... (16) **The men arose from there** and looked down toward Sodom, and Avraham walked with them to see them off.

Regarding the timing of the events in this song to *Pesah*, our *paytan* R. Elazar ha-Kalir relies on the position of the *Mekhilta de-Rabbi Yishmael*, cited in the previous comment. (In *Rosh ha-Shana* 11a, there is a differing view that all this occurred on Sukkot. Indeed, much has been written about this dispute. But our task is to explain the *piyut*, so we will remain focused.) The *mekhilta* posits that the three angels (in v. 2) arrived at Avraham's tent on *Pesah* day, the 15th of *Nisan*. But from the above *pesukim* it is clear that their arrival was shortly after God himself in v. 1 came to visit – or as R. Elazar ha-Kalir puts it: "knocked on Avraham's door." Hence this too occurred on *Pesah*, the 15th of *Nisan*. The baking of cakes in v. 6 and the preparation of the meat in v. 7 were also on the same day. The *mekhilta* explicitly says that the good tidings of Yitzhak's birth (v. 10) was also on *Pesah* day – the 15th, though we could have surmised this from the proximity of the verses in the text. Since v. 10 states that Yitzhak would be born "a year from today," Yitzhak was also perforce born on the first day of *Pesah*, as the *mekhilta* concludes. For future purposes, it is also important to stress that the angels leave Avraham while it is still day, also on *Pesah* day – the 15th of *Nisan*. More on this in a few lines.

Turning now to the present line of the poem, God's anthropomorphic knocking on the door may simply be a poetic way of describing His visit to Avraham. However, the poet's use of "knocking on his

זוֹעֲמוּ סְדוֹמִים וְלוֹהֲטוּ בָּאֵשׁ   בַּפֶּסַח.
חֻלַּץ לוֹט מֵהֶם וּמַצּוֹת אָפָה בְּקֵץ   פֶּסַח.
טִאטֵאתָ אַדְמַת מֹף וְנֹף בְּעָבְרְךָ   בַּפֶּסַח.
וַאֲמַרְתֶּם זֶבַח פֶּסַח.

---

doors" suggests that He was in a way asking permission to enter. R. David Silverberg (SALT, Parashat Vayera, 5777/2016) cites Song of Songs where the beloved knocks on the door repeatedly asking permission to enter. So too, says R. Silverberg, God only enters one's life if He is invited in. R. Nachum Bronznick (Ma'ayan 5769) comments on the *piyut's* use of the plural form *delatav* – "his doors." This corresponds to *Haza"l*'s (*Midrash Sekhel Tov*, Gen. 18:2) description that Avraham's tent was strategically placed with an opening in each direction. R. Bronznick also notes that Kalir's teacher, Yannai uses the idiom *va-Yidfok... dalta* – a euphemism for removing mother Rachel's barrenness. Hence the student R. Elazar ha-Kalir may be referring here to the angels' tiding/blessing that Sarah's barrenness will end and she and Avraham will have a child.

הִסְעִיד נוֹצְצִים עֻגּוֹת מַצּוֹת בַּפֶּסַח

ha-Kalir now turns to Genesis 18:6 (see previous comment), where Avraham asks Sarah to prepare for the guests *ugot* – "cakes." Firstly, these guests, later (Gen. 19:1) identified as angels, are referred to by the paytan as *notzetzim* – "sparkling," presumably based on Ezekiel's description of angels (Ezekiel 1:7): *ve-notzetzim ke-ein nehoshet kalal* – "their sparkle was like the luster of burnished bronze." But, the *paytan* makes another critical change. Ha-Kalir writes that Avraham asked Sarah to prepare *ugot Matzot* – "Matza cakes"! The *Paytan* is undoubtedly following the known tradition of *Haza"l* in both the *Mishna* (*Kiddushin* 4:14) and Talmud (*Yoma* 28b) that Avraham kept the Torah in its entirety. Since, as shown above, the visit of the angels occurred at *Pesah*-time, the 15th of *Nisan*, Sarah could not have prepared *hametzdik* cakes for the guests, but rather *ugot Matzot* – "*Pesahdik* Matza cakes." These were probably round soft Matza – like those prepared to this day by many sefaradic and Yemenite Jews. Indeed, the Torah itself (Ex. 12:39), regarding the matsot eaten in Egypt: "And they baked the dough

The Sodomites angered God and were burned up with fire on Pesah. Lot was rescued from them and he baked matzot at the end of Pesah. You swept the ground of Moph and Noph [Egypt] when You passed through on Pesah.

And you shall say: this is the Pesah sacrifice.

---

that they had taken out of Egypt as unleavened cakes (*ugot Matzot*)..." The word *uga* means round and circle-like (rather than elongated like a loaf), and says nothing about its degree of leavening.

וְאֶל הַבָּקָר רָץ זֵכֶר לְשׁוֹר עֵרֶךְ פֶּסַח

Commentaries have struggled with this otherwise simple line because of two problematic words: *Zekher* and *Erekh*. Dr. Avi Schmidman [cited in *Haggada Shirat Miriam* by R. Yosef Zvi Rimon] has suggested a novel interpretation of this line based on a few recently discovered facts. Firstly, the Torah reading was called *Erekh* by the early *paytanim*. In addition, we know from R. Kalir's other *piyutim*, that for the first day of *Pesah* in Israel, the portion read was *Shor o kesev o ez ki yivaled* (Lev. 22:27), though nowadays we read *Mishkhu u-kehu* (Ex. 12:21). Thus, this line of the *piyut* should be understood as follows: As shown in our comments to דְּלָתָיו דְּפַקְתָּ כְּחֹם הַיּוֹם, it was on the first day of *Pesah* that the guests arrived and Avraham ran to the cattle (which include **oxen**) to feed the guests meat. The paytan indicates that we remember this incident (*zekher le-shor*) by reading about the ox in the Torah portion for Passover (*Erekh Pesah*) (which is *Shor o kesev o ez*).

זֹעֲמוּ סְדוֹמִים וְלֹהֲטוּ בָּאֵשׁ בַּפֶּסַח. חֻלַּץ לוֹט מֵהֶם וּמַצּוֹת אָפָה בְּקֵץ פֶּסַח

This couplet deals with the destruction of Sedom, and Lot's salvation. Part of the difficulty with these lines is that the events are a bit jumbled and not in chronological order. To make order and understand what all this has to do with *Pesah*, let us read a selection of verses from Genesis 19 – which picks up with Avraham's angelic guests where Chap. 18:16 left off (see our comments to דְּלָתָיו דְּפַקְתָּ כְּחֹם הַיּוֹם).

> (1) The two angels arrived in Sodom **towards evening**, as Lot was sitting at the gate of Sodom... (3) But he urged them strongly, so

they turned his way and entered his house. He prepared a feast for them and **baked unleavened bread, and they ate**. (4) They had not yet lain down when the people of the city, the people of Sodom – young and old alike, the whole assembly without exception – gathered about the house. ... (6) So Lot went out to them to the entrance and shut the door behind him. ... (10) But the agents stretched out their hands and pulled Lot into the house with them. ... (15) **As dawn broke**, the messengers urged Lot on..." (16) Still he delayed. So the agents seized his hand, and the hands of his wife and his two daughters – in the Lord's mercy on him – and brought him out and left him outside the city. ... (23) **As the sun rose upon the earth** and Lot entered Zoar.

In our comments to דְּלָתָיו דָּפַקְתָּ כְּחֹם הַיּוֹם, we read from Genesis 18 that the angels left Avraham while it is still daytime and make their way to Sedom. *Mekhilta de-Rabbi Yishmael* indicated that their visit with Avraham occurred on the 15th of *Nisan* (*Pesah*). We now read that two of the angels arrive in Sedom *ba-erev* – "**towards** evening" of that first day of *Pesah*. Metzudot David (Yehoshua, 5:10) comments that *ba-erev* only means in the late afternoon, but not yet nighttime. And this is also the view of R. Sa'adya Gaon. Yehuda Kil (*Da'at Mikra*, 19:1) posits that from the story it is clear that there still was a good deal of time after eating until people went to sleep. Thus, even the attack of the Sodomites on the angels could have been before nightfall! Based on the above approach, the arrival of the angels to Sedom, their invitation to Lot's home, the baking of the *Matzot*, and even the attack of the Sodomites on the angels – could all have occurred before nightfall on the 15th of *Nisan*. Note, however, that as is clear from v. 15, 16, and 23, the destruction of Sodom and Lot's salvation from that city clearly occurred on the next day, the 16th of *Nisan*.

This analysis corresponds to what R. Elazar ha-Kalir writes at the end of this couplet: *u-Matzot afa be-ketz Pesah* – and he [Lot] baked *Matzot* at the end of [the first day of] *Pesah*." Thus, it was towards the end of the 15th of *Nisan* when Lot baked and ate *Matzot* with the angels (see: R. Yedidiah Tiah Weil, *Haggada Marbeh le-Sapper*; R. Asher Weiss, *Haggada Minhat Asher*). Rashi (19:3) also writes that Lot baked Matza because *Pesah haya* – "it was *Pesah*." As surprising as this may seem, this story shows that Lot was strongly influenced by Avraham's righteousness and was worthy of being saved. After all, he did *gemillut hassadim* – acts of kindness by welcoming and later protecting the angels – despite the fierce anger of his neighbors. He also baked and fed his guest *matzot* on *Pesah* – which was undoubtedly a tradition he picked up from his uncle Avraham, and reflects his commitment to family traditions and values.

Let us now return to explain the first verse of our couplet: *Zo'amu Sedomim ve-lohatu ba-esh be-Pesah*. The word *Zo'amu* is a strange construction and is commonly understood to mean: "The men of Sodom **angered** God, and were therefore burned in fire." We much prefer the translation in The Koren Sacks *Haggada* which uses instead: "The men of Sodom **raged**" or better yet "were **enraged**." The verse then becomes: The inhabitants of Sodom were enraged (by Lot's warm and protective reception of the angels on the 15th of *Nisan*, **and as a result** of such wickedness,) they were burned in fire (on the 16th).

The next verse reads: *Hulatz Lot me-hem u-matzot afa be-ketz Pesah*. As just pointed out, the saving of Lot referred to could not have been from the city of Sodom, since that occurred on the 16th of *Nisan*. Rather it must refer to Lot's salvation from the Sodomites by the angels. Hence, the second verse of the couplet should be translated as: "Lot was saved from them [from the vicious attack the **men** of Sodom, **because** of his righteous] baking of *matzot* at the end of [the first day of] *Pesah*." According to this explanation, the order and chronology of R. Elazar ha-Kalir's verses are vindicated. A variety of other interpretations have been given for the biblical text; but again, our focus is on explaining the *piyut*. More discussion of Lot's *Pesah* observance of Matza can be found in our "Introductory Essays" # 8.

טאטאת אדמת מף ונף בעברך בפסח

Moph and Noph (both identified in the Septuagint as Memphis) are Egyptian provinces mentioned in Hoshea (9:6) and Isaiah (19:13), respectively. They were swept clean on *Seder* night in the last plague of either firstborn children or of idolatry, as the verse (Ex. 12:12) says: "For on that night [15th of *Nisan*] I will go through the land of Egypt and strike down every firstborn in the land of Egypt, both human and

יָהּ. רֹאשׁ כָּל אוֹן מָחַצְתָּ בְּלֵיל שִׁמּוּר	פֶּסַח.
כַּבִּיר. עַל בֵּן בְּכוֹר פָּסַחְתָּ בְּדַם	פֶּסַח.
לְבִלְתִּי תֵּת מַשְׁחִית לָבֹא בִּפְתָחַי	בַּפֶּסַח.

וַאֲמַרְתֶּם זֶבַח פֶּסַח.

מִסְגֶּרֶת סֻגָּרָה בְּעִתּוֹתֵי	פֶּסַח.

---

beast; and I will mete out punishments to all the gods of Egypt, I am *Hashem*." *Mekhilta de-Rabbi Yishmael* (ad loc.) explains the latter as follows: "Idols of stone crumbled; of wood, rotted; of metal, rusted."

יָהּ. רֹאשׁ כָּל אוֹן מָחַצְתָּ בְּלֵיל שִׁמּוּר פֶּסַח

This line (and the next two) also refers to the night of *Makkat Bekhorot*. The word *On* means strength, potency, and virility. Reuven the firstborn of Yaakov is referred to as *Reshit oni* (Gen. 49:3). *Seder* Night is called (Ex. 12:42): *Leyl shimurim* – a night of watching/vigil/protection. See our discussion above to וַיְהִי בַּחֲצִי הַלַּיְלָה and שְׁפוֹךְ חֲמָתְךָ (כוס של אליהו).

כַּבִּיר. עַל בֵּן בְּכוֹר פָּסַחְתָּ בְּדַם פֶּסַח

Almighty, you skipped over the Israelites who are your firstborn, as written (Ex. 4:22) *Beni bekhori Yisrael*, because of the paschal sacrifice blood placed on the lintel and doorposts (Ex. 12:7).

לְבִלְתִּי תֵּת מַשְׁחִית לָבֹא בִּפְתָחַי בַּפֶּסַח

This line is based on Exodus 12:13: "And the blood on the houses where you are staying shall be a sign for you: when I see the blood I will pass over you so that no plague will destroy you (*ve-lo yihiyeh bakhem negef le-mashhit*) when I strike the Land of Egypt."

מִסְגֶּרֶת סֻגָּרָה בְּעִתּוֹתֵי פֶּסַח

The next historical event that occurred at *Pesah* time was the conquest of Jericho, which is described in detail in Yehoshua (Chap. 5 and 6). The text (Yehoshua 5:10) makes it clear that the Israelites camped at Gilgal

God, You crushed the head of every firstborn on the watchful night of Pesah.
Powerful One, You skipped over Your firstborn by merit of the blood of Pesah.
So as not to let the Destroyer enter my threshold on Pesah.
And you shall say: this is the Pesah sacrifice.

The besieged city [Jericho] was besieged at the time of Pesah.

---

on the plains of Jericho and celebrated *Pesah* there on the eve of the 15th of *Nisan*. Immediately thereafter, we are told (Yehoshua 6:1) that, out of fear of the Children of Israel: *ve-Yeriho sogeret u-mesugeret…* – "Jericho was shut tightly because of the Israelites; no one could leave or enter." In the next verses, Yehoshua was famously commanded to circle the city for six days, – and eventually conquer it on the seventh after the walls fell – which he did. What is important to our understanding of this *piyut* is that the conquest of Jericho itself began **after** the first day of *Pesah* (16th to 22nd of *Nisan*). Nevertheless, the city was already locked before that – over the 15th of *Nisan*, when the Israelites gathered outside Jericho to celebrate *Pesah*. It seems to us that, while the crumbling of the walls was a resounding miracle, it was on the preparatory lock-down – not the wondrous conquest – that R. Elazar ha-Kalir focuses. This is because that lock-down occurred on the 15th, like the other events in this poem.

Interestingly, ha-Kalir writes that the city was closed **be-itotei** *Pesah* – at *Pesah* **time**. He presumably used this terminology because the Israelites undoubtedly arrived at the plains of Jericho **before** the 15th, perhaps on the 13th or 14th of *Nisan*. We only know for sure that they were there for the *Seder* – the 14th at night; hence to be exact, the poet uses a vaguer term. Also interesting is the author's use of the double verb *mesugeret sugara*. On the one hand, it might simply be a poetic variation of the Tanakh's *sogeret u-mesugeret* – meaning **really** closed off. Alternatively, it might mean that the *mesugeret* – closed city – *sugara* – was "handed over" to the Israelites by God – *be-itotei Pesah* – around *Pesah* time. This would be around the 22nd of *Nisan*, rather than on the 15th like the rest of the poem; hence, as above, we disfavor this approach.

נִשְׁמְדָה מִדְיָן בִּצְלִיל שְׂעוֹרֵי עֹמֶר   פֶּסַח,

שׂוֹרְפוּ מִשְׁמַנֵּי פוּל וְלוּד בִּיקַד יְקוֹד   פֶּסַח,

וַאֲמַרְתֶּם זֶבַח פֶּסַח.

עוֹד הַיּוֹם בְּנֹב לַעֲמוֹד עַד גָּעָה עוֹנַת   פֶּסַח,

נִשְׁמְדָה מִדְיָן בִּצְלִיל שְׂעוֹרֵי עֹמֶר פֶּסַח

This refers to the incident of Gideon (Judges Chap. 7) to which we have already related at length above in our discussion of Yannai's *va-Yehi ba-Hatzi ha-Layla* (see above comments to בְּקוּמָם בַּלַּיְלָה). This line of the *piyut* refers to a Midianite soldier's nightmare of a tumbling *Tzlil lehem se'orim* – "barley cake" which destroyed their tents. The nightmare panics their forces, who lose the battle against Gideon's small select army. As explained, the battle began on the 15th of *Nisan*. *Midrash Rabba* (*Lev. Emor, Parasha* 25:6), however, adds that the text specifying *Tzlil lehem se'orim* (tumbling **barley** cake) suggests that the battle was won because of the Israelites' sacrifice of the barley *Omer* on the 16th of *Nisan* (which presumably occurred during the battle). For the same reason, ha-Kalir indicates that it was the *Omer* that destroyed Midian.

שׂוֹרְפוּ מִשְׁמַנֵּי פוּל וְלוּד בִּיקַד יְקוֹד פֶּסַח. עוֹד הַיּוֹם בְּנֹב לַעֲמוֹד עַד גָּעָה עוֹנַת פֶּסַח

Here we return to a miracle also discussed above by ha-Kalir's teacher Yannai in *va-Yehi ba-Hatzi ha-Layla* (see comments to יָעַץ מְחָרֵף לְנוֹפֵף אִוּוּי). This couplet of verses corresponds to the Hebrew letters *samekh* and *ayin*, although – as is very common – the *paytan* uses the similar sounding letter *sin* to replace *samekh*. The verses deal with the miraculous defeat of Sancherib (Kings II, Chap. 19) – though chronologically the verses are interchanged to preserve the alphabetic order. This couplet should therefore be translated as (Sancherib's) Elite soldiers of Pul and Lud were burned **on** (the night of) *Pesah*, **even though** earlier that day the troops had rushed to get to Nov (at the outskirts of Jerusalem) **before** the arrival time of the *Pesah* holiday.

The storyline is concisely reviewed by Rashi in his commentary to Isaiah (10:32): Sancherib was informed by his astrologers that he would only succeed in conquering King Hizkiyahu and Jerusalem if he

Midian was destroyed through a barley cake, from the Omer of Pesah. The mighty nobles of Pul and Lud [Assyria] were burnt in a great conflagration on Pesah.

And you shall say: this is the Pesah sacrifice.

Still today [Sanheirev] would be standing at Nov, before the arrival time of Pesah.

---

attacked **before** the 15th of *Nisan* – since *Pesah* was a particularly propitious time for the People of Israel. Hence, Sancherib pushed his army hard to arrive before that deadline. When he successfully arrived on the 14th of *Nisan* at Nov overlooking Jerusalem, he was totally unimpressed with the size of the city, and contravening his advisors decided to sleep over in Nov, rest up his army, and only then attack the next day. The *Tanakh* (Kings II, 19:35) relates: "And it occurred **that** night (*va-yehi ba-layla hahu*...) that an angel of the Lord went out and struck down one hundred and eighty-five thousand soldiers of the Assyrian camp, and the following morning they were all corpses." (We have seen several times already that "That night" is identified as the 15th of *Nisan* by *Midrash Panim Aherim*, Second Version, Chap. 6.) Our *Paytan* suggests that these were Sancherib's most elite or "fattened" Assyrian soldiers. *Haza"l* (as cited by R. David Kimchi) describe their death as wondrous: "The burning of the soul (within the body), but the body itself remained intact."

עַד גְּעָה עוֹנַת פֶּסַח

See our previous comments. This phrase should be translated as follows: "Before the arrival time of the *Pesah* holiday." We note that ha-Kalir here has created the word *ga'a* which does not exist in Hebrew. In his comments on the *Tisha be-Av Kinnot*, R. Joseph B. Soloveitchik (*Kinot Mesorat ha-Rav*, pp. 386–387) has commented on the creative language used in those elegies written by R. Elazar ha-Kalir. He points out that this *Paytan* attempted to make the Hebrew language more flexible and malleable – converting verbs to nouns and nouns to verbs (as was already commonplace in other languages). Here he took the infinitive *le-hagi'a* – "to arrive" and converted it to the yet unknown noun *ga'a* – "arrival."

פַּס יָד כָּתְבָה לְקַעֲקֵעַ צוּל	בַּפֶּסַח.
צָפֹה הַצָּפִית עָרוֹךְ הַשֻּׁלְחָן	בַּפֶּסַח.

וַאֲמַרְתֶּם זֶבַח פֶּסַח.

קָהָל כִּנְּסָה הֲדַסָּה לְשַׁלֵּשׁ צוֹם	בַּפֶּסַח.
רֹאשׁ מִבֵּית רָשָׁע מָחַצְתָּ בְּעֵץ חֲמִשִּׁים	בַּפֶּסַח.

פַּס יָד כָּתְבָה לְקַעֲקֵעַ צוּל בַּפֶּסַח

The next two verses refer to the famous feast of the last Babylonian King Belshazzar. Yannai, in the poem *va-Yehi ba-Hatzi ha-Layla* (comments to מִשְׁתַּכֵּר בִּכְלֵי קֹדֶשׁ above), also related to this incident. At the royal party that night, the King sinned by using the First Temple goblets and was assassinated by Persian conquerors (Daniel 5). The end of his kingdom was predicted by a mysterious writing appearing on the party room wall *mene mene tekel u-farsin*, which was correctly interpreted by Daniel (Daniel 5:25). That this event occurred on the 15th of *Nisan* may be based on wording of the verse in the Book of Daniel (5:30) which reads: **Bei be-leila ketil Balshatzar**– "**On that night**, Belshazzar was assassinated." Daniel Ernst Goldschmidt (cited in *Otzar Meforshei ha-Haggada*) has suggested that since *Bei be-leila* is the Aramaic equivalent to *ba-Layla ha-hu*, it too indicates that this event occurred on the 15th of *Nisan* (see comments to יָעַץ מְחָרֵף לְנוֹפֵף אִוּוּי above).

צָפֹה הַצָּפִית עָרוֹךְ הַשֻּׁלְחָן בַּפֶּסַח

This verse is based on the description of the Prophet Isaiah (21:5) relating to Babylonia. Just before Belshazzar sat down to his royal feast (described in our previous comment), he made sure the guards were in place to verify that the armies of the Persians and the Medes would not carry out a surprise attack. The table was set and everything was moved into place. Belshazzar was, nevertheless, assassinated by Darius and Koresh – who took over. As elucidated in the previous note, all this took place on *Seder* night, the 15th of *Nisan*.

A hand inscribed the destruction of Tzul [Babylon] on Pesah.
As the watch was set, and the table on Pesah.

And you shall say: this is the Pesah sacrifice.

Hadassah [Esther] assembled a congregation for a three-day fast on Pesah.
The head of the wicked clan [Haman] You crushed, through a gallows of fifty cubits, on Pesah.

קָהָל כִּנְּסָה הֲדַסָּה לְשַׁלֵּשׁ צוֹם בַּפֶּסַח

The next couplet of verses refers to the *Purim* story, which was also included by Yannai in the poem *va-Yehi ba-Hatzi ha-Layla*. As discussed previously, the *Megilla* informs us that on the 13th of *Nisan*, horsemen are sent out with orders to kill all the Jews of the Kingdom on the 13th of Adar. R. Yaakov Emden and others posit that Mordechai learns quickly of the plan and immediately notifies Esther, who initiates a three-day fast. According to this view, the fast of Esther occurred on the 13th, 14[th,] and 15th of *Nisan* – namely on *Pesah* proper. This is what this verse of this poem means when it says that they completed their three-day fast on *Pesah*.

רֹאשׁ מִבֵּית רָשָׁע מָחַצְתָּ בְּעֵץ חֲמִשִּׁים בַּפֶּסַח

As indicated in our discussion of *va-Yehi ba-Hatzi ha-Layla* (See our comments to שִׂנְאָה נָטַר אֲגָגִי, וְכָתַב סְפָרִים בַּלַּיְלָה above) R. Elazar ha-Kalir, like his teacher Yannai, followed the tradition of the *Targum* to *Megillat Esther* (6:1) and *Midrash Panim Aherim* (Second Version, Chapter 6), that the sleepless night of King Ahashverosh (Esther 6:1) occurred on the 15th of *Nisan*, *Seder* Night. Thus, Queen Esther's second party (Esther 7:1) took place on the afternoon thereafter – also occurred on the 15th of *Nisan*, *Pesah* day. At that party, Haman is exposed and King Ahashverosh commands that Haman (Esther 7:9) be hung on the same 50 *Amot* high tree he had set aside for Mordechai. The order was immediately carried out (Esther 7:10) which suggests that Haman's execution too occurred on the afternoon of the 15th of *Nisan*. This then is what the *Paytan* refers to when he writes: "You crushed the head of the wicked (Agagi) family (Haman) on a fifty Amot tree on *Pesah*" (cf. Habakuk 3:13 and Abravanel ad. loc.)

שְׁתֵּי אֵלֶּה רֶגַע תָּבִיא לְעוּצִית בְּפֶסַח.
תָּעוֹז יָדְךָ תָּרוּם יְמִינְךָ כְּלֵיל הִתְקַדֵּשׁ חַג פֶּסַח.
וַאֲמַרְתֶּם זֶבַח פֶּסַח.

שְׁתֵּי אֵלֶּה רֶגַע תָּבִיא לְעוּצִית בְּפֶסַח

The penultimate verse in this song is a turn towards a hopeful future. The prophet Isaiah (47:9) relates that at the end of days before the final redemption, Utsit (Edom) will suffer from a double calamity, loss of her present and future: its spouse and children. Our tradition (*Rosh ha-Shana,* 11a) teaches that according to R. Yehoshua *be-Nisan nigalu, be-Nisan atidin le-higa'el* – "The Israelites were redeemed in *Nisan*, and in *Nisan* they will be redeemed in the future as well." Hence, our poet assumes that the final destruction of Utsit/Edom will occur on *Pesah* – followed by our final redemption, described in the last line.

תָּעוֹז יָדְךָ תָּרוּם יְמִינְךָ כְּלֵיל הִתְקַדֵּשׁ חַג פֶּסַח

Midrash Rabba (*Shemot Bo, Parasha* 18:12) states: "Why did the Torah (Ex. 12:42) see fit to call the 15th of *Nisan* "a night of vigil?" This is because the Almighty did great acts for the righteous – just as he had done for the Jews in Egypt. Indeed, on this night He rescued Hizkiyahu [from Sennacherib], and on it, He rescued Hanania and his fellows [Mishael and Azariah], and on it, He rescued Daniel from the lion's den, and on it, **Eliyahu and the Messiah will become great…**" We pray in this final line of the *piyut* that in the final redemption, God's hand will be as glorious as when *Pesah* first became sanctified by the Redeemer's miracles.

וַאֲמַרְתֶּם זֶבַח פֶּסַח

As discussed above, the first two songs of *Nirtza, va-Yehi ba-Hatzi ha-Layla* and *ve-Amartem Zevah Pesah,* are historical poems which document God's involvement in salvation throughout the generations. Reading them is an inspirational, intellectual, and educational

Double will You bring in an instant upon Utsis [Edom] on Pesah.
Let Your hand be strengthened and Your right arm be uplifted, as on that night when You made holy the festival of Pesah.
And you shall say: this is the Pesah sacrifice.

---

experience. We conclude on a high note of hope for the Almighty's pending salvation for the Jews. God has saved us throughout the generations – particularly on *Pesah* night – and through the generations we have maintained the undying hope that the ultimate redemption will happen this year. Our task and tale are not yet done! As R. Jonathan Sacks has written ("In Search of the Why," *Covenant and Conversation*, *Behukotai* 2018/5778):

> The most often quoted of all Nietzsche's remarks – indeed one of the most quoted sentences of all in recent times – is his statement that "One who has a 'why' to live for, can bear almost any 'how'" (popularized by Viktor Frankl, *Man's Search for Meaning*). If life has a meaning, if our own life has a purpose, if there is a task we have yet to fulfill, then something within us gives us the strength to survive suffering and sorrow. The call of the future helps us get through the pain of the present and the trauma of the past. ... To be a Jew is to have faith that our individual lives and our collective history have meaning. God is there even if we cannot feel him. He hears us even when we do not hear Him. That is the blessing. It gave our people the courage to survive some of the worst blows ever to befall a people. It is what gives us, as individuals, the strength to come through "the slings and arrows of outrageous fortune" (Hamlet, Shakespeare). Lose that faith and we lose that strength.

Nirtza helps us to maintain or restore that faith! (See more in our discussion of *Had Gadya* below.)

אדיר במלוכה

כִּי לוֹ נָאֶה, כִּי לוֹ יָאֶה.

1. אַדִּיר בִּמְלוּכָה, בָּחוּר כַּהֲלָכָה, גְּדוּדָיו יֹאמְרוּ לוֹ:
לְךָ וּלְךָ, לְךָ כִּי לְךָ, לְךָ אַף לְךָ, לְךָ ה' הַמַּמְלָכָה.
כִּי לוֹ נָאֶה, כִּי לוֹ יָאֶה.

אַדִּיר בִּמְלוּכָה

The next pair of songs, *Adir bi-Melukha* and *Adir Hu*, extol the praises of an omnipotent, miraculous God who will change the course of history, return us to Jerusalem and build the Temple. The experience here is meant to be an emotional one, where we excitedly await the Almighty's wondrous intervention – may it come speedily in our days!

Though the author of *Adir bi-Melukha* is unknown, the 15th-century R. Shimon ben Tzemach Duran (*Tashbetz Katan* 99) reports it was found in the *Haggada* of the 13th-century Maharam of Rothenburg. The poem is made up of 8 stanzas (3 lines per stanza) – which contain three "fill-ins" in alphabetical order. The first fill-in is a descriptor of God as King (e.g., *adir, gadol, zakai* – powerful, distinguished, pure). The second fill-in is a more general quality of the Almighty (e.g., *bahur, hadur, hasin* – distinguished, glorious, mighty). Finally, the third fill-in describes one of the Creator's loyal subjects – alternating between angels, and the People of Israel – who sing God's praise. Thus, in verses 1, 3, 5, and 7 the angels are referred to as: 1. *gedudav* – companies (as soldiers or guards); 3. *tafserav* – princes; 5. *sevivav* – entourage; 7. *shinanav* – snow-white (pure) creatures). By contrast, in verses 2, 4, 6, and 8, the People of Israel are referred to as: 2. *vatikin* – pious; 4. *limudav* – learned ones; 6. *tzadikav* – righteous ones; 8. *temimav* – perfect ones. Each of Hashem's praises and those of His hosts has a source in Tanakh – except for *vatikav* which refers to the People of Israel. Nevertheless, this is a term that appears widely in Rabbinic literature (see *Berakhot* 25b, 26a) and refers to those who are worthy, pious, and observant.

כִּי לוֹ נָאֶה, כִּי לוֹ יָאֶה

The central words in the chorus are *na'eh* and *ya'eh*, which are synonyms

To Him [Praise] is Becoming; to Him [Praise] is Fitting

1. Mighty in Kingship, perfectly distinguished, His companies say to Him: Yours and Yours, Yours because it's Yours, Yours even Yours, Yours is the kingdom, O Lord.
   To Him [praise] is becoming; to Him [praise] is fitting.

---

meaning *yafeh* – which can be translated as: proper, fitting, appropriate. The linguist Yaakov Etzion (*Mekor Rishon* 2013) points out that the word *na'eh* per se does not appear in *Tanakh*, though the variation *na'ava* does, as in (Song of Songs 1:5) *Shehora ani ve-na'ava*. Nevertheless, *na'eh* appears extensively in *Haza"l*, most famously in (*Ketubot* 17a) *Kalla na'ah ve-hasuda* – "The bride is fair and attractive." On the other hand, the word *ya'eh* appears only once in *Tanakh* (Jeremiah 10:7) and infrequently in *Haza"l*. The word *ki* has a variety of meanings in Hebrew, but in this case, it is widely understood to mean "because." Thus, the chorus can be simply translated as: [We sing of God's many attributes] **because** To Him (Hashem) it is proper and fitting.

David Kessler prefers, however, to understand the word *ki* as *ka'asher* – when. Indeed, we find the Psalms recited in *Kabbalat Shabbat* (Chapters 95–99 and 92–93) talk about a time at the end of days when God will take over control of the world, judge the nations and reveal Himself as the true master of the universe. We will sing of Him *ki va lishpot ha-aretz* – "**when** He comes to judge the world (Psalms 98:9)." Similarly, the author of the song *Adir bi-melukha* is referring to the same period – **when** God finally reveals Himself openly as the true master of the universe – "**when** it is proper and fitting." That is when it will be proper for all of creation to refer to Him as *Adir bi-melukha, bahur ke-halakha* and for *gedudav* – the angels – to recite His praises as the One in control of all.

לְךָ וּלְךָ, לְךָ כִּי לְךָ, לְךָ אַף לְךָ, לְךָ ה' הַמַּמְלָכָה

Thus far we've worked our way through the praises of God and state that the hosts – be they angels or *Klal Yisrael* – praise Him as well. But what exactly do these hosts say? *le-Kha u-le-Kha; le-Kha ki le-Kha; le-Kha af le-Kha; le-Kha Hashem ha-mamlakha* This verse translated literally into English can be rendered: "Yours and Yours, Yours because it's Yours, Yours even Yours, Yours is the kingdom, O Lord." Sadly, this makes no more sense in English than it does in Hebrew. Over the generations, this verse has been loved for its tongue-twisting character and poetic beauty. But it remains a puzzle, nevertheless, and several explanations have been suggested.

R. Michel Shurkin (*Harerei Kedem*, II, sec. 103, end) posits that when the Almighty carries out salvation, He does so via one of three modes: (1) The first is *le-Kha u-le-Kha* – "Yours **and** Yours": You, God, do everything and man is merely an observer. Examples of this are the splitting of the Red Sea and the drowning of the Egyptian army therein. Alternatively, there is the destruction of 185,000 soldiers of Sennacherib's army. (2) The second mode is *le-Kha af le-Kha* – "Yours **even** Yours": Man and God are partners in carrying out the victory or action. An example would be the conquest of Jericho. The miracle was clearly God's, but the task was not complete until the Israelite army conquered the city. (3) Finally, there is *le-Kha ki le-Kha* – "Yours **because** it's yours": There are times when it seems that man does it all, but that is only because God's assistance is hidden from the eye. Examples of this are Gideon's battle with Midian, Devora and Barak's victory over Sisera, the victory of the Hasmoneans, and the War of Independence in 1948. This is also the Almighty's battle because we fought in His name and know He was there – even though His assistance was via the laws of Nature. But irrespective of the mode of action, we know that: *le-kha Hashem ha-mamlakha* – "Yours is the kingdom, O Lord." In other words, we reject the suggestion that *Kohi ve-otzem yadi asa li et ha-hayil hazeh* – "My own power and the might of my hand have won me this wealth." (Deut. 8:17).

But the most likely explanation was presumably first suggested by R. Don Isaac Abravanel (see: R. Menahem Mendel Kasher, *Haggada Sheleima*). He proposes that this tongue-twister is an abbreviated form of three *pesukim* – as shown in the table below. Each of these verses talks about the Creator's dominion over the world and the propriety of praising Him.

Abbreviated Verses	Complete Verses
(1) לך ולך	לך דמיה תהלה אלהים בציון, ולך ישלם נדר (תהלים סה:ב) Silence is **Your** praise, O' God in Zion; and for **Your** sake, the vow is fulfilled. (*Rashi*: Every attempt to enumerate Your wondrous attributes is futile. Hence, silence is the best form of praise.) What's more, "for **Your** sake," i.e., out of awe for You, those who make oaths – keep them.
(2) לך כי לך	לך ה' הגדלה והגבורה והתפארת והנצח וההוד – כי כל בשמים ובארץ. לך ה' הממלכה והמתנשא לכל לראש (דה"א כט:יא) **Yours**, O Lord, is the greatness, and the power, and the glory, and the victory, and the majesty; **for** all that is in the heaven and in the earth [is **Yours**]; **Yours** is the kingdom, O Lord, and You are exalted as head above all.
(3) לך אף לך	לך יום. אף לך לילה (תהלים עד:טז) **Yours** is the day; **also** the night is **Yours** או "לך שמים. אף לך ארץ" (שם פט:יב) **Yours** are the heavens; **also** the Earth is **Yours**
(4) לך ה' הממלכה	לך ה' הגדלה והגבורה והתפארת והנצח וההוד – כי כל בשמים ובארץ. לך ה' הממלכה והמתנשא לכל לראש (דה"א כט:יא). [Verse 2 above].

Another composite verse in widespread use in Jewish ritual is, *Hashem melekh. Hashem malakh, Hashem Yimlokh le-olam va'ed* which is made up of three verses: **Hashem melekh** *olam va-ed*... (Psalms 10:16); **Hashem malakh** *ge'ut lavesh*... (Psalms 93:1); and **Hashem yimlokh le-olam va'ed.** (Ex. 15:18). The 13th century R. Zedekiah ben Abraham Anav ha-*Rofeh* (*Shibbolei ha-Leket, Shabbat* 76) cites a tradition that "this text is recited by the angels."

2. דָּגוּל בִּמְלוּכָה, הָדוּר כַּהֲלָכָה, וָתִיקָיו יֹאמְרוּ לוֹ:
לְךָ וּלְךָ, לְךָ כִּי לְךָ, לְךָ אַף לְךָ, לְךָ ה' הַמַּמְלָכָה,
כִּי לוֹ נָאֶה, כִּי לוֹ יָאֶה.

3. זַכַּאי בִּמְלוּכָה, חָסִין כַּהֲלָכָה, טַפְסְרָיו יֹאמְרוּ לוֹ:
לְךָ וּלְךָ, לְךָ כִּי לְךָ, לְךָ אַף לְךָ, לְךָ ה' הַמַּמְלָכָה,
כִּי לוֹ נָאֶה, כִּי לוֹ יָאֶה.

4. יָחִיד בִּמְלוּכָה, כַּבִּיר כַּהֲלָכָה, לִמּוּדָיו יֹאמְרוּ לוֹ:
לְךָ וּלְךָ, לְךָ כִּי לְךָ, לְךָ אַף לְךָ, לְךָ ה' הַמַּמְלָכָה,
כִּי לוֹ נָאֶה, כִּי לוֹ יָאֶה.

The major problem with this *piyut*, *Adir bi-Melukha* – and for that matter the next *piyut*, *Adir Hu*, as well – is the abundance of praises used. The Talmud (*Berakhot* 33b and *Megilla* 25a) records the following incident:

> A particular individual descended before the ark as *Ḥazan* in the presence of Rabbi Ḥanina. He extended the first benediction of the *Amida* and said: "God, the great, mighty, awesome, powerful, mighty, awe-inspiring, strong, fearless, steadfast and honored." Rabbi Ḥanina waited for him until he finished and asked him: "Have you concluded all of the praises of your Master? Why do I need [to say] all of this superfluous praise? Even these three praises that we recite: 'The great, mighty and awesome,' had Moshe our teacher not said them in the Torah and had the members of the Great Assembly not incorporated them into the *Amida* prayer, we would not be permitted to recite them. And you went on and recited all of these. It is comparable to a king who possessed many thousands of golden dinars, yet they praised him for silver ones. Isn't that deprecatory?"

2. Prominent in kingship, perfectly glorious, His faithful say to Him: Yours and Yours, Yours because it's Yours, Yours even Yours, Yours is the kingdom, O Lord.
   To Him [praise] is becoming; to Him [praise] is fitting.

3. Worthy in kingship, perfectly immune, His princes say to Him: Yours and Yours, Yours because it's Yours, Yours even Yours, Yours is the kingdom, O Lord.
   To Him [praise] is becoming; to Him [praise] is fitting.

4. Unique in kingship, perfectly powerful, His learned ones say to Him: Yours and Yours, Yours because it's Yours, Yours even Yours, Yours is the kingdom, O Lord.
   To Him [praise] is becoming; to Him [praise] is fitting.

This source was the basis of a major dispute among the Halakhacists – with a broad spectrum of opinions. Some, like the Maharal of Prague, (*Netivot Olam, Netiv ha-Avoda* 12:3) forbade the recitation of excessive praises including *Anim Zemirot* and *Shir ha-Yihud* – with the possible exception of the *piyutim* of praise on *Yom Kippur*. Others held like the Rashba (*Berakhot* 33b) and were very lenient outside of the *Amida*. Still, a third school only forbade extra praises in the opening benedictions of the *Amida* (R. Joseph Te'omim, *Rosh Yosef. Megilla* 25a) and this is the prevalent custom. See also R. Barukh Epstein's related discussion of "ישתבח" at the end of *Hallel*.

דָּגוּל בִּמְלוּכָה

The noted Israeli linguist Avshalom Kor indicates the word *degel* appears in Song of Songs (2:4) …*ve-diglo alai ahava* – "…his look upon me is a look of love." We also find in Song of Songs (5:10) *Dagul me-revava* – "the prominent/preeminent one that ten thousand look at." A *degel* is a piece of cloth that all look at for direction and inspiration. Thus, *dagul bi-melukha* means "prominent in His kingship" – to which all can look for leadership.

5. מוֹשֵׁל בִּמְלוּכָה, נוֹרָא כַּהֲלָכָה, סְבִיבָיו יֹאמְרוּ לוֹ:
לְךָ וּלְךָ, לְךָ כִּי לְךָ, לְךָ אַף לְךָ, לְךָ ה' הַמַּמְלָכָה,
כִּי לוֹ נָאֶה, כִּי לוֹ יָאֶה.

6. עָנָיו בִּמְלוּכָה, פּוֹדֶה כַּהֲלָכָה, צַדִּיקָיו יֹאמְרוּ לוֹ:
לְךָ וּלְךָ, לְךָ כִּי לְךָ, לְךָ אַף לְךָ, לְךָ ה' הַמַּמְלָכָה,
כִּי לוֹ נָאֶה, כִּי לוֹ יָאֶה.

7. קָדוֹשׁ בִּמְלוּכָה, רַחוּם כַּהֲלָכָה, שִׁנְאַנָּיו יֹאמְרוּ לוֹ:
לְךָ וּלְךָ, לְךָ כִּי לְךָ, לְךָ אַף לְךָ, לְךָ ה' הַמַּמְלָכָה,
כִּי לוֹ נָאֶה, כִּי לוֹ יָאֶה.

8. תַּקִּיף בִּמְלוּכָה, תּוֹמֵךְ כַּהֲלָכָה, תְּמִימָיו יֹאמְרוּ לוֹ:
לְךָ וּלְךָ, לְךָ כִּי לְךָ, לְךָ אַף לְךָ, לְךָ ה' הַמַּמְלָכָה,
כִּי לוֹ נָאֶה, כִּי לוֹ יָאֶה.

עָנָיו בִּמְלוּכָה

R. Michel Shurkin (*Harerei Kedem*, sec. 103) is troubled by the description of Hashem as "modest in His kingship." Isn't it self-contradictory? The answer seems to be that with a human king, we are told (Sanhedrin 19b) that a king cannot set aside his honor, because his honor is that of the nation – not his own. But by God, His honor is His own! Hence, He can choose to set aside His honor and tolerate the rebellious, sinful, dishonorable, and improper behavior of sinners. He can be patient and tolerant. That is *anav bi-melukha*.

5. Commanding in Kingship, perfectly awesome, His surrounding [angels] say to Him: Yours and Yours, Yours because it's Yours, Yours even Yours, Yours is the kingdom, O Lord.
   To Him [praise] is becoming; to Him [praise] is fitting.

6. Modest in kingship, perfectly the Redeemer, His legions say to Him: Yours and Yours, Yours because it's Yours, Yours even Yours, Yours is the kingdom, O Lord.
   To Him [praise] is becoming; to Him [praise] is fitting.

7. Holy in kingship, perfectly merciful, His snow-white angels say to Him: Yours and Yours, Yours because it's Yours, Yours even Yours, Yours is the kingdom, O Lord.
   To Him [praise] is becoming; to Him [praise] is fitting.

8. Resolute in kingship, perfectly supportive, His perfect ones say to Him: Yours and Yours, Yours because it's Yours, Yours even Yours, Yours is the kingdom, O Lord.
   To Him [praise] is becoming; to Him [praise] is fitting.

אַדִּיר הוּא

אַדִּיר הוּא יִבְנֶה בֵּיתוֹ בְּקָרוֹב. בִּמְהֵרָה, בִּמְהֵרָה, בְּיָמֵינוּ בְּקָרוֹב.
אֵל בְּנֵה, אֵל בְּנֵה, בְּנֵה בֵּיתְךָ בְּקָרוֹב.

בָּחוּר הוּא, גָּדוֹל הוּא, דָּגוּל הוּא יִבְנֶה בֵּיתוֹ בְּקָרוֹב.
בִּמְהֵרָה, בִּמְהֵרָה, בְּיָמֵינוּ בְּקָרוֹב.
אֵל בְּנֵה, אֵל בְּנֵה, בְּנֵה בֵּיתְךָ בְּקָרוֹב.

אַדִּיר הוּא

As in the case of *Adir bi-Melukha*, the author of *Adir Hu* is also unidentified. This is a seemingly very simple song that can be summarized as follows: You God have all these magnificent attributes. We pray you will build the third Temple soon, indeed very soon, in our time! Most of the attributes have already been mentioned in the previous *piyut*, which has led some scholars to suggest that the author of both is the same. In any case, several qualities need some clarification, and we will do so below.

אַדִּיר הוּא יִבְנֶה בֵּיתוֹ בְּקָרוֹב

In this seemingly simple song there is a complicated issue which we touched upon above in our comments to שְׂמֵחִים בְּבִנְיַן עִירֶךָ וְשָׂשִׂים בַּעֲבוֹדָתֶךָ in *Birkat Asher Ga'alanu*. It relates to how the third *Bet ha-Mikdash* will be built. There are three basic approaches:

(1) Rashi (Sukka 41a, s.v. *I Nami*) maintains that the third Temple will suddenly appear, fully built by Heaven. One commentary (R. Shimon Bezalel Neiman, *Haggada* with *Yalkut Shimoni*) suggests that the first line of this song should be read not as a prayer, but as a declaration: *Adir – Hu yivneh beito be-karov!* – The Almighty – He will build His house soon!

(2) Maimonides, on the other hand, maintains that the building of the Temple is a human venture (*Sefer ha-Mitzvot*, Positive commandment 20). In the future, it will be carried out under the leadership of the Messiah, as he writes (*MT, Melakhim* 11:1).

He is Mighty

He is mighty.
May He soon rebuild His House, speedily,
yes speedily, in our days, soon.
God, rebuild, God, rebuild, rebuild Your House soon!

He is distinguished, He is great, He is renowned.
May He soon rebuild His House, speedily,
yes speedily, in our days, soon.
God, rebuild, God, rebuild, rebuild Your House soon!

In the future, the Messianic king will arise and renew the Davidic dynasty, restoring it to its initial sovereignty. **He will build the Temple** and gather the dispersed of Israel. Then, in his days, the observance of all the statutes will return to their previous state...

According to this view, when we assert that the Almighty "will build His house," our intention is that He will create the conditions that will finally allow **us** to serve as His intermediaries.

(3) The third school is the hybrid view of R. Yehoshua Leib Diskin and others (discussed above in our comments to שְׂמֵחִים בְּבִנְיַן עִירֶךָ וְשָׂשִׂים בַּעֲבוֹדָתֶךָ in *Birkat Asher Ga'alanu*). They maintain, like Rashi, that the basic physical Temple will come down from Heaven, as suggested by Rashi (above). But it will not be complete, leaving room for *Klal Yisrael* (the Nation of Israel) to be partners with God in completing the structure and fulfilling our biblical obligation as indicated by Maimonides. R. Dov Zvi Karlestein suggests that is the meaning of the words in the holiday *Mussaf* davening: *ve-Harenu be-vinyano ve-samhenu be-tikuno* – "Let us see it built [like Rashi] and let us rejoice in fixing it up and making the last touches [like Maimonides]."

(4) The last school is that of R. Yaakov Etlinger (*Arukh la-Ner, Sukka* 41a, s.v. *I Nami*). He posits that the physical Temple will indeed be built by man (as suggested by Maimonides) – in fulfillment of God's divine command. However, a spiritual Temple will indeed come from heaven, and infuse the cold man-made structure with a dynamic spiritual life and character of its own.

הָדוּר הוּא, וָתִיק הוּא, זַכַּאי הוּא יִבְנֶה בֵּיתוֹ בְּקָרוֹב.
בִּמְהֵרָה, בִּמְהֵרָה, בְּיָמֵינוּ בְּקָרוֹב.
אֵל בְּנֵה, אֵל בְּנֵה, בְּנֵה בֵיתְךָ בְּקָרוֹב.

חָסִיד הוּא, טָהוֹר הוּא, יָחִיד הוּא יִבְנֶה בֵּיתוֹ בְּקָרוֹב.
בִּמְהֵרָה, בִּמְהֵרָה, בְּיָמֵינוּ בְּקָרוֹב.
אֵל בְּנֵה, אֵל בְּנֵה, בְּנֵה בֵיתְךָ בְּקָרוֹב.

כַּבִּיר הוּא, לָמוּד הוּא, מֶלֶךְ הוּא יִבְנֶה בֵּיתוֹ בְּקָרוֹב.
בִּמְהֵרָה, בִּמְהֵרָה, בְּיָמֵינוּ בְּקָרוֹב.
אֵל בְּנֵה, אֵל בְּנֵה, בְּנֵה בֵיתְךָ בְּקָרוֹב.

נוֹרָא הוּא, סַגִּיב הוּא, עִזּוּז הוּא יִבְנֶה בֵּיתוֹ בְּקָרוֹב.
בִּמְהֵרָה, בִּמְהֵרָה, בְּיָמֵינוּ בְּקָרוֹב.
אֵל בְּנֵה, אֵל בְּנֵה, בְּנֵה בֵיתְךָ בְּקָרוֹב.

פּוֹדֶה הוּא, צַדִּיק הוּא, קָדוֹשׁ הוּא יִבְנֶה בֵּיתוֹ בְּקָרוֹב.
בִּמְהֵרָה, בִּמְהֵרָה, בְּיָמֵינוּ בְּקָרוֹב.
אֵל בְּנֵה, אֵל בְּנֵה, בְּנֵה בֵיתְךָ בְּקָרוֹב.

רַחוּם הוּא, שַׁדַּי הוּא, תַּקִּיף הוּא יִבְנֶה בֵּיתוֹ בְּקָרוֹב.
בִּמְהֵרָה, בִּמְהֵרָה, בְּיָמֵינוּ בְּקָרוֹב.
אֵל בְּנֵה, אֵל בְּנֵה, בְּנֵה בֵיתְךָ בְּקָרוֹב.

לָמוּד הוּא

Lamud is normally translated as "learned," and indeed in the previous *piyut*, *Adir bi-Melukha*, we applied it to the People of Israel described as *limudav* – "learned ones." However, it is problematic to apply it to the Almighty who is omniscient. Hence, there is nothing for Him to learn. Indeed, R. Moses Sofer (Gloss of Hatam Sofer to *Shulhan Arukh*, O.H., sec 480) suggests changing the text to *lohem hu* – "He is a fighter." To avoid this problem some scholars have suggested that

He is glorious, He is faithful, He is worthy,
May He soon rebuild His House, speedily,
yes speedily, in our days, soon.
God, rebuild, God, rebuild, rebuild Your House soon!

He is gracious, He is pure, He is unique,
May He soon rebuild His House, speedily,
yes speedily, in our days, soon.
God, rebuild, God, rebuild, rebuild Your House soon!

He is powerful, He is learned, He is majestic,
May He soon rebuild His House, speedily,
yes speedily, in our days, soon.
God, rebuild, God, rebuild, rebuild Your House soon!

He is awesome, He is sublime, He is all-powerful,
May He soon rebuild His House, speedily,
yes speedily, in our days, soon.
God, rebuild, God, rebuild, rebuild Your House soon!

He is the Redeemer, He is righteous, He is holy,
May He soon rebuild His House, speedily,
yes speedily, in our days, soon.
God, rebuild, God, rebuild, rebuild Your House soon!

He is merciful, He is Almighty, He is forceful.
May He soon rebuild His House, speedily,
yes speedily, in our days, soon.
God, rebuild, God, rebuild, rebuild Your House soon!

---

lamud can also mean skillful and experienced as in the expression *lamud be-milḥama* – "skillful and experienced in war" (see Chronicles I, 5:18). To my mind we should understand *lamud* in the same way we understand *barukh*. God is the **source** of blessing, so how can we say *Barukh Ata Hashem*? The answer is that this phrase doesn't mean that God **should be** blessed, but rather that God **is** blessed! Thus, *Barukh Ata Hashem* means: "Blessed **art** Thou…" Similarly, *Lamud Hu* means: You are the source of learning and wisdom!

אחד מי יודע

אֶחָד מִי יוֹדֵעַ? אֶחָד אֲנִי יוֹדֵעַ: אֶחָד אֱלֹהֵינוּ שֶׁבַּשָּׁמַיִם וּבָאָרֶץ.

נוֹרָא הוּא

Nora can mean causing fear as in awful. But it can also mean awesome or awe-inspiring, like in Yaakov *Avinu's* statement after seeing the angels rising and descending the ladder (Gen. 28:17): *Ma nora ha-makom ha-ze* – "How awesome is this place!"

אֶחָד מִי יוֹדֵעַ

This song was added to the *Haggada* relatively late, in the 16th century. There is a handwritten manuscript of the Prague *Haggada* from 1526 which contains *Ehad Mi Yode'a*. The first printed *Haggada* is also the Prague *Haggada* dated to 1590. The song appears in Hebrew and is accompanied by a Yiddish translation and colorful illustrations. *Haggadot* outside of Ashkenaz (Germanic) communities, did not know of this song until the 19th century. Interestingly, in 1972, Prof. Shimon Sharvit discovered Cairo Geniza fragments which had verse 12 of *Ehad Mi Yode'a*. We cannot date this fragment but it does suggest that the origin of this poem might be from a more Sefardic background and lay generally hidden. In any case, the author is unknown. *Ehad Mi Yode'a* is described as a "cumulative song" in which a simple verse structure is modified by progressive additions so that each successive verse is longer than the verse before it.

But we still need to understand the special connection between this beloved song and *Pesah*. If it is merely a song that deals with Jewish faith and tradition, then it would be appropriate all year round. Indeed, in Cochin, *Ehad Mi Yode'a* was long sung as a riddle at wedding feasts! One fundamental reason for singing it specifically at the *Seder* is related to why we were redeemed from Egypt. As noted repeatedly above, God did not say to Pharaoh: "Let My people go," but *Shalah et ami ve-ya'avduni* – "Let My people go **so that** they may **serve Me**" (Ex. 7:16; 7:26; 9:1; 9:13). Serve Me in the Temple; serve Me in prayer; serve Me by learning Torah (written and oral traditions) and by doing My *mitzvot*. Our willing acceptance of *ol malkhut Shamayim ve-ol mitzvot* (the yoke of Heaven and commandments) is one of the major goals of the *Seder*.

Who Knows One?

Who knows one? I know one: One is our God, in heaven and on earth.

Hence, as the *Seder* comes to a close, we find it imperative to review and reaffirm – in a fun way appropriate for all ages – the fundamentals of our faith, the centrality of our traditions, and Torah learning.

R. Yissocher Frand ("Emunah on *Seder* Night," Parashat Bo 5777) has a slightly different take:

> The ultimate purpose of reading the *Haggada* every year on the *Seder* night is to leave the *Seder* bigger *ma'aminim* [believers]. … The *Seder* is supposed to implant certain automatic word associations into our minds. When we hear the word *Ehad* [One], our automatic reaction should be *Ehad Elokeinu she-ba-shamayim u-va-aretz*. When we hear the word, "two" we think of "the Two Tablets of Stone." "Three?" The Three Patriarchs. "Four?" The Four Matriarchs. "Five?" The Five Books of the Torah. This means that on the night of the *Seder*, we become so attuned to *Emunah* in the *Ribono shel Olam* that our word associations become hardwired – such that everything we hear brings to mind the basic components of Judaism.

Education through a fun song is the best pedagogic technique, and *Ehad Mi Yode'a* does not seem at all burdensome and has stood the test of time. On the contrary, it is one of the highlights of the *Seder* – for people of all ages. These verses – each in their own way is simple, yet quite pithy and profound – as we shall see. The number 13 itself reminds us of the 13 Maimonidean principles of faith. My brother R. Shael Frimer pointed out that the "question and answer" style of *Ehad Mi Yode'a* is based on the *Haggada*'s instruction to the parent: *At petaḥ lo* – initiate the conversation with your child by bringing points of interest to his/her attention.

אֶחָד אֱלֹהֵינוּ שֶׁבַּשָּׁמַיִם וּבָאָרֶץ

Here we affirm that God is not only *Ehad, Yahid u-Meyuhad* – "One, Indivisible and Unique" (R. Hamai Gaon, *Sefer Iyun*; R. Moshe Hayim

שְׁנַיִם מִי יוֹדֵעַ? שְׁנַיִם אֲנִי יוֹדֵעַ: שְׁנֵי לֻחוֹת הַבְּרִית. אֶחָד אֱלֹהֵינוּ שֶׁבַּשָּׁמַיִם וּבָאָרֶץ.

Luzzato, *Derekh Hashem*, IV:4). Thus, *Ehad Elokeinu* asserts the unity of God and the rejection of polytheism – even a trinity or divided/composite Godhead. But we also assert that He is the ruler of Heaven and Earth. Polytheists could accept one god of heaven, another of the sea, and yet another of the land. *Pesah*, however, demonstrated that the Almighty controlled all the forces of Nature – above and below. The poetic style of counting backward in each subsequent verse naturally emphasizes the centrality of אֶחָד אֱלֹהֵינוּ שֶׁבַּשָּׁמַיִם וּבָאָרֶץ – "One is our God in Heaven and on Earth" as a fundamental principle of faith.

There are reports (*Otzar Meforshei ha-Haggada*) of early *Haggadot* in which the song was prefaced by the verse *Shema Yisrael: Hashem Elokeinu Hashem ehad*. R. Shlomo Aharon Wertheimer suggests that since it is preferable to start the *Seder* shortly after nightfall – so the children will be awake – this preface might be a reminder to those who *davened ma'ariv* early before dark to recite *Shema* again at its proper time. More simply, this preface indicates where this basic principle of faith (God's unity) appears in the Torah and our daily liturgy. Moreover, it emphasizes Israel's special relationship with Him. The mystics observe that the Hebrew word אחד in *gematria* (1+8+4) is 13, the same value as the word (13=1+5+2+5) אהבה. Indeed, there exists a mutual bond of love between the One God and the Jewish people. God chose Israel out of love, as we say before the morning recitation of *Shema*: *Barukh…ha-Boher be-amo Yisrael be-ahava* – "Blessed is [He] Who chose Israel out of love." We, in turn, reciprocate by declaring *ve-Ahavta et Hashem Elokekha* – "You shall love the Lord your God." This reciprocal relationship between God and Israel is cited in *Midrash Rabba* (Deut. 6:4, *s.v Shema Yisrael*): "You chose me, and I too choose you." It is also an idea made famous in the form of two jingles. The first is that of British Journalist William Norman Ewer, who wrote: "How odd of God, to choose the Jews." To this Hebrew University philosopher Leon Roth responded: "It's not so odd – The Jews chose God."

Who knows two? I know two: two are the Tablets of Covenant; One is our God, in heaven and on earth.

שְׁנֵי לֻחוֹת הַבְּרִית

R. Ari Kahn (*Haggada*) cites an interesting insight of R. Joseph B. Soloveitchik. It is commonly thought that the importance of the *Shenei luhot ha-berit* – "the two Tablets," is that they are the physical representation of the experience of *Ma'amad Har Sinai* – the Sinaitic revelation. This was a revelation (*hitgalut*) experienced by upwards of three million people: 600,000 males ages 20–50, an equal number of females between 20–50, and at least two million children below 20 and adults above 50. But that is true primarily for the first set of *Luhot*. R. Joseph B. Soloveitchik reminds us that the second set – the *Luhot Sheniyot* – represents much more. They are emblematic of God's forgiveness after the sin of the Golden Calf and His desire to renew the covenant with Israel. R. Joseph B. Soloveitchik proves this point by an intriguing analysis of the breaking of the first Tablets, which follows.

Many commentaries on the Torah say that Moshe shattered the *Luhot* on purpose so that the sinners would not receive the Torah. This approach would seem to agree with the *peshat* (simple understanding) of the verses. Others are of the opinion that Moshe broke the *Luhot* because he could no longer hold them aloft after viewing the scene of the people rejoicing around the Golden Calf. The *Yalkut Shimoni* quotes that the letters etched on the *Luhot* – which until that point had miraculously supported its weight – floated away in the air (*otiyot porhot ba-avir*). Though Moshe struggled to maintain his grip on the *Luhot* despite their much-increased weight, he failed – and they accidentally fell from his hands and shattered.

This dropping of the *Luhot* troubled R. Joseph B. Soloveitchik. After all, we find that Hashem commanded Moshe to carve out a new set of stone tablets and carry them up the mountain to receive the second set of *Luhot*. Now, it should be easier to carry an object down a mountain than up. Thus, if Moshe was able to carry two *Luhot* without script **up** Mount Sinai, he should have been able to carry the *Luhot*, even after the etchings floated away from the stone, **down** Mount Sinai. So why did he drop them?

שְׁלֹשָׁה מִי יוֹדֵעַ? שְׁלֹשָׁה אֲנִי יוֹדֵעַ: שְׁלֹשָׁה אָבוֹת, שְׁנֵי לֻחוֹת הַבְּרִית, אֶחָד אֱלֹהֵינוּ שֶׁבַּשָּׁמַיִם וּבָאָרֶץ.

The answer is that when Moshe ascended the mountain to receive the second *Luḥot*, he went to receive the forgiveness of Hashem for the People of Israel. Moshe ascended the mountain on that early morning, full of anticipation of his rendezvous with Hashem and the forgiveness he would receive. He was ecstatic about receiving the *Luḥot* that he would triumphantly carry back. In his exhilaration, Moshe was able to easily carry heavy stones, stones without etchings, up the mountain. However, when Moshe descended Mount Sinai for the first time and saw how the people had sinned, he became emotionally deflated. He was unable to control his descent or that of the *Luḥot* – and they fell and shattered.

Thus, the *Luḥot* (primarily the first Tablets) represent Hashem's revelation of His covenant with Israel at *Har Sinai*. But the second Tablets remind us of God's willingness to forgive Israel and re-establish his covenant with them – despite their sins. This was not only true for a repentant *Klal Yisrael* as a whole at Sinai, but is relevant to the repentant individual, as well. Indeed, the gates of *Teshuva* (repentance) are always open. These concepts are fundamental to Judaism and hence are present in the *Eḥad Mi Yode'a*. In this regard, R. Jonathan Sacks has written (*Covenant and Conversation*, *Aharei Mot–Kedoshim*, "Sprints and Marathons," 5781):

> The day Moshe descended the mountain with the second tablets was to be immortalized when its anniversary became the holiest of days, *Yom Kippur*. On this day, the drama of *teshuva* and *kappara*, repentance and atonement, was to be repeated annually. This time, though, the key figure would not be Moshe but Aharon, not the Prophet but the High Priest. That is how you perpetuate a transformative event: by turning it into a ritual. Max Weber [*Economy and Society*] called this "the routinization of charisma." A once-and-never-again moment becomes a once-and-ever-again ceremony.

Who knows three? I know three: three are the Patriarchs; two are the Tablets of Covenant; One is our God, in heaven and on earth.

שְׁלֹשָׁה אָבוֹת

(a) The noted linguist Avshalom Kor (*be-Ofen Miluli*, August 2020) indicated that there are indeed a few examples in the Bible of plural feminine endings for masculine gendered words, and *av/avot* is one classical example. Nevertheless, in the *Mishna* this is commonplace. See for example:

אב/אבות. אילן/אילנות. חלון/חלונות. ממון/ממונות. פעוט/ פעוטות. שולחן/שולחנות. תינוק/תינוקות.

(b) One can ask why the author of this song chose our Three Patriarchs for the number three. After all, there are several other "threes" in Jewish tradition which he might have chosen: the three *Regalim* – *Pesaḥ*, *Shavu'ot*, and *Sukkot*; the three central national Jewish values: *Am Yisrael, Eretz Yisrael, ve-Torat Yisrael* – the People of Israel, the Land of Israel, and the Torah of Israel. One simple answer is that regarding the number "four" there are only limited options – with the Four Matriarchs as the likely choice. Therefore, the author chose the couple: *Arba Imahot, Shlosha Avot*. R. Judah Shaviv (*ha-Tzofeh*, Nisan 14, 5763) posits, however, that the three *Regalim*, our three *Avot*, and the three values are all similarly aligned! Thus, (1) **Pesaḥ** is the holiday identified with our national physical redemption and it was in Egypt that we became a People, *Am Yisrael* – as Pharaoh himself declares (Ex. 1:9): "And [Pharaoh] said to his nation, 'Look, the Israelite people are much too numerous for us.'" Similarly, of the *Avot*, Avraham is the biological and spiritual father of our people. (2) On **Shavu'ot** we received the Torah of Israel – most identified with Yaakov, as God declares (Ex. 19:3) to Moshe just prior to *Matan Torah*: "Thus shall you say to the house of Yaakov and declare to the children of Israel." (3) Finally, **Sukkot** recalls our travels to the Land of Israel and the "Four Species" which grow therein. *Eretz Yisrael* is most strongly identified with our forefather Yitzhak who never left the country and plowed, sewed, reaped, dug wells, and struck roots in the Land. Thus, *Shlosha Avot* incorporates

אַרְבַּע מִי יוֹדֵעַ? אַרְבַּע אֲנִי יוֹדֵעַ: אַרְבַּע אִמָּהוֹת. שְׁלשָׁה אָבוֹת. שְׁנֵי לֻחוֹת הַבְּרִית. אֶחָד אֱלֹהֵינוּ שֶׁבַּשָּׁמַיִם וּבָאָרֶץ.

---

within it all three sets of three: three *Regalim*, three *Avot*, and the three Jewish national values.

אַרְבַּע מִי יוֹדֵעַ

Even though the numbers in the other questions in this song are male-gendered, this one is feminine, undoubtedly because the subject of the answer is the feminine *Arba Imahot*.

אַרְבַּע אִמָּהוֹת

In his "A Tribute to the Rebbitzen of Talne," (Tradition 17:2, Spring 1978, pp. 73–83), R. Joseph B. Soloveitchik links the three Patriarchs with the four Matriarchs, as we do here in *Ehad Mi Yode'a*. He posits that we have two *Masorot*, two traditions, two communities, and two complementary chains of transmission (*shalshalot ha-kabbalah*) – the *mesora* community of the fathers and that of the mothers. *Haza"l* (*Mekhilta*, cited by Rashi to Exodus 19:3) see this reflected in the verse (ibid.): "Thus shall you say to the House of Yaakov [i.e., the women] and tell the Children of Israel [i.e., the men]." Similarly, the wise King Solomon counseled (Proverbs 1:8): "Hear my son the instruction of your father [*mussar avikha*] and forsake not the teaching of your mother [*torat imekha*]." What is the difference between those two *masorot*?

Traditionally, though certainly not exclusively, it is the father who teaches his children Torah; it is after all his ultimate obligation (*Kiddushin* 29a). An individual commonly learns from one's father how to read a text – be it Bible, Mishna, Talmud, or Halakha – how to comprehend, how to analyze, how to conceptualize, how to classify, how to infer, how to apply, etc. One also learns from a father what to do and what not to do, what is morally right and what is morally wrong. Father teaches the son the discipline of thought as well as the discipline of action. Father's tradition is an intellectual-moral one. That is why it is identified with *mussar*, which is the Biblical term for discipline.

Who knows four? I know four: four are the Matriarchs; three are the Patriarchs; two are the Tablets of Covenant; One is our God, in heaven and on earth.

What is *torat imekha*? What kind of a Torah does the mother pass on? At this point, R. Joseph B. Soloveitchik drew upon his personal experiences. He used to have long conversations with his mother about matters of the day. He watched her arranging the house in honor of a holiday. He used to see her recite prayers; he used to watch her recite the *Parasha* every Friday night in a nostalgic tune. Most of all he learned that Judaism expresses itself not only in formal compliance with the law but also in a living experience. She taught him that there is a flavor, a scent, and warmth to *mitzvot*. He learned from her the most important thing in life – to feel the presence of the Almighty, and the gentle pressure of His hand resting upon her frail shoulders. Without her teachings, which quite often were transmitted to him in silence, "I would have grown up a soulless being, dry and insensitive."

The laws of *Shabbat*, for instance, were passed on to him by his father; they are a part of *mussar avikha*. The *Shabbat* as a living entity, as a queen, was revealed to him by his mother; it is a part of *torat imekha*. The fathers **knew** much about the *Shabbat*; the mothers **lived** the *Shabbat*, experienced her presence, and perceived her beauty and splendor. The fathers **taught** generations how to observe the *Shabbat*; mothers taught generations how to **greet** the *Shabbat* and how to **enjoy** her twenty-four-hour presence. Both are ideally required in raising a wholesome complete Jewish child.

R. Joseph B. Soloveitchik further argues (*Shi'urei ha-Rav, The Covenantal Community*, pp. 51–53) that Hashem's covenant with Israel, therefore, involves both man and woman. We can see this through the relationship of Avraham and Sarah – both were equal parties to the covenant with Hashem. In Genesis (17:18–21), Avraham asks that God pass the covenant on to Yishmael, resigning himself to remaining childless with Sarah. The Almighty answers that Sarah, his wife, will bear him a child to be called Yitzhak, and it is only **this** child, the product of both Sarah and Avraham, who will be the worthy recipient of the covenant. Ishmael cannot be the recipient of the covenant, because he represented only one side of the Covenant – Avraham – but not Sarah. Thus, the *Arba Imahot* and

חֲמִשָּׁה מִי יוֹדֵעַ? חֲמִשָּׁה אֲנִי יוֹדֵעַ: חֲמִשָּׁה חוּמְשֵׁי תוֹרָה, אַרְבַּע אִמָּהוֹת, שְׁלֹשָׁה אָבוֹת, שְׁנֵי לֻחוֹת הַבְּרִית, אֶחָד אֱלֹהֵינוּ שֶׁבַּשָּׁמַיִם וּבָאָרֶץ.

Shlosha Avot are intimately linked and pivotal in perpetuating our covenantal relationship with God. (Based in part on R. Ari Kahn, *Haggada Od Yosef Hai*, http://arikahn.blogspot.com/2013/03/blog-post_8.html).

אַרְבַּע אִמָּהוֹת, שְׁלֹשָׁה אָבוֹת

One fundamental question that needs to be asked is: How do we know that the *Avot* are limited to three: Avraham, Yitzhak, and Yaakov – and do not include the twelve sons of Yaakov, Moshe, Aharon, or King David? Similarly, why are *Imahot* limited to four: Sarah, Rivka, Rachel, and Leah – what about Bilha and Zilpa who were also the biological mothers of four of the Tribes? Our response begins with the Talmud's statement in *Berakhot* (16b; see also *Semahot* 1:14): "The Sages taught in a *baraita*: One may only call three people patriarchs: Avraham, Yitzhak, and Yaakov – but not Yaakov's children. And one may only call four people matriarchs: Sarah, Rivka, Rachel, and Leah." The Talmud continues (ibid.) that "the reason the sons of Yaakov are not called patriarchs is … because until Yaakov they are significant enough to be referred to as patriarchs, but beyond Yaakov, they are not." The thirteenth-century Italian *Rishon,* R. Isaiah di Trani (the Elder), further explains that "four matriarchs" specifically excludes Bilha and Zilpa, but he doesn't indicate why. The Talmudic discussion cited above regarding the Patriarchs suggest that these two were not considered sufficiently "significant"! Several pieces of evidence confirm this: (a) Rav Hai Gaon confirms that the Talmud's statement in *Berakhot* is the reason that in Jewish tradition we find the encomium: *Sarah Imenu, Rivka Imenu, Rahel Imenu,* and *Leah Imenu* but not *Bilha Imenu* or *Zilpa Imenu*. (b) Sarah, Rivka, and Leah are all buried next to their husbands in *Me'arat ha-Makhpela*, while Yaakov apologizes to Joseph for not doing so for his mother Rachel. We know nothing about the burials of Bilha or Zilpa. (c) The fundamental reason for their relative lack of significance is that they were *Shefahot* – maidservants, who were given as concubines to Yaakov by their mistress Rachel and Leah for the purpose of procreation. They were never formal wives. (The same was true for

Who knows five? I know five: five are the Books of the Torah; four are the Matriarchs; three are the Patriarchs; two are the Tablets of Covenant; One is our God, in heaven and on earth.

Hagar, Sarah's maidservant.) We see this clearly in Genesis 31:4. When God tells Yaakov to leave Lavan's house and return to Israel, Yaakov consults with his **wives** (see Malbim *ad loc.*) Rachel and Leah. Only they are significant in the family leadership. Similarly, at the end of the Book of Ruth, when the elders and people bless the union of Boaz and Ruth, they say: "May the Lord make the woman who is coming into your house like Rachel and Leah, both of whom built up the House of Israel!" They speak only of Rachel and Leah as the builders of the House of Israel. For completeness, we should mention one midrashic source (*Shir ha-Shirim Rabba* 6:4) which refers to six matriarchs, but the song *Ehad Mi Yode'a* certainly reflects the weight of tradition that Bilha and Zilpa played only a minor role in determining the character of *Kelal Yisrael*.

Let me conclude by quoting the comments of former Israeli Chief R. Yisrael Meir Lau. He notes that the name *Yisrael* – which identifies us all – is made up of the initials of the *Shlosha Avot* and *Arba Imahot* as shown below. It was these seven who set the moral tone for the People of Israel.

י-ש-ר-א-ל: י' – יצחק, יעקב; ש' – שרה; ר' – רבקה, רחל; א' – אברהם; ל' – לאה

חֲמִשָּׁה חוּמְשֵׁי תוֹרָה

This is followed in the next verse by שִׁשָּׁה סִדְרֵי מִשְׁנָה: This is a statement of the centrality of both The Written Torah (*Torah she-bi-khetav*) and The Oral Torah (*Torah she-be-al peh*). Regarding the former, the author of this song is emphasizing that the Written Torah is broken down into *Hamisha Humshei Torah* – five books. This is significant since each of these *Humashim* (Pentateuch volumes) tells us something unique.

Bereshit (Genesis) emphasizes the God of Creation and His Covenant with the Patriarchs (*Brit Avot*) – that our relationship and covenant with the Creator did not begin at Sinai but with the three Patriarchs: Avraham, Yitzhak, and Yaakov. A pivotal part of that covenant is *Brit Mila* which suggests that God commanded the Israelites to perfect

שִׁשָּׁה מִי יוֹדֵעַ? שִׁשָּׁה אֲנִי יוֹדֵעַ: שִׁשָּׁה סִדְרֵי מִשְׁנָה, חֲמִשָּׁה חוּמְשֵׁי תוֹרָה, אַרְבַּע אִמָּהוֹת, שְׁלֹשָׁה אָבוֹת, שְׁנֵי לֻחוֹת הַבְּרִית, אֶחָד אֱלֹהֵינוּ שֶׁבַּשָּׁמַיִם וּבָאָרֶץ.

שִׁבְעָה מִי יוֹדֵעַ? שִׁבְעָה אֲנִי יוֹדֵעַ: שִׁבְעָה יְמֵי שַׁבַּתָּא, שִׁשָּׁה סִדְרֵי מִשְׁנָה, חֲמִשָּׁה חוּמְשֵׁי תוֹרָה, אַרְבַּע אִמָּהוֹת, שְׁלֹשָׁה אָבוֹת, שְׁנֵי לֻחוֹת הַבְּרִית, אֶחָד אֱלֹהֵינוּ שֶׁבַּשָּׁמַיִם וּבָאָרֶץ.

---

themselves through *mitzvot*. (We will talk more about this below in the verse *Shemona yemei mila*.)

Shemot (Exodus) talks about the God of History and Revelation. It emphasizes the importance of the Tabernacle (*Mishkan*) and Divine Service as well as *Teshuva* (repentance) and God's forgiveness.

Va-Yikra (Leviticus) celebrates holiness (*Kedusha*). We become Holy (*Kedoshim*) by linking up with the source of holiness – the *Kadosh* – by fulfilling His *mitzvot*. Thus, the holiday liturgy says: *kadshenu be-mitzvotekha* – "sanctify us through Your commandments." The first half of *va-Yikra* emphasizes sanctity in the *Mishkan* – The House of the Lord. The second half of *va-Yikra* (Lev. 19ff), stresses the importance of creating holiness at home, and even in the marketplace, by following Jewish law.

Be-Midbar (Numbers) recounts the Israelite 40-year journey to the Promised Land. It emphasizes God's *hashgaha* – watchful supervision over man, as well as the centrality of the Land of Israel in our life.

Finally, *Devarim* (Deuteronomy) records the transmission of the Torah and *Mesora* from the generation of the Exodus and Sinaitic revelation – to the second generation which is about to enter the Land. This emphasizes the importance in each generation of renewing the covenant first made at Sinai. Indeed, the *Pesah Seder* is part of this renewal process, in which we pass on our unique history, our ever-vibrant present, and our beckoning future to **our** next generation in story, food, action, and song.

This is the important message of *Hamisha Humshei Torah*: it's not just the one-time experience of Sinai – but also the ongoing history of the subsequent 38 years and their varied lessons. And it is through the

Who knows six? I know six: six are the Orders of the Mishnah; five are the Books of the Torah; four are the Matriarchs; three are the Patriarchs; two are the Tablets of Covenant; One is our God, in heaven and on earth.

Who knows seven? I know seven: seven are the days of the week; six are the Orders of the Mishnah; five are the Books of the Torah; four are the Matriarchs; three are the Patriarchs; two are the Tablets of Covenant; One is our God, in heaven and on earth.

Shisha Sidrei Mishna – the distillation of **The Oral Torah** (appearing in the next verse) – that we can interpret and apply the Torah to the realities and exigencies of evolving life down through the Ages. That these two are bound together and binding on Jews is indeed one of the fundamentals of the Jewish Faith.

שִׁשָּׁה סִדְרֵי מִשְׁנָה

As pointed out in the previous comment, the *Shisha Sidrei Mishna*, edited by R. Yehuda ha-Nasi (around the year 200 C.E.), was perhaps the first authorized distillation of the *Torah she-be-al peh*, the Oral Law. This orally transmitted tradition included rules of interpretation and derivation of the Torah (the Written Law) – as well as various specific laws and judicial decisions. A much fuller presentation of the interpretive discussions based on the *Mishna* was edited around 500 CE and is called the Talmud. It was this Oral Law that allowed us to interpret and apply the Torah to the realities and exigencies of evolving life down through the Ages. That the Written Torah and the *Oral Law* are bound together in this song is indeed appropriate. That their acceptance is both binding on Jews is indeed one of the fundamental principles of the Jewish Faith.

שִׁבְעָה יְמֵי שַׁבַּתָּא

Most English *Haggadot* translate this verse as: "Seven are the days of the week." This rendering is problematic for several reasons: (1) Firstly, one needs to ask regarding this translation: "What is uniquely Jewish about the week that it should be in *Ehad mi Yode'a*? Secondly, the

שְׁמוֹנָה מִי יוֹדֵעַ? שְׁמוֹנָה אֲנִי יוֹדֵעַ: שְׁמוֹנָה יְמֵי מִילָה, שִׁבְעָה יְמֵי שַׁבַּתָּא, שִׁשָּׁה סִדְרֵי מִשְׁנָה, חֲמִשָּׁה חוּמְשֵׁי תוֹרָה, אַרְבַּע אִמָּהוֹת, שְׁלֹשָׁה אָבוֹת, שְׁנֵי לוּחוֹת הַבְּרִית, אֶחָד אֱלֹהֵינוּ שֶׁבַּשָּׁמַיִם וּבָאָרֶץ.

Aramaic word for week is שבועתא (see for example Talmud *Nidda* 30a and Jastrow Aramaic Dictionary). (3) Finally, *Shabbata* in Aramaic generally means the Sabbath – and only rarely "week" (see Jastrow).

(1) One possibility is that the correct translation is connected to the formula we say before reciting the *Yom* (the daily Psalm) at the end of *Shaharit*: *ha-Yom Yom Rishon/Sheni/Shlishi… ba-Shabbat*. Thus, Nahmanides (Ramban, Commentary to Ex. 20:8) writes:

> **Remember the Sabbath day, to keep it holy**: …And in the Mekhilta we find: "Rabbi Yitzhak says: 'You should not count [the days of the week] as others count them. Rather you should count them with reference to the Sabbath.'" The meaning of this is that other nations count the days of the week in such a manner that each is independent of the other. Thus, they call each day by a separate name or by the name of the ministers [in heaven, such as Sunday, which means "sun's day," Monday which means "moon's day," etc.], or by any other names which they call them. But Israel counts all days with reference to the Sabbath: "one day after the Sabbath," "two days after the Sabbath." This is of the essence of the commandment which we have been **obligated** always to remember the Sabbath every day [of the week]. This is the literal meaning of the verse, and so did R. Abraham ibn Ezra interpret it.

Ramban comments on the verse (Ex 12:2) – "This month (*Nisan*) will be the first in your count of the months" – that there too we count from the [month of] redemption which we are **obligated** to constantly recall. Thus, according to Ramban *Shiva yemei Shabbata* more correctly means: "Seven are the days in the count from *Shabbat* [to *Shabbat*]" – or briefly, "Every seventh day is *Shabbat*." This count bears witness that God was the Creator of Heaven and Earth in six Biblical days and rested on the seventh, as the text says (Ex 20:11): "For in six days God made heaven and earth and sea, and all that is in them and then rested on the seventh day; therefore, God blessed the Sabbath day and sanctified it."

Who knows eight? I know eight: eight are the days to circumcision; seven are the days of the week; six are the Orders of the Mishnah; five are the Books of the Torah; four are the Matriarchs; three are the Patriarchs; two are the Tablets of Covenant; One is our God, in heaven and on earth.

---

(2) There is, however, the possibility that there is something "uniquely Jewish" about the week being seven days! To understand why, we point out that astronomically a lunar month is ca. 29.5 days. The Egyptians, Chinese, and Greeks chose to have a 30-day month containing three ten-day weeks. The ancient Scandinavians and other nations counted six weeks of five days, again a 30-day month. The Assyrians had four 7-day weeks for their 28-day months. For the Babylonians, months went back and forth between 29 or 30 days and basically contained three seven-day weeks, followed by a final week of eight or nine days. This broke the continuous seven-day cycle but kept the total number of days linked to lunation.

Jewish months also alternate between being 29 and 30 days long – referred to as *Haser* (missing) and *malei* (full) months, respectively. Nevertheless, each week is exactly seven days long. The Jews were, thus, the first nation to have a calendar in which the length of the week was fixed and disconnected from the month. This, Judaism did consciously, of course, based on the "Seven Days of Creation" (*Shivat Yemei Bereshit*), and thereby downplayed the role of the Moon and the influence of Moon worship. (Based on *Segula Magazine*, 2019)

שְׁמוֹנָה יְמֵי מִילָה

My comments below are based in large part on the writings of R. Jonathan Sacks (see: https://www.rabbisacks.org/covenant-conversation/tazria/the-eighth-day/). The centrality of *brit mila* stems from the fact that throughout Jewish history, circumcision has been the sign of God's covenant with our people beginning from forefather Avraham (Gen. 17:1–14). Why circumcision? And why on the eighth day? Interestingly, the inauguration of the Mishkan – the Tabernacle – also took place on the eighth day. Is there a connection between these two quite different events?

The place to begin is a fascinating *Midrash Tanhuma* (*Tazri'a* sec. 5) which records an encounter between Rabbi Akiva and the tyrannical Roman governor Quintus Tineius Rufus. Rufus asks Rabbi Akiva, "Whose works are better, those of God or man?" Surprisingly, the rabbi replied, "Those of man." Rufus responded, "But look at the heavens and the earth. Can a human being make anything like that?" Rabbi Akiva replied that the comparison was unfair. "Creating heaven and earth is clearly beyond human capacity. Give me an example drawn from matters that are within human scope." Rufus then said, "Why do you practice circumcision?" To this, Rabbi Akiva replied, "I knew you would ask that question. That is why I said in advance that the works of man are better than those of God." The rabbi then set before the governor ears of grain and cakes. The unprocessed grain is the work of God. The cake is the work of man. Is it not more pleasant to eat cake than raw ears of grain? Rufus then said, "If God really wants us to practice circumcision, why did He not arrange for babies to be born circumcised?" Rabbi Akiva replied, "God gave the commandments to Israel to refine our character." This is a very odd conversation, but a deeply significant one. To understand why, we have to go back to the beginning of time.

Haza"l (*Midrash Shohar Tov*, Psalms 92:1; *Pesahim* 54a) relate that Adam and Eve sinned by eating the forbidden fruit already on Friday Erev *Shabbat* – the day of their creation, and were sentenced to immediate exile from the Garden of Eden. However, God delayed the execution of the sentence for a day, to allow them to spend *Shabbat* in the garden. As the day came to a close, and darkness descended, God took pity on them and showed them how to make fire by striking two stones together. That is why we light a special candle at *Havdala*, not just to mark the end of *Shabbat* but also to show that we begin the workday week – with the light God taught us to make. The *Havdalah* candle, therefore, represents the light of the eighth day – which marks the beginning of **human creativity**. Just as God began the first day of creation with the words "Let there be light," so too at the start of the eighth day He showed humans how they too could make light. *Human creativity is thus conceived in Judaism as parallel to Divine creativity, and its symbol is the eighth day.* That is why the Mishkan was inaugurated on the eighth day when we celebrate the human contribution to creation. That is also why circumcision takes place on the eighth day to emphasize that the act that symbolizes entry into the covenant is a human one. Male children were born uncircumcised, said Rabbi Akiva, because God deliberately left this act, this sign of the covenant, to us. God wants partners in Creation. Unlike the Greeks and Romans, we do not believe that nature is perfect.

This central idea is hinted at in the final verse of creation (Gen. 2:3): *va-Yevarekh Elokim et yom ha-shevi'i va-yekadesh oto, ki vo shavat mi-kol melakhto asher bara Elokim la'asot*. This verse is commonly translated as: "And God blessed the seventh day and sanctified it because He rested on it from all the work God had created to do." This English translation cannot be accurate since it has not translated the last word of the sentence: *la'asot*. This should be understood as: "...that God had created **to do**." To do what? The answer, says R. Joseph B. Soloveitchik (*Chumash Mesorat ha-Rav*, Gen 2:3; *Halakhic Man* p. 101) is that Creation is **not** complete, nor is it perfect. Mankind's mission is to do just that: to complete himself and complete the world. (See also the end of our comments to בָּרֵךְ above).

Now we begin to understand the full depth of the conversation between Rabbi Akiva and the Roman governor Tineius Rufus. The Romans found circumcision strange because it was unnatural. Why not celebrate the human body as God made it? God, said Rabbi Akiva, values the work of humans. God left creation unfinished so that we could become partners in its completion; he left man incomplete so that man could complete himself. God asks us to be co-creators, with Him, of human nature. As R. Abraham Mordechai Alter of Ger (*Likkutei Yehuda*) said: "When God said (Gen. 1:26), 'Let us make man in our image,' He was speaking to man himself. God said to man, Let us – you and I – make man together." The symbol of that co-creation is *Brit Mila* on the eighth day. And it indicates that our divine mission is to be partners with God in the ongoing creation and perfection of the world.

תִּשְׁעָה מִי יוֹדֵעַ? תִּשְׁעָה אֲנִי יוֹדֵעַ: תִּשְׁעָה יַרְחֵי לֵדָה, שְׁמוֹנָה יְמֵי מִילָה, שִׁבְעָה יְמֵי שַׁבַּתָּא, שִׁשָּׁה סִדְרֵי מִשְׁנָה, חֲמִשָּׁה חוּמְשֵׁי תוֹרָה, אַרְבַּע אִמָּהוֹת, שְׁלֹשָׁה אָבוֹת, שְׁנֵי לֻחוֹת הַבְּרִית, אֶחָד אֱלֹהֵינוּ שֶׁבַּשָּׁמַיִם וּבָאָרֶץ.

עֲשָׂרָה מִי יוֹדֵעַ? עֲשָׂרָה אֲנִי יוֹדֵעַ: עֲשָׂרָה דִבְּרַיָּא, תִּשְׁעָה יַרְחֵי לֵדָה, שְׁמוֹנָה יְמֵי מִילָה, שִׁבְעָה יְמֵי שַׁבַּתָּא, שִׁשָּׁה סִדְרֵי מִשְׁנָה, חֲמִשָּׁה חוּמְשֵׁי תוֹרָה, אַרְבַּע אִמָּהוֹת, שְׁלֹשָׁה אָבוֹת, שְׁנֵי לֻחוֹת הַבְּרִית, אֶחָד אֱלֹהֵינוּ שֶׁבַּשָּׁמַיִם וּבָאָרֶץ.

תִּשְׁעָה יַרְחֵי לֵדָה

What is it about pregnancy and birth that renders it uniquely Jewish? (a) Perhaps it is that procreation is a mitzva and that that Jews are very careful about their lineage. This was evident in Egypt under slavery, where exact lineage was known (see Pentateuch and Chronicles), even through the fathers, going back several generations. The family went down to Egypt as twelve tribes of Israel and emerged as twelve tribes – *shneim asar shivtaya*; (b) Alternatively, *Tisha yarhei leida* plays tribute to the "righteous women" – *nashim tzidkaniyot* in Egypt (see our comments above regarding אֶרֶץ דֶּרֶךְ פְּרִישׁוּת זוֹ .עָנֵינוּ אֶת־וַיַּרְא) who *Haza"l* tell us seduced their husbands. The men were hesitant to bring children into a world of slavery, suffering, and oppression, but the women believed in God's promise of redemption – and acted to make sure there would be a nation to redeem! (c) My brother R. Shael Frimer commented that many of the Matriarchs and other women of note like Hanna were barren. Hence the *tisha yarhei leida* was for them miraculous – worthy of our appreciation and recognition. It is the *Tisha yarhei leida* that enables other *mitzvot* like *Peru u-Revu, Brit Mila, Pidyon ha-Ben, ve-Shinantam le-Vaneka,* and *ve-Higadeta le-Vinkha*. Hence it is a natural process with deep Jewish significance. (d) Finally, Leonard Gamss has proposed that the significance of *Tisha yarhei leida* can be understood in light of the comments of R. Jonathan Sacks regarding *Shemoneh yemei mila* (see the previous comment). Thus, "Seven" celebrates the Almighty's creation of the world in seven days. The crown of these creations was man who was made "in God's image." "Eight" celebrates man's partnering with Hashem in the creative process – in particular, in completing himself

Who knows nine? I know nine: nine are the months of the pregnancy; eight are the days to circumcision; seven are the days of the week; six are the Orders of the Mishnah; five are the Books of the Torah; four are the Matriarchs; three are the Patriarchs; two are the Tablets of Covenant; One is our God, in heaven and on earth.

Who knows ten? I know ten: ten are the Ten Commandments; nine are the months of the pregnancy; eight are the days to circumcision; seven are the days of the week; six are the Orders of the Mishnah; five are the Books of the Torah; four are the Matriarchs; three are the Patriarchs; two are the Tablets of Covenant; One is our God, in heaven and on earth.

---

through circumcision. Finally, in "Nine," we proceed one step further and celebrate how man too, like God, can become a creator by bringing a new life into the world.

עֲשָׂרָה דִבְּרַיָּא

It's fascinating that although we have already mentioned *Shenei luhot ha-Berit* – the two covenantal tablets, the *Aseret ha-Dibrot* – Ten Commandments also appear. As commented above (regarding שְׁנֵי לְחוֹת הַבְּרִית), the *Shenei Luhot ha-Berit* emphasize the centrality of the Sinaitic revelation – our direct interaction and connection with the Creator. However, as R. Joseph B. Soloveitchik has pointed out, the second set of *Luhot*, in particular, also represents repentance and forgiveness after the sin of the Golden Calf. The 10 Commandments are not general goals or philosophy, but specific orders to each one of us regarding idolatry, swearing, honoring our parents, and caring for our fellow. These are independently important and deserve a special mention. We also heard these commandments directly from the Creator, which shows that we had a direct relationship with God – not intermediated by Moshe.

We should point out that the singular of *dibrot* is *diber* and male-gendered. A *ya* suffix is male plural in Aramaic; thus, we have *dibraya*, *kokhvaya*, and *shivtaya*. Similarly, it is *asara dibraya* (male) and not *eser* (female).

אֶחָד עָשָׂר מִי יוֹדֵעַ? אֶחָד עָשָׂר אֲנִי יוֹדֵעַ: אֶחָד עָשָׂר כּוֹכְבַיָּא, עֲשָׂרָה דִבְּרַיָּא, תִּשְׁעָה יַרְחֵי לֵדָה, שְׁמוֹנָה יְמֵי מִילָה, שִׁבְעָה יְמֵי שַׁבָּתָא, שִׁשָּׁה סִדְרֵי מִשְׁנָה, חֲמִשָּׁה חוּמְשֵׁי תוֹרָה, אַרְבַּע אִמָּהוֹת, שְׁלֹשָׁה אָבוֹת, שְׁנֵי לֻחוֹת הַבְּרִית, אֶחָד אֱלֹהֵינוּ שֶׁבַּשָּׁמַיִם וּבָאָרֶץ.

שְׁנֵים עָשָׂר מִי יוֹדֵעַ? שְׁנֵים עָשָׂר אֲנִי יוֹדֵעַ: שְׁנֵים עָשָׂר שִׁבְטַיָּא, אֶחָד עָשָׂר כּוֹכְבַיָּא, עֲשָׂרָה דִבְּרַיָּא, תִּשְׁעָה יַרְחֵי לֵדָה, שְׁמוֹנָה יְמֵי מִילָה, שִׁבְעָה יְמֵי שַׁבָּתָא, שִׁשָּׁה סִדְרֵי מִשְׁנָה, חֲמִשָּׁה חוּמְשֵׁי תוֹרָה, אַרְבַּע אִמָּהוֹת, שְׁלֹשָׁה אָבוֹת, שְׁנֵי לֻחוֹת הַבְּרִית, אֶחָד אֱלֹהֵינוּ שֶׁבַּשָּׁמַיִם וּבָאָרֶץ.

אֶחָד עָשָׂר כּוֹכְבַיָּא

R. Moses Sofer (*Hatam Sofer al ha-Torah*, sec. 192) asks the almost obvious question: If *kokhvaya* refers to the *mazalot* – constellations, we know there are twelve! Hence, these stars must be referring to the eleven stars in Yosef's dream (Gen. 37:9): "And [in this dream], the sun, the moon, and eleven stars were bowing down to me." Why does Yosef's dream have eleven stars and not twelve? Because Yosef the dreamer was alienated from his brothers and the eleven stars bowed down to him. Why is this important? Because the separation of the twelve brothers into eleven plus one – was one of the major factors that caused the Israelites to leave Canaan and go down into the Egyptian Exile. This is not at all trivial; after all, the *Avot* knew about the *Berit Bein ha-Betarim* (Gen. 15:13–14) where God foretells to Avraham that his offspring will be enslaved and afflicted in a "foreign land." Yaakov presumably knew what awaited them in Egypt, and, therefore, resisted initial attempts to draw him to the Land of the Nile. But the Almighty forced his hand with the proverbial "carrot and stick." The "stick" was the pressing famine in Canaan, while the "carrot" was an opportunity to reunite with his beloved Yosef, who also assured them of their economic safety and the pending blessings of plenty. *Ahad asar kokhvaya* further demonstrates the principle of "divine intervention" (*hashgaha pratit*) – that, despite man's freedom of choice, God is ultimately in control of the fate of individuals and nations as they go through history.

Who knows eleven? I know eleven: eleven are the stars [in Yosef's dream]; ten are the Ten Commandments; nine are the months of the pregnancy; eight are the days to circumcision; seven are the days of the week; six are the Orders of the Mishnah; five are the Books of the Torah; four are the Matriarchs; three are the Patriarchs; two are the Tablets of Covenant; One is our God, in heaven and on earth.

Who knows twelve? I know twelve: twelve are the tribes [of Israel]; eleven are the stars [in Yosef's dream]; ten are the Ten Commandments; nine are the months of the pregnancy; eight are the days to circumcision; seven are the days of the week; six are the Orders of the Mishnah; five are the Books of the Torah; four are the Matriarchs; three are the Patriarchs; two are the Tablets of Covenant; One is our God, in heaven and on earth.

שְׁנֵים עָשָׂר שִׁבְטַיָּא

(a) As discussed above, *Ahad asar kokhvaya* represents the alienation of Yosef from his brothers, while *Shneim asar shivtaya* reflects the reunification that ultimately occurred in Egypt. As R. Joseph B. Soloveitchik ("Joseph the Ruler" in *Vision and Leadership*, Ktav 2013, p. 28ff) writes:

> The genuine mission [of the brothers in the marketplace of Egypt] did not consist of buying food; the real mission was to renew brotherhood, to bring about the great conciliation between an alienated brother and themselves. The departure for Egypt was meant to reunite all twelve brothers in order that their brotherly bond be transformed, in the course of a long sojourn, into a great union… [The verse says: "Now the sons of Yaakov were twelve" (Gen. 35:22).] We learn from here that only twelve may comprise *Knesset Yisrael* (the Jewish People). Eleven could not do the job, and ten certainly not. All twelve tribes together must merge to create *Knesset Yisrael* – The Nation of Israel, that strange community with which the Almighty has concluded a covenant.

(b) The problem with the assertion that there are **only** Twelve Tribes of Israel is that from, time to time, we find a count of the tribes which suggests that there are thirteen! Thus, in Genesis 48:5–6, we see that

שְׁלֹשָׁה עָשָׂר מִי יוֹדֵעַ? שְׁלֹשָׁה עָשָׂר אֲנִי יוֹדֵעַ: שְׁלֹשָׁה עָשָׂר מִדַּיָּא, שְׁנֵים עָשָׂר שִׁבְטַיָּא, אַחַד עָשָׂר כּוֹכְבַיָּא, עֲשָׂרָה דִבְּרַיָּא, תִּשְׁעָה יַרְחֵי לֵדָה, שְׁמוֹנָה יְמֵי מִילָה, שִׁבְעָה יְמֵי שַׁבַּתָּא, שִׁשָּׁה סִדְרֵי מִשְׁנָה, חֲמִשָּׁה חוּמְשֵׁי תוֹרָה, אַרְבַּע אִמָּהוֹת, שְׁלֹשָׁה אָבוֹת, שְׁנֵי לֻחוֹת הַבְּרִית, אֶחָד אֱלֹהֵינוּ שֶׁבַּשָּׁמַיִם וּבָאָרֶץ.

Yaakov gives the sons of Yosef, Ephraim and Menashe, an equal standing with the other tribes regarding portions in the Promised Land: "Ephraim and Menashe shall be mine no less than Reuven and Shimon." Nevertheless, shortly after that (Gen. 49), Yaakov blesses the tribes before his death and the text lists only the twelve brothers, not Ephraim and Menashe. The blessings conclude (Gen. 49:28): "All these were the tribes of Israel, twelve in number…" The noted commentator, R. David Kimhi suggests (ad loc.) that Ephraim and Menashe were tribes only in matters related to *halukat ha-Aretz* – the division of the Land of Israel. They stepped in to complete the number twelve because Levi did not receive a portion. And, indeed, if one surveys the various instances where Levi is not counted among the twelve, for whatever reason, Ephraim and Menashe are in – thus maintaining the count of twelve tribes. For example, in the dedication of the *Mishkan*, Levi is excluded – because they are subsidiary to the Tabernacle – and Ephraim and Menashe appear. In the desert, twelve tribes (including Ephraim and Menashe) camp around the periphery, while Levi was in the center with the Tabernacle and Ark. When spies are sent into the Holy Land, which was in preparation for the subsequent inheritance of the Land of Canaan, Levi is excluded and Ephraim and Menashe were included.

Two points need to be emphasized. The fact that they entered Egypt as twelve tribes and departed as twelve tribes, reaffirms that they guarded their lineage and for the most part did not intermarry. In addition, they entered Egypt as eleven tribes – *ahad asar kokhvaya* and were there united with Yosef's tribe, melding together to form *shneim asar shivtaya*. That Israel is a **united** nation of twelve tribes, is one of the messages of *Ehad Mi Yode'a*.

Who knows thirteen? I know thirteen: thirteen are the attributes of God; twelve are the tribes [of Israel]; eleven are the stars [in Yosef's dream]; ten are the Ten Commandments; nine are the months of the pregnancy; eight are the days to circumcision; seven are the days of the week; six are the Orders of the Mishnah; five are the Books of the Torah; four are the Matriarchs; three are the Patriarchs; two are the Tablets of Covenant; One is our God, in heaven and on earth.

שְׁלֹשָׁה עָשָׂר מִדַּיָּא

(a) The word *midaya* is presumably the Aramaic translation of the Hebrew word *midot*. The *Even-Shoshan Dictionary* indicates that *mida* can have three possible meanings: (1) It can mean a "measure" of length, volume, weight, etc. – not relevant here. (2) Alternatively, *mida* can refer to a "trait or attribute," and that is how it is used in the phrase: *Shlosh esrei midot shel rahamim* – the thirteen Divine attributes of mercy. The latter list – *Hashem Hashem kel rahum ve-hanun*... (Ex. 34:6) – is recited in the liturgy whenever we pray for the Almighty's mercy and forgiveness. (3) Finally, *mida* can refer to a "rule or principle" and that is its meaning in the phrase: *Shlosh esrei midot she-ha-Torah nidreshet ba-hen* – The thirteen hermeneutical rules of Rabbi Yishmael (*Sifra*, Introduction) for deriving new laws from the Torah. It is not at all clear which *Midot* are being referred to here: the "**Attributes** of Hashem" or the "**Rules** of R. Yishmael." Most translations presume it to be the former: attributes.

(b) The fact is that the word *midaya* is problematic on several accounts. Firstly, the Aramaic equivalent for *mida* is *mekhilta* or *mashahta* – not *midaya*. The latter does not exist in Aramaic, except in the song *Ehad Mi Yode'a*. But even assuming that the word does exist, the male *ya* suffix of *midaya* is inappropriate since *mida* is female-gendered. We have seen the male *ya* suffix in Aramaic with *dibraya, kokhvaya*, and *shivtaya*, while a *ta* suffix is female. Since *midot* is feminine, it should have taken a *ta* suffix, i.e., *midata* in Aramaic. Furthermore, the number also needs to be female-gendered. Hence, this line of the song should have been *shlosh esrei midata*. Shimon Sharvit (The Academy of the Hebrew Language) suggests that the author purposely corrupted this last verse so that it would nicely rhyme with the previous three verses *dibraya, kokhvaya*, and *shivtaya*.

אחד מי יודע – תרגומים עממיים לשפות שונות

Ehad Mi Yodea – Popular Translations into the Vernacular

(1) English: Who Knows One?

Who knows thirteen? I know thirteen! Thirteen are the attributes of *Hashem*. And twelve are the tribes of Is-ra-el. And eleven are the stars in Yosef's dream. And ten are the [*Wave hands*] Ten Commandments! And nine are the months 'til a baby's born. And eight are the days 'til the *Brit Mila*. And seven are the days of the week [*clap, clap*]. And six are the books of [*clap*] *Mishna*. And five are the books of [*clap*] Torah. And four are the Mommas and three are the Pappas. And two are the Tablets that Moshe brought. And one is *Hashem*, one is *Hashem*, one is *Hashem* – in the Heavens and the Earth! Ooh Ah, Ooh Ah Ah; I said: Ooh Ah, Ooh Ah Ah.

אֶחָד אֱלֹהֵינוּ שֶׁבַּשָּׁמַיִם וּבָאָרֶץ

My niece Tzviya Frimer-Zeid brought to my attention that, with one exception, the numbers in *Ehad Mi Yode'a* come as pairs. Thus, numbers **1** (*Elokeinu*) and **13** (Attributes of *Hashem*) are both focused on the Almighty; **2** (Tablets) and **10** (Commandments) are a set; **3** (*Avot*) goes with **4** (*Imahot*); **5** (Written Torah) is connected to **6** (Oral Torah); **8** (*Mila*) and **9** (Pregnancy) deal with babies; and **11** (brothers without Yosef) and **12** (brothers with Yosef) both focus on the Yosef story. Only the number 7, which focuses on *Shabbat* as the seventh day – lacks a partner. This immediately brings to mind the beautiful *Midrash* in *Midrash Rabba* (Gen. 11:8):

> Why did God bless *Shabbat*? R. Berekhia says: "Because it has no partner. The first day of the week has the second, the third has the fourth, the fifth has the sixth, but *Shabbat* has no partner." … R. Shimon bar Yohai taught: *Shabbat* pleaded with the Holy One, blessed is He, saying: "Everyone else has a partner, but I have nothing!" God answered saying: "The community of Israel will be your partner." Hence, when Israel stood before Sinai, God said to

them: "Remember what I said to *Shabbat*, that the community of Israel is your partner," as scripture says: "Remember the Sabbath day and keep it holy" (Ex. 20:8).

Yael Levine has written an analog of *Ehad Mi Yode'a* ascribing the various numbers to events that occurred to leading women in Jewish tradition, based on various Midrashic works. See below: "Additions to the *Haggada*," Sec. 3.

תרגומים עממיים לשפות שונות

It is a widespread custom to sing the popular songs **Ehad Mi Yode'a** and **Had Gadya** in translation, often accompanied by hand signs and sound effects. For a rich collection, of translations of these two songs in various languages, see: https://www.jewishlanguages.org/who-knows-one and https://www.jewishlanguages.org/chad-gadya, respectively. Indeed, one of the earliest manuscripts we have of **Ehad Mi Yode'a** is the Prague *Haggada* from 1592 where each verse appears first in Hebrew and then in Yiddish. One of the major reasons suggested for this custom is to encourage the children to remain awake to the *Seder*'s end. But the appeal here is much more general, and the likely reason for this custom is the desire to end the *Seder* with a smile and a sense of exhilaration. After all, as we remarked in "Introductory Essays" #4 above, the *Seder* is an educational seminar. It is about keeping the memory of our special history, lineage, and relationship with God alive. It's about doing *mitzvot*, it's about convincing the *Seder* participants to identify with Judaism's goals and Jewish history past, present, and future. It's about us, our parents, and our children. Hence, we want the experience to be a positive happy one – *avodat Hashem be-simha* – serving God with joy. It is important to mention in passing that every translation is to some extent an interpretation. In addition, we will see that the translations often reflect a slightly different basic tradition regarding the various elements of the song.

English: Who Knows One?

English translations of *Ehad Mi Yode'a* were popularized by various groups. The present version is the one sung at the Frimer Family Seder. This song when done well with enthusiasm – turns into a loud happy

מה אספרה, מה אדברה: Yiddish (2)

מה אספרה, מה אדברה, אוי ווי צ"ירי בים בם . ווער קען צײלן, ווער
קען ריידן, וואָס דרייצן באַטייט? וואָס דרייצן באַטייט? דרייצן זענען
די מידות (י"א: איז מען בר מצווה), און צוועלף זענען די שבטים. און
עלף זענען די שטערן, און צען זענען די געבאָטן, און ניין זענען די
מאנאטין, און אַכט טעג ביז שניידן, און זיבעטער טאָג איז שבת (זיבן
זענען די וואָכנטעג), און זעקס זענען די משניות, און פינף זענען די
חומשים, און פיר זענען די אימהות (י"א: מוטערס), און דרײַ זענען די
אבות (י"א: פאָטערס), און צוויי זענען די לוחות, און איינער איז דער
גאָט, און גאָט איז איינער, אחוץ אים איז קיינער.

---

cheer – leaving a smile on everyone's face! To eliminate redundancy, we begin with **Thirteen**. Of import is the rendering of *Slosha asar midaya* as "The thirteen Divine attributes of mercy," rather than "The thirteen hermeneutical rules/principles of Rabbi Yishmael." Similarly, "Seven are the days of the week," rather than "the seventh day is *Shabbat*."

Yiddish: מה אספרה, מה אדברה

The Yiddish translation of *Ehad Mi Yode'a* is one of the earliest and appears in the first printed *Haggada* – Prague, 1590. It was widely sung in Europe and Russia with slight variations. Note that for **Thirteen** there is an alternate version that associates it with becoming Bar Mitzva. We will see that a similar aberration is found in the Ladino and Arabic translations, suggesting that there may have been a different tradition in the Hebrew version. Alternatively, the original Hebrew song ended at **Twelve** and was expanded to **Thirteen** only after the basic song had spread. Similarly, seven in one Yiddish version is rendered: "The seventh day is *Shabbat*." The version here is essentially what I learned in summer camp (Camp Munk) as a non-Yiddish-speaking youth. The English translation of the Yiddish is mine as well.

Regarding the Yiddish version, there is a very moving Reb Shlomo Carlebach story dating back to 1970, when he traveled to the Soviet

391 / Insights and Commentary on the Haggada

English Translation of Yiddish

What can I say? What can I tell? Oy vey! Cherri bim bom! Who can say, who can tell, what is the meaning of thirteen? Thirteen are the attributes (or: At thirteen one is Bar Mitzva), twelve are the tribes, eleven are the stars, ten are the Commandments, nine are the months (you're carried), eight days until the cutting (*brit*), the seventh day is *Shabbat* (or: seven are the days of the week), six are the books of the *Mishna*, five are the books of the Torah, four are the Mothers, three are the Fathers, two are the Tablets, and one is God, and God is one, and there is no other.

Union. This is the description transcribed by Yaakov Brown:

> In 1970, Reb Shlomo Carlebach traveled to the Soviet Union where he performed for tens of thousands of Jews in Moscow's Red Square. (It was on this trip that Carlebach composed his forever-famous tune, *Am Yisrael Chai*.) After completing a song on stage, Reb Shlomo felt a tug on his pant leg. He looked down and saw a boy, maybe around 7 years old, looking up at him. Reb Shlomo immediately stopped the concert and bent to hear what the boy had to say. The small boy wanted Reb Shlomo to sing, **Zibin Iz Der Heilige** *Shabbos* but Reb Shlomo, who knew hundreds and hundreds of *nigunim* from all over the world, didn't recognize the song that he was being asked to sing. Of course, Reb Shlomo was very curious as to what Shabbos song the boy was referring to, so he lovingly asked the boy to sing it for him. After taking a moment to collect himself, the boy closed his eyes and began to sing, in Yiddish, the famous *Seder* song *Echod Mi Yodea*. The boy only knew it starting from seven and so he slowly began, **Zibin** iz der heilige Shabbos, **Zeks** zenen deh Mishnayes, **Finf** zenen deh Humashim, **Feer** zenen deh Mames, **Drai** zenen deh Tates, **Tzvei** zenen deh Luhos, Un **Eins** iz doch Ah Gott, Un Gott iz Einer, Un veiter keiner. Reb Shlomo joined him and together with the entire crowd, they sang over and over again, *un* **Eins** *iz doch Ah Gott, un Gott iz Einer, un veiter keiner, un* **Eins** *iz Doch Ah Gott, un Gott iz Einer, un veiter keiner*…. This turned out to be the highlight of the night.

(3) Judeo-Spanish / Ladino

Elokenu she-ba-shamaym,	(Our God in Heaven)
Nos iremos a Yerushalayim,	(We will go to Jerusalem)
Kon la karavana grande	(With a great caravan)
Kualo son los tredje?	(What is thirteen?)
TREDJE anyos de **Bar Mitzva**.	(13 years for Bar Mitzva.)
DODJE tribus de Israel.	(12 tribes of Israel.)
ONZE hermanos sin Yosef.	(11 brothers without Yosef.)
DYEZ los mandamiento de la ley.	(10 commandments.)
MUEVE meses de la prenyada.	(9 months of pregnancy.)
OCHO dias de la milá	(8 days for circumcision.)
SIETE dias kon shabat.	(7 days with *Shabbat*.)
SEISH dias de la **semana**.	(6 days of the week.)
SINKO livros de la ley.	(5 books of the law.)
KWATRO madres de Israel.	(4 mothers of Israel.)
TRES muestros padres son.	(3 are our fathers.)
DOS Moshe y Aharon.	(2 Moshe and Aharon.)
UNO es el kri'ador,	(1 is the Creator,
Barukh hu u'varukh shemo.	Blessed is He and His name)

We see how *Ehad Mi Yode'a* with all its childish simplicity succeeded in keeping the flame of Judaism alight amid the darkness of the former Soviet Union.

Judeo-Spanish / Ladino

The Ladino translation has several variations from the Hebrew. In this tradition, the number two replaces the Tablets with Moshe and Aharon. They are of course the stars of the Exodus story, but also appear in *Haza"l*'s midrashic interpretation of *Shir ha-Shirim*, wherever pairs are mentioned (see for example *Shir ha-Shirim* 4:5). Thirteen represents different themes in different locations. In the Turkish tradition, it is connected to Bar Mitzva, while elsewhere the Thirteen Maimonidean Principles of Faith. In Salonica thirteen is the twelve brothers with Dina. The number twelve sometimes represents the Tribes of Israel

(4) Judeo-Arabic (Halabi Syrian)

Who knows, who understands	מן יְעלַם וּמן יְדרי
God Lord of the universe	אַללה רב אל מדגללי
(What is 13?)	הֶדה הִגֵּן אל תלתעש

תלתעש אל בר-מִצוָה (י"א לֵבֵס תְּפִילין)

(13 for Bar Mitzva or Dons *Tefillen*)	
(12 tribes of Israel)	תנעש שבטי ישְׂרָאֵל
(11 stars in the sky)	חדעש כּוכּב בּשַׁמַה
(10 commandments of Torah)	עשר קלמת אתּוֹרה
(9 months of pregnancy)	תשעת אשהוֹר אל חבלה
(8 days for *mila*)	תמן-ת-איים אל מילה
(7 days of *Hupa*)	שבעת-איים אל חוּפּה
(6 orders of *Mishna*)	סתי סדאדיר אל משׁנה
(5 books of Torah)	כּמשה מסאחף אתּוֹרה
(4 Matriarchs)	ארבּעה אמתנה
(3 Patriarchs)	ותלתה אבּתנה
(2 are Moshe and Aharon)	ותנֵן מוסה ואהַרן
(God is the only Creator)	ואחד יאלי-כלאנה

אללהו אללהו לא אלה אללה הוא

(God, God, there is no God but God)

---

or "The brothers **with** Yosef" – while eleven is "The brothers without Yosef." Six is the days of the week, while seven is the weekdays with *Shabbat*.

Judeo-Arabic (Halabi Syrian)

The Judeo-Arabic translation also contains two of the Ladino changes: two is Moshe and Aharon and thirteen is Bar Mitzva (or donning *Tefillin*) – and this may well suggest a common development. In addition, the Arabic tradition has seven, not as the days of the week or *Shabbat* as the seventh day, but as the seven days of the wedding

חַד גַּדְיָא

חַד גַּדְיָא, חַד גַּדְיָא דְזַבִּין אַבָּא בִּתְרֵי זוּזֵי, חַד גַּדְיָא, חַד גַּדְיָא.

וְאָתָא שׁוּנְרָא וְאָכְלָה לְגַדְיָא, דְזַבִּין אַבָּא בִּתְרֵי זוּזֵי. חַד גַּדְיָא, חַד גַּדְיָא.

וְאָתָא כַלְבָּא וְנָשַׁךְ לְשׁוּנְרָא, דְאָכְלָה לְגַדְיָא, דְזַבִּין אַבָּא בִּתְרֵי זוּזֵי. חַד גַּדְיָא, חַד גַּדְיָא.

וְאָתָא חוּטְרָא וְהִכָּה לְכַלְבָּא. דְנָשַׁךְ לְשׁוּנְרָא. דְאָכְלָה לְגַדְיָא, דְזַבִּין אַבָּא בִּתְרֵי זוּזֵי. חַד גַּדְיָא, חַד גַּדְיָא.

וְאָתָא נוּרָא וְשָׂרַף לְחוּטְרָא. דְהִכָּה לְכַלְבָּא. דְנָשַׁךְ לְשׁוּנְרָא. דְאָכְלָה לְגַדְיָא, דְזַבִּין אַבָּא בִּתְרֵי זוּזֵי. חַד גַּדְיָא, חַד גַּדְיָא.

וְאָתָא מַיָּא וְכָבָה לְנוּרָא. דְשָׂרַף לְחוּטְרָא. דְהִכָּה לְכַלְבָּא. דְנָשַׁךְ לְשׁוּנְרָא, דְאָכְלָה לְגַדְיָא, דְזַבִּין אַבָּא בִּתְרֵי זוּזֵי. חַד גַּדְיָא, חַד גַּדְיָא.

וְאָתָא תוֹרָא וְשָׁתָה לְמַיָּא, דְּכָבָה לְנוּרָא. דְשָׂרַף לְחוּטְרָא. דְהִכָּה לְכַלְבָּא. דְנָשַׁךְ לְשׁוּנְרָא, דְאָכְלָה לְגַדְיָא, דְזַבִּין אַבָּא בִּתְרֵי זוּזֵי. חַד גַּדְיָא, חַד גַּדְיָא.

וְאָתָא הַשּׁוֹחֵט וְשָׁחַט לְתוֹרָא. דְשָׁתָה לְמַיָּא. דְכָבַף לְחוּטְרָא. דְהִכָּה לְכַלְבָּא. דְנָשַׁךְ לְשׁוּנְרָא, דְאָכְלָה לְגַדְיָא, דְזַבִּין אַבָּא בִּתְרֵי זוּזֵי. חַד גַּדְיָא, חַד גַּדְיָא.

וְאָתָא מַלְאָךְ הַמָּוֶת וְשָׁחַט לְשׁוֹחֵט. דְּשָׁחַט לְתוֹרָא. דְשָׁתָה לְמַיָּא. דְכָבָה לְנוּרָא. דְשָׂרַף לְחוּטְרָא. דְהִכָּה לְכַלְבָּא. דְנָשַׁךְ לְשׁוּנְרָא. דְאָכְלָה לְגַדְיָא, דְזַבִּין אַבָּא בִּתְרֵי זוּזֵי. חַד גַּדְיָא, חַד גַּדְיָא.

---

celebration. The pervasiveness of thirteen being something other than מדיא in the various translations suggests that the song אחד מי יודע may

Had Gadya – One Little Goat

One little goat, one little goat,
that father bought for two zuzim, one little goat, one little goat.

And then came a cat and ate that goat
that father bought for two zuzim, one little goat, one little goat.

And then came a dog and bit the cat, that ate the goat
that father bought for two zuzim, one little goat, one little goat.

And then came a stick and beat the dog, that bit the cat, that ate the goat
that father bought for two zuzim, one little goat, one little goat.

And then came a fire and burnt the stick, that beat the dog, that bit the cat, that ate the goat
that father bought for two zuzim, one little goat, one little goat.

And then came some water and put out the fire, that burnt the stick, that beat the dog, that bit the cat, that ate the goat
that father bought for two zuzim, one little goat, one little goat.

And then came an ox and drank the water, that put out the fire, that burnt the stick, that beat the dog, that bit the cat, that ate the goat,
that father bought for two zuzim, one little goat, one little goat.

And then came a slaughterer and slaughtered the ox, that drank the water, that put out the fire, that burnt the stick, that beat the dog, that bit the cat, that ate the goat
that father bought for two zuzim, one little goat, one little goat.

And then came the angel of death and slew the slaughterer, who slaughtered the ox, that drank the water, that put out the fire, that burnt the stick, that beat the dog, that bit the cat, that ate the goat
that father bought for two zuzim, one little goat, one little goat.

---

have originally ended at 12, with thirteen developing later – differently in varying locations.

וְאָתָא הַקָּדוֹשׁ בָּרוּךְ הוּא וְשָׁחַט לְמַלְאַךְ הַמָּוֶת. דְּשָׁחַט לְשׁוֹחֵט. דְּשָׁחַט לְתוֹרָא. דְּשָׁתָה לְמַיָּא. דְּכָבָה לְנוּרָא. דְּשָׂרַף לְחוּטְרָא. דְּהִכָּה לְכַלְבָּא. דְּנָשַׁךְ לְשׁוּנְרָא. דְּאָכְלָה לְגַדְיָא. דְּזַבִּין אַבָּא בִּתְרֵי זוּזֵי. חַד גַּדְיָא, חַד גַּדְיָא.

חַד גַּדְיָא

We have finally reached the final song of the *Seder*. The song appears for the first time in print in the Prague *Haggada* of 1590, but we do not know the identity of the author. Like *Ehad Mi Yode'a*, it is an example of what is called a "Cumulative Poem" in which every subsequent verse adds some new information. These types of poems are well-known worldwide among children's nursery rhymes. An example is "There once was an old woman that swallowed a fly." Before we get into the themes and messages of the song, two technical comments are in order,

(a) As indicated above, scholars know neither the identity nor the credentials of this beloved poem's author. But it seems that he did not know Aramaic well, because he mixes in a large amount of Hebrew. In addition, there are a variety of linguistic errors and we will mention two. (1) If the intended meaning of **de-Zabin Aba** is "that my father **bought**," the correct Aramaic word should have been **di-Zeban** (see for example the scientific Haggadot of R. Menahem Mendel Kasher and R. Daniel Goldschmidt). The word *de-Zabin* actually means "sold." (Nevertheless, the classic translation remains "bought.") (2) The second verse reads: *ve-Ata shunra ve-akhla le-gadya*. It turns out that *shunra* is a male cat while a female cat would be *shunrita*. Nevertheless, the verb used almost universally in this song is *ve-akhla* and feminine, while for a male cat, it should have been *ve-akhal* as in Hebrew! Interestingly, here too, R. Menahem Mendel Kasher gives the correct reading without comment: *ve-Ata shunra ve-akhal le-gadya*.

b) Because **de-Zabin** means "sold," R. Yekhiel Mikhel HaLevi Epstein, in his *Haggada Leyl Shimurim* suggests that *Had Gadya* is all about the **Sale** of Yosef – which is why the Israelites went down to Egypt in the first place. The goat we are talking about is the goat that the brothers of Yosef killed to trick Yaakov, their father, into thinking that Yosef was dead – and the cause of the Egyptian exile. The word

And then came the Holy One, Blessed is He, and killed the angel of death, who slew the slaughterer, who slaughtered the ox, that drank the water, that put out the fire, that burnt the stick, that beat the dog, that bit the cat, that ate the goat
that father bought for two zuzim, one little goat, one little goat.

Aba not only refers to a father but also connotes importance. The brothers sold Yosef for 20 silver pieces, which divided among the 10 brothers is 2 *Zuz* a piece. Thus, *de-Zabin Aba bi-trei zuzei* means, they sold the important one (Yosef) for 2 *Zuz* each. The rest of the song deals with various aspects of the Exodus and Jewish history (see below).

Returning now to the poem, from the get-go some made fun of this song, claiming that it had no redeeming value and was merely a child's nursery rhyme. Yet others, like the noted authority R. Chaim Joseph David Azulai (*Resp. Chaim Sha'al*, I, sec. 28), argued that *Had Gadya* is an allegory replete with profound ideas and educational messages. Indeed, most commentaries have understood this poem on one level to be a summary of Jewish history through the ages, with the various powerful nations attacking Israel. R. Jonathan Sacks in his *Haggada*, suggests that the young goat represents Israel. The "father" who bought it for two coins is God, who redeemed Israel from Egypt through His two representatives, Moshe and Aharon. The cat is **Assyria**, which conquered the northern kingdom of Israel (722 BCE). The dog is **Babylonia**, which defeated the southern kingdom of Judah (601 BCE). The stick represents **Persia**, which replaced Babylonia as the imperial power (539 BCE). The fire corresponds to the **Greeks**, who defeated the Persians in the days of Alexander the Great (330 BCE). The water is **Rome**, which superseded ancient Greece (63 BCE). The ox stands for **Islam**, which defeated the Romans in Palestine (636–641). The slaughterer is **Christianity** – specifically the Crusaders (1099–1291), who fought Islam in Palestine and elsewhere, murdering Jews on the way. The Angel of Death is the **Ottoman** Empire, which controlled Palestine until the First World War (1516–1922). The song concludes with an expression of faith that "this too shall pass" and the Jewish people will return to their land. (And so it has been in our days). In this regard, R. Moses Sofer (*Derashot* II, p. 278) correctly points out that while the cat in the second line of *Had Gadya* "eats" the goat, it does **not** devour it, i.e., it does not eat it up or kill it. Rather, the feline attacker eats from it. The goat remains alive throughout to bear witness to the occurrences, as the chorus assures us at the end of each succeeding line: *Had Gadya, Had Gadya*. The goat is still around.

But *Had Gadya* is much more than a history lesson. As R. Azulai maintained, it transmits at the same time, a variety of important *hashkafic* and theological lessons. We now discuss a few of these.

(1) **The Miracle of Jewish Survival** (*ve-Hi she-Amda*) – R. Moses Sofer's observation above that the goat remains alive from chorus to chorus and from one historic event to another, brings us to the first lesson of *Had Gadya*. *Had Gadya* is very much in the spirit of *ve-Hi she-Amda* in its recognition that Jewish survival from generation to generation is not a fluke, but the protective hand of the Almighty intervening in history. Thus, the poem concludes: *ve-ata ha-Kadosh Barukh Hu ve-shahat le-malakh ha-mavet*. This idea is also found in the commentary of the 15th-century Italian Biblical scholar R. Ovadia Seforno (Gen. 25:26), who writes:

> **And he called his name Yaakov**: The word Yaakov (Jacob) means: He will remain at the heel and the tail-end. Our sages say that **God** gave him this name because, after the destruction of all the other nations, only Yaakov and his descendants will remain. Our sages base all this on Jeremiah 46:28: "I will make an end of all nations… but I will not make an end of you."

Indeed, the secret of Jewish survival has astounded thinkers for centuries. The renowned American author and humorist Samuel Clemens (Mark Twain, "Concerning the Jews," *Harper's Magazine*, 1899) has asserted:

> The Egyptian, the Babylonian, and the Persian rose, filled the planet with sound and splendor, then faded to dream stuff and passed away; the Greek and the Roman followed and made a vast noise, and they are gone; other peoples have sprung up and held their torch high for a time, but it burned out, and they sit in twilight now, or have vanished. The Jew saw them all, beat them all, and is now what he always was, exhibiting no decadence, no

infirmities of age, no weakening of his parts, no slowing of his energies, no dulling of his alert and aggressive mind. All things are mortal, but the Jew; all other forces pass, but he remains. What is the secret of his immortality?

R. Jacob Emden (Introduction, *Siddur Bet Yaakov*, *Sulam Bet El*) writes:

By my Life! When I consider the existence of our people in the exile, one sheep surrounded by seventy wolves, it is greater in my eyes than all the miracles that were done for our ancestors in Egypt, and on the Red Sea, and in the Land of Israel." (See also our comments to וְהַקָּדוֹשׁ בָּרוּךְ הוּא מַצִּילֵנוּ מִיָּדָם).

The import of this miraculous survival was the subject of a mesmerizing debate on January 31, 1961, between then-Israeli Ambassador to Canada Yaacov Herzog and British Historian Arnold Toynbee. See: https://www.youtube.com/playlist?list=PLzexu4Ywu3KkupX7u-OUHAavt3lVxotv5.

(2) **God has a relationship with man** – The second moral is that the Creator cares about the world and does become involved, if only surreptitiously. Since He also gave us the *mitzvot*, we as Jews assert that there is an ongoing relationship with Him. This idea is eloquently presented by R. Eliezer Berkovits (*God, Man, and History*, Shalom Press, 2004): "The foundation of religion is not the affirmation that God **is**, but that God **is concerned** with man and the world; that, having created the world, he has not abandoned it, leaving it to its own devices; that he cares for his creation. … Beyond any doubt, biblical religion bases itself on the possibility of a relationship between God and man."

(3) **God punishes Evil** – The third teaching is that (*Midrash Rabba*, Gen. 26:6): *Yesh din ve-yesh dayan* – "There is a Judge and there will be a judgment." Thus, in **Had Gadya** the various animals (nations) are punished by other animals. In retrospect, we realize that this is the hand of God working through the forces of nature and history. This song emphasizes our belief that evil is punished, which is why the Song ends with the Almighty slaughtering the Angel of Death. It's not simply that death ceases, but rather that God takes charge and punishes evil. In the end, God's role in running the world becomes eminent and

clear. We reiterate that throughout Jewish liturgy vengeance is not Israel's task – but God's. But it is our task to be cognizant of that fact, especially *Seder* night.

My teacher R. David Cohen (Cong. Gvul Yaavetz) cites in this regard Maimonides' (*Sefer ha-Mitzvot*). There, Rambam asserts that there is a special obligation at the *Seder* to mention God's revenge on evil nations, as we do in *ve-Hi she-Amda* and *Had Gadya*:

> In Positive Commandment 157, God commanded us to tell about the Exodus from Egypt at the beginning of the night of the fifteenth of Nissan, according to the speaker's abilities. And it is even better that one extends the discussion, by magnifying that which God did for us, and **what the Egyptians did to us in terms of injustice and oppression, and how God avenged us upon them**, and to thank Him, may He be exalted, for all of the good with which He benefitted us. As it is written [in the *Haggada*], "Anyone who is expansive in his describing the Exodus from Egypt is praiseworthy."

(4) **Rejection of Death Cults or Devil Worship** – Another message can be learned from the very fact that the ultimate victor is *ha-Kadosh Barukh Hu* – The Holy One, blessed is He – and **not** the מלאך המוות – the Angel of Death. In societies that have suffered massive numbers of deaths from plague, war or starvation, there often develops a death cult. Thus, a ballet called the "Green Table" was created by choreographer Kurt Jooss in 1932. It is a chilling commentary on the futility of war and the horrors it causes. The only true winner is "Death" who triumphantly and relentlessly claims his victims. Here in **Had Gadya** the ultimate champion is the Creator, indicating that He is the one who is in control throughout. Even death will end and is not inevitable.

(5) **Awareness of God's Presence** – The fifth approach is articulated by R. Zvi Romm ("Looking Past the Everyday" Pesah-to-Go, 5779). He argues that we are meant to walk away from the *Seder* with our eyes opened to the presence of God in the world around us. Thus, *Nishmat* and *Hallel ha-Gadol* are focused on God's role in facilitating miracles covertly through the natural events of everyday life. This point is reiterated in *Had Gadya*. The goat, cat, and dog of this allegory represent

nothing more than the common and mundane experiences of this world. It is only at the very end of *Had Gadya* that God Himself suddenly appears on the scene. The message is that God is really behind all the seemingly mundane events in the world.

(6) **Jewish Refusal to Give up Hope** – R. Norman Lamm ("Ideology of Neturei Karta," *Tradition*, fall, 1971) has asserted that "Messianism … bespeaks an optimistic view of life, an imperishable hope for a happy ending to history, a powerful faith in the divine promise of redemption for His exiled people." Similarly, R. Jonathan Sacks (*Haggada*) posits:

> This song, disarming in its simplicity, teaches the great truth of Jewish hope: that though many nations (symbolized by the cat, the dog, and so on) attacked Israel (the goat), each in turn has vanished into oblivion. At the end of days, God will vanquish the Angel of Death and inaugurate a world of life and peace, the two great Jewish loves. *Had Gadya* expresses **the Jewish refusal to give up hope**. Though history is full of man's inhumanity to man – dog bites cat, stick hits dog – that is not the final verse. The *Haggada* ends with the death of death in eternal life.

Indeed, *Had Gadya* reflects an undying hope or optimism that things will get better, that *Mashi'ah* will eventually come. As stated in *Ani Ma'amin*: "…*ahakeh lo be-khol yom she-yavo* – I will await for the Messiah whenever he should come." It is with this belief and declaration that we Jews end the *Haggada*. In essence, *Had Gadya* serves the same function as "Next year in Jerusalem!" that follows *Hasal Siddur Pesah*, the formal ending of the *Seder*. We end upbeat, happy, and hopeful.

(7) **The Dignity of Purpose** – *Had Gadya* reflects Judaism's assertion that life has a divine purpose; world occurrences are not merely random coincidences. We maintain that there is an element of Divine *hashgaha* and supervision that somehow "gently" guides our personal and communal actions and choices. (I say "gently" because Judaism also asserts that we have freedom of choice – *behira hofshit*. How these interact is one of life's great mysteries.) In *Had Gadya*, the Almighty reveals himself at the end but it is understood that He was guiding history all along.

This characteristic of Judaism has been noted by many prominent thinkers including the 20th century Christian historian Paul John. In the Prologue to his classic work, *A History of the Jews* (Harper Perennial, 1988), he writes:

> This book gave me the chance to reconsider objectively the most intractable of all human questions: What are we on earth for? Is history merely a series of events whose sum is meaningless? Or is there a providential plan of which we are, however humbly, the agents? No people has ever insisted more firmly than the Jews that history has a purpose and humanity a destiny. The Jews, therefore, stand right at the center of the perennial attempt to give **human life the dignity of purpose**.

Similarly, R. Jonathan Sacks ("Moving Forwards," *Covenant & Conversation, va-Yehi* 2021/5781) wrote:

> "I am your brother Yosef, the one you sold into Egypt! And now, do not be distressed and do not be angry with yourselves for selling me here, because it was to save lives that God sent me ahead of you." (Gen. 45:3–8) This establishes the idea of Divine Providence. **History** is not, as Joseph Heller called it, "a trash bag of random coincidences blown open in the wind." [*Good as Gold*, 1979, p. 74] It has a purpose, a point, and a plot. God is at work behind the scenes. "There's a divinity that shapes our ends," says Hamlet [Act 5, scene 2], "rough-hew them how we will." Yosef's greatness was that he sensed this.

R. Jonathan Sacks ("In Search of the Why," *Covenant and Conversation, be-Hukotai* 2018/5778) makes another profound observation:

> Nietzsche (*Twilight of the Idols*) has famously said "One who has a 'why' to live for, can bear almost any 'how.'" If life has a meaning, if our own life has a purpose, if there is a task we have yet to fulfill, then something within us gives us the strength to survive suffering and sorrow. The call of the future helps us get through the pain of the present and the trauma of the past… To be a Jew

is to have faith that our individual lives and our collective history have meaning. God is there even if we cannot feel Him. He hears us even when we do not hear Him. That is the blessing. It gave our people the courage to survive some of the worst blows ever to befall a people. It is what gives us, as individuals, the strength to come through "the slings and arrows of outrageous fortune." (Hamlet, Shakespeare) Lose that faith and we lose that strength.

This is also the message of *Had Gadya*.

(8) **Seeing the Hand of God in Retrospect** – In their *Haggada* commentaries, R. Yisrael Meir Lau and R. Shalom Rosner each remark that our personal and national lives are a puzzle and most often we see only part of the puzzle. It is often hard to comprehend why a specific event transpired, given our limited perspective. It is only at the end of the whole process that details begin to make sense. The events of Jewish history seem to be a tale of *Had Gadya* – full of nonsensical twists and turns, ups and downs. Only when we look backward do we see patterns and direction: *ve-Ata ha-Kadosh Barukh Hu ve-shahat le-malakh ha-mavet* – that God himself has been guiding the events to a specific goal.

(9) **Jewish Perception of Time** – Also related to the previous discussion of "The Dignity of Purpose" is an important lesson on the Jewish perception of time. There are fundamentally two perceptions of time: cyclical (or natural time) vs linear (or historical) time. R. Jonathan Sacks ("Counting Time," *Covenant & Conversation*, Emor 5768 – and elsewhere) indicates that ancient civilizations tended to see time as a circle – cyclical time. That is how we experience time in nature. Cyclical time is time as a series of eternal **recurrences**. Beneath the apparent changes, the world remains the same – man is essentially locked in. What was is what will be. The Hebrew Bible is the first document to see time as cyclical, **but also** as linear, as an arena of change. Tomorrow need not be the same as yesterday. Man tomorrow can be different than he is today. Time is a journey with a starting point and a destination, or a story with a beginning, middle, and end. This is time – not as it is in nature – but as it is in history. The Hebrew prophets were the first to see God in history. Linear time allows for hope, growth, a bright future, and the possibility of changing ourselves (*teshuva* – Repentance)

and the world. Some have described the hybrid Jewish conception of time as "helical." We, indeed, return yearly to the High Holidays and the Festivals, but hopefully, we have changed and grown in the meantime. Focusing now on *Had Gadya*, the song does describe a "cycle of violence," but time has linear elements and things can change. Thus, the song ends with God taking control. History progresses upward toward a Divine goal and ultimate redemption.

(We note in passing that the popular Israeli *Had Gadya* sung by Chava Alberstein (1989) focuses on the "cycle of violence," but totally removes the Almighty which concludes the poem. For her, time is purely cyclical and violence once started is nigh unstoppable. As we have argued above, this is by no means the message or worldview of the *Seder*'s *Had Gadya*.)

In summary, R. Chaim Joseph David Azulai – cited at the beginning of this comment – was indeed correct when he argued that *Had Gadya* is no simple children's poem, but an allegory replete with profound ideas and educational messages. This surely should be the case because *Had Gadya* is in a real way the summary statement of the *Seder*'s educational seminar.

וְאָתָא הַקָּדוֹשׁ בָּרוּךְ הוּא

R. Yosef Chaim of Baghdad (*Haggada Ben Ish Hai*) asks a well-known question (usually presented with a smile – one should never take an allegory too literally). If the cat attacks the innocent goat, then the dog seems justified in punishing the cat for his wrongful act. The stick, then, has acted improperly for striking the cat, but the fire acted correctly for punishing it. The water in turn is not justified and the bull is. The *shohet* is not justified and the *Malakh ha-Mavet* is. Why then does Holy One, blessed is He, slaughter the Angel of Death? R. Yosef Chaim answers that the dog was not justified in attacking the cat, because it wasn't a fight that he had any relevance to. Thus, the dog was wrong, the stick was right, the fire was wrong and, ultimately, so was the Angel of Death; God is vindicated!

And this, says the *Ben Ish Ḥai*, explains why we read *Ḥad Gadya* at the end of the *Seder*. We do so to address the question: why were the Egyptians punished for enslaving the Israelites? After all, it was already decreed by God in the *Brit bein ha-Betarim* ("Covenant of the Parts"). Following Maimonides (see comments above to וְגַם אֶת־הַגּוֹי אֲשֶׁר יַעֲבֹדוּ דָּן אָנֹכִי), the answer is that although the Jewish People were destined to be enslaved, the covenant says nothing about **who** was assigned that task; it could have been accomplished by a different nation. Hence, the Egyptians do bear guilt for their actions.

While the *Ben Ish Ḥai*'s moral is undoubtedly correct, there seems to be a basic flaw in the original argument. For, if the dog erred in becoming involved in a quarrel not his, so did all the other characters! Fortunately, there turns out to be a simple solution. In an article on *Ḥad Gadya* (*Maḥanayim* 55, 140–144, *Pesaḥ* 5721), Abraham Meir Habermann reports that a manuscript from the 15th or 16th century (found in the Historical Society of Israel) has one additional character: *Akhbera* – a mouse. The text of the first three lines reads as follows:

חַד גַּדְיָא. חַד גַּדְיָא דְּזַבֵּן אַבָּא בִּתְרֵי זוּזֵי. חַד גַּדְיָא. חַד גַּדְיָא.

וְאָתָא עַכְבְּרָא דְּאָכַל לְגַדְיָא. דְּזַבֵּן אַבָּא בִּתְרֵי זוּזֵי. חַד גַּדְיָא. חַד גַּדְיָא.

וְאָתָא שׁוּנְרָא דְּנָשַׁךְ לְעַכְבְּרָא. דְּאָכַל לְגַדְיָא. דְּזַבֵּן אַבָּא בִּתְרֵי זוּזֵי. חַד גַּדְיָא. חַד גַּדְיָא.

Thus, with one more player in this song, the Almighty is undoubtedly vindicated! (Pay attention to the use of *de-zevan* and a male verb for *shunra*, as discussed above).

הוֹסָפוֹת לְהַגָּדָה

(1) הַשְׁלָמָה לִדְרָשׁוֹת "אֲרַמִּי אוֹבֵד אָבִי", הַצָּעַת הָרַב דָּוִד מִישְׁלוֹב

לִפְנֵי "כַּמָּה מַעֲלוֹת טוֹבוֹת" מוֹסִיפִים - בְּאֶרֶץ יִשְׂרָאֵל:

וַיְבִאֵנוּ אֶל הַמָּקוֹם הַזֶּה, וַיִּתֶּן לָנוּ אֶת הָאָרֶץ הַזֹּאת, אֶרֶץ זָבַת חָלָב וּדְבָשׁ
(דְּבָרִים כו. ט).

*וַיְבִאֵנוּ אֶל הַמָּקוֹם הַזֶּה – זֶה בֵּית הַמִּקְדָּשׁ. כְּמוֹ שֶׁנֶּאֱמַר: "לִהְיוֹת עֵינֶיךָ פְתֻחוֹת אֶל הַבַּיִת הַזֶּה לַיְלָה וָיוֹם. אֶל הַמָּקוֹם אֲשֶׁר אָמַרְתָּ יִהְיֶה שְׁמִי שָׁם', לִשְׁמֹעַ אֶל הַתְּפִלָּה אֲשֶׁר יִתְפַּלֵּל עַבְדְּךָ אֶל הַמָּקוֹם הַזֶּה; וְשָׁמַעְתָּ אֶל תְּחִנַּת עַבְדְּךָ, וְעַמְּךָ יִשְׂרָאֵל, אֲשֶׁר יִתְפַּלְלוּ אֶל הַמָּקוֹם הַזֶּה, וְאַתָּה תִּשְׁמַע אֶל מְקוֹם שִׁבְתְּךָ. אֶל הַשָּׁמַיִם, וְשָׁמַעְתָּ, וְסָלָחְתָּ" (תְּפִלַּת שְׁלֹמֹה הַמֶּלֶךְ בַּחֲנֻכַּת הַמִּקְדָּשׁ. מְלָכִים א. ח. כט-ל).

דָּבָר אַחֵר: וַיְבִאֵנוּ אֶל הַמָּקוֹם הַזֶּה – אַתָּה מוֹצֵא בְּיַעֲקֹב שֶׁרָאָה אוֹתוֹ בָּנוּי, וְרָאָה אוֹתוֹ חָרֵב, וְרָאָה אוֹתוֹ בָּנוּי, שֶׁנֶּאֱמַר (בְּרֵאשִׁית כח. יז): "וַיִּירָא וַיֹּאמַר: מַה נּוֹרָא הַמָּקוֹם הַזֶּה" – הֲרֵי בָּנוּי. "אֵין זֶה" – הֲרֵי חָרֵב. "כִּי אִם בֵּית אֱלֹהִים, וְזֶה שַׁעַר הַשָּׁמָיִם" – הֲרֵי בָּנוּי וּמְשֻׁכְלָל לֶעָתִיד לָבֹא (סִפְרֵי דְּבָרִים. פִּסְקָא שנב).

הוספות להגדה

The *Haggada* in general, and *Nirtza* in particular allows for great creativity and encourages attempts to make the text come alive. We include in this section the creative efforts of those who have tried to enrich the *Haggada* and make it more relevant to our generation.

השלמה לדרשות

In our comments to אֲרַמִּי אוֹבֵד אָבִי above, we cited R. Joseph B. Soloveitchik (*An Exalted Evening*) who hypothesized that at the time of the Temple, the fifth verse of *Arami Oved Avi* (Deut. 26:9) was also said at the *Seder* and analyzed. However, with the destruction of the Temple and the scattering of the Jews throughout the diaspora, this verse

ADDITIONS TO THE *HAGGADA*

(1) Completion of the Exegesis of "*Arami Oved Avi*," Proposed by R. David Mescheloff

To be added – in Israel – before Kamma Ma'alot Tovot (Dayenu):

"And He brought us to this place and He gave us this land, a land flowing with milk and honey." (Deut. 26:9)

*And He brought us to this place – This is the *Bet ha-Mikdash* (The Jerusalem Temple), as is written: "May Your eyes be open day and night to this House, to the place of which You have said, 'My name shall abide there'; May You hear the prayers that Your servant will offer toward this place. And when You hear the supplications that Your servant and Your people Israel offer toward this place, give heed in Your heavenly abode – give heed and forgive."

King Solomon's prayer inaugurating the Temple (I Kings, 8:29–30)

Additionally: And He brought us to this place – You find with Yaakov, that prophetically he saw the Temple built, and he saw it in ruin, and he saw it rebuilt, as it says (Gen. 28:17): "And he was awestruck and said: 'How awesome is this place' – built; This is not' – it is in ruin; '[is not] other than the house of God, and this is the gate of Heaven'" – rebuilt and perfect in time to come. (*Sifri* Deut., 352)

---

was no longer relevant to the overwhelming majority of Jewry. R. David Mescheloff has suggested, however, that this verse should be reinstituted with appropriate *derashot* now that close to half of the world's Jewish population lives in the vibrant Land of Israel (https://www2.biu.ac.il/JH/Parasha/pesah/mis.html). R. Mescheloff has prepared a text for this purpose to be added just before *Kamma ma'alot tovot la-Makom alenu* (i.e., *Dayenu*). It is reprinted here with his permission. R. Mescheloff has indicated that the text should be said only in the Land of Israel, where the verses are directly relevant. The English translation was prepared by R. Aryeh Frimer and reviewed by R. Mescheloff.

דָּבָר אַחֵר: וַיְבִאֵנוּ אֶל הַמָּקוֹם הַזֶּה – יָכוֹל זֶה אֶרֶץ יִשְׂרָאֵל? כְּשֶׁהוּא אוֹמֵר: "וַיִּתֶּן לָנוּ אֶת הָאָרֶץ הַזֹּאת" – הֲרֵי אֶרֶץ יִשְׂרָאֵל אֲמוּרָה! וּמָה תַּלְמוּד לוֹמַר "וַיְבִאֵנוּ אֶל הַמָּקוֹם הַזֶּה"? בִּשְׂכַר בִּיאָתֵנוּ "אֶל הַמָּקוֹם הַזֶּה", נָתַן לָנוּ "אֶת הָאָרֶץ הַזֹּאת" (ספרי דברים פיסקא שא).

*וַיִּתֶּן לָנוּ אֶת הָאָרֶץ הַזֹּאת – מְלַמֵּד שֶׁחָפֵץ בָּנוּ יְיָ, כְּמוֹ שֶׁנֶּאֱמַר: "אִם חָפֵץ בָּנוּ יְיָ, וְהֵבִיא אוֹתָנוּ אֶל הָאָרֶץ הַזֹּאת וּנְתָנָהּ לָנוּ: אֶרֶץ אֲשֶׁר הִיא זָבַת חָלָב וּדְבָשׁ" (במדבר יד, ח).

דָּבָר אַחֵר: וַיִּתֶּן לָנוּ אֶת הָאָרֶץ הַזֹּאת – יָכוֹל הִיא הַפְּסֹלֶת שֶׁל שְׁאָר הָאֲרָצוֹת? תַּלְמוּד לוֹמַר "אֶרֶץ זָבַת חָלָב וּדְבָשׁ" – אֶרֶץ שֶׁפֵּרוֹתֶיהָ שְׁמֵנִים כְּחָלָב וּמְתוּקִים כִּדְבַשׁ – לְלַמֶּדְךָ שֶׁאֶרֶץ יִשְׂרָאֵל גְּבוֹהָה וּמְתוּקָה וּמְשֻׁבַּחַת מִכָּל הָאֲרָצוֹת (ילקוט שמעוני ישעיהו רמז תא).

*אֶרֶץ זָבַת חָלָב וּדְבָשׁ – רַבִּי אֱלִיעֶזֶר אוֹמֵר: "חָלָב" – זֶה חֲלֵב הַפֵּרוֹת, "דְּבַשׁ" – זֶה דְּבַשׁ תְּמָרִים. רַבִּי עֲקִיבָא אוֹמֵר: "חָלָב" – זֶה חָלָב וַדַּאי, "דְּבַשׁ" – זֶה דְּבַשׁ הַיְּעָרוֹת (מכילתא דרשב"י יג, ה).

פַּעַם אַחַת נִכְנַס רַבִּי לִבְנֵי בְרַק, וּמָצָא שָׁם אֶשְׁכּוֹל רוֹבֵץ כְּעֵגֶל בֶּן שָׁלֹשׁ שָׁנִים. פַּעַם אַחַת הָלַךְ רַבִּי יְהוֹשֻׁעַ לִסְכְנִין, וּמָצָא עֵז רְבוּצָה תַּחַת הַתְּאֵנָה, וְחָלָב שׁוֹתֵת מִמֶּנָּה, וּדְבַשׁ יוֹצֵא מִן הַתְּאֵנָה וּמִתְעָרְבִין זֶה בָּזֶה (מדרש תנאים לדברים).

דָּבָר אַחֵר: אֶרֶץ זָבַת חָלָב וּדְבָשׁ – אֵין עַם יִשְׂרָאֵל מִתְבָּרֵךְ אֶלָּא בָּאָרֶץ הַזֹּאת, כְּמוֹ שֶׁנֶּאֱמַר: "הַשְׁקִיפָה מִמְּעוֹן קָדְשְׁךָ מִן הַשָּׁמַיִם וּבָרֵךְ אֶת עַמְּךָ אֶת יִשְׂרָאֵל וְאֵת הָאֲדָמָה אֲשֶׁר נָתַתָּה לָּנוּ, כַּאֲשֶׁר נִשְׁבַּעְתָּ לַאֲבֹתֵינוּ – אֶרֶץ זָבַת חָלָב וּדְבָשׁ" (דברים כו, טו).

"אֲשֶׁר נִשְׁבַּע לַאֲבֹתֶיךָ" – הַכֹּל בִּזְכוּת אֲבוֹתֶיךָ (מכילתא דרשב"י יג, ה).

וּמַמְשִׁיכִים "כַּמָּה מַעֲלוֹת טוֹבוֹת".

Additionally: And He brought us to this place – Perhaps it refers to the Land of Israel?! [No, for] when the text says "and He gave us this land" the Land of Israel is already mentioned. How, then, am I to understand: "And He brought us to *this place*"? [As the Temple! "And He brought us to this place and He gave us this land"]: As a reward for our coming to *this place*, we were given *this land*. (*Sifri* Deut., 301)

*****And He gave us this land** – This teaches us that God wants us, as is written: "If the Lord wants us, He will bring us into this land and give it to us, a land that flows with milk and honey." (Num. 14:8)

Additionally: And He gave us this land – Perhaps it is the refuse of other lands?! This is why the text says: "A land flowing with milk and honey" – a land whose fruits are as rich as milk and as sweet as honey – to teach you that the Land of Israel is higher and sweeter and more praiseworthy than all other lands. (*Yalkut Shimoni*, Isaiah, *Remez* 401)

*****A land flowing with milk and honey** – Rabbi Eliezer says: "Milk" is the milk of the fruits, "honey" is the honey of dates. Rabbi Akiva says: "Milk" – this is real milk, "honey" – this is the honey of the forests (bees). (*Mekhilta de-R. Shimon bar Yohai* 13:5)

Once *Rebbi* (Rabbi Judah the Prince) went to Bnei Brak and found a cluster of grapes lying there the size of a three-year-old calf. Rabbi Yehoshua once went to Sakhnin, and found a goat lying under a fig tree – milk was dripping from the goat, and honey was coming out of the fig – and they mixed together. (*Midrash Tannaim*, Deut. 26:9)

Additionally: A land flowing with milk and honey – The Nation of Israel is blessed only in this land, as it says (Deut. 26:15): "Look down from Your holy abode from heaven and bless Your people Israel and the land that You gave us, as You swore to our ancestors – a land flowing with milk and honey."

"That He swore to your ancestors" (Ex 13:5) – It is all in the merit of your ancestors. (*Mekhilta de-R. Shimon bar Yohai* 13:5)

Continue with *Kamma Ma'alot Tovot* (*Dayenu*)

(2) תוספת לפיוט "וַיְהִי בַּחֲצִי הַלַּיְלָה" – מאת יעל לוין

בְּרִית הִבְטַחְתָּ אֶת רֹאשׁ הָאִמָּהוֹת לַיְלָה
מוּבֶלֶת לְבֵית פַּרְעֹה וְלַאֲבִימֶלֶךְ הִצַּלְתָּ לַיְלָה
מְשׁוּלַת שׁוֹשַׁנָּה יָעֲצָה לְהַחֲלִיף הַבְּרָכוֹת בַּלַּיְלָה
וַיְהִי בַּחֲצִי הַלַּיְלָה

צַעֲקַת הַיּוֹלֶדֶת וְהִכִּיתָ רֵאשִׁית אוֹנִים לַיְלָה
בְּכוֹרָה מִלַּטְתָּ לֹא יִכְבֶּה נֵרָהּ בַּלַּיְלָה
הֲדַסָּה עֲסוּקָה הָיְתָה בִּסְעוּדָתוֹ שֶׁל הָמָן בַּלַּיְלָה
וַיְהִי בַּחֲצִי הַלַּיְלָה

תוספת לפיוט וַיְהִי בַּחֲצִי הַלַּיְלָה

Yael Levine has composed two additional verses for *va-Yehi ba-Hatzi ha-Layla* describing events that occurred to women on *Seder* night, based on various Midrashic collections (*JOFA Journal*, Spring 2004 – *Nisan* 5764). The text and the translation are hers, while the sources below are based for the most part on the author's comments to the verses.

בְּרִית הִבְטַחְתָּ

Sarah was also included in the *Brit Bein ha-Betarim* (Covenant between the Pieces) (*Midrash Sekhel Tov*, Gen. 15:18). According to various sources, this Covenant was established on the first night of Passover (see: *Mekhilta de-Rabbi Yishma'el, Bo, Masekhta de-Pisha*, Chap. 14). Sarah is called *Rosh le-khol ha-Imahot* (the Head of all the Matriarchs) in *Bereshit Rabbati* (23:1)

מוּבֶלֶת לְבֵית פַּרְעֹה

Pirkei de-Rabbi Eliezer (Chap. 26) states that Sarah was taken by Pharaoh (Gen. Chap. 12) on the night of the 15th of *Nisan*. Regarding her abduction by Avimelekh (Gen. Chap. 20), *Midrash Rabba* (Num. 20:12) posits that this too occurred on the night of the 15th of *Nisan*; see comments to דָּנַתָּ מֶלֶךְ גְּרָר above.

(2) IT WAS IN THE MIDDLE OF THE NIGHT by YAEL LEVINE

You promised a covenant to (Sarah) the head of the Matriarchs at night.

She (Sarah) who has been taken to Pharaoh and Avimelekh you have saved at night.

She (Rivka) who is likened to a rose suggested exchanging the blessings at night.

It was in the middle of the night.

The mother who gave birth (Rachel, granddaughter of Shutelah) cried out and you smote the firstborn at night.

You saved a firstborn (Bitya, daughter of Pharaoh), her candle did not extinguish at night.

Hadassah (Esther) was busy with the feast of Haman at night.

It was in the middle of the night.

מְשׁוּלַת שׁוֹשַׁנָּה

According to *Pirkei de-Rabbi Eliezer* (Chap. 31), the switching of the blessings between Yaakov and Esav took place on Passover night at Rivka's initiative. Rivka is compared to "a rose among the thorns" (Song of Songs 2:2) because she remained pure despite growing up in a corrupt household (*Midrash Rabba* Lev. 23:1).

צָעֲקָה הַיּוֹלֶדֶת

Pirkei de-Rabbi Eliezer (Chap. 47) relates the plight of Rachel, granddaughter of Shutelah, an Israelite woman in Egyptian bondage. Although she was about to give birth, the Egyptians still forced her to make bricks by treading clay. (This *Midrash* maintains that the Israelites worked until the Exodus itself. There is another opinion in *Rosh ha-Shana* 11a-b that they stopped working the *Rosh ha-Shana* before.) Her child was born and became stuck in the bricks. Rachel's cry of horror ascended to the Throne of Glory, and that very night the angel Michael came down to earth and took the brick mold containing the baby up to God. The Almighty then descended "on that very night (*ba-Layla ha-hu*)," and smote the firstborn of the Egyptians. Thus, it was Rachel's cry that triggered the Plague of the Firstborn and the Exodus. The term *reshit onim* is based on the depiction of the Exodus in Psalms 78:51.

(3) פִּיּוּט "אַחַת מִי יוֹדֵעַ" – מאת יעל לוין

שְׁלֹשׁ עֶשְׂרֵה מִי יוֹדֵעַ? שְׁלֹשׁ עֶשְׂרֵה אֲנִי יוֹדֵעַ.

שְׁלֹשׁ עֶשְׂרֵה אוֹתִיּוֹת הָאִמָּהוֹת (שָׂרָה, רִבְקָה, רָחֵל, לֵאָה).

שְׁנֵים עָשָׂר חָדְשֵׁי מֵרוּק אֶסְתֵּר.

אַחַד עָשָׂר בְּמַרְחֶשְׁוָן (יוֹם פְּטִירַת רָחֵל).

עֲשָׂרָה זָהָב מִשְׁקָל צְמִידֵי רִבְקָה (שֶׁקִּבְּלָה מֵאֱלִיעֶזֶר עֶבֶד אַבְרָהָם).

תִּשְׁעָה יַרְחֵי לֵידָה.

בְּכוֹרָה מְלַטְתָּ

Bitya, daughter of Pharaoh (Chronicles I 4:18, Megilla 13a), who saved Moshe by night, was not killed in the plague of the firstborn although she was a firstborn child (*Midrash Rabba* Ex. 18:3).

הֲדַסָּה עֲסוּקָה

We commented above, that in his *piyut* va-Yehi ba-Hatzi ha-Layla (see our discussion of בַּלַּיְלָה סְפָרִים וְכָתַב אֲגִי, נָטַר שְׂנְאָה), Yannai relied on the tradition of the *Targum* to *Megillat Esther* (6:1) and *Midrash Panim Aherim* (Second Version, Chap. 6), that **ba-Layla ha-hu** nadeda shenat ha-Melekh (Esther 6:1) occurred on the 15th of *Nisan, Seder* Night. It follows that Hadassah (Esther) was occupied that very night with preparing the second feast for King Ahasuerus and Haman – which was scheduled for the next day.

פיוט אַחַת מִי יוֹדֵעַ

Yael Levine has written this analog of *Ehad Mi Yode'a* connecting the various numbers to events that occurred to leading women in Jewish tradition, based on various Midrashic works. The sources below are based mainly on the comments of Yael Levine to her verses (*Ahat Mi Yodei'a*, *Shabbat* section of *Makor Rishon* Newspaper, April 15, 2011, https://tinyurl.com/54fhnx3v). The text and translation are hers and reprinted with permission.

שְׁלֹשׁ עֶשְׂרֵה

There are a total of thirteen letters in the names of the *Avot*: אברהם, יצחק,

(3) *Ahat Mi Yode'a* by Yael Levine

Who knows thirteen? I know thirteen.

Thirteen are the number of letters of the matriarchs' names (שָׂרָה, רִבְקָה, רָחֵל, לֵאָה);

Twelve are the months of Esther's anointing;

Eleven is the eleventh of *Marheshvan* (the day of Rachel's death);

Ten shekels is the weight of Rivka's gold bracelets (received from Eliezer the slave of Abraham);

Nine are the months until a baby's birth;

---

and יעקב – and the same is true for the *Imahot*: רחל, שרה, רבקה and לאה. Ramban (*ha-Emuna ve-ha-Bitahon*, Chap. 13) notes that the sum of letters is 26 – equivalent to the numerical value of God's ineffable name י-ה-ו-ה.

שְׁנֵים עָשָׂר

Esther 2:12 records that: "When each girl's turn came to go to King Ahasuerus at the end of the twelve months' treatment prescribed for women – for that was the period spent on anointing and beautifying them: six months with oil of myrrh and six months with perfumes and women's cosmetics."

אַחַד עָשָׂר

This date of the passing of the matriarchs is not mentioned in the biblical text. Nevertheless, *Yalkut Shimoni* (Ex. 162) gives the birthday of Benjamin as the eleventh of *Marheshvan*. The text does indicate that his mother Rachel died in his birth.

עֲשָׂרָה

Genesis 24:22 states regarding Eliezer: "When the camels had finished drinking, the man took a gold nose-ring weighing a half-shekel, and two gold bands for her arms, ten [shekels] in weight." That the weight was in shekels is stated by R. Abraham Maimonides and R. David Tsvi Hoffman.

תִּשְׁעָה

This already appears in *Ehad Mi Yode'a*.

שְׁמוֹנָה בְּנֵי מִלְכָּה,

שֶׁבַע נְבִיאוֹת (שָׂרָה, מִרְיָם, דְּבוֹרָה, חַנָּה, אֲבִיגַיִל, חֻלְדָּה וְאֶסְתֵּר),

שֵׁשׁ (קַבִּין) הַשְּׂעוֹרִים שֶׁל רוּת (שֶׁקִּבְּלָה מִבּוֹעַז),

חָמֵשׁ בְּנוֹת צְלָפְחָד (מַחְלָה, נֹעָה, חָגְלָה, מִלְכָּה וְתִרְצָה),

אַרְבַּע נָשִׁים יְפֵיפִיּוֹת (שָׂרָה, רָחָב, אֲבִיגַיִל, וְאֶסְתֵּר),

שָׁלֹשׁ שֶׁהִצִּילוּ בַּעֲלֵיהֶן (אֵשֶׁת אוֹן בֶּן פֶּלֶת, מִיכַל בַּת שָׁאוּל, וְשֶׂרַח בַּת אָשֵׁר),

שְׁתֵּי מְיַלְּדוֹת עִבְרִיּוֹת (שִׁפְרָה וּפוּעָה),

אַחַת הִיא יוֹנָתִי תַמָּתִי.

שְׁמוֹנָה

Genesis 22:20–23 records that following the Akeda, Avraham receives news that his sister-in-law Milca gave birth to eight sons, the last being Betu'el, father of Rivka.

שֶׁבַע

The names of seven prophetesses are listed in *Megilla* (14a–b).

שֵׁשׁ

Chapter 3 of the Book of Ruth describes the clandestine meeting of Ruth and Boaz. In verse 15 the text states: "And he said, 'Hold out the shawl you are wearing.' She held it while he measured out six barley..." Ralbag, Seforno, and Malbim (ad loc.) indicate that "six barley" does not mean six **stalks** of barley but six *kav* [measures] of barley, which is ca. 7 liter – a sizable and respectable amount.

חָמֵשׁ

The matter of the five daughters of Zelophad is mentioned in Num. 27:1–11 and 36:1–13.

אַרְבַּע

The four beautiful women are recorded in Megilla (15a).

Eight are the sons of Milca;

Seven are the prophetesses of Israel (Sarah, Miriam, Debora, Hanna, Abigail, Hulda, and Esther);

Six are the number of kav measures of Ruth's barley (received from Boaz);

Five are the daughters of Zelophad (Mahla, No'a, Hogla, Milca, and Tirza);

Four are the beautiful women (Sarah, Rahab, Abigail, and Esther);

Three are the women who saved their husbands (On ben Pelet's wife, Michal daughter of Saul, and Serah daughter of Asher);

Two are the Hebrew midwives (Shifra and Pu'a);

One and Unique is my undefiled dove (Israel).

שָׁלֹשׁ

The three women who saved their husbands' lives are recorded in *Midrash ha-Gadol* Num. 16:32. (a) On ben Pelet was originally part of Korah's revolt but recanted. To prevent him from being called to action by his confederates, On's wife intoxicated him allowing him to oversleep the confrontation with Moshe. The full tale is presented in Talmud Sanhedrin 109b–110a. (b) As recorded in Samuel I, Chap. 19, King David's wife, Michal, daughter of Saul, lowered her husband with a rope, allowing him to escape her father's emissaries. (c) The tale of Sheva son of Bikhri's revolt against David is described in Samuel II, Chap. 20. Sheva hides in the city Avel, which David's army attack and threatens to destroy. The city dwellers are saved by a "wise woman" who has Sheva's head thrown over the wall. *Midrash Rabba* (Gen. 94:9) posits that the "wise woman" was Serah, daughter of Asher.

The two Israelite midwives were Shifra and Puah (Ex. 1:15), and identified as Yokheved and Miriam in *Sota* 11b and various *Midrashim*; see also Rashi to Ex. 1:15.

אַחַת

This is a quote from Song of Songs 6:9. According to the Midrashic tradition, these words of praise are said by the Lover (God) about his beloved (*Kenesset Yisrael*, the People of Israel).